The Victorian City

Judith Flanders, a Senior Research Fellow at the University of Buckingham, is the author of the bestselling *The Victorian House: Domestic Life from Childbirth to Deathbed* (2003); the critically acclaimed *Consuming Passions: Leisure and Pleasure in Victorian Britain* (2006); *A Circle of Sisters* (2001), which was nominated for the *Guardian* First Book Award; and, most recently, *The Invention of Murder* (2011). She lives in London.

ALSO BY JUDITH FLANDERS

The Victorian House: Domestic Life from Childbirth to Deathbed
Consuming Passions: Leisure and Pleasure in Victorian Britain
A Circle of Sisters: Alice Kipling, Georgiana Burne-Jones, Agnes Poynter and Louisa Baldwin
The Invention of Murder

The Victorian City

EVERYDAY LIFE IN DICKENS' LONDON

JUDITH FLANDERS

ATLANTIC BOOKS
LONDON

First published in Great Britain in 2012 by Atlantic Books,
an imprint of Atlantic Books Ltd.

This paperback edition published in 2013 by Atlantic Books.

1 2 3 4 5 6 7 8 9

A CIP catalogue record for this book is available
from the British Library.

Paperback ISBN: 978-1-84887-797-9
E-book ISBN: 978-0-85789-881-4

Designed and typeset in Adobe Garamond by Lindsay Nash
Printed in Great Britain by CPI Group (UK) Ltd, Croydon, CR0 4YY

Atlantic Books
An imprint of Atlantic Books Ltd
Ormond House
26–27 Boswell Street
London
WC1N 3JZ

www.atlantic-books.co.uk

For Ravi
With thanks

One may easily sail round England, or circumnavigate the globe. But not the most enthusiastic geographer…ever memorised a map of London…For England is a small island, the world is infinitesimal amongst the planets. But London is illimitable.

FORD MADOX FORD, *The Soul of London*

Cityful passing away, other cityful coming, passing away too: other coming on, passing on. Houses, lines of houses, streets, miles of pavements, piled up bricks, stones. Changing hands. This owner, that. Landlord never dies they say. Other steps into his shoes when he gets his notice to quit…Pyramids in sand. Built on bread and onions. Slaves. Chinese wall. Babylon. Big stones left. Round towers. Rest rubble, sprawling suburbs, jerrybuilt…built of breeze. Shelter for the night.

No one is anything.

JAMES JOYCE, *Ulysses*

CONTENTS

PART FOUR: SLEEPING AND AWAKE

ACKNOWLEDGEMENTS

This book is the product of a lifetime of London-loving and Dickens-loving, and I must first and foremost thank those great London and Dickens scholars who have enriched my reading: Peter Ackroyd, Philip Collins, John Drew, Madeline House, Susan Shatto, Michael Slater, Graham Storey and Kathleen Tillotson.

As always, I am indebted to the members of the Victoria 19th-century British Culture and Society mailbase for their tolerance of my seemingly random queries, and for their vast stores of knowledge. And to Patrick Leary, list-master *extraordinaire*, go not merely my thanks for creating such a congenial environment, but also for pointing me towards the Regent's Park skating disaster.

I am grateful to my agent Bill Hamilton for his skill, and for his patience and tolerance.

I thank, too, all those at Atlantic Books, past and present: Alan Craig, Karen Duffy, Lauren Finger, Richard Milbank, Sarah Norman, Bunmi Oke, Sarah Pocklington, Orlando Whitfield and Corinna Zifko. My thanks too to Jeff Edwards, Douglas Matthews, Lindsay Nash, Leo Nickolls and Tamsin Shelton. The wonderful pictures were found by Josine Meijer, while Celia Levett, with her sensitive and rigorous copy-editing, improved every sentence of the text.

Finally, I owe my career to Ravi Mirchandani, now my publisher but, before I became a writer, my friend. 'Stop talking about it,' he told me then. 'Write it.' So I have. This book is for him.

A NOTE ON CURRENCY

Pounds, shillings and pence were the divisions of the currency. One shilling is made up of twelve pence; one pound of twenty shillings, i.e. 240 pence. Pounds are represented by the £ symbol, shillings as 's', and pence as 'd' (from the Latin, *denarius*). 'One pound, one shilling and one penny' is written as £1 1s 1d. 'One shilling and sixpence', referred to in speech as 'one and six', is written as 1s 6d, or 1/6.

A guinea was a coin to the value of £1 1s 0d. (The actual coin was not circulated after 1813, although the term remained and tended to be reserved for luxury goods.) A sovereign was a twenty-shilling coin, a half-sovereign a ten-shilling coin. A crown was five shillings, half a crown 2/6, and the remaining coins were a florin (two shillings), sixpence, a groat (four pence), a threepenny bit (pronounced 'thrup'ny'), twopence (pronounced tuppence), a penny, a halfpenny (pronounced hayp'ny), a farthing (a quarter of a penny) and a half a farthing (an eighth of a penny).

Relative values have altered so substantially that attempts to convert nineteenth-century prices into contemporary ones are usually futile. However, the website http://www.ex.ac.uk/~RDavies/arian/current/howmuch.html is a gateway to this complicated subject.

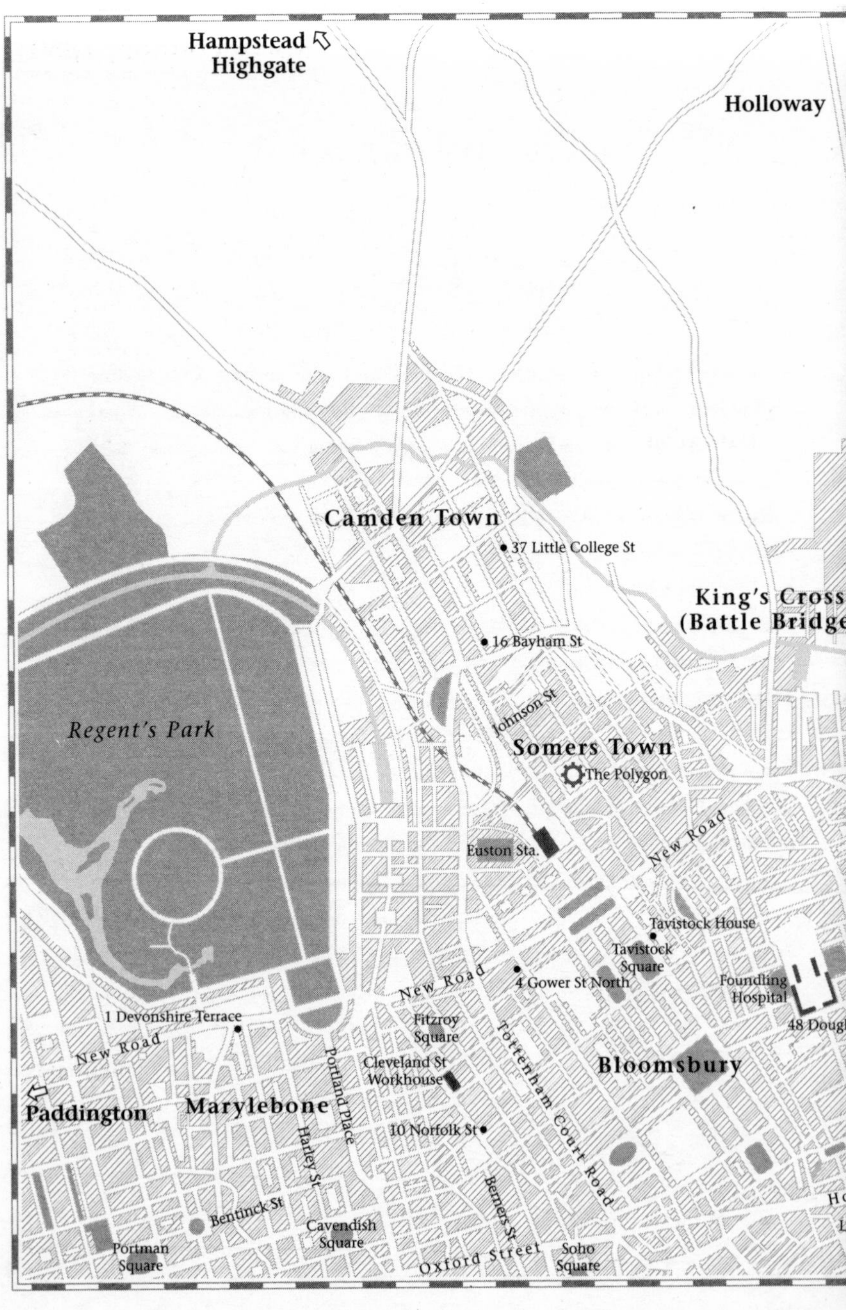
Hampstead
Highgate
Holloway
Camden Town
37 Little College St
King's Cross
(Battle Bridge
16 Bayham St
Johnson St
Regent's Park
Somers Town
The Polygon
New Road
Euston Sta.
Tavistock House
Tavistock
Square
New Road
4 Gower St North
Foundling
Hospital
1 Devonshire Terrace
Fitzroy
Square
New Road
Portland Place
Cleveland St
Workhouse
Tottenham Court Road
Bloomsbury
Paddington
Marylebone
Harley St
10 Norfolk St
Berners St
Bentinck St
Cavendish
Square
Portman
Square
Oxford Street
Soho
Square

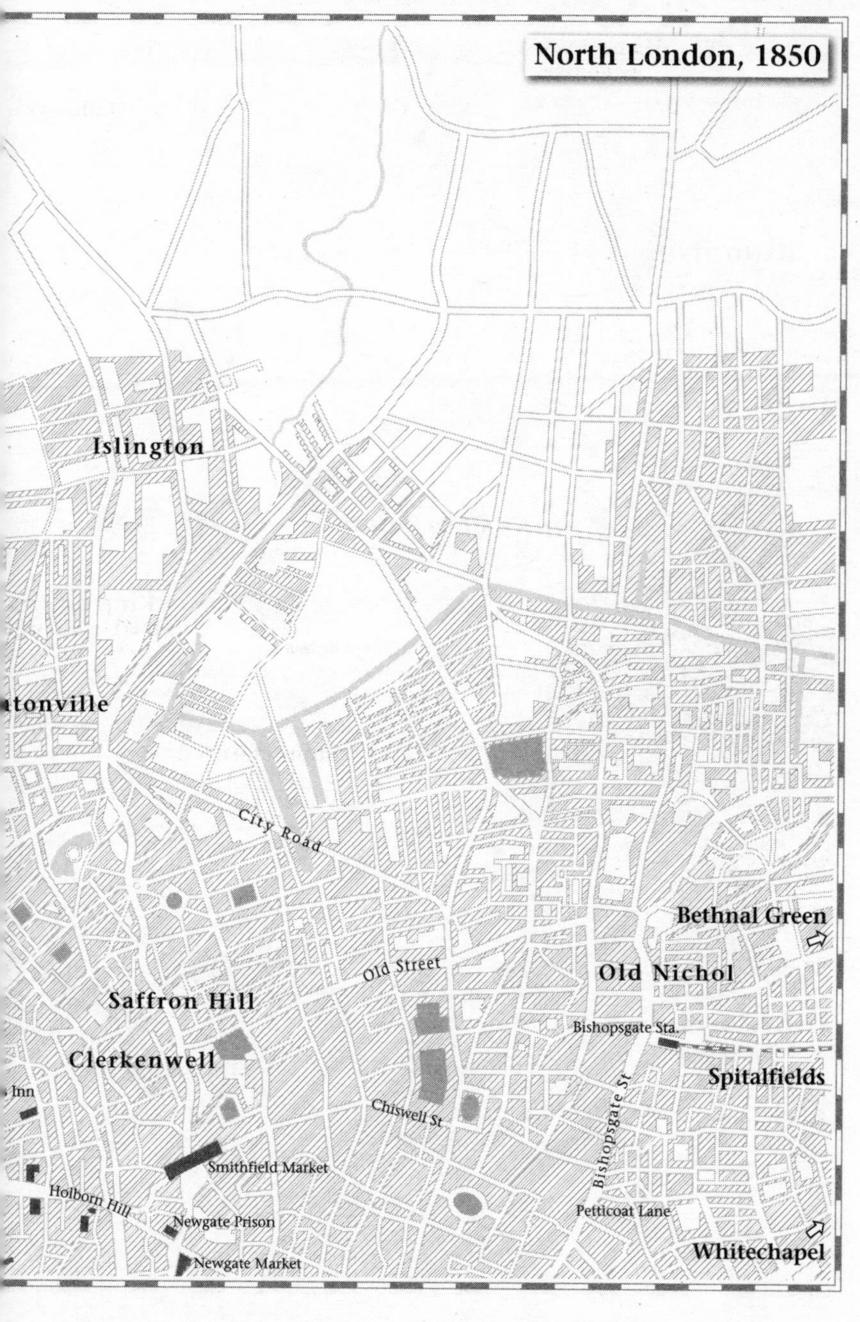

North London, 1850
Islington
tonville
City Road
Bethnal Green
Old Street
Old Nichol
Saffron Hill
Bishopsgate Sta.
Clerkenwell
Spitalfields
Inn
Chiswell St
Bishopsgate St
Smithfield Market
Holborn Hill
Newgate Prison
Petticoat Lane
Whitechapel
Newgate Market

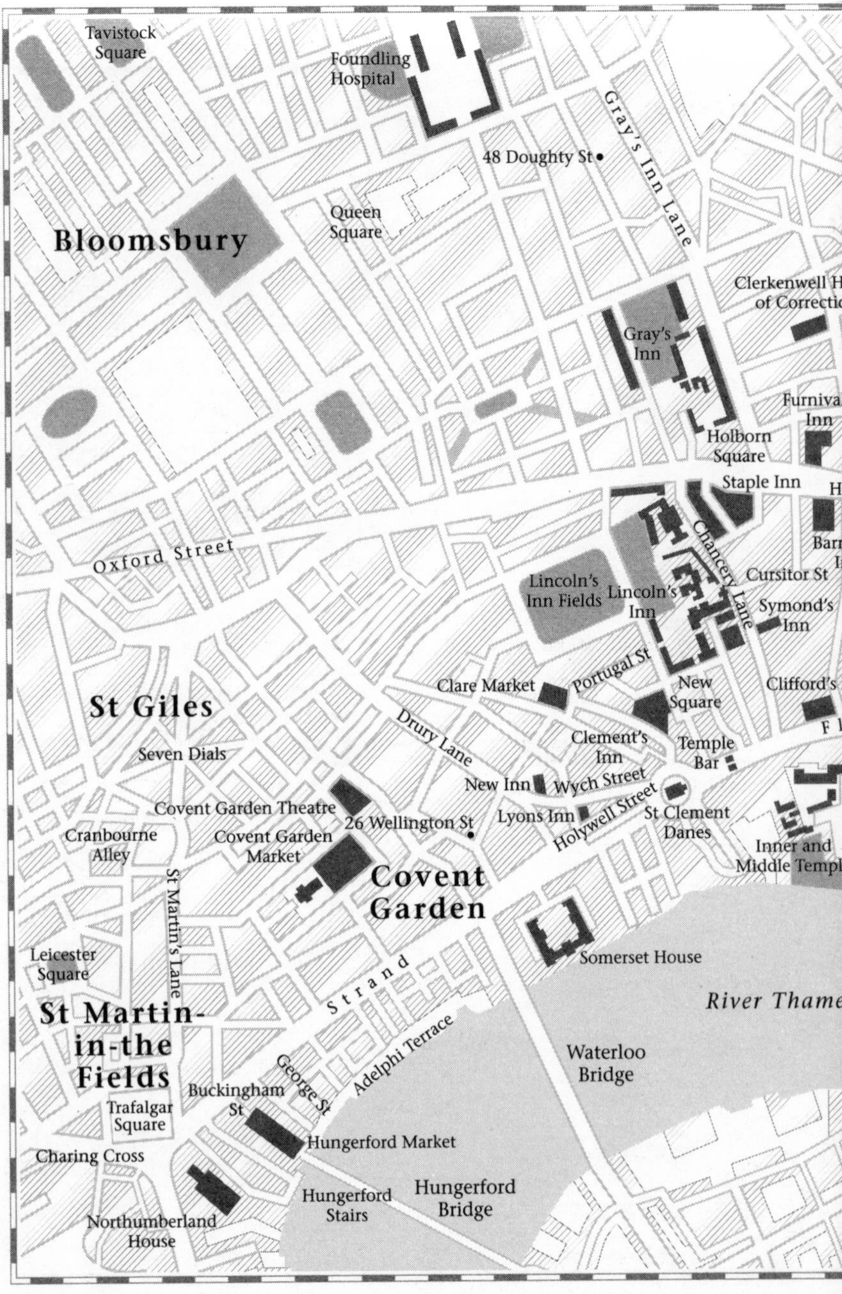

Tavistock Square
Foundling Hospital
Gray's Inn Lane
48 Doughty St
Queen Square
Bloomsbury
Gray's Inn
Holborn Square
Staple Inn
Oxford Street
Chancery Lane
Cursitor St
Lincoln's Inn Fields
Lincoln's Inn
Symond's Inn
Portugal St
Clare Market
New Square
St Giles
Drury Lane
Clement's Inn
Temple Bar
Seven Dials
New Inn
Wych Street
Covent Garden Theatre
Lyons Inn
Holywell Street
St Clement Danes
26 Wellington St
Cranbourne Alley
Covent Garden Market
Covent Garden
St Martin's Lane
Somerset House
Leicester Square
Strand
St Martin-in-the Fields
Adelphi Terrace
Waterloo Bridge
George St
Buckingham St
Trafalgar Square
Hungerford Market
Charing Cross
Hungerford Stairs
Hungerford Bridge
Northumberland House

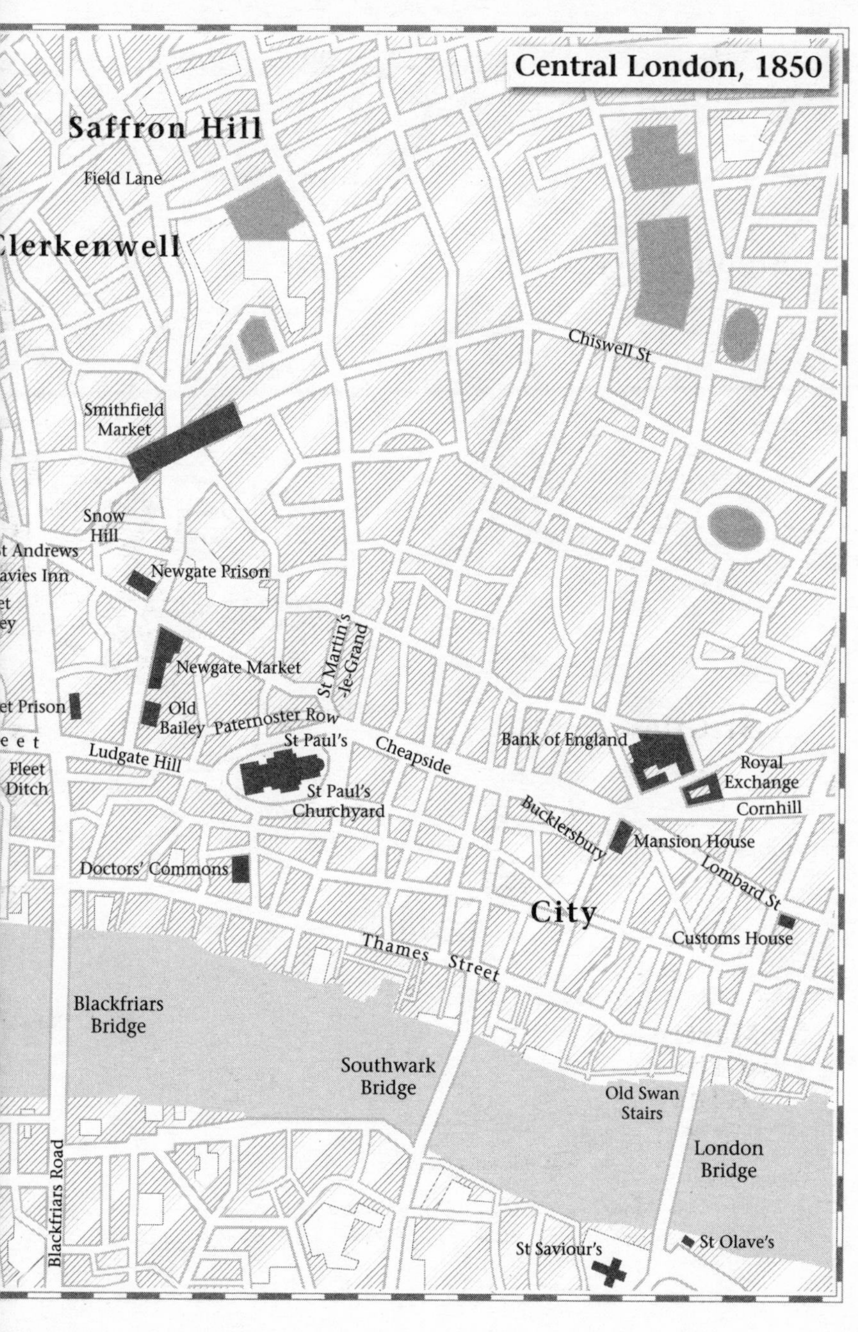

Central London, 1850
Saffron Hill
Field Lane
Clerkenwell
Chiswell St
Smithfield Market
Snow Hill
Newgate Prison
St Martin's-le-Grand
Newgate Market
Old Bailey
Paternoster Row
St Paul's
Cheapside
Bank of England
Royal Exchange
Cornhill
Ludgate Hill
Fleet Ditch
St Paul's Churchyard
Bucklersbury
Mansion House
Lombard St
Doctors' Commons
City
Customs House
Thames Street
Blackfriars Bridge
Southwark Bridge
Old Swan Stairs
London Bridge
Blackfriars Road
St Saviour's
St Olave's

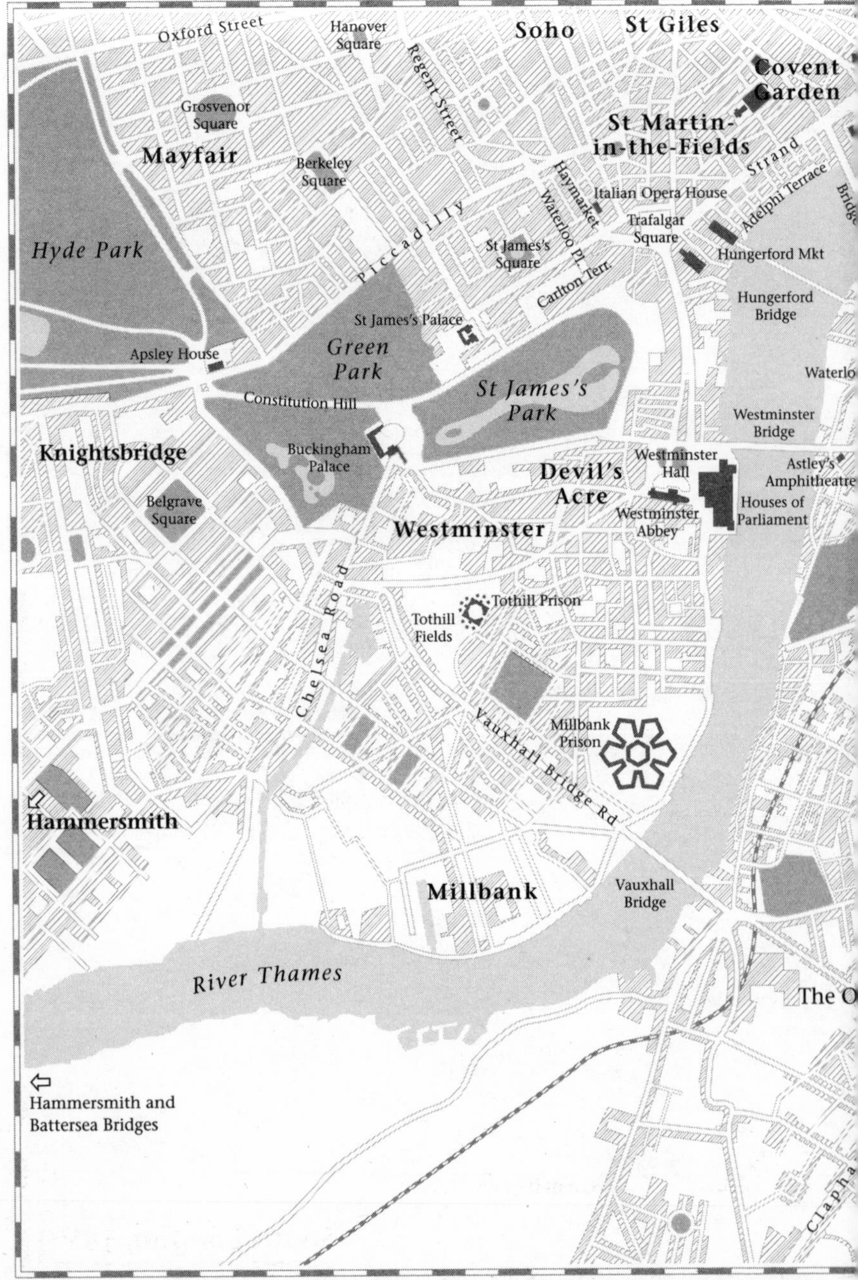

Oxford Street
Hanover Square
Soho
St Giles
Covent Garden
Regent Street
Grosvenor Square
St Martin-in-the-Fields
Mayfair
Berkeley Square
Strand
Haymarket
Adelphi Terrace
Italian Opera House
Waterloo Pl.
Trafalgar Square
Piccadilly
Hyde Park
St James's Square
Hungerford Mkt
Carlton Terr.
Hungerford Bridge
St James's Palace
Green Park
Apsley House
Waterlo
St James's Park
Constitution Hill
Westminster Bridge
Knightsbridge
Buckingham Palace
Westminster Hall
Devil's Acre
Astley's Amphitheatre
Houses of Parliament
Belgrave Square
Westminster Abbey
Westminster
Chelsea Road
Tothill Prison
Tothill Fields
Millbank Prison
Vauxhall Bridge Rd
Hammersmith
Millbank
Vauxhall Bridge
River Thames
The O
Hammersmith and Battersea Bridges

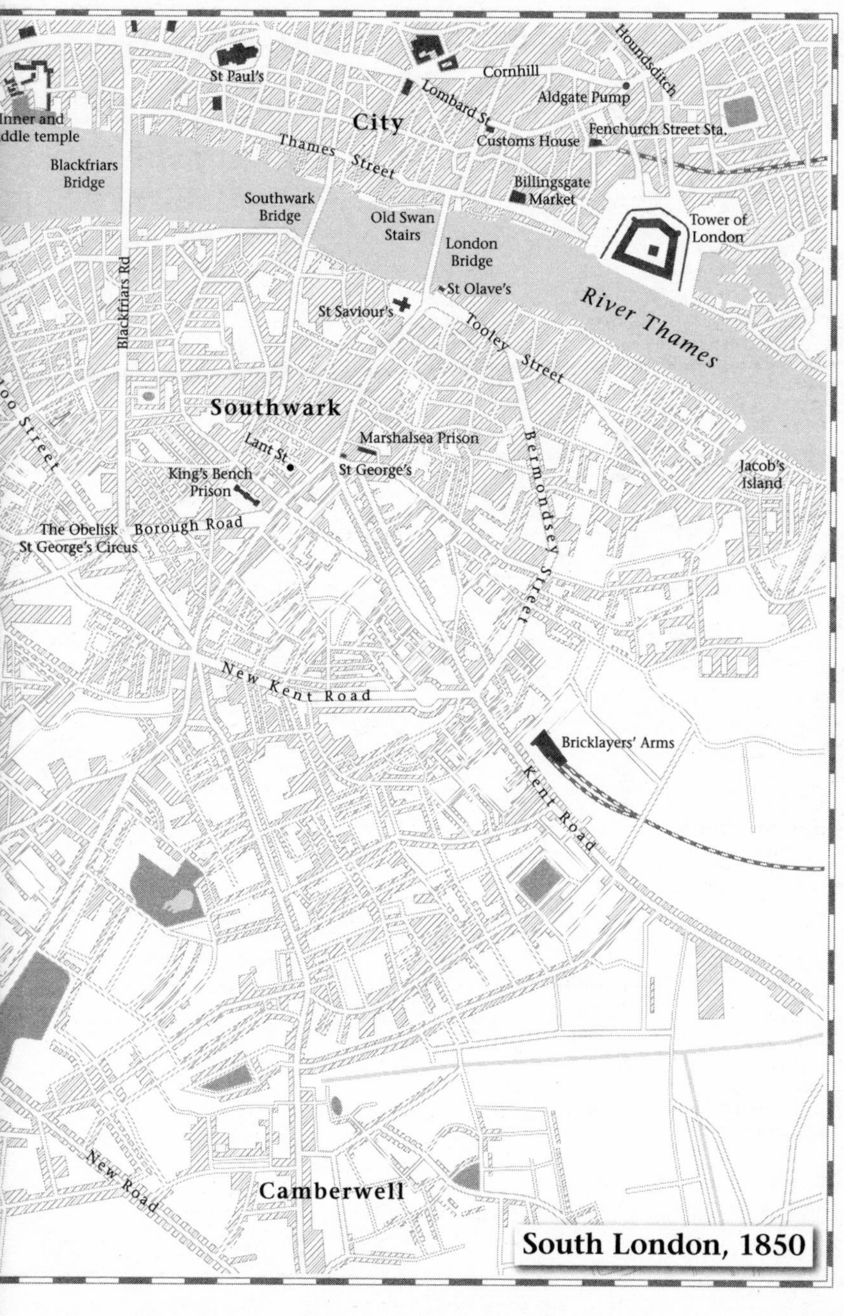

St Paul's
Cornhill
Houndsditch
Lombard St
Aldgate Pump
Inner and
ddle temple
City
Fenchurch Street Sta.
Customs House
Thames Street
Blackfriars
Bridge
Billingsgate
Market
Southwark
Bridge
Old Swan
Stairs
Tower of
London
London
Bridge
St Olave's
St Saviour's
River Thames
Blackfriars Rd
Tooley Street
Southwark
Marshalsea Prison
Bermondsey Street
Lant St
St George's
Jacob's
Island
King's Bench
Prison
The Obelisk
St George's Circus
Borough Road
New Kent Road
Bricklayers' Arms
Kent Road
New Road
Camberwell
South London, 1850

LIST OF ILLUSTRATIONS

Colour Plates

16. George Scharf, *The Strand from Villiers Street*, 1824. Watercolour. British Museum (© The Trustees of the British Museum)

17. Henry Alken, *Funeral Car of the Duke of Wellington*, 1853. Coloured engraving. (Victoria & Albert Museum, London/Bridgeman Art Library)

18. William Heath, *Greedy Old Nickford Eating Oysters*, late 1820s. Hand-coloured etching. British Museum. (© The Trustees of the British Museum)

19. Henry Alken, *Bear Baiting*, 1821. Coloured engraving. (Mary Evans Picture Library)

20. Rowlandson & Pugin, *Charing Cross Pillory*, 1809. Aquatint. (Mary Evans Picture Library)

21. George Cruikshank, *Acting Magistrates Committing Themselves being Their First Appearance on this Stage as Performed at the National Theatre Covent Garden*, 1809. Hand-coloured etching. British Museum. (© The Trustees of the British Museum)

INTRODUCTION

'A Dickensian scandal for the 21st century' blares one newspaper headline. 'No one should have to live in such Dickensian conditions,' says another. Today 'Dickensian' means squalor, it means wretched living conditions, oppression and darkness.

Yet Dickens finished his first novel with a glance at the sunny Mr Pickwick and his friends: 'There are dark shadows on the earth, but its lights are stronger in the contrast. Some men, like bats or owls, have better eyes for the darkness than for the light. We, who have no such optical powers, are better pleased to take our last parting look at the visionary companions of many solitary hours, when the brief sunshine of the world is blazing full upon them.' The brief sunshine of the world blazed out in full in Dickens' work and, early in his career in particular, that was the way his contemporaries saw it. For them, 'Dickensian' meant comic; for others, it meant convivial good cheer.* It was not until the twentieth century, as social conditions began to improve, that 'Dickensian' took on its dark tinge. In Dickens' own time, the way that people lived was not Dickensian, merely life.

The greatest recorder the London streets has ever known – through whose eyes those streets have become Dickensian – was not born in London at all, but in Portsmouth, on 7 February 1812, where his father, a clerk in the navy pay office, was working. Apart from a brief foray to the capital as a toddler,

* The first citation given in the *Oxford English Dictionary* is from 1881, eleven years after Dickens' death. But newspapers were using the term 'Dickensian' in 1842, when the author was just thirty years old and had yet to publish his greatest works.

Dickens moved to the city that gave meaning to his life and his fiction only when he was ten, arriving from Chatham, where his father had been posted, on the Commodore stagecoach, 'packed, like game – and forwarded, carriage paid', at the coaching inn in the heart of Cheapside, in the City of London.* In 1815, he and his family had lodged in Norfolk Street, near Tottenham Court Road, just steps away from the grim-faced Cleveland Street Workhouse. On their return to London in 1822, they moved to the newly developing, lower-middle-class district of Camden Town slightly to the north. Bayham Street was still rural enough for grass to grow down the centre of the road, and the houses that lined the street were new. This is not to say the Dickenses lived lavishly. Dickens' parents, five children, a servant and the stepson of Mrs Dickens' deceased sister were all crammed into the little two-storey, yellow-brick house. Dickens' authorized biographer and lifelong friend, John Forster, called Camden Town 'about the poorest part of the London suburbs' and described the house as a 'mean small tenement, with a wretched little back-garden abutting on a squalid court'. (The word 'court' in nineteenth-century London always meant a dead-end alley that housed slum lodgings.) Yet the residents listed by one of Dickens' childhood neighbours – small shopkeepers; the local building contractor – do not bear this out, nor does the rent of £22 per annum – well beyond the reach of the washerwoman Forster claimed was their nearest neighbour. It seems as if, unconsciously, 'Dickensian', meaning the dark without the light, was retrospectively being imposed on Dickens himself.

The dark came soon enough. In December 1823, the Dickens family moved to Gower Street North, to a house double the size of the one in Bayham Street. Mrs Dickens was hoping to start a school for young ladies to supplement John Dickens' income. While not poor, the Dickenses had by now an even larger family – seven children – and could never manage to live within their income. In the quasi-autobiographical *David Copperfield*,

* I will use City with a capital 'C' to mean that area of London that is more or less confined geographically within the old medieval walls governed by the Corporation of the City of London, which now represents the financial district of London; the city, in lower case, refers to London more generally.

Mr Micawber – a surprisingly affectionate portrait of John Dickens from an author more usually exasperated or enraged by his feckless father – famously pronounced, 'Annual income twenty pounds, annual expenditure nineteen nineteen six, result happiness. Annual income twenty pounds, annual expenditure twenty pounds ought and six, result misery.'*And despite the comically pompous tone, the Dickenses' lives were indeed made miserable, particularly young Charles's. As the debts mounted, Mrs Dickens' step-nephew offered to help. He was the new office manager of Warren's Blacking Factory, near the Strand, which manufactured shoe polish and the blackleading applied to fire grates and kitchen ranges.

And so, sometime around his twelfth birthday, Charles was taken out of school and sent to work in a factory for 6s a week. Less than a month later, his father was arrested for debt, and by April 1824 the household in North Gower Street was broken up. The novice child-worker lived alone in lodgings in Little College Street in Camden Town, while, to save money, the rest of the family moved into the Marshalsea prison nearly four miles away, where John Dickens was already incarcerated. David Copperfield once more speaks for the boy Charles, abandoned as he appeared to be: 'I know enough of the world now, to have almost lost the capacity of being much surprised by anything; but it is matter of some surprise to me, even now, that I can have been so easily thrown away at such an age. A child of excellent abilities, and with strong powers of observation, quick, eager, delicate, and soon hurt bodily or mentally, it seems wonderful to me that nobody should have made any sign in my behalf. But none was made; and I became, at ten years old, a little labouring hind.'†

The labouring hind had no idea when, or even if, this purgatory, his being 'thrown away', was ever to end. There was every possibility that he would be a factory-hand for the rest of his life. At some point later on Dickens attempted to write an autobiography. It was never finished, but he

* For an explanation of pre-decimal currency, see p. xiii.

† Hind was an obsolete word for a servant by the time Dickens was writing, but 'labouring hind' was a phrase regularly used in poetry and translations, and would have been recognized as such.

handed what he had written to John Forster, to be used in his friend's biography of him after his death. In this fragment, in his novels and, most likely, in his own mind, Dickens backdated the episode so that it occurred not when he was twelve, but when he was ten, making him more pathetically defenceless still. The trauma to the child endured. That terrible year, 1824, is the central date not only of the child labour episode in *David Copperfield*, but also of key sections of *Little Dorrit* and *Great Expectations*. For Dickens, until the old market at Hungerford, where Warren's was located, had been rebuilt (see Plate 14), until 'the very nature of the ground changed, I never had the courage to go back to the place where my servitude began...For many years, when I came near...I crossed over to the opposite side of the way', while the route past the Marshalsea 'made me cry' long into adulthood. It may be that the confusion over the status of Bayham Street can be attributed to this long-lasting distress. When the Dickens family lived there, it was a respectable lower-middle-class street; by the time John Forster saw it, it had become a slum. Dickens knew that it had been different in his childhood, but the worse it was perceived, the more he had achieved: the squalor of the area was a mark of how far he had come.

By 1825, John Dickens had been released from prison and the family was once more in decent lodgings in north London, with Charles back at school. But within two years John Dickens was in financial difficulties again, and the young Dickens, still only fifteen, left school for the final time. This time, his prospects were more hopeful. Mrs Dickens' family was again called on, and her aunt's lodger, a young solicitor named Blackmore, hired the boy as a clerk. Now his fierce determination to put the blacking factory behind him had an outlet. After leaving the Navy Office, John Dickens had found work as a parliamentary reporter, and in 1828 Charles followed suit, becoming successful enough in less than a year to leave clerking behind and set up as a freelance shorthand-writer. In 1833, when he was just twenty-one, his first story, 'A Dinner at Poplar Walk', was published in the *Monthly Magazine*. The would-be author had sent it in anonymously, and when he found it printed, 'I walked down to Westminster Hall, and turned into it for half an hour, because my eyes were so dimmed with joy and pride.' Soon he was producing newspaper and magazine sketches regularly, under the pseudonym Boz. (Boz, pronounced today with a short 'o', was probably pronounced by Dickens as 'Boze'. He had given his youngest brother the nickname Moses, which the toddler then mangled as 'Boses', and soon the family shortened it to Boz.)

In 1834, at the age of twenty-two, Dickens started work at the *Morning Chronicle*, ultimately earning five guineas a week, or £273 per annum, a decent middle-class salary.* In 1836, his first novel, a series of comic sketches about the doings of Mr Pickwick and his friends, was published. The additional £14 a month that it brought in gave him the security he needed to marry Catherine Hogarth, the daughter of the editor of the *Evening Chronicle*, who was publishing his 'Sketches of London' (later expanded into *Sketches by Boz*). By June 1836, the serial had become an unprecedented triumph: each issue, which had initially sold 400 copies monthly, was now selling 40,000. In July, Boz was revealed to be Charles Dickens and, as Byron had done before him, he awoke to find himself famous.

Dickens now did something extraordinary. Nine months before he finished *Pickwick Papers*, this man of prodigious energy, only twenty-five years old, began to write *Oliver Twist*, one of the world's most famous novels, whose 'Please, sir, I want some more' is familiar even to the millions who have never read it. And then, five months after he completed *Pickwick*, he started his third novel, *Nicholas Nickleby*, before *Oliver Twist*, his second, had reached its halfway point.†

This energy, this amazing outpouring of imaginative literature, suited the age. *Oliver Twist* was being read while William IV was still on the throne, for Dickens, contrary to our easy assumptions, was not a Victorian, or not solely a Victorian. He was born in the reign of George III, although by 1812

* Income and class, inextricably linked, are difficult to compare directly with modern income and social status. However, as a rule of thumb, between £100 and £150 was considered the entry-level income for the lower middle classes for most of the nineteenth century, and £500 was at the upper end of the middle-class scale. Although professional men who earned more (sometimes as much as £1,000) were still considered middle class, they emulated the lifestyles of the upper classes. In turn, the lower echelons of the upper classes, the gentry, often got by on £500 or even less.

† A list of Dickens' major works, with the dates of serial and one-volume first publications, appears on page 425.

the old king was permanently mad, as well as deaf and blind: the Regency had been declared the previous year, and the Prince Regent set the rackety and louche tone of the upper reaches of society. In 1820, when Dickens was still a boy in Chatham, the Prince Regent inherited the throne as George IV; Dickens was nineteen when the old stone London Bridge, a symbol of London for 600 years, was replaced. Even as his writing career took off, the new era had not properly begun: as Bill Sikes is hunted down at the end of *Oliver Twist*, his pursuers demand that a door be opened 'in the king's name'. By the time the eighteen-year-old Victoria came to the throne in 1837, Dickens was twenty-five, an established author, a magazine editor and a married man with a family. And when he died in 1870, the Victorian age still had thirty years to run. But although he was therefore not purely Victorian, Dickens' life – and Dickens' London – form a perfect optic through which to see the city's transformation. His was the London of dubious beginnings, of Regency grandiosity, as well as of early Victorian earnestness and endeavour, expansionism and technological advancement.*

Dickens would describe all these qualities as though no one had ever seen them before. And after he described them, no one would be able to see them again except through his eyes. Throughout his life, peripatetic residentially as well as psychologically – living at over two dozen London addresses in a half-century – Dickens covered the whole of London, from the East End and the City, north to Camden, through Westminster and west to Hammersmith, south along the shores of the river. Even when he was officially settled, he frequently maintained several addresses at once, some known to his friends and family, others more or less kept hidden. In the 1850s, the Dickens family home was in Bloomsbury, with a country house in Kent. Dickens was proprietor and editor of the magazines *Household Words* from 1850 to 1859, and of *All the Year Round* from 1859 to his death in 1870. Both magazines had offices in Covent Garden with rooms where he stayed overnight; and Ellen Ternan, his secret mistress, lived at first

* It is for this reason that I have cheated slightly, using 'Victorian' in my title, even though Dickens' dates, and the period I cover, begin earlier, and finish earlier, than the period when Victoria reigned (1837–1901.)

close to his early childhood home in Camden Town, then in the suburbs south of the river. Dickens could be different people at different times in different places, changing en route as he strode from one to another.

Dickens' London was a place of the mind, but it was also a real place. Much of what we take today to be the marvellous imaginings of a visionary novelist turn out on inspection to be the reportage of a great observer. In 1853, Dickens published an essay, 'Gone Astray', in which the narrator tells of a day when, as 'a very small boy indeed', he is taken to see St Giles' Church, lying between Covent Garden and the present-day Charing Cross Road, then on the edge of the fearsome slum of St Giles. From there his adult companion takes him to Northumberland House, which closed off the south side of what became Trafalgar Square, in a 'narrow, crowded, inconvenient street'. There the boy-narrator loses his accompanying adult and is off on his own, walking along the Strand, down Fleet Street, past Temple Bar – the Wren-designed stone gateway where the Strand and Fleet Street meet, which was the formal demarcation line between the West End and the City – seeing from there the great dome of St Paul's.* He wanders through the City, past the Royal Exchange, then the Mansion House, home of the City's Lord Mayor, and finally reaches Whitechapel: 'This is literally and exactly how I went astray.' It also, 'literally and exactly', covers the heart of Dickens' London, the streets he walked compulsively, obsessively, before transforming them into art until his death at only fifty-eight. One journalist, a protégé of Dickens, described how the author regularly appeared like the pantomime demon, popping up anywhere and everywhere: 'A hansom whirled you by the Bell and Horns at Brompton, and there he was, striding out, as with seven-league boots, seemingly in the direction of North-end, Fulham. The Metropolitan Railway sent you forth at Lisson-grove, and you met him plodding speedily towards the Yorkshire Stingo [pub]. He was to be met rapidly skirting the grim brick wall of the prison in Coldbath-fields,

* Temple Bar, which narrowed one of London's busiest roads to a mere twenty feet, was dismantled in 1878 after nearly a century as a traffic menace, and was purchased by a brewer to create the entrance to the grounds of his house near Enfield. In 2004, the house having long since become a conference centre, Temple Bar was returned to the City and inserted into the new development at Paternoster Square, beside St Paul's.

or trudging along the Seven Sisters-road at Holloway, or bearing, under a steady press of sail, underneath Highgate Archway, or pursuing the even tenor of his way up to the Vauxhall-bridge-road.'*

The younger man found Dickens' appearance as he walked the streets 'decidedly "odd"', delighting as he did in bright colours and clothes cut with dramatic flair. This was frequently commented on later in the nineteenth century by younger men who were unaware that Dickens had retained to the end of his life the Regency's love of bright colours and dandified attitudes. (He shared this trait with another colourful dresser, Disraeli, eight years his senior.) As he walked along, this small, fine-boned man presented himself with a 'slight flavour of the whipper-snapper', a dashing air, and 'remarkably upright' carriage. Over the years, the impression he made on the street shifted from that of a 'pretty-boy-looking sort of figure' to 'A man of sanguine complexion, deeply lined & scantily bearded…countenance alert and observant, scornful somewhat and sour'; yet even then, when he was ageing, he kept his 'light step and jaunty air'. With a 'brand new hat airily cocked on one side', he continued to march along at breakneck pace through the city streets well into his final years.

These walks were in part a way of processing his work, thinking out his fiction with his feet. In Switzerland, he lamented to John Forster, 'The absence of any accessible streets continues to worry me…at night I want them beyond description. I don't seem able to get rid of my spectres unless I can lose them in crowds.' The narrator who opens *The Old Curiosity Shop* has much in common with his author: 'Night is generally my time for walking…it affords me greater opportunity of speculating on the characters and occupations of those who fill the streets…a glimpse of passing faces caught by the light of a street-lamp or a shop window is often better for my purpose than their full revelation in the daylight.'

But other types of walks had other purposes. There was the 'straight on end to a definite goal at a round pace' walk, and the 'objectless, loitering,

* Dickens prided himself on keeping up a regular pace of four and a half miles per hour. Over a mere five miles, this was a 'breather'; friends learnt to be wary of his 'busters', which lasted up to thirty miles.

and purely vagabond' walk: walking to get places, and walking for the fun of it, for looking, and for being looked at. Many people did both, but it may be that Dickens wrote more about walking and wandering than anyone else. 'Whenever we have an hour or two to spare, there is nothing we enjoy more than a little amateur vagrancy – walking up one street and down another, and staring into shop windows, and gazing about as if, instead of being on intimate terms with every shop and house... the whole were an unknown region to our wandering mind.' According to his contemporaries, he was 'on intimate terms' with almost every district. A man who had worked with him when he had been an adolescent solicitor's clerk said, 'He knew it all from Bow to Brentford.' Four decades later, at the end of his life, they were saying the same: give Dickens the name of almost any street and he could 'tell you all that is in it, what each shop was, what the grocer's name was, [and] how many scraps of orange-peel there were on the pavement'. His London, in the words of a reviewer, was described 'with the accuracy of a cabman'.

Walking kept the author himself anchored to the great city. In his youth, Dickens described 'lounging one evening, down Oxford-street'; later, as a magazine editor, he recommended to his journalists that they actively choose their subjects in the city that he still found a daily novelty: 'Suggest to him Saturday night in London, or London Markets... the most extraordinary men... the most extraordinary things... the strangest Shows – and the wildest'. In the decade before his death, he assumed the guise of 'The Uncommercial Traveller' (a 'traveller' being a travelling salesman), 'always on the road... I travel for the great house of Human Interest Brothers... I am always wandering here and there... seeing many little things, and some great things, which, because they interest me, I think may interest others.'

Previous essays about London, by authors such as Charles Lamb and Leigh Hunt, had been filled with history, with learned asides, with a great panoply of education. Dickens, from the first, with *Sketches by Boz*, truly did sketch what he saw: the people of the streets and the world that these people lived in. *Pickwick Papers* had originally been planned as a series of vignettes 'illustrative of manners and life in the country', as the Londoner Mr Pickwick makes tours into different parts of the country. In the fourth instalment the cockney servant Sam Weller appeared at the White Hart Inn, in the Borough, south of the river. His knowledge of London was much like that of his creator, 'extensive and peculiar', and with him Dickens found his subject and his audience – for it was with this issue that sales took off and success was assured.

For the rest of his career, Dickens continued to find his subjects in the streets, or in journalistic descriptions of the streets. In *Dombey and Son*, Rob the Grinder is a working-class boy sent to a school through a charity that obliged him to wear a specific old-fashioned uniform. The *Illustrated London News* printed engravings of these outfits four years before the novel was begun. In *Our Mutual Friend*, Gaffer Hexam, who dredges corpses out of the river, the dustmen who collect household waste and Betty Higden, the itinerant pedlar, all have their street equivalents in Henry Mayhew's great compendium of the London street workers, *London Labour and the London Poor*. And in *Household Words* Dickens remembered a woman who had roamed Berners Street in his childhood, and who was said to have lost her mind when abandoned by her fiancé, wearing her wedding dress ever after – the inspiration for Miss Havisham in *Great Expectations*, found on the London streets.

These streets that Dickens drew on his whole life were a hive of activity, a route for commuters, a passage from home to work and from work to home. But they were also a place of work itself, as well as one of leisure and amusement. The streets had purpose to them; they were a destination as well as a means of reaching a destination.

'The streets' were not, however, a stable entity throughout the century. They, like London, were undergoing an unprecedented transformation: they were old, with much of London dating to its reconstruction after the Great Fire of 1666; and they were new, as modernity gathered pace and changed the face of the city, bringing railways, street lighting and other innovations; they were constantly renewing – London was, for most of the century, one never-ending building site. In 1800, London was already the largest city ever known, double the size of Paris with more than 1 million inhabitants, living in 136,000 houses; by 1851 nearly 3 million people occupied 306,000 houses;

at the end of the century, that figure had more than doubled again, to 6.5 million people, and 6 million houses had gone up over the previous seventy-five years. These statistics omit the new roads that had been constructed, the shops that had been built, the offices, the railway and underground stations, the sewers, the water mains and all the other infrastructure of modernity that had been added to the essentially seventeenth-century city that London had been in 1800.

And within the single entity called London, many Londons existed simultaneously. At two in the morning at a street vendor's coffee stall, young men on a night out might look for prostitutes, among the milliners' drudges returning home after another sixteen-hour day, who themselves had passed street children sleeping on doorsteps and under the railway arches. They, in their turn, foraged for their breakfast at four in the morning among market refuse, nimbly avoiding the carriages of the wealthy, who were returning home from assemblies and balls. These vehicles crossed the paths of the watercress sellers heading for the markets before dawn, so that they could be on their suburban selling routes by six, to supply breakfast greens to the households of the now-sleeping young men. Similarly London could be measured in time as well as space, physically and metaphorically. Covent Garden was the location of the market and the thriving vice trade; it was the centre that fed the populace and the location of two of London's most important theatres. Drury Lane, behind the market, was a byword for poverty and filth, while the Lowther Arcade, a few hundred yards away, was the haunt of the wealthy who lounged their days away shopping for luxury goods.

The economist and journalist Walter Bagehot encapsulated Dickens' encyclopaedic embrace of the city in a neat metaphor: 'London is like a newspaper. Everything is there, and everything is disconnected...As we change from the broad leader to the squalid police report, we pass a corner and we are in a changed world.' Dickens' critics complain that his characters are caricatures, with mannerisms and tics substituting for personality and emotion. But Dickens was capturing actual people as they flitted along the streets, their phrases overheard, their characters snatched on the hoof as they passed each other in London's hurly-burly. He created, he said, a 'fanciful photograph in my mind'. 'I couldn't help,' he wrote, 'looking upon my mind...as a sort of capitally prepared and highly sensitive [photographic] plate. And I said, without the least conceit... "it really is a pleasure to work with you, you receive the impression so nicely".'*

Whilst these impressions were real, they were also radically reworked by Dickens' imagination to create new realities, well recognized by his fellow artists. Henry James described Dickens' type of fiction, with its real places and real street names, as having the 'solidity of specification'; Ralph Waldo Emerson spoke of Dickens' 'London tracts'. So real were these tracts that when the American historian Francis Parkman arrived in London, 'I thought I had been there before. There, in flesh and blood, was the whole host of characters that figured' in Dickens – the people, the traffic: everything, he marvelled.

Details that Londoners didn't even notice they were noticing were given a place in the sharp-eyed author's books. Like foreigners, Dickens noted the native customs: he reproduced them faithfully for the locals, just as the visitors reported them to their audiences at home. In *À Rebours* (1884), by the French decadent novelist J.-K. Huysmans, the hero drifts into a daydream in an English bar in Paris, peopling the Parisian cellar with customers culled from his favourite Dickens novels. 'He settled down comfortably in this London of the imagination...believing for a moment that the dismal hootings of the tugs behind the Tuileries were coming from boats on the Thames.' As Walter Benjamin quoted half a century later, 'Dickens did not stamp these places on his mind; he stamped his mind on these places.' Dickens created London as much as London created Dickens.

As the city changed, what was imagination and what reportage has blurred and become hard to distinguish. Jokes that Dickens' readers understood, dry asides on the streets that he and they walked so regularly, for us lie deeply buried. This book is an attempt to bring these details to the surface once more, to look at the streets of London as Dickens and his

* It is worth remembering that the great illustrator of Dickens' work named himself 'Phiz', which was slang for face, from 'physiognomy'; the two men together captured the faces that passed them daily, giving the anonymous crowds characters.

fellow Londoners saw it, to examine its workings, to take a walk, in effect, through the city as it appeared in Dickens' lifetime, from 1812 to 1870.

Mr Micawber, the young David Copperfield's feckless but faithful friend, offered his services on David's first day in London: 'Under the impression…that your peregrinations in this metropolis have not as yet been extensive, and that you might have some difficulty in penetrating the arcana of the Modern Babylon…in short…that you might lose yourself – I shall be happy to call this evening, and install you in the knowledge of the nearest way.'

The arcana of the modern Babylon: like Mr Micawber, Dickens reveals to his readers the occult secrets of London, installing in us, his readers, the knowledge of the nearest, and best, way. The least we can do is follow him.

PART ONE

The City Wakes

1810: The Berners Street Hoax

Early one morning in November 1810, long before breakfast, a chimney sweep knocked at the basement door of a respectable house in Berners Street, just north of Oxford Street. He had been sent for, he said. Mystified, the residents said they had no need of a sweep and closed the door. That was the last moment of peace they had that day, for soon the house was besieged by sweeps, all claiming they had been summoned. They were swiftly followed by dozens of wagons bringing coal that the drivers said had been ordered, and by legions of fishmongers with the day's catch, also apparently required by the house's mistress, one Mrs Tottenham.

Soon came 'piano-fortes by dozens, and coal-waggons by scores – two thousand five hundred raspberry tarts from half a hundred pastry-cooks – a squad of surgeons – a battalion of physicians, and a legion of apothecaries – lovers to see sweethearts; ladies to find lovers – upholsterers to furnish houses, and architects to build them – gigs, dog-carts, and glass-coaches, enough to convey half the free-holders of Middlesex to Brentford'. Before this horde had retreated, on came an endless stream of tradespeople:

> Invitations and orders were sent in her name,
> (In truth, I must own, 'twas a scandalous shame)
> To milliners, wine-merchants, lawyers, musicians,
> Oculists, coal-merchants, barbers, opticians,
> Men of fashion, men cooks, surgeons, sweeps, undertakers,
> Confectioners, fishmongers, innkeepers, bakers,
> Men-midwives – the man who exhibits a bear,
> And, O worse than all! to his *lordship the mayor*.
> All were earnestly begged to be at her door
> Precisely at *two*, or a little before,
> The surgeons first, armed with catheters, arrive
> And impatiently ask is the patient alive.

> The man servant stares – now ten midwives appear,
> 'Pray, sir, does the lady in labor [sic] live here?'
> 'Here's a shell,' cries a man, 'for the lady that's dead,
> 'My master's behind with the coffin of lead.'
> Next a waggon, with furniture loaded approaches,
> Then a hearse all be-plumed and six mourning coaches,
> Six baskets of groceries – sugars, teas, figs;
> Ten drays full of beer – twenty boxes of wigs.
> Fifty hampers of wine, twenty dozen French rolls,
> Fifteen huge waggon loads of best Newcastle coals –
> But the best joke of all was to see the fine coach
> Of his worship the mayor, all bedizen'd, approach;
> As it pass'd up the street the mob shouted aloud,
> His lordship was pleased, and most affably bow'd,
> Supposing, poor man, he was *cheered* by the crowd...

These were followed by rows of carriages bearing the city's grandees, all invited to a party. Then came the chairman of the East India Company and the Governor of the Bank of England, both of whom had been promised information on supposed frauds on their companies; even royalty was summoned, in the person of the Duke of Gloucester, who arrived to hear the deathbed confession of an aged family retainer.

The street now teemed with people, their anger at having their time and money wasted dissipating as tradesmen who had been turned away stayed to watch the next batch of hopefuls arrive, to shouts of laughter. But the Lord Mayor was not amused, driving off to the Marlborough Street Police Office to lay a complaint before the magistrates.

> ...his lordship, it seems, is no friend to such jokes...
> In sooth 'twas a shame (not withstanding 'twas witty)
> To make such a fool of the *lord of the city*...
> Away drove his lordship, by thousands attended,
> The people dispersed, and thus the hoax ended...

The magistrates ordered their officers out to disperse the crowds, but by then even more had arrived, this time great numbers of servants who had received letters offering them positions. It was long after dark before Mrs Tottenham was left in peace.

Those in the know had, almost from the first, suspected that this was a trick perpetrated by Theodore Hook, a composer, farceur and man about town. Today his main claim to fame is that one of his plays was mocked by Byron in *English Bards and Scotch Reviewers*, but at the time the author of *Teleki* was famous in his own right, for pranks and practical jokes as much as his writing. Rumour immediately attributed this hoax to Hook, claiming that he had sent out hundreds – some said thousands – of letters ordering goods and services, answering advertisements for lost or found items, and directing all to 54 Berners Street, before hiring rooms in the house across the road so he and his friends might watch the fun in comfort.

Nancy Mathews – the wife of the actor Charles Mathews and a great friend of Hook – claimed after his death, that it was not he who had perpetrated this hoax at all: it had been, she said, 'designed and executed by a young gentleman, now a high, and one of the most rigid Churchmen in the kingdom'. (The reality of an unnamed person is always slightly suspect, but it is worth noting that Hook's brother, also conveniently deceased by this time, had been Dean of Worcester, and the dean's son was a High Churchman with decidedly Tory leanings.) Mrs Mathews' chief point was that this famous hoax was not the original. Hook, she said, had not been the perpetrator of the Berners Street Hoax, but had instead been responsible for an earlier hoax, which she said occurred in Bedford Street. For weeks, she claimed, he had assiduously replied to classified advertisements in the newspapers: 'everything *lost* had been found by Mr. — of Bedford Street. Every thing found had been lost by Mr. — of Bedford Street. Every servant wanting a place, was sure to find an excellent one in the family of Mr. — of Bedford Street. If money was to be *borrowed*, it would be lent on the most liberal terms, by Mr. — of Bedford Street. If money was to be *lent*, it would be borrowed, on most advantageous interest, by Mr. — of Bedford Street.'

And sure enough,

> on the following day, punctual as a lover, came... *honest men* leading the animals they had *found*, expecting their reward... and disconsolate owners

> of missing pets, hoping to regain the favourites they had lost. Men and maids... eager for '*sitiwations*', – congregated in such numbers, that there was not a place left... by and bye came carts, with large teams... with many a cauldron of coal, labouring up the narrow slanting street, followed by pianoforte carriages – crates of china and glass... rolls of carpeting – potatoes and firewood... trays of turtle – bags of flour – packages of flannel and linen – packing cases and trunks of every dimension – chariots and horses – asses – dogs – brewers' drays and butchers' trays – confectionery and books – wheel-barrows, surgeons' instruments and mangles – sides of bacon – boots and shoes – bows and arrows – guns and pistols, &c. &c.

As with Berners Street later, when the hoax was discovered at first everyone was enraged, until a change of mood overcame the crowd, and each person hoaxed remained for the sheer amusement of seeing their successors being imposed upon in turn: 'on each arrival a loud huzza from the assembled crowd proclaimed "*a brother won!*"'

Whether the site was Bedford Street, or Berners Street, the hoax took place in public, to be enjoyed by the public, not by a discerning, self-selecting group, such as would buy a book, or a newspaper, or go to a play, but by the indiscriminate pedestrian, the random passer-by. The perpetrator of the hoax, whether Hook or the high and rigid churchman, saw the streets not as a place to pass through on the way from one building to another, but as a place worth being in. Two months later, an epilogue to a play staged at the Lyceum included a mention of a '*Hoax*' that had 'set London in a grin' for the pleasure of giving 'gazing mobs a treat'. The enjoyment was not for the perpetrators but for the participants: those in the street.

The streets of London in the nineteenth century were, in many cases, the same ones we walk today. But not only did they look different, their purpose was different; they were used differently. It is that use, that idea of purpose, that needs to be recaptured.

1.

EARLY TO RISE

It is 2.30 in the morning. It is still night, but it is also 'tomorrow'. By this hour at Covent Garden market, in the centre of London, the streets are alive. Long lines of carts and vans and costermongers' barrows are forming in the surrounding streets. Lights are being lit 'in the upper windows of public houses – not the inhabitants retiring to rest, but of active proprietors preparing… for the new day… The roadway is already blocked up, and the by-streets are rapidly filling.'

By dawn, the streets leading into London were regularly filled with carriages, with carts laden with goods, and with long lines of men and women (mostly women), plodding down Piccadilly, along Green Park, on their way to Covent Garden, carrying heavy baskets of fruit on their heads as they walked from the market gardens in Fulham several miles away. More approached Covent Garden from the south, from the market gardens that lined the south-west side of the river.

Interspersed with these suppliers and produce sellers were many more who made their living around and in the markets. The coffee-stall keepers appeared carrying cans of coffee from yokes on their shoulders, the little smudge-pot charcoal fires already lit underneath, winking in the diminishing darkness. Then 'a butcher's light chaise-cart rattled past… with the men huddled in the bottom of the vehicle, behind the driver… dozing as they drove along', followed by 'some tall and stalwart brewer's drayman… (for these men are among the first in the streets), in his dirty, drab, flushing jacket, red night-cap, and leathern leggings'.

These early risers had woken long before daybreak with the aide of various stratagems. Alarm clocks had not yet been invented (wind-up alarm

The lithographer George Scharf sketched street traders and market porters in 1841, showing the many different ways they transported their wares.

clocks did not appear until 1876), and even clocks were beyond the reach of most workers.* In the first three decades of the century, the watch patrolled the streets nightly, dressed in long, drab greatcoats and slouch hats, carrying rattles and calling out the half-hours. For a small fee, these men stopped at houses along their routes, to waken anyone who needed to be up at a specific time. Later this job of knocking up, as it became known, was taken on by the police – a useful way to earn a little extra cash, as well as an aid to good community relations. As the constables walked their beats, they

* It was for this reason that street clocks were common. The lack of timepieces generally was the source of the running joke, renewed by Dickens in *Bleak House*, where 'we met the cook round the corner coming out of a public-house, wiping her mouth. She mentioned, as she passed us, that she had been to see what o'clock it was.'

tapped on the window with a long stick, or banged the knocker as they passed, waiting for an 'All right!' to be shouted from indoors in acknowledgement. The very poor, who could not afford the requisite penny or two a week, paid a halfpenny or so to an equally poor fellow worker who woke his friends on his way home from nightwork.

Among the first people out on the street each morning were the coffee-stall keepers. Today, eating out is more expensive than cooking at home, but in the nineteenth century the situation was reversed. Most of the working class lived in rooms, not houses. They might have had access to a communal kitchen, but more often they cooked in their own fireplace: to boil a kettle before going to work, leaving the fire to burn when there was no one home, was costly, time-consuming and wasteful. Water was a rare and precious commodity in working-class housing, which did not begin to see piped water (usually just to the basement kitchens) until late in the century. The nearest running water might be a street pump, which functioned for just a few hours a week. Several factors – the lack of storage space, routine infestations of vermin and being able, because of the cost, to buy food only in tiny quantities – meant that storing any foodstuff, even tea, overnight was unusual. Workers therefore expected to purchase their breakfast on their way to work.

After getting up in the dark and the cold, wrote Thomas Wright, an ex-labouring man,* 'the gleam from the hot-coffee stall comes like a guiding star... Here you get warmth to your hands on the outside of the cup, and for the inner man from the liquid, which you get piping hot, for the proprietors of the stalls are aware that that quality is regarded by their morning customers before strength or sweetness.' These stalls mostly appeared at the edges of the city and in the centre, with fewer in the suburbs: in Camberwell, in the late 1850s, one memoirist says that there were 'street refreshment stalls at night in some localities, but I never saw one'. On the major routes, however,

* Thomas Wright (1839–1909) was the son of a blacksmith who became a tramping worker (see pp. 164–5), before finding employment as a manual labourer in an engineering firm. He studied on his own, and in 1872 became one of the first national school-board visitors, a huge step up in status, if not in pay. He wrote widely on the world of the working man into which he had been born.

these stalls were everywhere, ranging from the simplest makeshifts to elaborate structures. Some consisted of a board laid over a pair of sawhorses, a can of coffee kept hot by a charcoal burner, and a few plates of bread and butter; if the owner could manage a blanket over a clothes horse to protect a bench from the wind, all the better. Others were more robust. The journalist George Augustus Sala described one Covent Garden stall as 'something between a gipsy's tent and a watchman's box'.* At Islington, a regular coffee stall by a pub was erected nightly: out of a hand-barrow came benches, a table and 'a great bright tin boiler with a brass tap', heated by a coke fire, and all enclosed in a cosy canvas tent. A lamp was lit, the table was covered with a cloth and laid with cups, saucers, a loaf and a cake, and in fifteen minutes a snug little booth was ready for customers.

Who the customers were, and which the busy times, varied by location and cost. A cup of coffee and 'two thin' – two thin pieces of bread and butter – was a penny in the West End and City; around the docks, where the customers were entirely working class, it was half that. Street sellers of food, walking to the markets to get their supplies for the day from about 3 a.m., were early visitors; later the night-workers heading home crossed with the day-workers, and at working-class stalls there was generally 'some thinly clad, delicate-looking factory boy or girl' standing by hopefully. The 'popular belief among working men', said Wright, is that 'a fellow is never any poorer' for buying something hot for those even worse off than themselves.

The journalist James Greenwood spent a night with a coffee-stall holder in Islington, watching the customers come and go.† The stall was set up at 11.30, just as the tavern near by was closing. In the first hour there were only

* G. A. Sala (1828–95) was ostensibly the child of a dancing master who died soon after his birth, although it is likely that his real father was an army officer. Sala was raised by his mother, a singer and teacher, and first became an artist providing illustrations for penny-dreadfuls. It was in 1851, with the essay 'A Key to the Street', published in Dickens' journal *Household Words*, that he came to prominence as one of 'Dickens' Young Men', before later becoming a well-known foreign correspondent.

† James Greenwood (early 1830s–1927) was a successful children's author before he turned to investigative journalism in the 1860s. He was one of, if not the, first to dress to blend in with those on whom he was reporting, most famously for a stay in a workhouse's casual ward, for which he became known as the 'Amateur Casual' (see pp. 198–9).

two paying customers, a night cabman and 'an unfortnight' (unfortunate – the standard polite term for a prostitute), plus a beggar. Then came a blind boy who sang in pubs and his father, four street-sweepers and three 'tipsy gents'. From 1.30 to 2.30 a.m., a number of men dropped by to sober up; then the 'very worst sort of customers' appeared: those who had nowhere to sleep, and eked out halfpenny cups of coffee by the charcoal fire for as long as they could; others did not even have the halfpence, but were allowed by the soft-hearted stall-keeper to sit by the fire all the same. Between 2.30 and 3.30, three more unfortunates stopped by, and two labourers asking the way to the Uxbridge road: they had, they said, been three days searching for work, and were returning home, having had no luck. One of the unfortunates made the offer: 'pitch into the bread and butter and coffee; I'll pay,' and, the stall-keeper reported, 'I'm proud to say that they used her like honest chaps, eating a tidy lot, certainly, but not half, no, nor a quarter as much' as they obviously wanted to, after which they thanked her politely and refused the 6d she tried to give them. They were followed by a cabman with a drunken passenger. By 3.30 the cattle-drovers began to arrive, filling the space with their dogs, 'which makes it uncomfortable', said the stall-keeper, but he knew that if he remonstrated they would upend his trestle-boards and destroy his livelihood: 'I'm thankful I only have their company two mornings in the week.' From then it was more prostitutes until around five, when the daily workers arrived. From this the stallholder earned around £30 a year for an eight- or nine-hour workday, six days a week, fifty-two weeks of the year: about average for a street seller.

An hour or so after the workmen set out in the morning, it was the turn of the office workers. Every morning it was the same, a thick black line, stretching from the suburbs into the heart of the City; every evening the black line reversed, dispersing back to its myriad points of origin, as hundreds of thousands of men tramped steadily to and from work, the 'clerk population of Somers and Camden towns, Islington, and Pentonville ... pouring into the city, or directing their steps towards Chancery-lane and the Inns of Court. Middle-aged men ... plod steadily along ... knowing by sight almost everybody they meet or overtake, for they have seen them every morning

(Sunday excepted) during the last twenty years, but speaking to no one.' Thus wrote the young journalist Charles Dickens.

These middle-aged clerks were sober in white neckcloths and black coats, although their neckcloths were often yellow with age, while the black dye of their coats had turned rusty brown. The secret ambition of the clerk Reginald Wilfer in *Our Mutual Friend* was to be able to afford an entirely new suit of clothes all at once. There were also younger, unmarried clerks, 'dashing young parties who purchase the pea-green, the orange, and the rose-pink gloves; the crimson braces, the kaleidoscopic shirt-studs, the shirts embroidered with dahlias, deaths' heads, racehorses, sun-flowers, and ballet-girls... the shiniest of hats, the knobbiest of sticks'. In *Bleak House*, when Mr Guppy proposes to Esther, he puts on a new suit, 'a shining hat, lilac-kid gloves, a neckerchief of a variety of colours, a large hot-house flower in his button-hole, and a thick gold ring on his little finger'.

Of whatever type, 'each separate street, pours out its tide of young men into the City. From the east and the west, the north and the south, on it comes... clerks of all ages, clerks of all sizes, clerks from all quarters, walking slowly, walking fast, trotting, running, hurrying'. This implies variety, but in reality these commuters moved in an extraordinarily regimented way. In an age when traffic was not constrained by any regulations – with no rules about which side of the street to drive on; no one-way streets – walking was, by contrast, 'reduced to a system', with everyone walking on the right. One worker living south of the river bought the *Morning Star* every day at a tavern near his house, and 'So orderly was the traffic throughout that route that I could, by keeping to the right, read my paper the whole way' as he walked the three miles to the City.

The scale made it a sight, but walking was the most common form of locomotion throughout the nineteenth century. By mid-century it was estimated that 200,000 people walked daily to the City; by 1866 that figure had increased to nearly three-quarters of a million. These were numbers worth catering to. By seven, or even six o'clock, depending on the trade, many shops had taken down their shutters. Bakers were among the first to open, supplying servants and children sent to fetch breakfast bread and rolls, as well as the passing lines of walkers, serving them with breakfast on the hoof, just as earlier the labourers had bought theirs from the coffee stalls. The poet Robert Southey early in the century asked a pastry-cook-shop owner why all their windows were kept open, even in the rain. 'She told me, that were she to close it, her receipts would be lessened [by] forty or fifty shillings a day' as commuters reached in to buy a loaf or a bun as they passed – 40s equating to 480 penny loaves, or around 500 customers buying a daily walking breakfast from that one shop alone.

It was not only the working classes and the clerks who travelled on foot, however. In our time of public and private mass transport, the walkability of London has almost been forgotten. But in the nineteenth century, Londoners walked, without much differentiation between economic groups. In 1833, the children of a middle-class musician living in Kensington walked home from a concert in the City. Two decades later, Leonard Wyon, a prosperous civil servant, and his wife shopped in Regent Street, then walked home to Little Venice. In 1856, the wealthy Maria Cust returned from her honeymoon, walking with her husband from Paddington to Eaton Square. And according to Dickens (in a letter he may have coloured somewhat for comic effect), a child who got lost at the Great Exhibition in Hyde Park was found by the police in Hammersmith, 'going round and round the Turnpikes – which he still supposed to be a part of the Exhibition'. All except the first journey are, to the modern eye, surprisingly short, less than three miles. Even the longest, to Kensington from St Paul's, is only four and a half miles.

Put in this context, the amount of walking done by the characters in Dickens' novels is not as unusual as it appears today. In *Bleak House*, Peepy, a small child living in Thavies Inn, near Gray's Inn Road, is 'lost for an hour and a half, and brought home from Newgate market', a mile away, having most likely walked through the slum of Saffron Hill. The more prosperous characters in the novel also walk across London, the women alone at night sometimes taking hackneys, but not always even then. The Jarndyce cousins go to the theatre by fly (rented coach) when they are staying in lodgings in Oxford Street, but in the daytime they walk to Holborn, to Westminster Hall and, on 'a sombre day', with 'drops of chilly rain', to Chancery Lane. Mr Tulkinghorn walks from the Dedlocks' house, probably in Mayfair (this is the one place in the novel not given a specific location), to his own chambers in Lincoln's Inn Fields, and even Lady Dedlock follows him there and back on foot. Even at 4 a.m., Esther and Mr Bucket walk from Cursitor Street to Drury Lane, which probably takes them less than a quarter of an hour, but much of their route is through Clare market and Drury Lane slums. The lower-middle-class or working-class characters walk even further afield. Prince Turveydrop, a dancing master, walks from Soho to Kensington; Mr George from Mount Pleasant, in Clerkenwell, over Waterloo Bridge, then to the Westminster Bridge Road; he returns, again on foot, to Leicester Square. What is today even more unexpected is the number of middle-class women walking alone in Dickens' novels. In *Our Mutual Friend*, Bella Wilfer walks from Holloway to Cavendish Square without comment; people look at her only when she reaches the City, where few women were to be seen on the streets. In *Little Dorrit*, Amy Dorrit, at this point in the novel wealthy, walks from the Marshalsea prison, south of the river, to Brook Street in the West End. None of these walks is commented on as unusual – there is no mention that the women concerned tried and failed to find a coach, or that a carriage was not available. Walking was the norm.

Many of those walking long distances then worked twelve-, fourteen- or sixteen-hour days, at the end of which they then walked home again. The great journalist of working-class London, Henry Mayhew, noted in passing what he considered 'the ordinary hours' of employment: from six to six.* At Murdstone and Grinby's wine warehouse, the eight-year-old David Copperfield works until 8 p.m., walking to and from his lodgings in Camden Town. Many people worked much longer hours. Shifts for drivers of hackney cabs were always long: the shorter shifts lasted eleven or twelve hours, the long shifts from fourteen to sixteen hours, sometimes more. (The horses could work nothing like these hours: two or three horses

* Henry Mayhew (1812–87) was a journalist and social reformer. As well as being one of the founders of the comic magazine *Punch*, he compiled a monumental study of street workers, *London Labour and the London Poor* (1851, with additions until the early 1860s), based on hundreds of interviews initially conducted for a series of essays he wrote for the *Morning Chronicle* between 1849 and 1850. Scholars have since discussed methodological flaws in this work, but no study of nineteenth-century working-class street life could manage without it.

were needed for a twelve-hour shift.) Even worse were the hours of many omnibus employees: frequently drivers and conductors (known as 'cads', probably from 'cadet', that is, the junior partner of the team) worked twenty hours at a stretch, beginning at 4 a.m. and ending at midnight, with an hour and a half off during that time. The industry average, however, was fifteen hours: 7 a.m. to midnight, with seven minutes for dinner, and ten minutes between journeys at the termini.

Shop assistants worked equally long hours. One linen draper told his fellows at the Metropolitan Drapers' Association that he had started to close his shop at 7 p.m. instead of 10 – thus working an eleven-hour day – and had found it saved money: 'so cheerful and assiduous' were the staff made by these short hours that he could manage with fewer employees. Henry Vizetelly, later a publisher, worked his apprenticeship as a wood-engraver, walking ten miles daily from Brixton to Judd Street in Bloomsbury and back, leaving his lodgings at about six and arriving home again around ten. And, he pointed out in his memoirs, he was lucky: City hours were longer. The description of the Cheeryble brothers' City firm in *Nicholas Nickleby* accords with his recollection. Their manager opens up the office six days a week at 9 a.m. and locks up again after the last employee goes home at 10.30 p.m., 'except on Foreign Post nights', when the letters abroad go late, to catch the last post; then the office closes at 12.20 a.m.* The Cheeryble employees thus work an eighty-five-hour week. Yet their business is presented to the reader as the epitome of benevolence and good employment practices.

* By mid-century, every night was a foreign post night, but in 1839, when *Nicholas Nickleby* was appearing, the post office sent out post to different countries on set days to coincide with ships' sailing dates: France daily, Belgium four times a week, Holland and northern Europe twice a week, but southern Europe and Malta only once a fortnight. Post to the United States went once a month, to the Caribbean twice a month. So 'Foreign Post nights' varied from office to office, depending on where they did business abroad.

2.

ON THE ROAD

When Nancy decides to betray Fagin and Bill Sikes, so that Oliver Twist can be rescued to live a better – a middle-class – life, she rushes from Bill Sikes's room in Bethnal Green, in the east of London. It is a quarter to ten at night, yet as 'She tore along the narrow pavement' she found herself 'elbowing the passengers from side to side; and darting almost under the horses' heads, cross[ing] crowded streets, where clusters of persons were eagerly watching their opportunity to do the like'. It is only when she reaches the West End that the streets become less crowded, and even then there are plenty of people about who turn to watch this frantic woman running along.

That the London streets were always busy, always teeming with humanity, is a regular feature of travellers' accounts of the city. In 1852, Max Schlesinger, a German journalist who spent much of his life in London, said 'there is not a single hour in the four and twenty' when the main streets were empty. When Charlotte and Anne Brontë had planned their first visit to London 'in the quiet of Haworth Parsonage', they had expected to walk from their lodgings at the Chapter Coffee House in Paternoster Row, near St Paul's, to their publisher in Cornhill, a few hundred yards away. But once in London, 'they became so dismayed by the crowded streets, and the impeded crossings, that they stood still repeatedly, in complete despair', the journey taking them the best part of an hour. Locals were as overwhelmed as strangers. Henry Mayhew, born and bred in London, compared the sound of the city to the 'awful magnificence of the great Torrent of Niagara … if the roar of the precipitated waters bewilders and affrights the mind, assuredly the riot and tumult of the traffic of London at once stun and terrify'.

It was that continuous sound that struck most people – the 'uninterrupted and crashing roar'.

This roar made it difficult, sometimes impossible, to hear, often indoors as well as out of doors. An American clergyman in the early 1820s attended a service at St Clement Danes, sitting near the pulpit, but even so found the sermon inaudible because 'The church... is most unfortunately situated for hearing, being placed in the middle of the Strand.' Suburban householders suffered too. In 1834, Jane Carlyle, wife of the historian Thomas Carlyle, wrote from her new home, in a side street in Chelsea: 'I... have an everlasting sound in my ears, of men, women, children, omnibuses, carriages, glass coaches, street coaches, waggons, carts, dog-carts, steeple bells, door bells.' The noise was, if anything, worse in a coach. When the characters in Dickens' novels want to have an important conversation, they 'stop... the driver... that we might the better hear each other'.

Dickens commented on the noise directly from time to time, but more often it runs under the surface of his novels. Again and again when his characters walk through the city, they stop and turn onto side streets to talk. In particular, this noise is notable when they are near Holborn. In this heart of legal London, and the heart of Dickens-land, they frequently veer off into one of the Inns of Court as a refuge from the sound. The Inns of Court – Lincoln's Inn, Gray's Inn, and Inner and Middle Temple – were where barristers trained, lived and practised.* Traditionally, each Inn comprised a cluster of buildings, with a dining hall, a chapel or church, a library and chambers, laid out around private gardens, and each represented a legal society, as did the Inns of Chancery – Furnival's Inn, Lyon's Inn, Clement's, Thavies', Barnard's, Staple's, Symond's, Clifford's and New Inn – for solicitors. (Only the Inns of Court survive as functioning entities today, although a small section of Staple's Inn still stands.) The importance of the Inns had declined as training and accreditation was taken over by the Law

* Dickens' employers in 1827, Ellis and Blackmore, were located in Holborn Court (now South Square), Gray's Inn, later also the address of Tommy Traddles, David Copperfield's struggling attorney friend. The square having been heavily damaged in the Blitz, today almost all the buildings are reconstructions. The single original building is, happily, number 1, once the offices of Ellis and Blackmore.

Society from 1825, and so many of their chambers were let out in lodgings. These buildings were densely populated by Dickens' fictional characters, as well as by Dickens himself, who lived for nearly four years in Furnival's Inn. (The massive late-Victorian Prudential Building stands on the site in Holborn today.)

On Holborn, one of the largest east–west routes, the Inns were oases of quiet. After leaving Ellis and Blackmore, Dickens began work as a shorthand parliamentary reporter. For this he took a room in Doctors' Commons, off St Paul's Churchyard, where 'Before we had taken many paces down the street...the noise of the city seemed to melt, as if by magic, into a softened distance.'* This magicking away of the clamour was a repeated refrain in his works. In the early 1840s, in *Martin Chuzzlewit*, Tom Pinch passes 'from the roar and rattle of the streets into the quiet court-yards of the Temple'. In the 1860s, in *Our Mutual Friend*, Mr Boffin is accosted by Mr Rokesmith outside the Temple: 'Would you object to turn aside into this place – I think it is called Clifford's Inn – where we can hear one another better than in the roaring street?' And in Dickens' final work, *The Mystery of Edwin Drood*, left unfinished at his death in 1870, Staple's Inn 'is one of those nooks, the turning into which out of the clashing street, imparts to the relieved pedestrian the sensation of having put cotton in his ears, and velvet soles on his boots'.

The roar of the city was not a single noise, but was made up of a multiplicity of noises. In 1807, Robert Southey published a series of letters in the voice of a visiting Spanish nobleman, who on his arrival in the capital wonders that a watchman, calling loudly, goes past his house every half-hour the whole night long: 'A strange custom this, to pay men for telling them what the weather is every hour during the night, till they get so

* Doctors' Commons, between Knightrider Street and Upper Thames Street (a plaque on Faraday Building on the north side of Queen Victoria Street now marks the site) was not an Inn of Court but the location of various arcane areas of law, including the ecclesiastical courts of appeal, the offices that provided marriage licences and the places where wills were probated. The lawyers here were also in charge of divorce, which until 1857 required an Act of Parliament to dissolve each marriage individually. After 1857, when divorce became part of common law, Doctors' Commons ceased to function, and in 1867 the secluded courtyard was demolished.

accustomed to the noise, that they sleep on and cannot hear what is said.'* But a single voice was not going to make much difference to the tumult of London, with its street sellers, sweeps and dustmen, its street musicians, its 'hundred churches...chim[ing] the hour...in a hundred different tones'. And each area created its own industrial sounds as well. At the docks, 'the clicking of the capstan-palls, the chains of the cranes, loosed of their weight, rattle as they fly up again; the ropes splash in the water; some captain shouts his orders through his hands; a goat bleats from a ship...and empty casks roll along the stones with a hollow drum-like sound'. Behind everything lay 'the rumbling of the wagons and carts in the street...and the panting and throbbing of the passing river steamers...together with the shrill scream of the railway whistle'. For it was, above all, transport that created noise, 'the steady flow' that 'rises and falls, swells and sinks, but never ceases day nor night'.

This was no exaggeration. In 1816, a French visitor, Louis Simond, wrote that between six and eight in the evenings the volume of the carriages shook the pavements and even the houses, worsening after ten, when 'a sort of uniform grinding and shaking, like...a great mill with fifty pair of stones' began, continuing until after midnight, when it finally faded before beginning again with the dawn.† The main ingredient in the din was traffic, and the reason was basic mechanics. One factor was the horses' hooves and the iron wheels on granite paving stones; another was 'the boxes of the wheels striking the arms of the axeltrees' of the carts and carriages. The chief problem was that for much of the century the majority of streets were either paved poorly or not at all.

Retrospectively, we assume that one of two surfaces were used: cobblestones, a word rarely used at the time, or macadam. But there was in fact

* Despite being replaced by the Metropolitan Police in 1829, a few of the old watch hung on in unexpected places: the Temple, private land owned and run by the Inns of Court, had a watchman calling the hours until 1864.

† Louis Simond (1767–1831), a shop owner, had emigrated to the USA before the French Revolution, where he married an Englishwoman, before visiting England in 1809 and remaining for nearly two years. One contemporary historian has described his journal as 'cranky and hostile'.

a plethora of choices: asphalt, granite setts (the contemporary term for cobblestones), flint and gravel, wood, even cast iron were all tried out. The aim was to produce a surface that horses did not slip on, that was not too hard on their legs at a trot, that was easily cleaned and that did not turn into a swamp in the rain – yet each set of circumstances required a different solution.

Macadam began to be laid in the 1820s, and the first macadamized road in London was in St James's Square, one of the most exclusive locations of the aristocratic West End. The surface then spread to St George's parish, around Hanover Square, equally exclusive, before Piccadilly too was macadamized. Officially, macadam was a mix of tiny (less than two-inch) granite stones, spread over a prepared surface and then rammed home by 'huge iron or stone cylinders painfully hauled by ten or a dozen big navvies' or labourers (a name originally given to the men, the 'navigators', who dug the canals), after which 'Stone blocks or sets were driven home by files of men wielding great wooden rammers which they lifted and let fall in unison.'*

When the surface was properly laid, the roads were good. The problems came when corners were cut. Some contractors used bigger stones, which failed to cohere into the necessary smooth surface. Some created an initially smooth surface by placing sand and gravel on top of the stones, which quickly deteriorated under traffic and poor weather. Others failed to ram or roll the foundations adequately, leaving the traffic to press the stones sideways, creating ruts and forcing the horses to work harder to pull their loads on the unstable surfaces. And even on well-laid macadam, quantities of surface dirt formed when the streets were warmed by the sun and the friction of traffic: 'the mud becomes sticky, the carriage wheels draw the stones out, and the road becomes broken up.' When it rained, the 'macadamized streets, mixed into a sickening decoction, formed vast quagmires' of a glutinous mud known as 'licky'. (Less often, but no less importantly, the licky streets provided ammunition for 'the mob to revenge themselves on the police' in times of unrest.)

* Nineteenth-century macadam bears only an ancestral relationship to twentieth-century 'tar-macadam', or tarmac, which incorporates tar and creosote to bind together the surface.

Granite roads were the main competition to macadam. In the 1820s, Thomas Telford, the engineer, recommended that the major arteries be paved with granite setts between eleven and thirteen inches long, half as wide and nine inches deep, set tight over a level of ballast. But again, what was recommended and what was actually done were different things: many contractors used poorly shaped stones and filled in the gaps with mud, which soon left an irregular surface on which horses routinely stumbled and fell; others used stones only a quarter of the recommended size, while less important streets were paved with the offcuts, or the discarded, worn stones from the main streets. Even when the setts were in good condition, granite was difficult for horses, being extremely slippery; grit had to be spread for their hooves to grip, but in its turn grit reproduced all the problems of macadamized surfaces.

On London Bridge, remembered the engineer Alfred Rosling Bennett of his childhood in the 1850s, it was necessary to have navvies periodically hammer away at the road with mallets and chisels, to roughen the surface for the horses.* In snow even this was not enough and, to gain purchase on the roads, riding horses had 'Four sound large-headed nails' driven into their hooves, while wagon- and carriage-horses had their hooves 'calk[ed] at heel and toe'. (Another danger from the macadam and granite roads apparently occurred only in sensationalist fiction. Wilkie Collins, Dickens' younger contemporary and friend, killed off one of his characters in his first novel, *Basil* (1852), using the new street surface: 'As I dug my feet into the ground to steady myself, I heard the crunching of stones – the road had been newly mended with granite. Instantly, a savage purpose goaded into fury the deadly resolution by which I was possessed. I shifted my hold to the back of his neck, and the collar of his coat; and hurled him, with the whole impetus of the raging strength that possessed me, face downwards, on to the stones.' The man's body is later found, having 'fallen on a part of the

* Alfred Rosling Bennett (1850–1928) worked on the first Indian government telegraph, and then in electrical engineering, establishing the first experimental overhead telephone line. He was noted for his great personal charm, which is amply borne out in his delightful memoir of his childhood.

road which had been recently macadamised; and his face, we are informed, is frightfully mutilated by contact with the granite'.)

Wooden road-surfacing seemed to solve many of the more mundane problems. Blocks were dowelled together in factories and then assembled on site like parquet, which made them quick to lay and ensured a uniform quality. The surfaces were grooved, which in dry weather gave the horses

Road surfacing in 1838 and 1842: *top*, the men are paving a road with granite setts; *above*, wooden paving is being assembled on site.

a good grip, but the main selling point of wood was that it muffled the noise of the hooves and the wheels. Residents and businesses in busy parts of the city clamoured to have their streets resurfaced in wood, and parts of Holborn, Regent Street and Oxford Street were all wood paved by the early 1840s: 'The shopkeepers state that they can now hear and speak to their customers,' even, some noted in wonder, when their windows were open.

Within a year, doubts were widespread. The blocks degenerated with fatal speed: three years was the average. By 1843, the City magistrates had already asked for a police report on the number of accidents on one stretch of wooden road in the City, and discovered that nineteen horses had fallen there in four days. Frost also made wooden roads impassable for horses, and furthermore wood could not be used at all on hilly streets. By 1846, wood pavements were being replaced by granite across London; even Cheapside, where the shopkeepers and residents had petitioned to have wood put down just four years earlier, had had to be resurfaced. Soon only a few locations where noise abatement was essential were still wood paved: outside the Central Criminal Court, the Old Bailey, and a few churches and public buildings. (Nevertheless, there was a revival in wood paving post-1870, with the surface surviving on some roads into the twentieth century.)

While many locals complained about the roads, visitors were generally impressed. In the early 1830s, a New Yorker thought the London streets were 'incomparably superior' to those of Paris, 'being broad, dry, clean, and extremely well paved'. The guidebooks proudly echoed this, one stating flatly that 'All the streets in London are paved with great regularity.' The London of tourists and guidebooks, however, bore little relation to most of the metropolis. New Oxford Street, the continuation of Oxford Street that had been driven through the slum of St Giles to create a major artery between the West End and Holborn, was opened to traffic in 1846; yet it was not until 1849 that it 'is [now] being paved'. If a main road could be considered finished three years before it was paved, the slums, the small courts, alleys and passageways of the poor districts were certainly not paved 'with great regularity', or even paved at all.

In 1848, Hector Gavin, surgeon to the Bethnal Green Workhouse and a lecturer in public hygiene, drew up an alley-by-alley record of the sanitary failings of Bethnal Green. He listed 397 streets in the parish, of which 40 per cent were paved: a long way from 'all'. This was true of the more prosperous districts too, not only of the slums. One middle-class writer lived 'on the western outskirts' of London, 'where they were building on what had been still largely pleasant fields' around mid-century. Five minutes from his house was a new road connecting two main roads where both roads and pavements were 'of coarse gravel', that is, unpaved. This type of half-built suburban development was common. In Anthony Trollope's 1860 novel, *Castle Richmond*, he describes 'a street of small new tenements, built, as yet, only on one side of the way, with the pavement only one third finished, and the stones in the road as yet unbroken and untrodden. Of such streets there are thousands now round London... in every suburb.'

Trollope uses 'pavement' to mean the road, not the area designated for pedestrians. By the time he was writing, the segregation of the two areas was complete, but it was a relatively recent innovation. In 1800, a memoirist recalled how in the previous century 'the broad flagging on each side of the streets was not universally adopted, and stone posts were in fashion to prevent the annoyance of the carriages.' Within a decade Louis Simond, freshly arrived from America, noticed 'The elevated pavement on each side of the streets full of walkers', keeping them 'out of the reach of carriages', the phrasing suggesting that the idea was new to him. The reports of other visitors agree that at this early stage segregated spaces for pedestrians may have been unusual even in London. In 1824, the American clergyman Nathaniel Wheaton described coaches pulling up 'in the throng of foot passengers', the drivers giving warning to pedestrians by an 'accustomed *heigh!* in a tone so sharp, as to put the most heedless on their guard'. Even in 1835 a guidebook still felt the need to explain to its readers that streets were 'divided into a carriage-way and a foot-path... finished with a kirb [sic] raised a few inches above the carriage-way'. Separate provision for pedestrians arrived fully only with macadam. Earlier paving methods had created kennels, or gutters, down the centre of each street, leaving the dry areas on either side to be used by all. Macadam roads were impermeable, and were therefore built with a camber from the centre for the rainwater to run off into gutters on either side, creating, inadvertently, borders that divided those mounted from those on foot. The terminology was not yet set, however: 'pavement' frequently meant the road, that is, the paved area, while 'footpath' indicated the flagstoned section given over to pedestrians. Dickens used 'pavement' to mean sometimes one, sometimes the other, throughout his life.

By mid-century, the intensity of traffic had made pedestrian areas necessary in the busiest streets. These were demarcated by posts, or, as one visitor understood them, 'a circle of upright cannon, where a person can take refuge'. Max Schlesinger gave them a more modern name, visualizing them as 'an island of the streets'. The watery metaphor appealed to many: a visitor from Salem, Massachusetts, compared the view from the top of a bus along Fleet Street or the Strand to 'the breaking up of one of our great rivers in the spring by some sudden flood...here moving in a swift torrent, there circling in some rapid eddy, and presenting only a picture of indescribable confusion, and yet all hastening on, with a steady and certain progress'.

At the beginning of the century, the land on the northern edge of the city, still mostly tenanted by market gardeners, was eyed by its owner, the Crown, as ripe for redevelopment. In order to make this viable it was essential, wrote John Fordyce, the Crown surveyor, to build a road to connect the new suburb with the fashionable West End. 'Distance is best computed by time,' he advised, 'and if means could be found to lessen the time of going from Marybone [sic] to the Houses of Parliament, the value of the ground for building would be thereby proportionately increased.' In London distance was more a matter of traffic than of horsepower, for the city's streets were unbearably congested. In *Little Dorrit*, set in the 1820s, Mr Dorrit's coachman travels from the City to the West End not in a direct line – which would have taken him along Fleet Street and the Strand, two of the most heavily used streets in London – but instead by crossing the river at London Bridge, driving along the south bank to Waterloo, and recrossing the river: the trip is nearly double the distance, but still faster.

Many factors contributed to the traffic problem. From 1830 to 1850, the population of London grew by nearly 1 million. The number of stagecoaches increased by 50 per cent, while the number of hackney carriages more than doubled. The arrival of the railways from the 1840s further increased road usage, as goods, instead of being manufactured and sold in one place, now underwent different manufacturing stages in different locations, being transported by rail but beginning and ending their journeys by cart. One of the biggest – and most intractable – causes of traffic obstructions was an official one: the toll gates. In the eighteenth century, many of Britain's main roads had been built by groups of businessmen who advanced the capital to build the roads; in return for their investment, they were permitted by Parliament to levy tolls on all road users. The main arteries in and out of London that Dickens knew as a young man were all toll roads, with turnpike gates blocking access to the west in Knightsbridge, at Hyde Park Corner; in Kensington, at the corner of the Earls Court Road; at Marble Arch, at Oxford Street; and in Notting Hill (the toll was the 'Gate' in Notting Hill Gate, just as it was the 'bar' in Temple Bar). On the northern side of the city there was one at King's Cross; on the eastern side, at the City Road near Old Street, and at Shoreditch, in the Commercial Road. On the south side of London there were three turnpike gates in the Old Kent Road; another at the Obelisk at the Surrey Theatre, where Lambeth Road and St George's Road meet; with another at Kennington Church, then Kennington Gate.

These toll gates were substantial blockages. The one at Old Brompton, by the Gloucester Road, consisted of a 'house-shed on one side of the road, a pillar on the other', with a heavy pole running between them. In the 1820s, the Oxford Street turnpike, then still known as the Tyburn turnpike, was sited on the corner of Oxford Street and the Edgware Road where the gallows stood until 1783, at what is now the north-east corner of Hyde Park.* At right angles to the Tyburn gate was another one that closed off the Edgware Road, and one man operated both, standing in the centre between the two, dressed in a white apron 'with pockets in the front of it, one for halfpence and one for tickets'.†

* At one time the spot, on a traffic island in the centre of Oxford Street, where it nears the Edgware Road, was indicated by three brass markers, but at some point in the recent past they seem to have disappeared.

† 'Pockets' were not what we mean by pockets, which were surprisingly late to develop. In the eighteenth century, pockets in clothes were still mostly decorative, and working men

The ticket was important. One payment gave each vehicle access through that gate for twenty-four hours (except for vehicles carrying goods for sale, in which case every individual load required a fresh toll to be paid). As midnight struck, the next day's ticket came into operation, and everyone had to pay again. The keepers slept in little lodges built beside each bar and were always on duty, required to rise at shouts of 'Gate, gate!' Many couldn't be bothered and left the bar open all night. Others kept late-night travellers, who had already paid that day, waiting at the gate until midnight, so that they could be charged again, the toll keeper skimming off some of the day's proceeds. This was so common that one man at least took his revenge. He paid again, then walked his horse up and down the road near by until he judged the keeper had gone back to sleep. At this point he returned, shouting 'Gate!' to rouse the keeper, before showing his new ticket. Then he idled up and down on the other side of the gate once more, before returning to rouse the keeper. This procedure was repeated again and again until the keeper admitted defeat and returned the money.

From the 1830s, turnstiles began to be fitted with clockwork mechanisms, inaccessible to the keepers, recording how many times the gate was lifted. (According to Dickens, the machine had been invented by the prop-master of the Drury Lane theatre.) Other toll keepers, long after the mechanisms were the norm, continued to cheat somehow. One told Dickens in the 1850s that, when poor people asked to cross but didn't have the requisite penny, 'If they are really tired and poor we give 'em [a penny ourselves] and let 'em through. Other people will leave things – pocket handkerchiefs mostly. I *have* taken cravats and gloves, pocket knives, toothpicks, studs, shirt pins, rings (generally from young men, early in the morning), but handkerchiefs is the general thing.' It is unclear whether the goods were left as a pledge against returning with the penny, or whether this was an informal system of pawning: the men who had lost all their money gambling handed over their handkerchiefs, which the

---

had a pocket only in their aprons. Women's pockets tied on with strings around their waists, like market sellers' or waiters' money pouches today. In the nineteenth century, pockets were made in coats and waistcoats more generally, but tie-on pockets remained commonplace.

toll keepers then pawned, paying the penny toll from the proceeds and keeping the rest themselves.

If there were annoyances and delays in passing through just one gate, the system became cumbersome and ferociously expensive when undertaking a drive of any distance:

> A man…starts from Bishopsgate Street for Kilburn. The day is cold and rainy…He has to pull up in the middle of the street in Shoreditch, and pay a toll; – he means to return, therefore he takes a ticket, letter A. On reaching Shoreditch Church, he turns into the Curtain-road, pulls up again, drags off his wet glove with his teeth, his other hand being fully occupied in holding up the reins and the whip; pays again; gets another ticket, number 482; drags on his glove; buttons up his coats, and rattles away into Old-Street-road; another gate, more pulling and poking, and unbuttoning and squeezing. He pays, and takes another ticket, letter L…he reaches Goswell-Street-road; here he performs all the ceremonies…a fourth time, and gets a fourth ticket, 732, which is to clear him through the gates in the New-road, as far as the bottom of Pentonville; – arrived there, he performs one more of the same evolutions, and procures a fifth ticket, letter X, which…is to carry him clear to the Paddington-road…[He] reaches Paddington Gate, where he pays afresh, and obtains a ticket, 691, with which he proceeds swimmingly until stopped again at Kilburn…where he pays, for the seventh time, and where he obtains a seventh ticket, letter G.

If he were planning to return, the driver had not only to keep all these tickets, but to find the right one to present at each gate in turn. In *Oliver Twist*, when Noah Claypole is disguised as a waggoner by Fagin, in addition to the usual smock and the leggings, he is given 'a felt hat well garnished with turnpike tickets' for that final touch of verisimilitude.

Toll gates therefore constricted trade as well as slowing down traffic, and in 1829 an Act was passed to transfer the costs of upkeep from the turnpike trusts to the local parishes. On 1 January 1830, a few (very few) turnpikes were abolished: Oxford Street, Edgware Road, the New Road, Old Street and Gray's Inn Lane all became toll free. By the 1850s, there was one toll gate left in Westminster and none in the City. But most of the surrounding areas, and the roads leading into and out of London, kept theirs: there were 178 toll bars charging between 1d and 2s 6d in the surrounding suburbs and on the bridges. This cost had to be taken into account by traders, individual sellers and big companies alike, and had to be included even in the cost of a night's entertainment. One of the reasons Vauxhall pleasure gardens declined in popularity was the expense: not just the 2s 6d for admission, nor even the price of a cab to get there, but the cost of 'the bridge-toll and a turnpike – together ninepence'. Yet the campaign to abolish all the turnpikes had still not achieved its goal. A deputation of MPs noted tartly that a Select Committee had recommended that the number of gates be reduced; instead it had increased, from 70 to 117 around London. '(Laughter.)' The prime minister, Palmerston, as is the way of all politicians, ordered another inquiry. In 1857, 6,000 people turned out at a 'Great Open-air Demonstration' to object to the toll that was being imposed on the bridge about to open between Chelsea and Battersea. The toll, they protested, would prevent the working classes having free access to Battersea Park – a park that had recently been created at public expense precisely to provide a recreation space for the people who were suddenly being priced out of it. The

The Kennington turnpike gate, just before it was abolished in 1865, at the corner of Brixton Road (*left*) and Clapham Road (*right*). The left-hand gate has been propped open, and the turnpike keeper may be standing in the foreground.

government ministers whipped into action: they set up another committee. It was not until 1864 that the last eighty-one toll gates within fifty miles of London on the Middlesex (northern) side of the river were abolished.

Four months later, Southwark Bridge, underwritten by the City of London, began an experiment in going toll free. This was the bridge that in *Little Dorrit* is called the 'Iron Bridge'. Little Dorrit prefers it to London Bridge, precisely because the penny toll ensures that it is quieter, while Arthur Clennam uses it when he finds 'The crowd in the street jostling the crowd in his mind'. Dickens had a fondness for the old toll bridges: when night walking, he liked to go to Waterloo Bridge 'to have a halfpenny worth of excuse for saying "Good-night" to the toll-keeper... his brisk wakefulness was excellent company when he rattled the change of halfpence down upon that metal table of his, like a man who defied the night'.

The toll gates were a major traffic obstacle, but not the only one. For much of the century there were, legally, no rules for traffic in most streets. In the 1840s, buses were equipped with two straps that ran along the roof and ended in two rings hooked to the driver's arms. When passengers wanted to get down on the left side of the road, they pulled the left strap, for the right, the right strap, and the buses veered across the roads to stop as requested. Some streets had informal traffic arrangements. The newsagents, booksellers and publishers who comprised most of the shopkeepers in Paternoster Row mailed out their new magazines and books on a set day each month – 'Magazine Day' – and on that day, 'the carts and vehicles... enter the Row from the western end, and draw up with horses' heads towards Cheapside'. Even there, from time to time a carter 'hired for the single job, and ignorant of the etiquette... will obstinately persist in crushing his way on the contrary direction'. It was 'etiquette', not law, that made Paternoster Row into a one-way system one day a month. In 1852, the police first issued a notice that, because of severe traffic problems at Marble Arch, on the north-east side of Hyde Park, 'Metropolitan stage-carriages are to keep to the left, or proper side, according to the direction in which they are going, and must set down their company on that side. No metropolitan stage-carriage, can be allowed to cross the street or road to take up or set down passengers.' The word 'proper' still suggested etiquette, but the involvement of the police was new: the press carried furious debates on this intrusion into what had up to now been an entirely private matter.

As late as 1860, traffic was still segregated in a variety of ways, different for each road, with no overarching rules. When the new Westminster Bridge opened in 1860, 'Light vehicles are to cross the bridge each way, on the western side; omnibuses, waggons, &c., on the two tramways, on the eastern side', while the old bridge was reserved for 'foot-passengers, saddle horses, trucks [hand-carts], &c'. There was still no separation for traffic moving in opposite directions. (It is interesting to see that riding horses were categorized with pedestrians, not with wheeled vehicles.) In 1868, a lamp was erected near Parliament Square that 'will usually present to view a green light, which will serve to foot passengers by way of caution, and at the same time remind drivers of vehicles and equestrians that they ought at this point to slacken their speed': a proto-traffic light. (It exploded and wounded a policeman, which put an end to that experiment for the time being; a plaque marks the spot.) The following year the police first took on the duty of directing traffic, even though the public continued to query whether they had the legal authority to enforce drivers to act in certain ways. The author of an 1871 treatise on how to improve traffic referred to the 'rule of the road', where vehicles were expected to stay 'as close to the "*near* side" as possible', but then went on to say that no one actually complied: traffic converged naturally on the best part of the road, the central line. In some countries, he added, it was part of the duty of the police 'to chastise any driver they might see transgressing, or fine him', but in England there would be 'objections... against such power being given to the police'.

The nature of horse transport meant that some slowdowns were inevitable. The logistics of horses and carts required endless patience. Even important streets, such as Bucklersbury in the City, were too narrow for many carts to be able to turn, and their horses had to back out after making deliveries. Railway vans, transporting goods to and from stations, weighed two tons, their loads another thirteen; brewers' vans carried twenty-five barrels of beer weighing a total of five tons; the carts that watered the streets held tanks of water weighing just under two tons. Manoeuvring these great weights, and the large teams of horses needed to pull them, required time as well as skill, as did the ability to handle a number of animals. Brewers habitually used three enormous dray horses harnessed abreast, while other carters with heavy loads might use six harnessed in line one in front of the other. Extraordinary events required even more: in 1842, the granite for Nelson's Column was shipped by water to Westminster and was then transported up to Trafalgar Square in a van pulled by twenty-two horses. Even when not conveying these vast loads, drivers of heavily laden carts often needed to harness an extra horse to deal with London's many hills. Some bus and haulage companies kept additional horses at notoriously steep spots, such as Ludgate Hill, the precipitous side of the Fleet Valley. But otherwise individuals went to the aid of their fellow drivers on an ad hoc basis. A carter seeing another carter in difficulty would stop, unharness one or two of his horses and lend them to the passing stranger, who yoked up the animals to his cart, then stopped at the top of the hill to unharness them and return them to their owner, who was presumably blocking traffic while he waited. Tolls and turnpikes caused more delays – particularly where goods for sale were brought into the city, as their tolls were calculated by weight, and carts had to stop at each weighing machine.

Road layouts were also a major cause of delays, especially as the roads themselves were narrow. Temple Bar, that divider between the West End and the City, was just over twenty feet across, while almost all carriages were more than six feet wide, and carts often much more. In other streets, centuries of building accretions did not help. Until the early 1840s, the Half-way House stood in the middle of Kensington Road, the main route into London from the west, narrowing it to two alleys on either side, while Middle Row in Holborn was just that: a double-row sixty yards long of sixteenth- and seventeenth-century houses occupying the middle of the street. (Dr Johnson was said to have lodged there briefly in 1748.) This row of shops, lawyers' offices and pubs narrowed one of London's busiest roads at the junction of Gray's Inn Lane (now Gray's Inn Road) to just ten yards. The caption to an 1820s engraving of Holborn at Middle Row reads, 'The part here exhibited is perhaps the widest and best of the whole line of street.' One can imagine what the rest of it looked like. Middle Row was demolished only in 1867, widening the street to nearly twenty-five yards.

The main problem for traffic, however, was a historic one. London had developed on an east–west axis, following the river, with just three main routes: one that ran from Pall Mall via the Strand and Fleet Street to St Paul's; one from Oxford Street along High Holborn; and the New Road (now the Euston Road). Yet none ran clear and straight. Along the Holborn route, the slum of St Giles necessitated a detour before New Oxford Street was opened at the end of the 1840s. A few hundred yards further on lay the obstacle of Middle Row, and 500 yards beyond that was the bottleneck of the Fleet Valley, whose steep slopes slowed traffic until Holborn Viaduct was built across it in 1869. The Strand had its own problems: the western end, until Trafalgar Square was developed in the 1830s, was a maze of small courts and lanes, while at its eastern end Temple Bar slowed traffic to a crawl, as did the street narrowing at Ludgate Hill. It must be remembered that these were the good, wide, east–west routes. North–south routes could not be described as bad, because they didn't exist. Regent Street opened in sections from 1820, and the development known as the West Strand Improvements began to widen St Martin's Lane and clear a north–south route at what would become Trafalgar Square. But otherwise there was no Charing Cross Road nor Shaftesbury Avenue (both of which had to wait until the end of the century); there was no single route through Bloomsbury, as the private estate of the Duke of Bedford was still being developed; there was no Kingsway (which was built in the twentieth century); and what is today the Aldwych was until the twentieth century a warren of medieval lanes, many housing a thriving pornography industry.

Plans for improvements were made. And remade. And then remade again. The Fleet market was cleared away in 1826 to prepare the ground for what would ultimately become the Farringdon Road; the Fleet prison too was pulled down; but still nothing happened. A decade later only one section, from Ludgate Circus to Holborn Viaduct, had been constructed. Similarly, in 1864 the *Illustrated London News* mourned that, after decades of complaints, narrow little Park Lane still had not been widened: 'The discovery of a practicable north-west passage from Piccadilly to Paddington is an object quite as important as that north-west passage from Baffin's Bay to Behring's [sic] Strait…The painful strangulation of metropolitan traffic in the small neck of this unhappy street... is one of the most absurd sights that a Londoner can show to his country cousins.'* Even the river blocked the north–south routes: the tolls on Southwark and Waterloo Bridges ensured that the three toll-free bridges – London, Blackfriars and Westminster – were permanently blocked by traffic.

Almost any state or society occasion caused gridlock. As early as the 1820s, when the king held a drawing room – a regular event at which he received the upper classes in a quasi-social setting – carriages were routinely stuck in a solid line from Cavendish Square north of Oxford Street, all the way down St James's to Buckingham Palace, a mile and a half away. 'The scene was amusing enough' to one passer-by, looking in at the open carriage windows and discovering that the elaborately dressed courtiers were 'devouring biscuits', having come prepared for what was then known as a 'traffic-lock' of several hours' duration.

Everyday traffic was every bit as bad. One tourist reported a lock made up of a number of display advertising vehicles (see pp. 246–7), a bus, hackney coaches, donkey carts, and a cat's-meat man (who sold horsemeat for household pets from a handcart), whose dogs got caught up in the chaos. All was in an uproar until a policeman came along, who 'very quietly took the pony by the head, and drew pony, gig, and gentleman high and dry upon the side-walk. He then caused our omnibus to advance to the left, and made room for a clamorous drayman to pass', who did so with a glare at the bus and a shake of his whip. Dickens was dubious about such actions, maintaining that policemen rarely did anything except add to the confusion, 'rush[ing] about, and seiz[ing] hold of horses' bridles, and back[ing] them into shop-windows'.

Worse than these situations were the locks caused by accidents, usually a fallen horse. Max Schlesinger watched the combined efforts of two policemen, 'a *posse* of idle cabmen and sporting amateurs, and a couple of ragged

* In 1866, a political group was refused permission to hold a rally in Hyde Park, and the infuriated crowd tore down the park railings. The newspapers tsk-tsk-ed about the 'mob', but, added the *Illustrated London News* cheerfully, 'One useful result' of the civic unrest was that Park Lane had been involuntarily widened.

urchins' needed to get one horse back on its feet. Frequently the fallen horse was beyond help, and licensed slaughterhouses kept carts ready to dash out, deliver the *coup de grâce* and remove the animal's body. People, too, were often badly injured, or killed, in these locks and on the streets more generally: between three and four deaths a week was average. More commonly, though, Schlesinger observed, 'Some madcap of a boy attempts the perilous passage from one side of the street to the other; he jumps over carts, creeps under the bellies of horses, and, in spite of the manifold dangers...gains the opposite pavements.' It took a foreigner to notice this, for hundreds of boys earned their livings by spending hours every day actually in the streets: the crossing-sweepers.

One of Dickens' most compelling characters is Jo, the crossing-sweeper in *Bleak House*, who lives in a fictional slum called Tom-all-Alone's, which has been variously sited. An accompanying illustration shows the Wren church of St Andrew's, Holborn (destroyed in 1941 in the Blitz); but there are suggestions in the novel itself that it might be located in the slum behind Drury Lane, or even in St Giles. These seem to be more likely, as Jo eats his breakfast on the steps of the nearby Society for the Propagation of the Gospel in Foreign Parts* before taking up his post at his crossing 'among the mud and wheels, the horses, whips, and umbrellas'.

Jo and his kind were necessary. In the rain even a major artery 'resembled a by-street in Venice, with a canal of mud...flowing through it. And as often as [the crossing-sweeper] swept a passage, the bulwarks of mud rolled slowly over it again until they met.' The crossing-sweepers were performing an essential service, confining the mud to the sides of the roads, clearing away the dung, the refuse and the licky mac, making a central route for people to cross. All day, every day, this was the task of the old, the infirm and the young, all coatless, hatless and barefoot. Most busy corners had a regular sweeper, who held his position as of right; he was known by sight and even by name to many who passed daily, as the mysterious Nemo in

* This is a private joke of Dickens, who does not name the building, but for those who recognized it, he silently contrasted the Society's zeal for exporting religious education abroad while ignoring the illiterate crossing-sweeper on its doorstep.

Bleak House knows Jo. Residents relied on their sweeper to run errands and do small chores, and in turn gave him cast-off clothes or food.* There were also morning-sweepers who stood at the dirtiest sections of the main roads, sometimes half a dozen or more over a mile, to sweep for the benefit of the rows of clerks walking into work, enabling them to arrive at their offices with clean boots and trousers. By ten o'clock the morning-sweepers had dispersed, going to other jobs. Sweepers were often approved by the police, either outright – sometimes sweepers checked at the local stations before they took up a pitch – or if the local beat-constable saw a sweeper was honest and helpful, he made sure that he kept his pitch, seeing off rivals for a good corner. Some large companies paid a boy or elderly man to act as their own sweeper, both to ensure that their clerks arrived looking respectable as well as to provide the same service for their customers.

Apart from these individuals, there were also civic attempts to keep the roads clean. A Parliamentary Select Committee in the 1840s recorded that three cartloads of 'dirt', almost all of it animal manure, were swept up daily between Piccadilly Circus and Oxford Circus alone – 20,000 tons of dung annually in less than half a mile. In addition to this, every day more refuse was cleared, most of which had fallen from the open carts constantly trundling by: coal dust, ash, sand, grit, vegetable matter, all ground to dust by the horses' hooves and the carts' iron wheels. In wet weather, it was shovelled to the sides of the roads before being loaded on to carts by scavengers employed by the parishes, with the busiest, most traffic-laden streets cleared first, before the shops opened, when traffic made the task more difficult. Dustmen also appeared on every street, ringing a bell to warn householders to close their windows as they drew near. Traditionally they wore fantail hats, which resembled American baseball caps worn backwards, with a greatly enlarged leather or cloth bill, the back flap protecting their

* I use the word 'him' because most sweepers were male, although the wives of regular sweepers frequently stood in for their husbands when they ran errands, or were ill. In the 1860s, the diarist Arthur Munby noted a fourteen-year-old girl working as a sweeper in Charing Cross, dodging deftly between the horses and the wheels. He evidently spoke to her, as he noted that she wanted to be an orange-woman when she grew up; the very fact that he noted this, however, suggests the rarity of girl sweepers.

necks and shoulders. Wearing short white jackets and, early in the century, brown breeches or, later, like Sloppy in *Our Mutual Friend*, red or brown cotton trousers, they carried huge wicker baskets and a ladder that allowed them to climb up the side of their carts and deposit their loads.* (See Plate 1, where fantail, red trousers and bell are all shown.)

There were attempts throughout the period to mechanize the street-cleaning process. In 1837, a footman named William Tayler, who lived in Marylebone, wrote in his diary: 'saw a new machine for scrapeing the roads and streets. It's a very long kind of how [sic]...One man draws it from one side of the street to the other, taking a whole sweep of mud with him at once...There are two wheels, so, by pressing on the handles, he can wheel the thing back everytime he goes across the street for a hoefull.' By 1850, the streets were 'swept every morning before sunrise, by a machine with a revolving broom which whisks the dirt into a kind of scuttle or trough'.

With so many unpaved roads, and as many poorly paved ones, dust was as much a problem in dry weather as mud was in wet. When David Copperfield walked from the Borough, in south London, all the way to Dover, he arrived 'From head to foot...powdered almost...white with chalk and dust'. Because all the roads surrounding London were as dusty in hot weather, when heading for the Derby, 'Every gentleman had put on a green veil' while the women 'covered themselves up with net': 'The brims and crowns of hats were smothered with dust, as if nutmegs had been grated over them'; and without the veils the dust combined with the men's hair-grease, turning it 'to a kind of paint'. Street dust also spoilt the clothes of pedestrians, and could even insinuate itself indoors, damaging shopkeepers' stock and furniture in private households.

Water not only kept down the dust in dry weather but also helped prolong the life of macadam surfaces, so by the end of the 1820s most parishes maintained one or more water carts, filled from pumps at street corners. The pumps were over six feet high, with great spouts that swung

* Dustmen strictly removed only 'dust', the remains from coal fires. However, the word was frequently used more elastically, and many called the men whose job it was to remove human waste 'dustmen'.

Streets were watered daily to keep down the dust. Here a water cart is being filled at a street pump in Bloomsbury. On the cart on the left a lever is being pulled, and the water squirts out behind.

out over the wooden water troughs on the carts.* By the 1850s, the rumbling of 'tank-like watering-carts' marked the arrival of spring as they rolled out across the city. When the driver pressed a lever with his foot, it opened a valve in the water trough, and the water squirted out of a perforated pipe at the back of his cart as he slowly drove along, 'playing their hundred threads of water upon a dusty roadway'.

That is, he drove along if driving were possible. Traffic was not the only problem. For much of the century, London was one large building site. On a street-by-street basis, the creation of the infrastructure of modernity meant that the roads were constantly being dug up and relaid, sometimes for paving but more often for what we would call utilities, but then didn't even have a name.

Responsibility for street lighting, originally a private matter, had devolved over the centuries to the parishes and finally to the civic body. In the early

* The pumping was very hard work, said Alfred Bennett. His childhood home was directly across the road from a pump, and to this proximity he and the neighbouring children 'owed our first introduction to swear words'. Note in the drawing above that the man pumping has taken off his hat and coat, which hang on the railings. He seems to have replaced his colleague, who sits on the kerb, mopping his forehead.

1700s, parish rates were used to pay for a tallow light to be lit in front of every tenth building between 6 p.m. and midnight, from Michaelmas to Lady Day (29 September to 25 March). But these created little more than an ambient glow, and the more prosperous called on what was, in effect, mobile lighting: linkmen who carried burning pitch torches and who, for a fee, lit the way for individual pedestrians. Even this was not ideal. By the late eighteenth century the poet and playwright John Gay expressed a common fear:

> Though thou art tempted by the link-man's call,
> Yet trust him not along the lonely wall;
> In the mid-way he'll quench the flaming brand,
> And share the booty with the pilf'ring band.

In the same vein a print from 1819 (Plate 6) shows three linkboys, where the one on the right is picking a pocket. Gay therefore recommended, 'keep [to] the public streets, where oily rays, / Shoot from the crystal lamp, o'erspread the ways'. These 'oily rays' were oil lamps, which, in winter and when there was no full moon, householders hung on the front of their buildings, to be tended by a parish-paid lamplighter. Even when the number of lamps in the City had risen five-fold, the amount of light they gave depended, as *The Pickwick Papers* recorded, on 'the violence of the wind'. And when the lamps were alight, grumbled Louis Simond, the West End streets were nothing more than 'two long lines of little brightish dots, indicative of light'.

But change was coming, and quickly. In 1805, Frederick Winsor demonstrated a new method of lighting, fuelled by gas, outside Carlton House – the residence of the Prince of Wales, later the Prince Regent – between Pall Mall and St James's Park (at what later became the south end of Regent Street).* For the birthday of George III he created a display of coloured

* Frederick Winsor (1763–1830) was born Friedrich Winzer in Brunswick. He was an entrepreneur rather than an engineer or inventor, bringing to the home of the Industrial Revolution discoveries that were not much regarded in France. Like many entrepreneurs, his promotional skills were better than his managerial ones, and more pragmatic men soon forced him out of the company he formed.

gas-burners, including four shaped like the Prince of Wales feathers, and an illuminated motto. (For more on illuminations, see pp. 363–9.) By 1807, thirteen lamp-posts had been erected along Pall Mall, with three gaslights in each, for a three-month experiment. Awed visitors filled the street every night to gaze at the sight of one gas lamp-post giving more light than twenty oil lamps. The caricaturist Thomas Rowlandson drew a cartoon of the wondering citizens (Plate 5): a comic foreigner overcome by the marvels of modernity in London, a preacher who warns of ignoring religion's 'inward light' in favour of this outward show, and a prostitute worrying that, with no dark corners left, 'We may as well shut up shop.' (Her customer shares her concern.)

Whitbread's brewery in the City, which had installed its own gas plant in the same year as Winsor's first exhibition, offered to light part of nearby Golden Lane and Beech Street. These eleven lamps gave a light 'so great that the single row of lamps fully illuminate both sides of the lane' – which is a telling insight into the feebleness of oil lamps, unable to shed their light across a narrow passage. By 1812, there was gas lighting in Parliament Square and four of the surrounding streets, and in 1813 Westminster Bridge was lit by gas. These new lights also made it possible to establish more firmly the separation between pedestrians and wheeled transport: 'it has been proposed... [that] to mark the distinction between the two pavements, lamps should be placed on stone pedestals.' (Iron was substituted for stone for practicality, so the pipes could be accessed.)

In the days of oil, the lamplighters filled their small barrels at oilmen's shops before hoisting them on their backs and, carrying a small ladder and a jug (to transfer the oil from barrel to lamp), jogging swiftly along to complete their route in the brief period between dusk and darkness, then doing the same in reverse to extinguish the lamps in the mornings. To light each lamp they placed their ladders against the iron arms of the lamp-posts, ran up, lifted off the top, which for convenience's sake they temporarily balanced on their heads, trimmed the wick with a pair of scissors they carried in their aprons, refilled the reservoir, lit the wick, replaced the top and ran on to the next post. With the arrival of gas the job became easier. No longer was it necessary to carry heavy oil barrels, nor to refill each lamp;

instead they just ran up their ladders, turned a stopcock and lit the gas with their own lamp.

Central London and the main routes in and out of the city swiftly became brightly lit: by the 1820s, 40,000 gas lamps were spread over 200 miles of road. As early as 1823, the Revd Nathaniel Wheaton described arriving in London by stagecoach from Hammersmith to Kensington, 'all the way for miles brilliant with gas-light'. But the brightness was confined to the capital. The stage before Hammersmith was Turnham Green, where 'we could neither see nor feel any thing but pavements' – it was still entirely unlit. And in the late 1830s, the sexual predator Walter roamed the roads 'between London and our suburb' on the western side of the city, perhaps Isleworth. As the roads there were 'only lighted feebly by oil-lamps', prostitutes frequented 'the darkest parts, or they used to walk there with those who met them where the roads were lighter'.*

The new technology, however, came at the price of long-term civic discomfort. The *Oxford English Dictionary* dates the first use of the term the roads being 'up' – to mean the road surface having been removed for work to be carried out – to 1894, but as early as the 1850s Sala wrote that in his private opinion the paving commissioners enjoyed repeatedly taking the 'street up'. When the gas mains were laid in Parliament Square, sewer pipes were also renewed, and the water companies took the opportunity to exchange their antique wooden pipes for iron – for MPs, at least, everything

* 'Walter' is a conundrum. He is the pseudonymous author of the eleven-volume *My Secret Life* (published 1888–94), a supposedly autobiographical account of his, shall we say, ebullient erotic life. The book is pornography, and those sections have, no doubt, all the verisimilitude of that genre, but there follow three possibilities: (1) that Walter was indeed a man with an exhausting private life, and the autobiographical elements he includes are true, or nearly so; (2) that Walter imagined his private life, but that he did indeed live the life of the middle-class professional man he claimed to be; or (3) the entire book is a work of fiction. If (1) or (2) are the case, then *My Secret Life* is useful for the light Walter throws on many aspects of the London sex trade (for more on this subject, see pp. 393–424), and equally so for his passing descriptions of daily life; if (3), the former becomes less reliable, but there is still no reason to believe that the author did not describe daily life as he knew it. If we take Walter's biographical hints at face value, he was born in the 1820s and died after 1894. I have based my reading of his book on this chronology. Walter does, unusually for an unknown person, have an entry in the *Oxford Dictionary of National Biography*, which offers suggestions as to who the real Walter may have been.

was done at once. For most of the population it was a different matter. In the thriving south London suburb of Camberwell, the first gas company was established in 1831; three years later, twenty miles of street had been torn up to receive new mains. Over the next two decades, competition between the local gas companies meant that 'occasionally as many as ten sets of pipes would be laid in one street'. This became a chronic problem. In 1846, Fleet Street was closed for five weeks for repaving, the previous road having been partially destroyed when a new sewer was laid; immediately afterwards the road was once more reduced to single file while first gas mains and then water pipes were replaced. Until 1855, each parish looked after its own streets, or, even worse, this was the responsibility of each district within a parish, sometimes with different commissions to deal with paving, lighting, water and soon telegraph too, so roads were endlessly being taken up and resurfaced. In 1858, 150 shopworkers and residents of the Strand petitioned the London Gasworks company, complaining that the entire street had been closed to traffic at the peak season. They also noted, bitterly, 'the short hours at which the men have for the most part worked' and the poor quality of the resurfacing once they had finished.

This particular incident did not occur in isolation: street construction elsewhere was an ongoing process. From the very earliest part of the century, when Regent Street was created to connect St James's Park with the new Regent's Park a mile and a half to the north (see pp. 264–6), new roads, road widening and 'improvements' in general were part of the never-ending shape-shifting that London was prone to. The new centre of London, Trafalgar Square, was itself constructed out of a site of mews, stables, a workhouse and an inn. Trafalgar Square and Regent Street were both the fruit of great municipal plans. Far more of London was constructed, designed, reconstructed and redesigned by private individuals, whether large landowners or small contractors. Because so much building was private, the construction process might be especially quick, or it might drag on for decades, speeding up as money became available and the possibility of profitable returns increased, or slowing down when hard times hit. In Bloomsbury, Gordon Square took three decades to complete, while Fitzroy Square, begun in the eighteenth century, was nearly five decades in construction.

For the first half of the century, road widening was planned by major landlords, or was something local businesses and residents agreed on together and then carried out. In one example of many, in 1850 the residents and shopkeepers around Chancery Lane felt so strongly that widening the north end of the street would improve their lives and businesses that they were willing to pay for it themselves. Several benchers (senior members) from Gray's Inn offered to contribute, as did Pickford's moving company, 'whose great traffic was seriously impeded by the present confined thoroughfares'. Within two weeks, discussions had been held with the parish paving board, and approval had been received for a house to be purchased and knocked down at the Holborn end of the street.

Other projects were the responsibility of the civic authorities, whether the Corporation of the City of London, or the Commissioner for Woods and Forests (the Crown Estate, used as a loose synonym for the government). London Bridge had stood in one form or another since 1209, but more than half a millennium later it was not just replaced by a new structure, but re-sited upriver, and nine streets, a Wren church and 318 houses were razed to build the new approach street to the bridge. Other demolitions were managed on a parish-by-parish basis, as when in 1842 it was decided that seven large warehouses that projected into Upper Thames Street, narrowing the carriageway by about twenty feet and producing a bottleneck where two carriages could not pass, needed to be demolished. Some similar projects never came to pass because various parishes were at odds. The plans for widening Piccadilly were endlessly postponed because of arguments between the parishes of St Martin-in-the-Fields and St George's Hanover Square as to who was to pay for the upkeep.

By mid-century this patchwork planning was no longer viable. 'The Wants of London', said the *Illustrated London News*, were fourfold: London lacked sewers and drains; it lacked sufficient river crossings; it lacked sufficient major thoroughfares for traffic; and, most importantly, it lacked a unifying plan to achieve all that was needed. In 1855, Parliament created the Metropolitan Board of Works to deal with building or widening, paving and maintaining the streets. The Metropolitan Board of Works was also in charge of rationalizing the numbering and naming of streets. In the first decades of the century, many buildings were unnumbered, and even streets were often unnamed except to locals. Addresses were descriptive: 'opposite the King's Head Public House in a Street leading out of Winfell Street being the first turning from the Black Hell Flash House there' or 'at a Potatoe Warehouse next door to a Barley Sugar Shop about 30 Houses from the beginning of Cow Cross [Street]'. Dickens described how in the 1820s he had walked from the blacking factory to his lodgings next to the Marshalsea via 'that turning in the Blackfriars-road which has Rowland Hill's chapel on one side, and the likeness of a golden dog licking a golden pot over a shop door on the other'. What today sounds like a piece of descriptive writing was the contemporary way of giving an address. By the 1850s, although all the streets were named, the names were rarely indicated on signs. In 1853, the parish of St Mary's, Islington, was commended for painting a street name on every corner: 'a course which would be a great accommodation to strangers, if generally adopted'.

Even if the name of the street was known, that was not always a help. In 1853, London had twenty-five Albert and twenty-five Victoria Streets, thirty-seven King and twenty-seven Queen Streets, twenty-two Princes, seventeen Dukes, thirty-four Yorks and twenty-three Gloucesters – and that was without counting the similarly named Places, Roads, Squares, Courts, Alleys or Mews, or even the many synonyms that designated squalid back-courts: Rents, Rows, Gardens, Places, Buildings, Lanes, Yards and Walks. One parish alone had half a dozen George Streets. Once the Metropolitan Board of Works got into its stride, orders were given for parishes to rename duplicates, or even merge many small sections of a single stretch of a road, each of which had had its own name. Charlotte Street, Plumtree Street and one side of Bedford Square were subsumed into Bloomsbury Street; Maiden Lane, Talbot Road, York Road and 'several terraces, villas, and places' all became Brecknock Road. Thirty-six street names were lost to create the East India Road, while 'The name of Victoria-road being so numerous... the Metropolitan Board of Works proposes to abolish... the one at Pimlico, and to call the whole line of thoroughfare, from Buckingham Palace to Ebury Bridge, Pimlico-road.' As these roads were renamed, a wholesale renumbering of the buildings also took place.

London was, to many, a great map that mapped out the impossibility of mapping. There had been many maps of the city, but it was only at this time of renaming that the first official map of London was produced. That was precipitated not by the Metropolitan Board of Works' desire for regimentation, but by a cholera epidemic. In 1848, the need to improve the sanitation of London was no longer a matter for debate (for more on sanitation, see pp. 194–6; on cholera, pp. 216–8), but the most basic element, the knowledge of the locations of the sewers, was entirely lacking, and so the army was called in to map out all the city streets for planning purposes. Today the 'ordnance' in the Ordnance Survey maps has become detached from its meaning, but it was the army's ordnance division, the sappers and miners of the engineering corps, who covered Westminster Abbey with scaffolding, from which they surveyed London in a radius of twelve miles around St Paul's, at twelve inches to the mile. The results were published in 1850, in an unhelpful 847 sheets, reinforcing the sense of London's mammoth unknowability.

The size of the city impressed itself on its residents – Byron thought it 'A mighty mass of brick, and smoke, and shipping…as wide as eye / Could reach'. But far more did the size impose itself on strangers. A visitor from Philadelphia, not itself a small town, walked to the West End from St Paul's in 1852. By the time he reached the relative quiet of Pall Mall, he was, he wrote, 'tired of omnibuses, and hacks, and drays, and cabriolets…without number, and the ceaseless din and interminable crowd, that kept increasing as we went', for 'No matter where [a man] goes, or how far he walks, he cannot get beyond the crowd.' In this he was one of many. In the decade following, a visitor from Russia spent a week in London, a city he thought was 'as immense as the sea', feeling dazed and overwhelmed by 'the screeching and howling of machines…that seeming disorder…that polluted Thames; that air saturated with coal dust; those magnificent public gardens and parks; those dreadful sections of the city like Whitechapel, with its half-naked, savage, and hungry population' – a surprisingly restrained description, perhaps, from Fyodor Dostoyevsky.

Many others, repulsed by the city's great size and consequent anonymity, equated it with alienation. The German poet Heinrich Heine, in 1827, found himself on Waterloo Bridge, so 'sick in spirit that the hot drops sprang forcibly out of my eyes. They fell down into the Thames...which has already swallowed up such floods of human tears without giving them a thought.' Certainly the essayist Thomas de Quincey would have understood: 'No man ever was left to himself for the first time in the streets...of London, but he must have been saddened and mortified, perhaps terrified, by the sense of desertion, and utter loneliness, which belongs to his situation. No loneliness can be like that which weighs upon the heart in the centre of faces never-ending, without voice or utterance for him; eyes innumerable...and hurrying figures of men weaving to and fro...seeming like a mask of maniacs, or oftentimes, like a pageant of phantoms.'

Dickens saw the unknowability of London differently. For much of his life he was excited by it, and one of his earliest eulogists, the political commentator Walter Bagehot, got to the core of that excitement: the size and variety, and therefore the scope, were 'advantageous to Mr. Dickens's genius. His memory is full of instances of old buildings and curious people...He describes London like a special correspondent for posterity.' This was what his contemporaries saw as they looked around a city that was expanding in speeded-up motion, even if they couldn't report, or write, like Dickens. The old sat cheek-by-jowl with the new; yet around the corner, something that had stood for hundreds of years had vanished overnight. By the 1840s, vast civic construction was a routine sight. In that decade alone, 1,652 new streets were constructed, covering 200 miles. In 1869, the Metropolitan Board of Works announced proudly that it had approved an average of 100 new streets a year since its formation, but the number was accelerating: 202 new streets had been approved in the previous twelve months. Queen Victoria Street had been created, ploughing through smaller neighbourhoods; Cannon Street, Farringdon Street, Garrick Street, New Oxford Street and Clerkenwell Road had all been built. The consequent loss of variety and individuality can be seen in one small area of Westminster. A hive of government buildings – the Foreign, India, Home and Colonial Offices, erected from 1873 – stand on what was once a warren of tiny streets. Bridge Street, underneath the Treasury, originally contained Ginger's Family Hotel and Denton's Hotel, as well as a pub. King Street, once running between Downing Street and Great George Street, had a baker, a bootmaker, a cheesemonger and the Britannia Coffee-room. Until 1839, Downing Street was the home of 'A dirty public-house [and]...a row of third-rate lodging houses', as well as the prime minister.

The greatest changes, however, were driven by the arrival of the railways. In 1836, London's first station opened at Spa Road, not far from London Bridge, with a line running to Deptford. By 1837, trains ran from Chalk Farm to Harrow, Watford and Boxmoor; and the following year the line was extended to Euston station, the second railway station to be built in London.* This development had personal resonance for Dickens. He had lived near by as a child, and now Wellington House Academy in Hampstead Road, the school he had attended after leaving the blacking factory, was obliterated: 'the Railway had cut it up root and branch. A great trunk-line had swallowed the play-ground, [and] sliced away the schoolroom.' The fictional upheaval in *Dombey and Son* was even greater, as Staggs's Gardens stood in for the very real Somers Town neighbourhood that had been eaten up by the London–Birmingham line: 'Houses were knocked down; streets broken through and stopped; deep pits and trenches dug in the ground; enormous heaps of earth and clay thrown up...Everywhere were bridges that led nowhere; thoroughfares that were wholly impassable; Babel towers of chimneys, wanting half their height; temporary wooden houses and enclosures, in the most unlikely situations; carcases of ragged tenements, and fragments of unfinished walls and arches, and piles of scaffolding, and wildernesses of bricks, and giant forms of cranes, and tripods straddling above nothing.' This fictional construction work accurately represented the reality, indicated by the startling statistic that by the 1860s more than 10 per cent of the adult male population of London was employed in the building trade.

These huge enterprises didn't just alter the appearance of the city. At a geographical level they fundamentally changed the topography of London. There had once been a hill between Half-Moon Street and Dover Street

* Because the gradient was nearly 1 in 77, until 1844 the trains to and from Euston were pulled up or winched down by a cable to and from the engine house in Camden.

in Piccadilly, which was flattened out in the mid-1840s. The 150 yards of Oxford Street that lay between Bond Street and South Molton Street ran at 'a rapid decline', steep enough to trouble horses, which was similarly filled in. More ambitiously, 'a series of quicksands, mudbanks, and old peat-bogs' was drained from the old Grosvenor Basin behind Buckingham Palace, later to become Victoria. The land had long been considered too marshy for building, but the railways made the substantial and expensive investment worthwhile for the private Grosvenor Estate.

But it was principally via the Metropolitan Board of Works that great swathes of London were changed from the ground up. One of its first ventures, nearly a decade in the making, was building a bridge across the Fleet Valley. This, the Holborn Viaduct, was one of the biggest engineering projects in a century of big engineering projects. In January 1864, Arthur Munby took the train between the new Charing Cross station on the day it opened ('Temporary stairs, a temporary platform: the great building in the Strand...yet unroofed,' he groused) and the 'miserable makeshift station' at

The coming of modernity was obtrusively visible: the construction of Holborn Viaduct, for example, reduced one of London's busiest streets to a single lane for traffic and pedestrians for three years.

London Bridge, before walking back, 'passing on my way another tremendous excavation on each side of Ludgate Hill'.* The *Daily News* bitterly reported that Holborn had been turned into 'a waste and howling wilderness' of hoarding, with, behind it, 'ruin and desolation' for 500 yards. For more than three years, Holborn, one of the busiest roads in the city, was reduced to a single lane for both traffic and pedestrians. 'The remainder of the roadway...is in the same condition as that of so many other parts of London at the present time – a place given up to contractors, diggers, and builders, to navvies and bricklayers, to carts and wheelbarrows, to piles of materials for masonry, and huge frames of timber.'

London was taking on the lineaments of modernity before its inhabitants' eyes, although sometimes it had been hard to discern while it was happening.

* Arthur Munby (1828–1910) was a civil servant in the ecclesiastical commission, but he is know today for the diaries he kept between 1859 and 1898, in which he recounted in detail his long relationship with (and ultimately marriage to) Hannah Cullwick, a servant, as well as wonderfully detailed descriptions of a fast-changing London.

3.

TRAVELLING (MOSTLY) HOPEFULLY

The technicalities of the creation of the roads, and their maintenance, were of less interest to most Londoners than how to navigate the city, and by what means. The ways to cross London evolved as rapidly as the roads had done. At the top of the tree, those with good jobs went on horseback. This required the feeding and stabling of a horse at home and also near the place of work. Only Dickens' most prosperous characters, like the merchant prince Mr Dombey, and Carker, his second-in-command, ride to work. The playwright and journalist Edmund Yates worked for twenty-five years in the post office. As a young clerk he walked from St John's Wood to his office behind St Paul's: later, as he rose in the hierarchy, the combination of his increased salary, his income from playwriting, and also the fact that he was living with his mother, enabled him 'in the summer, [to] come on horseback through the parks'. Even then, he didn't ride all the way, paying exorbitant City livery rates. Instead he left his horse in Westminster and continued on into the City by boat.

For centuries, the Thames had been the 'silent highway', the major artery into London and the principal east–west transport route from one side of London to the other. At the start of the nineteenth century, it was possible to cross the river within London at only three fixed points: by London Bridge (where a crossing in some form or another had existed since Roman times), by Blackfriars Bridge (built 1769) and by Westminster Bridge (1750). There were also two wooden bridges over the river at Battersea (1771–2) and Kew (1784–9), but both were then on the very edges of London. By the time Victoria came to the throne in 1837, five new bridges had opened – Vauxhall (1816), Waterloo (1817), Southwark (1819), Hammersmith (1827, the first suspension bridge in London) and the new London Bridge (1831, sixty yards upriver from the old location). These were later followed by Hungerford (1845), Chelsea (1851–8), Lambeth (1862), Albert and Wandsworth Bridges (both 1873) and Tower Bridge (1894), trebling the number of crossings between one end of the century and the other.

Because of the lack of crossings at the start of the nineteenth century, about 3,000 wherries and small boats were regularly available for hire to carry passengers across the river. Even in the 1830s the shore was still lined with watermen calling out, 'Sculls, sir! Sculls!' In *Sketches by Boz*, Mr Percy Noakes, who lives in Gray's Inn Square, plans to 'walk leisurely to Strand-lane, and have a boat to the Custom-house', while as late as 1840, the evil Quilp in *The Old Curiosity Shop* is rowed from where he lives at Tower Hill to his wharf on the south side of the river.

From 1815, when the *Margery*, the first Thames steamer, ran from Wapping Old Stairs to Gravesend, steamers had been used for excursion travel, and to take passengers downriver. By the early 1830s, the steamers had also become commuting boats within London, ferrying passengers between the Old Swan Pier at London Bridge and Westminster Pier in the West End, stopping along the south bank of the river at the bridges as well as at some of the many private wharves, quays and river stairs in between. (One map in 1827 showed sixty-seven sets of river stairs in the nine miles between Battersea and Chelsea in the west, and the Isle of Dogs in the east.)

Old Swan Stairs or the Old Swan Pier (the name varied; it was roughly where Cannon Street railway bridge is now) was one of the busiest landing places, the embarkation point for steamers to France and Belgium as well as the river steamers. Yet for decades it was just a rickety under-dock, reached by wooden stairs so steep they were almost ladders. Even in the 1840s, by which time it had been renamed the London Bridge Steam Wharf and had a high dock made of stone, its wooden gangway still led down to a small floating dock. Old London Bridge had been a notoriously dangerous spot on the river. The eighteen piers under the bridge, widened over the centuries to support the ageing and increasingly heavy structure, had become so large that they held back the tidal flow and created a five-foot difference in water levels between the two sides. Passengers disembarked at the Old

Swan Stairs and walked the few hundred yards to Billingsgate Stairs before re-embarking, leaving the boatmen to shoot the rapids without them. After the new London Bridge opened in 1831, for many years the steamers' routes continued to mimic the old pattern: three steamer companies ran services above-bridge, to the west of London Bridge, and two below-bridge, to the east, with the change made at the Old Swan Stairs. In *Our Mutual Friend*, set in the 1850s, the waterman Rogue Riderhood's boat is run down by a 'B'low-Bridge steamer'. Long after the new bridge removed the danger, 'steamers...dance up and down on the waves...[and] hundreds of men, women, and children, [still] run...from one boat to another'.

Hungerford Stairs was typical. Passengers walked down a narrow passage lined with advertisements 'celebrat[ing] the merits of "DOWN'S HATS" and "COOPER'S MAGIC PORTRAITS"...We hurry along the bridge, with its pagoda-like piers...and turn down a flight of winding steps.' On the floating pier, 'The words "PAY HERE" [are]...inscribed over little wooden houses, that remind one of the retreats generally found at the end of suburban gardens', and tickets were purchased 'amid cries of "Now then, mum,

The Old Swan Stairs at London Bridge, the embarkation point for steamers to Europe, was for decades nothing more than a rickety wooden flight of stairs leading to an equally rickety under-dock.

this way for *Cree*morne!" "Oo's for Ungerford?" "Any one for Lambeth or Chelsea?" and [you] have just time to set foot on the boat before it shoots through the bridge.' In *David Copperfield*, Murdstone and Grinby's wine warehouse stood in for Warren's blacking factory, which, until it was razed for the building of Hungerford market, had been 'the last house at the bottom of a narrow street [at Hungerford Stairs], curving down hill to the river, with some stairs at the end, where people took boat'.

By 1837, small steamers owned by the London and Westminster Steam Boat Company shuttled between London and Westminster Bridges every day between 8 a.m. and 9 p.m., with sometimes an extension loop out to Putney in the western suburbs. Their boats, the *Azalea*, the *Bluebell*, the *Rose*, *Camellia*, *Lotus* and other floral tributes, departed every fifteen minutes, for journeys that lasted up to thirty minutes, depending on the number of intermediary stops. All but the smallest boats had hinged funnels, which folded back as they passed under the bridges. The boats were only about ten feet wide, with 18-horsepower engines and crews of five, and the boilers and the engines occupied most of the space. The skipper, wearing a top hat, stood on the bridge if there was one, or on the paddlebox itself. A call boy, 'Quick of eye, sharp in mind, and distressingly loud in voice', stood at the engine-room hatch and transmitted the skipper's hand signals to the engineer below 'with a shrillness which is a trifle less piercing than that of a steam-whistle': 'Sto-paw!' ('Stop her'), 'E-saw!' ('Ease her'), 'Half-a-turn astern!' Because of this method of communication, signs everywhere on board warned, 'Do not speak to the man at the wheel.'

At first it looked as though the arrival of the railways from the late 1830s would destroy this new transportation system almost before it had begun, but for the next decade the competition instead drove frequency up and fares down. By the 1840s, at least one steamer ran from London and Westminster Bridges every four minutes. The river had become 'the leading highway of personal communication between the City and the West-end', with thirty-two trips an hour, 320 a day, carrying more than 13,000 passengers daily: this '*silent highway* is now as busy as the Strand itself'. The London and Westminster Steam Boat Company reduced its 4d price to 2d for a return ticket between London Bridge and St Paul's, and soon penny steamers were the norm. Competition was guided solely by price, for the boats were neither luxurious nor even pleasant. There was barely any seating and no shelter on board; in the rain passengers huddled in the lee of the wheelhouse, holding up 'mats, boards, great coats, and umbrellas' for protection. The boats were, in addition, 'diminutive ungainly shelterless boats...rickety, crank little conveyances' and 'filthy to a degree'.

At the same time, the number of companies proliferated. Operating above-bridge, in addition to the London and Westminster Steamboat Company, were the Iron Boat (which named its steamers for City companies: the *Fishmonger*, *Haberdasher*, *Spectacle-maker*), the Citizen (which used letters: *Citizen A*, *Citizen B*), and the Penny Companies. Below-bridge operators included the Diamond Funnel (the largest company, with twenty steamers, its biggest called the *Sea Swallow*, *Gannet* and *Petrel*; the medium-sized the *Elfin* and *Metis*; and the smallest, which were still larger than any above-bridge boats, the *Nymph*, *Fairy*, *Sylph* and *Sybil*), the Waterman (named for birds: the *Penguin*, *Falcon*, *Swift*, *Teal*) and the General Steam Navigation Company (its *Eagle* was known as 'the husbands' boat', since it ran to the seaside resorts of Margate and Ramsgate on Fridays).

In 1846, two halfpenny steamers, the *Ant* and the *Bee*, began to run from Adelphi Pier (between present-day Charing Cross and Waterloo Bridge) to Dyers' Hall Wharf, west of the Swan Stairs: with no intermediary stops, and double-ended boats which had no need to turn around for the return trip, the journey time as well as the price was halved. They were, rejoiced one user, 'cheaper than shoe-leather'. But cheapness and speed had a fatal price. A year later, the *Cricket*, the company's third boat, was berthed at the Adelphi Pier with about a hundred passengers on board. Without warning 'a sudden report' was heard, followed immediately by a huge explosion: such was its force that pieces of the *Cricket*'s boiler were found 300 yards away, and tremors were felt in houses at 450 yards' distance. Immediately 'skiffs, wherries and boats of all kinds' put out to rescue the passengers, who had been hurled into the river. Six died, twelve were seriously injured and many more had minor injuries. It was later revealed that the engineer had tied down the boat's safety valves so they couldn't cut off the build-up of steam while he went for an illicit break. When the boiler overheated, there was nothing to prevent the devastating explosion. (The engineer was convicted of manslaughter.)

This was a shocking accident, but in the period between 1835 and 1838, when steamers were at their peak, twelve were involved in serious collisions in which forty-three people drowned: nearly one fatality a month. In *Our Mutual Friend*, the owner of a riverside pub hears shouting and is told, 'It's summut run down in the fog, ma'am...There's ever so many people in the river...It's a steamer,' to which a world-weary voice replies, 'It always IS a steamer.' It was not just on the water itself that danger lay. The piers were built by the steamer companies, or by the owners of the private wharves, at a time when there were no building or safety regulations, nor requirements for crowd control. One pier, at Blackfriars, gave way in 1844 when a large number of people crushed onto it in order to watch a boat race. Thirty fell into the river, of whom four may have died.

Shortly after Max Schlesinger moved to London in 1852, he already understood that 'Among the middle classes...the omnibus stands immediately after [fresh] air, tea, and flannel, in the list of necessaries of life.' Omnibuses by that date appeared to have always been part of the life of the city, but they were an innovation of only two decades' standing. Until the mid-1830s, the short-stagecoach, often referred to as the short-stage, had been the main method of transportation between suburbs and centre. These coaches were similar to the stagecoaches that made longer journeys across country (see pp. 90–101), but tended to be the older, smaller and less comfortable models. By 1825, London had 418 short-stagecoaches making over a thousand journeys daily, transporting the residents of Kilburn, or Bayswater, or Paddington, to and from the centre. Dickens' fiction teems with characters using the short-stage: in *Pickwick Papers*, set in the late 1820s, Mrs Bardell and her friends go from Pentonville 'in quest of a Hampstead stage' in order to take tea at the famous Spaniards Inn on Hampstead Heath. In *David Copperfield*, Agnes takes the stage from Highgate to Putney, and then from Putney to Covent Garden. In *Great Expectations*, Pip takes the stage to Hammersmith from Barnard's Inn, where he was lodging in Holborn; Estella travels to Richmond by the City short-stage.

The short-stages were notoriously unreliable. In Dickens' very first published short story, 'A Dinner at Poplar Walk', Mr Minns gets into a coach 'on the solemn assurance... that the vehicle would start in three minutes'. After a quarter of an hour, Mr Minns leans out the window and asks when they are going to start: '"Di-rectly, sir," said the coachman, with his hands in his pockets, looking as much unlike a man in a hurry as possible.' Dickens' readers must have laughed ruefully. Twenty years earlier, Louis Simond had lamented his experience on the short-stage from Richmond to the West End: 'We stopped more than twenty times on the road' and it took two hours to cover seven or eight miles.

Yet they also offered a convenient and personal service. After dinner at Mr Minns' friend's house, 'as it was a very wet night' the nine o'clock stage comes by to see if anybody wanted to go to town. This was no fictional device. In the 1820s, the driver of the short-stage for a neighbourhood such as Peckham proceeded along his route each morning, house by house, picking up his regulars, and if they were not ready he waited. (Mr Minns, not being a regular, does not get the same courtesy and the coachman drives off, saying Mr Minns can 'run round' and meet him at the inn.) When the coaches arrived at their destinations, passengers told the coachman whether or not he should wait for them on his return trip in the afternoon. The short-stage, starting late in the mornings and returning early to the suburbs, was of no use to working men, but suited their employers, whose office hours were much shorter; the class of passenger was reflected in the price, with many suburban journeys costing 2s.

In 1828, a mourning-coachbuilder named George Shillibeer saw omnibuses on a visit to Paris and thought they might work in London. He shipped one over and had it running by December, but it was the following summer before there was a regular service, which ran from Paddington Green to the Bank, pulled by three horses harnessed abreast, and carrying twenty-two passengers.* (It was no coincidence that this first bus route was

* An 1893 book claims that Shillibeer's buses each contained 'a library' of books to entertain the passengers. I would like to believe that this were the case, but the many reports on the darkness of the early buses make it seem implausible.

along the New Road, one of the earliest of the arteries to free itself from the turnpikes.) The buses were an immediate success: they averaged six miles an hour and the fare for the route swiftly dropped from 1s to 6d, a quarter of the cost of the short-stage. The original French three-horse buses were too wide and too clumsy for London – two could not pass each other at Temple Bar, while at St Paul's nothing could pass a bus, not even the narrowest cab – and they were quickly replaced by smaller buses, pulled by two horses. All the buses had names: some, like the Bayswater, were known by their destinations, but most were named for the famous, or the legendary – the Nelson, for example, or the Waterloo, or the Atlas – while a few were named for their owners. The *Times* omnibus was owned by the newspaper, and the Bardell belonged to the Bardell omnibus company.

Inside, there were twelve seats, with another two beside the coachman (a few models had four, but this was rare). These box seats were for favoured regulars, who tipped the driver to ensure that places were kept for them. When they arrived, depending on which seat was empty, the cad shouted 'near side' or 'off side', and the driver offered the passenger the end of a leather strap. Grasping it with one hand, and a handle on the side of the bus with the other, the passenger put his foot on the wheel and then swung himself up, using a single step halfway between the wheel and the driver's footboard to mount the box. When the box passengers were ready to dismount, the driver banged with his whip on the board behind his head to alert the cad, who collected the fares from the passengers as they left.

From 1849, there was also seating on top of the bus, reached by a set of iron rungs at the back, which led to a knifeboard, a T-shaped bench where passengers sat back-to-back, facing outwards (see Plate 2). The outside was the preserve of men: no woman in skirts could have managed the ascent to the seat beside the driver, and even if their clothing had permitted them to climb the iron rungs to the top – and there was no rail to hold on to on the way up, only a leather strap – once they were aloft there were no panels along the side, so their legs would have been exposed to passers-by below. The inside was low-roofed, and so narrow 'that the knees of the passengers, near the door, almost effectually prevent their comrades from entering and departing'. Straw was laid on the floor, to keep out the damp and cold, but it was ineffective, and usually filthy. In the 1850s, the ladders were replaced by a little iron staircase and what were called decency boards were placed along the length of the roof. After that, said one Frenchman appalled by the 'narrow, rickety, jolting, dusty and extremely dirty' interiors, no one rode inside 'if there is an inch of space unoccupied outside; women, children, even old people, fight to gain access to the top'.

The driver surveyed the world from his perch, wearing a white top hat, 'a blue, white-spotted cravat, with a corresponding display of very clean shirt-collar, coat of dark green cloth...his boots well polished...There is...an easy familiar carelessness...a strange mixture of *hauteur* and condescension, as much as to say: "You may keep your hats on, gentlemen."' According to Alfred Bennett, at least in the 1850s, the drivers always wore a rose in their buttonholes, too. In the rain, they shared with the box-seat passengers a leather covering that went over their laps, while the remaining 'outsides', as the passengers on the top deck were known, took shelter under their own umbrellas.

The buses devastated the short-stage business. By 1834, the number of short-stagecoaches had fallen by a quarter, to 293, matched by 232 buses. By 1849, buses ran from London Bridge to Paddington, and from the old coaching inn, the White Horse Cellar in Piccadilly, to Fulham; the New Conveyance Office in Paddington had an hourly bus service leaving from coaching inns on the New Road and Oxford Street, and from the Bank via Oxford Street among others. At first they were no more for the working classes than the short-stages had been, as none ran first thing in the morning: until the early 1850s, no bus reached the City before 9.30. They were, said the *Penny Magazine* in 1837, for those 'whose incomes vary from £150 to £400 or £600 and whose business does not require their presence till nine or ten in the mornings, and who can leave it at five or six in the evening'. But soon their popularity meant that routes from the suburbs started earlier and ran later, as well as more frequently. In 1856–7 the London General Omnibus Company, an amalgam of many of the early companies, carried 37.5 million passengers, and Gracechurch Street, equidistant between the Bank and London Bridge in the City, had become a hub for buses running south of the river to the suburbs.

The stops were then, as they had been for the stagecoaches before them, at a series of inns. In their sometimes days-long journeys, stagecoaches had stopped at coaching inns and public houses for their passengers' comfort. When short-stages appeared, they continued to wait at inns and taverns, in great part because of the availability of stabling for the horses and, to a lesser degree, for the convenience of the drivers and conductors; by the time buses arrived, it simply seemed to be the order of things that public transport stops were near hostelries.*

While no one knew any longer how they had managed without this splendid system of transportation, they found plenty to complain about nonetheless. The bus conductor, in top hat and with a flower in his buttonhole, stood one-footed on a tiny step beside the door at the rear, raised about a third of the way up the bus so that he could see whether seats were vacant on top, and could tell new passengers which side to climb up. He also leant over, when crinolines were in fashion, to hold down the women's hoops as they squeezed through the narrow doorway. Otherwise he swayed in place, holding on to a leather strap hanging by his shoulder and taking fares from departing passengers, his eyes always darting to find the next, as passengers hailed the buses anywhere along their routes.

Initially, there were no tickets and thus no check on the takings, apart from the word of the cad and the driver; they both therefore had a great incentive to stop for as many passengers as possible while admitting to the bare minimum at the end of the day. Wits claimed that perfectly innocent pedestrians were virtually kidnapped by the cads: they could, said a character in *Sketches by Boz*, 'chuck an old gen'lm'n into the buss, shut him in, and rattle off, afore he knows where it's a-going to'. For the same reason, no cads ever admitted to being full up: 'Plenty o' room, sir,' they cried jovially, shouting 'All right,' and thumping on the roof to signal the driver to move off so the passenger couldn't jump down when he saw that he would more or less have to sit on someone's lap. Or, as Sophia Beale, a doctor's young daughter from Kensington, wrote in 1850, 'he...shouts

* Some tube stations today – the Angel, Royal Oak and Swiss Cottage – are still named for pubs, just as London buses continue to move between fare *stages*.

"Kilburne, Kilburne, come along mam, sixpence all the way" then he stops and runs back and pulls the lady along and stuffs her in and slams the door and begins to shout again "Kilburne, sixpence all the way".' That is, he did so until it rained, and then he charged passengers extra, from which he creamed off the surplus. A snowfall made matters even worse: an extra horse was needed for each bus, and that, together with the increased feed and hay prices in bad weather, sent fares up to 9d.

The drivers also competed for fares. An 'old gentleman elevates his cane in the air, and runs with all his might towards our omnibus; we watch his progress with great interest', Dickens had a passenger report in *Sketches by Boz*; 'the door is opened to receive him, he suddenly disappears – he has been spirited away by the opposition.' This was comedy, but court records indicate that many drivers raced along the streets to get ahead of the other buses and increase their chance of finding passengers: reckless driving was a regular charge. In 1844, two drivers were sentenced to a month's hard labour

At places like Holborn Hill, before the Viaduct was built across the steep Fleet Valley, bus companies stabled extra horses to harness on to each bus before it began the ascent. Mud, ice, rain and snow all made accidents more likely.

after a policeman testified to seeing them galloping down Regent Street; when they reached Pall Mall, one forced the other on to the pavement, where, nothing daunted, he continued at speed 'for some time'. However, once a system of tickets was instituted, the complaints were the reverse: that the drivers dawdled along, while the cads became wilfully blind, 'indifferent to shouts, threats, and entreaties of those who hail them from the road', since they made no profit from the increased work.

Even when drivers behaved responsibly, the streets of London, the weather and technology all made driving perilous. Holborn Hill, with its steep gradient across the Fleet Valley, was a well-known black spot for horses: extra horses were stabled at the bottom of the hill, to be harnessed on to each bus before it attempted the ascent. The bus companies also had men stationed at the top of the hill to thrust skids under the wheels of the buses as they started back down, slowing the motion of the wheels, both as a brake and to prevent the vehicle crashing against the horses' heels. (As it was, bus drivers were strapped to a post behind their seat, which allowed them to throw their full weight on to the drag as they went downhill.) At the bottom of Holborn Hill more men were posted to dart into the road to remove the skids as the buses passed. And everywhere the rain and the mud routinely caused problems, making 'horses sink slowly on their sides or knees, amid the greasy mud, and, having sunk, make fruitless endeavours to rise'. Accidents to the vehicles were so common that people wrote casually of an entire bus tipping over, as a matter of course. When there was a hard frost, no horse-drawn vehicles could go out at all (although small boys rejoiced, as they skated along the suddenly emptied roads).

Even with these drawbacks, buses were one of London's great conveniences. In the early days, they, like the short-stages, gave personal service. In *Nicholas Nickleby*, the omnibus calls for Miss La Creevy, who is visiting friends in Bow. She makes a protracted farewell, 'during which proceedings, "the omnibus", as Miss La Creevy protested, "swore so dreadfully, that it was quite awful to hear it"' – but still it waits. For prosperous men with a workday routine, the bus went even further. The journalist Charles Manby Smith described a typical suburban street in the late 1840s, where at 8.30 and 9.30 every morning, two buses appeared to collect their regular passengers.

After that the street saw no more buses until they returned in the evening: it was not a regular route, and 'the vehicles diverge from their…course in order to pick them up at their own doors'.

Methods of inner-city mass transit were increasing at a furious rate: after the steamers and the buses came the underground, confusingly also called the 'railway'. It was long in the planning. In 1830, the first part of a new major north–south road, from Ludgate Circus to Holborn Viaduct, had been completed, and in 1838 the City Corporation obtained powers to extend this new Farringdon Street further, up to Clerkenwell Green. Partly it was to improve the flow of traffic across the Holborn area. More importantly, the aim was to clear the slum district of Clerkenwell, Saffron Hill and around the Fleet prison. (For more on slum clearance, see pp. 188–92.) A Clerkenwell Improvement Commission was established in 1840, which oversaw the relocation of the Fleet market and the demolition of the prison in 1848, but did nothing further, with the result that for decades the north end of what was to become Farringdon Road lay in a pockmarked, rubble-strewn landscape. Fresh impetus came in 1850 with the arrival of the Great Northern Railway at Euston. The following year, plans were presented to widen the road, finish it off and have a railway running underneath, from Farringdon Street to King's Cross. Just when it appeared the project might actually move ahead, the Crimean War made its financing impossible. (All railways then were private enterprises.) It was not until, in despair, the Corporation of the City of London bought £200,000-worth of shares that building could begin in 1859.

Although people had become used to the wasteland of Farringdon Road over the decades, the construction that followed proved even worse. One newspaper asserted that the word 'underground' implied an air of 'mole-like secrecy', but 'Those who have had the misfortune to live, or whose business has called them frequently along the line of its operations, know too well that this is a great mistake. No railway works were ever more painfully plain…For the best part of three years a great public thoroughfare has been turned into a builders' yard…Many long patches of what was once a broad open roadway were enclosed with boarding; filled with mountains of gravel, brick, and stone…temporary wooden footways, greasy with wet clay, were erected across echoing caverns.' This was no exaggeration. A photograph of later excavations for the District Railway in Parliament Square shows what resembles a bomb site, London during the Blitz, perhaps, or some hideous natural disaster.

Enough disasters, natural and man-made, did occur during the construction. In November 1860, a locomotive exploded, killing two people; in May 1861, there was a landslide; and in 1862, the River Fleet – long filled with sewage, covered over as the Fleet Ditch, and known as the 'Black River of North London' – ruptured. By this time, the work on the underground alongside the new Fleet sewer was moving into its final stages, with the train tunnel being laid parallel to it (see Plate 10). The first intimation of looming catastrophe came when water was discovered seeping into the cellars of houses in Clerkenwell; three days later when a rush of water was spotted beside the sewer, it became clear that the Fleet Ditch was going to burst. Most of the workmen were evacuated; several others were lowered in baskets on ropes, to breach the brickwork to allow the water to escape. But even as they descended, they saw the foundations give way. They were hauled to safety minutes before the wall supporting the western embankment of the railway, a massive brick structure over eight feet thick, 'rose bodily from its foundations as the water [from the Fleet] forced its way beneath... breaking up into fragments' and scattering down 'scaffolding, roadway, lamps, pavement and "plant" of every description'. A hundred feet of wall was swept away, and through the next twelve hours the water rushed north and west to King's Cross and Paddington, a distance of two and a half miles. The water also poured into a mausoleum that had been created to take the human remains from the churchyards that had been destroyed in the construction of Farringdon Road, washing the bodies out into the excavation. It was to be another ten days before the engineers, damming the railway tunnel and creating a trench to divert the water, regained control.

Nonetheless, the Metropolitan Railway – the first line of the tube – opened on 10 January 1863, running between Paddington and Farringdon Street, with six intermediary stations. The previous day, a group of grandees had been transported along the track in open wagons, although Palmerston, the seventy-nine-year-old prime minister, had refused to go, on the grounds that at his age it was advisable to stay above ground as long as possible (or so it was said). A photograph of this preliminary voyage, with Gladstone sitting prominently at the front, is today often captioned to suggest these were the first-class passenger vehicles. In reality, the first-class carriages were 'luxuriously fitted up', with six compartments each seating ten. Even second- and third-class compartments were lit with gas stored 'in long india-rubber bags, within wooden boxes' that were located on top of the carriages. Fares were 6d, 4d and 3d. The first day 30,000 people took the opportunity to travel underground. That evening 'the crush at the Farringdon-street station was as great at the doors of a theatre on the first night', and in the following week another 200,000 passengers ventured underground.

Such was the line's success that extensions were planned westward and eastward, to South Kensington and to Blackfriars. Work on the Hammersmith and City line began in 1864, starting from Green Line (now Westbourne Park), travelling through Porto Bello (sic), Notting Barn (also sic) and ultimately to Hammersmith Broadway. The Circle line began excavations in 1868, the District line the following year (it used part of the old Kensington Canal as its tunnel). By the 1870s, the Metropolitan line alone was carrying 48 million passengers annually.

Not that it was always, or even often, an enjoyable experience. An American visitor was at first disappointed with the reality of travelling under the surface of the earth: 'It was to be nothing but going through a tunnel,' he wrote. But soon he realized that, between the smoke and the lack of ventilation, travelling by underground 'was more disagreeable than the longest tunnel the writer had ever passed through... With a taste of sulphur on his lips, a weight upon his chest, a difficulty of breathing as he climbed out of the station at which he stopped, and with a firm determination to encounter ten [traffic] jams on Ludgate Hill, rather than make another trip on the underground rail of London, the writer got into the open air, and found the smoky atmosphere of London equal by comparison to that of Interlachen.' Yet such was the convenience that soon everyone was travelling that way. In 1875, in Trollope's *The Way We Live Now*, even Hetta Carbury, an upper-class girl, 'trusted herself all alone to the mysteries of the Marylebone underground railway, and emerged with accuracy at King's Cross'.

Such were the numbers of new lines and stations, and the complexities of changing, that even local residents got lost: 'How many Kensington stations there may be... I do not know; but I know... that the officials always send you to the wrong one... All very well to say that we should look at the map at home and ascertain our route: firstly, there is no map.' (After that 'firstly', surely the writer needed no other objections.) Even the station staff were bewildered: 'The folk at the booking-offices are not... uncivil; but... If they do attempt to advise you, take some other ticket than the one recommended, and the chances against you are reduced.'

For those who could afford it, the century had brought with it a new form of city transport that was neither entirely public nor completely private: the cab. Hackney coaches had operated in the early decades of the century. These were four-wheeled carriages, usually second-hand private carriages repurposed as hackneys, with the driver's seat moved to a little outcropping on the side, beside the passengers' seats. Only 1,100 were licensed until the monopoly was broken in 1832. The fare in the 1820s was 1s a mile per passenger, and the carriages seated four with a squeeze. From 1836, four-wheeled broughams appeared too, which could carry 'a large quantity of luggage on the roof, besides six persons'.

It is hard to overstate how poor the hackneys' reputation was. An American tourist in 1832 was appalled at the condition of his hackney: 'all tattered and torn – dirty straw... [on the floor]... amidst greased and filthy rags of lining within, and broken panels, broken springs, and broken pole... for horses, two miserably jaded beasts... every limb presenting a skeleton of bone, with the skin here and there rubbed off'. The coaches were also difficult to get into and out of, because of the peculiar, add-on configuration of the driver. It was easy, Dickens joked: 'One bound, and you are on the first step; turn your body lightly round to the right, and you are on the second; bend gracefully beneath the reins, working round to the left at the same time, and you are in the cab.' And as to getting out, it is 'rather more complicated in theory, and a shade more difficult in its execution'. But, he added as consolation, there was no point worrying about how to get out, because in all likelihood the cab would overturn and the passengers would be pitched into the street. In Holborn and Fleet Street, he solemnly declared, one saw 'a hat-box, a portmanteau, and a carpet-bag, strewed around' every few yards and, on asking if anybody was hurt, one would be given the reassuring response, 'O'ny the fare, sir.' Even without accidents, the experience was generally miserable. If the passenger wanted the window open, it was invariably stuck shut; if the passenger wanted it closed, the glass was broken; the doors refused either to close or to open; the check-string, used to tell the driver to stop, never worked, which meant that to do so the passenger had to lean out of the window instead, whereupon the driver was so close that if he 'had been indulging in liquor, onions, tobacco, &c., you had the full benefit'. The carriages were known as growlers, for the bad temper of the drivers.

But it was the coaches' lack of speed that most irritated passengers. 'If the horse is wanted, it is sure to be eating; if the cabby is wanted, he is equally sure to be drinking,' grumbled Max Schlesinger. When one arrived at a cabstand, it was necessary 'to bawl with might and main' to locate the waterman and wake the driver.* In theory residents could open their front doors and shout 'Coach!' whereupon the waterman led the horses over and called for the coachman. But in either situation the horses had to be woken, or their feedbags removed; the steps had to be lowered and the waterman paid. The standard joke response to a cabman soliciting by asking 'Coach, sir?' was, 'No, thank you: I'm in a hurry.'

In 1823, a new type of conveyance, a two-wheeled, one-horse cab, appeared on the street. ('Cab' was short for *cabriolet*, French for a little leap, describing the vehicle's bouncing motion.) These carried two people, with the driver up front; by 1830 there were 165 of them in London, charging 8d a mile instead of the hackney coaches' 1s. Then, after a few experiments

* These watermen were not the same as those who earned a living on the river. The waterman on a cabstand was so-called for the water he used to wash down the cabs, rather than for the more obvious watering of the horses, although this was also one of his duties: the watermen kept order generally, ensuring there was no ill-usage of the horses, feeding, watering and attempting to keep them warm. He also helped passengers and their baggage in and out of the cabs. For this he was paid 1d by each driver as he joined the rank, and another ½d from the driver when he was hired by a fare. (He also stood hopefully by, expecting to be tipped another 1d by the passenger.)

with form, came the 'Hansom patent safety cab', the invention of Joseph Hansom, an architect.* The 'safety' element was the larger wheels and an axle and body nearer to the ground, giving a lower centre of gravity, which made the vehicle less likely to overturn. After a few modifications on the original design, the driver sat perched up high to the rear of the roof of the cab,† with passengers behind half-doors and a little window. For the first time, passengers could see where they were going while remaining under cover, and the primary sensation was of being cocooned: the passenger 'is in the midst of the roar and the conflict, but he is safe and quiet'. However, perhaps because the cabs were lighter and the journeys therefore faster, cab drivers were proverbial for their recklessness: 'he's a havin' two mile o' danger at eight-pence,' says Sam Weller of Mr Pickwick when he is 'cabbin' it'. Although the cabs turned over less than the coaches, accidents were still common, especially to the horses. The *Illustrated London News* even set out instructions on what to do when a cab horse fell: 'The first measure...ought to be to release the horse from the shafts and draw the vehicle quite away...so that he may sweep the ground freely with both hind-feet, and gain a space...to plant them upon as he endeavours to lift his body,' it began. Even so, the cabs' convenience was undeniable, and their numbers soared: by the early 1830s there were 1,265 cabs in London; a decade after that, 2,500; by 1863 this figure had risen to 6,800, or roughly 1 for every 413 residents. (This is not far different from today, when London's black cabs number approximately 1 per 300 residents.)

Cabs, cabstands, cab drivers and watermen were sources of constant complaints, bitter jokes and fear. The cabstand itself was hard to miss. Horses, cabs, the pump for the horses' water and the equipment to service men, horses and cabs: all took up far more space than the equivalent taxi

* Hansom (1803–82) spent a lifetime producing innovative work that he could somehow never make pay: he and his architectural partner built the Town Hall in Birmingham, but went bankrupt by underestimating costs; he founded *The Builder* magazine, but was forced to give it up, again through underestimation of costs; and although he patented his enormously successful safety cab, he never received the many thousands of pounds the rights were ostensibly sold for.

† The original version had the driver on a perch on the right of the cab, as can be seen in an illustration in Chapter 2 of *Pickwick Papers*.

stands do today and, as Dickens noted in 1851, cabstands might hold as many as fifteen cabs at a time. But the real complaint of Dickens and many others was the condition of the stands, where horse manure was churned into the fallen oats, chaff and hay, and the whole made wet and swilly by water from the pump in the summer, or in winter was piled up around the pump to insulate it from frost. Straw, too, was used as insulation, both for the pump and for the horses themselves, who stood all day in the cold and the rain. Piles of, theoretically, fresh and dry straw helped keep the animals minimally warm, but the straw was usually as damp and dirty as they were, while the buckets for watering the horses rolled across the road and the pavement, a danger to traffic and pedestrians alike. (Many suburban watermen kept chickens on their stands too, to add to the noise and dirt.)

The watermen were poorly dressed, in 'a sackcloth coat, and apron of the same', and their tickets – their licences – around their necks; the watermen's

While providing a useful service, cab ranks also were an annoyance: cabs and horses took up a great deal of space, and the ever-present swilly mix of dropped feed, water and manure underfoot was a constant hazard to pedestrians.

ankles, said Dickens, were 'curiously enveloped by hay-bands', a reference to the men's sheepskin gaiters, worn for warmth. While hackney drivers were also considered to be stereotypically shabby, hansom-cab drivers were generally represented as smartly dressed. A print in 1850 showed a driver in a snappy brown coat instead of the coachman's heavy multiple-caped outfit, pale green striped trousers, short boots and top hat, the reins held daintily in his gloved hands. Both cab and coach drivers wore top hats, but cabbies of a sporting bent later switched to bowlers, and in summer donned bright checked outfits.

Some stands were said to be better than others, the term 'better' implying they were cleaner and less intrusive into the neighbourhood, but mainly referring to the quality of the drivers and the watermen. Of the 200 authorized stands in London in the 1850s, the ones outside the theatres, or south of the river, and in Westminster, were considered to be the worst, while those outside railway stations – where the drivers were fined by the railways if passengers complained of 'insolence' or overcharging, or were banned outright for repeated offences – were 'the top post in the trade'. At a properly run large cabstand, such as that outside Euston, there were two watermen on duty on the fifteen-hour day-shift, two on the nine-hour night-shift, taken week by week in turn, while smaller stands had one man on each shift. The water on better stands was provided free by the water companies, but on smaller or less reputable stands the waterman was responsible for paying the fee to the water company, which could be up to £4 annually, or 2½d a day. Many watermen needed other forms of income as well, running errands for nearby residents, or cleaning pots or boots or drawing water for the local pubs, where they spent a lot of their time anyway. Even for sober watermen, pubs were good places to wait out of the cold and wet. More often, watermen were drivers who had lost their licences, usually for drunkenness, and they naturally gravitated to the pubs.

'Bucks', or drivers who had lost their licences but continued to drive illegally, were ubiquitous: many were drunks, with no family or settled life, sleeping in the cabs at night, and dozing in pubs and coffee rooms during the day. Their ability to find employment is unsurprising, for the economics of cabs were harsh. A hansom cost up to £50 to purchase, a horse up to

£20 and a harness perhaps £5, while a cab licence was £5 a year. Duty was payable at a rate of 10s a week and the driver's licence cost another 5s a year. This meant a capital outlay of £75 and ongoing payments of 12s a week, not including maintenance costs for the cab, or the horse's feed, stabling and medical bills. A horse, furthermore, could work for only half a shift at a time, so two per shift were the minimum. Over a single shift a cab driver averaged 9s a day in fares in the off-season, and up to 14s during the season. If the drivers were not owners, but leased their cab from a master, as most did, they were, by the 1860s, obliged to hand over 15s of their earnings daily for the long-day shift, with night cabs paying 9s. If they failed to earn the agreed sum, they had to make up the difference themselves. A night driver took home, at best, 18s a week, or £46 a year.

To boost their income, licence-holders sublet their cabs to bucks, who gave the driver 1s for every 1s 6d or 2s he earned. Fares were set down by law: so much per mile. But at the end of each journey, how many miles a journey had taken was easily disputed, and many drivers expected to bully and threaten their way to a higher fare. Dickens and his *Household Words* colleagues fantasized about a world in which 'eightpence were understood to mean not more than a shilling, and three-quarters of a mile not more than a mile', but until that happy day arrived, bucks could in effect extort what they liked. If the passenger complained to the police and had the driver brought up before the magistrates, as did happen with some regularity, when the licence-holder arrived the passenger would have to acknowledge that this was not the man who had driven him. From 1853, legislation was enacted to regulate the situation: the driver had to display a table of fares, with the legal distances between specific points.

Yet the question of fares remained ugly. In snow, when cabs had to be drawn by both the driver's horses at once, passengers were charged vastly inflated sums – legitimately, the drivers thought, as the horses tired more quickly, and they had no extra horses to continue with when the pair tired, forcing them to work a short day. For many passengers, the problem was nothing more than an irritant. Max Schlesinger shrugged it off: the simplest solution was 'to pay and have done' with it, but, he added, even those who knew London intimately would at some point in their lives have to 'appeal to the intervention of a policeman' to deal with cabbies. In his fiction Dickens portrayed the very real fears of, particularly, women travelling alone when confronted with these aggressive and often drunken men. Genteel Miss Tox, in *Dombey and Son*, makes 'systematic' arrangements before entering a cab, loudly requesting the footman of the grand house she is leaving to note down the cab's number, before instructing, 'He's to drive to the [address on the] card, and is to understand that he will not on any account have more than the shilling…Mention to the man…that the lady's uncle is a magistrate.'

Even with these problems, cabs quickly became popular as a speedy, efficient and relatively inexpensive means of transport for the middle classes. They were now necessities, even if they were necessities that had to be rationed. In Trollope's *Phineas Redux* (1873), the middle-class but not rich Mr Maule had to make choices. When the weather is fine he walks to save money, but when it is wet, or at night, 'A cab…was a necessity; – but his income would not stand two or three cabs a day. Consequently he never went north of Oxford Street, or east of the theatres, or beyond Eccleston Square towards the river': that is, he confined himself to the fashionable West End, Mayfair and Belgravia.

Most people could not imagine ever owning a private carriage. It was not just the cost of the carriage itself, or the horse and its accoutrements – harnesses and so on – but the running costs: the feed and care of the horse, the stabling, as well as the taxes that were imposed on carriages throughout the century. If a carriage were needed regularly, or the family was large, more than one horse might be required. The needs of the animals constrained people's movements. In *Our Mutual Friend*, when Mr Veneering campaigns for a parliamentary seat, his friends dash about in their carriages to spread the word, but after a certain amount of time 'pails of water must be brought from the nearest baiting-place' to cool the horses before they can set off again. Dickens used this for comic effect, but other novels simply reported these requirements as a natural event. In *London by Night*, a racy novel of about 1862 concerned with fallen women, two prostitutes go out in their brougham in the evening, to drink in a saloon and pick up men. Six hours later, when they are ready to return home, one says, 'I sent the [coachman] home to change his horse, but it must have returned some time [ago]' – horses could not stand about for hours, and visits, even to saloons brimming with loose women, had to be planned. By mid-century there were only 10,000 private carriages in London – 1 for every 260 people, and this number included jobbing carriages, which were actually commercial vehicles, hired out by the day or hour. So low did the number sink that by the 1860s builders no longer routinely built mews behind even prosperous streets, for their owners were unlikely to need stables.

A major component in the cost was the staff needed to service a carriage: the coachman and possibly a tiger, or groom. Footmen stood on the back step, ready to jump down to help the passengers into and out of the carriage.* Footmen were also known for the flamboyant manner in which they knocked on doors while their masters waited in the carriages. When Tom Pinch first arrives in London in *Martin Chuzzlewit*, no one answers his polite little rap at a door, at which Tom concludes, 'I am afraid that's not a London knock.' Foreigners were amazed to discover that there was a recognized, if unspoken, hierarchy of doorknocks in the city. The German journalist Max Schlesinger viewed the knocker as

> the most difficult of all musical instruments. It requires a good ear and a skilful hand...The postman gives two loud raps in quick succession; and for the visitor a gentle but peremptory *tremolo* is *de rigueur*. The master of the house gives a *tremolo crescendo*, and the servant who announces his master, turns the knocker into a battering ram...Tradesmen, on the other hand...are not allowed to touch the knockers – they ring a bell which

* According to *The Traveller's Oracle* of 1828, those households that did not keep a footman would be wise to fit their carriages with a set of spikes at the rear: '*Do not permit Strangers to place themselves behind your Carriage* at any time, or under any pretence whatever,' as they will either rob you or steal bits off the carriage, including the 'Check Braces, and Footmen's Holders' (the lead-strings by which passengers notified the driver they wanted to stop, and the leather straps that the footmen on the steps at the rear held on to) 'in half the time that your Coachman can put them on'. Therefore, 'unless you think that two or three outside passengers are ornamental or convenient, or you like to have your Carriage continually surrounded by Crowds of Children, incessantly screaming, "Cut! Cut behind!"', the 'Spikes are indispensable'. This may have been no exaggeration: the illustration on p. 384 shows children clambering unmolested across the top of a coach.

> communicates with the kitchen. All this is very easy in theory but very difficult in practice. Bold, and otherwise inexperienced, strangers believe that they assert their dignity, if they move the knocker with conscious energy... They are mistaken for footmen. Modest people [who knock softly], on the contrary, are treated as mendicants.

As well as their salaries and their keep, all of these servants were liveried, that is, they wore a uniform, each household having its own distinctive colours to identify their servants. Livery for footmen was essentially court-dress of the 1770s frozen in time: knee-length coats with metal buttons and braid, long striped waistcoats, breeches, stockings and buckled shoes. Coachmen too wore breeches, waistcoats and coats with parti-coloured collars, facings and cuffs. Tigers, usually boys, wore tight, jockey-like outfits, and their name derived from their striped livery. In *Martin Chuzzlewit*, Bailey the tiger wears white cord breeches, big top-boots, and 'A grass-green frock-coat... bound with gold! And a cockade in your hat!'

The technology of carriages advanced out of all measure from the 1820s: they became safer, more comfortable and easier to drive. As with cabs, the wheels were larger and the body set lower, making them less likely to overturn, as well as rendering the interior accessible by a double step, instead of the three-fold ladder steps that had previously been needed. Better springs gave a smoother ride, while a strengthened undercarriage improved safety. Different types of carriages had their own strengths and weaknesses, and were liked or disliked for their perceived stylishness or indications of status and income, as cars are today. Broughams were either singles – with one seat holding two people, and a space for a footman behind, pulled by one or two horses – or doubles, always pulled by two horses, with two facing seats – although the one facing backwards was small – accommodating three passengers, plus the footman. Victorias were more 'modern and stylish': also four-wheeled, they carried two, with a fold-down leather hood at the back, and were open at the front. Four-wheeled carriages were difficult to turn, unlike the two-wheeled cabriolets, which became more common from the late 1830s. Cabriolets also carried two people, with a boy behind if wanted, and were generally considered more stylish, less bourgeois. They were also less expensive to run, as one of the passengers drove from inside the cab, doing away with the need for a coachman, a footman or even a boy. However, cabriolets were not particularly easy to drive, and the ride was very rough; as the carriages were heavy to pull, the quality and strength of the horses was crucial. The Tilbury was promoted as easier on the horses, because it was lighter, but it was badly hung, giving a bumpy ride, which in turn made it hard to control the horse.

Another drawback was that, unlike coaches, the cabriolets did not make much noise. This today seems to be a positive, not a negative, but it was the noise that alerted drivers to an oncoming vehicle after dark. By mid-century the London streets were lit by gas street lamps on average just over 200 feet apart: closer on Oxford Street, further apart on secondary roads, and entirely absent on small streets or in impoverished districts. Before this, there were even fewer, so travelling in the dark at a rate of up to ten miles an hour (horses' top speed when being ridden: less when pulling a carriage) was hazardous. Drivers on the roads into London relied on the ambient light from the numbers of mailcoaches entering and leaving the city, many having five or six lamps, and the guard, 'especially on thick [foggy] nights', making 'free use of his horn to avoid collisions'. In town, by mid-century, the hansoms helped light up the streets, having 'a bright speck of light fixed in front of the hood'.

Otherwise carriage lighting developed slowly. In the 1820s, carriage lamps consisted of a candle in a glazed container with a spring at the bottom to push the candle up as it burnt, keeping the flame level; behind it were mirrored reflectors to direct the light outwards, around the carriage, to warn oncoming traffic. These lights were placed below and slightly behind the driver, so that he had relatively little light spilt on him: it was important to keep his eyes adapted to the dark. By the late 1830s, the household Argand lamp had been adapted for carriage driving, its main benefit being a clear glass funnel that did not become blackened with soot as the wick burnt. It is indicative of how dirty the older style of glass must have been that in the opinion of one journalist these new lights made coaches look as if they were carrying 'two harvest moons'. Yet by today's standards, the lighting was exiguous. In 1855, an engraving of Queen Victoria in a long procession at the Arc de Triomphe in Paris showed her own carriage as the only one with a light.

Lights were not always seen as a positive addition on the roads. Many horses were spooked by these ghostly moving lights, and to make matters worse, 'The presence of a number of coaches carrying powerful lights…[has] the tendency of throwing small carriages without lamps into the shade…making it more difficult to see them.' Smaller vehicles, such as donkey carts, pushcarts and all other manner of barrows, were easily overlooked and ridden down. The minor streets in London could be as dangerous as the major roads leading to the metropolis with their much greater traffic. Steamers, omnibuses, tubes, cabs and carriages represented the triumph of mass transport in London itself. Getting into and out of London required something altogether different.

4.

IN AND OUT OF LONDON

One of the more idiosyncratic sights of London was by Smithfield market and Newgate prison, in the centre of the City, where the coachyard of the Saracen's Head Inn boasted a 'portal guarded by two Saracens' heads and shoulders…frowning upon you from each side of the gateway'. Another Saracen's head frowned down from the top of the inn's yard. On the boots of all the red coaches waiting there, more miniature Saracens' heads similarly glared away.

One of these red stagecoaches was the daily 8 a.m. Yorkshire coach, ready to take Nicholas Nickleby to the dreaded Dotheboys Hall school. When Dickens travelled north in 1838 to look at schools as source material for the novel, he took the 'Express' coach, which was not actually an express at all, but a slow or heavy coach. The heavy left the Saracen's Head an hour later than the stage, at 9 a.m. every day, travelling first to the Peacock in Islington (today marked by a plaque on a very drab building across from the Angel tube station), then continuing to Bedfordshire, sixty miles on. There it stopped to light its lamps, for by then it was nearly evening, and it would be another full day before the heavy reached its destination at Greta Bridge in County Durham. Dickens travelled in leisurely fashion, taking several overnight breaks, unlike Nicholas and his poor freezing companions, who travelled as outsides on the top of the coach for thirty-two hours straight.

The stage and the heavy were just two of the many regular coaches. The most old-fashioned method as the century began was the post-chaise, which was a smaller, lighter carriage than a stagecoach, usually with four wheels (some had two), pulled by two or four horses harnessed in pairs and with the lead horse ridden by a postboy, or postilion.* When real speed was needed, each pair had its own postilion. The two-wheeled post-chaise carried two passengers, while a four-wheeled chaise held one extra passenger in a dickey or rumble, an open back seat at the rear. A post-chaise was always hired privately, to the passenger's own schedule, but the chaise, horses, driver and postboys all belonged to the coaching inn or a local proprietor. Travelling post was expensive and, as the stagecoach network grew, it declined in popularity. In 1819, a guidebook needed two pages, with sixty-nine entries, to list the London stables and inns that hired out post-chaises; the 1839 edition listed none. In 1827, when Mr Pickwick and his friends chase after the eloping Miss Wardle, they take their host's gig to the local inn, where they rush in shouting, 'Chaise and four directly! – out with 'em!' and Wardle roars out that there will be a reward if the driver covers the next seven-mile stage in less than half an hour. (Mr Pickwick, more cautious by temperament, frets about moving at that rate in the dark: 'Pretty situations...strange horses – fifteen miles an hour – and [at] twelve o'clock at night!')

There were less expensive ways to travel into and out of London. A system of mailcoaches had been running since 1785: these were stagecoaches that carried the post to guaranteed schedules, and which also had space for a limited number of passengers. The mailcoaches were painted brown or mauve below, with black above and on the boot at the rear; the wheels and the undercarriage were all bright red, with the royal arms on the doors, gilt initials on the front boot and the number of the coach on the rear. The driver and an armed guard, who sat behind, were resplendent in royal livery, as carriers of the royal mails: this meant gold-braided scarlet coats for both with, later, blue lapels, linings and waistcoats, and gold braid on the guards' hatbands. The guard was responsible for ensuring the bags reached their destination and were not pillaged, as well as for keeping the coach to

* The word 'shay', often heard on the street and sometimes used in literature, was a back-formation from chaise, created under the impression that 'chaise' was plural: one shay, two chaise. A chaise was an all-purpose word to describe many types of carriage: it could have two or four wheels, was generally open (although it might have the folding hood known as a calash), and often simply meant a light carriage or cart used for pleasure rather than work.

schedule and taking the fares from passengers who joined on the road; if the coach broke down, it was his job to keep the mail moving.

The mailcoaches were expected to travel at a steady ten miles an hour. One minute was scheduled for the tired horses to be taken out of harness and replaced by fresh ones at coaching inns along the way, although some ostlers prided themselves on achieving the feat in even less. The American visitor Alexander MacKenzie described the change over on the Dover–London mail in the 1830s. When the bugle of the guard was heard, the barmaid automatically drew a drink, usually a 'heavy wet', or malt, for the coachmen. As the wheels sounded in the yard, out ran the 'inn-keeper, bar-maid, stable-boys, mischievous urchins, and all the idlers of the neighbourhood. The horses were pulled back upon their haunches, and stopped as if shot; the reins were thrown down on either side; the whip given unceremoniously to the envied occupant of the box-seat; and the coachman descended, with a princely air of condescension.' If the coach was full, a third pair of horses, with a postilion, was harnessed at every hill. Even this 'occasioned no delay; each horse had its attendant hostler... and the business of changing was managed with admirable despatch. A wooden block... was thrust under the hind wheel the instant we drew up... the coachman would nobly toss off the foaming tankard presented to him... and ere a minute had flown by, the guard would say "All right!" as he ascended the back of the coach, the block be withdrawn, and the horses... dart[ed] away at a gallop.'

For outward journeys from London until 1828, passengers booked seats and began their journey at the inn where the horses were stabled, travelling on to the main post office at Lombard Street, where the mailbags were collected and locked in the boots as the coaches clogged up the street, drawn up in double ranks. From 1829, the new, very large main post office at St Martin's-le-Grand became the starting point, and from there the coaches roared out. Crowds stood by to watch their departure every evening, one of the sights of London. Their speed was proverbial, both a marvel and a worry. In *Little Dorrit*, a man is knocked down by a mailcoach, and all the bystanders agree: '"They ought to be prosecuted and fined, them Mails. They come a racing out of Lad Lane [now Gresham Street] and Wood Street at twelve or fourteen mile a hour, them Mails do. The only wonder is, that people ain't killed oftener by them Mails"..."*I* see one on 'em pull up within half a inch of a boy, last night"..."*I* see one on 'em go over a cat, sir – and it might have been your own mother."' But it was precisely because of this speed that fares were higher than for a regular stagecoach: from 4½d to 5d per mile outside, or 8d to 10d per mile inside.

The mails became woven into the fabric of life, not merely as a symbol of modernity, nor even later of nostalgia, though they were both at different times, but also as a symbol of national pride. The essayist Thomas de Quincey described how during the French wars, from the battles of Trafalgar (1805) to Waterloo (1815), it was primarily the mails that broke the news of each victory. Traditionally, boards had been affixed to the sides of the mails, announcing events of national importance, such as the death of a monarch, to those towns and villages through which they passed without stopping. But during the decade of allied victories in Europe, it was considered a privilege to ride on top of a coach that was carrying the glad tidings. On such a night the 'horses, men, carriages, all are dressed in laurels and flowers, oak-leaves and ribbons'. The streets around the post office filled with even more excited spectators than usual, who shouted 'continual hurrahs' as the mails moved out: 'what a thundering of wheels! – what a trampling of hoofs! – what a sounding of trumpets! – what farewell cheers – what redoubling peals of brotherly congratulations, connecting the name of the particular mail – "Liverpool for ever!" – with the name of the particular victory – "Badajoz for ever!" or "Salamanca for ever!"...all night long, and all the next day...many of these mails, like fire racing along a trail of gunpowder, will be kindling at every instant new successions of burning joy.'

As they passed through the towns and countryside, everyone who saw the coach understood the symbolism of the oak leaves and ribbons, while 'rolling volleys of sympathising cheers run along us, behind us, and before us'. As private carriages approached the mails, passengers could see comprehension dawning: 'See, see!' the oncomers seemed to be saying, 'Look at their laurels!' The box-seat passenger on these victory runs was always supplied with a stack of the London papers, each one carefully folded so that the headline – 'GLORIOUS VICTORY' – was uppermost as he tossed a copy into each carriage as it passed in the opposite direction.

Not every run could be this thrilling, although even the regular stagecoaches had a glamour of their own. The drivers, unlike the drivers of the mails, were not in livery but usually wore white coats with, over them, great travelling cloaks, often with several capes attached. Tony Weller, the stagecoach driver in *Pickwick Papers*, wore 'a crimson travelling shawl...over this he mounted a long waistcoat of broad pink striped pattern, and over that again a wide-skirted green coat, ornamented with large brass buttons...His legs were encased in knee-cord breeches and painted top boots and a copper-watch-chain...dangled from his capacious waistband.' Unlike the mails, the stage was not legally compelled to travel as fast as ten miles an hour, although that was still the aim, and some even 'push their speed to twelve miles'. (This was proudly contrasted to Dutch or French diligences, which were said – although possibly only by the British – to travel at less than half that rate.) The coaches were named to reflect their speed: the Quicksilver, the Comet, the Rocket, the Greyhound, Lightning, Express and Hirondelle all became commonplace. It was not just speed, but scheduling, and keeping to those schedules, that were the stages' selling points. In the 1830s, a coachman on the Cambridge–London route kept a brass clock on his box to ensure that he did his daily hundred-mile round-trip in eleven hours precisely. On the highly competitive London–Brighton run, with two or three proprietors running twenty or so coaches between them every day, several owners promised to refund fares if the coaches were late.

The heavy-stage, or night-stage, was less expensive than the ordinary stage. The heavy was usually an older stage demoted to night duty, so it was also less comfortable, and it stopped more frequently. It was also used by locals outside London as a short-stagecoach, as well as carrying passengers to and from London at reduced fares. When Dickens took the heavy to Yorkshire he was a successful author, but not yet a rich one, and he had a growing family. In *Martin Chuzzlewit*, Pecksniff and his daughters travel to London by the heavy stage: either he is less prosperous than he suggests to the world, or he is miserly, making his daughters travel in some discomfort as, unlike Dickens, they made no overnight stops. The young David Copperfield, too, after his mother's death, is sent away to school 'not by the mail, but by the heavy night-coach, which was called the Farmer'. (What a difference between a coach called the Farmer and one called the Flyer!)

As with the mails, crowds, especially boys, regularly gathered to watch the arrival and departure of the stages at the main coaching inns in London. Thomas Trollope, the brother of the novelist, remembered in his 1820s childhood going to the White Horse Cellars in Piccadilly (originally on the south side, where the Ritz Hotel now stands next to Green Park; later in the century it was on the north) to watch the arrivals and departures: 'I knew all their names, and their supposed comparative speeds.' This too was where Esther Summerson in *Bleak House* first arrives in London, having been sent, by arrangement of a lawyer, 'for^{ded}, carriage free'. Like the Saracen's Head near Newgate, the White Horse was tavern, hotel and inn combined, providing services to visitors who were staying for some time, to those passing through and to locals.

The façades of the coaching inns were deceptively modest for the size of the businesses behind them. Often the only indication of an inn was a large

The great coaching yard of the Swan with Two Necks on Lad Lane was one starting point for the great procession of mailcoaches setting off daily. (Note the royal arms on the coach's door, indicating the Royal Mail.)

archway to the street. The main focus of the inns were the great courtyards at the rear, where coaches were loaded, and the one important element on the street side was the travellers' room, which from early days had large windows, so passengers could keep an eye out for their coach. Memories tinged with nostalgia recalled these rooms as wonderfully welcoming places, but in reality, claimed Dickens, they were 'mouldy-looking'; in the *Pickwick Papers*, the White Horse Cellar's travellers' room 'is of course uncomfortable; it would be no travellers' room if it were not', while at the Blue Boar even the poker was removed 'to preclude the possibility of the fire being stirred'.

Guidebooks in the 1820s set out the system for coaching. The fare was approximately 2½d to 3d per mile outside, or 4d to 5d inside. Seats were booked on payment of half the fare at the inn where the coach started, or at any of the inns where the horses were changed en route, with the balance of the fare payable at the beginning of the journey; alternatively a traveller could wait at a crossroads and flag down a passing stage. Outsides were expected to tip the coachman and the guard 1s each, with 3d to the porter at the inn where they set off; the tip for insides was 2s, to the outrage of many tourists. The stages carried four passengers inside, and ten or twelve outside, who perched up on benches on the roof. This was more than the mails could accommodate, as they didn't have to make space for the postbags, which by the 1820s were heaped four or five layers high on the roof. One lucky outside passenger got the box seat beside the coachman. This was the most desirable outside seat, and dashing young men tipped the booking clerk well to reserve it for them. Theoretically, the stage was more comfortable than the mailcoaches, with cushioned outside seats, while the mailcoaches offered only bare boards.

Seating, inside and out, was on a first come, first served basis, so passengers generally arrived a little before departure time to reserve a particular seat. Once that seat had been taken, no matter how many changes and rest stops there were, etiquette required that each passenger always returned to the same place. Trunks and boxes were then handed over; it was advisable for passengers to ensure that they were stowed on the right coach, or were not left sitting in the coaching yard. Likewise at any stops on long trips when the coach was changed, seasoned travellers watched out for their bags at the transfer point. If passengers arrived at the inn to find that the stage had left early, a not infrequent occurrence, they were entitled to order a post-chaise to chase down the slower-moving vehicle. It was stipulated that 'the Proprietors pay the Expense of your Ride'.

There were many little habits and routines specific to the stages. The Revd Heman Humphrey from the United States observed that when two coachmen passed on the road, without fail 'they exchange salutations, very significantly, by raising the elbow to a horizontal position, at a sharp angle, and turning it out toward the other'. Dickens concurred that there was a greeting 'strictly confined to the freemasonry of the craft', but he described it differently: it was more 'a jerking round of the right wrist, and a tossing of the little finger into the air at the same time'.

While this freemasonry did not extend to the passengers, they too fell into recognizable patterns of behaviour. In *The Pickwick Papers*, 'The outsides did as outsides always do. They were very cheerful and talkative at the beginning of every stage, and very dismal and sleepy in the middle, and very bright and wakeful again towards the end.' There was always one young man who smoked endlessly; another who pretended to be an expert on cattle, while another was the real thing. These were interspersed by locals, familiar to the guard and 'invited to have a "lift"'. And, most familiarly, 'there was a dinner which would have been cheap at half-a-crown a mouth, if any moderate number of mouths could have eaten it in the time,' for there were constant sardonic jokes about the lack of time to eat at stops along the route. Many passengers suspected collusion between the inns and the coachmen, the former bribing the latter to cut the stops short, so that they could serve up several times in the course of a day the same meal that no one had had time to eat.

Despite all its drawbacks, coaching was regarded as glamorous. Fashionable men dressed in caped greatcoats in imitation of the coachmen, 'ornamented with enormous mother-o'-pearl buttons as big as crown-pieces, with pictures on them of mail-coaches going full speed'. Some upper-class young men even paid coachmen to let them drive on their routes. The playwright Edmund Yates remembered 'my astonishment at my father shaking hands with the coachman' of the Brighton coach, until it was revealed that he was in fact a titled gentleman. One upper-class man recounted how, when he was passing the White Horse Cellar, 'a coachman had familiarly tapped him on the shoulder with his whip'. He had been enraged by this insolence from a working-class man, until he looked more closely at the supposed driver and recognized his own nephew.

Similarly, the author of *Old Coachman's Chatter*, a nostalgic look at coaching days, described seeing, in 1837 or 1838, the 'Taglioni' leave the White Horse Cellars: it was painted blue, with a red undercarriage, the family colours of Lord Chesterfield, who together with Count d'Orsay and Prince Bathyani paid for the privilege, and supplied their own horses.* The aristocratic 'coachman' wore a scarf in the same colours, with 'Taglioni' embroidered on it 'by the Countess's own hands'. This reality had fictional antecedents: in the 1821 novel *Real Life in London*, Bob Tallyho drives 'about twice a week' on the Windsor–London stage, 'tipping coachy a crown for the indulgence', acquitting himself well, apart from 'two overturns only...and...the trifling accident of an old lady being killed, a shoulder or two dislocated, and about half a dozen legs and arms broken, belonging to people who were not at all known in high life': 'nothing worthy of notice', the author concludes with a wink to the reader.†

Such satires apart, coaching was dangerous. When it was not dangerous it was uncomfortable, so much so that its discomforts became proverbial: it was said that the painter Constable, known for his sunny good nature, could manage to remain 'a gentleman even on a coach journey'. Sitting

* The dancer Marie Taglioni (1804–84) was in the 1830s at the height of her fame, having starred in Paris in Meyerbeer's ground-breaking opera, *Robert le Diable*, leading the famed 'dance of the nuns', and dancing ballet's first Sylphide in her father's *La Sylphide* in 1832. In London she dazzled audiences, with Princess Victoria an ardent fan.

† Two picaresque novels of London life fought it out in 1821: Pierce Egan's *Life in London, or, the Day and Night Scenes of Jerry Hawthorn, esq., and his elegant friend, Corinthian Tom, accompanied by Bob Logic, the Oxonian, in their rambles and Sprees through the Metropolis*, with illustrations by George and Robert Cruikshank, and Jonathan Badcock's *Real Life in London, or, The Rambles and Adventures of Bob Tallyho, Esq., and His Cousin, the Hon. Tom Dashall, Through the Metropolis; Exhibiting a Living Picture of Fashionable Characters, Manners, and Amusements in High and Low Life*, with illustrations by Thomas Rowlandson. Egan's won, but both stories of young rich men out on the razzle are useful guides, if not to authentic London life, at least to how most readers *wanted* to see the city.

facing the rear caused queasiness in many, but insides in front-facing seats were at the mercy of the wind and rain unless the window was kept closed, in which case the queasy insides complained, or even let their 'Stick or... Umbrella fall (accidentally) against one of the Windows'. Many passsengers considered paying for a breakage preferable to hours in an increasingly fetid atmosphere, but if it rained the insides became nearly as wet and muddy as the outsides. Straw was scattered on the floor for insulation against the cold although, as with the omnibuses, it was usually dirty and wet. Some coaching inns supplied a '*Calefacient*', a pewter container that could be refilled with hot water at each stop, to put under the feet and mitigate the cold.

And yet, inside was a considerable improvement on outside. *Tom Brown's Schooldays* (1857) described a ride on the Tally-ho stage with 'your feet dangling six inches from the floor. Then you knew what cold was, and what it was to be without legs, for not a bit of feeling had you in them after the first half hour.' Tom rides on a fairly empty stage, and the guard helps him pack his feet in straw for warmth, as well as giving him a piece of sacking to cover himself with. A queasy passenger complained that on his first stagecoach ride, in 1835, the choices were sitting facing the horses, 'but without anything against my back (for the iron bar... four inches above the seat, can hardly be called a resting-place)', or facing backwards, 'but secured from falling over... and breaking my neck'.* In either case, all that protected him from the bare boards was a cushion, which 'is, alas, soaking from the previous day'. This misery was replicated in fiction. When Mr Pickwick and his friends take a stage to Birmingham, Bob Sawyer ends up with rain 'streaming from his neck, elbows, cuffs, skirts, and knees... his whole apparel shone so with the wet, that it might have been mistaken for a full suit of prepared oilskin'.

Whilst a wetting was miserable enough, Dickens' novels are filled with much more serious stagecoach accidents. In *Nicholas Nickleby*, the

* The passenger, Friedrich von Raumer (1781–1873), was a professor of both history and political science, at the universities of Breslau and then Berlin. He travelled widely in Europe between 1816 and 1855.

London–Yorkshire stage overturns, with the result that 'the lady inside had broken her lamp, and the gentleman his head... the two front outsides had escaped with black eyes, the box [passenger] with a bloody nose, the coachman with a contusion on the temple, Mr Squeers with a portmanteau bruise on his back'. In *Martin Chuzzlewit*, a storm made the horses uneasy even before they set off; once on the road, 'they gradually became less and less capable of control; until, taking a sudden fright at something by the roadside, they dashed off wildly down a steep hill, flung the driver from his saddle, drew the carriage to the brink of a ditch, stumbled headlong down, and threw it crashing over,' while a boy is 'thrown sheer over the hedge... and was lying in the neighbouring field, to all appearance dead'.

Dickens had extensive experience to draw on, for his career as a journalist for the *Morning Chronicle*, from 1834 to 1835, had been in the surprisingly short golden age of coaching, from the spread of macadamized roads in the mid-1830s to that of the railways in the early 1840s. In 1841, in Scotland, he found himself in a coach with a broken drag, forcing the passengers to get out 'every now and then' and hang on to 'the back of the carriage to prevent its rolling down too fast'. It was, naturally, also raining, even before the carriage broke a spring, and was 'in a ditch and out again, and [having] lost a horse's shoe. And all this time it never once left off raining.'

Other natural hazards included fog. In 1840, one coaching enthusiast remembered 'seven or eight Mails following one after the other' in a particularly dense fog: the guard on the first coach held up a flare at the rear of his coach, which could just be seen by the driver of the next, whose guard in turn held up his own flare, 'and so on till the last'. In this manner one ten-mile stretch took three hours, instead of the more usual one, and even then one coach ended up in a ditch, where its wheelers – the pair of horses nearest the stage's wheels – drowned, while the outsides were 'thrown into the meadow beyond', and the insides 'extricated with some difficulty'.

Even without fog, writers listed an array of accidents: from obstructions on the road that could not be seen by the driver; to horses that ran up a bank, upsetting the coach into the road; broken reins; a broken pole, which tipped the coach over; horses that jammed together and, with their heads turned the wrong way, could no longer be controlled by the coachman; a lead horse falling, and the wheelers in turn stumbling over it; a driver hitting his head on an overhanging branch and falling off, upon which the horses then bolted; a driver being jounced off the coach by a rut or an obstacle; outsides falling off regularly ('It's like helping an outside passenger up ven he's been pitched off a coach,' says Tony Weller in *Pickwick* aphoristically); or horses shying and running off. All of which makes Dickens – 'I do verily believe I have been upset in almost every description of vehicle known…I have been…belated on miry by-roads…in a wheelless carriage, with exhausted horses and drunken postboys' – seem positively understated.

The romance nonetheless survived. In 1860, Dickens recalled his childhood: 'The coach that had carried me [to London as a child], was melodiously called Timpson's Blue-Eyed Maid, and belonged to Timpson, at the coach-office up-street; [while] the locomotive engine that had brought me back [as an adult] was called severely No. 97, and belonged to S. E. R. [the South-Eastern Railway], and was spitting ashes and hot-water over the blighted ground.' Dickens never quite made up his mind about trains. He used them frequently, travelling to seaside holidays, to the continent, to his house in Kent; and then relentlessly once he started his famous reading tours, repeatedly criss-crossing the country. Yet long before he was in a terrible train crash in 1865 – in which ten people died just outside Staplehurst, in Kent, and which left him with a fear of train travel that lasted the rest of his life – long before this, while he welcomed the railways as a convenience and a sign of modernity, he also regretted them as symbols of a time that was passing, or past.

Thackeray, his elder by a year, wrote elegiacally: 'what a gulf between now and then! *Then* was the old world. Stagecoaches…riding-horses, pack-horses, highwaymen, knights in armour, Norman invaders, Roman legions…all these belong to the old period…But your railroad starts the new era and we of a certain age belong to the new time and the old one.' Looking both backwards and forwards from the start of his career as an author, writing in 1836–7, Dickens set his first novel, *Pickwick Papers*, a decade earlier, opening in 1827, before the arrival of the railways, but one chapter was nevertheless entitled 'Strongly illustrative of the Position, that the Course of True love is not a Railway'. Ten years later in *Dombey and Son*, he was still looking both ways: he described the savage destruction that the building of the railways caused, but he also saw that 'The miserable waste ground, where the refuse-matter had been heaped of yore, was swallowed up and gone; and in its frowsy stead were tiers of warehouses, crammed with rich goods and costly merchandise... the new streets... formed towns within themselves, originating wholesome comforts and conveniences... Bridges that had led to nothing, led to villas, gardens, churches, healthy public walks.' Even so, he finishes: 'But Staggs's Gardens had been cut up root and branch. Oh woe the day when "not a rood of English ground" – laid out in Staggs's Gardens – is secure!'

In some ways, the arrival of the railways didn't shrink London, but made it appear to be expanding at the seams. Trains made areas seem suburban that had previously been rural, while suburbs became part of the city; Dickens wrote in 1847, 'places far apart are brought together, to the present convenience and advantage of the Public'. At a time when an exasperated commuter claimed that it was quicker to walk the two and a half miles from London Bridge to Trafalgar Square than to take a bus, Max Schlesinger praised the marvels of the suburban line, 'a miraculous railway' that ran from Blackwall and Greenwich in the east and over the northern section of the City to north-west London: every quarter of an hour, 'from early morn till late at night', the ten-mile journey took twenty minutes. Schlesinger was not alone in his attitude. Within a quarter of a century, 160 million journeys a year were made by rail within London itself. Many places that had recently been quiet suburbs were heavily visited. After the Great Exhibition in 1851, the Crystal Palace was relocated to Sydenham and, with new, elaborately laid out gardens, it opened to the public in 1854. At first trippers had to take the train to the suburb of Penge and walk up a hill, but such was the volume of visitors that the Crystal Palace company set up its own railway branch line. This was so successful that it was soon taken over by the London and Brighton Railway, which built a substantial station, linked to Crystal Palace 'by long glass corridors embellished with flowers and climbing plants'. By the 1860s, Crystal Palace afternoon concerts were drawing audiences brought by special express trains from Kensington, over twelve miles away.

The railways also transformed people's notion of what could be considered a commuting distance. Until 1844, trains were too expensive, even in third-class, to be used by the working classes for their daily commute. In that year, however, the government, in exchange for lifting a tax on third-class carriages, laid down that all railway companies had to run at least one train daily with fares of no more than 1d per mile. Even so, average fares still mounted up to £1 weekly, the entire weekly income of many skilled, well-employed artisans. But slowly workers did begin to move out of the city centre, as these so-called parliamentary trains (also known as working-men's trains) gradually made it possible for them to live in slightly more salubrious conditions for the price of an inner-city slum rent, or perhaps even less, funds that could then be reallocated to travel. Even so, these working-men's trains were not attractive in and of themselves. Officially they were required to travel at a minimum of twelve miles per hour, but they were notorious for being regularly shunted on to sidings to give priority to trains carrying first- and second-class passengers. The companies initially saw these working-men's trains as a political gesture and did not expect them to make a profit. The day's single parliamentary train was usually scheduled to arrive

By mid-century a day out and the railways were inseparable. Here holiday crowds leave the Crystal Palace in Sydenham.

at the London stations well before dawn, to get the legal requirement out of the way, with the service from Ludgate Hill to Victoria, for example, departing at 4.55 a.m. and arriving at Victoria at six.

For the privilege of being shunted aside, until the 1850s the passengers in the third-class carriages stood in cars without benches or even roofs, exposed to rain, sleet and snow as well as the soot and smoke from the engine. There were no doors either, but as in cattle-cars a flap on one side of the carriage folded down to provide access. (The conditions gave rise to a series of jokes along the lines of 'A man was seen yesterday buying a third-class ticket... The state of his mind is being inquired into.') These carriages were more dangerous than the trains in general – in 1841, eight labourers from the building site at the new Houses of Parliament were thrown out of their open wagon and killed when the train they were travelling on ran into a landslide.* Some passengers actively enjoyed this form of travel: 'the jolly part was coming down in the train we were in an open carrage the thurd class... but some times the sparks flu about and one woman got a hole burnt in her shawl. there was no lid to our carrage like some of them.' However, the author of this paean was Sophia Beale, aged eight, to which she added the proviso, 'I should not like to go in these carrages in winter.' Second-class was little better, with bare benches holding five a side facing each other. Ventilation came via a small square of wooden louvres on the door, sometimes, but not always, covered by a pane of glass. 'Smoking, snuff-taking, tobacco-chewing are all allowed,' said one visitor sourly. Despite these habits, he added, only the 'nobility and the wealthy' travelled first class, as it was so expensive. In 1856, a ticket from Liverpool to London on the accommodation train – that is, a stopping train, not an express – cost 37s, or nearly a week's salary for a well-paid clerk. Even

* The old Palace of Westminster, consisting of the medieval buildings where Parliament sat, together with the Royal Courts of Justice, burnt down in 1834. (For more on the fire, see p. 331.) The only surviving buildings were Westminster Hall, the Cloisters of St Stephen's, St Mary Undercroft Chapel and the Jewel Tower. The new Palace of Westminster, today's Parliament buildings, was designed by Charles Barry with Augustus Pugin, after Barry won the competition for the design. Building began in 1840, and in 1847 the new House of Lords was used for the first time, although further building work continued for decades.

Until the 1850s, third-class passengers had no seating at all; after that wooden benches were provided, although there were no other comforts. The windows were simply openings, with wooden shutters to keep out bad weather: the choice was darkness and lack of air, or rain and cold.

the best-selling novelist Harriet Beecher Stowe declared, 'first-class cars are beyond all praise, but also beyond all price,' although she conceded, 'their second-class are comfortless, cushionless, and uninviting.' In first class, the passengers sat in 'luxuriously upholstered' seats in 'nicely carpeted' compartments, with plate-glass windows to let in the daylight, while after dark these carriages were lit first by rape-oil lamps, later with gas.

Omnibus travel and mailcoaches had increased the average speed of travel to nearly six miles an hour; with the railway this figure rose to over twelve, sometimes double that. By the late 1840s, therefore, areas that had traditionally been on the edges of London now housed commuters: Bow, Greenwich, Blackheath, Croydon, Woolwich, Gravesend and Charlton. By 1856, a town known as 'Kingston on Railway' made its priorities clear. (It later changed its name to Surbiton.) In 1851, there were 120 trains daily carrying commuters to and from Greenwich alone. Early railway lines, built to transport freight from Camden to the East and West India Docks, were soon transformed into commuter lines and promoted an east–west spread, via Canonbury, Kingsland, Homerton and out to Bow. By 1851, this North London Railway transported 3.5 million commuters annually, half of whom were City commuters.

The first London station opened on the south side of London Bridge, and its twelve-minute trip to Greenwich replaced a one-hour coach journey. In 1837, Euston station opened, followed by a series of others: in 1838, Paddington and Nine Elms; in 1840, the Shoreditch/Bishopsgate terminus, which carried passengers to Romford, in Essex; in 1841, the station at Fenchurch Street in the City. In 1846, one contemporary estimated that, at the height of railway fever, if every company that had wanted to run a railway line into London had been given permission, over 30 per cent of the city would have been excavated for the purpose. To prevent even a fraction of this, in 1848 a Royal Commission on Metropolitan Termini drew a circle around the inner city, past which no railway would be permitted to run. In a shorthand description, it ran: Euston Road, City Road, Borough Road, Kennington Lane, Vauxhall Bridge Road, and Park Lane up to the Euston Road again. This boundary was breached almost immediately by a line from Nine Elms, at Battersea, to York Road (which became Waterloo) in 1848, but this was south of the river, and so somehow, mystically, to the West End and City men, it didn't quite count. And despite two further breaches – Charing Cross (1864) and Liverpool Street (1874) – that line has held for 165 years: instead of lines coming into the city, as in most other European centres, London is ringed by railways.* (The underground, too, silently conforms to this loop.)

Initially, money was lavished on the construction of the railway lines, not on the stations. While many of London's railway stations today have some Victorian elements remaining, they are all from the later part of the century. In the 1830s and 1840s, the stations started off very humbly indeed. Euston in 1838 had two platforms: the 'arrival stage' and the 'departure stage'

* The remaining Victorian stations built after the 1848 fiat were: King's Cross (1852), the Brunel station at Paddington (1854), Victoria (1860), Broad Street (1865), Cannon Street (1866) and St Pancras (1868), Holborn Viaduct (1874, becoming Thameslink in 1990), St Paul's (1886, becoming Blackfriars in 1937) and, just at the close of the century, Marylebone (1899).

(note the coaching word), from which three outward and three inward trains arrived and departed daily. ('Inward' and 'outward' were quickly superseded by 'up' and 'down' trains, meaning to and from London respectively, terms that survived until sometime after World War II.) In 1850, the Great Northern Railway's station at Maiden Lane (the street is now York Way, while the station has become King's Cross) was a temporary structure with two wooden platforms on the down side, between a gasworks and the tunnel for the new line. London Bridge in the 1860s had three stations: the Brighton station, the South-Eastern station and the Greenwich Railway station, the latter 'a mean structure'.

As trains became more heavily used, attention turned to the stations. In 1849, Euston opened its Great Hall, a concourse and a waiting room, all poorly designed, because when they were planned no one quite knew how a railway functioned, nor what needs had to be served. (Most stations, for example, found space for stands on which were chained large Bibles, 'for the use of the passengers while waiting for the train'.) At Euston, the new hall was vast – 125 by 61 feet, and 62 feet high – but the booking office was tucked into a cramped corner, with a secondary booking hall separated from the main concourse by the parcels office. Initially tickets could not be purchased on the train, and in some stations the booking office opened for just fifteen minutes before each train's departure, causing great bottlenecks. At Euston a large area was given over to the Queen's Apartments, a lounge for the use of the royal family should they be happening to pass through. It was rarely used and soon came down in the world with a bump, to become the 'additional parcels office'.

Passengers too needed to learn how the system operated. Guides instructed them that, once they were on the train, 'A glove, a book, or anything left on a seat denotes that [a seat] is taken'. Luggage, it was explained, was placed on the roof of each carriage (it was not until the early 1860s that specially designated luggage vans appeared). Until the 1880s, each carriage had doors opening only on to the platforms, with no connection from one carriage to the next. As a result all trains halted somewhere along the line to permit the conductor to walk along the track from carriage to carriage to check tickets. On the trains coming into Waterloo, the pause was made 'on the high viaduct over the Westminster Bridge Road'; by Euston 'outside the engine-house' (the Roundhouse at Camden); while outside London Bridge they stopped 'close to the parapet of the 20-feet-high viaduct' in Bermondsey. The Frenchman Francis Wey, in the 1850s, complained that his train was stopped while the tickets of nearly 2,000 passengers were checked: in third-class carriages, which were still mostly open-sided carts ('in a country where it rains perpetually', he wailed), the passengers were forced to wait 'unprotected in the broiling sun between a rock and a brick wall'.

No matter how uncomfortable and inconvenient railways were, however, they were synonymous with modernity: by 1852, Dickens referred to the world he was living in as 'the moving age'. Even a more prosaic man that same year acknowledged that he was 'work[ing] at a railroad pace' – that is, like a steam engine. For life was moving faster and faster, and even leisure was speeding up.

PART TWO

Staying Alive

1861: The Tooley Street Fire

By five o'clock on the evening of Saturday, 22 June 1861, the workmen in a row of warehouses were preparing for the Sunday shutdown in the repositories for the many goods traded in the City, sitting snugly along the river by London Bridge, near where the Borough High Street met Tooley Street. Scovell's Warehouse was filled with hemp, saltpetre, tallow, cotton, rice, sugar and tea, and spices including ginger, pepper, cochineal and cayenne. Next to it stood Cotton's Warehouse, then, further along the row of wharves, Hay's Wharf, then Chamberlain's Wharf, which traded in sulphur, tallow, saltpetre, jute, oils and paint.

Almost everyone had left for the day when a fire began, no one knew how, in the counting house at Scovell's Warehouse. In minutes it had spread to four nearby buildings, quickly igniting the next four: 'owing to the great quantity of tallow on the premises' it raced through those too. Without pause, the flames then leapt the walls, reaching Cotton's Warehouse and engulfing Hay's Wharf. At last it set alight Chamberlain's Wharf, with its lethal combination of wares.

> There was fire north, south, east, and west, fire everywhere; red lurid flames in dense masses, not like the thin tongues which leap themselves picturesquely round the devoted building, but broad, glaring, gleaming masses, which rose and floated like clouds of fire over the doomed wharves. From whatever point of view it was seen the spectacle...was grand and terrible – a mighty element in the full tide of its power, defying all the puny efforts of man. From the opposite side of the river it appeared like some volcano, throwing up its flames, reddening the sky, and illuminating all public buildings with the shade of an unnatural-looking autumnal sunset...the masts and flags and rigging of the ships in the river glowed as though they were in a red heat; the water reflected the towering flames of the burning ships, till the very Thames itself seemed on fire.

In truth, the very Thames itself not only seemed, but actually was, on fire. The tallow and oil from the burst barrels in the warehouses had poured out into the river, and the surface of the water was burning fiercely. Mr Hodges, the owner of a distillery near by, took it upon himself to act as fire-marshal until the arrival of the professionals of the London Fire Engine Establishment under their famous superintendent, James Braidwood. (For more on fires, see pp. 325–32.) Distilleries were dangerous places and often maintained their own private fire brigade, as did other manufacturers dealing with flammable goods, such as Price's Candles (the company is still in Vauxhall today). Hodges brought out his two engines and was soon joined by another handful of private brigades. When the official fire brigade arrived, the groups worked together under Braidwood, as was customary. The London Fire Engine Establishment's floating river-engine soon appeared, but it was almost low tide, and the water was not sufficiently deep for its pumps to operate. On the street side, too, the firefighters were

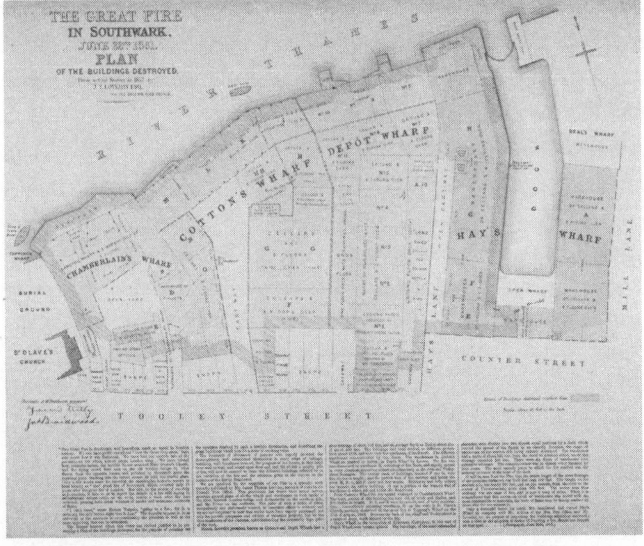

The vast extent of river-frontage destroyed by the Tooley Street fire can be seen here, running from the road next to St Olave's Church on the left, to Hay's Wharf on the right – eleven acres in total.

hampered. The same tallow and oil stores that had flowed into the river had also escaped into the street, where they were burning ankle deep. The firemen were forced back even further as the spice warehouses caught fire, the pepper-smoke blowing towards them in blinding clouds.

Fifteen miles away, Arthur Munby was on a train between Epsom and Cheam when he saw from the window 'A pyramid of red flame on the horizon, sending up a column of smoke that rose high in the air & then spread...At New Cross [four miles away] the reflection of the firelight on houses & walls began to be visible; & as we drove along the arched way into town, the whole of Bermondsey was in a blaze of light.'

By now the warehouses of eight companies were ablaze, and clearly beyond rescue. The firemen went to work instead on drenching the surrounding streets and buildings, to prevent the fire spreading – but in vain. Their new engine, which pumped more strongly, via steam power rather than manual labour, was being repaired at a works in Blackfriars Road. Hodges went to retrieve it, returning with the steam engine and extra hose. Supervising this himself, he managed temporarily to prevent the fire from leaping to the next range of warehouses, as his men and the fire brigade were joined by members of the Royal Society for the Protection of Life from Fire, bringing their own engines.

Still the fire roared on. The floating engine on the river was almost engulfed: 'the flames were so great, the explosions so frequent, the surface of the river being at the same period covered...with ignited tallow, and the flames rising 27 feet over the floating engine' that it was forced to retreat to the Customs House Stairs on the far side of the river. For several hundred yards, the south bank of the Thames was on fire: burning barges floated across on burning water as the oil and tallow poured 'in cascades' from the wharfs.

Braidwood, the great hero, the man who had professionalized the service, was everywhere at once, advising, controlling, encouraging his brigade. At 7.30 he was seen by the wall of a warehouse behind Tooley Street, working out a plan and giving his exhausted men rations of brandy. Suddenly from behind the wall came a huge explosion of saltpetre. The wall burst outwards, and the last anyone saw of James Braidwood was as fifteen feet of burning brickwork rained down on him and four or five others, burying them completely. 'Any attempt to rescue, or even recover the body, or what might remain of it, was quite impossible.' Instead, his men carried on as he had trained them.

Sometime after eleven o'clock that evening, the houses fronting Tooley Street caught fire. The fear was that a warehouse behind Cotton's Warehouse would be engulfed: it was said to contain 'several thousand barrels of tar'. By this time, 'thousands' of gallons of oil were on fire and pouring out in 'liquid flames'. Each building that contained some form of fuel or fat – and there were many – was quickly set alight: 'the flames rose high... in all sorts of colours – first there was a brilliant vermilion hue, which seemed to tip the pinnacles of the Tower of London, and the water side of the Custom-house' across the river, then 'the fire changed to a bright blue, and, at the same time, immense volumes of white and black smoke rolled over the house tops'.

The fire rapidly jumped over to granaries close to St Olave's Church, near London Bridge. Behind the church, on the river, were moored 'several schooners filled with barrels of oil, tar, and tallow'. Efforts had been made to tow them out to the middle of the river, but the steam tugs attempting this operation at low tide had themselves caught fire, 'and in a short space of time were burnt down to the water's edge', while the cargoes of the schooners drifted 'out blazing into the river... the blazing barrels of tar floating in a line along the banks of the river about a quarter of a mile in length and one hundred yards across... forming as it were a complete firing of flame twenty feet high'. At this point the wind shifted eastward, towards more tallow warehouses. By one in the morning the warehouses and shops in Tooley Street were given up for lost.

It was not until three o'clock, ten hours after the fire began, that it was finally contained in one area, although within that section buildings still burnt fiercely, punctuated by explosions as caches of saltpetre, gunpowder or sulphur were ignited. From St Olave's Church to Battle Bridge Stairs, just under 1,000 feet from east to west, and from the Thames extending another 1,000 feet inland, to Tooley Street, the fire continued to burn: over eleven acres were completely razed.

And throughout these long hours, as the men, exhausted, grimy, choking, their leader dead, continued their struggle, sightseers arrived en masse. Only hours after the first flames had been seen, when it had become clear that this was a major fire, sellers of beer, ginger-beer, fruit, cakes and coffee crowded the streets, hoping to pick up extra trade when the pubs closed, although many pubs, seeing the number of spectators, stayed open all night.

As Munby's train neared London, 'Every head was thrust out of window,' and at London Bridge he found 'The station yard, which was as light as day, was crammed with people: railings, lamp posts, every high spot, was alive with climbers. Against the dark sky…the façade of S. Thomas's Hospital and the tower of S. Saviour's…both were fringed atop with lookers on.' A few omnibuses were still waiting for passengers, and men fought for places, 'offering three & four times the fare', not to get away from the danger zone, but 'for standing room on the roofs, to cross London Bridge' and watch the fire. Munby was among them, 'and we moved off towards the Bridge…with the greatest difficulty. The roadway was blocked up with omnibuses, whose passengers stood on the roofs in crowds; with cabs and hansoms, also loaded *outside*; with waggons pleasure vans & carts, brought out for the occasion and full of people; and amongst all these, struggling screaming & fighting for a view, was a dense illimitable crowd.' Across the river, 'every window and roof and tower top and standing space on ground or above, every vessel that hugged the Middlesex shore for fear of being burnt, & every inch of room on London Bridge was crowded with thousands upon thousands of excited faces, lit up by the heat. The river too, which shone like molten gold…was covered with little boats full of spectators, rowing up & down in the overwhelming light', as watermen at the Customs House Stairs charged 1s to take people along the river, despite the great chunks of burning tallow choking the surface of the water.

It took Munby's bus half an hour to inch its way across London Bridge. From nine in the evening until nearly dawn, 'London-bridge and the approaches thereto presented all the appearance of the Epsom road on Derby day. Cabs were plying backwards and forwards on the bridge, carrying an unlimited number of passengers on the roof, at 6d per head. Omnibuses, licensed to carry 14 outside, were conveying double that number,' while the railway stations were so full of sightseers that passengers could neither reach nor leave their trains. On the north side of the Thames, 'the Custom-house quay, Billingsgate Market, the various private quays, the Monument, the roof of the Coal Exchange, and every available place from which a sight could be had, was filled with people, and the strong reflection from the burning mass on the opposite side of the river on their eager and upturned faces, presented a most singular appearance to the spectator at a distance'. At 3 a.m., many 'thousands... were still congregated on the bridge and in its neighbourhood'. The police had arrived to keep the crowds back, but as the numbers increased, they needed reinforcing with army regiments. Not only London Bridge, but also Waterloo and Westminster Bridges – in fact, any bridge from which even a glimpse of the fire could be caught – were thick with spectators.

Two hundred police continued on duty the next morning, as did the entire fire brigade. For days the fire continued to burst out at various points, walls still threatened to topple and explosions were constant as the heat of the smouldering fires found new barrels of explosives. On the 26th, four days after the fire began, 'an immense body of fire suddenly shot up' and took two hours to control. On the night of the 30th, engines were needed to pump water on new outbreaks. On 2 July, a full ten days after Scovell's Warehouse first caught fire, leaseholders and owners were still stripping the surrounding buildings of goods and fittings, for fear that flare-ups might engulf them too. It was to be another ten days, one day short of three weeks, before the fire was finally judged to be contained, although even then large areas continued to smoulder.

Meanwhile, many were taking advantage of the fire's largesse. Munby watched as 'all the women and girls of the neighbourhood turned out with the boys and men, to gather the fat which floated in vast cakes down the river... For days and weeks it went on... many women & girls waded up to their necks in mud and water... Some too went up the great sewers hereabouts for the same purpose.' Boat-owners were also busy collecting the valuable fats. 'For days afterwards, as far afield as Erith', twelve miles downriver, the 'banks and mud flats were coated with grease' assiduously gathered by 'hordes of men, women and children'.

For months, the courts were bursting with people charged with stealing the salvaged fats, which, in the view of the magistrates, continued to belong to their original owners, despite having been dissipated along the river and down the sewers. One second-hand dealer was accused of buying more than a ton of this stolen fat. The fat's legal owners, however, were more pragmatic, arranging salvage sales at knock-down prices for the mounds of tallow that blocked up the roads around Tooley Street: 'the conditions of sale being an immediate clearance'.

Meanwhile, tourists continued to gather, from all levels of society. Two days after the outbreak of fire, 'The burning ruins have been visited by the Earl of Stamford and lady, the Lord Mayor, and many other eminent gentlemen and their ladies,' followed the next day by the Duke of Buccleuch, the Earl and Countess of Cardigan, Earl Spencer, Lord Alfred Paget and Lady Gower. Disraeli and his wife were initially barred when the policeman on duty failed to recognize him. It was a week before things began to return to normal. The gawpers on London Bridge thinned, forming a single line of spectators gazing at the devastated site, while the traffic once more ran smoothly as crowds no longer blocked the way, with no extra buses or cabs now driving back and forth at a walking pace to give the best views. Watermen, too, no longer found sightseers wanting to be rowed out, and the quays on the opposite shore were 'comparatively free from intruders'.

The first concern, the day after the fire was brought under control, was to recover the body of James Braidwood. It was known where he had been standing when the wall collapsed, but such was the devastation that it was to be three days before his body was located. When it was, 'The crowds of persons who blocked up every avenue leading to the ruins manifested the greatest eagerness to catch a glimpse of the spot where the unfortunate gentleman fell, and when it was known that his body had been disinterred the excitement became very great... almost every person within the barriers flock[ing] to the fatal spot.' More touchingly, Fire Engineer Tozer, who was in charge of Tooley Street station and had previously worked directly under Braidwood as his chief clerk, cut off Braidwood's epaulettes and buttons from his uniform, giving them to the foremen of the fire service as a memento of their great chief.

Braidwood's funeral became a civic mark of appreciation of the man who had modernized the fire service, who had, in that age of chimney fires and dangerous workshops, done so much to keep the city safe. The fire service planned an elaborate public procession, but even they were taken by surprise by the public response. On 29 June, crowds of bystanders staked out positions long before the procession formed at Watling Street, in the City. Shops had closed; shutters and blinds were drawn as a sign of respect. Every bell in every City church rang a funeral peal (apart from St Paul's, which was reserved for funerals of the royal family, or the serving Lord Mayor). 'No one had anticipated that the ceremony of burying the lamented chief of the Fire-Brigade would excite an almost unprecedented degree of public interest. The police seemed bewildered to know how to manage the vast host that lined the thoroughfares…From the very first step a difficulty was experienced in obtaining a clear passage for the *cortège*, and although vehicles were turned into bye-streets, and the roadways stopped up against fresh comers, yet the struggle was incessant, and the long line was compelled to halt many times during the afternoon.'

The funeral of the London Fire Engine Establishment's superintendent, James Braidwood, killed while fighting the Tooley Street fire. So great were the crowds that lined the streets to pay their respects that it took the procession three hours to travel four miles.

The Times gave the order of the funeral procession as it left Watling Street for Abney Park Cemetery, in Stoke Newington:

A body of the City Police.

The London Rifle Brigade, with its band...
to the number of about 700.

The 7th Tower Hamlets...with various other
Volunteer Rifle Corps, to the number of about 400.

Friends of the deceased in mourning.

Metropolitan Police.

Superintendents.

Inspectors.

Constables of the various divisions, to the number of about
1,000 (four abreast).

City Police.

Inspectors.

Constables of the various divisions, 350 (four abreast).

The Waterworks Companies.

Superintendents.

Inspectors.

East London. } Turncocks. { West Middlesex.
New River. } { Lambeth and Vauxhall.

Band of the Society for the Protection of Life from Fire.

The Secretary, Mr. Low, Sen.

Fire Escape Conductors (four abreast).

Charles Henry Firth,

Captain of the West Yorkshire Fire Brigade Guard Volunteers,
accompanied by two privates and a deputation from the
Lancashire and Yorkshire Fire Brigades.

Private Fire Brigades: –

Mr. Hodges's, Lambeth,

Mr. Burnet's, Lambeth,

Messrs. Price's, Vauxhall,

Messrs. Beaufoy's, Vauxhall,

Messrs. Lennox and Co.'s, Millwall.

Local Brigades: –
Hackney. West Ham.
Shoreditch. Crystal Palaces.
Islington. Whitechapel.
Bow. Wapping.
Stratford. Greenwich.

Superintendent White, of the Gravesend Police and Fire Brigade and others.

Pensioners and Friends

London Fire Engine Establishment.

Junior Firemen.

Senior Firemen.

Sub Engineers.

Engineers (two abreast).

The Ward Beadle of Cordwainers' Ward.

The Undertaker.

Two Mutes.

The Pallbearers:

Mr. Swanton, engineer.	Mr. Gerrard, engineer.
Mr. Fogo, foreman.	Mr. Henderson, foreman.
Mr. Bridges, foreman.	Mr Staples, foreman.

A plume of feathers.

THE HEARSE.

The Chief Mourners:

Mr. James F. Braidwood	Mr. Lithgow Braidwood
Mr. Frank Braidwood	Mr. Charles Jackson

Fifteen Mourning Coaches

Containing the relatives, friends, and committees of the London fire engine establishments.

Private carriage of the Duke of Sutherland.

Private carriage of the Earl of Caithness.

Private carriage of Dr. Cumming [the officiating clergyman].
And other private carriages.

Most unusually, in an age when sending an empty carriage was considered to be a significant mark of respect, the Duke of Sutherland and the Earl of Caithness were actually present.

The procession moved slowly through an 'immense multitude' that had gathered in homage to Braidwood; 'in the front of the Royal Exchange, and all round this space the roofs and windows were thronged. As the procession slowly approached, the troops with arms reversed, and the bands slowly pealing forth the Dead March, the mass of spectators, as if by an involuntary movement, all uncovered [their heads], and along the rest of the route this silent token of respect was everywhere observed.' The crowd was so thick that, despite an escort of mounted police, the cortège took three hours to cover the four miles to the cemetery in Stoke Newington, with thousands of silent onlookers lining the route the entire way.

At Abney Park, the body of James Braidwood, aged sixty-one, was laid to rest beside his stepson, also a fireman, who had died on duty six years earlier. Braidwood Street, off Tooley Street, today continues to commemorate both the worst fire London had seen since the Great Fire of 1666, and the heroic service rendered the city by the founder of the modern fire brigade.

5.

THE WORLD'S MARKET

Saturdays were Covent Garden market's biggest day, when the costermongers stocked up with produce to sell over the coming week, up to 5,000 of them heading for the market with donkey carts, with shallow trays or with head-baskets.* By the 1850s, London's main produce market had long overspilled its bounds, covering not just the Piazza it was designed to occupy, but spreading over an area 'From Long Acre to the Strand…from Bow-street to Bedford-street', for several hundred yards in either direction: 'along each approach to the market…nothing is to be seen, on all sides, but vegetables; the pavement is covered with heaps of them waiting to be carted; the flagstones are stained green with the leaves trodden underfoot…sacks full of apples and potatoes, and bundles of brocoli [sic] and rhubarb are left…upon almost every doorstep; the steps of Covent Garden Theatre are covered with fruit and vegetables; the road is blocked up with mountains of cabbages and turnips.'

This description came a quarter of a century after the new market had first been planned. In 1678, the Dukes of Bedford, who owned the land, had been granted a 250-year lease for a market, and for nearly two centuries what had been called a market had been merely a collection of wooden sheds and stalls. In the early 1820s, with the lease due to expire, the Bedford Estate received permission to build permanent structures in the centre of the Piazza, expanding beyond the original square itself, and soon sellers operated in a landscape of half-built premises. By 1858, there was a central

* Costermongers, or costers, sold fruit, vegetables and fish from carts on the streets. For more on street sellers, see pp. 140–62.

structure of wrought iron. The old Piazza Hotel, which had backed on to Covent Garden theatre, and had long served as the entrance to the pit and box seats in the theatre, had been demolished. In its stead Floral Hall, a building to house the flower sellers, was being constructed in the style of the Great Exhibition's Crystal Palace. (In a neatly circular fashion, Floral Hall once again serves not the market but the theatre, providing the Royal Opera House's box office and refreshment bars. One section of the Piazza's central structure was rescued when the market was demolished in the 1970s, and in the early twenty-first century was re-erected in the Borough market.)

Before dawn the traffic converged on the streets surrounding the main markets. The waggoners were recognizable by their countrymen's smocks, with velveteen breeches and leggings, or their gaiters, made of canvas, linen, wool or leather, tied below the knee and again at the ankle, or buttoned or buckled on, all designed to prevent the roads' endless mud from making a pair of stockings unwearable after a single outing (see Plate 4, top row right, and bottom row third from right). Carts were an ongoing problem: slow to arrive, cumbersome to turn, difficult to leave while their drivers took their goods into the market. As a result queues up to a mile long were not unusual. In the late 1840s, one enterprising boy carved out a job for himself by offering a solution. Like many homeless street children, Bob had haunted the market, running errands and fetching and carrying for stall-holders in return for food, or a penny. Winning their trust, he promoted himself to the self-created position of 'market-groom': now when the carts had been driven as close to the market as possible, the waggoners were met by Bob, who held their whips as a sign of authority and then kept watch, preventing the donkeys and horses from wandering off, or straggling into the roadway, or entangling themselves with other carts. He also stopped the street children from pilfering from the carts, as well as ensuring that the animals themselves didn't pilfer, by munching the produce of the cart in front of them.

Business, in summer, started before three o'clock, when 'the crowd, the bustle, the hum' of the morning really began. There were three official market days at Covent Garden – Tuesdays, Thursdays and Saturdays – but for most of the century the market was in operation every morning. The market traders who walked in from the country wore smocks covered by a thick blue or green apron; if their job were of a particularly messy or unpleasant type – skinning rabbits, for example – this apron was in turn covered by a piece of sacking tied on top. In the main square were the flower, fruit and vegetable sellers. Potatoes and 'coarser produce' were on one side, with more delicate fruit and vegetables set apart, and potted plants also given their own section. Cut flowers were displayed separately, where 'walls' (wallflowers), daffodils, roses, pinks, carnations and more could be found in season. The size of the market and the variety of colour were dazzling. When Tom Pinch and his sister come up from the country in *Martin Chuzzlewit*, they stroll through the market, 'snuffing up the perfume of the fruits and flowers, wondering at the magnificence of the pineapples and melons; catching glimpses down side avenues, of rows and rows of old women, seated on inverted baskets, shelling peas; looking...at the fat bundles of asparagus with which the dainty shops were fortified as with a breastwork'.

Fruit and vegetables were the main focus, while around the sides subsidiary sellers set up, selling to other traders: horse-chestnut leaves to put under exotic fruit displays; ribbons and paper to make up bouquets; or tissue paper 'for the tops of strawberry-pottles', those conical wicker baskets shaped like witches' hats, without which, it appeared, no strawberry could be sold. (See illustration on p. 22: the couple at top right carry two pottles.) On the railings at the edge of the Piazza hung many more baskets for sale, usually watched over by Irishwomen 'smoking short pipes' and calling out, 'Want a baskit, yer honour?' In the 1840s, these women wore loose gowns looped and pinned up out of the dirt, showing their thick underskirts and boots; on their heads were velveteen or straw bonnets, with net caps underneath. Men and women alike wore luridly coloured silk 'kingsman' kerchiefs around their necks.

Many other sellers had no fixed pitches, but walked around selling from trays or baskets: 'One has seedcake [for birds], another...combs, others old caps, or pig's feet.' Dodging among them, essential to keep the goods moving in and equally essential to purchasers to get the goods back out, were the market porters, identifiable by their porters' knots: a piece of fabric strapped across the forehead and hanging down over the nape of the neck, ending in a knot that secured the edge of their baskets or crates as they carried them on their backs, to distribute the weight. Some modified the fantail hats worn by workers in particularly dirty occupations, padding the fantails to provide a two-for-the-price-of-one porters' knot and dust protection.

Covent Garden was known for its luxury imports. Other markets had their own specialities. Like Covent Garden, Billingsgate fish market on the riverside, between London Bridge and the Tower, had first been established in the seventeenth century, although fish had been sold less formally on the site even earlier. Yet, unlike Covent Garden, at mid-century Billingsgate was still nothing but a 'collection of sheds and stalls – like a dilapidated railway station', and even the sheds were a fairly recent addition. Despite being the world's largest fish market, Billingsgate had been held in the open street for the previous two centuries, moving indoors only in 1849.

In the early part of the century, the market sold the local catch: in 1810, 400 boats fished the river between Deptford and London Bridge, providing Thames roach, plaice, smelts, flounder, salmon, eel, dace and dab. But by 1828, the run-off from the new gasworks near by, combined with ever more factory effluent, had destroyed the fisheries, and instead fishing boats from downriver or from coastal waters were pulled up the Thames by tugboats, with particularly delicate fish, such as turbot, brought in alive in tanks on deck. Rowboats then ferried the fish from the boats to the market. By 1850, Dutch fishing boats supplied the market with eels, while other vessels continued to bring catches from the North Sea, but the system had otherwise been modernized. The fishing boats stayed in their home waters, discharging their catch on to the faster clippers, which brought them upriver. Fish that went off quickly, like mackerel, were dropped off at the railway stations, to be put on the mail trains; having arrived by 6 a.m., they could be processed through the market to reach the fishmongers' shops within sixteen hours of being caught.

By 4 a.m. daily the Billingsgate workers had assembled. Here the porters wore jerseys, old-fashioned breeches, porters' fantails and thigh-high boots as they prepared for the auctions. The auctioneers themselves wore frock coats and waistcoats, street clothes, to indicate they were middle class – Dickens called them 'almost fashionable' – but, as a nod to practicality, over their coats they tied heavy aprons. For much of the century these were made of flannel or coarse wool, usually serge – in *Our Mutual Friend*, set in the 1850s, the fishmonger's men 'cleanse their fingers on their woollen aprons'. It was only later that canvas replaced wool, while many at Billingsgate switched to oilskin.

Many of the auctioneers met at the start of the day at Billingsgate's most famous tavern, the Darkhouse, to compare notes on quality and discuss prices over coffee or 'the favourite morning beverage…gin mingled with milk'. At five the bell rang to announce the opening of the market, when buyers immediately headed towards their favourite stalls. Now everything was a blur of action: 'Baskets full of turbot…skim through the air…Stand on one side! a shoal of fresh herrings will swallow you up else.' Crowds gathered by each auctioneer as the porter set out plaice, sole, haddock, skate, cod, ling and 'maids' (ray) in doubles – oblong baskets 'tapering at the bottom, and containing from three to four dozen of fish' each – while sprats were sold by the tindal – a thousand bushes – or in offals, which held 'mostly small and broken' fish, to be sold off cheaply. No examination was permitted, the porter hefting each double on to his shoulder as all over the market bidding began by Dutch auction, with the auctioneer setting a high opening price, then dropping down by increments until someone made an offer. Each type of fish was sold first to the 'high' salesmen, who bought in bulk and then sold on to middlemen, known as bummarees, at whose stands the doubles and tindals were broken up and the contents sold off in smaller quantities to individual shopkeepers or to costermongers.

The other great market, Smithfield, was, for the first half of the century, a running sore in the City. Dickens could hardly bear it, but neither could he bear to leave it alone. This market appears again and again in his journalism, and in his novels. On market mornings, he wrote, 'The ground was covered, nearly ankle-deep, with filth and mire…the whistling of drovers, the barking dogs, the bellowing and plunging of the oxen, the bleating of sheep, the grunting and squeaking of pigs, the cries of hawkers, the shouts, oaths, and quarrelling on all sides; the ringing of bells and roar of voices… the crowding, pushing, driving, beating, whooping and yelling; the hideous and discordant din that resounded from every corner of the market… rendered it a stunning and bewildering scene, which quite confounded the senses.'

Smithfield cattle market had been held in the heart of the City since 1638. For five or six centuries even before that, a horse and livestock market had convened on the same spot, half a mile north-east of St Paul's and a few hundred yards from the old redoubt of the City, the Barbican. By mid-century over 2,500 cattle and nearly 15,500 sheep traversed the traffic-choked streets twice weekly, before their purchasers drove them back out once more; on Friday, horses were sold; and three times a week there was a hay market. The streets leading to all the City markets were narrow and difficult to navigate: Newgate market near by had only two access roads, one just ten feet wide, one slightly less. Add the animals to the traffic and the streets became chaotic. One American resident in London said he avoided the spot on market days, because he loathed the 'fiendish brutality of their drivers', with calves 'piled into a cart… and transported twenty or thirty miles, – their heads being suffered to hang out of the cart at each end, and to beat against the frame at every jolt of the vehicle'.

Smithfield itself was merely a city square measuring three acres. (In 1824, Thomas Carlyle, seeing it for the first time, was so overwhelmed by the heaving mass of animals, stench and noise that he estimated the ground it covered was ten times its actual size.) Owing to the large number of animals to be compressed into this small space, extreme cruelty was routine. 'To get the bullocks into their allotted stands, an incessant punishing and torturing of the miserable animals [occurs] – a sticking of prongs into the tender part of their feet, and a twisting of their tails to make the whole spine teem with pain.' All around were animals bellowing in agony as drovers 'raved, shouted, screamed, swore, whooped, whistled, danced like savages; and, brandishing their cudgels, laid about them most remorselessly… in a deep red glare of burning torches… and to the smell of singeing and burning'. Cattle were tied to the rails 'so tightly, the swelled tongue protruded', before being hocked: 'tremendous blows were inflicted on its hind legs till it was completely hobbled'. For lack of space many more were pressed into ring-droves, circles where they stood nose to nose, wedged against the next ring-drove, driven into this unnatural formation, and kept there, by sharp goads. The goads were used so freely, were so savagely stuck into the animals, that good tanners rejected hides from Smithfield cattle, referring to them contemptuously as 'Smithfield Cullanders', that is, colanders, or sieves.

By the time Dickens wrote this, it was news to no one: there had been parliamentary inquiries about the horrors of Smithfield in 1828, in 1849 and in 1850, but nothing could move the obdurate Corporation of the City of London. Smithfield made a lot of money for the City, on average £10,000 per annum in fees from the sellers. As the obvious solution to the problem was to move the market to a less crowded part of London, which meant outside the City, they stalled as long as possible.

The population at large, however, could not close its eyes to the problem simply by avoiding Smithfield. The animals were driven in and out of the market through city streets clogged with 'coaches, carts, waggons, omnibuses, gigs, chaises, phaetons, cabs, trucks, dogs, boys, whooping, roarings, and ten thousand other distractions'. By the time they were sold, they had been twenty-four hours without water or food, and it was scarcely surprising that the beasts ran amok regularly.

In *Dombey and Son*, small Florence Dombey and her nurse are walking towards the City Road on a market day when 'a thundering alarm of "Mad Bull!"' was heard, causing 'a wild confusion…of people running up and down, and shouting, and wheels running over them, and boys fighting, and mad bulls coming up'. That was Dickens in fiction. A decade later, in the 1850s, he watched in reality when, in St John Street, in Clerkenwell, the same shout of 'Mad bull! mad bull!' was heard: 'Women were screaming and rushing into shops, children scrambling out of the road, men hiding themselves in doorways, boys in ecstasies of rapture, drovers as mad as the bull tearing after him, sheep getting under the wheels of hackney-coaches, dogs half choking themselves with worrying the wool off their backs, pigs obstinately connecting themselves with a hearse and funeral, other oxen looking into public-houses.' The owner pelted along behind the animal until he finally found his bull in 'a back parlour…into which he had violently intruded through a tripe-shop'. This sounds more like fiction than the fiction itself, but similar reports routinely appeared in the journals.

Non-cattle-market days were no quieter. Friday afternoons were costermongers' day at Smithfield, when the costers purchased the tools of their trade: 200 donkeys were sold on a concourse about eighty feet long while a smaller area held ponies. Barrows and carts were offered for sale, as were spare parts – wheels, springs, axles, seats, trays, or just old iron for running repairs. Harnesses, bridles and saddles were hung from posts or spread on sacking on the ground, as were smaller necessities, such as whips, lamps, curry-combs and feed-bags. Even at this much smaller market, Smithfield was ill suited for the number of people who attended. The concourse itself was paved, but the surrounding selling areas became so churned up and mixed with animal dung that the policemen on duty habitually wore thigh-high fishermen's or sewermen's boots; the costers accepted that their trousers would be 'black and sodden with wet dirt'.

Finally, in 1852, the Smithfield Removal Bill was passed in Parliament, and the live meat market was closed in 1855, moving to Copenhagen Fields in Islington. In 1868, the old Smithfield ground, now called West Smithfield, was re-established, this time as a dead-meat market – that is, for butchered meat, not live animals – complete with an underground station to bring in the goods for sale. (The hay market survived at Smithfield because officials had forgotten to allow space for it in the new market in Islington; it continued until 1914, when the rise of the car made it redundant.) No longer would the cry of 'Mad bull!' run through the City. The new market was iron-roofed, gaslit, with wooden stalls: the epitome of modern trade elegance, complete with restaurants and drinking establishments, and rooms for dining, meeting, or reading the newspaper. Other markets had to wait longer for renovation. Leadenhall had been the largest market in Europe, selling dead meat, skin and leather; herbs and 'green'-market goods; pigs, and poultry, in three separate yards, from 1400. Gradually poultry became its main item (in *Dombey and Son*, Captain Cuttle hires 'the daughter of an elderly lady who usually sat under a blue umbrella in Leadenhall Market, selling poultry'), and in 1871 an Act was passed to prevent the old market from continuing to sell hides or meat.

These specialist markets serving the whole of London were the exception. Many neighbourhoods supported a small market of one sort or another, and most had several. In the streets around Oxford Street, for example, there were Carnaby market, 'now but a small provision market'; Oxford market, near Portland Street, which sold vegetables and meat; Portman market, for hay, straw, butter, poultry, meat and 'other provisions'; St George's market, at the western end of Oxford Street, primarily for meat, but with many nearby vegetable stalls; Mortimer market, 'a very obscure market'; and Shepherd's market, on the south side of Curzon Street, for provisions generally, 'a convenience for this genteel neighbourhood, and... not a nuisance'. (It is notable that only in this very exclusive district does the compiler of this list consider that a market might be a 'nuisance'.)

Around the Strand and Covent Garden was Hungerford market (underneath what is now Charing Cross station), which sold fish, fruit, vegetables and dead meat. It also had a number of poulterers' shops, with live cockerels

There had been a market at Hungerford Stairs (where Charing Cross station now stands) for 200 years, but in 1830 a modern three-storey market was built. It was only after this, when 'the very nature of the ground changed', that the adult Charles Dickens felt able to revisit the spot where the blacking factory had once stood.

and hens, their black beady eyes peeping through the wicker baskets. Beside these basics, according to one author mid-century, the market was also known for its penny ices, advertised as 'the best in England'. Hungerford had been covered over since the seventeenth century, but in 1830 it was expanded and rebuilt on three levels, with a fish market below and fruit and vegetables above. Dickens was spotted here one day in 1834, behind a coal-heaver carrying a child who peeked shyly over his father's shoulder at the young journalist. Dickens promptly bought a bag of cherries and, walking along, posted them one by one into the child's mouth without his father being aware, 'quite as much pleased as the child'.

Nearby was Lumber Court market, in Seven Dials, selling fish, and some vegetables and meat. Newport market, off Great Newport Street, west of Long Acre, sold butchers' meat, and also had a large number of slaughtermen: around 400 bullocks, up to 700 sheep and 100 calves were slaughtered there weekly. In 1837, one author noted that most butchers slaughtered the animals in their cellars, tipping the blood down the drains – perhaps as much as 12,000 barrels of blood annually. Things altered little: thirty years later James Greenwood, a journalist of London's underbelly, claimed that one firm slaughtered 1,000 sheep weekly behind its market stall, in a shed 'no larger than a drawing-room, in which were eight men gory to the elbows'.

Clare market, between the Strand and Lincoln's Inn Fields (where the Aldwych is today), sold butchers' meat, vegetables, tripe, dogs'- and cats'-meat. Although smaller than many markets it was still 'a nuisance', owing to its twenty-six butchers, who between them weekly slaughtered 400 sheep, up to 200 bullocks and an unknown number of calves, 'in the market, or in the stalls behind, and in cellars'. On Saturday nights, therefore, the market-goers found themselves 'tramping about in... a rich compost of dead rats, sickening offal, and decaying vegetable matter, which changes its colour only where the red stream from the shops has formed into stagnant pools, offending the sight as terribly as the surrounding nastiness annoys the nostrils'. In the late 1850s, one street there housed six slaughterhouses within a few yards of each other, as well as a tripe boiler and a livery stables, all next door to three small houses, in which lived four families of five to six people.

These small-scale slaughterhouses situated cheek-by-jowl with private houses were a fact of life, and for the most part they were unquestioned. In Farringdon, one William Waight was prosecuted in 1847, not because he slaughtered sheep and cattle on his premises, but because he allowed the resulting 'dung and filth' to sit in his yard for three years. A cease and desist order was handed down, but Waight, who failed to show up for the hearing, 'continues to slaughter as heretofore'. Even Dickens' magazine, usually so compelling in its outrage over the squalid living conditions of the poor, commented apropos of the slum of St Giles, not far from Clare market, that 'There are no trades in the district that affect in a remarkable degree the health of its inhabitants; there is nothing worse than the fifteen not ill-managed slaughterhouses.' This was not the way Dickens himself wrote. Earlier, in a polemic against Smithfield cattle market, he broke off to inquire satirically why there should be any reason not to have 'cattle-driving, cattle-slaughtering, bone-crushing, blood-boiling, trotter-scraping, tripe-dressing, paunch-cleaning, gut-spinning, hide-preparing, tallow-melting... in the midst of hospitals, church-yards, workhouses, schools, infirmaries, refuges, dwellings, provision-shops, nurseries, sick-beds, every stage and baiting-place in the journey from birth to death'?

This was the reality, for markets also sustained subsidiary industries that were deeply offensive, such as the licensed slaughterhouse in Smithfield, where animals unfit for human consumption ended up. To those venturing into the yard, 'the sense of smell is not only assailed, but taken by storm, with a most horrible, warm, moist, effluvium'. Much worse lay next door, where 'you will find the largest sausage manufactory in London', owned by the 'brothers, we believe' of the slaughterhouse owner. The best of the diseased animals were quietly slipped over to the sausage machine, 'to be advantageously mixed with the choppings of horse-flesh' and 'sold to the poor, in small lots by gas-light, on Saturday nights, or in the form of soup; and to the rich, in the disguise of a well-seasoned English German-sausage'. It was well known that the retail markets sold diseased meat; Newgate market was more corrupt only in that it sold it wholesale.

For most of the century, and for most of the population, it was the smaller, unmodernized markets that were their primary shopping locations.

There were dozens of working-class markets, many if not most held on a Saturday night and again on Sunday mornings. Wages were paid at the end of the working day on Saturdays, and a family's main purchases were made that evening, after six or seven, with the markets lit up dazzlingly. By the 1850s, a variety of lighting was used on the stalls, from 'the new self-generating gas-lamp' through the 'old-fashioned grease lamp' down to various makeshifts: a candle stuck in a bundle of sticks, or even in a turnip, or just a wick wrapped in a piece of brown paper, which flared up nicely before burning down. The shops themselves relied on gas, 'Great jets...flaming and roaring far out into the thoroughfare, stretching like some fiery sword across the pavement, waving to and fro at each gust of wind'. In larger markets, such as Whitechapel, 'The gas...flaring from primitive tubes, lights up a long vista of beef, mutton, and veal. Legs, shoulders, loins, ribs, hearts, livers, kidneys, gleam in all the gaudy panoply of scarlet and white on every side.' Outside on the pavement was an informal set of pitches and itinerant sellers, almost another market as pedestrians navigated the 'trucks, barrows, baskets, and boards on tressels [sic], laden with...Oysters, vegetables, fruit, combs...ballads, cakes, sweetstuff, fried fish, artificial flowers...chairs, brushes and brooms, soap, candles, crockery-ware, ironmongery, cheese, walking-sticks, looking-glasses, frying-pans, bibles, waste-paper, toys, nuts, and fire-wood'.

The glare was matched by the noise. Each seller had his own cry, and called out regularly, enticing shoppers by the goodness or the cheapness of his wares. In the working-class market of St Luke's, Clerkenwell, one butcher shouted, 'Hi-hi! weigh away – weigh away! the rosy meat at three-and-half! Hi-hi!' The cries of Bethnal Green market, behind Shoreditch Church in east London, ran the gamut: 'Who'll buy a cock?' 'Almond nuts!' 'Hay'penny a lot, whelks; toss or buy!' And in the New Cut, in Bermondsey,

> the thousand different cries of the eager dealers, all shouting at the top of their voices...'So-old again'...'Chestnuts all 'ot, a penny a score'... 'An 'aypenny a skin, blacking'...'Buy, buy, buy, buy, buy – bu-u-uy!' cries the butcher. 'Half-quire of paper for a penny,' bellows the street stationer...'Twopence a pound grapes.' 'Three a penny Yarmouth

bloaters.' 'Who'll buy a bonnet for fourpence?' 'Pick 'em out cheap here! three pair for a halfpenny, bootlaces.' 'Now's your time! beautiful whelks, a penny a lot.' 'Here's ha'p'orths,' shouts the perambulating confectioner. 'Come and look at 'em! here's toasters!' bellows one with a Yarmouth bloater stuck on a toasting-fork. 'Penny a lot, fine russets'... 'Fine warnuts! sixteen a penny, fine war-r-nuts'... a double 'handful of fine parsley for a penny'... 'Ho! ho! hi-i-i! What do you think of this here? A penny a bunch – hurrah for free trade! *Here's* your turnips!'

The purchasers moved slowly along amid the noise and dazzle, while the sellers shouted enticements and encouragement. The main pathways were thronged with women with large market baskets, although some of them allowed their husbands to follow along 'as basket-bearers and light porters generally'. The first item to be purchased by the comfortably-off artisan's wife was the Sunday-dinner joint, and so the butchers' shops were slowly surveyed. A butcher offered his beef at 'three-and-six, that's under eightpence a-pound!', but any housewife worth her salt at this stage made a feint of leaving, allowing herself to be persuaded back, only to shift her attention to a joint of mutton. It too was, naturally, 'as good a bit as ever you had a knife in, I'll go bail... It ought to be nine-and-a-half [pence per pound], but, as I want to make a regular customer of you, we'll say nine.' The housewife made another sortie. 'Well, now, come, what *will* you give?' asked the butcher in reply; her counter-offer of 8d a pound was rejected, before 8½d was finally agreed – if, the frugal shopper added in triumph, the butcher would throw in some suet as well. The butcher accepted, 'resignedly'. Then on to the butterman, where 'after smelling, tasting, and otherwise testing a large variety of samples', the housewife beat down the price once more, agreeing to buy all her butter, cheese and bacon from him for a discount. And so on, until around nine o'clock, when the major purchases had been made, and the housewives headed for home, their husbands trailing behind.

Sunday markets were considered less respectable, especially by the middle classes, who thought that decent people should be in church, not shopping for food. (The fact that most of the working classes finished work at 10 p.m. or later on Saturdays, and were not paid until then, leaving no time at all to shop, was skated over by the Sabbatarians.) One such market among many was in Brill Place, behind Euston station. In the 1850s, it was so crowded on Sunday mornings that the road became 'almost impassable'. The shoppers were for the most part very poor: many of the women couldn't even afford bags, but carried their purchases in their aprons, by gathering the corners together. Mayhew said that the men generally stood around and talked, while the women went from butcher to coal seller to baker, between stalls selling anything from 'Walnuts, blacking, apples, onions, braces, combs' to 'turnips, herrings, pens and corn-plaster'. When the church bells began to ring, the tempo speeded up to a frantic pace, to get everything bought in that last half-hour before the legally enforced closure during the hours of church services. Once the bells stopped, the only shops that remained open were the cookshops, which baked the meat and vegetables brought to them in their owners' dishes; these would be ready for collection when the other shops reopened after church. Whitecross Street market, another Sunday market, was much larger. Near Old Street, towards the Barbican, it opened at 7 a.m. on Sundays, with sellers including butchers, bakers, grocers, provision dealers, linen drapers, hosiers, milliners, furniture brokers, ironmongers, hardware and trinket shops, leather sellers and curriers. The working poor arrived first, but by nine the market was filling with the 'hungry, meagre, and unwashed'.

Many men spruced themselves up while their wives shopped. 'Sunday morning is always an exceedingly busy time in a barber's shop in a working-class neighbourhood,' as men had their weekly shave, or the 'swells' who were going out for the day came in 'to have their hair brushed and "done up"'. In *Nicholas Nickleby*, the barber in Soho is considered 'a highly genteel establishment – quite first-rate in fact', and yet the accompanying illustration makes plain that the 'shop' was nothing more than the front room of an ordinary house, as so many still were. But the main occupation there was local gossip, exchange of news and a look at the Sunday papers, as well as 'various cunningly concocted "revivers", which are euphemistically styled medicine', and were sold circumspectly to customers the barber knew personally, as they were in reality alcohol to cure Saturday-night heads.

There were also dozens of thriving second-hand clothes markets, the best known of which was in the East End of London, spread around Houndsditch and in Petticoat Lane. This was Rag Fair, the centre of the old-clothes market, which was said to be entirely run by Jews. The Exchange in Houndsditch was originally held on about an acre of ground, enclosed by wooden hoardings. Inside, there were four double rows of benches, where the sellers sat back to back with their wares laid out on the ground in front of them. Soon the selling area spread to encompass the neighbouring streets, and two distinct markets arose. The first had about ninety stalls by the late 1840s, where second-hand clothes were sold wholesale, for resale or renewing. These items appeared to have no use or value at all: some 'old tea-coloured stays, and bundles of wooden busks [the supports in corsets], and little bits of whalebone'; or boots with no soles; or just the ribs of umbrellas. But buyers were looking for goods for breaking, or taking apart, using the materials to produce other items; or for turning, making new versions of whatever they had been before. Goods that were past both these stages still had value, being sold for shoddy, a fabric made from old wool rewoven with new; worn-out shoddy was broken down for manure, or bleached and sold to paper mills.

The second area of the market, about a third smaller, was where renovated clothing was sold to second-hand dealers stocking their shops. Shopkeepers from as far afield as Marylebone Lane, Holywell Street, Monmouth Street, Drury Lane, Saffron Hill, the Waterloo Road and Shoreditch itself, all poor districts, bought from the Exchange. In the 1840s and 1850s, admission to both areas was ½d for buyers and sellers. A third area, with no admission charge, operated as a retail market in the afternoons. There sellers displayed their stock, purchased from unredeemed pledges from pawnbrokers' shops, or overstocks from military suppliers.

Boots were sold separately, in an area centred on Rosemary Lane (from 1850 renamed Old Mint Street), near the Tower, and around Monmouth Street in Covent Garden. Boots, pre-mechanization, were expensive. Those that had worn out were refronted and sold to clerks and others who needed to look respectable for work. Boots that were too worn out for that were 'translated': resoled, refronted once more and the leather painted to look (briefly) new. These were sold to the very poor. Mayhew counted 800 shops selling translated boots, but this was probably a vast underestimate, as many boots were sent to Ireland to be translated and then returned to London for sale in the cheapest shops.

In some ways, these markets were no more salubrious than the meat markets. The smell of the old clothes, the old shoes, 'together with, in the season, half-putrid hare skins, is almost overpowering': a 'peculiar sour smell blended with the mildewy'. For any smell to have overpowered Londoners, it must have been truly noxious, for the city was filled with stenches. Horses produced their own smells. Omnibuses at their peak utilized 40,000 horses in London, and each horse ate nearly twenty-one pounds of oats and hay daily, so the quantity of manure left behind on the streets can be imagined – and this was without taking into account the dray horses, carthorses, carriage horses, riding horses, or costermongers' donkeys and ponies, much less the cattle and sheep driven through the streets. Pickford's Removals, a moving company, alone kept 1,500 horses to pull its vans in 1870, and that same year 18 million tons of coal were delivered for domestic use, almost all by horse-drawn cart. No one knows how many horses there were in London before the twentieth century: they were so ubiquitous that no one ever thought to count them, but there can have been no district that did not smell of horses and manure.*

Horses in the afterlife caused further, and vastly worse, smells. In the 1820s, it was estimated that 400 horses a week were slaughtered via licensed horse-butchers (more commonly known as knackers' yards); by mid-century the number had risen to 1,000 horses weekly, and knackers' yards dotted the poorer districts – more prosperous neighbourhoods wouldn't dream of housing such a place as the 'sickening stench', said Mayhew, came 'leaking in through every crevice'. At Holborn Hill in Islington, Bermondsey, Whitechapel and Wandsworth, there were more than twenty all told.

* One small indication of their importance is seen in the number of pubs that have 'horse' in their name. In one 1851 list, there were twenty-one pubs named for Queen Victoria, but twenty-five named the Black Horse, twenty-seven named the Horse and Groom, fifty-four named the White Horse, plus additional ones with names like the Horseshoe, or the King on Horseback. There were also fifteen Watermen's Arms.

Smaller yards processed up to sixty horses weekly; the larger yards around 150. Live horses as well as dead arrived, and the biggest yards had contracts with brewers, coal merchants and omnibus companies, who used, and used up, horses at a great rate.

The yards boiled up the flesh in great vats, by law at night, so as to cause the least possible nuisance from the dreadful smell, and also because the cats'-meat men started their rounds first thing in the morning. In theory, horsemeat was not sold for human consumption, but most people were sure that it was. The tongues were also sold, in the guise of ox tongues, the hearts and kidneys masquerading as ox hearts and kidneys. The rest was not discarded, either: manes and tails were sold to upholsterers for horsehair upholstery; hooves went to glue-makers; shoes and nails were sold back to blacksmiths and ironmongers for reuse. Early in the century bones went to button manufacturers and, when mechanization later made that uneconomic, they were processed to make manure, while the fat was skimmed off and sold as harness oil and axle grease. The skins went to tanners, which were mostly situated in Bermondsey, and provided another stench, giving the district literally its own air.

6.

SELLING THE STREETS

The streets were a place to go to, not to go through, in the nineteenth century. There was a thriving shop trade, but for many people, purchases were made on the streets, both central and suburban. The sellers were rather like the horses: so ubiquitous that counting them was an afterthought. Mayhew estimated in the late 1840s and early 1850s that there were 30,000 adults, and an uncounted number of children, who sold goods and services on the streets. The census, by contrast, lists fewer than 3,700 street sellers in 1851. The reality, no doubt, is somewhere between the two. Even taking a halfway-house figure suggests that one out of every 150 people in London was selling something outdoors.

Street selling was, at best, a subsistence-level job. Mayhew suggested that averaged together, a street seller earned 10s weekly over the entire year: on £26 a year, no one was doing more than surviving. Earnings might rise to 30s a week in the summer, but winter was hard for almost all street sellers. Many of them lost entire days of income in the rain: this included most street entertainers; those who provided services on the streets – knife-grinders, tinkers who mended pots and pans, people who recaned chairs; or those reliant on the whims of passers-by – children selling lavender, or violet sellers, or those offering fruit and sweets. Rain drove ballad and broadsheet sellers under cover, too, as their entire stock could be wiped out by a sudden shower. Yet others prospered during bad weather. Those who sold staples such as vegetables and fish did well: housewives and servants were pleased to stay indoors and have their dinners walk past them. Umbrella pedlars, too, appeared when it rained, heading for theatres and pleasure gardens, or the pubs or doorways, where those who had unwisely set out unprotected were sheltering. In summer, and in good weather, these 'mush-fakers' (mush from mushroom, for the shape of the umbrella) switched from selling to buying, walking the poorer districts and calling, 'Sixpence for any old humbrellar,' and then in the better-off residential districts, arriving with a bag of supplies, calling, 'Humrellars to mend!'

At the poorest end of the food trade were the watercress sellers. Watercress was a fresh green that many bought daily in penny bundles at breakfast or teatime. There was little profit in it, and the start-up costs were correspondingly small: for a penny outlay a buyer got 'a full market hand, or as much as I can take hold of at one time without spilling; for threepence you should have a lap full enough to earn about a shilling off'. Cress sellers were therefore the very young or the very old. Girls started to sell cresses when they were about seven, moving after a few years into more profitable lines. Yet the work was not easy. Cresses were sold in bulk at Farringdon, Waterloo and Hackney markets. Farringdon and Waterloo were closer for the central London sellers, but Hackney was near the cress beds, and, for those who could manage the extra two- or three-mile walk in each direction, it was worth it: by cutting out the middleman at the city markets, they could earn an extra 3d to 4d a day.

The girls arrived at the markets daily by 4 a.m. Buying in the dark, by candlelight or gas, was a skilled job: it was not easy to see whether the produce was fresh, or whether the suppliers were passing off the previous day's wilted remainders. In winter, the damp produce froze solid on the walk back to town and could no longer be separated into penny bunches, so the new cresses had to be washed under the market pump, before being carefully mixed with the tired cresses left from the day before. The girls then walked back, either to stand in a favoured spot where commuters passed by, or headed for the residential districts, following a regular route, carrying the families' breakfast greens in a flat, shallow basket on their heads, while the very poorest used a tin tray suspended from their necks by a string. They sold until about 8.30 in the morning, before returning to their lodgings for a breakfast of tea and bread; or, if their parents were themselves already out selling, which was likely, the girls continued with their route until they had made the penny profit needed to buy coffee and bread and butter from a coffee stall. Then they started again, selling through the streets for the teatime and then the late-supper market, until about 10 p.m., at which point, having walked up to fifteen miles daily, they returned home to bed, to get up the next morning at three once more.

Henry Mayhew claimed that in 1850 he had walked forty-six miles of 'the principal thoroughfares' in London, and found on average fourteen stalls to the mile, of which a dozen sold fish or fruit. The main purveyors were the costermongers. Some were prosperous, with a pony or donkey, and a cart with a rail at the back to hold a tray of vegetables, and the rest of the stock in the cart; others had a cart with sides, front and back, that folded down to display the produce. Still others had a barrow with cords tied to the handle, pulled by a donkey; for the less successful, there was the handbarrow, some of which had rails, all sloping from back to front, with the goods placed on top on a wooden tray and sometimes marked by small, brightly coloured flags at the four corners. The least prosperous stood with a basket on the streets. One woman in the 1860s had a pitch in the gutter outside a pub in Lamb's Conduit Street in Bloomsbury. This had the advantage that, under the pub's flaring gaslight, she was visible to customers on their way home. (It probably also threw off a little residual heat, which she no doubt welcomed.) Her produce was routinely just a few lettuces and onions.

Many of the more successful costermongers employed a boy, aged between ten and sixteen, who, for 2d or 3d a day and his food, called the goods, his piping voice carrying further over the street noise. (The poor diet of the working classes delayed puberty; many sixteen-year-olds had voices that had not yet broken.) Costermongers and their boys started for the markets at four o'clock in the summer, six in the winter. Once their produce was prepared, they set off to sell it. If a coster had regular customers, he might finish his rounds by noon, after which he sent the boy out on his own, letting him keep any money he earned over a set sum, while he took up another line to sell. Most costermongers expected to start before dawn, sell 'greens of a morning, and go…round to the public [houses] with nuts of an evening, till about ten o'clock at night'.

Pubs were a popular selling site. Many sellers stocked food to be eaten with the drinks the customers had bought, and publicans welcomed those with 'relishes', whose sharp and salty tastes encouraged drinking. But many other sellers offered items that were quite independent of the setting. In the late 1840s, Henry Mayhew sat and watched the sellers in one pub: in seventy-five minutes he saw four selling sheep's trotters, three with shrimp, pickled whelks and periwinkles, two baked-potato men, eight with ballads and song-sheets, eight more selling matches and three selling braces. According to Mayhew, while he watched 'Not one of these effected a sale,' yet it is unlikely that so many sellers would return so frequently without some result.

Suburban dwellers marked the passing of the seasons by the variation of street sellers, not only of seasonal food, but of manufactured goods and of services. In autumn, red-flannel draught excluders were sold; in summer the men selling flypaper reappeared. The latter wore top hats encircled with strips of the paper dotted with dead flies, to show how well it worked, and they shouted, 'Catch 'em alive-o!' (Often they were trailed by small boys lobbing dead insects at their hats, to see if they could get them to stick.) In spring came the first of the root sellers, as they were called, women who sold potted plants, as well as children with bunches of sweetbriar or violets. Indeed, flowers were suddenly everywhere: 'The signs of spring-time that come to the Londoner's ear' included the women's 'shrill cry of "Two bunches a-penny – sweet wa-a-ll-flowers!"' The Londoner's eye was greeted by the sight of wagons, 'the tops of which are a bright canary-yellow, with their hundred roots of blooming primroses', while the barrow-men shouted, 'All a-blowing! All a-growing!' Equally springlike were the women crying, 'Any o-ornaments for your fire stove!', selling paper cut-outs and coloured shavings to fill the empty grates once the warm weather arrived. In summer came the gravellers, a man and a boy with a horse and cart: 'wherever he sees that the walks are grown dingy or moss-grown, he knocks boldly at the door, and demands to be set to work.' Householders might as well say yes at once, shrugged one resigned suburban resident, for otherwise the men would keep coming back until they 'bore[d] you into consenting'. In winter the same men reappeared to sweep snow off the paths and pavements, while costers and greengrocers turned themselves into ice sellers when there was a hard frost, going up to ponds on common land and chipping off enough to fill a basket or cart to sell around the neighbourhood.* In late December, many costermongers went 'Christmasing', cutting holly, ivy, evergreen boughs and mistletoe on common land and selling it to the cry of 'Holly! Holly!! Holly-o!!! Christmas Holly oh!' In April they sold lilac, in May, hawthorn blossom, and on the Saturday before Palm Sunday there were palm fronds in their carts.

Some suburban sellers had permanent pitches and a clearly understood arrangement with the local residents. Americans renting a house near Hyde Park were told that it was their house's responsibility to send out 'a cup of tea and a bit of something to eat' twice a day to an elderly apple-woman who sat outside their house. In exchange, these sellers did small jobs and ran errands for the householders, as the ballad seller Silas Wegg's sign offered in *Our Mutual Friend*:

Errands gone
On with fi
Delity By
Ladies and Gentlemen
I remain
Your humble Servt:
Silas Wegg.

(In Silas's case, his services were not called on 'half a dozen times in a year' by the owners of the house he regarded as 'his'.)

Most sellers, however, walked the rounds of the streets on a regular daily or weekly schedule, at set times, days or seasons. First every morning came the sweeps, calling, 'Sweep-o! Sw-e-e-e-p!', followed by the dustman, ringing his bell and crying, 'Dust-ho!' as he arrived to collect the ashes that had been swept out of fireplaces. The sweeps needed to do their work before the fires were lit for the morning hot water. Large houses with many fires that were kept up all day sometimes called the sweep in once a month;

* One report of these ice suppliers came at the height of London's worst cholera epidemic, although the water-borne nature of transmission was not yet recognized.

more often, for most of the middle classes, it was once a quarter; while the working classes tried to get by with once a year – chimney fires were a sign that the sweep had not been recently enough. It cost up to 1s 6d to have the chimneys swept in an ordinary terraced house and, as a perk, the sweep kept the soot, which he sold on to market gardeners, as fertilizer.

Sweeps and dustmen were followed by the milkmen and -maids. In the 1840s, one writer said that milkmaids were usually from Wales 'and did, until of late' wear national dress. More commonly, both men and women wore country smocks, usually white; the men had glazed pot-hats; the women white stockings, straw bonnets with white caps underneath, and woollen shawls. Men and women alike carried heavy wooden yokes over their shoulders, supporting milk-pails holding forty-eight quarts of milk, with a dozen or more supplementary cans hooked on the edges of the pails, ranging down from a quart size. The yokes were sometimes painted with the name of the dairy – 'Sims, 122 Jermyn Street' – and the names of an aristocratic customer as advertising. Arthur Munby, in Mayfair early one summer morning, noted one yoke boasting, 'Wreathall, milkman to His Grace the Duke of Northumberland', although another topped that with, 'Stevens, By appointment to the Queen'. As they walked, the milkmaids called, 'Milk-o,' or just 'Mi-o,' contractions of 'Milk, below,' their warning to those in basement kitchens that supplies were coming down. For households with few servants or none, whose inhabitants could not stop work for every tradesman or woman, the milkmaid had a length of string with a hook at the end that she attached to one of her smaller cans and lowered it through the railings. (The milkmaid in Plate 4 is doing exactly this.) The can in which she had delivered the previous day's milk was left hitched on to the area railings ready for collection. After the morning round, milkmaids walked the streets selling to passers-by, before returning for teatime and supper trades. One walked four miles to and from her dairy: after a 5.30 start she trudged her routes until 7 p.m., earning 9s a week and her meals.

The next sellers were the watercress girls, followed by the costermongers, then the fishmongers', the butchers' and the bakers' boys to take the daily orders. The cress girls and the costers wore the standard street-dress of the working poor. Early in the century, for the men, this was breeches, thereafter replaced by cord trousers, with shirts and waistcoats or smocks, sometimes a jacket, a cloth cap and always a silk kingsman neckerchief – a coster had to be very hard up not to have one. The girls wore cotton dresses, usually pinned up out of the mud, frequently with two aprons, a coloured one covered by a white one, with a shawl, a silk neckerchief if it was affordable, and a black velvet or straw bonnet, or, if they carried their goods on their heads, a folded handkerchief. Delivery boys all wore clothing that denoted their trade: bakers' boys in white, with aprons; the butchers' boys in light-blue smocks and dark-blue aprons (which matched the bright-blue ink with which butchers wrote out the orders), and all wearing caps.

After that, the day really began, with a procession that, daily or weekly, included the cats'-meat man, wearing a shiny black hat and waistcoat, with black sleeves, blue apron and corduroy trousers, and always with a blue-and-white spotted handkerchief tied around his neck, selling his horsemeat by the pound, or in small pieces on skewers for a farthing.* Other goods regularly available from itinerant sellers in the suburbs included: footstools; embroidery frames; clothes horses, clothes-pegs and clothes line; sponges, chamois leathers, brushes and brooms; kitchen skewers, toasting-forks and other tinware; razors and penknives; trays, keyrings and small items of jewellery; candlesticks, tools, trivets, pots and pans; bandboxes and hatboxes; blackleading for kitchen ranges and grates, matches and glue; china ornaments and crockery; sheets, shirts, laces, thread, ribbons, artificial flowers, buttons, studs, handkerchiefs; pipes, tobacco, snuff, cigars; spectacles, hats, combs and hairbrushes; firewood and sawdust. The hearthstone-brick

* Men rarely if ever wore short sleeves, no matter how dirty their work. Some indoor jobs allowed for rolled-up shirtsleeves (in *Our Mutual Friend* the potboy of the Six Jolly Fellowship Porters has 'his shirt-sleeves arranged in a tight roll on each bare shoulder'), or men sometimes held their sleeves up with a band. Copying clerks and those in inky trades, as well as those doing outdoor work, where men wore jackets, all wore calico oversleeves, almost always just called 'sleeves'. (Plate 18 shows a pair.) In *Bleak House*, Mr Snagsby, the well-to-do law-stationer, wore a grey shop-coat with black sleeves over it. Sleeves were tied on at the upper arm, with strings until the arrival of 'gutta-percha', or elastic. Most were black, although bakers and muffin men, among certain other trades, wore white sleeves as a badge of their 'clean' calling.

men (before detergent, abrasives were needed to clean floors and cooking utensils) also purchased old bottles and bones for resale.

For it was not a one-way trade, from the streets to the houses. Many of the traders were buying from, not selling to, the households. Sometimes, as with the hearthstone men, the trade was in both directions. Crockery sellers exchanged their wares for old clothes, trading a tea service for a suit of clothes, a hat and boots 'in decent condition'; an old coat might be exchanged for a sugar basin; a pair of wellington boots for a glass. One crockery seller started with crockery worth 15s and, on a good day, ended with 1s in cash, plus two or three old shirts, a couple of coats, a suit of livery, a dress, a pair of boots or two, and a waistcoat, carrying them all on his back, with his crockery balanced on his head, 'and werry probably a humberella or two under my arm, and five or six old hats in my hand'. Thus laden, he tramped up to twenty-five miles a day.

As with their colleagues in the second-hand clothes market, old-clothes men were said to be Jewish and were usually elderly. They carried a bag for the clothes, while whatever hats they had bought that day were perched on top of their own. Traditionally they made themselves known by carrying a small clock under one arm, the striker of which they twanged as they walked along, calling, 'Old clo'!' Many middle-class housewives considered selling clothes to be not quite respectable, and so the old-clothes men prided themselves on their discretion: 'A form, half-concealed by a curtain, appears at a window...a finger is hastily raised, and then the figure as hastily retires. It is enough; the Jew saunters across the road, glances with apparent carelessness around, and slips quietly into the house, of which the door is conveniently ajar, and the whole business is managed with that secrecy so greatly desired by penurious but highly respectable householders.'

Other purchasers were equally stealthy, not to save the face of the householders, but because the sellers were disposing of goods they didn't technically own. The least honest servants sold the family's food. In *Great Expectations*, the cook to the chaotic Pocket household is found lying 'insensibly drunk', with a packet of butter ready to sell beside her. Other servants saw various forms of recycling as their perquisites. Well-regulated households, according to advice books, produced no food waste: everything was reused in leftovers or transformed into other dishes, with the residue going to feed dogs, cats or chickens, or to fertilize the garden. But many servants sold on the waste, called wash, to dealers who purchased it as pig-feed (hence the word 'hogwash'). Some bought wash to feed their own pigs, kept in market gardens around the edges of the city or even in many inner-city slums (see p. 208); others were middlemen, buying wash in bulk from coffee houses, eating houses and cookshops. Dealers sold the wash for 4d to 6d per bucket, hiring boys to go door to door, for 2s a week plus their meals, or sometimes for as little as 1d a bucket. Cooks sold hare and rabbit skins after they had cut up the meat for cooking: at mid-century hare skins were worth up to 2s 2d each. There was even a trade in used tea leaves. In most households, after the tea had been made, the leaves were rinsed, dried and sprinkled on the carpets before sweeping, to help collect the dust. Once this had been done, some charwomen sold the leaves to unscrupulous dealers who mixed them with new tea leaves, selling the tea at bargain prices. It was these very women and their kind who were most likely to purchase the lowest-priced tea, and who were drinking what they had lately swept up.

Other street sellers offered not goods, but services. Tinkers routinely trawled the streets, calling, 'Pots and Kettles to Mend! – Copper or Brass to Mend', as they pushed a cart with a small fire-pot, over which they soldered items for repair. 'Chairs to mend' men carried a supply of canes and rushes, fixing broken rush-bottomed or cane seats on doorsteps and front gardens. 'Knives to Grind' men carried a grinder powered by a small foot-treadle in their carts. With this they sharpened scissors and knives for housewives (3s for a dozen table-knives, or carving knives at 4d each in 1827), honed cleavers at markets, and even whetted penknives for office workers in the days before steel-nibbed pens were common. Until the invention of stainless steel in the twentieth century, knives could not be immersed in water, as the pin holding the blade to the handle rusted and the knife fell apart. By the 1850s, men walked the streets with patent knife-cleaning machines: the knives were inserted blade first into a box and when a handle was turned the blades were buffed by emery paper. Other new services in the 1850s were less high-tech: the Ragged School – a charity that aimed to get children off the streets, educating them and finding them trades – organized for its little girls to 'attend the dwelling-houses of the neighbourhood every morning, and brush and wash the steps for 1d a door'.

Thus suburban streets, so quiet in the twenty-first century, were in Dickens' time a hubbub of noise from dawn until well past dusk, so much so that the never-ending din was a staple of comic writing. In *Punch* in 1857, 'Edwin the poet' is in the throes of inspiration:

Edwin (composing). Where the sparkling fountain never ceases –
Female Demon. 'Wa-ter-creece-ses!'
Edwin. And liquid music on the marble floor tinkles –
Male Demon. 'Buy my perriwinkles!'
Edwin. Where the sad Oread oft retires to weep –
Black Demon. 'Sweep! Sweep!! Sweep!!!'
Edwin. And tears that comfort not must ever flow –
Demon from Palestine. 'Clo! Clo! Old Clo!'
Edwin. There let me linger beneath the trees –
Italian Demon. 'Buy, Im-magees!'
Edwin. And weave long grasses into lovers' knots –
Demon in a white apron. 'Pots! Pots!! Pots!!!'
Edwin. Oh! what vagrant dreams the fancy hatches –
Ragged Old Demon. 'Matches! Buy Matches!'
Edwin. She opes her treasure-cells, like Portia's caskets –
Demon with Cart. 'Baskets, any Baskets!'
Edwin. Spangles the air with thousand-coloured silks –
Old Demon. 'Buy my Wilks! Wilks! Wilks!'
Edwin. Garments which the fairies might make habits –
Lame Demon. 'Rabbits, Hampshire Rabbits!'
Edwin. Visions like those the Interpreter of Bunyan's –
Demon with a Stick. 'Onions, a Rope of Onions!'
Edwin. And give glowing utterances to their kin –
Dirty Demon. 'Hare's skin or Rabbit skin!'
Edwin. In thoughts so bright the aching senses blind –
Demon with Wheel. 'Any knives or sissors [sic] to grind!'
Edwin. Though gone, the Deities that long ago –
Grim Demon. 'Dust-Ho! Dust-Ho!!'
Edwin. Yet, from her radient bow [sic] no Iris settles –
Swarthy Demon. 'Mend your Pots and Kettles!'

Edwin. And sad and silent is the ancient seat –
Demon with Skewers. 'Cat's M-e-a-t!'...
HERE – EDWIN GOES MAD.

In the 1820s, Rowlandson drew a street with a woman selling cucumbers from a wheelbarrow (the phallic implications of her vegetable also being clearly much on his mind); a man selling roasting jacks for kitchen fires; a seller of doormats, with his wares hanging from a long pole; and a man with teapots, flowerpots and chamber pots all laid out on the pavement. He carefully depicted each seller with his or her own specific method of transporting and displaying goods. Stationery, soap and remedy sellers carried boxes suspended from their necks by leather straps; rabbits and hares were sometimes transported in baskets or were more usually tied together and slung over a pole on the sellers' shoulders, as were bonnet- and hatboxes; mats, brushes, brooms, clothesline and rope, fire-irons and skewers were all carried on the sellers' shoulders. Knife-cleaners and grinders used barrows, as did men selling hearthstone and whiting, as well as cats'-meat men, whose carts were equipped with a little shelf in the front, used for chopping the meat to order. Shallow willow baskets with a strap at the waist were used by fruit women, while oval baskets with a handle were characteristically used by onion- or apple-sellers; 'prickles', narrow willow baskets, contained walnuts, holding about a gallon at a time, or were used by the wine trade for empties. The poorest sellers had old rusty tea trays: shoeblack boys kept their brushes and paste on these trays, while match sellers tied them around their necks with string. Even delivery boys had specialized containers: telegraph boys carried a 'despatch-box'; doctors' boys a 'little double-flapped market-basket'; milliners' boys baskets covered in oiled silk, to protect the contents from the damp. Vendors of every article or service under the sun passed through the centre of town. In Holborn in the early 1850s, Max Schlesinger saw within a short space of time a man selling coconuts and dates, a woman selling oranges, a man with dog collars 'which he had formed in a chain round his neck', a man offering to mark linen indelibly, another selling razor strops, as well as miscellaneous sellers of notebooks, cutlery, prints, caricatures and more: 'it seemed as if the world were on sale at a penny a bit.'

Street sellers and shopkeepers coexisted, supported each other and were at war, all at the same time. Streets that were renowned as luxury shopping destinations, such as Regent Street, also drew their fair share of street sellers. Three in the afternoon was the fashionable shopping hour, and it was therefore the time that the street sellers crowded from Piccadilly Circus to St Martin's Lane (that is, eastwards, away from the most fashionable section of the street). Not unnaturally the shopkeepers and the street sellers chafed on each other. In 1845, in one case out of many, a fruit-woman was arrested by a policeman at the behest of the shopkeepers in Shepherdess Walk, City Road, on the basis that they suffered 'serious injury…by the competition of cheap itinerant traders'. From 1839, the Police Act had entitled – although not obliged – police to keep the roads and pavements clear of goods and blockages. The shopkeepers interpreted this to mean that the street sellers should be moved on, but the magistrate threw the case out. There was no law forbidding street trading, he said, and 'If poor creatures like this are to be seized…merely because they use praiseworthy exertions to support themselves', then the parish would have to support them, which would benefit neither the traders nor the shopkeepers, whose rates as a consequence would go up. The battles continued, while street sellers went on finding new locations for their trade. When the underground opened in 1863, they colonized this new space too, soon making it seem a natural place to be selling goods: 'Let anyone wanting their Noise and Rubbish,' snorted *Punch*, 'go Underground for it.'

Some sellers concentrated on specific locations. Around the Covent Garden and Drury Lane theatres in the 1830s, when the playhouses stood in the midst of slums, visitors 'were assailed by needy wretches' running beside the coaches and selling programmes for the plays. Some sellers concentrated on becoming known as *the* purveyor of an item. Rhubarb, used as a drug because of its laxative properties, supposedly came from what was vaguely thought of as 'the East'. In the late 1850s, a seller in Clare market dressed as 'a genuine Turk', carrying a sign declaring that 'Hafiz Khan was made prisoner by the Russians [in the Crimean War, just ended]; and…after undergoing many barbarities by the cruel order of the Emperor, succeeded in escaping to England, and is now reduced to the dreadful alternative of selling rhubarb (received direct from Turkey), in the public streets.'

Often selling appeared more random. In *Sketches by Boz*, Dickens reported that stagecoach offices were well known for their miscellaneous sellers: 'Heaven knows why', it is considered 'quite impossible any man can mount a coach without requiring at least sixpenny-worth of oranges, a penknife, a pocket-book, a last year's annual, a pencil-case, a piece of sponge, and a small series of caricatures'. Later, with the coming of the railways, at least one item of street-selling became more directly linked to the voyage itself. Now one of the prerequisites for setting out on a journey was a penknife: newspapers and books all had uncut edges, and in every train compartment passengers had to be busy with their knives before they could settle down to read. In *Dombey and Son* the very wealthy Mr Dombey's office, off Leadenhall Street in the City, is situated in a court 'where perambulating merchants' sold 'slippers, pocket-books, sponges, dogs' collars, and Windsor soap; and sometimes a pointer or an oil-painting'.

Jewellery was sold on the streets from cases, as well as in pubs by sellers showing off a few chains held at arm's length or sticking a few pins decoratively in their own clothes – sailors treating their girls tended to be good customers. (The illustration on p. 358 shows a woman selling goods from a tub on the right.) Pubs were also good places for pedlars to persuade listeners of the efficacy of their magic potions: medicines for people and animals; salves to knit broken bones, heal cuts and bruises; or pastes to remove stains and soot. The pedlar in *Oliver Twist* sells one such product that removes 'rust, dirt, mildew, spick, speck, spot, or spatter, from silk, satin, linen, cambric, cloth, crape, stuff, carpet, merino, muslin, bombazeen, or woollen stuff. Wine-stains, fruit-stains, beer-stains, water-stains, paint-stains, pitch-stains, any stains...One penny a square!' Items of every kind were on offer: malacca canes, or the smallest Bible in the world, or a Punch and Judy squeaker, or a bird-warbler.

In the 1840s, a type of proto water pistol – flexible metal tubes filled with scented water, which young boys enjoyed squirting at passers-by – became such a nuisance that legislation was passed to prevent its sale by hawkers. However, this toy was probably not as annoying, if only because it was not as common, as a toy sold at Greenwich Fair, known as 'All the Fun of the Fair': 'a mischievous little wooden instrument, with a rasp or toothed wheel', which, when run down someone's back, made a noise that sounded like fabric being torn. 'These are for sale by thousands at every fair…Mr. B— and myself got scraped a dozen times the other day by the girls in the crowds as we passed along…You are obliged to take it with good humor, but I cannot say that I think it a very refined amusement.' Refined or not, the writer nonetheless soon found himself buying one, whereupon 'a couple of girls came up, and…wanted to know if I was not ashamed to be getting one, thinking, as well they might, that I was a little too gray and too bald to be amusing myself in that way; but if the jades had not fled in no time, I certainly would have scraped them in return.'

On a more sober and necessary note, ready and waiting on the streets leading into the City that were tramped every morning by ranks of City workers, were rows of shoeblacks: in the days before routine street paving, every respectable worker needed to have his shoes cleaned after walking to work. In the early part of the century, blacking, or shoe polish, came in liquid form, and boys equipped themselves with paintbrushes, enquiring, 'Japan your shoes, your honour?' Blacking paste became available in cake form from the 1820s. Dickens is irrevocably linked to this new product after his ordeal at Warren's Blacking Factory, at 30 Hungerford Old Stairs.* It was so easy to use that shoeblacks vanished from the streets, but in 1851 the Ragged School set up a Shoeblack Society, and soon their red-coated shoeblacks were seen throughout the city at fixed pitches. The charge was 1d for brushing a gentleman's shoes and trousers, from which the boys earned about 10s a week in summer but in the winter only half that. (This is surprising: one would have expected the wet season to require more shoe-cleaning, not less.) Of this, the boys kept 6d a day, about a third of their earnings; a third went to the Society for its overheads, while the remaining third was put into a savings account for each boy. Boys of good conduct were

* Warren's Blacking was the original company, based at 30 Strand, but Warren's brother set up in competition, advertising as '**Warren's Blacking, 30** Hungerford Stairs, **Strand**'. This latter was the company that employed the young Charles.

transferred from the lowest-earning pitch to more valuable ones. Because they were moved regularly, the value of each pitch was known, and the boys had to report their earnings honestly. In the first year, despite the Society having taken in twenty-seven boys with criminal records, only two had to be discharged for dishonesty. Five were given the fares to emigrate; five got good jobs; one was 'restored to his friends'; three left of their own accord; four were sacked for misconduct and two for incompetence; while the rest continued as shoeblacks. Twenty-five of these boys supported their parents on their earnings.

Children, especially boys, made up a large segment of the street-selling world, and the founder of the Shoeblack Society described the 'two currents' that ran along every street, one 'five or six feet above the pavement, one two feet below that', the boys creating the lower one. On this lower level, equally ubiquitous, were the newsboys, who permeated every street in the West End and the City. By 1829, London was served by seven morning papers and six evening ones. At mid-century, one newsboy described his day. It began three hours before dawn, when he left his home to walk to the alley off Fleet Street where the morning papers were printed. There he and the other newsboys collected the papers that his employer, a newsagent, had ordered, folding, packing and bundling up the regular country orders to despatch by the first morning post, then carrying them to the main post office at St Martin's-le-Grand, a few hundred yards away. After that they waited outside their masters' shops; when the owners arrived to open up, they took down the big wooden shutters, bundled up more papers and set off on their rounds.

Some people ordered a newspaper every morning; others, for a reduced charge, rented a paper for a set number of hours, at a cost ranging from 6d to 1s a week, depending on the length of time it was kept, and the more or less popular hours. To purchase *The Times* at mid-century cost 6d a day, or £8 per annum, while rental was as little as £1 6s a year. If that was still too expensive, it was possible to rent the previous day's paper by the hour, at half the price of the current day's paper. All these orders had to be organized, and collections and redeliveries made for the rentals. At about nine the boys stopped for breakfast before returning to the shop to collect more papers to sell in the streets or at railway stations: '*Times, Times* – to-day's *Times*! *Morning Chronicle*! *Post*! *Advertiser*! *Illustrated News*! Who's for to-day's paper? Paper, gentlemen! News, news! Paper, paper, paper!' At one they stopped for dinner, going home to their mothers if they lived near by. Many women performed piecework at home, either sewing for subcontractors, making matches or artificial flowers (both notoriously poorly paid), or sewing sacks and bags for the corn trade, the wool trade or other commercial uses. But many of the boys had mothers who were out at work all day, as charwomen, laundresses, market porters, street sellers or fishwomen; many more had no mother living. For these boys, lunch was a penny loaf eaten on the street, or perhaps bread and coffee at a stall, maybe even a pie if they were in funds.

After lunch they returned to their pitches, then it was back to the shop to prepare the afternoon papers for the evening mails. The rented newspapers had to be collected and reallocated, and – as any newspapers remaining unsold at the end of the day lost half their value and, after two days, all value – the boys ran an informal exchange programme. They met between four and five every afternoon on Catherine Street and at St Martin's-le-Grand and the calls began: '*Ad.* for *Chron.*', '*Post* for *Times*', '*Herald* for *Ad.*' But the trades were not always simple. Six o'clock was the hour that the last post left from the main post office, to reach the country that same afternoon. As posting time grew ever closer, the negotiations became more complex, with some chains involving three, four, or even as many as eight or ten papers. But timing was key. After the boys had amassed as many papers as they had orders for, and traded away as many as their employers no longer needed, they returned to their shops to make up the bags once more before heading to the post office. Policemen were always on duty outside the entrance to St Martin's-le-Grand, keeping the way clear for the last-minute rush – this was a known sight of the city, with guidebooks recommending it to visitors. (The painter George Elgar Hicks' *The General Post-Office, One Minute to Six* was a huge success when it was shown at the Royal Academy in 1860.) Newsboys who were old hands at the game sometimes made a great show, waiting down the road until the clock began to strike six – on the sixth stroke, the gate closed for the day – dashing up in fine style on the penultimate stroke, to the cheers of the crowd. With the final stroke, their day was over, until three hours before dawn the next morning.

Many boys, however, did not have an employer. They worked for themselves, standing outside offices, clubs and, especially, coaching inns or, later, railway stations and bus stops, selling a wide variety of items. Other children sold services. Much casual labour had to do with horses, in stables or on the streets. Boys hung about livery stables, where they helped the stable-hands for a few pennies, or for food. Dickens' fiction teems with boys like Kit Nubbles in *The Old Curiosity Shop* who goes out to 'see if I can find a horse to hold' so he can 'buy something nice'; another character in the same novel hands his pony and phaeton to a man 'lingering hard by in expectation of the job', while in *Dombey and Son* Mr Carker calls 'a man at a neighbouring way to hold his horse'. All these men and boys expected to earn a penny for standing with a horse for up to half an hour. (Any longer than that and the horse needed to be taken to a stable.) One boy, in fiction, was a bit more entrepreneurial. In the 1821 comic novel *Real Life in London*, a man leaves his horse with a boy while he visits his club. On his return he finds the boy hiring out his horse in penny rides to other street boys and this was, supposedly, his '*fifteenth* trip' – which, to work as comedy, must at least have held the possibility of truth.

More usual was the boy who was given some bread and butter for helping a shopboy to polish the brass on the door of a chemist's shop; or those who stood by the restaurants and saloons in the Haymarket late at night, hoping for pennies for opening cab doors 'and putting their ragged coat-tails against the muddy wheels to protect the dresses of those alighting'. A woman who sold sheep's trotters had a crippled son who cleaned knives for a family; although not paid, he was fed, which alone was enough to make a difference in mother and son's weekly accounts. During a frost, when pipes froze, boys knocked on doors in residential districts, offering to wait in line at the standpipe for the householders; or they marched along the streets calling, 'Water – water! any water wanted?' and for 2d filled the householders' buckets.

Boys haunted railway stations, carrying bags or helping porters push carts. Some were cab runners, waiting near the cabstands at stations, then running behind any cab that left loaded with luggage. When the cab reached the passenger's destination, the boy got the luggage down and (unless prevented by the passenger's own servants) carried it into the house, for which he was then tipped. Attitudes to these porters varied widely. One journalist claimed that the runners shouted abuse if they weren't permitted to take the luggage, preying in particular on women and servants; an American tourist, on the contrary, reported them waiting 'very humbly' for 'Anything y'r honor pleases'.

Running porters performed the same service for omnibus passengers, waiting at stops by the railway stations and following buses when passengers got on with luggage. A journalist in the 1850s watched as a group of six boys, ranging in age from about seventeen to twelve or thirteen, ran behind his bus from Paddington to the Bank, in the City. At each stop, when a passenger with luggage got out, one boy peeled off to carry the bag home for a tip. The final boy, aged about fourteen, had to fight off 'a half-drunken porter of forty' who was standing at the Bank omnibus stop, also waiting for passengers with luggage. These older men, frequently unemployable alcoholics, were one of the reasons the boys ran in packs. The boy who won this job earned a penny or two for carrying a bag half a mile, having already run five miles from the station, but as the boys took it in turn to serve the first passenger, some of their journeys were shorter. Altogether, the journalist was told, the boy averaged three trips a day, on a good day earning 1s 3d, on a bad one 8d or 9d. His lodgings cost him 6d a week, and his food consumed the rest: like the crossing-sweepers, he worked barefoot, unable to afford the wear and tear on his boots.

A grown-up version of these boy porters, and slightly better paid, were the ticket porters of the City, one of whom, the stalwart and faithful Trotty Veck, was created by Dickens in a Christmas story, *The Chimes*. Ticket porters – recognizable by their ticket, their badge of office, which had to be worn, and by their white aprons – were licensed by the City to function as letter carriers and messengers: when in *Bleak House* Esther needs to send an urgent message to her guardian, she writes it at a coffee house, and sends it by ticket porter. They were also licensed to carry goods weighing up to three hundredweight (136 pounds) within a radius of three miles. Across the City there were wooden pitching places, upright blocks on which parcels could be balanced while porters got their breath back. Despite these loads, the porters were stereotypically considered lazy. 'Trotty' was an exception, as his name suggests, but in *David Copperfield* Dickens presented the general view, as David watches a ticket porter dawdling along with a letter. 'He was taking his time about his errand, then; but when he saw me... he swung into a trot, and came up panting as if he had run himself into a state of exhaustion.'

Trotty's income is minuscule. Even when children lived with their parents, even for those earning well in their trade, and with a family all contributing to a group income, there was no give in the budget: one illness, or one week of bad weather, could destroy them all. If there was no money for rent, then the entire structure on which the family had built their life quickly disintegrated. Some, who were far worse off, were always in view as a warning, on the same streets, also selling. The really indigent were reduced to peddling matches.

Matches were paradoxical, being both cheap and highly valued in an age of fires, candles and gas. By the end of the eighteenth century, brimstone, or sulphur-tipped, matches were in use. These could be made by the vendors in their rooms: the cheap deal wood was split with a knife, a pennyworth of brimstone was heated over a fire to make it liquid, and the match tips were dipped in it. (If no fire was available, then sham matches could be made by dipping the wood in powdered sulphur, which looked the same but did not ignite; by the time the buyer found out it was too late.) Brimstone matches were lit by holding them to a candle or fire. In the absence of an open flame, a tinderbox was needed: a small wooden box divided in two, with a flint, a steel, the matches and some old linen rags on one side. The flint and steel were struck over the rags, creating sparks, which caused the rags to catch fire. The match was lit and held to a candle, to light whatever else was wanted, while the damper, a loose block that nestled into the other side of the box, was used to tamp out the rags.

Tinderboxes were overtaken in the 1810s by phosphorus bottles and matches dipped in chlorate of potash; when a light was needed, the match was dipped into the phosphorus and then rubbed against a cork until it ignited. By the 1830s, the congreve or 'congry' match appeared, which lit by friction when struck on any surface, making it easy to light, but causing many accidents by accidental friction. The names congreve and lucifer were used interchangeably, although the lucifer, also dipped in sulphur, was treated so that it ignited only when rubbed against sandpaper, leading to the matchboxes with sandpaper strips along the sides. Although lucifers smelt as foul as the brimstones, and were still dangerous, they were a great improvement on the old tinderbox method: 'the box we could never find when we wanted it; the tinder that wouldn't light; the flint and steel that wouldn't...strike a light till we had exhausted our patience'. This farrago had 'gone now; and, in its place, we have sinister-looking splints, made from chopped-up coffins; which, being rubbed on sand-paper, send forth a diabolical glare, and a suffocating smoke. But they do not fail, like the flint and steel, and light with magical rapidity.'

The constant presence of open flames in the nineteenth century meant that matches were not always necessary. In 1843, there was a gas explosion in Rosamond Street, Clerkenwell, when a man lit his cigar with a paper spill, or twist of paper, which he had held to a gaslight outside a shop. He tossed the spill away and it blew down a sewer grating: 'an instantaneous explosion of gas took place, resembling a discharge of artillery...about ten houses only have sustained injury, and these not to any great extent.' With less drama, this use of spills was routine. A novel of the 1850s depicts street children waiting in the Haymarket to run errands or fetch cabs for the men about town, and carrying paper 'to accommodate gentlemen whose cigars had gone out...if any such...chanced to approach, instantly the "spills" were lighted at the convenient jets at the café door'.

Congreves quickly became the standard match sold by street sellers, who offered two, sometimes even three, boxes for a penny, substantially undercutting the cigar shops, which sold penny boxes. The street sellers sometimes made a penny profit on a dozen or simply sold them at cost, which is why match sellers were classed not as street sellers, but as beggars.

Match selling was a byword for poverty. Most pictures of match sellers show either very small children or the very elderly – always an indication that there was little, if any, profit in a trade – and they are almost always depicted barefoot. The link between age, physical debility and matches occurs again and again. One journalist in the 1840s outside a gin palace reported seeing 'aged women selling ballads and matches, cripples, little beggar-boys and girls' – that is, those who physically could not earn a living. The architect, magazine editor and housing reformer George Godwin counted the residents of a slum court near Whitechapel Church in 1854, where sixteen rooms were home to 300 people. It was unsurprising to read that in one room lived a family of five match sellers, while the room above was occupied by a family of four whose wares were lucifers and onions.

In the first decades of the century, there was another, even more impoverished, group, 'the lowest classes to gain a livelihood'. It is noticeable that

Selling matches was the last resort of the ill, the very old and the very young. This photograph from the 1880s shows a fairly successful-looking seller: although the child is barefoot, he wears a cap, a sign of respectability.

for them, all interaction with the more prosperous classes, even by begging, was entirely absent. Mostly these people collected and resold waste that even the impoverished thought had no value. There were women who scavenged in Thames Street, known as the place where 'Lisbon merchants' sold imported citrus fruit, salvaging the squeezed lemon skins from the gutters and selling them to manufacturers who extracted the last vestiges of juice to make cheap lemon-drops. There were bone-pickers, who fought the dogs on the streets for discarded bones, which they sold to second-rate bone burners at 2s a bushel. Grubbers searched the cobblestones for bits of nails or other metal, which they sold to marine-stores dealers (see p. 239), while finders walked up to ten miles a day collecting the same sorts of metal, as well as rags and bottles. Grubbers earned on average between 2d and 3d a day, while finders, if the weather was wet, earned even less, as muddy rags had to be washed and dried before they could be sold. By mid-century, however, the modernization of manufacturing processes had made these ways of earning a living unviable.

These people were one accident or illness away from the fate of the man on whom an inquest was held in Walthamstow in that decade of economic depression, the Hungry Forties. The inquest jury heard that this man, 'name unknown, aged 52', had been out of work for weeks, but had managed to scrape a living selling congreves, until the police had threatened to arrest him as a beggar. Too frightened to go out selling in the streets again, he bartered his remaining stock of congreves for stale crusts and the dregs of tea, as well as a place to sleep on the floor in a room. Then he vanished for four days, until he was found crouched outside: he said he had moved out because he had nothing left to barter. His 'landlord' helped him in and gave him some gruel and ale, but he died the next day. Verdict: 'That the deceased died from want of the common necessaries of life and exposure to the cold.'

Many who were selling in the streets were doing so as a temporary measure to avoid precisely this fate. They were neither begging nor stealing, just tiding themselves and their families over a bad patch by making something from (almost) nothing. Early in the century one unemployed labourer and his son in Watford wove willow branches around pebbles to create children's rattles; they made a sackful of them and then walked the nearly twenty miles to St Paul's Churchyard to sell them at 6d each on that busy commercial thoroughfare. Groundsel and chickweed, to feed songbirds, were gathered freely from common land, and thus the sale of it was the preserve of the young or the very old: one old brush seller became a chickweed seller when rheumatism prevented his plying the more lucrative trade. He was known for having no cry and instead merely standing outside his regular houses, where the caged songbirds recognized him and began to cheep. Another man skimmed the weed off a pond in Battersea to sell to those who kept ducks in the slums, where residents raised fowl for sale. Simplers foraged in the woods on the edge of the city, gathering simples – medicinal herbs, mushrooms, dandelion greens and nettles – which they sold in markets, or collecting snails, leeches or vipers for simpling shops or herbalists. (Snails were recommended for consumptives, but vipers, says one writer in 1839, 'of late years ... are so little called for that not above one in a month is sold in Covent Garden Market'.) Boys cut grasses and reeds growing around the ponds on Hampstead Heath or in ditches near drains and sewers, selling it to costermongers as fodder for their donkeys.

The equation of street selling with poverty was complete, with it being generally understood as 'honest' or 'decent' poverty, in which people worked hard to support themselves. Yet by the 1850s, Mayhew, interviewing hundreds of street sellers, found a consistent belief among them that things had been easier decades earlier. No longer did housewives wait at home to hear a cry of 'Pretty pins, pretty women?' but instead went to the drapers; likewise, the men carrying barrels on their backs, with measures and funnels, and calling 'Fine writing-ink', had also lost business to the shops. Steadily modernity was changing the nature of the streets. The new office buildings in the City, the increase in bus (and soon underground) transport, the increasing size of London: all were making street selling less practicable, and necessitating more shifts to produce a bare living.

Street sellers were not alone in this. Most workers did not have a single job that sustained them, much less their family. Instead they patched together a series of jobs, either ones they held regularly, or seasonal work, to pay for basic sustenance and a room, or part of a room, to sleep in. A guidebook on London in 1852 contained a section entitled 'Banking'; in addition to information on the Bank of England, private banks, joint-stock banks and so on, it listed loan societies run by pubs for the poor, tallymen (pedlars who sold on instalment), and even pawnbrokers, who regularly lent money on the same goods, pawned and redeemed week after week as a family struggled from payday to payday. According to the guidebook, these makeshifts of the working classes were an integral part of the financial system.

Much of the battle to get work was visible on the streets. Many labourers, both skilled and unskilled, were hired by the day, or at best by the job. Skilled workers such as tailors and cobblers used pubs as trade clubs, a 'house of call', where 'the masters applied when they wanted workmen'. But in the earlier half of the century in particular, the hiring of unskilled labour took place out in the street: 'chairmen, paviers, bricklayers'-labourers, potato-gatherers, and basket-men' stood daily 'at their usual stands for hire' around the city: in Whitechapel, in Cheapside, on Oxford Street and at Tottenham Court Road among others.

The dockyards, some of the largest employers in London, used similar hiring practices. Skilled labourers such as coopers, rope-makers and carpenters held permanent jobs; until the 1850s, when the shipbuilding industries moved out of London, so did men working in iron foundries, sail yards and block-and-tackle shops. But two-thirds of the dockworkers were unskilled and were hired by the day. At 7.30 every morning a ragtag army a thousand or more strong stood waiting for a few hundred jobs, pushing and jostling for their favourite spots, where they thought the calling foreman looked most frequently. Once the foreman came out, 'Then begins the scuffling and scrambling, and stretching forth of countless hands high in the air, to catch the eye of him whose nod can give them work…some men jump up on the back of others, so as to lift themselves high above the rest and attract his notice. All are shouting.' After the foreman had filled his quota, many hung around in the waiting yard, in case a ship arrived late on the tide: a hundred or so men competing to be one of the half-dozen who might possibly be needed, to earn 4d an hour.

Even at the docks, weather affected the work – a prevailing easterly wind meant no incoming shipping; the seasons dictated the volume of ships arriving and leaving. Away from the docks, these factors affected many other kinds of labourers. Bricklayers, house painters, slaters, fishermen and watermen all suffered loss of earnings on rainy days, while pipe layers, sewer builders and some smaller building firms could not function when the ground was frozen. Luxury goods and services suffered badly when the social season ended and the rich shifted to their country houses. Even clerks, on the edge of the middle class, suffered then, as those who serviced the legal world had to survive the long summer vacation when the courts rose: 'it is starvation to the Scribe; it means the workhouse for many.' It was here that the true precariousness of life, and status, were made clear, where these men, hanging grimly on to the fringe of the lower middle classes, were forced to join the working classes, 'earning a scanty livelihood... picking hops' in Surrey and Kent. In Farringdon the Ragged School Dormitory for the indigent and homeless employed a night officer, whose job it was to sit on a dais every night from 9.30 p.m. to 6 a.m., to prevent assaults, thefts or other antisocial behaviour. The holder of this position in the early 1850s was a clerk by day, who put in another eight and a half hours through the night for the extra £1 it brought each week – and he had beaten 200 applicants to the post.

Those from the working classes whose trades slowed or ceased in summer found similar work, hop picking, or in market gardens. Pea picking was ideal for women with small children, as they could operate in rotation: families working together could sometimes make 4s a day in the ten-week season. Some had to juggle jobs not from month to month but from week to week. A stick seller offering whips, crops and walking sticks did a brisk trade in the parks and near excursion sites on Sundays in summer, but for the rest of the time needed to find another commodity more in demand.

Many more spent their lives 'on the tramp', a sort of forced moving on, as if in parody of the upper-class life of moving from home to home around the country. Trampers generally spent the summer and autumn in the countryside or suburbs, working as builders' labourers, brickmakers, navvies or agricultural labourers. In the winter, when no building work was done outside the capital, they headed back to London where they could find work, if not on building sites, then in subsidiary industries such as brickmaking,* or in gasworks, which required more labourers in the cold months, or in breweries after the hop harvest, or as chimney sweeps, who also had more work in winter. Showmen left London between March and April to tour the Easter fairs, returning to the city in October for the London fair season.

A shoemaker around 1810 walked daily from his half-room, as he called it (that is, the section of the room he rented from its primary tenant), to the Barbican, across Smithfield and onwards, going 'occasioning', where he went into each shoemaker's he passed, asking if any of them had occasion to hire him to do a day's work.† William Lovett, originally a Cornish rope maker, in 1821 came to London to find work, lodging with other Cornishmen by the docks and becoming an itinerant labourer. He and a friend got up at five every morning 'and walked about enquiring at different shops and buildings till about nine'; they paused to share a penny loaf before looking for work again until four or five in the afternoon, 'when we finished our day's work with another divided loaf'. After a fortnight three Cornish carpenters offered to find him work on a building site for a fee of 2s 6d. This was not avarice, just recognition that everyone was living at subsistence level, and a few pennies made a difference. Such trade-offs were not uncommon. At mid-century the sack- and bag-making trade was entirely supplied by women who collected canvas from the warehouses in Bermondsey by the river, carrying the bundles home on their heads to make up the bags as piecework. One woman earned a useful 6d a day by this trade, but being small and slightly built, 'she can't carry the sacks home as other gals do; so a strong young woman...carries them home for her, and charges her twopence for it'.

Trampers had a variety of places to stay, either overnight, weekly or for the season. Many were in the well-known slum areas: St Giles, Tothill Fields near Parliament, the Mint, south of the river; some lay in the suburbs, near

* In the ever-growing city, brickmaking should be understood for the huge industry it was. Like the 'horse' names for pubs, there were fifteen Bricklayers' Arms in London in the early 1850s.

† This usage is not recorded in the *Oxford English Dictionary*, but the shoemaker used it as if the term were common enough; certainly his meaning is not in doubt.

the market gardens and other work areas. Notting Dale (later gentrified as Notting Hill) was one of the first tramp sites, settled by pig-keepers who had been driven out of Tyburn (later Marble Arch) as it moved upmarket. Lodging houses for trampers cost up to 3d a day at mid-century, 6d a day in later years, and were for those in skilled trades and regular employment. Many trampers slept outdoors, by the brickfields if possible (the kilns stayed warm all night); others haunted the markets, where could be found late-night coffee stalls, the chance of odd jobs or, at worst, shelter under a trestle after the market closed. One alternative was the 'Dry Arch Hotels', the vaults under the bridges and later the railway viaducts: the Great Eastern Railway's arches at Spitalfields regularly sheltered sixty men every night; while the 500 arches under the line from Rotherhithe along the south-east corner of London offered a refuge to almost a whole town's population.

Even people in employment lived in such places, for sometimes it was seen as an improvement on what they might find in one of London's great slums.

7.
SLUMMING

At the beginning of the nineteenth century, the word 'slum' was unknown. Instead, 'rookery' was the usual word for overcrowded living conditions – as many rooks build their nests in a single tree, so a court 'is known by the name of the "Rookery", (from there being a humble family in each room)'. That 'to rook' had long meant to cheat added a moralistic note: rookeries were where the dishonest and disreputable lived. The word 'slum' emerged gradually during the late 1820s, gathering pace as did the growth of slums themselves.

This growth was driven by the rapidly increasing numbers of London's inhabitants. Between 1800 and 1850 the population of England doubled. At the same time, agricultural work was giving way to advancing industrialization and factory labour. In 1801, 70 per cent of the population lived in the country; fifty years later, this figure had been reduced to just 49 per cent. Migration, particularly from Ireland during the Famine years towards the middle of the century, resulted in the eighteenth-century infrastructure of London being swamped by the huge mass of its nineteenth-century residents. Transport, sanitation, food distribution, housing: none could cope with the numbers pouring into the capital every day.

The changing attitude to the poor, and the consequent creation of the harsh new Poor Laws in the 1830s, must be seen against this background. At the beginning of the century, there was a general acceptance of the poor – some were good, some were bad, some lazy, some worked hard: just as with the wealthy. In a series of views of London, which Rowlandson illustrated between 1808 and 1810, the caption to a picture of the Westminster Workhouse, with its happy, well-fed paupers, reads: 'The establishment of a permanent and certain provision for the aged and the helpless, not of occasional bounty, but of uncontrovertible [sic] right, and the anxious care which has watched...over every abuse or neglect in the execution of them, may be placed in competition with the greatest of our national achievements.' Workhouses were shelter for the very aged or the ill; the healthy and working poor who could not make ends meet received 'outdoor relief' of both money and food, supplemented sometimes by clothes, shoes and assistance in finding apprenticeships for their children. By the 1830s, however, increasing urbanism, population and inequality of income, creaking infrastructure and the rise in evangelical morality helped to create a view that the poor were poor not because of misfortune, or because wages were too low, but because they were drunken and lazy, probably immoral and dissolute, and no doubt rogues and thieves to boot. Even those who were generously inclined, who did not believe that being poor by definition made a person bad, used language that suggested they saw the poor as different from themselves in essential ways. *Oliver Twist* was an outraged response to the new Poor Laws; even so, Dickens used the words 'wild' and 'voracious' – as of an animal – to describe the workhouse children. Mayhew, a decade later, in the equally sympathetic *London Labour and the London Poor*, saw the poor as a 'tribe', that is, a group that was distinct from both the author and his readers.

Dickens and Mayhew were representative of many, possibly most, of the middle classes in this feeling of them and us. Those who were far less sympathetic objected to the growing number of workers receiving money under the old Poor Laws, which, through cash payments linked to the price of bread, had long enabled employers to pay their workers less than a living wage. In response, the 1824 Vagrancy Act criminalized the state of being indigent: begging and sleeping out without visible means of support were made criminal acts. (Thus, in *Oliver Twist*, when Oliver runs away, he is breaking the law by being on the road with no money.) In 1832, a Royal Commission was established, heavily weighted towards the Utilitarian philosophy that was hostile to the notion of the state subsidizing employers in this fashion. Two years later the Poor Law Amendment Act established a system in which outdoor relief was first reduced, then ultimately abolished almost entirely. In Southwark and the East End, before 1830 each pauper received 3s a week; by the mid-1860s, those who had some other form of income received less than 1s a week. A poor person who was entirely dependent on the parish was forced into the workhouse.

The problems inherent in the new arrangements soon became obvious. The Poor Law Guardians, who oversaw the system, were elected by ratepayers who had a vested interest in keeping expenditure down. Initially, the workhouses were meant to create an orderly life – no alcohol nor tobacco, early to work and early to rise, but with nourishing food and decent living conditions – in which the impoverished worker would learn the habits of gainful employment. But it was feared that if the workhouses were warm and well lit, the paupers well fed and well clothed, then there would be no incentive to work. Thus the notion of making the workhouses less 'eligible', or desirable, became central, with workhouses rendered 'as prison-like as possible'. Families were separated: men lived on one side, women on the other, with school for the children and work for all – preferably grinding, repetitive, meaningless work to discourage people from entering the workhouse until they were *in extremis*. The paupers were allowed no personal possessions; they were dressed in deliberately unattractive uniforms; their hair was cut unbecomingly (they were, said Dickens, 'pollarded'); they had to ask permission to leave the premises; their food was insufficient, and of the coarsest kind. The entire aim was to make them unhappy, and to make the better-off despise them. For many, these aims were achieved. In *Little Dorrit*, Old Nandy is forced into the workhouse at the end of his life. 'It was Old Nandy's birthday, and they let him out. He said nothing about its being his birthday, or they might have kept him in; for such old men should not be born.' When Little Dorrit accompanies the old man in his workhouse clothes, she is berated by her sister for 'coming along the open streets, in the broad light of day, with a Pauper!'

The Master of a workhouse was expected to ensure that the workhouse functioned, that the paupers were diligent and disciplined, that the staff kept order, that the accounts balanced and no more was spent than was necessary. The ratepayers' primary demand on him was to keep costs down, and cutting staff in quality and quantity was the easiest way. Workhouses were therefore run by people who could not get better jobs, and the fact that cruelty abounded was hardly a surprise. Yet the very existence of the workhouses was used by many, as Dickens noted so savagely, as an excuse to do nothing for the most wretched in society. In *A Christmas Carol*, when some philanthropic men approach Scrooge for a contribution to help the 'Many thousands [who] are in want of common necessaries', Scrooge refuses: 'those who are badly off,' he declares, should take themselves off to the workhouse.

Dickens returned again and again to the attitudes that had permitted the creation of this injustice. Written three years after the passing of the new Poor Laws, *Oliver Twist*, with its depiction of the ravenous children in the workhouse, is today the most famous description of the horrors of this penal system disguised as charity. Dickens as a young man had lived in lodgings in Norfolk Street, now 22 Cleveland Street, steps away from the huge Cleveland Street Workhouse (still surviving today almost intact). In 1843, in *A Christmas Carol*, he made this tale of the miser Scrooge's reform another enraged commentary on the Poor Laws; he wrote memorably on the same subject in *Little Dorrit* in the mid-1850s. In *Our Mutual Friend* in 1865, five years before his death, he created Betty Higden, the poor woman who in old age becomes an itinerant pedlar to avoid being taken to the workhouse: 'Kill me sooner than take me there. Throw this pretty child under cart-horses' feet and a loaded waggon, sooner than take him there...Do I never read in the newspapers...how [the paupers] are grudged, grudged, grudged, the shelter, or the doctor, or the drop of physic, or the bit of bread?...Johnny, my pretty...You pray that your Granny may have strength enough left her at the last...to get up from her bed and run and hide herself...sooner than fall into the hands of those...that...worry and weary, and scorn and shame, the decent poor.' 'It is,' Dickens added savagely, 'a remarkable Christian improvement, to have made a pursuing Fury of the Good Samaritan.' From his second to his penultimate novel, the evils of the workhouse ran through everything he wrote. He was not alone in his views. Even that bastion of middle-class rectitude, *The Times*, condemned the laws as an 'appalling machine...for wringing the hearts of forlorn widowhood, for refusing the crust to famished age, for imprisoning the orphan in workhouse dungeons, and for driving to prostitution the friendless and unprotected'.

But many dismissed these views, claiming that all beggars were thieves living at the expense of the hard-working. In Pierce Egan's *Life in London*, as early as 1821, a crossing-sweeper, arrested for abusing a woman who refused to give him a tip, asks, 'Who would *work hard* for a few shillings...when, with only a *broom*...a *polite bow* and a *genteel appearance*...the *ladies* could be *gammoned* [fooled] out of pounds per week.' Instead of the bare living that the work in actuality provided, Egan's novel presents his sweeper as earning £1 a day regularly – the income of a small tradesman. Many people wanted to believe these myths for economic reasons. A journalist touring the slums of Bermondsey in the mid-1860s was told that the poor positively 'liked dirt, and wouldn't use water not if it was tapped and messed into every room of the place'. His guide finished triumphantly by saying there was no point complaining to the parish, because the vestrymen who determined how much could be spent on poor relief were also the owners of these slum dwellings.

The reality of nineteenth-century poverty, however, was such that many things had value that today we cannot imagine buying, selling or even giving away. Near the basin where glasses were washed in pubs was a 'saveall', a small ledge of pierced pewter-work, in which the dregs from the glasses were deposited, to be sold to 'the poorer customers' or (as an afterthought), 'given away in charity'. In *Dombey and Son* a woman attempts to snatch Florence Dombey on the street, to steal her clothes for resale. Dickens may have read of a case that occurred in 1843, three years before *Dombey and Son* began to appear. A woman applied to a workhouse for relief. The workhouse surgeon thought the three-year-old boy with her was in some way 'superior'. So puzzling did the child appear that he was, ultimately, interviewed by the Lord Mayor in his home, where the toddler recognized a piano and a watch-guard, notably middle-class objects. He said he had one mother in the country who was kind to him and called him Henry, as well as this woman, whom he called his strawyard mother (a strawyard was a night refuge for the indigent; see pp. 198–9), who had taken away his clothes, which he itemized, and which were the clothes worn by middle-class children.* This was the oddest, but not the only, instance of children being stolen for their clothes. Many workhouses marked even their ugly clothes: in the 1840s, the Camberwell Workhouse had 'Camberwell parish' and 'Stop It' painted across their uniforms, while lodging houses sometimes had 'STOP THIEF!' marked on their sheets. There were many incidents that indicated the poor's utter desperation. Children broke windows or street lights to get themselves arrested: in gaol, they would be warm and fed, and could sleep indoors. In 1868, when a man was sentenced to seven days' prison for breaking lights, he begged for fourteen, 'but the magistrate was inflexible': seven was all he would give him.

Since it was far more comfortable for many to believe in Egan's rich beggars, the conditions in workhouses grew worse and worse. In 1842, a Select Committee heard from a man who had applied for relief and was punished for his temerity by being confined for forty-eight hours with five others 'in a miserable dungeon called the Refractory-room, or Black-hole', a room with no windows. 'The weather then (August) being exceedingly warm...they complained...and...as a punishment, a board was nailed over the small air-hole.'

There was little difference between the workhouses and the prisons. There was no sense that prisons were places that should be tucked away: they were physically as well as mentally integrated into the fabric of London. Tothill prison, in what is today Victoria (it was demolished in 1854 to build Westminster Cathedral), was visible from fashionable Piccadilly, where it could be mistaken for a wing of Buckingham Palace, while from Belgravia it looked as if it were set in 'a very enviable grove of trees'. The Fleet prison, by the nineteenth century almost entirely used for debtors, even had a street number posted on the front entrance: those who did not want to admit to being incarcerated could have their letters sent to 9 Fleet Market and hope that the sender would be none the wiser.

* A search was instituted for the child's family, but without success. Henry was raised by the workhouse surgeon, with contributions made from 'private individuals' towards his education. In 1852, he appeared again before magistrates to get permission to join the surgeon, who had emigrated to Melbourne.

In 1800, there were nineteen prisons in London, which by 1820 had increased to twenty-one, and they were regarded, by those outside the walls, as just one more of the city's many sights. In *Great Expectations*, when Pip arrives from the country: 'I saw the great black dome of Saint Paul's bulging at me from behind a grim stone building which a bystander said was Newgate Prison.' While he declines to purchase a seat at a trial, one of the gaol's officials nevertheless shows him the gallows, the whipping post and 'the Debtors' Door, out of which culprits came to be hanged'. Sightseers gained entrance easily. In 1843, the splendidly named American

The prisons of London could not be ignored, embedded as they were in the very centre of the city. The Fleet prison, almost entirely a debtors' gaol by the nineteenth century, had an opening, *right*, where until the 1820s prisoners took turns to stand, rattling a tin and beseeching, 'Remember the poor debtors.' The money collected paid for their food and clothing.

visitor Thurlow Weed sent in his card to the governor at Newgate and was immediately given a tour around the entire prison.* In the list of 'Exhibitions, Amusements, &c.' in *Routledge's Popular Guide to London*, Newgate prison is listed after the National Portrait Gallery and before the 'Polygraphic Hall (Entertainment by Mr. W. S. Woodin)'. In the mainstream *Illustrated London News*, a regular feature entitled 'Public Improvements of the Metropolis' highlighted buildings of which a new and modern city should be proud: the Sun Fire-Office's office was one, Pentonville prison another. There was no difference in the magazine's attitude, both being considered as bringing the benefits of modernity.

Convict prisons remain with us, but debtors' prisons vanished in the nineteenth century. For much of the first half of the century, however, those who could not pay what they owed were imprisoned until their debts were met. When the debtor's creditors decided that they had no option but the law, a writ of execution was put in and the debtor was arrested. He or she was usually first taken to a sponging house (sometimes spunging house), so-called for its ability to squeeze money out of debtors, 'where, like a spunge, they soon begin, you / Find, to suck out whatever you've got in you!' There the debtor was held under the supervision of the bailiffs while, with luck, he might come to an arrangement with his creditors. These houses were commercial propositions run by private individuals, and living costs were charged just as they were in regular lodgings. According to one novel a small room cost 5s a day, while another claimed a fire was an additional 5s. Dickens priced the more luxurious front drawing room at 'a couple of guineas a day'. To survive decently as a debtor, one had to have money.

One of the best-known houses was Abraham Sloman's, at 4 Cursitor Street, off Chancery Lane. In Disraeli's novel *Henrietta Temple*, published in 1837, it was described as 'a large but gloomy dwelling', providing 'a Hebrew Bible and the Racing Calendar' for the 'literary amusement' of its inhabitants. In Thackeray's *Vanity Fair* (1847–8), Colonel Crawley is a regular

* He was a newspaper publisher and a politician, so perhaps his name was recognized, nevertheless, contrast that to the British Museum at the time, which permitted visitors to see the exhibitions only if they had a letter of introduction signed by a trustee.

visitor, passing through at least three times; his 'old bed', when he returns, has just been vacated by a captain of the Dragoons, whose mother left him to languish there for a fortnight before paying off his creditors, 'jest to punish him'. Dickens knew Sloman's in reality, not simply in literature. In 1834, three years before Disraeli's novel, John Dickens was arrested yet again for debt, and was taken to Sloman's to wait for his journalist son, now gainfully employed, to extricate him; that same son re-created the house the following year, as Solomon Jacob's, also on Cursitor Street, in one of his earliest short stories, 'A Passage in the Life of Mr Watkins Tottle', as well as, two decades later, more touchingly as Coavinses' Castle, in *Bleak House*.

If no one came forward to pay what the debtors owed, the prisoners were taken from the sponging house to a debtors' prison, where they were kept until the debts were paid – potentially for ever if the debtor had no means of settling. Like Mr Dorrit in *Little Dorrit*, a handful of prisoners were unable to untangle their affairs and spent the bulk of their lives in these institutions: when the Fleet closed in 1842, one prisoner had been there since 1814; another, still in the Queen's Bench prison in 1856, had been arrested for debt in 1812.* Although there were nine debtors' prisons in London at the beginning of the century, the ones we know best today are the Fleet and the Marshalsea, mostly thanks to Dickens' depictions of Mr Pickwick in the Fleet and Mr Dorrit in the Marshalsea. These two, with King's Bench, in Southwark, and Whitecross Street, in the City, held most of London's debtors.

Despite being places for people who were penniless, debtors' prisons required cash, and rather a lot of it. In the Fleet those who had money to spend lived on one side, where basic services were provided for a fee. In contrast, 'The poor side of a debtor's prison is, as its name imports, that in which the most miserable and abject class of debtors are confined.' Until the 1820s, the latter received the barest minimum of food and were expected

* The Fleet was shut down preparatory to a planned rebuilding, but Holloway prison was built instead, the beginning of the movement of prisons to the suburbs. In 1846, the Fleet was demolished and the site left derelict for over twenty years, before the land was sold to the London, Chatham and Dover Railway.

to beg in order to supplement their rations. Dickens described the opening on to the street, where prisoners stood in turns behind a grille, 'rattl[ing] a money-box, and exclaim[ing] in a mournful voice, "Pray, remember the poor debtors; pray remember the poor debtors."' But, Dickens added, 'Although this custom has [since] been abolished, and the cage is now boarded up, the miserable and destitute condition of these unhappy persons remains the same.' After that date, each prisoner with funds was charged 'footing' on entry, to provide food for the destitute inmates. For a 'chummage' fee to the chum-master – the prison officer in charge of lodgings – the prisoner was given a room, which, because of habitual overcrowding, always had at least one occupant already. Good chum-masters ensured that a prosperous debtor was quartered with an indigent one, whereupon the prosperous new arrival paid a weekly fee to the poorer to go and sleep elsewhere. The destitute prisoner in turn paid a portion of that fee to an even poorer prisoner for space in the corner of his cell, leaving a few shillings a week for food and other necessities. For the better-off, turnkeys let out furniture for a further sum. Food was brought into the prison by family members, or ordered from a local eating house for another sum; drink was similarly available. In a parody of university life, prisoners also 'subscribed', as 'collegians', to the cost of the fire in the taproom and the provision of hot water. As Mr Pickwick discovered very rapidly, 'money was, in the Fleet, just what money was out of it; that it would instantly procure him almost anything he desired'. The same held true in prisons for criminals: in Newgate, when the Artful Dodger is awaiting trial for pickpocketing, Fagin promises, 'He shall be kept in the Stone Jug...like a gentleman...With his beer every day, and money in his pocket.'

Tradesmen routinely conducted business in the prisons too, as they did outside. When Pip visits Newgate – a holding prison for those awaiting trial, as well as for convicted prisoners awaiting transportation or death – he sees 'a potman...going his round with beer' as such sellers did on the streets (see pp. 287–8; p. 292, top row, centre, shows a picture of one). Debtors were not necessarily kept off the streets altogether anyway. Around most of the debtors' prisons there was a designated area where, on payment of yet another fee to the prison officials, prisoners could work and even live within what were known as 'the rules'. They comprised, Dickens wrote in *Nicholas Nickleby*, 'some dozen streets in which debtors who can raise money to pay large fees, from which their creditors do NOT derive any benefit, are permitted to reside by the wise provisions of the same enlightened laws which leave the debtor who can raise no money to starve in jail'. One memoir claimed that the rules were so little policed that one prisoner deputed for the stagecoachman on the London–Birmingham route for an entire month without the prison officers being any the wiser. Many prisoners still worked at their old trades: in the 1830s, the cabinet-maker William Lovett was employed by a man who ended up in the Fleet, continuing to work for him in a workshop in the rules. Those in the Queen's Bench didn't even need to go outside the prison walls to resume their trades. On the ground floor of the gaol a number of indebted tradesmen turned their rooms into shops: butchers, greengrocers, a barber, tailors and so on. This group rather looked down on the row of rooms at the back of the building, where the poorer prisoners lived, and where 'there are shops of an humbler class': sausage seller, knife- and boot-cleaner and a pie seller.

When Dickens placed the Dorrit family in the Marshalsea prison off the Borough High Street, south of the river, he made it world famous, although at the time readers were unaware of his own intimate childhood experiences within its walls. By the time he began *Little Dorrit* in 1855, most of the debtors' prisons had been closed down – the Marshalsea was emptied in 1842 – and there were only 413 debtors imprisoned in London. It is not surprising, given the author's youthful scarring, that the novel was set during the years that the Dickens family too had suffered. William Dorrit enters the Marshalsea in about 1805, but most of the scenes there take place when he has already been imprisoned for two decades, almost exactly coinciding with the date when John Dickens was there – 1824.

The prison, wrote his son, was 'an oblong pile of barrack building, partitioned into squalid houses standing back to back… environed by a narrow paved yard, hemmed in by high walls duly spiked at [the] top'. But the novel barely scratched the surface of the reality that was the Marshalsea. Just over a decade after his father's imprisonment, Dickens, in *The Pickwick Papers*, had been more passionate about the conditions in the Fleet: 'poverty and debauchery lie festering in the crowded alleys; want and misfortune are pent up in the narrow prison; an air of gloom and dreariness seems...to impart...a squalid and sickly hue.' Even this was an understatement. The prisoners' lodgings in the Marshalsea consisted of fifty-six rooms measuring ten feet, ten inches square, each of which comfortably held one bed, although each routinely housed three prisoners. The narrow paved yard that Dickens mentions was really an alley, five yards wide at the widest point. There was, for the 150-odd prisoners and any additional family members who moved in for lack of funds to live elsewhere – as Mrs Dickens and their younger children had been forced to do – a single water pump, a single cistern to hold the drinking and washing water, and two privies. The yard was flooded with waste water, the open drains were 'choked and offensive', the dusthole, where rubbish and fire ashes were thrown, smelt, although not as badly as the privies: they were emptied only once every two months, and their stench carried to the kitchen.

Little Dorrit presents a rather orderly, domestic image of the prison, where families lived according to middle-class norms as best they could. But the rules of the prison suggest otherwise: there were fines for taking other people's property; for throwing urine or faeces out of the windows or into other people's rooms; for making noise after midnight; for cursing, fighting, dirtying the privy seat, urinating in the yard, stealing from the taproom and singing obscene songs. Rules, by their prohibitions, tell us what people really do, as there is no need to create rules for things people do not do. The Marshalsea was clearly not a pleasant place to live.

Early in the century, like the Fleet and the King's Bench, inmates could live within the rules outside the Marshalsea, in an area a later writer on prison reform referred to as covering 'nearly half the south side of London'. The Marshalsea also had a system of 'liberty tickets', whereby the indebted prisoner, for sums ranging from 4s 2d to 11s 10d, purchased between one and three days' leave from the prison entirely. This, however, was abolished once the Marshalsea moved to its new site, and there living conditions mirrored those of any slum.

Throughout the century there were ongoing attempts to improve conditions. Pentonville, a prison for convicts and for those awaiting transportation, opened in 1842 as a 'model' prison. Cells were generously sized, ventilated 'on the newest scientific principle' and heated by 'warm air', while inmates were supplied with good bedding and food. But others, such as Millbank, also for convicts, remained a blot on the landscape, no matter how good the intentions. Millbank was the largest prison in England, made up of six buildings spread over sixteen acres. (Tate Britain now stands on the site.) The ground in this historically poor district was marshy and considered to promote fevers. One journalist claimed that 'Here the cholera first appears'. Although cholera had first reached London via the docks (see pp. 216), Pimlico somehow had that feel about it as Dickens describes in *David Copperfield*:

> The neighbourhood was a dreary one…as oppressive, sad, and solitary by night, as any about London…A sluggish ditch deposited its mud at the prison walls. Coarse grass and rank weeds straggled over all the marshy land in the vicinity. In one part, carcases of houses…rotted away…Slimy gaps and causeways, winding among old wooden piles, with a sickly substance clinging to the latter, like green hair…led down through the ooze and slush to the ebb-tide. There was a story that one of the pits dug for the dead in the time of the Great Plague was hereabout; and a blighting influence seemed to have proceeded from it over the whole place

Even more blighted, and just as intermingled in the life of the streets, were the prison hulks, which had been established during the American Revolution, when criminals could no longer be shipped off to the colonies. Here prisoners were held in decommissioned ships berthed at Woolwich and other navy yards, in theory on a temporary basis during wartime. But long after transportation to Australia had replaced transportation to the former colonies, the hulks continued to be used. Sometimes prisoners were held on the hulks while awaiting transportation, as was the case with Magwitch in *Great Expectations*. All the prisoners on those in London worked in the navy yards alongside regular employees, providing free labour that the government found invaluable, loading and unloading ships, hauling coal and doing whatever heavy unskilled work was necessary in tandem with paid workers.

Thus prisons and slums were equated in people's minds: the prisons housed the criminally poor; the slums the merely poor. Throughout the century, as many journalists toured the slums as the prisons, describing for their readers what they saw. While these generally middle-class accounts are reports from outsiders looking in, they are with few exceptions all we have.

For poor children, like Oliver Twist, it was often but a short step from poverty to crime, with the punishment being prison, transportation or worse. Accounts of the homeless – particularly homeless children – pervade Dickens' work, fiction and non-fiction alike.* Partly this was to do with his own feeling of having been, as he later called it, 'thrown away' as a child, when, 'but for the mercy of God, I might easily have [become], for any care that was taken of me, a little robber or a little vagabond'. There is little difference between this response and that of the semi-autobiographical David Copperfield. When David finally finds his aunt after having been thrown away himself, he says, 'I thought of all the solitary places under the night sky where I had slept, and…I prayed that I never might be houseless any more, and never might forget the houseless.' The great nineteenth-century creator of the idea of 'home' was driven by this childhood sense of homelessness.

Dickens' horror at the destitution he saw all about him appears over and over in his accounts of his long night walks, barely changing over the decades. On one evening, in 1856, in a piece he carefully entitled 'A Nightly Scene in London', he spotted five 'bundles of rags' sleeping on the pavement in the rain outside the Whitechapel Workhouse. Being Dickens, he

* The list of those without homes in Dickens' fiction includes: Oliver Twist's mother, who ends in the workhouse, as well as the children who work for Fagin; Nicholas and Smike after they run away from Dotheboys Hall in *Nicholas Nickleby*; Nell and her grandfather in *The Old Curiosity Shop*; the prostitutes Martha and Little Em'ly in *David Copperfield*, and David himself on his way to find Betsey Trotwood; Jo the crossing-sweeper, a nameless woman passed by Esther and Inspector Bucket, and even Lady Dedlock on her final flight, in *Bleak House*; both Stephen Blackwood and his wife, and Tom Gradgrind in *Hard Times*; nameless homeless people 'coiled up in nooks' in *Little Dorrit*; Magwitch in his youth in *Great Expectations*; Betty Higden, and the 'half-dozen' who die of starvation in the street that Mr Podsnap dismisses as 'not British' in *Our Mutual Friend*.

of course went to question the Master and, being Dickens, he also received a truthful answer: 'Why, Lord bless my soul, what am I to do? What can I do? The place is full. The place is always full – every night. I must give the preference to women with children, mustn't I?' One of the women outside said she hadn't eaten all day, apart from refuse picked up off the ground at the market. Dickens gave her and her companions 1s each to buy some food and get a few nights' lodging. A crowd of starving collected around him as he did this, but 'the spectators…let us pass; and not one of them, by word, or look, or gesture, begged of us…there was a feeling among them all, that their necessities were not to be placed by the side of such a spectacle; and they opened a way for us in profound silence, and let us go.'

On another night, this respect, or perhaps resignation, was absent:

> I overturned a wretched little creature, who, clutching at the rags of a pair of trousers with one of its claws, and at its ragged hair with the other, pattered with bare feet over the muddy stones. I stopped to raise and succour this poor weeping wretch, and fifty like it…were about me in a moment, begging, tumbling, fighting, clamouring, yelling, shivering in their nakedness and hunger. The piece of money I had put into the claw of the child I had over-turned was clawed out of it, and was again clawed out of that wolfish grip, and again out of that, and soon I had no notion in what part of the obscene scuffle in the mud, of rags and legs and arms and dirt, the money might be.

The visceral response that is so close to the surface is not just born of his sympathy for these people 'thrown away', but derives from the knowledge that, had life turned out only a little differently, he might have been one of them.

Much of the middle-class disdain for the poor was the result of incomprehension, owing to the increasing separation of the classes. Previously, the rich and poor had lived in the same districts: the rich in the main streets, the poor in the service streets behind. As London expanded, to meet the needs of the growing numbers of workers and residents in the City and the West End the houses of the poor were demolished (up to 25 per cent vanished between 1830 and 1850 alone). Their residents were forced into areas that were already slums, or would soon become so through overcrowding, while the prosperous, in turn, moved out of the city centre to the new suburbs.

Slums developed for a range of reasons. In some areas, where speculative building had failed – huge houses were built in Notting Dale for the prosperous who never came, put off by the nearby piggeries and brickfields – the houses were divided up into lodgings for the poor. Some areas failed to attract the affluent for reasons no one quite understood. Portland Town, on the north-east corner of Regent's Park, never had the cachet of St John's Wood next door; Pimlico, on the edge of Belgravia, should have been a desirable location for the middle classes, but was not, perhaps because of its marshy ground; Chelsea, despite being near the country and with good roads into town, was low-lying and prone to flooding. Other areas degenerated as employment patterns changed: in Spitalfields, as the weaving industry was destroyed by industrialization and the abolition of import duties on foreign textiles, the once-prosperous workers' houses were subdivided among multiple tenants. By 1851, Hampstead housed 5.3 people per acre and Kensington 16.2 per acre, while Chelsea accommodated 65.4, Westminster 71.5, St Martin-in-the-Fields 80.8, Marylebone 104.5, St Giles 221.2 and the Strand 255.5. The poor had become an alien race.

At the beginning of the century, there were a dozen or so large slum districts. In the centre of town, St Giles – sometimes known as the Holy Land, possibly for its large number of Irish residents – ran south from Tottenham Court Road and Bloomsbury, with Soho on its western edge, down to Seven Dials on the east; St Martin-in-the-Fields ran westwards from the church to Swallow Street, off Piccadilly; the Devil's Acre, around Tothill Fields, and Old and New Pye Streets, clustered near Parliament. Heading east, Clare Market ran from High Holborn to the Strand; Saffron Hill or Field Lane were two names for one slum, in Clerkenwell, bordering the Fleet Ditch. Smithfield held more tenements and back-courts, as did the area around Golden Lane and Whitecross Street. Further east still, around Shoreditch, Old Nichol was a slum district, as were increasing areas of Bethnal Green. In Spitalfields, Rose Lane, Flower Street, Dean Street and Petticoat Lane were the centre of another slum; in Whitechapel, the slum areas developed around Rosemary Lane. South of the river, the slums of Old Mint lay in Bermondsey, as did Jacob's Island, which was not an island at all but a swampy area where the River Neckinger met the Thames.

Several of these districts were used in *Oliver Twist*: Fagin's 'ken' is 'in the filthiest part of Little Saffron-Hill', and his second hideout is 'in the neighbourhood of Whitechapel', while Sikes lives in Bethnal Green, possibly in Old Nichol Street itself, while his final hideout was Jacob's Island. The tone was set for readers when Oliver first walks into London: the route he follows is 'across the classic ground which once bore the name of Hockley-in-the-hole', which many would have then recognized as a district in *The Beggar's Opera*, that eighteenth-century celebration of rogues and thieves.

These areas were presented to middle-class readers as a voyage into the unknown, with myriad references to the confusion created by the mazes of courts and alleys. In *Sketches by Boz*, a stranger in Seven Dials is faced with alleys that 'dart in all directions' before they vanish into an 'unwholesome vapour', like a ship at sea moving into the foggy distance. Anyone even attempting to navigate the courts, warned Sala, was liable to become 'irretrievably lost'; despite living in Great St Andrew Street (roughly where Charing Cross Road is today), he wrote: 'I declare that I never yet knew the exact way, in or out of that seven-fold mystery.' And the way itself was always presented as dangerous. Donald Shaw, a sporting upper-class gent with a military background, described going to the 'dens of infamy' in the 1860s, where he enjoyed himself enormously by imagining that the 'motley groups' of drunken sailors he passed all had 'deadly knives at every girdle', watched by 'constables in pairs' – that is, these were supposedly places where constables were not able to patrol singly because of the danger. He and his friends were taken to an East End pub said to be 'the most dangerous of all the dens', and he was thrilled to be told, 'We've got a mangy lot here tonight; they won't cotton to the gents. If they ask any of their women to dance it will be taken as an affront, and if they don't ask them it will be taken as an affront.' Yet the leader of his clique, the Marquess of Hastings, had only to shout out, 'What cheer... my hearties,' and everyone settled down amicably to drink together. (Shaw appears not to notice that this rather invalidates his shivery thrill at the danger.) More realistic was

Dickens, mocking that sort of fearful gloating when he wrote to a friend: 'I...mean to take a great, London, back-slums kind of walk tonight, seeking adventures in knight errant style.'

Field Lane was renowned as being 'occupied entirely by receivers of stolen goods, which...are openly spread out for sale. Here you may *re*-purchase your own hat, boots, or umbrella.' Thomas Trollope claimed that in 1818, aged eight, he had visited the notorious street, drawn by adult stories of its wickedness. It is notable that, if his story is true, an eight-year-old child could venture there without hindrance, much less violence. Dickens was sharp on the notion of no-go areas. Even in failing health, in the year before he died, he routinely visited these districts with no trouble at all: 'How often...have I been forced to swallow, in police-reports, the intolerable stereotyped pill of nonsense, how that the police-constable informed the worthy magistrate how that the associates of the prisoner did...dwell in a street or court which no man dared go down.' He was aware, however, that both the public and many magistrates believed such stories.

Dickens walked at night for journalistic purposes, and in his sympathetic portrait of a night-walking doctor in *Bleak House* – 'he often pauses and looks about him, up and down the miserable by-ways. Nor is he merely curious, for in his bright dark eye there is compassionate interest; and as he looks here and there, he seems to understand such wretchedness and to have studied it before' – it is hard not to see a portrait of the night-walking author. In *Household Words* the previous year, he had described going to St Giles to see a tramps' lodging house, where, as the door opens, the visitor is 'stricken back by the pestilent breath that issues from within': 'Ten, twenty, thirty – who can count them! Men, women, children, for the most part naked, heaped upon the floor like maggots in a cheese!'* These lodging houses were different from 'lodgings'. Many of the comfortably

* 'Naked' in the nineteenth century generally meant wearing only underclothes, but it also had a less formal secondary use: to describe people in the street as 'naked' appears to have meant that they were not wearing outdoor clothes – no hats, and the men might have had no jackets. It seems likely that here 'naked' means that in mixed company the men were in shirtsleeves and the women possibly were not wearing their neck handkerchiefs, leaving their *décolletage* uncovered bare over low-cut dresses.

middle class, and even rich, lived in lodgings, or rooms rented in a house, while lodgings for working people were single rooms converted for a whole family, perhaps several families. In *Nicholas Nickleby*, in the poor clerk Newman Noggs' lodgings, 'the first-floor lodgers, being flush of furniture, kept an old mahogany table – real mahogany – on the landing-place...On the second storey, the spare furniture dwindled down to a couple of old deal chairs...The storey above, boasted no greater excess than a worm-eaten wash-tub; and the garret landing-place displayed no costlier articles than two crippled pitchers, and some broken blacking-bottles.' (The blacking bottles were Dickens' own secret poverty indicator, a reminder of his days in the blacking factory.)

Lodging houses, by contrast, provided beds that were rented by the night, each room having several beds occupied by people who were strangers to each other. In *The Pickwick Papers*, written in 1836, Sam Weller told of a 'twopenny rope' in some lodging houses where the beds were made of coarse sacking, stretched across ropes: 'At six o'clock every mornin' they let's go the ropes at one end, and down falls the lodgers.' While I have found no mention of this outside fiction, many lodging houses were brutally basic in their amenities, as well as desperately overcrowded.

Often, lodging houses were regular small terraced houses, letting out beds in a few rooms. In the 1840s, one lodging house comprised a shop in its front room; a parlour behind, which the lodgers used as a communal kitchen; two rooms with two beds at 6d each for married couples; and two rooms for single people, housing altogether twenty-four lodgers (plus children, uncounted, sleeping on the floors). Another small house offered six rooms, for men only: two rooms with six double beds, sleeping three each, at 2d per person, and four rooms sleeping ten each, at 3d. Most people in lodging houses were transients. For their nightly 3d-worth in a vast, hundred-bed house in Holborn, lodgers received a rushlight in a piece of broken crockery to light them up to their rooms (or the first forty did: the remainder presumably had to make do with reflected light, as there were only forty available). They had the use of a communal kitchen, as well as access to the fire, a pot, a gridiron and a toasting-fork, plates, benches, and two or three deal tables; in the yard behind was a shed with water and a sink.

In 1868, Arthur Munby went to see what was called the Thieves' Kitchen, in Fulwood's Rents, also off Holborn: 'Up an alley… through an iron gate, down a narrow passage, down a rude old stair, across a rude lobby; and opening a door, we entered at the dark end of a large long antique cellar.' There he found a dozen men and boys, while upstairs he counted 180 beds, with one bedroom containing eleven beds and nothing else. As late as the 1870s, even after legislation had been passed regulating the number of people per room, in Flower and Dean Street in the East End, thirty-one lodging houses were occupied by 902 lodgers paying 4d a night, or 2s a week, two to a bed. Of these, sixty-eight, or one out of every dozen residents, were aged under fourteen, living there without a parent.

The words 'rents' or 'courts' were enough to identify a slum in nineteenth-century London, meaning as they did housing built behind other buildings, using the passageway that had originally been designed to give access to stabling, 'a covered alley, not wider than an ordinary doorway', or even half that, compelling visitors 'to walk in sideways'. The entrance to Frying-pan Alley, one of Field Lane's nearly three dozen courts, measured two feet six inches across – not wide enough to get a coffin through,

The very worst lodgings offered nothing more than patches of floor space. Children often lived together, as protection. In the 1870s, in two streets in the East End, one in every dozen lodgers was an abandoned or orphaned child.

exclaimed a scandalized reporter. Twenty feet long, the court nevertheless contained twenty houses, with more courts beyond. Around these dead-end courtyards stood 'black and crumbling hovels, forming three sides of a miserable little square', built against three walls, and so having windows on just one side. Sometimes behind these courts more buildings were thrown up, in what had been the yards of the houses opposite: buildings, therefore, with no windows at all. Having windows that received some ambient light after dark was a luxury. In *Bleak House*, when the orphaned twelve-year-old Charley locks her baby brother and sister in their room while she is at work, she notes with pride, 'When it comes on dark, the lamps are lighted down in the court, and they show up here quite bright – almost quite bright.' The fact of its being 'almost quite bright' made their room a desirable one and not a slum at all, but ordinary working people's lodgings.

By the time Dickens wrote this, the separation of many of the middle and upper classes from the lives, and locations, of the working poor, was complete. When in *Bleak House* the lawyer Mr Tulkinghorn tells Sir Leicester and Lady Dedlock of the death of the pseudonymous Nemo in his barren lodgings (not a lodging house, but a respectable lodging for those with steady if small incomes, like Charley), Sir Leicester's response is that even to mention 'this sort of squalor among the upper classes is really – really – ', while Lady Dedlock asks whether the man's name had not been known to whoever had 'attended on him'. Sir Leicester wants to reject all knowledge of even honest poverty; Lady Dedlock cannot imagine a world where a person has no one to 'attend' on them – that is, no servant. The Dedlocks live in a fashionable but unnamed location, probably Mayfair, but little that happens in the novel occurs more than half a mile or so away. Nemo's rat-infested graveyard is a matter of steps from the austere beauty of Lincoln's Inn Hall, which in turn is around the corner from the home of Mr Tulkinghorn, lawyer to the grandest families, which itself is hard by the slum of Tom-all-Alone's, and Charley's and Nemo's lodgings off Holborn.*

* Mr Tulkinghorn's address was also a private joke: Dickens' friend Forster lived at 58 Lincoln's Inn Fields, and it is either his house, or the one next door (designed by Inigo Jones), that Dickens describes.

The quarantining of the poor soon became more consciously planned. Two words were used regularly to describe the destruction of neighbourhoods where the poor predominated: 'improvements' and 'ventilation'. Both involved the building of wide new streets through a poor district, to allow the prosperous access to better areas on either side and, more specifically, to drive the poor out. As early as 1826, the author of *Metropolitan Improvements* boasted that 'Among the glories of this age, the historian will have to record the conversion of dirty alleys, dingy courts and squalid dens of misery...into stately streets...to palaces and mansions, to elegant private dwellings,' and forty years later the *Times*' leader writer still took the view that 'As we cut...roads through our forests, so it should be our policy to divide these thick jungles of crime and misery.' He could not, he said, understand why the poor chose to live in such squalid conditions and locations: it must be the 'attraction of misery to misery'.

Like the *Times* writer, few considered where the poor were to go once they were pushed out of these newly tidied-up areas. There was no expectation that mixed neighbourhoods would develop: indeed, the purpose of the 'improvements' was to separate even further the prosperous from the poor. At best, the hope was that by 'ventilating' the slums, by running new roads through previously tiny back-courts, according to the Select Committee on Metropolis Improvement in 1840, these once-hidden areas would be opened to inspection by their social superiors, which through their judicious oversight would lead to improvements. In 1845, the route of the new Victoria Street in Westminster was approved to take 'the channel of communication in a direction further south [than was originally suggested], into a more imperfectly drained, a more densely peopled, and consequently a more objectionable portion of the district', obliterating much of the slum around Westminster Abbey and the Houses of Parliament known as the Devil's Acre.

Once an area 'improved', however, its original residents were priced out, and the problem was simply moved elsewhere. Without inexpensive public transport, workers were forced to live within walking distance of 'their bread': if labourers were not near their work, they were not in work. As late as 1900, 40 per cent of Westminster residents were costers, hawkers and cleaners living near their employment. Clearances simply increased crowding in nearby neighbourhoods, turning them into slums in turn, or worsening their conditions if they were slums already. In 1841, in Church Lane, in St Giles, 655 people were crammed into twenty-seven houses; six years later, after Victoria Street had been built, the same number of houses were occupied by 1,095 people. And throughout the city the pattern was repeated. Between 1838 and 1856, the first major incursion into the slums – New Oxford Street, to ventilate St Giles – saw up to 5,000 people left homeless. Victoria Street encompassed the destruction of 200 houses, displacing nearly 2,500 people. Commercial Street, to ventilate Spitalfields market and Whitechapel, caused 250 houses to be razed; and Farringdon Street, Queen Victoria Street and Cannon Street, to ventilate City slums, laid to waste hundreds more. Dickens raised the issue in *Household Words*: 'What must be the results of these London improvements, when the roofs of a hundred wretched people are pulled down to make room for perhaps ten who are more prosperous'? His answer came with Jo the crossing-sweeper in *Bleak House*, which was written at the culmination of this destruction:

> 'This boy,' says the constable, 'although he's repeatedly told to, won't move on – '
>
> 'I'm always a-moving on, sar,' cries the boy, wiping away his grimy tears with his arm. 'I've always been a-moving and a-moving on, ever since I was born. Where can I possibly move to, sir'...
>
> 'He's as obstinate a young gonoph as I know.* He WON'T move on'...
>
> 'Well! Really, constable, you know,' says Mr. Snagsby wistfully, and coughing behind his hand his cough of great perplexity and doubt, 'really, that does seem a question. Where, you know?'
>
> 'My instructions don't go to that,' replies the constable.

* The OED's earliest usage of 'gonoph', to mean pickpocket, from the Yiddish 'thief', is attributed to Dickens in this novel. But in the previous decade *The New Swell's Night Guide to the Bowers of Venus* tells of 'having put the green culls fly to the fakements of the mots and the *gonnifs*' (that is, 'having made the innocent dupes aware of the trickery of the whores and thieves'). This book is a guide to brothels (see pp. 404–6), and I am not suggesting that this is where Dickens learnt the word, just noting that it was already current.

For 'we make our New Oxford Streets, and our other new streets', Dickens had written, 'never heeding, never asking, where the wretches whom we clear out crowd.' Jo, and the many thousands like him, were driven as were the cattle at Smithfield, which, 'over-goaded, over-driven... plunge, red-eyed and foaming, at stone walls, and often sorely hurt the innocent and often sorely hurt themselves. Very like Jo and his order, very like.'

Some, like *Our Mutual Friend*'s Mr Podsnap, refused to believe that anyone was starving. When 'a stray personage of a meek demeanour' makes a

> reference to the circumstance that some half-dozen people had lately died in the streets... It was clearly ill-timed after dinner... It was not in good taste.
>
> 'I don't believe it,' said Mr Podsnap, putting it behind him.
>
> The meek man was afraid we must take it as proved, because there were the Inquests and the Registrar's returns.
>
> 'Then it was their own fault,' said Mr Podsnap...
>
> The man of meek demeanour intimated that truly it would seem from the facts, as if starvation had been forced upon the culprits in question – as if, in their wretched manner, they had made their weak protests against it – as if they would have taken the liberty of staving it off if they could – as if they would rather not have been starved upon the whole, if perfectly agreeable to all parties.

Podsnap was considered by many to be a portrait of Dickens' friend, John Forster (who was, happily, apparently entirely unaware of the resemblance). But perhaps Dickens was also having a little fun at the expense of Sir Peter Laurie, a magistrate and once Lord Mayor, who had claimed that Jacob's Island, which Dickens had described in *Oliver Twist*, 'only existed in a work of fiction, written by Mr. Charles Dickens'. In *Oliver Twist*, he had painted it as a place of 'Crazy wooden galleries... with holes from which to look upon the slime beneath; windows, broken and patched... rooms so small, so filthy, so confined, that the air would seem too tainted even for the dirt and squalor which they shelter... dirt-besmeared walls and decaying foundations'. But Jacob's Island, that spit of land in Bermondsey, truly existed: in the same year that Sir Peter rejected its existence, Henry

Mayhew visited and found 'The water of the huge ditch in front of the houses is covered with a scum...and prismatic with grease. In it float large masses of green rotting weed, and against the posts of the bridges are swollen carcasses of dead animals, almost bursting with the gases of putrefaction. Along the banks are heaps of indescribable filth...In some parts the fluid is almost as red as blood, from the colouring matter that pours into it from the reeking leather-dressers close by...the air has literally the smell of a graveyard.'

Oliver Twist was concluded in 1839; Mayhew reported in the *Morning Chronicle* in 1849; both descriptions were very much part of the political discussion. In 1847, the Town Improvements Clauses Act gave parishes the right to demolish any buildings they judged to be insanitary, and further Acts provided ways of using taxpayers' money to do so. St Giles, in the centre of the West End, was one of the first areas where an attempt was made to eradicate a slum district entirely. The area covered sixty-eight acres,

The slum district of Jacob's Island, where Bill Sikes made his last stand in *Oliver Twist*, was a warren of 'crazy wooden galleries' hanging over a slimy, stagnant ditch filled with dead animals and effluent from the nearby tanneries. The residents, for lack of alternatives, used the ditch to dispose of their waste – as well as for their drinking water.

with 90 per cent of the population living in multiple-occupancy housing. And that housing was poor: particularly around Drury Lane, many of the buildings were over a hundred years old, some dating back to before the Great Fire in 1666, possibly even to the sixteenth century.

Here the young Dickens walked along 'streets of dirty, straggling houses, with now and then an unexpected court composed of buildings as ill-proportioned and deformed as the half-naked children that wallow in the kennels'. This was no journalist's exaggeration – or if it was, it afflicted all journalists in the same way. In the previous decade, Flora Tristan had seen children in St Giles 'without a stitch of clothing…nursing mothers with no shoes…wearing only a tattered shift which barely covered their naked bodies…young men in tatters…dismayingly thin, debilitated, sickly'.* Yet, as Dickens reported, the inhabitants might not conform to the usual expectations. In one house a shopkeeper's family lived in the shop and the back parlour, with an Irish labourer and his family in the back kitchen, and a 'jobbing man – carpet-beater and so forth' and his family in the front kitchen.† 'In the 'front one-pair' lived another family, and, in the back one-pair 'a young 'oman as takes in tambour-work [embroidery], and dresses quite genteel'; another family occupied the front attic, and 'a shabby-genteel man' in the back attic. Every single one of them was in employment. They were not, by any means, the type of people that most writers, and most readers, thought of when they heard the word 'slums': the unnuanced idea of a seething population consisting entirely of layabouts, drunkards and thieves.

A look at a small slum in Kensington at mid-century affirms what Dickens found in St Giles. In Jennings' Buildings – made up of eighty-three

* The French social critic and activist Flora Tristan (1803–44) made two stays in London, one in the 1820s, one the following decade, which together formed the basis for her *London Journal*. I use her reports with some caution: her material was chosen to heighten her political and socio-economic points; in some places it is demonstrably taken from other writers whose reliability I question. (See p. 408.)

† In a middle-class home, the back kitchen was the scullery, most commonly where the pump was to be found; a front kitchen was where the range was, and the cooking was done. In the next sentence, the front one-pair is the front room on the first floor, that is, up one pair of stairs.

two-storey late-eighteenth-century houses built around five small courts off Kensington High Street – 1,000 residents lived with no running water, no drains and forty-nine privies between them.* The inhabitants were mostly Irish: the men seasonal labourers, the women laundresses and other daily workers. Despite being unskilled, many were long-term employees, not casual labour, and the courts supported social clubs, pubs and a savings club. The residents resorted to the magistrates to bring cases against neighbours who were behaving in a manner considered unacceptable – that is, they saw themselves not as the middle class saw them, as an unruly and potentially dangerous underclass, but as part of the law-abiding majority. There was almost no record of arrests for prostitution connected with these residents; children were baptized and couples married at the local Catholic church. Nevertheless the density of overcrowding was appalling, and there was no running water of any sort until 1867 (when a cholera epidemic finally compelled the vestry to provide outdoor standpipes). But slum conditions did not necessarily mean criminality, except, perhaps, to journalists.

Even among the gainfully and regularly employed poor, thirty or more people might live in six or eight rooms, and as their jobs waxed and waned, they too might occasionally have to take in lodgers. In Bemerton Street, off the Caledonian Road, in King's Cross, at mid-century there lived in one eight-room house: in the basement, an old man and his wife in the front room, with two lodgers at the back; in the two rooms on the ground floor, a couple and their eight children; on the first floor in the front room, a couple and their baby, plus their lodgers: in the back, two sisters and sometimes their mother, two women and their three children; on the second floor, in the front, a couple, their two adult sons, a baby 'and a brood of rabbits', with two women and two boys in the back. The cellars were generally the worst, being at best both damp and dark; in particularly bad lodgings, the liquids from the cesspools seeped up into them. In a court in Nichol Street,

* Jennings' Buildings was across the road from St Mary Abbotts, near where what used to be Barkers department store stood for a century, and is now the *haut-bourgeois* Whole Foods market.

in Bethnal Green, a cellar had a single opening for a window, measuring three feet by 4.5 inches. The mildewed walls ran with water; the ceiling, six feet high, was half fallen-in. This was home to nine, who between them paid rent of 3s a week. A Covent Garden porter lodging near by earned 3s a week in a good week: a fraction of a room was all he could ever hope to afford, and that only for as long as he was strong enough to work.

Even for those not in cellars, sanitation was an insuperable problem. In *Oliver Twist*, Oliver washes himself 'and made everything tidy by emptying the basin out of the window', as directed by Fagin. This no doubt raised a smile in middle-class readers, but what else was Fagin to do in his Clerkenwell slum? Few houses had any drainage, water supplies ranged from scarce to non-existent, and there were few privies. It was not what the residents wanted, but what the landlords supplied, and most inhabitants made efforts to keep their living quarters as clean as possible, given their meagre resources. Sometimes landlords let an elderly or infirm person have a bed (rarely a room) rent-free in return for washing down the privy daily. When the landlord made no such provision, the residents arranged for the most impoverished of them to take on the task and as payment 'the people what lives there *gives her their cinders*' – the broken bits of leftover coal. No matter how clean the inhabitants may have wanted to be, it was a losing battle. In one alley behind Farringdon Street as late as the 1860s, there was one privy for a court with 400 residents. Landlords who thought 400 people needed only one privy were not going to pay to have it emptied regularly. In 1849, a letter signed by fifty-four people appeared in *The Times*:

> Sur, – May we beg and beseach your proteckshion and power, We are Sur, as it may be, livin in a Willderniss, so far as the rest of London knows anything of us, or as the rich and great people care about. We live in muck and filthe. We aint got no priviz, no dust bins, no drains, no water-splies, and no drain or suer in the hole place. The Suer Company, in Greek St., Soho Square, all great, rich and powerfool men, take no notice watsomedever of our cumplaints. The Stenche of a Gully-hole is disgustin. We all of us suffur, and numbers are ill, and if the Colera comes Lord help us.
>
> Some gentlemans comed yesterday, and we thought they was comishoners from the Suer Company, but they was complaining of the

> noosance and stenche our lanes and corts was to them in New Oxforde Street. They was much suprized to see the seller in No. 12, Carrier St., in our lane...and would not beleave that Sixty persons sleep in it every night...but theare are greate many sich...Sur, we hope you will let us have our cumplaints put into your hinfluenshall paper, and make these landlords of our houses and these comishoners...make our houses decent for Christions to live in.
>
> Preaye Sir com and see us, for we are living like piggs, and it aint faire we shoulde be so ill treted.
>
> We are your repeckfull servents in Church Lane, Carrier St., and the other corts.*

This particular court lay in St Giles, just steps away from Tottenham Court Road, and the letter was written after the area had been 'improved' – in fact, the courts' single privy had been removed to make way for the improvements. *The Times* followed up this letter and recorded, in one room, a child naked but for a sack, eaten up with fever, watched helplessly by his parents, and lying next to a woman with cholera. 'A strange boy' was also sleeping in the room; no one knew where he had come from, or what his name was: 'He had had nothing to eat for two days except a crust of bread given him by a woman who pitied him, though she could ill-spare the morsel.' It is hard to imagine that Dickens, with his confirmed interest in slums and living conditions, did not see this *Times* article; *Bleak House*, with its picture of the slum of Tom-all-Alone's, and the fever-racked Jo helped by the brickmakers' wives who can ill spare him food, springs obviously to mind.

Population growth, the Famine, the Hungry Forties: all contributed to this state of affairs, with the result that the poor lived 'like piggs'. But the precipitating factor was the slum clearances themselves. Most people failed, or refused, to make the connection. *The Illustrated London News*, antipathetic to the Poor Laws and sympathetic to the poor, nevertheless strongly approved of the 'improvements' (always their word), even as they

* One contemporary historian has suggested that the publication of this letter was arranged – and possibly part written, or at least elaborated – by Charles Cochrane, a sanitary-health agitator. Perhaps, but it is no less heartrending.

condemned the increasing misery they saw in the streets. In one week in February 1847, they reported that up to 4,000 starving people had arrived nightly at just three Asylums for the Houseless Poor. The following week, the magazine noted with exasperated relief that 'finally' the work to eradicate the Devil's Acre slum was about to begin.

From the 1840s, the railways drove these clearances at an ever faster pace. St Giles and Saffron Hill were no longer the worst parts of London; the new slums had all been created by the railways. Property owners and long lease-holders were compensated if their buildings were destroyed, but those who rented day to day, or even week to week, received nothing. They simply had to shift for themselves, finding new lodgings, which were likely to become more expensive as nearby cheap rooms became scarcer. In 1846, a Parliamentary Select Committee heard that 'the rents of the wretched hovels of the poor increased 10, 15, 20 and 25 per cent in all the surrounding districts where these improvements have taken place.' Behind Farringdon Street station, a resident of an alley claimed that 'a thousand houses have been pulled down for the railway within half a mile', and those residents had all moved into his street, 'because there's nowhere else'.

Other 'improvements' were created as London was transformed from an eighteenth-century city to a modern one. In the 1860s, 500 people were displaced from Ship Yard, off the Strand, with more from the surrounding courts, as the area was cleared for the preliminary groundwork for the building of the new Royal Courts of Justice (which still stand). Four months later, another 4,000 were evicted. Ultimately eight acres were completely razed: thirty-three streets, 343 houses, 170 or so stables, plus numerous warehouses and shops. The newly homeless, crowding in with their neighbours, were no doubt unmoved that the Courts, when they were completed fifteen years later, were impressive, as were the buildings lining the many new wide roads that had displaced the homes of the poor. The slums continued to exist but were just better hidden and broken up by streets that the respectable were happy to walk down.

By the 1860s, the harsh times of the Hungry Forties had returned once more. Newspapers reported on the hundreds of starving in the street, even of instances when 'thousands' broke into bakers or eating houses, not to rampage, but to get bread to keep them alive. The Poor Law had 23,000 paid officers and produced 12,000 annual reports, but whatever relief the system had once offered, had now broken down entirely. As a result, 'Dorcas societies, soup-kitchens, ragged-schools, asylums, refuges' and other benevolent societies were 'strained to the utmost', attempting to ameliorate the very worst conditions.*

Charities such as the Ragged School concentrated on trying to educate the poor so that they could support themselves. The first Ragged School had originally been a single schoolroom in a back-court in Saffron Hill in 1841; a decade later there were 110 schools, where nearly 2,000 children were taught trades, and dormitories were available to those who attended school regularly. Here around 200 boys and men slept together, in 'narrow pathways' that had been 'partitioned off into wooden troughs, or shallow boxes without lids'. Similar accommodation was offered by the privately endowed Asylums for the Houseless Poor, sometimes also known as the Refuges for the Destitute. These were set up in 1820, with branches near Blackfriars, Smithfield and Marylebone. In the early 1850s, on winter nights 'a large crowd of houseless poor [are] gathered about the asylum at dusk, waiting for the first opening of the doors...with their blue, shoeless feet, ulcerous with the cold, from long exposure to the snow and ice in the street...To hear the cries of the hungry, shivery children, and the wrangling of the...men assembled there to obtain shelter for the night, and a pound of dry bread, is a thing to haunt one for life.'

Then there were Night Refuges, privately supported and open only in winter, where residents could stay for up to a month, coming and going as they pleased. Casual Wards, or strawyards, were subsidiaries of the workhouses, and just two nights' stay was allowed at one time. By the 1850s, these Casual Wards had become a matter for journalistic examination. Mayhew visited one and listed one night's residents, by age. The youngest was six, with another twenty-four boys and girls under fourteen; altogether, there were 152 children, half of whom had no parents. In 1865, the journalist

* Dorcas societies were named for the woman who 'was full of good works and almsdeeds' in Acts 9:36; they were organizations of church ladies who met to make clothes for the poor.

James Greenwood, possibly the first journalist to go undercover, visited a Casual Ward in Princes Road, Lambeth, in the guise of a labourer out of work. He and his fellow indigents had their clothes taken away, and, dressed only in their shirts, were sent out to a yard where thirty men were given bags of hay to sleep on, in a shed closed in on only three sides. He was too late to get dinner, but one boy told him he had missed a treat: 'There's skilly [gruel, or thin porridge], nights as well as mornin's now...and spoons to eat it with, what's more.' There was a single pail of drinking water (and if there was another to serve as a chamber pot, Greenwood was too reticent to tell his readers). At seven in the morning they were roused to wash and dress in their own clothes, before waiting in the yard for a breakfast of bread and skilly. Then, before they were permitted to leave, they were forced to take turns cranking a flour mill. This was make-work, intended to inculcate the indigent in middle-class ways of industry, for the flour that resulted was too poor in quality to be used. The idle did as little as they could get away with, while the men who truly wanted to look for work were prevented from doing so: by the time they were released, the day-workers had all been chosen at the casual hiring stands.

Greenwood's report caused a sensation, even toned down as it had been by the *Pall Mall Gazette*'s editor, 'to avoid suspicion of exaggeration'. Much of the discussion focused on the institutionalized contempt shown to the inmates, the sham work forced upon them, the cruelty through regimentation, such as making men stand barefoot and in nightshirts outdoors. But these men had at least managed to gain admittance, and were fed.

The conditions in the 1860s for many were no better than when Oliver asked for 'more' in 1838. In the 1840s, the *Illustrated London News* reported numerous inquests on those who had died after being refused relief by the parish. Twenty years later, over a third of the children at the Great Ormond Street Hospital suffered from that disease of malnutrition, rickets. Dickens saw these walking dead and, through the decades of his writing life, made sure his readers saw them too. In 1852, at a Ragged School dormitory, an elderly alcoholic printer was dying of starvation and next to him 'was an orphan boy with burning cheeks and great gaunt eager eyes, who was in pressing peril of death too'. Both were taken to the workhouse to die. Or, as

Dickens addressed the authorities directly, after Jo dies in *Bleak House* of a similar fever: 'Dead, your Majesty. Dead, my lords and gentlemen…Dead, men and women, born with heavenly compassion in your hearts. And dying thus around us every day.'

8.

THE WATERS OF DEATH

Death from lack of food was ever-present for the majority of London's population. However, death from water was even more likely, and not by drowning in it, but by drinking it. The rivers of London have so far vanished from sight that today it is hard to remember how much they defined London's shape and history. In 1810, a labouring man visiting London for the first time went to see 'the metropolitan curiosities...a glimpse of the public buildings, the river, and the shipping; together with the docks and their warehouses', before walking up to Hampstead to view 'the noble river, with its "forest of masts"', and then rowing out to see Greenwich Hospital from the river. For him, the sights of London revolved around the Thames, as Dickens' fiction emphasizes: three out of his fifteen novels – *Bleak House, Great Expectations* and *Our Mutual Friend* – begin with a scene on the river.

Had the visiting labourer but known, in going to Hampstead from his lodgings he was crossing even more rivers, for London, built on a flood plain, is saturated with rivers that debouch into the Thames. By the nineteenth century most of them had been built over and made invisible. On the north side of the river, from west to east, Stamford Brook runs from Wormwood Scrubs to Chiswick; Counters Creek covers the same districts; the Westbourne runs from Hampstead to Chelsea; the Tyburn, along part of its route renamed the Aye, from Hampstead to Westminster; the Fleet, from Highgate and Hampstead to the City; the Walbrook, from Islington to Cannon Street; the Black Ditch, from Stepney to Poplar; and Hackney Brook from Hornsey to the River Lea. South of the river, from west to east, Beverley Brook runs from Wimbledon to Barnes; the Wandle, from

Merton to Wandsworth; the Falconbrook, from Tooting to Battersea; the Effra, from Norwood to Vauxhall; the Peck, joined by Earl's Sluice to the Neckinger, from East Dulwich to Bermondsey and Rotherhithe; and the Ravensbourne from Bromley to Deptford.

Most of these rivers have entirely disappeared, both from our sight and from our consciousness, except for small breaks where from time to time one briefly surfaces, or when perhaps the name of a street or district reminds us of what lies underneath. For in London, these names are legion, evidence that the ground beneath our feet is rarely as solid as we think. Many roads or districts are named for the rivers they are built over or beside: Fleet Street, Place and Road, Effra Road, Neckinger Street, the districts of Wandsworth ('Wandle-worth') and Peckham. There is also more generic naming, such as Angler's Lane, Creek Road, Pont Street, and Brook Street, Brook Green and Brook Drive. Conduit Street, Mews, Place, Drive and Way all mark river culverting. Then there are Bayswater and Coldbath Fields, and all the 'bournes' and 'burns': Bourne Street, Marylebone (a corruption of Mary-le-bourne), Kilburn, Holborn, Langbourne, Westbourne Grove. There are 'bridge' names: the generic Bridge Street, Place, Road and Lane, and Knightsbridge, Uxbridge and Stamford Bridge (originally Stanbridge, or 'stone bridge', it became Sandford, indicating the ford in the river, then Stamford); as well as all the 'fords', too: Hungerford, Dartford, Deptford, Romford and Brentford. Dozens of springs are marked by their surface eruption as wells: Wells Street, Way, Terrace and Mews; Chadwell Street, Amwell Street, Sadler's Wells, Bagnigge Wells, Shadwell, Camberwell, Stockwell, Clerkenwell, Bridewell, Muswell Hill.

Much of London's physical topography too was created by rivers, which carved out great valleys that were still visible in the nineteenth century but are less so today as infill has been used to minimize the difficulties created by the steep gradients. The main one in London was the Fleet Valley, 'once almost a ravine'. Although the ground level has risen over thirteen feet since the nineteenth century, part of the hill from King's Cross still has a gradient of 1 in 17. 'Fleet', deriving from the Anglo-Saxon for 'inlet', indicates that this river was originally large enough to be navigable at its mouth. The Fleet has two sources: the ponds on the west side of Hampstead Heath (today's mixed-bathing ponds), from where it runs down Fleet Road to Camden Town; and the ponds in the grounds of Kenwood and those on the east side of the Heath (today's men's and women's bathing), whose waters run down Highgate Road. The two sources meet north of Camden, at Kentish Town Road – and such is the volume of water here, that when the Fleet flooded it created a pool sixty feet across. The river then runs under the Regent's Canal, past St Pancras Church, to Battle Bridge (now King's Cross), where it was channelled into a brick conduit, to become the Fleet sewer. This runs almost exactly parallel to Farringdon Road, which was built at the same time as the sewer, and then along the valley that bears its name, spanned by Holborn Viaduct, before it ultimately reaches the Thames as a tidal inlet at Blackfriars.

The Tyburn runs from Hampstead, too, from Shepherd's Well, through Swiss Cottage and down to Regent's Park, where it meets a tributary running from Belsize Park. It is carried by aqueduct at Regent's Canal and then reappears as the boating lake on the southern side of the park. Marylebone Lane was originally the left bank of the stream, which explains its meandering path. After the Tyburn crosses Oxford Street, it runs under Grosvenor and Berkeley Squares, under Piccadilly and then towards Green Park, where it gets lost on the marshy lands heading for the river. (Tyburn, now Marble Arch, was not actually near the River Tyburn at all; it was built beside a tributary of the Westbourne known as Tyburn Brook, the brook taking its name in this instance from the gallows it ran past.)

Only slightly smaller than the Fleet, the River Westbourne also rises up on Hampstead Heath but then heads south-west, meeting more tributaries near Kilburn and running towards Bayswater Road, into Hyde Park, where it bubbles up into Londoners' consciousness as the Serpentine, where the river had been dammed in the previous century. After that, it leaves the park via Knightsbridge and can be seen in outline once again at Sloane Square tube station, where a metal culvert carrying the river runs over the District and Circle line platforms. From there it is diverted to a reservoir for the Chelsea Waterworks and debouches as the Ranelagh Sewer, which as late as the 1960s was still visible in the Thames at low tide. Until 1834, the Ranelagh sewer discharged its effluent into the Westbourne. At that point a collateral sewer was built to divert the waste away from the Serpentine, but 'a communication' was left between the two. By the mid-1840s, the 'effluvia from under the arches' of the Serpentine's bridge 'were so offensive' that they had to be closed off, while the Serpentine itself was said to be 'nine feet of mud' under a mere 'eighteen inches of water', and 'not mud of an ordinary description, but a compound of decayed animal and vegetable refuse' – that is, sewage. 'The Serpentine has been, in fact, transformed into a vast metropolitan laboratory of cholera.' Despite this, as late as the end of the 1840s the Serpentine was piped as drinking water to many Londoners, including the inhabitants of Kensington Barracks, Buckingham Palace and Westminster Abbey.

One of the effects of the watery nature of the capital was frequently visible, as well as oppressive. There had always been fogs in London, but as the population increased and coal fires spread, so a pall of dark smoke, by the early 1830s estimated at nearly thirty miles across, regularly hung over the city. By the 1860s, the 2 million residents, the animals, the gasworks, the industry and the home fires combined to make London two to three degrees warmer than the surrounding countryside. We take it for granted today that this is what happens in dense population centres; then it was a new phenomenon.

The fogs were seasonal, arriving in late autumn, persisting through the worst of the winter and lifting somewhat in the spring. But most contemporary accounts portray them as omnipresent, and the fogs became a part of almost every description of London, by visitor or resident, from the start of the century. As early as 1805, the artist Benjamin Robert Haydon saw London's 'smoke' as a 'sublime canopy that shrouds the City of the world', but he also wrote that it 'drifted', so it appears that at this date it remained a relatively gentle component of the weather. By the 1820s, it was permanent enough for Byron to think of it as architectural: a 'huge, dun Cupola'. A visitor in the same decade confirms this: London, he wrote, was covered with a dense cloud of smoke 'as usual'.

Yet the fog was still not the smothering menace of later years. Dickens may have backdated his memories in some of his fiction. *A Christmas Carol,* set in the 1820s, was written in 1843, and in Scrooge's counting house 'it had not been light all day...The fog came pouring in at every chink and keyhole, and was so dense...that...the houses opposite were mere phantoms.' In *Bleak House*, which Dickens started to write in 1852 but which was set during the 1830s, fog also epitomizes the city. When Esther arrives in London from Reading, she asks 'whether there was a great fire anywhere? For the streets were so full of dense brown smoke that scarcely anything was to be seen.' But no, she is told, it is just 'a London particular'.*

The fog in turn created a city of black buildings. The Portland stone façade of St Paul's was not well suited to the London atmosphere, but then, 'it is difficult to conceive of *any* colour except black, which can long preserve its identity, in an atmosphere perpetually charged with coal-smoke, which would speedily tarnish a palace of gold.' Dickens described the cause as well as the effect of this blackening, as he watched 'Smoke lowering down from chimney-pots, making a soft black drizzle, with flakes of soot in it as big as full-grown snowflakes – gone into mourning, one might imagine, for the death of the sun.'

From the late 1830s, it was the colour of the fog rather than the buildings that fascinated and disturbed. It was most commonly the same shade as coal smoke, and smelt of coal smoke too, but then suddenly it changed, becoming bottle-green, or 'a dilution of yellow peas-pudding'. In *Our Mutual Friend*, in the 1860s, Dickens was even more precise: in the countryside the fog was grey, at the edges of the suburbs it became dark yellow, 'and a little within it brown, and then browner, and then browner, until at the heart of the City...it was rusty black'. The American novelist Nathaniel Hawthorne, however, described it as 'very black indeed, more like a distillation of mud than anything else; the ghost of mud, – the spiritualized medium of departed mud, through which the dead citizens of London probably tread'. In 1858, Dickens took an Italian friend to the Crystal Palace: 'I asked him to try to imagine the Sun shining down through the glass, and making broad lights and shadows. He said he tried very hard, but he couldn't imagine the

* This term, when applied to fog, was apparently invented by Dickens in this novel. Previously it had referred to a type of Madeira.

sun shining within fifty miles of London under any circumstances.'

Even after gas lighting arrived in the streets (see pp. 53-55), the fog physically swallowed up most of the illumination, by depleting the oxygen and causing the gas to 'burn on dim, yellow and sulkily', while candles gave 'a haggard and unwilling' light. The smothering lack of oxygen, too, made breathing difficult, and many more deaths among those with respiratory illnesses were registered during periods of extreme fog. Even the young and healthy found it troublesome: 'Dear me, you're choking!' says Mr Grewgious to Edwin Drood in the novel of the same name: 'It's this fog…it makes my eyes smart, like Cayenne pepper.'

For those like the comfortably-off Mr Grewgious, who stayed at home and had his supper delivered to his chambers, the fog was a nuisance, no more. The real problem was for those who had to navigate the streets, whether commuting to work, or working in the streets themselves. In *Bleak House*, Dickens described 'Implacable November weather' with 'Dogs, undistinguishable in mire. Horses, scarcely better; splashed to their very blinkers. Foot passengers, jostling one another's umbrellas in a general infection of ill temper, and losing their foot-hold at street-corners'. As the fog thickened, street conditions worsened: 'You step gingerly along, feeling your way beside the walls, windows, and doors, whatever you can, until at least you tumble headlong into some cellar,' or run against some 'respectable old gentleman, with whom you have a roll or two in the gutter, thankful that you did not fall on the other side, and stave in the shop-front…Porters with heavy burdens, women and men with fish, watercresses, &c., you run against every few minutes…As for your watch…you saw the fellow's arm that dragged it out of your pocket, and that was all; it was a jerk amid the deep fog…you might as well hunt for a needle in a bottle of hay, as attempt to follow the thief in that dusky, woolly, and deceptive light.' Meanwhile, on the river, the boats could not run, while 'Many lives have been lost through foot-passengers mistaking the steps at the foot of some of the bridges for the…bridge itself, and…rolling head-foremost into the river.' Ultimately, there was nothing to be done but make a joke of it: many Londoners swore that in a fog the quickest way of getting to Temple Bar from Charing Cross, a twenty-minute walk eastwards in normal circumstances, was to set off due south and 'walk...without once turning your head. In three hours or so, 'you would be pretty sure of reaching the point aimed at, should you not be run over'.

As the quality of air deteriorated through the century, so did the water, a process that began at the beginning of the century, from a combination of factory waste, contamination from gasworks, the dockyards releasing 'copper and other ingredients', and dozens of other industries flushing out their own chemical brews into the Thames. As early as 1821, an inquiry presided over by the Lord Mayor looked at river water near the gasworks. Live fish were put into buckets of locally collected water: the flounders died within a minute of immersion, while eels lasted four minutes.

The problem of industrial waste was dwarfed by the problem of human waste. Too many people living in one place were all discharging their effluent into the Thames. By 1828, nearly 150 sewers were disgorging into the Thames between Vauxhall Bridge and Limehouse alone, and by the 1850s the city's central sixty sewers daily flushed 260 tons of raw sewage directly into the river. And because the Thames is tidal, this pollution was being washed right back twice a day: as the tide ebbed, shorelines of 'mud' 125 yards wide were revealed, 'mud' that was raw sewage.

Summoning the political will to deal with the problem took decades, long after the increase in population had overwhelmed the civic infrastructure. The Bill of Sewers legislation – defining sewers purely as conduits for rainwater and entirely prohibiting their connection to house drains – had passed three centuries earlier and was still in force. According to the law, cesspools, not sewers, were for sewage. For centuries, therefore, cesspools under houses had been where all human waste was disposed. Even if cesspools were cleaned regularly, in densely populated districts they were still offensive; when they were not cleaned regularly, they were almost beyond imagining. The latter was often the norm: cesspools were expensive to clean and the process was unpleasant. To minimize the disruption, by the middle of the century emptying cesspools was confined to the hours between midnight and 5 a.m. Five night-men were usually required to clean one cesspool. A holeman descended to fill the tubs lowered by the ropeman;

two tubmen then carried the tubs back and forth out to the street, where the fifth man emptied the loads into an open cart. (In most London houses, few of which had rear access, these tubs were carried one by one through the interior.) Until 1848, this waste was taken to nightsoil yards, where it was mixed with exhausted (used) hops, bought cheaply from the breweries, and spread out to dry, wafting its scent across the neighbourhood until it was in a condition to be sold as fertilizer.

Those with less money, or those in rental properties whose landlords wanted to scrimp, had their cesspools cleaned infrequently; the poor, or those with bad landlords (which was often the same thing), never had them cleaned at all. By the late 1840s, there were so many cesspools under even the most expensive housing in the West End, that the walls between them frequently collapsed, and so fashionable London was perched on top of what one sanitary reformer called not cesspools but 'cess-lakes'. These noxious lakes filled up and overflowed, the liquids soaking into the ground and ultimately contaminating the water, while the solids slowly seeped into neighbouring cellars and streets, oozing up through the bricks every time it rained. In St Giles, 'whole areas of the cellars were full of nightsoil to the depth of three feet' and yards were 'covered in nightsoil…to the depth of nearly six inches'.

The number of animals in the city added to the filth. Many city dairies kept cows, often in cellars, where they were fed through hatches, with their waste removed the same way. In 1829, the student Hékékyan Bey went to look at lodgings in Parliament Street: on finding that half the courtyard was given over to four dairy cows he declined, but such arrangements were not unusual.* By 1837, a guidebook suggested there might have been as many as 10,000 cows in London dairies, fed not on hay but on spent mash from the breweries. A decade later, this figure had doubled; many animals were kept under the newly built railway arches by the Thames, forty or fifty cows

* Joseph Hékékyan, or Hékékyan Bey, as he was known (1807–75), an Armenian, was the son of a translator for the Khedive of Egypt, who paid for his education, first at Stonyhurst, then as an engineer. He returned to Egypt in 1830 and became president of the Board of Health, before becoming a pioneering archaeologist, most notably at Memphis.

per arch, and fed on market sweepings. At mid-century, Westminster, near one of the slums around St James's, was home to '14 cow-sheds, 2 slaughter houses, 3 boiling houses [most likely boiling horses for glue], 7 bone stores, [and] 1 zincing establishment'.

Animals were found throughout the city. At Millbank prison, once surrounded by a moat, a cow was kept in the 1850s to crop the ditch's grass; Westminster Abbey and Green and Hyde Parks all had sheep and cattle to keep the grass down. (Hyde Park leased its grazing rights to butchers, and the odd goat, too, was to be found there.) Throughout both town and suburbs, many people kept chickens and other fowl. As well as those owned by the watermen on cabstands, fowl routinely pecked and scratched outside the Old Bailey on Sundays, when there was less traffic, while Thomas Carlyle in Chelsea was tormented by the night-time crowing of a cockerel next door. Dickens placed chickens outside the fictional Newman Noggs' Soho lodgings in *Nicholas Nickleby*, and David Copperfield's aunt suspects all London chickens to be cellar-reared and exercised at the local hackney stands.

At least those who owned chickens annoyed their neighbours with nothing more than droppings with a powerful smell of ammonia. Many of the working-class population also raised pigs at their lodgings. Notting Dale was notorious for the smell of piggeries, while Jacob's Island was just notorious for the smell. Here there was no way of dispersing the waste from the pigs, or even from the humans, for the privies were built over a huge ditch, 'the colour of strong green tea', into which the waste dropped, and from which the residents then drew their drinking water. They had begged the landlords for piped water, but for more than two decades the reply was that the lease was about to expire, so it wasn't worth the expenditure.

Flush lavatories, which had at first appeared to be the solution for the problem of human, if not animal, waste, in actuality worsened the situation. By adding water to the waste as it was flushed, cesspools filled up 'twenty or more times as fast', and with liquids rather than solids, which made them more difficult to clean. In 1844, the Metropolitan Buildings Act reversed the prohibition on house drains being connected to the sewers: now such a connection was mandatory, to wash the waste from the city into the river, and from there out to sea. But all that happened was that 'The Thames is now made a great cesspool instead of each person having one of his own.' To compound the problem, by mid-century urban sprawl had pushed the market gardens that took the waste-turned-fertilizer ever further away and the economic returns of transporting it were diminishing. When in 1847 guano, concentrated bird excrement, began to be imported as fertilizer, the market for normal waste collapsed, with prices halving. Soon farmers found they could refuse to pay for waste entirely, the nightsoil men being pleased to find anyone at all to take it.

Before flush lavatories could become commonplace, one thing was needed: running water. Until the 1870s, after Dickens' death, a household's water supply was a private contract, rather than a civic right. In 1847, of 270,000 houses in the City, 70,000 had no piped water. In less prosperous and more rural Fulham, in 1856, of 1,009 houses, only 147 paid for company water to be pumped into their houses. By then the Waterworks Clauses Act had been in force for a decade. It laid down that constant piped water had to be supplied to all dwellings in London, but that meant only that mains had to pass near by; it was up to individuals to connect their houses to those mains. 'Constant', even for the mains supply, was a matter of interpretation: there was no mechanism for enforcing the legal requirement, so the water companies did as they pleased. In 1874, 0.3 per cent of Chelsea houses had running water twenty-four hours a day, and the average across the city was 10.3 per cent. It was not until the twentieth century that a citywide figure of 100 per cent was reached.

Throughout the century, therefore, street pumps were ubiquitous. In 1860, behind fashionable Bond Street, in Savile Row – then the location of prosperous doctors, as Harley Street is today – Dickens watched outside Albany, a stylish set of chambers, as the doctors' menservants pumped up supplies for the maidservants of local tradesmen. In less prosperous neighbourhoods, those without servants to pump up water at the street pumps or collect it from the standpipes had to do it themselves. In 1854, one shopkeeper was found to have stolen his neighbours' water. The mains passed through his shop, and he had bored a small hole in the pipe so that he no longer had to join the crowds 'struggling and fighting' for access to the pump in those hours when the water was running: 'there being so many of them, and so little water'.

Those with no alternatives had good reason to struggle and fight. Some companies, like the East London Water Company, provided what was considered to be a good supply: two hours, three times a week. Standpipes were placed in better streets every three or four houses, but in the courts and alleys they were to be found 'every 8, 12, 20, or even 30 houses'. In such places the standpipes tended to have no taps: when the water company turned on the water for the requisite hours, the water gushed out until it was turned off at the mains again. In paved streets this ensured the paving was regularly washed, but in the unpaved courts two hours of running water created lagoons of mud, which ran into the nearby privies and in turn swilled the waste back out.

Even the best water companies supplied water for only a couple of hours a day, two to three times a week. Middle-class houses had cisterns to store supplies, but for the working classes in lodgings, every household receptacle needed to be utilized during those precious few hours to provide enough water to keep them going until the taps were turned on again.

As the water ran at fixed hours, if the householders were out at work at the time, then they had to do without. Even if they were at home, they needed to have enough utensils to hold a forty-eight-hour supply of water. Many courts shared a single communal cask that filled up when the mains water ran, but these were generally uncovered and, for lack of any other space, were situated near the privies. They also had no taps: all the residents dipped in their own, necessarily unwashed, receptacles to collect their share. For one house in Rose Street, Covent Garden, with forty inhabitants, their 110-gallon cask was filled three times a week, meaning each resident had a ration of just under three gallons of water a day, for washing themselves, their clothes, their houses and their privies, for cooking and for drinking.* They were, they said, better off than most. Water companies were obliged by law to turn on the water if there was a fire, for the fire engines. The sanitary reformer George Godwin said that in one backstreet slum 'while he was talking to a woman, an alarm of a house on fire resounded through the street. She exclaimed suddenly with pious gratitude, "Thank God... We will soon get some water."'

Public baths, which began to appear in the 1840s and often included laundry facilities, were a partial solution for some. In the previous decade, prosperous men had enjoyed their own luxury version (without the laundry facilities), where they indulged in cold plunges, warm baths, sea-water baths, 'tepid swimming-baths', 'medicated vapour', 'warm, cold, shower and chalybeate' (medicinal spring-water) baths – ranging in price from 1s to an astronomical 7s 6d. Some baths listed additional enticements, including 'shampooing', or massage. In the 1860s, the Jermyn Street Baths were the latest in opulence, with cushions on the floor, 'divans, sofas, and all sorts of luxurious seats', an 'oblong marble tank filled with clear water', around which bathers lay sleeping; a hot and a very hot room, a sluice room for post-massage, a cool room and a plunge pool. After all the massaging, sweating and sluicing, visitors were dressed 'à la Turque', complete with turban, before finishing off the visit with a pipe and a cup of coffee.

* In the UK in 2008, the average person used thirty-three gallons daily.

Baths for gentlemen, of greater or lesser opulence, were to be found across London: south of the river in Camberwell, north in Albany Place, York Road, near Regent's Park, and particularly in areas around the clubs: in Suffolk Place, Pall Mall East and at Mivart's Hotel (later renamed Claridge's). These baths were sometimes called 'hummums', or 'hammams'. The Hummums, with a capital H, referred to an establishment in Russell Street, Covent Garden, which had started off as a baths, but had transformed itself into a hotel, although one where irregular hours were the norm, 'chiefly for bachelors'; Pip in *Great Expectations* knows that 'a bed was always to be got there at any hour of the night'.

The poor were not regaled with Turkish costumes and coffee, but baths provided welcome help. In 1845, the first baths for the destitute of the East End were opened in Glasshouse Yard; more opened in 1846 near Euston Square. Here alone, within the first two years, 111,788 baths had been taken and 246,760 laundry-washes done. The following year an establishment designed by sanitation experts opened in Goulston Square, Whitechapel, with first-class and second-class facilities: cold and warm second-class baths for 1d and 2d, or cold and warm first-class baths for 3d and 6d. In the same year the Baths and Washhouses Act permitted parishes to set aside funds for building bathhouses, some of which opened their laundries 'Gratuitously to the very Poor during the prevalence of the Epidemic'.*

For the bathhouses were above all a health measure. In 1830, when Dickens turned eighteen, the average life expectancy of an upper-middle-class professional man was forty-four; for a tradesman or a clerk (the class in which Dickens was born), it was twenty-five; and for a labourer, twenty-two. Of course, by the time a clerk like Dickens was eighteen, he no longer expected to die at twenty-five. Life expectancy was so starkly foreshortened because of infant and child mortality rates: 150 out of every 1,000 children died before the age of five. Once people reached sixteen, in the 1840s their life expectancy went up to fifty-eight years (which was the age at which Dickens died); and when they reached twenty-five, their life expectancy

* One of the baths built after this Act was passed, the Old Castle Street bathhouse, in Whitechapel, is today the Women's Library of London Metropolitan University.

rose to sixty-one. The mortality returns in 1869 gave a fairly standard range of deaths in one winter week: 40 per cent of them were among children under five, of everything from childhood illnesses – measles, whooping cough and so on – to typhus and fevers, to specific infant ailments such as diarrhoea, or the mother's lack of breast milk and premature birth. Of the adults, the deaths were listed as being from infectious diseases, as well as many lung problems, cancer, kidney disease, diabetes and childbirth. Just 5 per cent died of old age.

Many of these illnesses were exacerbated by overcrowding. In 1858, in the industrial cities, men of all ages died at a rate of 12.4 per 1,000; in the general population it was 9.2 per 1,000; in the countryside, only 7.7 per 1,000. For the soldiers of the Foot Guards living in barracks a decade later, the rate was 20.4 per 1,000. The *Illustrated London News* pooh-poohed the notion that the increasing numbers of deaths in army living quarters were 'supposed' to be caused by overcrowding and poor ventilation. As the men had no 'healthy stimulus to exertion; their minds prey on their bodies', and this was why, it reasoned triumphantly, the Dragoons and the Cavalry had lower death rates than the Foot Guards: in looking after horses they have 'cheerful occupation' and 'escape...some of the killing ennui'.

It was not yet understood how fevers and infections were transmitted, and it took decades of work by campaigners to convince the government that social care was an important aspect of public health. When the first cholera epidemic arrived in Britain in 1831, the government's response was neither scientific nor medical, but the declaration of a Day of Fasting and Humiliation, to pray for a remission of the fever. It was not until the Vaccination Act of 1840, enforcing the vaccination of infants, that the government accepted it had a role in maintaining the health of its citizens. As Sir John Simon, from 1848 the original Medical Officer to the City of London, later remembered, before that Act, 'the statute book contained no general laws of sanitary intention.* The central government had nothing to say in regard to the public health and local authorities had but the most indefinite relation to it.'

* Simon (1816–1904) was the descendant of French immigrants and gave his last name the French pronunciation.

Edwin Chadwick, a non-practising barrister and formerly secretary to the Utilitarian philosopher Jeremy Bentham, was in 1834 made Secretary to the Poor Law Commissioners.* From this position he argued for sanitary reform, stressing that it would pay for itself, since epidemics increased the amount of poor relief that needed to be paid from the rates. In 1842, his hugely influential *Report into the Sanitary Conditions of the Labouring Population of Great Britain* linked insanitary conditions to disease, showing how much it cost the country. He wrote, 'The sewerage of the Metropolis... will be found to be a vast monument of defective administration, of lavish expenditure and extremely defective execution.' It was not long before the General Board of Health was established.

In 1846, the Diseases Prevention Act authorized sanitary improvements under the General Board of Health's auspices. In 1848, the Metropolitan Commission of Sewers Act and the City, with its own parallel Act, gave parishes responsibility for sanitation, drainage and water supplies; this permitted them to appoint health officials and inspectors, as well as to condemn and close houses and entire civic spaces, such as cemeteries (see below). Very soon Chadwick was universally loathed: the poor hated him because their houses were condemned and they were evicted; the Poor Law Guardians and civic authorities detested him for the increased burden on rates; and everyone agreed that he was quarrelsome, vindictive, arrogant and entirely lacking in collegial abilities. Chadwick was sacked and in 1858 the General Board of Health was dissolved, to be replaced by a governmental Board of Health. However, his legacy remained: the involvement of local and state government in the health of the nation.

Everyone knew what the problems were. They could hardly help but know. Even the new Houses of Parliament, the pride of modern London, were in 1848 found to have defective sewers. The main sewer had been run under the length of the building, so digging it up again was a major undertaking. Then, when it was opened, the released air was so foul that

* Chadwick (1800-90) was one of the instigators of the idea that workhouses be made less 'eligible' than poverty (see p. 169): he was a dedicated social reformer, but one with a fairly robust distaste for the masses.

it extinguished all the lamps. Finally, it was discovered that the pipes had not been laid on an incline, so the sewage had failed to drain away: the new Parliament was sitting over a single enormous cesspool. This was, in microcosm, the predicament faced by the whole city. And solutions were excessively complicated. In 1848, the rector of Christchurch, Regent's Park, had asked the Board of Health what could be done about sewage issues in his parish. The answer was that there were sixteen paving boards in St Pancras parish alone, operating under twenty-nine Acts of Parliament, and all would have to be consulted before 'an opinion could be pronounced' on what the possibilities were – a decision on what was to be done would take much longer. Although the government knew action needed to be taken, the vested interests in both Westminster and the City vigorously protected their own powers. This was the golden age of localism, and by 1855 London was governed by 300 separate legislative bodies, operating under 250 Acts.

What finally changed attitudes were the successive waves of epidemics: two influenza epidemics between 1831 and 1833; the first cholera epidemic in 1831, which killed 52,000 across the country; scarlet fever in 1834, which killed another 50,000; then more influenza. In 1837, the footman William Tayler reported, 'There were to of [sic] been fifty persons buried at St John's Wood bureying ground in one day this week,' and the following month, 'every day the streets are regularly crowded with funerals and mourning coaches, herses and such like... The undertakers in London are [usually] very particular in having all black horses to attend funerals but now there are so many wanted they are glad to get any colour.' This epidemic was in turn followed by waves of smallpox, typhus and typhoid, before 1848 saw the return of cholera, together with more typhus and typhoid.*

Medical orthodoxy held that many diseases were caused by fermenting particles of decomposed matter that were spread through the air in a

* Typhus and typhoid were recognized as distinct diseases only in 1869. Typhus, or gaol fever, is transmitted by lice or fleas, and was therefore linked to poverty; typhoid is water-borne, transmitted by ingesting food or drink contaminated with faeces. It was the latter that was said to have killed Prince Albert in 1861, although stomach cancer is today suggested as the cause: there were no other reported cases of typhoid in the area, and he had suffered for four years from an undiagnosed stomach ailment.

miasma, or poisonous vapour, identifiable by its foul smell. This miasma theory, as it was known, triggered the Building Act of 1844, obligating houses to be connected to the city sewers: by flushing the decaying matter away from the houses and into the river, it was thought that disease would also be flushed away. Many City aldermen were landlords of extremely profitable slum buildings, however, and they saw no need for expensive sewerage in these properties. The City, protested one official response, already had 'complete house-drainage, with sewerage and all necessary provisions'. But the Health of Towns Association, on whose board sat the indefatigable John Simon, the City's Medical Officer, countered that, on the contrary, the City sewers and drains were 'in fact and effect, nothing but elongated cesspools'. He added for good measure that an extra 58,961 children under five had died in the City, owing to its crowded, insanitary state, compared to the population of Lewisham. As a final riposte, he reminded them that in his testimony to the Health of Towns Association, the City Surveyor to the Commissioners had confessed: 'I am a very incompetent witness on this subject, for I cannot smell.'

While this was being fought out, the epidemics continued their deadly work. In Spitalfields Workhouse, which held 1,500 inmates, even before cholera arrived in 1831, 'eight and ten persons were often placed, head to feet, in one bed'. One man with a fever was put in a bed from which another man, who had died of fever, had just been removed, without the bedding being changed. When a formal complaint was made to the police, the police inspector sent the Master a note telling him to deny everything. (Unfortunately for the Master, he mistakenly sent the policeman's note to the complainant, who then handed it over to the crusading editor of the medical journal *The Lancet*.) The practice of bed-sharing was little different from what went on in the homes of most labouring families, who through the century lived and died together. In one case of many, which took place in the Minories, in the City, in 1847, the body of a man who had died in a fever hospital was returned to his family for burial. For lack of any other place, it remained in the single room in which they all slept and ate for eight days, until the funeral could be arranged. The dead man's mother, wife and child all died soon after, as did the doctor who treated the poor in the area.

. Benjamin Robert Haydon's *Punch, or May Day* (1829) encompassed the entire world in a painting he riginally intended simply to entitle *Life*. On a corner of the New Road (now the Euston Road) a Punch and udy show, *left*, amuses both rich (in the shape of the two horsemen behind) and poor (the crossing-sweeper, *entre*, and the barefoot apple-woman on the pavement). *Right*, chimney sweeps celebrate Mayday in traditional ashion, with their 'Queen' dressed in her best, and a Jack-in-the-Green wearing his wicker frame covered by reenery and May flowers. Haydon depicts every stage of life from cradle to grave: a baby is held up to watch unch; a wedding party, identifiable by the favours in their hats, comes out of St Marylebone Parish Church; at he rear a funeral passes, identified by the 'weepers' the coachman wears around his hat. City and country folk are epresented by the farmer, *centre*, with his dog, and the police officer; the honest (the policeman, the sailor and he guardsman, whose uniform indicates he is a Waterloo veteran) and the dishonest (the boy picking the farmer's ocket) mingle on the canvas as in the streets.

2. *Ludgate Circus*, by Eugène Louis Lami (1850), *above*, shows a traffic 'lock', or jam, when the mass of unregulated street transport was brought to a dead halt. To the left and right are omnibuses, with a costermonger's cart centre front. The conductor, or cad, stands on his step at the back of the bus on the left; his comparative height makes clear how low-ceilinged and cramped the bus interiors were.

3. *Pool of London from London Bridge*, by William Parrott (1841), shows how small the passenger steamers were that chugged up and down the river every dozen minutes or so, making the Thames a great commuter highway.

4. George Scharf, a German lithographer who spent his entire working life in London, illustrated scientific ournals by day. But street-life in London was his passion, and he walked the city by night and by day, sketching ndlessly. *Betwen 6 and Seven O'Clock morning, Sumer* (his English spelling remained erratic), shows, *top row, econd from right* and *bottom row, third from left*, a milkman and a milkmaid, and *bottom row, right*, a dustman vith his cart. The small boy, *fourth left, top row*, may be a muffin seller: his white clothes and flat cap suggest it, lthough he carries a deep basket rather than the more usual flat covered tray, and the object in his right hand loes not appear to be the muffin-seller's bell.

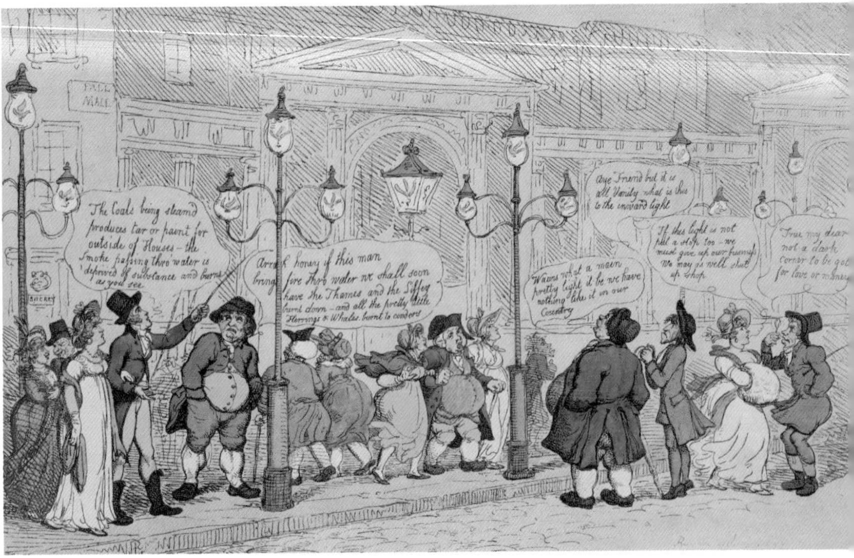

5. & 6. *A Peep at the Gas Lights in Pall Mall*, Thomas Rowlandson, *above*. Awestruck Londoners come to gaze at the first gas streetlights, which appeared in 1807. Meanwhile coal fires, population growth and climate combined to create the legendary 'London particulars', or pea-soup fogs, *below*, in George Cruikshank's *Foggy Weather* (1819).

. Dozens of warehouses along the southern riverbank were destroyed in the Tooley Street fire of 1861. In the entre is the London Fire Engine Establishment's river-engine, while sightseers take up any available viewing ation, whether along the north shore, in small boats or on London Bridge.

8. *Covent Garden Market* (*c*.1829), by Frederick Christian Lewis. A market had been held on this site for two centuries, but only in the 1820s, when this was painted, were permanent structures built to house the sellers. He the canopy is only half-built, and the central area remains open, with makeshift stalls on the right.

9. *Hungerford Stairs*, by George Shepherd (1810), shows the pre-Embankment shore, now covered by Charing Cross station. Fourteen years after this was painted, The Old Fox pub on the right had become Warren's Blacking Factory, where the child Charles Dickens laboured. On the left was the fictional location of the 'dirty, tumble-down public house' where the Micawbers lodged in *David Copperfield* before they emigrated to Australia.

). The great dust-heaps that Dickens describes in *Our Mutual Friend* were not the product of a novelist's nagination: here, at Battle Bridge (now King's Cross), in 1837, a single heap is painted, towering over the nearby ouses and the district's market gardens. Although the artist only shows one, Battle Bridge was home to many ws of such heaps.

11. The great projects of the industrial age were often built by low-tech means – manual labour. Here, in 1825, George Scharf sketched the workers building the new Fleet sewer.

Deaths of this kind confirmed the notion of a miasma of infection: slums smelt and more people died there; the better areas did not smell and fewer people died there.

These were cases of general fevers, but in 1831 a new terror had appeared: cholera. The medical community had been warning of its coming for more than a decade, after an outbreak of 'Asiatic cholera' in Lower Bengal in 1817. But it was another six years before it reached Europe, when 144 deaths were recorded in Astrakhan. In 1829, in Russia, 1,000 died before the disease again resurfaced in Astrakhan, and this time 25,000 may have died. By 1831, the disease had spread to the Baltic ports, and then it was only months before it reached Britain via the shipping routes: in October, the first British death from cholera was recorded in Sunderland. A medical officer who had worked in India recognized the symptoms and warned the authorities, but the local doctors refused to accept the fact, recording the death as 'English cholera'.* Another 201 deaths did little to change their minds or to prepare the rest of the country. The Westminster Medical Society continued to 'vehemently contest' the diagnoses, even as by 1832 the first cases reached London, spreading along the river, from St Anne, Limehouse, to Rotherhithe, Whitechapel, with its dock workers and sailors, then away from the Thames' path, to Clerkenwell and the City, to Marylebone, St Pancras, St Giles and Bermondsey. In four months there were over 9,000 cases, of which 4,266 ended in death. By December 11,020 cases in London had been diagnosed in the previous six months and 5,275 died.† The poor, as always, suffered most. In the epidemics of 1832, of 1848–9 and 1853–4, the districts south of the river, consistently poorer than those to the north, were worst affected.

How people viewed the outbreaks was in great measure dictated by the political climate during the first epidemic, which occurred against the background of political agitation for the Reform Bill. The large number of arrests of working men following the Chartist uprisings and protests for

* In the nineteenth century, the terms English or summer cholera referred to symptoms that today are grouped together as gastroenteritis – fever accompanying gastric illness.

† The nearly 50 per cent mortality rate was terrifying, but so too was the speed with which cholera killed. It was reported that one-third of deaths occurred less than a day after the symptoms first appeared, two-thirds within forty-eight hours.

reform meant that gaols were more than usually overcrowded: in that first cholera year, 12,543 men were committed to Coldbath Field prison, which had a capacity of 1,200. When cholera hit, prison conditions were almost designed to spread the disease, and 15 per cent of the inmates were affected. (The impact was such that prisoners who volunteered to work in the infirmary had their sentences remitted and were even given cash payouts.) Then cholera broke out on board the hulks, the prison ships moored in the Thames. Even by prison standards, conditions in the hulks were repellent. As late as the second epidemic a decade later, the *Warrior*, theoretically a hospital ship, had no regular supply of clean linen; the majority of prisoners were verminous and on average were given a change of clothes only every five weeks; no one could say when the bedding had last been washed; there were no towels or combs, and not enough sheets; the privies were 'imperfect and neglected', and the smell 'almost insupportable'. Of the 638 convicts on board, 400 were stricken with cholera. Little more care was accorded the convicts after death. Their chaplain refused to conduct a funeral service until the dead numbered at least half a dozen, and even then he declined to accompany the bodies on their last journey, reading the burial service to himself on board and signalling to the burial party onshore when he reached 'dust to dust' by dropping his handkerchief.

The 1854–5 outbreak was the one in which John Snow, a Soho doctor, famously disabled the Broad Street pump and in so doing stopped the spread of cholera in that district. (Broad Street has become Broadwick Street, and a pub, the John Snow, marks the location of the pump.) This was not a sudden insight. During the previous epidemic, in 1849, Snow had already indicated the disease might be water-borne. Contradicting Chadwick and other proponents of the miasma theory, he suggested that the new lavatories flushing sewage into the river were facilitating the transmission of the disease. Few were persuaded, even as late as 1855, when in Soho 'The gutters were flowing with a thick liquid, partly water and partly chloride of lime… "front parlours" were taken by dozens in every old and stuffy street for the preparations of coffins that could not be supplied fast enough, and the peculiar sharp tap of the undertaker's hammer could be heard above the muffled sound of voices.'

The number of burials from the epidemics was bringing to crisis point a problem that had been growing throughout the century: what to do with the dead. In 1860, Dickens wrote, 'It was a solemn consideration what enormous hosts of dead belong to one old great city, and how, if they were raised... there would not be the space of a pin's point in all the streets and ways... the vast armies of dead would overflow the hills and valleys beyond the city, and would stretch away all round it.' His summation came three decades after he and the rest of the city were forcibly made aware of how the dead were encroaching on the space of the living. As early as the late 1830s, Dickens was already voicing his concern. In *Oliver Twist* he described a pauper burial in a graveyard so full that each grave contained multiple coffins, and 'the uppermost coffin was within a few feet of the surface'. This was based on a graveyard he had seen near Chatham, but the overcrowding of the dead in London preoccupied him as much as the overcrowding of the living, and he returned to the subject within the year. In *Nicholas Nickleby*, Ralph Nickleby walks past a City burial ground, 'a dismal place, raised a few feet above the level of the street', where the dead 'lay, parted from the living by a little earth and a board or two... no deeper down than the feet of the throng that passed there every day, and piled high as their throats'. This was a reality for Londoners. In Drury Lane and Russell Court, churchyards belonging to St Martin-in-the-Fields and St Mary-le-Strand had originally been sunken patches of ground: by the date of *Nicholas Nickleby* (1838–9) they reached their neighbours' first-floor windows.

Most cemeteries in London had been over capacity for years, if not decades, but they continued to function for the same reason Smithfield market did: they made money for their owners. Furthermore, there were no regulations, no supervision and no fear of repercussions. And, like the markets and the prisons, the graveyards were right in the centre of the city, beside virtually every London church. Dr George Walker, whose practice was in the capital's heartland of Drury Lane, determined to change things, gathering evidence from gravediggers as well as from those who lived next to the graveyards. In 1842, an ex-gravedigger for St Ann's burial ground, in Soho, testified to a Parliamentary Select Committee, telling them that when new bodies arrived for burial, the old ones were dug up, the coffins chopped up for firewood and the bodies, if they were too recent to have decomposed, were broken up with spades. The coffin nails and plates were sold to second-hand shops; the old bones piled in corners or burnt, or sometimes sold off, presumably to those who bought animal bones for fertilizer.

Inside many churches, the situation was no better. On the Strand, in St Clement Danes' vault, the air was so putrid that there was not enough oxygen for candles to stay alight. The crypt needed to be aired for days before each burial, to make it safe for the mourners. (Perhaps not coincidentally, at the same period the well on the eastern side of the church had to be blocked off owing to the quality of its water.) Dickens was mild in his comment: the City, he wrote, smelt of 'rot and mildew and dead citizens'.

As Walker saw it, it was a straightforward mathematical equation. New Bunhill Fields burial grounds, in the City, covered two-thirds of an acre and on average just over 1,500 bodies a year were interred there; in the epidemic year of 1842, that figure had risen to 21,000.* Similarly the burying ground at St Martin-in-the-Fields had operated from at least the sixteenth century, and over 300 funerals a year were conducted there. Having heard the stories, the family of a Mr Foster, of Chapel-court, Long Acre, went to supervise his interment personally. When they arrived, the proposed grave was only two and a half feet deep, which they said was not acceptable. The gravediggers, not remotely perturbed, took their pickaxes to the coffin underneath, lifting out the corpse, breaking it up and shovelling it away, before assuring Mr Foster's friends that if the grave were still too shallow, the two coffins remaining could be removed in the same fashion. These corpses had sometimes been interred just a few years earlier, sometimes a matter of months or even weeks.

The gravedigger for the Portugal Street burial ground, by Clare market (now underneath the London School of Economics), testified that frequently the corpses were fresh enough that the gender of the dead could still be determined; but they were nonetheless 'chopped and cut up', and placed

* This site had been burying Dissenters since *c.*1665. Today it is famous as the last resting place of William Blake, Bunyan, Daniel Defoe, Isaac Watts and George Fox, although one wonders how much of their remains in reality survived Victorian burial methods.

under the boards on which the mourners of that day's funeral service stood, to 'be thrown into the recent grave' again after they left. When Scrooge is shown his own grave in a City churchyard in Dickens' 1843 *A Christmas Carol*, the area is typically 'choked up with too much burying; fat with repleted appetite', which sounds very much like the Portugal Street churchyard walls, which seeped a 'reeking' fluid.

Undertakers and church officials all agreed that nothing of the sort could possibly have occurred under their supervision. One undertaker protested that he visited the cemeteries once, sometimes even twice, a week and would have noticed such improper practices. One of these graveyards, as Walker dryly annotated, had records stating that, while that same undertaker had been in business, 9,500 burials had taken place in a space that could comfortably accommodate 900. But nothing anyone said could cover up the Enon Chapel scandal. Enon Chapel was not far from the Portugal Street burying grounds, halfway along the west side of Clement's Lane, a turning off the Strand (now under the Royal Courts of Justice). It opened as a chapel in 1823, with a burial vault underneath measuring fifty-nine by twenty-nine feet. Over the next sixteen years, up to 12,000 bodies were buried there, with nothing but a wooden floor between them and the worshippers in the chapel above. The children in its Sunday school became accustomed to seeing what they called 'body bugs', the flies that hatched in the decomposing corpses. When the scandal finally broke, in 1844, a dustman testified that he had removed sixty loads of 'waste'. After the chapel's forced closure, the speculators who bought the building advertised: 'Dancing on the Dead – Admission Threepence. No lady or gentleman admitted unless wearing shoes and stockings.' In 1847, the owner opened up the vault to the public, charging them for the privilege.

Enon Chapel was at least closed down; few of the civic authorities had legal powers to close graveyards. In 1845, when a pawnbroker complained that his Exmouth Street premises were virtually uninhabitable because of the 'continual stench' from the 1,500 people buried annually in the neighbouring workhouse burial ground, he was told that he would have to petition the Poor Law Guardians, who had control of the two-acre site. If they refused to act, then he could go to the Poor Law Commissioners; after that, there was nothing for it but to petition the Secretary of State: no one else could oblige them to cease using the grounds.

To deal with this impasse, in 1850 the Metropolitan Interments Act was passed, enabling the Board of Health to supervise new cemeteries, to close churchyards that were full and to purchase private cemeteries if necessary. In June 1850, a parody in *Household Words*, 'Address from an Undertaker to the Trade', satirized the undertakers' hostile response to this bill. It was science that was to blame, they protested, for showing people 'that they are drinking their dead neighbours'. In case the message was lost, six months later the journal published a poem on the churchyards' 'half-unburied dead':

> I saw from out the earth peep forth
> The white and glistening bones,
> With jagged ends of coffin-planks,
> That e'en the worm disowns;
> And once a smooth round skull rolled on,
> Like a football, on the stones...

In 1853, Dickens preserved for ever St Mary-le-Strand's churchyard in Drury Lane, by burying Nemo there in *Bleak House*, in 'a hemmed-in churchyard, pestiferous and obscene...a beastly scrap of ground'. As in reality, in the novel Jo watches as 'They was obliged to stamp upon [Nemo's coffin] to git it in.' In the year *Bleak House* was published, this churchyard was formally closed, but readers would have been aware that Dickens was describing an ongoing problem, and he returned to it a decade later, in *Our Mutual Friend*, when Lizzie and her brother Charlie meet in a City churchyard, with its 'raised bank of earth about breast high...Here, conveniently and healthfully elevated above the level of the living, were the dead.'

In an attempt to take the pressure off the city centre, new suburban cemeteries were authorized from the 1830s. Kensal Green cemetery became the first 'garden' cemetery, opening during the first cholera epidemic. It was here in 1837 that Charles and Catherine Dickens arranged for the burial of Mary Hogarth, Catherine's seventeen-year-old sister, whose sudden death so traumatized the author that an instalment of *Oliver Twist* had to be delayed.* The previous year, an Act had been passed 'for establishing cemeteries for the Interment of the Dead, Northward, Southward, and Eastward of the Metropolis by a Company to be called The London Cemetery Company'. In 1837, the South Metropolitan Cemetery in Norwood opened, with Highgate Cemetery following in 1839, and Abney Park Cemetery in Stoke Newington and Brompton Cemetery in 1840. (The land for Brompton Cemetery included part of the Kensington Canal, and the original plan was for water-borne coffins.)

The return of cholera in 1853–4, this time in the West End, led to the Metropolis Land Management Act, which in turn created the Metropolitan Board of Works, which was given statutory powers to remove any civic 'nuisances', be they street pumps or graveyards. Yet even then Parliament failed to endow the Board with the one thing it needed – the authority to create a London-wide system of sewers, to drain the city that was almost a single cesspool of waste. That took the Great Stink of 1858.

In an essay in *Household Words* in 1850, a narrator imagines he tours the river with Father Thames: 'may I inquire,' he says, 'what that black, sluggish stream may be which I see pouring into you from a wide, bricked archway'? Replies a proud Father Thames, 'that's one of my sewers...and a fine, generous, open fellow, he is...[there is] one generally near every bridge.' He indicates the different-coloured currents swirling about: 'That one belongs to a soap-boiler...next to it, is from a slaughter-house...[others] are from gas-factories, brewhouses, shot-factories, coal-wharfs, cow-houses, tan-pits, gut-spinners, fish-markets, and other[s].' He benevolently advises his interviewer not to be confused by the 'scum derived from barges, and limeworks, and colliers, and the shipping...and bone-grinders, and tar-works, and dredging-machines, and steamers...and floating remains of creatures from knackers' yards'. Or, as Dickens put it more succinctly in *Little Dorrit*, 'Through the heart of the town a deadly sewer ebbed and flowed, in the place of a fine, fresh river.'

* She was followed there by many others of the Dickenses' acquaintance: Thomas Hood, Leigh Hunt, Thackeray, John Leech, Anthony Trollope, Wilkie Collins and George Cruikshank.

In 1857, the same year that novel was finished, the stench from the Thames had become so overwhelming that the government authorized quantities of chloride of lime to be dumped in the river in an attempt to mitigate the smell. An unusually dry, hot summer the following year rendered even that measure useless. The water was its usual black mass, and now the shrunken river revealed a bed of rotting, putrescent waste, which soon began to ferment in the sun. By 19 June conditions were, said Dickens, 'head-and-stomach distracting'. Despite the ninety-degree heat, every window of every building overlooking the Thames remained closed, 'and, as the smell rushes up the streets that lead from the river to the Strand, passers-by utter maledictions on the Government, the City authorities, the Central Board, and all who can or are supposed to be able to interfere'. By the end of the month, all were pointing a single finger of blame: 'The causes of the nuisance are perfectly clear, so are the means of cure; but... no Minister has the courage to demand [what it will cost]. If it were a question of arming ships, or embarking soldiers, there would not be a day's hesitation in asking for ten times the sum – it is so much better to spend money in killing our neighbours than in keeping ourselves alive and well.' 'Nobody knows what is to be done,' wrote Dickens; 'at least everybody knows a plan, and everybody else knows it won't do.'

But he was wrong: nothing makes funds available more quickly than the discomfort of the ruling class, and the Houses of Parliament sit directly on the river. One hot day there was a 'sudden rush' of MPs, all dashing from a committee room: Disraeli, the Chancellor of the Exchequer, had 'papers in one hand and... his pocket handkerchief clutched in the other', holding it 'closely to his nose, with body half bent' as he fled, followed by Gladstone and his colleagues, all choking, their eyes streaming. Twelve days later Disraeli sponsored a bill to give the Metropolitan Board of Works the funds and, for the first time, the legal authority to undertake a city-wide, sewage-building project. The Metropolis Local Management Act for the Purification of the Thames and the Main Drainage of the Metropolis was passed one day short of a month after parliamentarians were forced to flee their own offices. 'Parliament,' said *The Times*, 'was all but compelled to legislate upon the great London nuisance by the force of sheer stench.'

The Metropolitan Board of Works and its engineer, Joseph Bazalgette, had long been attempting to get approval for their plans to build intercepting sewers to run along the bank of the Thames, collecting waste from the street sewers and shipping it off to four pumping stations, then to great outfall sewers at Beckton and Crossness, near Abbey Wood, where at high tides it would be released to be swept out to sea. And this was what happened: only five years after the Great Stink, intercepting sewers were taking much of London's waste as far as Barking Creek; in 1865, the Crossness pumping station was opened by the Prince of Wales. And in 1866, with eighty miles of sewering laid, the benefits were visible to all: a fourth epidemic of cholera arrived in London, but this time only the East End, not yet connected to the great new sewage system, was affected. Once the Abbey Mills station was opened in 1868, there were no further cholera outbreaks in London.

Sewers and sewerage became a subject of fascination to the reading public. In 1861, *All the Year Round* took readers along the sewers from Finchley Road in north London to Vauxhall Bridge, showing the different types of waste: blood sewers under the meat markets, where 'you could wade in the vital fluid of sheep and oxen'; 'boiling-sewers' near sugar bakers, where the effluent was always hot; 'open rural sewers that were fruitful in watercresses, and closed town sewers whose roofs are thickly clustered with edible fungi'; and 'sewers of different degrees of repulsiveness' near chemical works and factories. (Informed that he was underneath Buckingham Palace, the reporter's 'loyalty was at once excited, and, taking off my fan-tailed cap, I led the way with the National Anthem, insisting that my guides should join in the chorus'. The sewer workers' response is not recorded.) By 1866, the sewers were so much part of daily London life that they had almost ceased to seem dirty. In *The Wild Boys of London*, an 1866 adventure story for boys, a gang of orphans and outcasts live in a sewer that somehow has no smell and no waste: 'It's nothing when you get used to it. We gets wet, and we gets dry again; the mud makes us dirty, and the water makes us clean.'

There was one single delay. Parliament had deliberately closed its eyes to the fact that the Thames would have to be embanked for Bazalgette's plan to function in full, and not until 1862 did the government accept that the money would have to be found for this too. Another couple of years elapsed before the various plots of land along the river were purchased. The Duke of Buccleuch, for example, had a newly built house on land leading down to the river, and his case for compensation took eight years to grind its way through the courts. There was more delay as elaborate plans were developed to utilize the opportunity to create a new road, as well as a mass of underground support systems, including what became the District and Circle lines of the tube, water and gas pipes, and service access tunnels. This slowed things down, but everyone understood that it was worth doing properly.

The idea of embanking the river, building out into the Thames to create additional shore, was not new: the Adelphi Terrace to the west of Waterloo Bridge, and Somerset House to the east, had both built on embankments in the eighteenth century. Waterloo Bridge in the early nineteenth century had banked in the area underneath the new span to link up these two pieces of land. There were also embankments where the Temple gardens stood;* by Blackfriars Bridge, created in 1769, when the bridge was built; and at Chelsea Hospital, the remains of an older, failed embankment. The new Houses of Parliament, which were built between 1837 and 1852, had created an 850-foot embankment, its buildings jutting out into what had previously been the river. So the new Embankment was new only in scale; the entire length of the river, running for five miles on the north side of the river from Chelsea to Blackfriars, was embanked. On the south side the land by Lambeth was embanked to prevent the regular floods that the low-lying south bank had always been subject to, creating the reclaimed land on which St Thomas's Hospital was built.

For many Londoners, the building of the Embankment was an ordeal to be survived. The city had become the site of what was in effect a military campaign, in which 'a series of fortifications, mostly surmounted by huge scaffolds…arose in our chief thoroughfares'. Arthur Munby felt the full

* The Temple gardens were much more than simply a nice square of green: they covered three acres in the middle of the busiest part of London.

force of this campaign. He lived in Fig Tree Court, Inner Temple, and the buildings on the south side of his courtyard were all demolished for the work, as he noted dismally in his diary:

> APRIL 1864: 'On my way home, went to look at the great mound of earth, now an acre in extent, which carts are outpouring...at the foot of Norfolk Street, for the Embankment.'
> MAY 1864: The embankment seen from Middle Temple garden is now 'outlined by the scaffold beams and dredging engines ranged far out in the river opposite'.
> SEPTEMBER 1864: 'The embankment grown a more horrible chaos than ever.'

And so it went on for him, year by dreary year:

> APRIL 1866: 'The walls of the Embankment begin to appear: piles for new bridges block up the Thames everywhere.'

Before the Thames was embanked, low-lying areas of London flooded regularly. Here, with the new Chelsea Embankment nearing completion in 1874, and plans under way for the Embankment Gardens, residents could look forward to drier and more pleasant living conditions after years of building work.

Unlike Munby, Dickens did not live by the river, and so he saw less the devastation of the present than hope for the future. In 1861, he wrote, 'I thought I would walk on by Mill Bank, to see the river. I walked straight on *for three miles* on a splendid broad esplanade overhanging the Thames... When I was a rower on that river it was all broken ground and ditch, with here and there a public-house or two, an old mill, and a tall chimney. I had never seen it in any stage of transition.'

Finally, in 1869, the Embankment opened, and even Munby was awed:

> January 1869: 'The bright morning sun shone on the broad bright river, and the white walls of the Embankment, which stretch away in a noble curve to Westminster, under the dark contrasting masses of the bridges. There is silence, except for the tread of passersby; there is life and movement, almost noiseless, on the water... What a change from the vulgar riot of the Strand! Here is stateliness and quiet, and beauty of form and colour.'

Today the gardens that covered much of the reclaimed land are gone, or are cut off by a four-lane road of whizzing cars, somehow becoming invisible. One historian suggests that this is because we view the Embankment from the wrong viewpoint: it was designed by people who still thought the entrance to London was by water, whereas we approach it from land. This part of London would benefit from a return to stateliness, quiet, and beauty of form and colour.

PART THREE

Enjoying Life

1867: The Regent's Park Skating Disaster

In the *Pickwick Papers*, Sam Weller and the fat boy 'cut out a slide' on the ice, and 'all' go sliding – Wardle, Pickwick, Sam, Winkle, Bob Sawyer, the fat boy and Snodgrass. Mr Pickwick in particular slides over and over, enjoying himself enormously. But when 'The sport was at its height…a sharp smart crack was heard. There was a quick rush towards the bank, and a wild scream from the ladies' – who are not skating, but watching admiringly – as 'A large mass of ice disappeared, the water bubbled over it, Mr Pickwick's hat, gloves, and handkerchief were floating on the surface, and this was all of Mr Pickwick that anybody could see.' This being a comic novel, nothing worse happens than Mr Pickwick getting a ducking and rushing indoors for a hot bath and his bed to ward off a cold.

And that too was how the vast numbers of men who skated regularly on the frozen waters of the London parks regarded the hazards, although this was hardly a risk-free pastime. On one day in 1844 over 5,000 people were counted on the Serpentine, even after 'the icemen of the Royal Humane Society' had warned that the ice was dangerously thin; another 2,500 were counted on Long Water, the area north of the Serpentine Bridge, while 1,500 skated on the Round Pond in Kensington Gardens. The Humane Society, established for 'the recovery of persons apparently drowned or dead', had set up its first receiving house in 1794 beside the Serpentine, where bathers were taken in summer, skaters in winter. In that one afternoon, by four o'clock the ice had broken under at least ten people on the Serpentine. At St James's Park, the iceman working for the Humane Society went to the aid of seven or eight skaters who went through the ice there, saving five, while another fifteen got a ducking at the Buckingham Palace end of the water.

The risks slowed few down. In 1855, at St James's Park, 'the Express Train came off': between 300 and 400 men formed a line, each holding on to the coat of the man in front, starting off with 'some whistling the railway overture, and others making a noise resembling the blowing off of the steam of a locomotive'. Some of the Foot Guards joined in and soon they 'glided over the ice at the rate of three-quarters of a mile per minute'. In Regent's Park, 'hundreds' of men skated along the canal tunnel between Aberdeen Place and Maida Hill, racing through 'in imitation of express trains, with appropriate noises and whistlings'. One weekend there were so many wanting to go through the tunnel that the police barred the entrance; but the next day 'the trains' were permitted to go through the tunnel 'as usual'.

On 6 January 1867, the Serpentine's ice 'was about three inches thick, and, with the exception of a small portion at the eastern end, perfectly safe'. A large number of skaters were out, and only five people went through the ice, of whom four were not seriously hurt; the final man 'was rescued after considerable difficulty' and put into a warm bath in the Humane Society's receiving house. St James's Park, by contrast, warned its skaters of the 'irregular' ice, and 'several immersions' needed the Humane Society's assistance. Other parks reported no problems: Kensington Gardens, Clapham Park, Hampstead Ponds 'and the London, Chatham, and Dover Railway Company's ponds at Brixton' were all 'crowded with sliders and skaters. Several accidents occurred, but not of a serious nature.'

The same could not be said of Regent's Park. The lake in the park was partially fed by the Tyburn, and there were dangerous currents. Between three and four o'clock a man, possibly employed by the Humane Society, told one spectator the ice was 'in a very unsafe condition, and that there would be a terrible accident very soon'; she watched as park employees broke up the ice by the Long Island. After the event no one knew why this had been done: an iceman from the Humane Society said he had done so because 'It has been done ever since I was a boy.' The park superintendent claimed that the ice was being broken only by the islands, to protect the vegetation and the birds, and no one, he said, had ever suggested it was dangerous. This was contradicted by the Secretary to the Humane Society, who replied that it was very clearly dangerous. The Society's men had asked the police to keep people away, but were told they had no such powers: it might have been dangerous to go on the ice, but it was not illegal.

The ice was 'tessellated', cracked in squares a yard or more across, with water oozing up between the cracks. Suddenly, near the island, the water abruptly rose up in 'spurts'. This prompted a sudden rush as everyone headed for the banks, but many were cut off by the quickly cracking surface. Ladders were pushed out along the ice, but some people fell off and disappeared through the ice. Panic ensued, as 'they skated back towards the centre of the ice, and as they did so they fell, and the whole surface suddenly gave way, and all of them went into the water'.

A huge sheet of ice had broken off, plunging about 250 people into the lake, with hundreds more scrambling to safety. The water, dropping away to the natural bed of the river, was up to twelve feet deep in places and without a firm bottom. Some who were tipped off the ice became trapped underneath. Others lay flat on the surface, clinging to isolated pieces of ice, screaming for help, as the thousand or so spectators on the banks began to scream too. The ten Humane Society icemen did their best. They had 'the usual appliances': ropes, wicker ice-boats, a sledge, ladders, drags, boat-hooks, ice axes and cork belts. But the ice was not firm enough for the Humane Society's sledges to be launched; the boats were blocked by the large chunks of floating ice; the ropes that were thrown out saved some, but others snapped. And all the while, women and girls stood on the shore, watching as their husbands, sons and brothers, dressed in sodden, woollen, three-piece suits and overcoats, held on to smaller and smaller pieces of ice, finally letting go and sinking, frozen, as the fragments disintegrated. Several men onshore grabbed ropes and jumped in, attempting to rescue their children, brothers or fathers, or complete strangers.

In January, darkness falls by four o'clock, and although flares were lit and placed around the water, it was too dark to continue the search, which had to be given up for the night. By this time nearly 200 men and boys had managed to reach the shore, or were dragged out by hooks and ropes before they drowned, or died of cold. Two surgeons were regularly on call near by for the Humane Society. More doctors and surgeons from the surrounding area rushed to the spot and, in makeshift premises, in the Humane Society's receiving house and on the open ground, they worked to revive those who had been pulled from the water, while bodies beyond rescue were carried past.

None of those who died in the water that afternoon had any identification on them whatsoever. Almost every one of them was in their teens or twenties; five were children and only two were older men. The bodies were all taken to the nearby Marylebone Workhouse, where they were laid out for relatives and friends to identify. Small objects that might help – a hat with the maker's name, a letter beginning 'Dear Richard' – were placed beside them.

Shirley Brooks, a journalist, and later editor of *Punch*, who lived in Kent Terrace, in the ring of houses surrounding the park, wrote in his diary:

> Day of the hideous disaster in the Regents Park…I had gone to the Garrick [Club] to meet [the musician] German Reed. I walked, on my way, about 2.15 through the 'Ornamental' [Garden, near the water], & great numbers were skating. It was a fine day. I had half decided on hiring skates, & trying whether I had forgotten the work – I could skate fast in old days; but I thought my shoes were unsuitable, & I went on. Reed was late, & when I left him to walk home it was 5.10. At the Clarence gate I saw several cabs & carriages, & some groups, but it was dark, & being in a hurry, I asked no questions. On getting into the hall Reginald rushed out[.] 'O papa, there has been a dreadful accident, the ice broke, & at least 30 are drowned.' Then I had the details from poor Emily, who had been fearfully frightened. The boys had gone to see the skating in the Botanic [Garden, on the other side of the park], & at their prayers, she had at last relaxed the order not to go on the ice. Mrs. Linton called, & while they were talking…Hawkins rushed in – 'the ice had broken, where were the boys.'…Of course she dashed out with Mrs L. & hurried among the crowds, saw the frightful scene, heard the women shrieking & wailing, & witnessed many agonies – and though told by several that her boys were all right, was convinced that no one really knew. She went into the Humane Tent, where was a boy, in bed, but a moment told her he was not hers, & she went out again. At last she met them, strolling leisurely up to the scene. She was soon crying over them by her fireside. I returned to hear all this…After [dinner]…went into…the tent. That work was over – all who were in that lake were dead – but eight or ten bodies had been taken out…Rego cried – Cecil was silent, he would not eat, & scarcely slept. That night Emily & I thanked God for the children.

The next morning, volunteers arrived to break up the ice, to try to find the bodies under the surface; they were watched by as many as 3,000 on the shore. Even as the light faded once more, 1,000 still kept watch, Shirley Brooks and his wife among them: 'We saw the cutting, the dragging, & the bringing out a body, a man, in black, his arms extended & bent – they brought him across the island, to our very feet. The crowds were great. Four bodies have been got out today up to the time I write (12). *Two boys* in Hanover Terrace, next to us, are *dead*...'

Three days later, bodies were still being taken from the water, and forty men were hired at 2s a day to help. On the following Monday, another 104 were employed, and still another 207 on the Tuesday, a full week later, as the search continued. And still the spectators stood on the banks, even if their numbers were 'considerably less' than the week before. It was not until 22 January, seven days after the accident, that the list of the forty dead could be compiled:

Frederick Beer, 21, paper-hanger
R. Born, 13, the stepson of a publican
John Broadbridge, aged 10
John Bryant, 29, costermonger
Thomas Chadwick, 22, porter
James Crawley, 28, coach-joiner
William Davies, 22, medical student
Henry Gamble, aged 14
Harold Giles, 15, schoolboy
Frank Glanfield, 15, son of a butcher
James Griffin, 28, orange-seller
Henry Hardiman, 17, cabinetmaker
Richard Harnack, aged 10
Thomas Harries, 29, gentleman
Thomas Harvey, 17, medical student
James Justice, 21, corn-chandler
James Jobson, 35, painter

Charles Jukes, 9, the son of a carpenter

C. E. Luckman, 24, warehouseman

Donald Macintyre, aged 26, silk-merchant

James Mitchell, 26, organ-builder

David North, aged 13

Samuel Olley, 20, wood-turner

William Parkinson, 18, organ pipe-maker

Edward Pullan, 25, commercial traveller

George Rhodes, 20, paper-hanger

William Robertson, 33, dentist

Robert Edwin Scott, 29, clerk

Charles Smith, 13, son of a coachman

Thomas Wilson Spencer, 25, solicitor

Arthur Reginald Stevens, 16, the son of an army officer

Edward Thurley, 30, butler

John Vincent, aged 10

Joseph Waite, 22, clerk

Charles William Wake, 20, law student

John Thomas Whatley, 14, schoolboy

H. Woodhouse, 16, son of a colonial broker

John Spencer Woods, 18, upholsterer

unnamed, aged 13

unnamed, 20, gas-fitter

9.

STREET PERFORMANCE

In the 1830s, a building running between Oxford Street and Regent Street was turned into a 'bazaar', a warren of small luxury-goods shops. The Pantheon, as it was named, boasted vestibules filled with sculptures, a hall, a series of galleries, 'a species of atrium', a conservatory eighty-eight feet long 'in the Moorish style', complete with 'stands for parroquets', a fountain and goldfish.* Those who wanted to shop could do so, but the Pantheon was primarily used as a place to meet, walk, chat and watch the world, especially when it was raining. For there was a type of lounging about the fashionable streets, watching the world go by, that was the prerogative of the man about town. According to Thackeray, 'now a *stroll*, then a *look-in* [to a shop], then a *ramble*, and presently a *strut*' was the right way for a gent to occupy his day.

When the day was fine, the fashionable crowds came to Regent Street at the fashionable hours, between two and five o'clock, peaking around four. What today we call window-shopping was part of the life of the street, a performance participated in by those who could afford actually to go in and buy, as well as by those who could not. Thus window-shopping, and shopping itself, were different: one was part of the performance of street life, the other consumption. The former included the 'carriages... in groups in front of Swan and Edgars silk shop...gentlemen [on horseback] wishing to pay their respects to the ladies...The pavements...swarming with pedestrians,

* The building later became the National Institute to Improve the Manufactures of the United Kingdom, then a wine shop, and today it is a Marks and Spencer, for many years known as their 'Pantheon' store.

idlers, or shoppers bent on a visit to the gunmaker, the haberdasher's or the jeweller's.' The Regent Street shop windows were considered to be the most glamorous, displaying, wrote Dickens in the late 1830s, 'sparkling jewellery, silks and velvets of the richest colours, the most inviting delicacies, and the most sumptuous articles of luxurious ornament'. In the first half of the century, the street encompassed a wide range of shops, not merely those selling luxury goods, and their displays were enjoyed by all. In Regent Street alone, Sala itemized 'a delightful bird-stuffer's shop...with birds of paradise, parrots, and hummingbirds...[a] funeral monument shop, with the mural tablets, the obelisks, the broken columns, the extinguished torches, and the draped urns in the window', an 'Italian statuary shop' and a 'filter shop, with the astonishing machines for converting foul and muddy water...into a sparkling, crystal stream', in between bakers, staymakers, stationers, a grocer and an optician with a model of a steam engine in his window. Two decades later, the luxury trade had taken over, and the street was the home of 'Fancy watchmakers, haberdashers, and photographers; fancy stationers, fancy hosiers, and fancy staymakers; music shops, shawl shops, jewellers, French glove shops, perfumery, and point lace shops, confectioners and milliners'.

All this glamour was seasonal for the upper classes and depended on the parliamentary calendar, around which all social occasions were scheduled. When Parliament sat, towards the end of January or in February, the wealthy returned from country to town, although the more sporting did not appear until March, when the hunting season ended; the Royal Academy summer exhibition in April or May was the signal for entertainment to get under way at full tilt. In August, Parliament rose and, together with the partridge-shooting season, caused the main exodus back to the country. Many of the gentry and landed classes did not return to London until January, but professionals and businessmen took as holiday just the single month of August. The shops that supplied them, therefore, frequently closed for August too. In 1853, Dickens complained that 'The West End of London is entirely deserted...I went to three shops this morning...Blackmore the tailor was at Brighton. Butler the tailor was...in the bosom of his family. Only two subordinates were in attendance at Beale's the hosier's, and they were playing at draughts'. Shops that were open were staffed by temporary employees 'who are imperfectly acquainted with the prices of the goods, and contemplate them with unsophisticated delight'. The milkwomen didn't even bother to water down their milk they had so few customers. All the luxury trades were affected, even prostitutes, whose clients also vanished.

There were many shopping streets that were not as fashionable as Regent Street, and therefore did not suffer in the same way, even in the same fashionable West End districts, and yet the street life they promoted was every bit as lively. 'In secluded corners' near by, Dickens noted, there were many little shops 'withdrawn from public curiosity', shops that traded with servants, both selling them goods and buying their perquisites: the cook sold offcuts of food, the butler got rid of empty wine bottles, the valets and the lady's maids the second-hand clothes they had been given.

There were several types of second-hand shop, whose names supposedly indicated what they bought, although the names could be misleading and the goods in which they dealt often overlapped. Marine stores sold and bought nothing nautical, but stocked pretty much the same thing as the rag-and-bone shops. In *Bleak House*, Krook, who calls his shop a 'Rag and Bottle Warehouse', says he is also a dealer in 'Marine Stores', and he buys old furniture, paper, rags, bones, kitchen equipment and 'kitchen-stuff' (food waste), fire-irons, iron, old clothes, bottles, old books, pictures, tools and bits of metal. The paper was sold to tradesmen for wrapping goods; the dirty rags for breaking down for fertilizer, clean ones to paper mills; bones for soap or fertilizer; kitchen stuff to the pig-keepers; grease to tallow makers; old iron to manufacturers. Dripping and old clothes were sold either directly to the poor, or to wholesalers who resold them through the Rag Fair market.

A step above these were the pawnshops. In rich districts, pawnshops looked like ordinary jewellers, and only the notice at the door, announcing that money was advanced on goods and advertising a 'fireproof safe' in which to keep them, indicated their real function. Inside, instead of an open counter, as Martin Chuzzlewit discovered, many pawnshops were fitted with 'a series of little closets, or private boxes', so that each customer could remain hidden from his or her neighbour. Items pawned in the West

End might include decorative household objects such as drawings, vases, statuettes, or personal items like jewellery and cashmere shawls; in St Giles, by contrast, the pawned items were more likely to be petticoats, shirts and workmen's tools. Here the same items were pawned every week, 'not because the man is a drunkard or an idler', wrote Dickens sympathetically in *Household Words*, 'but because he is a poor jobbing carpenter, without a penny of monied capital: who, when he has a small job in hand, and has done the sawing part of it and wants [to purchase] the nails and glue to finish it, pawns the saw to provide them, until he is paid and can redeem it'. By 1850, there were more than 400 official pawnbrokers in London (and probably thousands more of the unofficial sort: see below).

On pawning a watch valued at, say, £2, its owner was given £2 and a pawn ticket. The watch could be redeemed any time over the next year by paying back the £2, plus interest, which usually ran to 15 or 20 per cent a year. If it were not redeemed within fifteen months, the pawnbroker was allowed to sell it. But there were many tricks of the trade. Unscrupulous pawnbrokers made customers take two tickets each for half the value of an item, since the interest was calculated from a base rate, and this way the value for an inexpensive item could be doubled. Some sewed a farthing into the lining of a coat: when customers making a purchase felt it, they chose that coat over others of better quality, imagining that someone had secreted a high-value coin there for safety and then forgotten about it. Other pawnbrokers were sympathetic to their clientele and accommodated their needs, whether it was routinely accepting carpenters' tools at a pawnshop by the dockyards, or in the West End allowing their regular customers, prostitutes, to take their jewellery out of hock for a night 'for a consideration'.

Many marine stores, Krook's included, hung a small black-faced doll in the window, to indicate they were dolly shops, that is, unlicensed pawnbrokers that offered money on goods considered too contemptible to be accepted by a regular pawnbroker. Dolly shops, said Dickens, took on the air of their neighbourhood by the accumulation of goods that were pawned. Around Drury Lane, the stock leant towards 'faded articles of dramatic finery, such as three or four pairs of soiled buff boots… worn by a "fourth robber", or "fifth mob"', while around the Marshalsea the clothes were of better quality than usual, having been pawned by formerly well-heeled debtors as money grew scarcer; near the docks, the main items were sailors' clothes. Below the dolly shops in the hierarchy came leaving shops, for items that even the dolly shops wouldn't take: a single knife or fork, or a baking dish to be redeemed on Saturday, payday, for the Sunday meal. This is the type of shop run by Pleasant Riderhood in *Our Mutual Friend*. She has other income – she lets rooms, and her father earns his own living – which makes the contents of her fictional shop slightly superior to a real one in a Southwark slum in 1858, kept by a paralysed ex-sewerman and his wife. Pleasant's window contains a couple of handkerchiefs, a coat, some 'valueless' watches, tobacco, pipes, sweets and a bottle of walnut ketchup. The sewerman's shop contained, as its entire stock, 'a handful of sugar candy, a few brandy-balls, four sugar-plums contained in pickle-bottles, three herrings and a half, five dip candles and a half... a quart of parched peas, in a broken plate'.

Just as Regent Street was *the* place for luxury goods, other streets had reputations as the places to go for specific items, even if on a less elegant scale. Cranbourne Alley, running between Leicester Square and St Martin's Lane, had nothing but bonnet shops, 'at the doors of which stood women, slatternly in appearance, but desperate and accomplished touters', according to one point of view. (Other writers said the women were not slatternly at all but 'of decent appearance'.) 'Man, woman, or child, it was all the same to them; if they had made up their minds that you were to buy a bonnet, buy one you were obliged to... Piteous stories were told of feeble-minded old gentlemen emerging from the "courts", half-fainting, laden with bonnet-boxes, and minus their cash, watches, and jewellery'. These touters were known as 'She-Barkers', as though they worked in fairs, and such was their fame that even children knew of their practices. Young Sophia Beale thought that the omnibus cads calling their route were like 'the milliners in Cranbourne alley who run at people passing and hold up bonnets and shout "buy, buy, only 5 shillings"'.

Even without a barker, or without the great plate-glass windows that the most expensive, modern stores could afford, smaller shops in the less fashionable districts had their own means of advertising their wares to the streets' passers-by. Many kept their street signs from the eighteenth century much longer than did the glossy Regent Street emporiums. In the 1820s, such signs were an everyday sight: 'The Pawnbroker decorates his door with three gold balls – the Barber…hangs out a long pole – the Gold-beater, an arm with a hammer in the act of striking – the Chemist, a head of Glauber, or Esculapius* – the Tobacconist, a roll of tobacco, and of late it has become customary for these venders [sic] of…snuff, to station a wooden figure of a Highlander, in the act of taking a pinch.' In *Little Dorrit*, the Chiverys' tobacco shop by the Marshalsea prison has its little Highlander. At Captain Cuttle's, in *Dombey and Son*, a wooden midshipman is affixed outside to indicate he is a ship's-instrument maker, and in *Martin Chuzzlewit*, written in the early 1840s, while not mentioned by Dickens, an illustration shows a pie shop with a massive pie sign.

As these fictional references suggest, sometimes the signs were painted boards, as the old ones had been and as pub signs are today; sometimes they were in the shape of the object they represented; and sometimes there were also wooden models, increasing in size as the century progressed. Pubs went in for elaborate renditions of their names: the Elephant and Castle Tavern used a vast model elephant bearing a howdah; the Swan Tavern in the same south London location 'had a large and well-proportioned bird' over its board. Smaller businesses also thought size mattered. One bootmaker's model boot was 'large enough for the Colossus of Rhodes', while in the same row of shops a gigantic dustpan indicated a tin-man's shop, a vast cigar a cigar divan (see p. 295) and a huge stick of sealing wax a stationer. Some traders stuck with elaborate painted images. Fishmongers went in for seascapes, while small grocers favoured pictures of tea parties 'of staid British matrons, assembled round the singing kettle', or 'a party of Bedouins in the Desert' sitting around a Staffordshire-ware tea service. The 'humbler sorts of coffee-shops and eating houses' favoured a picture of a loaf of bread, some butter, a piece of cheese and some bacon on a

* Johann Rudolf Glauber was a seventeenth-century alchemist; Esculapius (now more commonly Asclepius) the Greek god of medicine. I am not aware of the former being as common a motif as the latter as this passage implies.

blue-and-white plate, beside a cup of coffee. If they were teetotal, there would be nothing further; otherwise they would include a glass of ale or a tankard of porter, 'with a foaming top like a cauliflower…and perhaps a red herring, eloquent of a relish. Sometimes there are a couple of mice delineated in the act of nibbling the cheese.'

Aside from shop signs, painted exhortations to buy had begun to appear in the early 1830s. 'Warren's Blacking, 30, Strand' (the main firm, not Dickens' employers) was painted up 'in letters from six to eighteen inches long, on the brick walls along the public roads': coach passengers saw the reminders from miles away, over and over again. In one fictional treatment nearly two decades later, these painted signs on the road to London were 'great white invitations to "TRY WARREN'S", or, "DAY AND MARTIN'S BLACKING", loom[ing] through the darkness of the dead walls'. Sometimes Warren's even painted 'WARREN'S IS THE BEST' on the pavements.

These signs were insignificant in quantity when compared to the ever-present 'bills': sheets posted, or stuck up, on almost every flat surface, whether static or ambulant. Many Regency engravings show every temporary hoarding covered in bills, and through the century technology altered only their size and colours, 'a fresh supply of artistical gems' being posted anew every day. These included playbills, which were the most common, the contents lists from weekly magazines, or images of items with addresses where they could be purchased, whether pens, spectacles, dresses or men's suits. The bill-sticker was a regular sight, in 'fustian jackets with immense pockets', his tins of paste attached by a strap, with great bags holding the bills and long extendable sticks with a crossbar at the end, which made it possible for him to post the bills at any height.

Dickens wrote about these men in 1851, although unusually his report doesn't sound particularly authentic. The 'King of the Bill-Stickers' told him his father had also been a bill-sticker eighty years before, which in terms of life expectancy sounds unlikely in itself, while his statement that he himself earned 30s a week, 'including paste', defies belief. In *Bleak House*, the legal clerk Mr Guppy presents his salary of 40s a week as pushing him into the middle classes, and Mayhew's street sellers averaged 10s a week. The 'King' also tells Dickens he was 'the first that ever stuck a bill under a bridge!', although Max Schlesinger in the same year wrote that the bridges, running with damp, never had bills posted on them, but were instead painted: 'there is not an arch in a London bridge but has its advertisements painted on it.' He adds that, in 1851, every one of them was for the steamer companies. The question, however, must remain open. In 1858, the painter Augustus Egg in his triptych *Past and Present* showed the Adelphi arches papered with playbills as well as excursion advertisements.

These bills were all advertising well-established companies. Smaller businesses relied on another eighteenth-century survival, the handbill. These were given to customers in shops, and wrapped around purchases, but most often they were handed out in the street. By Temple Bar, wrote Southey, posing as a visiting Spaniard in 1807, 'I had a paper thrust into my hand [and] Before I reached home I had a dozen.' Just over a decade later, the fictional *Life in London* claimed handbills were so common 'that a man scarcely opens a coal-shed, or a potatoe-stall' without distributing handbills to all and sundry, 'frequently with great success'. Such handbills might advertise exhibitions, patent medicines, whisky, linen drapers' or giraffes at the zoo. Many handbills printed their advertising jingles in verse. In *The Old Curiosity Shop*, Mr Slum writes the text for handbills, with 'pathetic effusions' for goods purchased by 'private houses and tradespeople', parodies for pubs and lawyers' clerks, while he couched advertisements directed at girls' schools in moral educational verses. By the 1850s, bills were handed out by 'seedy personages' who could not earn a living in any other way.

Early in the century the hander-out was as much a part of the advertisement, and the street entertainment, as the handbill. Often such men wielded poles with banners, or some other noticeable ornament, as they took up their position in the street. In the early 1830s, by Regent Street, a man stood dressed in a red coat with epaulettes, 'having on his head a cocked hat, surmounted by the panache of a field-marshal. At his back and before him were suspended, so as to balance each other, a couple of boards, with printed placards... "Gentlemen should instruct their servants to use Brown's blacking!"' The awkward phrasing of this description makes it clear that the idea of a sandwich-board was new. Dickens was the first to create an edible metaphor, referring two years later to 'an animated sandwich, composed of a boy between two boards', and soon these 'Peripatetic placards' became 'a piece of human flesh between two slices of pasteboard'. When the *Illustrated London News* began publishing in 1842, it hired 200 sandwich-board men to promenade the streets, also publishing an engraving of this event that suggests they marched in one single long line, to make a bigger impression.

In the 1830s, odd costumes designed to attract attention became a feature of street life. Two men between them wore 'one huge garment of green moreen', with long, flowing, green sleeves, and just one hole for the face, 'surmounted by a dunce's cap'. For some inexplicable reason this two-for-one was advertising 'a new cure for the itch'. By the 1850s, strange clothing or pasteboard signs were no longer enough, being replaced by large papier-mâché representations of the product in question. One man wore a giant scarlet boot on his head; underneath it he 'was wrapped in a garment entirely composed of cardboard soles', while also somehow managing to carry a flag with a bootmaker's name and address. Even something as simple as a tradesman's moving premises received elaborate treatment. On Holborn, twelve men walked up and down carrying a huge table on which was painted 'MR. FALCON REMOVED' and the address of the new shop. As its sole purpose was to notify Mr Falcon's regular customers, the procession covered only a dozen yards of pavement, 'continually, silently, without ever stopping for rest...for many days and even weeks'.

Other forms of advertisements seem more natural today. By the 1830s, omnibuses were already carrying advertisements. By 1837, some bore portraits of Boz himself, as the author of *The Pickwick Papers*. (It is nice to think that perhaps the Bardell omnibus, whose name Dickens possibly borrowed for Mr Pickwick's landlady, carried advertisements for the very novel in which Mrs Bardell appeared.) From these, it was a short step to entire carts being dedicated to advertising, which were on the roads at about the same time, presenting complex scenarios to promote the excellence of various products. One cart carried a huge tub of water while behind it walked men bearing an enormous wellington boot suspended from a pole, repeatedly submerging it in the tub to prove its waterproof qualities. Carts might be seen with 'huge skeleton houses covered with handbills' or be disguised as imitation steamboats. One cart bore a giant hat, 'a hybrid between an Egyptian obelisk...and an English country-gentleman's gate', which advertised washable wigs; another displayed arched gothic windows in which dresses endlessly revolved on clockwork stands. In the 1850s, when such things were at their peak, a cart advertising a panorama was made up of 'three immense wooden pyramids', complete with hieroglyphics (thoughtfully translated into English), together with portraits of Isis and Osiris. Max Schlesinger, who watched this spectacle trundling down the street, noted that it was followed by another cart got up to look like a mosque, complete with cupola, and driven by a fair boy whose face had been artistically adorned with soot, to promote 'a most marvellous Arabian medicine, warranted to cure the bite of mad dogs and venomous reptiles generally'. Behind it, to promote Vauxhall Gardens, came 'a dark green chariot of fantastic make, in shape like a half-opened shell, and tastefully ornamented with gilding and pictures'.

Other advertisements required less capital and were of a more transient nature. Auctions of household goods were advertised by 'a breadth of stair-carpet' hanging out of a first-floor window, together with a printed notice on the door or gate. Barber's shops regularly posted similar printed notices announcing that they were selling '*on oath*, the pure grease of a fine large bear' as pomade for men's hair, and from time to time, to promote the freshness of their grease, the sign declared, 'We kill a bear this week,' frequently accompanied by a live bear itself, muzzled and tied up in the little area by the shop's basement. It was cynically assumed that the same bear was handed round from barber to barber, each one in turn displaying it while advertising its imminent demise, then sending it on to a colleague. The joke was so common that in *Nicholas Nickleby*, when a stagecoach is overturned and the passengers pass the time by telling stories, one concerns a German count who killed his own bear to grease 'his whiskers with him afterwards'.

Apart from greasing whiskers, shops, pubs and other public places offered wide-ranging street services. Shops were constant scenes of coming and going, and it was only in the backstreets that the shabbiest little ones had bells on the doors; the more prosperous shops always had at least one member of staff present, more often several, to provide goods and services. Tailors made running repairs to torn or damaged clothing, lending their customers something to wear while they sat and waited. In *Pickwick Papers*, Sam Weller buys from a stationer 'a sheet of the best gilt-edged letter-paper and a hard-nibbed pen', taking them to an inn, where he orders brandy 'and the inkstand'. Coffee rooms and taverns also acted as postal drops, taking letters and passing them on; personal newspaper advertisements gave these addresses as a *poste restante*. In *Great Expectations*, pubs also supply services that to us seem even more unexpected. When Magwitch is captured by the police on the river, he and Pip are taken to a nearby pub, where Pip purchases a full set of clothes, so that Magwitch won't have to go to gaol in his wet things.

Every shop delivered, whether they were expensive establishments with their own emblazoned carriage, or small local ones that despatched the goods by an errand boy in a small top hat and a big suit with shiny buttons. Even *The Pickwick Papers*' hard-up medical student Bob Sawyer, buying spirits in the unprosperous Borough for a little evening party, gets the alcohol delivered from the wine vaults, the glasses from the pub and oysters from the oyster shop: he carries nothing home himself. Refreshment rooms routinely stocked newspapers for their customers (see p. 301) and many also sent them out: in the late 1830s and early 1840s, a retired actor in Kentish Town had the *Morning Advertiser* delivered every day 'with the early dinner-beer'.

For those who couldn't afford that, there was still plenty of opportunity to read the news on the street. In part, the news was a constant street noise, as the newsboys cried out the latest headlines. But newspaper offices also pinned up copies of each edition outside their offices, where extraordinary events drew huge crowds, whether it was the 1848 revolutions in Europe or the Derby winners. The *London Gazette*, which printed the official list of bankruptcies, as well as army promotions and retirements* and other official notices, also produced 'an *Extraordinary Gazette*' during the Crimean War,

* It is for this reason that soldiers are 'gazetted': that is, their promotion is announced in the *Gazette*.

giving the official casualty lists. These were sent on to all the newspapers for reprinting, but since the *Gazette* had them first, crowds stood outside daily, waiting for the first copies to be pinned to the *Gazette* office wall in St Martin's Lane.

All of these buyers, sellers, touters and hawkers contributed to the many voices of the street, voices which in Dickens' fiction become fixed and create a sense that we know what these people sounded like. The most famous of them all was that of the cockney servant, Sam Weller: 'Vy didn't you say so before...For all I know'd he was one o' the regular threepennies...If he's anything of a gen'l'm'n, he's vurth a shillin' a day.' Or Sam describes his hat: ''Tain't a wery good 'un to look at...but it's an astonishin' 'un to wear; and afore the brim went, it was a wery handsome tile. Hows'ever it's lighter without it, that's one thing, and every hole lets in some air, that's another – wentilation gossamer I calls it.' It's almost all there – the Ws and Vs switching places, the irregular past tenses of verbs, the dropped Gs. Later, when Dickens created Jo in *Bleak House*, 'in course' instead of 'of course' appears; the addition of the 'g' ending on words like 'sovereign' joins the missing 'g' of Sam's 'astonishin'' and the final 'k' on 'nothink'. The Hs are added to words that begin with a vowel and are missing from words that begin with 'h', while the 'i' sound replaces 'oi' in words like 'spoil' – 'spile'.

Many have since claimed that Dickens invented the W/V slippage, but *Real Life in London*, published in 1821, when Dickens was just nine, claimed that Billingsgate fishmongers said, '*vat slippy valking...all the vay to Vapping Vall.*' This had disappeared by the 1850s: Alfred Bennett, writing of his childhood in that decade, claimed not to have heard it, but he agreed that Dickens' irregular past and present tenses – 'come' for 'came'; 'seed' for 'saw' – were a constant, as were double negatives – 'we ain't got no', 'without no'. By the end of Dickens' life the voices that one might today think he had imagined out of the ether had found their way on to the very real streets, as the bus conductors shouted out the destinations – 'Benk', 'Charin' Krauss', 'Pic'dilly'. People headed for Emma Smith [Hammersmith], Glawster Rowd [to rhyme with 'loud'], I [Hay] Street, Nottin Ill

Gite, Bizewater, Peddingten, Biker Street, Oldersgit Street, Ol'git, and Menshun Ouse.

The cockney voice was the most characteristic of the London accents, but it was not the only one. Other classes had their own idiosyncratic patterns. Dickens was particularly fond of lower-middle-class genteelisms. A lodging-house keeper in Bloomsbury shows her 'front parlior' to potential lodgers: 'the back parlior being what I cling to and never part with... Unless your mind is prepared for the stairs, it will lead to inevitable disapintmink.' Moving up the social scale, an 'affected Metropolitan Miss' created as many syllables as she could: she 'loves the ble-ue ske-i' and delights in being 'key-ind' to the poor. So snarled Mayhew in the 1850s, while noting similar pretensions among the upper classes: 'Your London exquisite, for instance, talks of taking – aw, his afternoon's *w*ide – aw – in *W*otton *W*o – aw – aw – or of going to the Ope*w*a – aw – or else of *w*unning down – aw – to the *W*aces – aw – aw.' (The stuttering vanished in perhaps the 1920s, although it has been suggested the R/W substitution still survives more among the upper than the working classes.) Not only did pronunciation vary between classes, but through the years changes occurred within each social group. Thomas Trollope, the son of a barrister and the grandson of a baronet, remembered that when he was a child in the 1810s older people pronounced Rome, 'Room', James, 'Jeames' and gold, 'goold', while 'oblige' was given the French pronunciation, 'obleege', a beef steak was a 'beef-steek', and the 'a' in words such as danger and stranger was pronounced as the 'a' in 'man'. Seventy years later, these pronuncitations had all vanished.

Even more than pronunciation, slang separated the various socio-economic groups, making each one as distinct on the street as their clothes did. 'The fast [cash-strapped] young gentleman positively *must* speak to his governor [father], and get the old brick [decent chap] to fork out [give] some more tin [cash], for positively he can hardly afford himself a weed [cigar] of an evening – besides he wants a more nobby crib [better lodgings], as the one he hangs out in now... really isn't the Stilton [done thing].' (The last phrase sounds remarkably like P. G. Wodehouse, born two decades after this was written.) Costermongers specialized in backslang, although it was 1860 before that word began to be used to describe their private language.

Long before it had a name, however, Mayhew supplied examples: a penny was a yenep, twopence owt-yenep, threepence erth-yenep and so on (except eight, which was 'teaich'). Backslang also gave 'on' for no, 'say' for yes, as well as 'cool the esclop', 'cool the namesclop' and 'cool ta the dillo nemo' – look at the police/policeman, the old woman. Other elements from various sources were mixed in: 'Vom-us! I'm going to do the tightener [have my dinner].' 'Vom-us' is from the (to us) familiar 'vamoose', which is in turn from the Spanish '*vamos*', 'let's go', while 'tightener' is not foreign, just colourful – when you eat well your clothes get tight.

Most of this has long vanished. What has survived is rhyming slang. Some attributed this new slang to thieves, others to ballad sellers and cheap-jacks, the travelling hawkers who used it in their sales patter. By the late 1850s, it was prevalent enough that mainstream middle-class publications gave their readers tasters, although they didn't yet have a name for it, but had to laboriously explain the method. It was, said Mayhew, 'arranged on the principle of using words that are similar in sound to the ordinary expressions for the same idea... the... cant words are mere nonsensical terms, rhyming with the vernacular ones'. He offered as an example a 'shallow cove' from St Giles who says, 'S'pose now... I wanted to ask a *codger* to come and have a *glass* of *rum* with me, and smoke a *pipe* of *baccer* over a game of *cards* with some *blokes* at *home* – I should say, *Splodger*, will you have a Jack-sur*pass* of finger-and-*thumb*, and blow your yard of *tripe* of nosey-me-*knacker*, while we have a touch of the *boards* with some other heaps of *coke* at my *drum*?' Other examples were Jimmy Skinner, dinner; Battle of the Nile, tile (a top hat); elephant's trunk, drunk; Epsom races, braces; over the stile, sent for trial. Although not using rhyming slang himself, Dickens unexpectedly gets a look-in when in a novel of 1858 a character says, 'leave the kid alone, or I'll put out my Chalk Farm (arm) and give you a rap with my Oliver Twist (fist).'

Mayhew realized that a great deal of the coster and more general working-class slang came from foreign languages. According to him, 'carser', for 'house', came from 'the organ boys', that is, from Italian (*casa*), while 'ogle' originated from '*oogelijn*' or 'little eye', brought to London, he suggested, by 'the Hollanders on board the Billingsgate eel-boats' (it does derive from

Dutch, but dates back two centuries earlier). 'Fogle', a handkerchief, he supposed came from from *vogel*, German for bird. (*Foglia*, Italian for pocket, seems more likely, as a fogle-hunter was a pickpocket: Oliver Twist was a 'young fogle-hunter' before he was rescued.) Dickens may have picked up some of these newly acculturated words. In *Oliver Twist* the undertaker Mr Sowerberry utters 'Gadso!' as an oath, although Dickens probably did not realize that it derived from *cazzo*, or 'prick' in Italian. Far more working-class slang came from Romany, although it was rarely recognized as the source. The most basic word, *bona*, good, Mayhew says comes from 'the old dancing dog men'. He believed that what he called 'thieves' slang was 'made up, in a great degree, of the mediaeval Latin', and he translated, 'Can you roker Romany' as 'Can you speak cant', without elaborating on the word Romany at all, or translating 'roker' as Romany for 'speak'.

More commonly heard on the street were the everyday expressions that boys shouted at each other or at passers-by, the catchphrases of a lively street life. Some – such as the phrase 'I believe you, my bo-o-o-y!', derived from a popular play – were the currency of professional entertainers, but no one knew where most of these sayings came from before the arrival of music hall, when snatches of a song or a comic's routine spread widely. But nonetheless, in the 1830s, 'One's ears were incessantly assailed with such cries as "What a shocking bad hat!" "There he goes with his eye out!" "How are you off for soap?" "Flare up! and join the union," "Does your mother know you're out?" or "It's all very fine, Mr. Fergusson, but you don't lodge here."' When the army Volunteer Corps was formed in 1859, mostly drawn from the ranks of the middle classes, their lack of professionalism provoked the sneer that all the Volunteers had ever managed to shoot were their own dogs; for years street boys shouted, 'Who shot the dog?' at any man in uniform. By the 1860s, there were more generic challenges to young men who were either excessively (in the boys' opinions) well dressed or merely out with a young woman: 'Who's your hatter?' or even 'How's your poor feet?'

Some expressions indicated disbelief – 'All my eye and Betty Martin' – while 'Do you see any green in my eye, as you pull down the lid?' meant, do you take me for a fool. The longest-surviving, and one of Dickens' favourites, was 'Hookey Walker!', sometimes shortened to 'Walker!' and often drawled out – 'Waa—alker!' This was the equivalent of the twentieth century's 'Pull the other one, it's got bells on.' In *A Christmas Carol*, when the newly reformed Scrooge leans out his window and tells a street boy to go and buy the biggest turkey at the poultryman's shop, the boy replies, 'Walk-ER!', Scrooge responds, 'No, no…I am in earnest.' In *David Copperfield*, little Miss Mowcher, also to express disbelief, says, 'Do you know what my great-grandfather's name was?…It was Walker, my pet…and he came from a long line of Walkers, that I inherit all the Hookey estates from.'

Even when they weren't shouting out these phrases, people found ways of indicating contempt. In *Pickwick Papers*, when the legal clerk for the shyster lawyer thinks Mr Pickwick is trying to pump him for information, he 'smiled once more upon the company, and, applying his left thumb to the tip of his nose, worked a visionary coffee-mill with his right hand, thereby performing a very graceful piece of pantomime (then much in vogue, but now, unhappily, almost obsolete) which was familiarly denominated "taking a grinder"'. A few years later, in *The Old Curiosity Shop*, another lower-middle-class notary's clerk gestures at a street boy 'with that peculiar form of recognition which is called "taking a sight"', that is, he put his thumb up to his nose and wiggled his fingers in what was later called cocking a snook.

Gestures and catcalls might seem like entertainment enough for passers-by and residents alike, but the streets were also the place for a whole raft of professional entertainers: Punch and Judy men, animal acts, peep-shows and tumblers were only the start. The most numerous were the street musicians. In Mayhew's view there were two types, 'the skilful and the blind', that is, those with abilities and those who were begging. Bands were classed either as 'English' or 'German'. The English players might be English and played in groups of up to twenty-five, usually made up of men who couldn't read music and therefore couldn't get jobs in theatres. The German bands were not necessarily German, or even foreign; 'German' indicated they were either brass bands or groups playing highlights from the operatic repertory. Then there were the instrumentalists: fiddlers, harpers, clarionet [sic] players and pipers, often accompanied by a dancing-girl.

The main street instrument, however, was the organ, and the nineteenth-century passion for classification categorized these in the mid-century. Hand organists were usually 'French', which sometimes just meant foreign; if the performers were any good they had regular rounds and pitches, but most weren't, and didn't. Monkey organists were generally Swiss or Tyrolese boys, on the top of whose organs perched a monkey or marmoset dressed in a red jacket and cap; if possible the animal played the organ and the boy danced, but sometimes it was the other way round. Those who couldn't afford a monkey had white mice, or a doll on a plank that 'danced' as they jerked a string tied to their knees.

Handbarrow organists were jeered at as 'some lazy Irishman' or 'sickly Savoyard' because they wheeled their instruments in a barrow. Because they couldn't grind and walk at the same time, they waited for a group of children or a crowd to collect and then made such a din that in effect they were paid to go away. The handcart organists were more enterprising, travelling in twos, threes or fours, with a complicated organ plus 'bells, drums, triangles,

George Scharf sketched dozens of London's street musicians – a sailor, a man with a baby, and a blind violinist among them – as well as a kerb-side letter-writer.

gongs, and cymbals'. Set out in front was 'a stage about five or six feet in width, four in height, and perhaps eighteen inches or two feet in depth', on which danced automaton figures, just over a foot tall, 'gorgeously arrayed in crimson, purple, emerald-green, blue, and orange draperies, and loaded with gold and tinsel, and sparkling stones and spangles'. They performed little stories: Daniel in the lion's den, a Grand Turk threatening a slave, Nebuchadnezzar eating painted grass 'with a huge gold crown on his head, which he bobs... every other bar'. At the front were figures of Napoleon, Tipu Sultan and his sons, and the Queen and Prince Albert.* Napoleon, Tipu and Victoria 'dance a three-handed reel, to the admiration of Prince Albert and a group of lords and ladies... who nod their heads approvingly' until 'the fiend in the corner rushes forth from his lair with a portentous howl. Away, neck or nothing, flies Napoleon, and Tippoo [sic] scampers after him, followed by the terrified attendants; but lo! at the precise nick of time, Queen Victoria draws a long sword from beneath her stays, while up jumps the devouring beast [from Daniel in the lion's den]... and like a true British lion... flies at the throat of the fiend,' just as the collection is made.

Ranking lower on the scale of attraction and approbation were the horse-and-cart organists, whose vast machines needed a cart drawn by two horses, crammed with 'every known mechanical contrivance for the production of ear-stunning noises'. The most numerous of all organs on the street were the ordinary piano grinders, which at least had the benefit of not being too loud. Many of their practitioners were Italians living in Leather Lane: they carried the instrument on their backs, holding a staff as they walked that later doubled as a support to the instrument when they played. Flageolet organists and pianists were 'the *élite* of the profession', usually to be found in the West End 'and on summer evenings... in the neighbourhood of some of

* Tipu Sultan (1750–99), ruler of Mysore, was a demon figure in nineteenth-century Britain. He had won a series of battles against the British, before being killed at the battle of Seringapatam. His attitude to the British can be seen in 'Tipu's Tiger', a half-life-sized clockwork tiger, which he commissioned. When wound up, the tiger savages a prostrate redcoat, to the accompaniment of growls from the tiger and squeaky wails from his prey. The piece was looted by the British after his defeat and is now in the V&A. It is too fragile to be played, but can be seen in action on vimeo.com/8973957.

the Inns of Court'. Hurdy-gurdy players came in two classes: 'little hopping, skipping, jumping, reeling, Savoyard or Swiss urchins, who dance and sing and grind and play...and men with sallow complexions, large dark eyes, and silver earrings, who stand erect and tranquil'. These men also played at 'extempore "hop[s]" at the door of a suburban public house on a summer night', or at some other form of working-class entertainment. Most bands settled around pubs and other entertainment venues, and were known to the locals: Dickens wrote that 'Stabbers's Band' performed every Monday morning outside a Camden pub. Women players existed but were few and far between. Arthur Munby saw a female cornet player in Westminster, but that was extremely unusual.

There were also singers, as individuals or in groups. Many singers performed because they had no skills, no tools of a trade, no choices. In the 1830s, Dickens saw near the Old Vic theatre a woman carrying a baby, 'round whose meagre form the remnant of her own scanty shawl is carefully wrapped', who warbled a popular ballad 'in the hope of wringing a few pence from the compassionate passer-by' – but failing. Munby watched the dancing and singing of five 'Ethiopian Serenaders' in Scotland Yard one day, the women with their 'hair decked with network and rolls of scarlet cloth: they wore pink calico jackets, petticoats of spangled blue, ending a little below the knee: and red stockings and red boots'. When he spoke to them, he realized they were English, blacked-up. They may have been inspired by Joseph Johnson, a black sailor in the early part of the century, who had been wounded during the French wars. He built a model of the *Nelson*, which he wore on his head and, by dipping and swaying, made it 'sail' as he sang. He was well known, walking as far afield as Staines, Romford and St Albans on his rounds. In the 1840s, another singer wore a similar ship on his head while carrying a baby on his back: one observer noted that he had seen him perform thus over a full decade, '*the Child being always the same*'. Other wounded sailors, usually dressed in a uniform, sang sea shanties and theatre songs of heroic tars. (Alfred Bennett added that as far as he could remember he had never seen a soldier in such circumstances.)

Most householders professed to be driven mad by the constant jumble of music cranked out on the streets. It is unsurprising therefore to find the magistrates courts filled with cases where residents attempted to have the musicians banned, with the musicians in turn applying to the courts for loss of earnings. An early cartoon by Robert Seymour, the original illustrator of *The Pickwick Papers*, showed a street musician refusing to be moved on for less than 6d: 'd'ye think I does n't know the walley o'peace and quietness?' The cartoonist John Leech, before his death, commented, 'Rather…than continue to be tormented in this way, I would prefer to go to the grave where there is no noise.' And even Dickens, otherwise so passionately absorbed in street theatre, dismissed these 'brazen performers on brazen instruments'.

There were, however, some who enjoyed the music. Since children adored performers of all sorts, many of the shows were geared towards them. Punch and Judy shows were generally elaborate street performances, requiring at

Joseph Johnson, a sailor injured in the French wars, made his living as a street musician. As he sang, he dipped and swayed his head to make his model of the *Nelson* 'sail' in time to the music.

least two men: one to work the puppets, one to play the drum and mouth-organ beforehand, and to collect the money during the action. In the 1840s, Mayhew spoke to one man whose first Punch and Judy show had consisted of 'twelve figures...Punch, Judy, Child, Beadle, Scaramouch, Nobody, Jack Ketch, the Grand Senoor, the Doctor, the Devil (there was no Ghost used then), Merry Andrew and the Blind Man...The heads...was all carved in wood...A set of new figures, dressed and all, would come to about fifteen pounds...A good show at the present time will cost three pounds odd for the stand alone...including the baize, the frontispiece, the back scene, the cottage, and the letter cloth.' Given this outlay, Punch and Judy shows stuck to the more prosperous areas. Dickens wrote that in Camden in his childhood, 'they knew better to do anything but squeak and drum...unless a collection was made in advance – which never succeeded'. Many did what they called 'dwelling on horders' (orders): performing outside a family's house by request, with the children watching from a window. If there were no orders they performed a 'long-pitch', or thirty-minute show, at a busy junction. Because it was a rich man's toy, in the summer 'Punch mostly goes down to the seaside with the quality.'

There were other kinds of puppet shows as well, including fantoccini, which were marionettes similar in size to Punch and Judy, wheeled about on a cart. Various types of dancing puppets also appeared, such as sailors doing a hornpipe, or a skeleton that came apart as it danced, until only the skull was left, 'footing it...merrily'. Most popular, with adults as well as children, were raree-, or peep-shows. The father of George Sanger (later 'Lord' George Sanger, the self-ennobled owner of one of the largest circuses in Europe) was an itinerant showman with a small peep-show: 'a large box carried on the back, containing some movable and very gaudy pictures, and having six peep-holes fitted with fairly strong lenses. When a pitch was made the box was placed on a folding trestle and the public were invited to walk up' and look at the various scenes depicted within. 'My father...could "patter" in the most approved style, especially about the battle of Trafalgar [he had served on the *Victory* with Nelson]...In his white smock-frock, beaver hat, knee-breeches, with worsted stockings and low-buckled shoes', he travelled the fairs in season and worked as a costermonger in the winter.

By 1833, he had bought a much larger box, with twenty-six holes in the side, for twenty-six simultaneous viewers, 'the pictures being pulled up and down by strings'; at night they were lit by candles inside the box. The most popular scenes for these raree-shows were battles, famous (or local) murders, the death of William IV, Napoleon's return from Elba, or at Waterloo, the death of Nelson and 'The Queen embarking to start for Scotland, from the Dockyard at Voolich', as well as famous scenes from popular melodramas and Christmas pantomimes.

Animal shows were also in demand. In the 1820s, there had been a famous dancing-bear and monkey team: the monkey, dressed as a soldier, danced on the bear's head, and the bear tumbled and danced. But this was unusual, and generally the animals used were more domestic. In the mid-1830s, George Sanger himself began to work, aged about eleven, buying canaries, redpoles and white mice, which he taught to do tricks: the birds drew and fired a cannon, rode in a miniature coach, walked a tightrope and danced; the mice climbed poles, fetched flags 'and other tiny tricks'. A few carts housed 'Happy Families', a number of unlikely animals living happily together in one cage: dogs, cats, monkeys, various types of bird, rats, guinea pigs and so on, which performed tricks. One Happy Family exhibitor even claimed to have been invited to show his 'Family' to Queen Victoria.

Some shows needed less money to set up. Street conjurors and acrobats travelled in pairs, dressed in overcoats, one carrying a drum, the other a ladder. If a crowd gathered, they put down the drum and rolled out a mat; then the conjuror brought out 'cards, cups and balls'. Their coats came off to display a red-and-white motley for the clown and 'a loose pair of white tights, garnished with strips of red and green tape' for the conjuror. They did a comic cross-talk act – Conjuror: 'Beat the drum.' Clown: 'Beat the donkey?' – after which the conjuror juggled, balanced balls, swords and sticks, and did card tricks, all the while keeping up his comic dialogue with the clown, who meanwhile had the important role of taking up the collection in the crowd. After ten or fifteen minutes, they picked up their mat, put on their coats and headed for a new pitch. Sometimes the group was larger, comprising a strong man, a juggler, 'a snake, sword, and knife-swallower' or a contortionist; sometimes the clown was dressed as a soldier, and his comic business consisted of riddles, jokes, songs and, 'where the halfpence are very plentiful', a funny dance.

As with the singers, many performers were street entertainers because they had no other way of earning a living. A showman's child in the 1830s did a 'Cackler Dance', skipping blindfolded between twenty eggs. Sala remembered a man who stood outside St Martin's-le-Grand with a piece of paper, shaping and reshaping it, calling out, 'It forms... now it forms a jockey-cap, now a church-door, a fan, a mat, the paddle-boxes of a steamer', hoping for a few coins. Profile cutters created paper silhouettes. Pavement chalkers were obviously beyond all possibility of work: one who had a pitch in the New Kent Road had been an usher (a junior teacher) until he had a stroke. Children danced, sang or turned cartwheels. Many congregated by the riverside pubs, hoping that sporting gentlemen sitting on balconies would throw pennies into the river for the amusement of watching the children dive for them. In the 1850s, children also stood under the viaduct at Bermondsey, where the Greenwich excursion train stopped for ticket inspection, shouting, 'Throw down your mouldy coppers!' Cheery and slightly drunk, the day-trippers obeyed.

The leisure industry and the street world intersected here informally, but more often the two worlds met in more planned ways.

10.

LEISURE FOR ALL

A morning walk in the park: what could be more ordinary? But London, today considered to be one of the world's cities most generously provisioned with public parks, did not historically have this largesse available to all. Its nineteenth-century development can be seen, in some ways, as a narrative of how green spaces were gradually made accessible to the masses. As late as 1855, in Trollope's *The Warden*, the Revd Mr Harding spends a day in London being constantly harried from place to place: there were few locations where one might sit without paying for the privilege by buying something to drink or eat. Gentlemen might walk in the park, but sitting on a bench was not respectable. Both St James's Park and Green Park were officially private Crown land, where access could be arbitrarily withdrawn.* In reality, even though their gates were locked nightly at ten, by the seventeenth century there were over 6,500 keys to the gates of St James's alone, and the walls were easily scaled, too. When George II lived at Kensington Palace in the eighteenth century, Kensington Gardens was open to the public only at weekends. After the court moved elsewhere, the public hours were increased, but regulations, enforced by park-keepers, were designed to keep the masses out.

Similarly, London's unique green spaces – its squares, so prominent a part of the city today – were either not open to the public or were not planned to

* Although the parks continued to be closed for the occasional civic event throughout the nineteenth century – Green Park was closed for the day of the Duke of Wellington's funeral, for example, so the gentry could watch in comfort – the last long-term closure was under Queen Anne (reigned 1702–14), when the public was barred from much of St James's Park.

be green. In the seventeenth century Inigo Jones designed the first London square, Covent Garden Piazza, in the Italianate style: as a paved space. After the Restoration, more paved squares were built, such as Lincoln's Inn and Leicester Fields (where, in 1760, George III, as he was soon to be, lived in Savile House; he was proclaimed king in the square itself). But throughout the late seventeenth and eighteenth centuries the paving gave way to grass as a vogue for planted squares spread: first in Soho Square, St James's Square and Panton Square, all in Westminster; in Bridgewater Square, near the Barbican; and in Queen Square in Bloomsbury. By the start of the nineteenth century, there were about fifty squares in London; forty years later there were 200; by 1928 the figure had risen to 461.

At the time, London's garden squares were an urban oddity, following the European tradition of a public space in a city centre, usually containing a church or civic buildings, but miniaturizing it and making it private. Even as the squares were being built, there was uncertainty as to their purpose, or indeed whether they even had a purpose. In 1819, *Leigh's New Picture of London* opined, 'they add so essentially to the healthful and pleasing appearance of so many parts of London'. By 1839, the same book had changed its mind: now the squares were valued for their history and 'peculiar beauty'. It is too easy to forget that not only were these squares created without a single overriding aim, but that there is an inevitable gap between how we see them and how they were viewed by their contemporaries. One contemporary garden historian suggests the squares of Bloomsbury are linked both by their ground-landlord (the Bedford Estate) and by colour, via their trees, visible from one square the next. So they are, in the present day. But at the time, as engravings show, the trees, newly planted, were completely invisible over the rooftops: the secret green spaces we know today are the unplanned by-product of nearly two centuries of growth.

While the idea of squares was taken up across the city, they were created by a wide range of builders and therefore in a wide range of styles. Great swathes of land were owned by wealthy landlords and either were developed directly in a unified style, or were leased out in parcels to be developed by builders, who either created entire districts themselves or subcontracted to smaller companies. The landowners were, in effect, in the building business, sometimes contracting out the work to the great builders of the day, as the Bedford Estate did in Bloomsbury from the late 1770s to about 1840, hiring first James Burton, then Thomas Cubitt to build to their own specifications, dictating street plans, building type, density and even the details of the façades, developing a series of squares on Georgian grid patterns, 'all comely, and some elegant, but all modern and middle class'.

As this guidebook quote suggests, the uniformity produced by these estates gave various neighbourhoods different socio-economic profiles, while leading contemporary observers to impose on them almost human characteristics. One book outlined its own readings. The West End squares were 'fashionable', so much was obvious, but the northern ones were 'genteel': a nice distinction. Holborn and Oxford Street on the south side were 'obsolete and antiquated spots', while on the north side Portman Square was considered 'as imposing' as that pinnacle of Mayfair-dom, Grosvenor Square. Moving down in the world were 'the respectable and genteel squares' in Bloomsbury and north of Oxford Street. After these come the City squares, 'old and desolate', which could be compared with the 'obsolete, or "used up" old Squares... which have mostly passed from fashionable residences into mere quadrangles, full of shops, or hotels, or exhibitions, or chambers', referring to Soho, Leicester and Golden Squares, Lincoln's Inn and Covent Garden. Finally, almost shame-facedly, came 'the pretentious *parvenu*-like suburban squares' in Chelsea, Kensington, Islington, Stepney and south of the river, neatly describing a ring around central London.

A closer examination shows that none of the squares was all, or only, one thing. Leicester Square was for most of the century a byword for raffishness, for slightly dodgy goings-on, or just for disrepair. In 1860, a conman at the Thames Police Court was referred to as 'a Leicester-square adventurer'. No evidence was presented to indicate that this was where he lived or operated; the term simply defined his shady activities. In *Bleak House*, when Dickens placed Mr George's shooting gallery (a place where men went to practise target shooting) in 'that curious region lying about the Haymarket and Leicester Square', he was giving his readers a hint that perhaps Mr George was not what he seemed. It has been suggested that the shooting gallery was in Panton Square (on the west side of Leicester Square, demolished in 1868).

The streets around Panton and Leicester Squares certainly are mentioned more than regularly in the memoirs of that erotomaniac 'Walter' as a site of brothels and accommodation houses. In 1853, an attempt was made to blackmail Gladstone simply for being seen here, talking to a woman alone on the streets. But at the beginning of the century, Leicester Square was mostly made up of private houses set around their own enclosed garden. The land was owned by one family, who leased it out to developers, and only slowly did it stop being residential: the house of the painter Joshua Reynolds, on the west side, became a bookseller's auction rooms; the house Hogarth had lived in on the opposite side became the Sabloniere Hotel. Savile House, long vacated by nobility, was turned into Lever's Museum, containing, among other items, Miss Linwood's Gallery of Needlework Pictures, in which famous works of art were reproduced in embroidery. The square became 'unlike the other squares of London', filled with 'hotels with foreign names', with 'Polish exiles, Italian supernumeraries of the opera, French figurantes of the inferior grades, German musicians, teachers and translators of languages, and keepers of low gaming-houses'. Then in 1865 a gas explosion destroyed all the buildings along one side of the square. Instead of being an opportunity for a fresh start, the decaying ruins and rubble were simply left. To add insult to injury, pranksters topped the statue of George I in the middle of the square with a dunce's cap before painting red spots all over his horse.

Even the great aristocratic redoubts of Belgrave and Berkeley Squares, routinely presented as solely the homes of the gentry and the moneyed, were not homogeneous. An 1844 guidebook stated flatly that Belgrave Square was entirely made up of detached villas, surrounded by gardens, even as its own engravings show a solid row of terraces all along the north and west sides (the south and west sides may have been occcupied by villas, but the engravings claimed to show the most exclusive housing). Neither mentioned in the guidebook nor revealed in the engravings was the fact that Belgrave Square was also the location of the Pantechnicon, 'a vast establishment, uniting a bazaar, exhibition-rooms, wine-stores, and carriage-repository', as well as a huge storage facility for furniture. Berkeley Square did indeed house some of the richest and the most aristocratic families in the country, but it was also the site of a row of shops, a hotel and Gunter's, a confectioner and caterer to the upper classes. In season the square was filled with delivery vans and carts, with 'thousands of white paper parcels' coming and going to the sounds of 'clatterings of china and glass, [and] cross porters swearing under their great trays'.

These squares – which were less unified architectural objects and more mixed environments in permanent flux – are useful reminders when studying the development of Regent's Park, for it too was a private commercial development by a landowning estate, in this case the Crown. 'The main object of the Crown, I conceive it to be,' wrote John Nash, the Prince Regent's architect, was 'the improvement of their own Estate.' Just as with the squares on the Bedford Estate in Bloomsbury, or the Grosvenor Estate in Belgravia, the main aim of the Regent's Park development was not to create a green oasis for public use, nor an area of beauty, but to maximize the landowner's revenue.

Most of the land in Marylebone had been leased out to farmers, market gardeners and other smallholders. As the leases expired in 1811, John Fordyce, the Crown surveyor, presented a plan to entice the prosperous classes to the area by creating, in a single scheme, a modern infrastructure. It would include churches, shops, sewers, lighting and, most important, a major thoroughfare to connect the residents to the sites of government and consumption in the West End. Regent Street was to run from the home of the Prince Regent – Carlton House, set at the end of what is now Lower Regent Street, between Pall Mall and the Mall – up to what was to become the new pleasure and recreation ground of Regent's Park, where the prince was to have a rustic summer pavilion surrounded by his friends' villas in a *rus in urbe* setting.

John Nash modified the original Georgian grid-plan by adding two circuses (in effect, round squares), plus crescents and avenues, to create a more countrified feel. Fordyce had imagined Regent Street as a straight line, ploughed through the slum and working-class districts that were Soho, but Nash moved the street eastwards, edging it around the slum in Swallow Street, neatly creating a border between the homes of the upper classes and the 'meaner', working-class districts. Piccadilly Circus and the beautiful swoop of Regent Street were the creation of social rather than aesthetic engineering. Within these constraints, Nash planned the street itself as one cohesive piece of architecture, giving the Quadrant, the swoop, a columned, arcaded walkway on both sides, lit from above by long skylights, to create an area for prosperous loungers and window-shoppers. Where Regent Street and Portland Place meet, before the straight run up to the Park, there is a kink in the road, caused by the refusal of a landowner to sell. Nash solved the problem by creating the little round All Soul's Church, its shape echoing his two circuses – the Regent's Circus (today's Piccadilly Circus) and Oxford Circus – along the new street.

The suburban market gardens of Marylebone were then redeveloped into Regent's Park. From the beginning, the Crown's plan – to create a countrified retreat for the Prince Regent's aristocratic friends, with middle-class housing in terraces surrounding the park – caused outrage. In Parliament, Lord Brougham denounced the Crown for 'trenching on the comfort of the poor for the accommodation of the rich'. Both Nash and the Surveyor General of the Crown Lands were shareholders in the company that was constructing the Regent's Canal, and both parties stood to make a profit from the enclosure of land to which the public had previously had access. Popular disgust forced the Crown to throw open 510 acres of land to the public, rather than constructing houses on it to be sold for its own profit. After peace with France was declared in 1815, a slump in the market led to the number of houses planned in the park diminishing from forty to twenty-six, then to eight, while the number of terraces around the park similarly dwindled; the prince's pavilion was never even begun, and one of the two barracks planned was replaced by a zoo.*

At the same time plans for the great ceremonial route at the south end of Regent Street began to go awry. Nash had expected the full-stop there to

* Little more than the ground-plan of Nash's great project survives. Every building Nash designed in Regent Street has long gone; the Quadrant lasted only decades, being demolished in 1848: it was 'both inconvenient and injurious to the inhabitants', as 'doubtful characters' lurked in its shelter; in the park itself, only the Holme, the house designed by Decimus Burton, even vaguely resembles its original construction, although substantial alterations and additions were made in the twentieth century; the other houses were razed

be Carlton House, with the spire of St Margaret's and Westminster Hall in the distance: royal, ecclesiastical and governmental power seen in a single glance. But in 1820 the Prince Regent became George IV and moved to Buckingham Palace, previously the residence of Queen Charlotte, the wife of George III, who had died in 1818, the year before her husband. Carlton House was demolished and Nash created on its site Carlton Gardens and Carlton House Terrace, and, from these streets a set of stairs leading down to the Mall and to St James's Park.

It took time before Nash's great creation was appreciated, much less admired. In the 1820s, an American tourist thought that 'Never, perhaps, was there so much bad taste displayed' as in Regent Street: 'everyone' agreed the buildings were 'preposterous'. Henry Vizetelly, the journalist and publisher, remembered the verses that had gone around in his childhood, when Nash's white stucco-fronted buildings were still startlingly new:

> Augustus at Rome was for building renowned,
> And of marble he left what of brick he had found.
> But is not our Nash, too, a very great master? –
> He finds us all brick and he leaves us all plaster!

Yet only a decade later, Regent Street was proclaimed 'one of the great routes' of the world, with 'an air of great magnificence'.

The discussion over access to Regent's Park was the first of the century, and it set in motion what in 1833 became a Parliamentary Select Committee, inquiring 'into the means of providing Open Spaces in the vicinity of populous towns as public walks and Places of Exercise'. North of Regent's Park, the open land at Primrose Hill was under threat from developers; the Select Committee recommended that fifty-eight acres be acquired for public recreation, to become the only public green space between Regent's

---

or completely rebuilt. The terraces surrounding the park are in the style of Nash, in that they are white stucco, but few are actually to his designs. All Soul's Church, Langham Place, still valiantly hangs on. Up close it is dwarfed by the BBC's loomingly vast new Broadcasting House, but from Oxford Circus it appears to be gently encircled, echoing Nash's curves.

Park and the East End. There was one park in Lambeth, south of the river, apart from Kennington Common, which was still unenclosed; north of the Thames the committee recommended that Copenhagen Fields be purchased (it later became Hackney Downs). But change came about slowly. It was not until 1846 that Victoria Park was created: the first royal park established specifically for the public. Kennington Common was finally enclosed in 1852; Battersea Fields was purchased in 1846, although it was nearly a decade before the park opened, and Finsbury Park had to wait until 1857.

Having access to parks for recreation was seen as desirable for all. Victoria Park, in the East End, was, unusually, designed for the working classes as well as in part by them: they had had some say in what facilities would be on offer, ensuring that a bathing pond was provided so that working men could cool off on their way home from work. In the more westerly, more fashionable parks, different provisions were made. The prosperous liked a ride or a carriage drive on this stylish route: slowly along Regent Street to see who was out; then up to the zoo, before heading for Hyde Park, where 'they join the press of carriages and riders crowding in hundreds about Kensington Gardens'. For those who kept neither horses nor carriages, walking in parks and green spaces was a regular feature of a happy bourgeois life. Leonard Wyon, engraver to the Royal Mint, recorded in his diary his quiet suburban life's many variations on this theme: 'walked through Regents Park to town', 'Walked for sometime... in Ladbroke Square Gardens', 'a short walk on the Kensall [sic] Green in the evening', 'walk to Hampstead Fields'. For many like Wyon, Sundays in the parks were enlivened by bands playing, and the numbers of those who went to listen are astonishing: on one Sunday in September 1855, 48,841 people were counted in Kensington Gardens, even though a heavy rain shower had stopped the performance; the previous week it had been 60,000. At the last concert of the summer season in 1856 in Regent's Park, 200,000 were said to have attended.

In the first decades of the century, the emphasis had been on ceremonial spaces. A subsidiary project, however, beginning as the humbly named 'West Strand Improvements', unexpectedly created a new focus to London altogether, eclipsing St Paul's as the ceremonial and mapping centre point of the city: Trafalgar Square. Before the railway arrived, Charing Cross had for centuries been the entry to Whitehall and thus to court and government, marked by a sculpture of Charles I on horseback.* Nash's original 1812 report had expressed the hope that, one day, 'Every length of street would be terminated by a façade of beautiful architecture.' 'To add to the beauty of the approach from Westminster', he suggested that either 'a Square or Crescent... might be built round the Equestrian Statue', to give 'a magnificent and beautiful termination of the street from Westminster'.

Initially, only modest changes were outlined. The King's Mews, the stable that served the royal household, had been on the site in some form for five centuries (Chaucer had once been employed there as a clerk of the works). It sprawled massively, from Charing Cross up to the south side of Leicester Square. Other buildings occupying the site included the Golden Cross Hotel, the coaching inn from which Mr Pickwick set out on his adventures; a workhouse, a barracks and a cemetery.† In addition, fronting a narrow and rather squalid lane, lay the church of St Martin-in-the-Fields and, behind it, a desperate warren of courts and lanes. The entire south side of the Strand was taken up by Northumberland House, the great Tudor palace belonging to the Duke of Northumberland, its gardens extending all the way to the river. Over its entrance was one of the landmarks of the city, a lion with its tail stiffly raised to the breeze, like 'the pigtail of an old sailor'. (When Northumberland House was demolished in 1874, the lion was moved to Syon House in Chiswick, where it lurks over the back elevation, a sad comedown

* The statue still remains *in situ* although now, dwarfed by Trafalgar Square and marooned on a traffic island, it has become so insignificant as to be virtually invisible. And it is worth noting here that the pretty story that Charing Cross was named for Edward I's *chère reine* Eleanor of Castile is just that, a pretty story. More prosaically, the medieval village of Charing derived its name from the Anglo-Saxon *cerr*, a turning, referring to the sweep of the Thames. The 'cross' outside Charing Cross station does stand on the spot where one of twelve markers indicated the resting places of Eleanor of Castile's coffin on its way to Westminster Abbey, but the original was demolished by the Puritans in 1647; today's cross is Victorian.

† The office block behind South Africa House is still named Golden Cross House, although one doubts whether its occupants know why.

from the days when an entire city passed beneath its gaze.) North of what is now the Admiralty building lay shops and exhibition spaces, a chapel and several large private houses, including Gun House, named for the two cannon, trophies from the battle of Salamanca, that sat on the front lawn.

By 1800, most of the leases were due to expire, and the king was planning a new stables in Pimlico; like the Regent Street development, it appeared the perfect opportunity for some civic improvements. The earliest plans sought to widen the Strand here, to create 'a more convenient communication between East and West ends of town'. But Nash never thought small, and he hoped to create 'a large splendid quadrangle...the West side of which would be formed by the College of Physicians and the Union Club House; the East side would correspond with that already existing; namely the grand portico of St. Martin's Church; and on the Northern side a new line of buildings would be erected'. He was of the view that a building to house the Royal Academy might sit nicely in the centre of the square, but others wanted an open piazza.

Northumberland House, the last great Jacobean palace in London, filled the south side of the Strand until its demolition in 1874. The lion over the entrance was one of the city's landmarks long before Nelson's Column was erected almost directly opposite.

While this was being discussed, in 1826 the southernmost section of St Martin's Lane, which ran down to Northumberland House, was demolished, opening up space in front of the church.* The graveyard was moved out of the district, and a new street, named Duncannon (after the soon-to-be Chief Commissioner of the Office of Woods, Forests, Land Revenues, Works and Public Buildings), was pushed through at an angle between St Martin's Lane and the Strand. This had the effect of clearing a small section of the larger slum, as well as creating an exit route for carriages. At the same time, a new road, Pall Mall East, was built to give a vista from Pall Mall to St Martin-in-the-Fields.

Three years later, the houses all along the north side of the Strand, from Charing Cross to Exeter Change, together with a gallery of shops and a menagerie, were razed, while the south side of the Strand remained a jumble of old buildings. That area (under what is now the Savoy hotel, Shell-Mex House and the surrounding buildings) had once been the grounds of a palace, then successively a charitable hospital under Henry VII, a barracks and, finally, a prison for deserters. It was hedged around with coal wharves and a few private houses, all blighted by a curious legal anomaly. In the thirteenth century, the Duchy of Lancaster had been made an independent Palatinate. As a result the landowner, the Duke of Lancaster, rather than the British government, was the ruler of this little patch, where the laws of the United Kingdom did not apply. This created an 'Alsatia' (after Alsace, that ambiguous borderland ruled alternately by France and Germany), a refuge for criminals who could not be arrested because British law had no remit there.† In 1816, the hospital, long closed, was demolished, leaving as its only trace a 'triple flight of steps (Savoy-steps)' down to the river, and its chapel,

* It is for this reason that the numbering of St Martin's Lane still today does not begin at '1': numbers 1 to 28 St Martin's Lane had stood in the section of the lane that was sacrificed to create the open area of Trafalgar Square.

† This was not London's only geographico-legal anomaly. Ely Place, in Clerkenwell, and the surrounding land belonged to the Bishop of Ely, and the land was technically governed by Cambridgeshire. Other Alsatias were in Whitefriars, between Salisbury Square and Hanging Sword Alley in the City, once owned by the Carmelites and therefore a religious sanctuary, but by the nineteenth century merely a place where thieves felt secure, as they did in the Alsatia in the Mint, south of the river.

which burnt down in 1864. Between the Savoy and the Temple Gardens stood what David Copperfield referred to as 'an old Roman bath…in which I have had many a cold plunge'.*

As the north side of the Strand was being 'improved', Nash was demolishing the King's Mews and some 'vile houses' near by in order to create a vista up Whitehall to what was agreed would become the National Gallery's new home (at the time it was still located in the founder-donor's house in Pall Mall). Nash proposed a design for that building, but was passed over in favour of the architect William Wilkins, who had already built the University Club House on the north-west corner of what was to be Trafalgar Square. His National Gallery was finished in 1838, to much derision at the time and ever since. It was not helped by a thrifty piece of governmental recycling, which forced Wilkins to reuse the columns from the recently demolished Carlton House. The front elevation of the Gallery, however, is seen from a low viewpoint, as the south side of Trafalgar Square drops away quite sharply, while the vantage point for viewing Carlton House was from rising ground. Wilkins had planned to raise the south side of the square, but Charles Barry, who completed the work after Wilkins' death, failed to incorporate this part of his scheme.†

Although by 1835 it had been agreed that the new square was to be named 'Trafalgar' in commemoration of the 1805 naval victory, it was not until 1837 that it was agreed that this was the right place for the 'Nelson Testimonial', and even then no one could decide what form the tribute was to take. The Duke of Wellington and Sir Robert Peel headed a committee to look at the proposals: one suggested a ninety-foot trident; another had Nelson balanced on a thirty-foot-high globe, surrounded by the figures of Fame, Neptune, Victory and Britannia. Another presented the idea of a cenotaph, with Nelson's gaze fixed on three mermaids who, in the words of two contemporary historians, were 'apparently playing water-polo'. The vast

* It still survives, under the care of the National Trust, behind the closed Aldwych tube station (although at least one historian has suggested that it is eighteenth century rather than Roman).

† A later architectural historian claimed that the domes are the problem, set out, he puts it, like pots on a mantelpiece.

scale of the square made any statue based on human proportions virtually invisible,* while a larger monument would block the view up Whitehall. So the tall thin colonnade by William Railton, an architect who was otherwise best known for designing vicarages, was chosen – and immediately decried: the column was too small for the statue, according to some; columns were to hold up buildings, not manikins, claimed others; it destroyed the vista, and so on. Even Nelson's bicorne hat was condemned: the public, it was said, had an image of the man 'as most frequently we see him [in engravings], bare-headed'.

Today Nelson's hat is his most characteristic feature, in part because head coverings have now vanished so completely that those of other times are more noticeable. It is difficult to bear in mind the importance of hats as not only markers of class and income, but also as indicators of respectability. Sala commented that 'every' man throughout the history of the world 'must, necessarily and habitually, wear some kind of covering to his head'. Postmen wore hats, small children wore hats, field labourers and market gardeners wore hats, cricketers, skaters – all sportsmen – wore hats. It was, self-evidently, impossible to go outdoors without one. When Jonas Chuzzlewit slips out of the house in *Martin Chuzzlewit*, in order to commit murder, 'he had purposely left his own [hat] up-stairs': if his hat was in the house, it indicated he must be too – alibi by hat. Those in professional occupations wore pot hats, as did clerks and all those with pretensions to middle-class status. Even doctors' delivery boys wore battered hand-me-down pot hats: 'the nap rusty, the band a mournful strip of tarnished

* And so it proved. Barry planned statues of William IV and George IV on the north side of the square, for the east and west corners, but the money was never forthcoming. George IV paid for his own, and the commission was eventually carried out. The north-western corner remains empty today, or, rather, a rotating series of contemporary pieces have been installed since 1998, most a useful means of uniting all passers-by in contempt. Much the same was felt at the time for the sculptures on the south side of the square: the statue of Sir Charles Napier, conqueror of Sindh in 1842 and later Commander-in-Chief of the army in India, was installed in 1856, and described by the *Art Union* journal as 'perhaps the worst piece of sculpture in England'; Sir Henry Havelock, who recaptured Cawnpore after the Indian Mutiny in 1857, joined him in 1858. But good or bad makes no difference: in the vast wastes of Trafalgar Square they are all barely noticeable.

lace; but still a Hat', which 'stamps him as being associated, in however slender a manner, with a learned profession'. Cloth caps were for labourers, for costers and for boys. One journalist in the 1880s, watching some men being released from prison, observed 'A big bullet-headed fellow' lurking until a friend in the crowd threw him a cap, which he carefully put on before he acknowledged his waiting family. Artisans wore caps made out of paper, which they folded themselves and so could easily replace as they became dirty. Dickens frequently passes social comments by indicating the condition of a cap. In *Martin Chuzzlewit*, a drunken, violent artisan wears a 'tarnished' paper cap, revealing his character, as he hasn't even bothered to make himself a clean one.

Work in Trafalgar Square continued for decades. The fountains were installed in the 1840s, after artesian wells were bored in Hemmings Row (now Orange Street, behind the National Gallery), which supplied the fountains themselves, as well as the Houses of Parliament, the government offices, Buckingham Palace and St James's Palace. (By the following decade the fountains had become, according to one novel, the street urchins' bathing spot, despite a 'film of soot and grease floating on the surface of the water'.) In 1843, the statue of Nelson, seventeen feet high, arrived at Charing Cross, and 100,000 people were said to have come to have a look at it before it was installed on its pedestal. Ten years later, however, the reliefs around the base of the column had still not been completed and, with the fiftieth anniversary of Nelson's death on the horizon, the newspapers were scathing. Had they but known, ten years later Landseer's lions would not be in position either, with the Commissioner of Public Works forced to admit 'he was sorry to say that he could not tell what Sir Edwin Landseer was about'.

Finally, in January 1867, Arthur Munby, walking past, 'saw the first pair of Landseer's lions...One of them had arrived yesterday, & was already in its place: the other had just come...Both were cased all over in white Calico, tightly wrapt; through which their proportions showed visibly grand and massive.' That was about as much of an arrival ceremony as they received. Everyone was so tired of the subject that the only people who gathered there for the unveiling were Lord John Manners, as Commissioner of Works,

Landseer himself, Baron Marochetti, who had cast the sculptures, and a few unnamed 'other gentlemen'. Manners twitched the covers off, the sculptures were inspected and that was that.

While the reality – the physical construction – had become a boring, endless story, the *idea* of Trafalgar Square now epitomized London, and the Nelson Column epitomized the square. When the playwright Dion Boucicault wanted to create a single image to stand for 'London' in *The Streets of London*, it was Trafalgar Square he chose: 'with its lighted lamps, its Nelson Column, its gleaming windows of Northumberland House'. This great street space had become part of everyone's outdoor sitting room.

One of the most popular ways to spend one's leisure hours was in a tea garden attached to a pub or tavern. In the 1830s, Dickens described the many tea gardens spread across London, and their mostly lower-middle-class customers: 'Gentlemen, in alarming waistcoats, and steel watch-guards, promenading about, three abreast... [and] ladies, with great, long, white pocket-handkerchiefs like small table-cloths, in their hands, chasing one another on the grass'. They drank ginger beer and tea, ate winkles and shrimps, and had a fine time. The Eagle pub on the City Road offered 'beautifully gravelled and planted' walks, outdoor wooden 'refreshment-boxes', or booths, and was brightly lit in the evenings for dancing to 'a Moorish band playing at one end of the gardens – and an opposition military band playing away at the other'. Highbury Barn could even boast that customers danced on a 'crystal platform'. In *Little Dorrit*, Old Nandy, the workhouse resident, dreams that when his ship comes in he will 'take a noble lodging' in a tea garden for his entire family, living happily 'all the rest of their lives, attended on by the waiter'.

Similar social groups patronized public houses in what had recently been outlying villages but were soon reached first by the short-stage, later by omnibuses or railway for weekend outings. Mrs Bardell – Mr Pickwick's landlady, who lives in Goswell Road, in Islington – goes on jaunts to Hampstead Heath; Hornsey Wood was another favourite place for a walk, for picnics, or a visit to a pub or an eel-pie house. Those with access to 'vans, coaches, carts, &c., &c.' might go to Epping 'and enjoy their beer and long pipes at High Beech or the Roebuck' pubs. By mid-century, 'The vehicular movement is prodigious... Four-wheelers, out for the day, abound. Here it is the comfortable tradesman who has been drudging all week... who on Sunday... takes his wife and children to Hampton Court or Beulah Spa'. It might equally be 'the greengrocer' who 'drives his Missus out in the spring cart which during the week... fetch[ed] the homely cabbage... from Covent Garden Market', while 'A group of clerks hires a dog-cart to drive down to Staines'.* With more visitors being transported by rail, the Old Welsh Harp in Hendon, on the Brent Reservoir, became accessible to day-trippers and was renovated in 1856, complete with the gardens, dancing and concerts that were now expected, plus fishing, pigeon shooting and more countrified pastimes. Such was its customer base that the Midland Railway found it economically sensible to open a nearby station, also named the Welsh Harp, for the area's main attraction.

All along the river, from Rotherhithe to Deptford and then on to Greenwich, 'a whole riverside full of tea-gardens' could be found flourishing. 'Here come, emphatically, the public; the working, toiling, sweating, patient' people with their families, out for a day's river excursion.

The river had long provided amusement. In *Great Expectations*, set in the 1820s, once Pip becomes prosperous he takes up sculling as a suitably gentlemanly pastime, something Dickens himself had done as a young man when he could afford it. Those with less cash went to riverside pubs such as the Dolphin and Swan taverns, both at Hungerford market, where customers 'used to drink and smoke, and pick periwinkles', sitting on the roof terraces and tossing pennies to mudlarks. Numerous regattas were held; occasionally there might be swimming matches (one, from London Bridge to Greenwich, in a week when 678 Londoners died of cholera). More commonly, rowing competitions, often for professional watermen, offered prizes by 'the ladies and gentlemen' of the neighbourhood. In the 1840s, a

* A dog cart was not drawn by dogs, but was a small open cart with a double bench running the length of the cart, with, underneath, space that was originally used in the country to transport hunting dogs. The carts therefore had a somewhat raffish, sporting air, hence these clerks hiring one. Because the carts were easy to drive, however, in the countryside upper- and middle-class women also frequently drove themselves in them.

Thames Watermen's Royal Regatta was a two-day event, while even after the Great Stink of 1858 two single scullers raced for the 'championship of the Thames' between Putney and Mortlake, watched by passengers from a dozen steamers, as well as from the banks, 'the trees being almost borne down by their living weight'. In addition there were the one-off events. In 1844, a clown from Astley's theatre announced he would make his voyage downriver from Vauxhall to Westminster Bridge in a washing-tub pulled by four geese. The crowd that turned out to watch 'was very great', lining the road past the new Houses of Parliament down Millbank, while across the river wharves and barges were filled with spectators. More followed his progress from boats that accompanied the clown, in full clown-suit, as he travelled downriver (having scheduled his trip so that he was more or less floated along by the tide).

Many amusements were to be found on the banks of the river. Middle-class men had long been accustomed to jaunts to Greenwich to eat fish dinners, the Trafalgar Tavern being the most famous destination. The arrival of steamers made that treat available to greater numbers, so that by the 1850s various river suburbs vied for custom. In Blackwall, Lovegrove's, the Brunswick or the Artichoke were the places to go. Other favoured establishments were the Star and Garter in Richmond, or inns at Hampton Court, Mortlake, Staines, Ouseley, Chertsey or Gravesend. Edmund Yates remembered that, in the 1850s on a Sunday, 'a serried phalanx of fifty or sixty...carriages, drags, barouches, cabriolets, broughams and hansoms' stood waiting outside the numerous hotels that specialized in these dinners. The type of transport is an indication of the diners' considerable financial resources.

Fish dinners were often organized by professional men to forge professional bonds, as well as pass a pleasant evening. Twenty pupils and assistants of the architect Sir Charles Barry gave such a dinner in 1850, with Sir Charles as the guest of honour, 'on the occasion of their forming a society or club among themselves for the purpose of continuing or increasing the[ir] friendship...and to evince their appreciation of the high talent of Mr. Barry'. The importance the participants placed on the gatherings can be seen from the fact that in 1854, during the Crimean War, cabinet ministers Lord John Russell, Lord Palmerston, Lord Canning, Lord Stanley and even

Sidney Herbert, then the Secretary at War, still turned out for their annual fish dinner at Greenwich.

In 1842, a dinner was given for Dickens at the Trafalgar Tavern in Greenwich, to mark his return from America. The dinner took very much the standard form, in which over two dozen men ate turtle soup and whitebait, with Frederick Marryat (author of *Mr Midshipman Easy* and *The Children of the New Forest*) in the chair, and the journalist William Jerdan his vice-chair. They sang in chorus and then each man did a solo turn, whether a comic skit, an impression, a recitation or a song. They toasted 'the Boz', who returned his thanks with a speech. The Revd Richard Barham (author of *The Ingoldsby Legends*) and the illustrator George Cruikshank then sang again. 'Mrs Boz', who was of course not present, was toasted, followed by more songs and more toasts, before all shook hands in friendship. This was an event involving the upper middle classes, taking place in private; but publicly Dickens also sent his financially stretched lower-middle-class characters for riverside dinners on special occasions. In *Our Mutual Friend*, Bella Wilfer and her father, a poor clerk, sneak away for a day out to Greenwich, where they eat 'dishes of fish'; when she marries the ostensibly poor John Rokesmith, this is where they return for the wedding breakfast.

Once steamer fares dropped, the trip itself became the focus of the day for many. Steamers ran from London Bridge (sometimes Westminster) to Gravesend, or nearby Rosherville, or Greenwich. In the late 1860s, the journalist James Ritchie described a jaunt to Sheerness and back in the *Princess Alice*. They left London Bridge at 10.30, and, as they went downriver, everyone had 'a good dinner on board, well served and at a very moderate price', supplemented by tea and shrimps later. Ritchie (who had a temperance streak) disapproved of the 'unnecessary demand for beer' and judged that 'smoking may be carried to excess', but added patronizingly that it was, after all, only a 'little wildness'. The 700 or 800 excursionists then spent an hour and a half in Sheerness before the return journey, with a band and dancing on board, before reaching London Bridge again at 9 p.m.*

* The number of passengers does not appear to be an exaggeration. In 1878, the *Princess Alice* foundered and sank on a similar excursion, killing 650, with nearly 200 more being rescued.

Dickens himself chartered a steamer as late as 1860, going from Blackwall to Southend and back with a group of friends for a day on the river.

But throughout the period, the main destination remained Greenwich. In the summer, people went there for the fish dinners, or the park, or the Observatory, or the many taverns, or simply for pleasant walks. At Easter, however, it was Greenwich Fair that drew the masses. Fairs declined through the first half of the century and in many cases ceased to exist as major civic events. In 1819, *Leigh's New Picture of London* listed eighty-six fair-days in nearly thirty locations around London. '[E]stablishments so popular, and so productive of honest joy,' it foresaw, 'will never be discountenanced by a wise legislature.' By the 1839 edition of the same guidebook, the sole surviving fair in central London was Bartholomew Fair, and 'this antique nuisance' was, the author shrugged in disdain, now a display of 'flagrant evils'.

Bartholomew Fair was held in Smithfield, with the market space 'entirely parcelled out in booths and standings'. In the centre were sellers of oysters and sausages, surrounded by rows of exhibitions; on the pavements behind were sellers of gilt gingerbread, a Barts speciality, and toys. At the beginning of the century, a number of major shows returned annually: Wombwell's Wild Beast Show, and his competitor Atkins, Ballard's Menagerie, Astley's and Clark's Equestrian Shows and Abraham Saunders' theatre troupe (as a child Edmund Kean was said to have appeared with Saunders, but this was probably a myth). Richardson's, Gyngell's and Scowton's theatres also mounted yearly productions, plus 'the usual variety of conjurors, wire-dancers, giants, dwarfs, fat children, learned pigs'. The stalls that housed these shows were vast – some twenty-five feet long, and all at least seven feet high – and they lined the streets for hundreds of yards around the square. But although the fair continued to be accorded prime status – it was opened by the City's Lord Mayor each year – by 1848 there were only three gingerbread stalls, 'a few beggarly stalls for the sale of oysters and fruit', and nothing else.

With the help of the steamers, Greenwich Fair maintained its status for longer. In 1838, when Bartholomew's Fair still drew 100,000 visitors, Greenwich attracted only half the number, dispersed over a much larger space, with the park covering more than two miles. Yet Bartholomew Fair's visitors eventually vanished, while Greenwich's returned every year. From the landing stage to the park gates, the 'road is bordered on either side with stalls, games, and hand-waggons, containing goods or refreshments'. In 1838, about forty stalls alone offered a variety of amusements, such as 'the holes and the sticks' game, in which a prize (a penknife, a snuffbox) was balanced on a staff, and for a penny participants got three sticks to try to knock them down. If that didn't appeal, there were sellers of 'Waterloo crackers and detonating balls…percussion guns, to shoot with at targets for nuts', or sellers of those rattles known as 'All the Fun of the Fair' (see p. 153). At the upper park gates were fortune-tellers and donkey rides, leading to a thoroughfare of orange stalls, food stalls, toy stalls and, to the puzzlement of the American novelist Nathaniel Hawthorne, a large number of weighing machines, leading him to speculate that perhaps Englishmen wanted to know 'how solid and physically ponderous they are'. There were also roundabouts* and swings, waxworks, peep-shows, freak-shows and shows with learned animals that counted, or knew the alphabet. Then came a row of theatre booths, with drummer boys, or 'brawny fighting-men', or jugglers, or 'posture-makers' (contortionists and acrobats), performing outside to draw the crowds.

Many other Greenwich amusements were both self-generated and free: the young and 'even staid men and women' rolled down One Tree Hill 'in giggling avalanches'; oranges were thrown at passers-by and were in 'nowise to be resented, except by returning the salute'. The favourite pastime was Kiss in the Ring: 'A ring is formed…into the centre of which steps an adventurous youth', who leads a girl to the centre, where he 'salutes her on the lips, and retires', while the girl then does the same with another boy, and so on. Sometimes a girl threw a handkerchief into the ring, and the boy who caught it was permitted to kiss her, 'always politely raising his hat at the critical instant'. At dusk the bands started to play, and by ten o'clock the dancing booths were filled to bursting.

* Roundabouts were powered either by the roundabout owners, or, when they could find them, by small boys: 'having no half-pennies of their own, [they] were always ready to push round their luckier companions for the reward of a ride later on'.

Both day and night, people danced, and ate, and drank. The road to the fair was lined with booths selling gingerbread, brandy snaps, shellfish, eels – 'pickled, stewed, and in pies' – puddings, cold fried fish and oysters ('in June!' shuddered one fastidious reporter). Outdoor eating, eating in the streets, was, after all, what most people did, most of the time.

2. One of the world's earliest photographs, *c.*1841, by Fox Talbot, captured the building of Nelson's Column in 'rafalgar Square. St Martin-in-the-Fields is to the left, with the new Morley's Hotel (where South Africa House ow stands) behind the column. The statue of George IV, *left*, is already in place, but the rest of the square is still wasteland behind the advertisement-laden hoardings.

13. & 14. Scharf carefully documented the many buildings that were about to be destroyed when, in 1830, the new London Bridge was re-erected 60 yards upriver from its old site. As well as memorializing the old, he also recorded the workers creating the new, giving singular view of their clothes and construction methods.

5. Scharf also painted the chimney sweeps dancing on their Mayday holiday. Here he shows the 'Queen' with er attendants. She holds the spoon into which, traditionally, donations were dropped, while behind her the Jack-n-the-Green in his beehive of foliage follows along.

16. Scharf drew the northwest end of the Strand in 1824, shortly before it was razed to create an access road to the new Trafalgar Square. Before the London Fire Engine Establishment was formed in 1833, fires were the responsibility of individual insurance companies, and the Sun Fire Office's man, wearing the Sun's red-and-gold uniform, directs his men pumping away at the green engine behind him. The Strand was one of London's busiest streets, yet even here the paving was erratic, with a pile of loose paving-stones visible beside the lamppost.

17. The funeral car of the Duke of Wellington. The carriage itself was bronze, and the canopy, seventeen feet high, had to be lowered en route, to allow it to pass under Temple Bar. (A trial run was carried out in the middle of the night to make sure the weight and height of the vehicle would not cause it to topple over, or stick in the mud – which it did, briefly, only once on the day.) On the carriage were the duke's many military honours, the collection dwarfing the red coffin at the top. This over-lavish display in 1852 was a turning point, and popular taste subsequently embraced less elaborate funerals.

18. *Greedy Old Nickford Eating Oysters*, by William Heath (late 1820s), *left*, caricatures the owner of Crockford's, an upper-class gambling-den, as the devil, swilling at a tub as rooks, symbolizing the young men being 'rooked', or cheated, fly towards him as he calls out to 'Brother Mace', mace being slang for a swindler. At *bottom right*, the oyster shells have been arranged to form a grotto, of the type children built on the first day of the oyster season, when they called out, 'Please to remember the grotto' as passers-by gave them pennies.

19. Upper-class men also amused themselves at animal-baiting. Here, in this 1821 watercolour, a tethered bear is set upon by terriers, and wagers are laid as to how long each one will last.

20. The caricaturist Thomas Rowlandson depicted two men in the pillory at Charing Cross, in 1819, by the equestrian statue of Charles I, which still stands on the south side of what is now Trafalgar Square. The man under the statue appears to be about to throw something, while the woman, *centre front*, in green, bends down to gather mud for the same purpose. Spectators watch from nearby windows, and also the rooftops. After 1816, the pillory was used only to punish perjurers, and the crowds – and violence – diminished. The punishment itself was discontinued after 1830.

21. The Riot Act is read from the stage of Covent Garden in 1809 in an attempt to end the Old Price riots, sparked by increased ticket prices when the theatre was reopened after a fire. The actor-manager John Philip Kemble, dressed for *Macbeth*, holds up his hands in supplication to the rioting audience, to no avail, as audiences singing Old Price songs, and dancing Old Price dances, made performances impossible for the next month.

11.

FEEDING THE STREETS

The eight-year-old David Copperfield, alone and adrift in London, buys his meals as most other working men, women and children did: on the street. He has a penny loaf and a pennyworth of milk for breakfast; with supper another penny loaf 'and a modicum of cheese'. On his way to work he passes 'the stale pastry put out for sale at half-price at the pastrycooks' doors', which he finds difficult to resist, even though it makes a large dent in 'the money I should have kept for my dinner'. If he succumbs, he either goes without his dinner, or reduces it to a roll or a slice of pudding (a suet and flour savoury dish, which survives as Yorkshire pudding, rather than today's sweet dishes). 'I remember two pudding shops, between which I was divided, according to my finances.' One puts currants in its puddings, and therefore charges double the price of the ordinary pudding, which is 'stout pale pudding, heavy and flabby'. Nonetheless, 'many a day did I dine off it'. On days when he rejects the allurements of the stale pastry, he has enough to dine 'handsomely' on a saveloy, or cold sausage – salami – and another penny loaf, or 'a fourpenny plate of red beef from a cook's shop; or a plate of bread and cheese and a glass of beer, from a miserable old public-house opposite our place of business... Once, I remember carrying my own bread (which I had brought from home in the morning) under my arm, wrapped in a piece of paper... to a famous alamode beef-house [see p. 296] near Drury Lane, and ordering a "small plate" of that delicacy to eat with it.' When in funds, David buys coffee and bread and butter from a coffee stall for his tea; otherwise he makes do with looking at the butchers' shops and the markets. 'I know,' he says simply, 'if a shilling were given me... I spent it in a dinner or a tea.'

Even for street urchins, therefore, the range of street food was wide and merged imperceptibly into indoor dining – taking one's own food to places where other items were prepared, or buying food outdoors that was then taken indoors to be eaten. A fair-sized section of the street-selling population devoted itself to prepared food, and much of it was available virtually round the clock, from pre-dawn breakfasts to post-theatre and post-drinking sandwiches and oysters.

Those selling cooked shellfish on the streets started early, to buy their stocks and prepare them. Hot eels, which were cheap and, because of their gelatinous consistency, filling, were a favourite of labourers and those who worked outdoors. The sellers bought the eels at Billingsgate; then their wives cut them in small pieces and boiled them, thickening the cooking water with flour and flavouring it with parsley and spices. This stew was sold in halfpenny cupfuls, with a dash of vinegar and pepper, from about 10.30 in the morning to about ten at night. Boys were the hot-eel sellers' most regular customers, and so popular was the dish that most sellers did not even have to shout their wares; the ones who did called, 'Nice hot eels – nice hot eels!' or 'Warm your hands and fill your bellies for a halfpenny!' Whelk sellers also began their preparations early: the whelks were boiled, drained, then covered with more boiling water and stirred with a broom handle to clean out the mud and dirt, and also make it easier to 'worm' them – remove the digestive tract – without damaging the shell. Having been shaken up in cold water, they were ready to set out in little saucers, for between two and eight whelks for a penny. Children were also the main customers for crab claws, which the sellers bought at Billingsgate and boiled up in the yards of their lodgings.

Oysters were legendary as a poor man's food. In *The Pickwick Papers*, Sam Weller says sagely, 'poverty and oysters always seem to go together…the poorer a place is, the greater call there seems to be for oysters…Blessed if I don't think that ven a man's wery poor, he rushes out of his lodgings, and eats oysters in reg'lar desperation.'* Many costers did a daily round selling

* It has recently been suggested that it is a mistake of our day to assume that oysters were once food for the poor, and that Sam Weller is suggesting that the desperation indicates

fruit and vegetables, later adding another round of oysters, purchasing a bushel at a time and going to poor neighbourhoods. After 6 p.m., when workers were walking home, the sellers shifted to the main streets to sell them a snack at the end of their workday. Alfred Bennett remembered many improvised corner stalls in his childhood, selling four oysters for a penny, 'opened, vinagared and peppered'. Monday was the best day, when workers still had their wages from Saturday; as the week progressed, business steadily declined.

From March to October, wink men also purchased their stock at Billingsgate, where they could have their periwinkles prepared for them by the dealer for an extra 4d a week. Periwinkles were profitable, and wink men made up to 12s a week in summer, but in winter, when winkles were out of season and they switched to mussels and whelks, their income dropped to about 5s a week. The wink men had one of the most eccentric cries, calling, 'Winketty-winketty-wink-wink-wink – wink-wink – wicketty-wicketty-wink – fine fresh winketty-winks wink wink'.* Servant girls were good customers, the wink men said: 'It's reckoned a nice present from a young man to his sweetheart.' Old people too 'that lives by themselves... and [have] nothing to do pertickler' also favoured winks, as extracting each one with a pin was 'a pleasant way of making time long over a meal'.

Among the most popular prepared-food sellers were the hot-potato men, who began to sell in the streets from the 1830s. The potatoes were cooked

---

the poor man is eating above his station. But I think that the differentiation is between poor and destitute. Mayhew's oyster seller is clear: her customers include men who look like 'poor parsons down upon their luck' or 'The poor girls that walk the streets' but her 'heartiest customers... are working people, on a Saturday night... The *very* poor never buy of me... A penny buys a loaf, you see, or a ha'porth of bread and a ha'porth of cheese... My customers are mostly working people and tradespeople': poor by middle-class standards, but not poverty-stricken.

* Sellers' mysterious cries were a running joke among the middle classes. A visiting American claimed that one woman regularly called 'Stur-ur-ur!' outside his window, to sell her watercresses. Other cries were just baffling: a seller near Portland Place called 'cats'-meat', but in fact he was selling cabbage plants, while a man calling 'chickweed' had watercresses for sale. The tourist thought that the cry didn't matter, as the sellers had regular beats and were recognized by the cry, not the content, but some of these calls do seem counter-productive.

in bulk in cookshops (see p. 291), for a fee of 9d for a hundredweight (112 pounds), and were then transferred in smaller quantities to a portable tin box with legs, square or oval, and sometimes brightly polished, sometimes cheerfully painted. A few had brass ornaments, or were even solid brass, with patriotic names emblazoned on them as if they were steam engines: 'The Royal Union Jack', 'The Royal George' and 'The Prince of Wales'. They had a hinged lid and a charcoal fire at the bottom under the main compartment to keep the potatoes hot, with a small pipe for the escaping steam. A recess on one side held salt, one on the other butter. The hot-potato season was August to April, and the hours of darkness were the best selling-time: one vendor told Mayhew that at ten o'clock on any given night he could walk down any street in the Borough in south London, a notoriously impoverished district, and sell 3s worth – thirty-six potatoes – right away.

Hot-potato men sold their wares from tin containers, the potatoes being kept warm by the charcoal fire underneath. The men expected to sell several dozen a night, so it is unsurprising that this illustrator stressed how heavy the containers were.

Equally popular were the muffin men, who patrolled the middle-class suburbs around teatime, ringing their small bells (except on Sundays: they still patrolled then but went bell-less on the Sabbath).* They carried their goods in oilskin-covered baskets wrapped in flannel or green-baize lining to retain the heat, either over their arms or on their heads. Muffin men were young boys or old men – that is, those who could not earn a better living in some other trade – for the muffins generally came from one manufacturer, and his 'lads' had to pay for their own uniform of white sleeves and white apron, as well as the basket, blanket and bell. (Among the few sellers to carry goods on their heads, they wore caps rather than hats.) They received 3d for every 1s-worth of muffins they sold, and they could carry only a single shilling's-worth before the muffins got cold. Given those geographical and physical limitations, and the fact that most people bought muffins only at teatime, being a muffin man was not profitable.

Neither was being a pieman. These men either had fixed pitches, or were flying piemen, walking the streets carrying a tray about three feet square, either on their heads or hanging from a strap around their necks. In the 1840s, the Corn Laws kept the price of flour high and, with it, the cost of pies.† To maintain their price at the expected penny, the piemen were forced to scrimp: their pies were made with cheap shortening, or had less filling, or poor-quality meat. Many of the legends of cats'-meat, or worse, in pies spring from this period. In 1833, Sam Weller advises the horrified Mr Pickwick, 'Wery good thing is weal pie, when you…is quite sure it ain't kittens,' but in summer 'fruits is in, cats is out'. The legend of Sweeney Todd, the barber who murdered customers for his neighbour to bake into

* Nineteenth-century muffins were, of course, not American cake-like muffins. The modern 'English muffin' (an American anomaly too) is the descendant of what was being sold here. Made from a yeast batter, they were cooked on a griddle rather than baked, then cut in half, and served hot, spread with butter.

† The Corn Laws were passed in 1815, as Britain moved to a peacetime economy after a quarter of a century of war. The import of grain (corn in this context generally meaning wheat, but legally all grain) from abroad was prohibited unless the home price rose above a certain – astronomical – level, to protect the home markets. Even though the laws brought immense hardship, repeal did not come until 1849, such was the hostility of the great landowners to competition from abroad.

pies, was also created in the Hungry Forties. Even the repeal of the Corn Laws did not help, because once flour became cheaper, pie shops began to open, which damaged the street-trade of the piemen even further.

Their customer base became confined almost entirely to boys, who worked in the streets, eating coffee-stall breakfasts, shellfish at lunch, hot eels or pea soup for dinner, perhaps with a potato, and a pie to fill in the gaps when they could afford it. What the boys loved about piemen was their method of charging. A pie cost a penny, but all piemen were willing to toss a coin for one: if the customer won, he got the pie free; if the pieman won, the pieman kept both pie and penny. Tossing for a pie was part of the language. Dickens used it regularly: in *Pickwick Papers* the stagecoach driver warns his passengers: 'Take care o' the archvay, gen'lm'n. "Heads," as the pieman says'. In *David Copperfield*, little Miss Mowcher is like 'a goblin pieman' as she tosses up the two half-crowns she is paid, as did Montague Tigg in *Martin Chuzzlewit*, spinning a coin 'in the air after the manner of a pieman'.

Pies were available all year round, but some foodstuffs were sold seasonally. Greenwich's Easter Fair saw the last of the men selling hot green peas, which they ladled out of a tin pot into basins in halfpenny servings, alongside other dishes that remained popular for longer: pickled salmon '(fennel included)', oysters, whelks and that fairground favourite, gingernuts. Fried fish, although becoming more popular in town, especially near pubs, was still mostly considered a racecourse delicacy. At Epsom in 1850 there were fifty fried-fish sellers, whose customers were mostly the boys who held the carriage-horses' heads and did odd jobs, or were themselves sellers of other goods. Fried-fish sellers charged a penny for a piece of fish and a slice of bread, sold from newspaper-lined trays that hung from straps around their necks.

Some vendors set up on Sundays at working-class excursion spots, such as Hornsey Wood House, or on roads near pubs in the suburbs. Gooseberries or pottles of strawberries were popular on steamer excursions downriver to Greenwich on a summer Sunday too: 'the working-people's Sunday dessert', they were sometimes called. The seller's cry for strawberries was, mysteriously, 'Hoboys!' and was a sign summer had arrived.

Many drinks, naturally, were seasonal. Hot elder wine was sold in the winter in penny and halfpenny measures, with a small piece of toast alongside, to dip into the wine. This, said one street seller, appealed to the working classes, 'but not the better order of them'. Peppermint water, too, was a winter drink: it was mint extract, purchased from a chemist, and diluted, sometimes with pepper added to give it more kick. Curds-and-whey sellers were occasionally still seen after the 1820s, although their drink was considered old-fashioned. There were also a few sellers of rice milk, which was four quarts of milk boiled to every pound of rice, sweetened and flavoured with allspice, and served hot, a cup for a penny. The customers for this were the very poor, who substituted it for a meal.

The weather had an effect on many other food and drink sellers' trades. Cold weather obviously improved the chances of selling warming items like pea soup or pease pudding. One freezing winter, the young George Sanger, living with his showman father in the off-season, bought sugar and oil of peppermint, borrowed some pans to boil it up in and made peppermint rock to sell to the skaters on Bow Common and Hackney Marshes at a penny a lump, making several shillings' profit in a few hours. Spring and summer brought the arrival of cooling drinks. Outside Rag Fair, in Houndsditch in the East End in the 1850s, a girl with 'a horse-pail full of ice' was selling something that looked like 'frozen soap-suds' in halfpenny eggcup sizes. In the same decade, ice cream first appeared, initially sold by Italian vendors, later by hokey-pokey men who were natives of Whitechapel and New Cut, with 'Neapolitan' ices that were rumoured to be frozen mashed turnip.*

More commonly available, outdoors as well as in, were ale, porter and stout, all sold by potboys employed by pubs and taverns. They walked the streets, smartly dressed in white aprons and white sleeves, usually carrying wooden frames divided lengthways into two compartments, into which they slotted their foaming cans, with a measuring jug hooked on the side, although some preferred long sticks with up to twenty cans dangling by

* The origin of the word 'hokey-pokey' is uncertain, but it is probably connected to the novelty of ice cream – milk (or turnip) is, 'hocus-pocus', magically turned into a delicious treat.

their wire handles. On weekday evenings these boys had set routes to supply local residents with their supper beer, but householders could also call to a potboy as he passed, as Dick Swiveller does in *The Old Curiosity Shop*. In the 1830s, Dickens wrote that at teatime householders opened their doors 'and screamed out "Muffins" with all their might', before retreating indoors until nine o'clock, when a potboy's passing produced a repeat performance.

After the beer was finished, the pots, which were the property of the pub, were hung on the house-railings outside, to be collected by the potboys early the following morning, just as the milkmaids collected their jugs from the same place. In *Nicholas Nickleby*, there is one square in Soho that is almost entirely let out in lodgings, in which 'every doorway [is] blocked up and rendered nearly impassable by a motley collection of children and porter pots of all sizes, from the baby in arms and the half-pint pot, to the full-grown girl and half-gallon can'. Even in the shabby-genteel, upper-middle-class neighbourhood of Miss Tox, in *Dombey and Son*, somewhere in a backstreet in Mayfair, 'the top of every rail... [is] decorated with a pewter-pot'.

Theatres were lucrative places for night-time food selling: many street sellers either specialized in ready-made food for theatregoers, or they doubled up, working one line during the day and another at night. The Britannia theatre in the East End, a working-class house that seated nearly 4,000 people, had 'no drink supplied, beyond the contents of the porter-can', observed Dickens. However, 'Huge ham sandwiches, piled on trays like deal in a timber-yard, were handed about for sale to the hungry, and there was no stint of oranges, cakes, brandy-balls, or other similar refreshments.' Ham-sandwich sellers, wearing white aprons and white sleeves, and carrying trays or flat baskets covered with white cloths, also stood outside the theatres, often selling until 4 a.m. to those out on the town.

After the theatres closed in the West End, many of the audiences in the 1850s headed for the ham-and-beef shop at the corner of Bow Street, calling out for ham, beef or 'German sausage sandwiches', 'half a pound of "cold round", or three-pennyworth of "brisket"'. It was possible to eat at the shop, but most people took their orders away, 'neatly rolled up in paper', to eat on the street or at home, as Martin Chuzzlewit did when he 'bought some cold beef, and ham, and French bread, and butter', returning to his tavern room to eat it. These shops served sandwiches and cold meat all day, with hot meals at set hours. In the 1820s, according to the fictional *Real Life in London*, there was a chain of 'fourteen to twenty' ham and beef shops, where hot boiled beef and ham were available 'at moderate prices', and the offcuts were served to the less prosperous for a penny. By the 1840s and 1850s, this type of shop had window displays to tempt the hungry: a 'long window-board lined with pewter, in which wells had been sunk like small baths to receive the puddles of gravy in which joints of meat were perpetually steaming... [together with] a pagoda of boiled beef... pegged into a pile with a metal skewer'. For 2d, a helping was put into a piece of newspaper, or customers brought their own dishes, 'and those who have basins take gravy away'.

Oysters were sold on the street during the day, but at night oyster houses came into their own, after the dancing saloons closed between two and four in the morning, opening when ordinary hard-working people were going to bed. (There were also oyster houses in the City, but these were closed in the evenings.) In the 1850s, the oyster houses in the West End were scattered around the Haymarket, the red-light district, as well as in the Strand and close to the theatres and other late-night locations: at the Opera Colonnade by the Haymarket, on the corner of Leicester Square, in Rupert Street and Coventry Street, and near the Argyle Rooms, the Haymarket theatre and the Opera House. More were on Holborn, such as the one described by Dickens in 1835 as being 'on a magnificent scale', with 'a little red box with a green curtain', behind which the customers could sit and eat.

In the 1820s, the oyster houses had been designed mostly as retail outlets, looking very much like fishmongers, with either plate-glass windows revealing trays of oysters, or with an open hatch to the street and a slab for displaying oysters and other food to passers-by. By the 1850s and 1860s, the 'best shell fish shop in the metropolis' was Scott's Oyster House, at the north end of the Haymarket, which had a counter at the front and behind it a range of shellfish: lobster, prawns, crabs, mussels and periwinkles. The owner, his wife and three men served the customers, who either took the oysters away to eat elsewhere, stood at the counter and ate them then and there, or went to the back room, where 'clerks, swells, men about town, Englishmen and foreigners' all mixed. Upstairs was 'more select', as well as the haunt of women supposedly of dubious reputation. Some oyster houses were simpler: 'lobsters, crabs, pickled and kippered salmon, bloaters, and dried sprats' were sold to customers who stood at the counter, eating and drinking and then 'contentedly wip[ing] their hands on the jack-towel on its roller afterwards'.

In the daytime, there was a wider range of choices. There were taverns, public houses, eating houses, chophouses, ham-and-beef shops, alamode beef houses, oyster rooms, soup houses, pastry-cooks, cookshops and coffee houses. Some of these places overlapped in terms of what, and whom, they served, but most had a distinct profile. What is perhaps noticeably absent from this list is the restaurant, which did not emerge on the London eating scene until the 1860s. The *Oxford English Dictionary* lists several usages before this date, but they all refer either to restaurants in Europe or compare English establishments with their European counterparts. Sala, for example, mentions the Haymarket 'restaurants' only to dismiss them as places where they give you things 'with French names'. Although initially all of these eating places seem not to be part of street life, their separation from the street was far more ambiguous than their names suggest.

Most closely linked to street life were the pastry-cooks and the cookshops. Pastry-cooks supplied not just pastry but a variety of cooked dishes. When David Copperfield gives his first dinner party, the roast chicken, stewed beef, vegetables, cooked kidneys, sweet tart and jelly all come from the pastry-cook. Twenty years later, Dickens listed a similar range of food in an essay on how the day visitor in London managed to feed himself. (If it was a 'herself' who needed feeding, it was even more difficult.) In a pastry-cook's window, Dickens' visitor sees two old turtle-shells with 'SOUPS' painted on them, a dried-up sample meal spread out for display, and a box of stale or damaged cut-price pastry on a stool by the door. The welcome, warned Dickens, would be as glum and dispiriting as the display: every pastry-cook employed 'a young lady...whose gloomy haughtiness...announced a deep-seated grievance against society'. A couple of years later a guidebook was more positive, recommending pastry-cooks for 'a good cup of tea and a chop', adding that 'for a light meal, when you have a lady with you, there are several admirably conducted houses'.

Cookshops, or bakeshops, although they often carried the same foodstuffs as the pastry-cooks, were regarded as places for the working classes, because earlier in the century they were where the working classes, without access to kitchen ranges or even kitchens, took their food to be cooked in a communal oven.* For a Sunday dinner, the housewife had an earthenware dish divided into two unequal parts; on one side she piled potatoes, with 'the modest joint' on top; into the other she poured the pudding batter before carrying it all to the cookshop in the early morning and collecting it a few hours later. Thomas Wright, the working-class engineer, disapproved of cookshops: the 'meat [is] burnt to a cinder outside, and red raw inside; and pies [have] scorched crusts and uncooked insides', not to mention the fact that the joints were returned with 'the marks of slicing', as part of the meat had been shaved off by the cookshop owners, or 'the print of the knife that has been used in lifting the tops of the pies, in order to toll the inside'. Happy were the artisans' families who did not need to resort to the cookshop, but they were few and far between. Cookshops did their best business on Sundays, and on Christmas Day Dickens made a habit of going to the 'shabby genteel' neighbourhoods of Somers Town and Kentish Town at Christmas to 'watch... the dinners' coming and going.

For the rest of the week, and the rest of the year, cookshops sold ready-cooked food, either to be eaten on the premises, or to be taken home. In *Little Dorrit*, there is 'a dirty shop window in a dirty street, which was made almost opaque by the steam of hot meats, vegetables, and puddings... Within, were a few wooden partitions, behind which [sat] such customers as found it more convenient to take away their dinners in stomachs than in their hands.' Beef, veal, ham, greens, potatoes and pudding were a typical menu. In Bethnal Green in the 1860s, offal was also available, with cows' heels and baked sheep's heads, which a family might eat on Saturday night, as well as food to supply 'the immediate wants' of passers-by: the same list of

* Working-class cookshops were also places where street sellers had their food cooked in bulk, as with the baked-potato sellers on pp. 283–4.

stodge-heavy offerings of puddings, pastry, pies and saveloys that David Copperfield had enumerated four decades earlier. For the main thing was to stave off the ever-present hunger. One street boy remembered a cookshop by Billingsgate market that specialized in pea soup, 'exposed most temptingly in a large tank in one of the windows'. The soup cost 3d a basin, or 1d for a half-basin, and the 'initiate' chose his day carefully: 'It was freshly made on Monday, and even then was good. On Tuesday, however, the thick residue at the bottom of the tank remaining unsold was left, and the usual

Scharf sketched the streets at Sunday dinnertime: the people in the top row are collecting their dinner beer, and a potboy with a wooden frame makes deliveries; the other two rows show dinners being carried home from the cookshops. Note the enthusiasm of the boy, centre right, who is carrying a pie.

ingredients...were added to it, making it much richer and more substantial. On Wednesday, this process was repeated, with the result that Wednesday's soup was a thick pureé [sic] in which a spoon would stand erect.' Street boys ordering a pennyworth of the Wednesday soup and a halfpenny-worth of bread 'could go in the strength of that meal for twenty-four hours'.

Coffee shops were of two sorts: those for the working classes and those for City gents. Some working-class coffee shops had a temperance tinge to them; many were used by working men as a meeting place, where communal newspapers could be read and political discussions held. Many workers tried to find a congenial regular spot between their lodgings and work, stopping there every morning instead of going to a coffee stall. It was a little more expensive, but it was warm, and there was a newspaper to read. In the late 1810s, there was one in Bear Street, leading into Leicester Square, where for 6d a month subscribers even had access to magazines. One man set up a coffee house in Greville Street, near Hatton Garden, in 1834; having ambitions for it, he offered his customers in addition to newspapers and magazines 'several hundred volumes' and 'a *conversation room*'. Unfortunately his morals got in the way: refusing to adulterate his tea and coffee to make them go further, which, he said, all coffee houses did, he went bankrupt. (The fact that he was a 'somewhat notorious' political radical didn't help him either.) Most coffee houses, however, did not aspire so high. Pierce Egan, in his novel *Life in London*, described one coffee shop as a haunt of 'drunkenness, beggary, lewdness, and carelessness', although this is more likely to be the middle class's view of poverty than necessarily the prevailing state of affairs. The accompanying picture shows a small room with one candle, wooden tables and benches, and a few stools by the fire. Many people used the coffee shops as somewhere to stay warm. Thirty years after Egan, Sala visited an early-morning coffee shop that before dawn was giving shelter to 'half a dozen homeless wretches' who had paid for a single cup of coffee in order to be allowed to sit and doze indoors.

The coffee houses clearly filled a need: from only a few dozen catering to artisans in 1815, they had increased in numbers by 1840 to nearly 2,000; there a full breakfast could be purchased for 3d. A coffee house in one working-class district served up to 900 customers a day, who had a choice of three rooms: the cheapest was open from 4 a.m. to 10 p.m., where customers could enjoy a breakfast of coffee, bread and butter for 1½d; the second-grade room offered coffee, a penny loaf and a pennyworth of butter for 3d; or, in the most expensive room, customers could order a dinner where the coffee shop supplied the bread and the coffee but the diner brought his own cooked meat. The customer bringing cooked food, or a raw chop or a herring, which the waiter put on the gridiron over the fire, was a routine service. Dickens described one such coffee house near Covent Garden in 1860, watching, enchanted, as 'a man in a high and long snuff-coloured coat, and shoes, and, to the best of my belief, nothing else but a hat...took out of his hat a large cold meat pudding'. The man was clearly a regular, because as soon as he sat down the waiter brought him tea, bread, and a knife and fork.*

City coffee houses were of a different order. Some were quasi-hotels, letting out rooms. The Brontës on their first foray to London stayed at the Chapter Coffee-House in Paternoster Row, while the nearby London Coffee House, on the north side of Ludgate Hill, is where the fictional Arthur Clennam lodges in *Little Dorrit*. The mysterious Julius Handford, in *Our Mutual Friend*, lodges at the Exchequer Coffee-House, Palace Yard, in Westminster. These establishments were the meeting places of businessmen,

* If Dickens is to be believed, men kept almost everything they owned in their hats. It is almost quicker to itemize those characters who did not use their hat as a handy man-bag. Those who did include: Mr Pickwick, who keeps his glove and handkerchief there when he goes skating; in *Oliver Twist* a hat is home to Mr Bumble's handkerchief; the Dodger brings hot rolls and ham for breakfast in his; his pickpocket colleague Toby Crackit puts a shawl in 'my castor' ['castor' = beaver]; in *Nicholas Nickleby*, Newman Noggs, flustered, tries to fit a parcel 'some two feet square' into his, as well as keeping at different times a letter there, 'some halfpence' and a handkerchief, while the moneylender Arthur Gride keeps large wedding favours (see p. 315) in his; in *The Old Curiosity Shop*, Kit's handkerchief is in his hat; in *Martin Chuzzlewit*, Montague Tigg keeps old letters, 'crumpled documents and small pieces of what may be called the bark of broken cigars' in his, while the stagecoachman uses his to store his parcels for delivery; in *Little Dorrit*, Pancks, the moneylender's clerk, keeps his notebook and mathematical calculations there; and finally, in *David Copperfield*, David puts a bouquet for Dora 'in my hat, to keep it fresh' – possibly the only fully middle-class person in Dickens' novels to use this caching spot. Much later in the century Sherlock Holmes notices a bulge in Watson's hat, which indicates he has stashed his stethoscope there, but there are few other mentions in fiction. I suspect it was a standard location for a man's handkerchief, and for all the other items Dickens merely thought it was funny.

and their decor matched their customers' prosperity, with 'cosy mahogany boxes' (booths)* and sanded floors in dark-panelled rooms always supplied with a vast range of newspapers: the New England Coffee-House had even the New York papers, 'dated only twenty-one days back: so rapidly had they been transported over 3000 miles of ocean, and 230 of land!' Specific trades patronized specific coffee houses. The Jerusalem Coffee House in Cowper's Court, Cornhill, was linked to the East Indies, China and Australia trades; Garraway's, in Exchange Alley, was linked to the Hudson Bay Company (and in *Martin Chuzzlewit* is called a 'business coffee-room'). Legal London had its own coffee houses around the Inns of Court and Holborn. George's was across from the new Royal Courts of Justice as well as near the solicitors clustered around Lincoln's Inn. John's Coffee-house, in a lane by the gatehouse of Gray's Inn, is where David Copperfield goes to look for his old friend Tommy Traddles. He gives the waiter Traddles' name and, because it is a legal haunt, the waiter knows off the top of his head which chambers Traddles is in, even though he is not particularly successful.

For the West End men, there were also cigar divans, usually behind or above a cigar shop. A 1s fee obtained a cigar and a cup of coffee, plus access to a comfortable room furnished like a drawing room, with magazines and books. Mr Simpson, before he opened a restaurant in the West End, owned a cigar divan on the Strand, considered 'one of the most attractive, and by far the most comfortable lounge in the metropolis'. By the 1850s, there was also Gliddon's Divan, next to Evans's Supper Rooms (see p. 358), which was 'conducted in the most gentlemanly style'; Follit's Old-Established Cigar Stores, near Portman Square; and the Argyle Divan, on Piccadilly. This last opened after the theatres closed, which gives a hint that the divans were not entirely respectable. In Trollope's 1855 novel, *The Warden*, Mr Harding, a clergyman from the country, tries to avoid his acquaintances and ends up in a cigar divan; the reader is intended to relish the incongruity of an unworldly cleric in such a place.

* Boxes appear to have been a recognized coffee-room feature. In an essay Dickens refers to the arrangements at a Ragged School, where 'each class was partitioned off by screens adjusted like the boxes in a coffee-room'.

The divans were financially well out of reach of most men. For those with less disposable income, particularly in the City, even lunch was a snatched meal. Edmund Yates said that in the 1840s he and his fellow junior clerks at the main post office were given a quarter of an hour to eat. In smaller offices the younger men 'merely skat[ed] out...for a few minutes...for a snack', while the married clerks brought bread and cheese from home or, as Reginald Wilfer does in *Our Mutual Friend*, got in a penny loaf and milk from a dairy to eat in the counting house. The most junior employees 'eat whatever they can get, and wherever they can get it, very frequently getting nothing at all'.

The 'impecunious juniors' from the post office went to Ball's Alamode Beef House, in Butcher Hall Lane (demolished together with Newgate), which sold 'a most delicious "portion" of stewed beef done up in a sticky, coagulated, glutinous gravy of surpassing richness', the same dish David Copperfield had chosen for his treat. Other alamode houses offered boiled beef with carrots, suet dumplings and potatoes: more cheap fillers. For these clerks were not much different from David Copperfield and the small boys buying pea soup: they were all trying to stave off hunger as cheaply as possible, and the alamode and boiled-beef houses catered to this need. In the 1820s, the Boiled-Beef House by the Old Bailey was already famous (its owner, later a theatre leaseholder, has come down to history as 'Boiled-Beef Williams'). By the 1860s, it was almost the definition of an alamode house, being 'on a much larger scale' than any others, apart from one near the Haymarket, on Rupert Street. Choice was limited, the waiters asking, '*Which* would you please to have, gentleman, *buttock* or *flank*, or a plate of *both*?' At lesser houses, the question was even briefer: 'a sixpenny' or a 'fourpenny'?

Soup houses were one step down the scale. In the window, basins, often blue-and-white, were displayed. Depending on the location of the soup house and the size of the portion, 2d or 3d would buy a bowl of soup, some potatoes and a slice of bread. Friedrich von Raumer strayed into a soup house in Drury Lane in 1835. The sign in the window said 'Soup', but he assumed that, while this was the speciality, other dishes would undoubtedly be served. He was rapidly disillusioned by both menu and decor: 'No table-cloth…[only] an oil-cloth; pewter spoons, and two-pronged forks; tin saltcellar and pepper-box'. For 3d he received a piece of bread, 'two gigantic potatoes' and 'a large portion of black Laconian broth' with some submerged items he dubiously identified as 'something like meat'.

Clerks who could afford it opted for a chophouse, as did their employers, who merely took care to frequent a superior one. In the 1830s and 1840s, chophouse food was 'principally chops, steaks, kidneys and sausages…leg of beef soup was a staple commodity, so were trotter, so was pease-pudding': again, meeting the main requirements of being filling and hot. As with the coffee houses, in some chophouses 'peculiar…to London', such as the Old Fleece and Sun Tavern, near the Stock Exchange, customers could bring their own meat. The Old Fleece was conveniently situated next door to

A City chophouse, fitted out with standard booth-style seating, or 'boxes', as they were known. The waiter looks anxious to serve: he was not an employee, but instead he paid the chophouse for his place, earning his living from tips.

a butcher's shop, from which the meat was purchased, to be handed in at the chophouse on the way to work, with information on the hour at which its owner planned to return. Patrons were charged 3d for 'bread, cooking and 'taters' any time between one and four, the remaining hours 'being devoted to serious drinking'. The Bay Tree, in St Swithin's Lane, also much patronized by clerks, was the only chophouse without seating, although in the 1840s 'a remarkably cheap and good lunch' could be bought and eaten standing at the counter: 'Huge joints of cold roast and boiled meats were cut up by two men...A medium-sized plate of meat, bread, and half a pint of porter or mild' was 6d, with vegetables, pickles, cheese and salad costing extra. There was a third room where 'hot joints, chops, and steaks' were available for those willing to pay more for the privilege of being able to sit down to eat.

Each day 500 or 600 customers might pass through each of these chophouses. The waiters were not paid a salary by the owners; rather, they paid the owner for their places, besides usually providing glasses and table linen, which they had to keep clean. Their tips, a standard penny per customer per meal, regardless of its cost, had to cover their weekly payments to the owners, the laundry of the table linen, and still provide their own upkeep.* According to Robert Seymour, the illustrator, successful waiters survived by making the customer feel special. If a customer ordered boiled beef, the waiter would say quietly, 'The beef won't do for *you*, Sir...it's bin in cut a hour.' Most of the customers were repeat visitors, eating in the same chophouse every day, and they got to know 'their' waiter or, in some chophouses, waitress (called a lady waiter). In *Bleak House*, young Smallweed, anxious to present himself as a man about town, makes sure to address the

* If a waiter served a third of the average 600 customers each day, even deducting half his earnings for his place and for the laundry and supplies, he would earn about 8s a day, which was a good enough wage. One book published in 1840 claimed that waitresses paid as much as 20s a day for their places, although it also claimed that a 2d tip was average, double the sum quoted in every other source. The waitress would thus need to serve 125 customers before her fee was covered (and much more likely 250). This seems feasible, but I think it's likely that her tips, too, were usually 1d, and given that the average working day in a coffee house was fifteen hours, it would therefore have been possible for her to earn her fee plus another 7–8s a day.

waitress by name. Calculating the price of the meal for himself and his two friends, he adds to the bill another 3d for Polly the waitress: 'Four veals and hams is three, and four potatoes is three and four, and one summer cabbage is three and six, and three marrows is four and six, and six breads is five, and three Cheshires is five and three, and four half-pints of half-and-half is six and three, and four small rums is eight and three, and three Pollys is eight and six.'* Chophouses that attracted less reputable customers may have demanded payment before the food was served, at least late at night: in 1842 a police court heard the case of two men who ordered soup at an eating house near St Andrews, Holborn, at 12.40 on a Sunday morning, and refused to pay when the waiter brought it to them. Respectable clerks on small budgets considered their menus carefully. Dickens describes the prototypical poor clerk in the 1830s at his 'usual dining-place': after enquiring 'What was up last?' – that is, what has been most recently cooked, so he doesn't get meat that has been sitting and steaming for hours – 'he orders a small plate of roast beef, with greens, and half-a-pint of porter. He has a small plate to-day, because greens are a penny more than potatoes, and he had "two breads" yesterday, with the additional enormity of "a cheese" the day before.'

Given that the waiter paid for laundering the table linen, it is unsurprising that the reputation for cleanliness in chophouses was poor. Yates said that all 'quaint old City chop-houses' had 'sanded floors, hard seats, and mustard blotched tablecloths'. Dickens baptized them more memorably in *Great Expectations* as 'geographical' chophouses, with their 'maps of the world in porter-pot rims on every half-yard of the tablecloths, and charts of gravy on every one of the knives'. As good a name as this is, the standard one for these poorer eating houses was even better: they were known as slap-bangs, for their method of serving and the speed with which the customers

* For those with an interest in pre-decimal sums, or food prices, this translates as: four servings of veal-and-ham at 9d each (3s), four servings of potatoes at 1d each (running total now 3s 4d), one cabbage at 2d (total 3s 6d), three servings of marrow at 3d each (total 4s 6d), six servings of bread at 1d each (5s), three servings of cheese at 1d each (5s 3d), four half-pints of half and half (porter and ale mixed) at 3d each (6s 3d), four glasses of rum at 6d each (8s 3d), tip for three diners at 1d each (or 8s 6d for lunch for three).

were in and out. Speed was a major selling point. An 1862 advertisement for George Reeves' City Luncheon Rooms in an alley between Cornhill and Lombard Street promised that, there, 'a Luncheon or Dinner can be procured of a *better quality* and in *less time* than at any other house', which was no doubt aimed at those workers with just a quarter-hour break.

The slap-bangs were almost all laid out in rows of wooden booths for four or six. On the wall by each booth was a rack, into which the men slotted their hats, hanging them upside down by the brim. (Although, in Guppy's slap-bang in *Bleak House*, the men hang their hats on the corner of their box.) One of the most famous slap-bangs was Izant's, in Bucklersbury, a single large room with thirty boxes.

> From twelve noon when business begins, until seven evening when it finishes, the room is crammed, and one incessant clatter of knives and forks pervades the place... No sooner are you seated, than you are espied by the head-waiter; that functionary is down upon you in a moment, and in the most mellifluous of voices pours the bill of fare into your ear. 'Roase beef, roase lamb, shoulder o' mutton and onion soss, roase veal and bacon, ham an' peas, stooed steak, mutton cutlets and Tummarter soss, jugged 'are, 'arrico mutton, 'ashed duck, sammon and lobster soss, peas and newpotatoes, sir' in one long-sustained coo.

By 1840, a guidebook was explaining to its readers that some places provided 'a printed bill-of-fare', which it approved of as 'the most systematic method'. For those who had never seen such a thing, it elaborated: 'all the dishes customarily prepared at the house are printed in certain groups, and the prices are *written* opposite those which are to be had hot on any particular day, so that a customer can at once see what provisions are ready, and how much he will have to pay.' The menu had just been invented. But most chophouses had no need for menus, priding themselves on serving one dish in particular: Dolly's 'has been distinguished for more than a century for its mutton-chops and beefsteaks... the Cock, near the Bank of England, for its ox-tail soup; and the Ship, in Leadenhall Street, for its turtle [soup]'.

Like coffee houses, chophouses too provided newspapers for their customers. Smallweed, at his favourite slap-bang, is familiar: 'He has his favourite box, he bespeaks all the papers, he is down upon bald patriarchs, who keep them more than ten minutes afterwards.' Dickens' readers would have smiled knowingly, for customers monopolizing the papers was a regular complaint. According to the unwritten code, customers should glance through each paper quickly and hand it on to the next customer, but the number of complaints and jokes suggest that many did no such thing. Sam Weller, two decades earlier, described a civil servant who was 'so uncommon grand' that he marched into his chophouse daily, demanding, 'Post arter the next gen'l'm'n' – that is, he was reserving the *Post* as soon as the person currently reading it had finished with it, ignoring the possibility that others had been waiting before him. To add to his rude behaviour, he also hoarded all the papers, which 'vorked the other customers up to the wery confines o' desperation and insanity, 'specially one i-rascible old gen'l'm'n as the vaiter wos alvays obliged to keep a sharp eye on at sich times, 'fear he should be tempted to commit some rash act vith the carving-knife'.

While the French restaurant was distrusted as a word, the French idea of the *table d'hôte*, or fixed menu at a fixed hour, was enormously popular. Places that followed this system were called ordinaries, and the most famous, as well as the one that led the way to restaurants establishing themselves in London, was a fish ordinary near Billingsgate, down Bell Alley, a thoroughfare so narrow that two people could not pass. A guidebook claimed it was of 'world-wide repute' in 1840, so it had evidently been established some time before that. By 1850, Dickens was writing about it in *Household Words* and calling it Simpson's, the name of its owner. Simpson served dinners at four o'clock, at one long table with a second smaller side-table for the overflow, and every seat was filled on a daily basis. After 'A hurried grace... the scramble began': 'Suddenly a fine salmon sparkled and twinkled like a silver harlequin before Mr. Simpson. A goodly dish of soles was set on lower down; then, in quick succession, appeared flounders, fried eels, stewed eels, cod fish, melted butter, lobster-sauce, potatoes', before 'Boiled beef, mutton, and a huge dish of steaks, were soon disposed of in like manner. Small glasses of brandy round, were gone... Cheese melted away. Crusts dissolved into air.' Then 'bunches of pipes were laid upon the table; and everybody ordered what he liked to drink, or went his way... Eighteen pence a-head had done it all – the drink, and smoke, and civil attendance [tip] excepted.' Dickens may perhaps have been recognized and therefore received better service, for another visitor warned that, to be served, 'Strangers had to look sharp, and, seizing a waiter by the tail of his once new swallow-tail coat, either implore or threaten.'

When Billingsgate was renovated, Simpson shut his ordinary, intending to retire, but he soon moved to a tavern, the Queen's Head, near Bucklersbury, and renamed it Simpson's. At the same time, Simpson's brother opened both a supper house called the Albion, near Drury Lane, and, in 1862, a cigar divan in the Strand. The Albion was both 'a revolution and a revelation. Large tables and comfortable chairs in place of boxes and benches; abundance of clean linen tablecloths and napkins; plated forks and spoons; electroplated tankards instead of pewter pots; finger-glasses; the joint wheeled to your side... a choice of cheeses, pulled bread, and a properly made-out bill: all these were wondrous and acceptable innovations', as was the quality of the food and the fact that 'the rooms were large and well ventilated; the attendants were clean, civil and quick'.*

But for all these institutions, eating on-site was only one option. Every eating place expected to deliver meals, complete with cutlery, dishes and even condiments, which were brought by waiters who then stayed on, if wanted, to serve. Endless processions of meals passed through the streets daily. In *Martin Chuzzlewit*, a man living in chambers is waited on by the local coffee-house waiter, 'a being in a white waistcoat, carrying under his arm a napkin, and attended by another being with an oblong box upon his head, from which a banquet, piping hot, was taken out and set upon the table'. Each stage of the meal is brought over hot by a second waiter, while the man in the white waistcoat stays and serves, before packing up the empties and 'vanish[ing], box and all'.

Large sums of money were not necessary for this service, although, as with the eating houses who demanded payment up front in some

* By 1875, the Albion had taken over the cigar divan and become Simpson's Divan Tavern, at 103 the Strand, where it remains as a restaurant today, although the building is more recent, and its street number is now 100.

neighbourhoods, they did tend to know their customers. In *The Old Curiosity Shop*, the indigent Dick Swiveller sends an order to the nearest eating house, but this establishment '(having experience of its customer) declined to comply, churlishly sending back for answer that if Mr Swiveller stood in need of beef perhaps he would be so obliging as to come there and eat it, bringing with him…the amount of a certain small account which had long been outstanding'. Not at all dismayed, Dick reorders at another place where he is not known, and is soon rewarded with 'a small pewter pyramid' of meat and drink.

Waiters also delivered to office workers. The post-office clerks were granted a cursory dinner break only because in the late 1840s the Post-master General of the day was 'annoyed by encountering strange persons wandering through the lobbies, balancing tin-covered dishes and bearing foaming pewter-pots'. He banned this influx of food from the streets, but other offices were not so particular: George Reeves' City Luncheon Rooms advertised 'All Goods delivered free of charge within Ten Miles'. Thus nearly all food might end up being street food, for at least part of its time.

12.

STREET THEATRE

When he was twenty-three, Dickens wrote: 'We have a most extraordinary partiality for lounging about the streets. Whenever we have an hour or two to spare, there is nothing we enjoy more...We revel in a crowd of any kind – a street "row" is our delight – even a woman in a fit is by no means to be despised, especially in a fourth-rate street, where all the female inhabitants run out of their houses and discharge large jugs of cold water over the patient, as if she were dying of spontaneous combustion, and wanted putting out. Then a drunken man – what can be more charming than a regular drunken man...?'

In this early piece Dickens used the editorial 'we' to signify the predilection of much of the populace. Even so, his own delight in a street row was considerable, and remained with him for ever. Twenty years later, when he was planning some private theatricals, he asked advice from Astley's, which staged theatrical extravaganzas with horses. The next thing he knew, 'an open phaeton drawn by two white ponies with black spots all over them (evidently stencilled)' rattled in at his gate at a great rate before circling 'round and round' the central flower bed, 'apparently looking for the clown'. This tickled the fancy of the established, middle-aged author as much as the drunken man had amused the hopeful young journalist. It was, he crowed, 'One of the finest things...I have ever seen in my life.'

The carriage had been followed by 'a multitude of boys', many of whom, Dickens thought, had run all the way from Astley's, south of the river, to his Marylebone house, nearly three miles in all. This was neither surprising nor unexpected. Amusement was found on the streets by rich and poor alike, and boys were at the forefront of what might be termed street theatre, creating drama, watching it and enhancing it. If they found nothing to entertain them, such as an artificially spotted pony, they were happy to manufacture their own amusement. When a tray of wedding rings was removed from a jewellery store window for customers' inspection, boys gathered outside and made ribald comments audible to the abashed couple inside. Men standing at oyster bars in the Haymarket and other nightspots were hardened to boys sharing their thoughts on their eating habits and manners: 'He don't take no winegar with his'n,' and, 'Look at that chap, he swallows 'em like soup!' Boys were not alone in openly showing curiosity. Adults of all sorts felt it entirely natural to take an interest in the goings-on in the streets. When a police van carrying prisoners became stuck in a traffic jam, the bus driver as a matter of course chaffed the van driver: 'What's yer fare...?' Meanwhile the cad added to the merriment by paraphrasing to the prisoners his standard request to his inside passengers: 'Won't any of your inside gents be so good as to ride outside to obleege a lady?' Prisoners being moved around the city were of abiding interest. A van daily transported prisoners from Bow Street magistrates court to the various gaols. Daily the street outside would be 'studded with a choice assemblage', just as the departure of the mailcoaches also summoned a throng.

Dickens might be thought to be indulging in novelistic fancy when in *Martin Chuzzlewit* the nurse Betsey Prig buys salad from a street seller in High Holborn, 'on condition that the vendor could get it all into her pocket', which is 'accomplished...to the breathless interest' of an entire hackney-coach stand full of people. Yet the journalist James Ritchie noted the same universal interest in the mundane: 'Hail a cab in any part of London,' he wrote, and 'you will observe that several grown-up persons and a large number of boys will stop to see you get in the cab.' When the Serpentine in Hyde Park was drained of its stagnant, sewage-infected water in 1869, 'a small army' could not have kept bystanders from gathering to watch as the park's fish were scooped up and transferred temporarily to the Round Pond. Crowds also gathered outside houses where some disaster had occurred: murder, violence, death. In *Dombey and Son*, when Walter miraculously returns long after being given up for dead in a shipwreck, 'groups of hungry gazers' could be found outside his uncle's house 'at any time between

Street theatre might spring from the most unlikely events. When Sir Robert Peel was injured in a fall from his horse, crowds gathered daily outside his house until he died. Not only did these people find staring at a house interesting; journals like the middle-class *Illustrated London News* thought that its readers would enjoy an engraving of it too.

sunrise and sunset', staring at its closed shutters. This too echoed reality. In 1850, when riding along Constitution Hill, Sir Robert Peel was fatally injured after being thrown from his horse and then crushed by the falling animal. For the few days that he survived, a great mass of people 'thronged' the 'little garden' at Whitehall, and even as night fell, 'respectful groups' remained standing outside well after 10 p.m.* Aside from miraculous returns from the dead and incidents involving famous statesmen, mundane events also drew huge gatherings. When in 1843 a family of ten was evicted from their room in Clerkenwell for non-payment of rent, 'an immense mob was forthwith attracted', numbering possibly a thousand people, to commiserate with the homeless and shout abuse at the landlord's men.

* Peel lived in Whitehall Gardens, which was on the river before the Embankment pushed out the shoreline (see p. 225ff.), behind the Banqueting House and more or less where the Ministry of Defence is now.

Sometimes street events might be more extraordinary still, lasting days or even weeks. At the beginning of March 1842, the *Morning Post* reported a 'Singular Delusion': 'for some weeks past... the lower classes of Irish residing in the metropolis' had believed that London was about to be hit by an earthquake 'which is to swallow up the capital' on the 16th. The other papers eagerly picked up the story, recounting how many of London's residents had left for the country, or gone to Ireland, or merely east of Stepney, 'on the supposition that the earthquake is not to extend beyond that'. A week later, 'popular credulity' suggested that 'St. Paul's Cathedral has already sunk five feet', prompting hundreds to turn out to see for themselves. The papers published over a hundred stories in the next four weeks, many running three or four of them a day. Some readers thought it a joke, some a Chartist plot (see pp. 375–6), but most took it as an opportunity to laugh at the credulity of the labouring Irish. Even so, by the 17th, the day after the earthquake had been scheduled to take place, it was clear that it was not only the poor who had been taken in. Certainly the slums were either unusually empty, or rang with 'frantic cries [and] the incessant appeals to Heaven'. However, the wharf for the Gravesend steamer at London Bridge was also 'thronged by crowds of decently-attired people', while Brighton experienced an influx of expensive carriages, and hordes gathered on the well-heeled heights of Hampstead, Highgate and Primrose Hill. When nothing happened, people sheepishly returned to their everyday lives, but took away no lasting lesson. In October, reports circulated that a ghost 'in snow-white apparel' was to walk through the churchyard of Whitechapel Church, and the surrounding streets became impassable for the best part of a week.

The middle classes enjoyed other types of one-off events in the streets, as when a crowd gathered in Hyde Park to watch the arrival of 'a huge truck drawn by forty of [brewer] Mr Goding's finest cream-coloured horses bedecked with green bays', co-opted to pull M. C. Wyatt's vast equestrian statue of the Duke of Wellington, which was to be placed on top of Decimus Burton's triumphal arch outside Apsley House.* Even preparations for a

* The arch now faces Apsley House, at Hyde Park Corner, but the statue was almost unanimously disliked from the outset, and by 1883, when the arch was moved to its current

public event drew multitudes. In 1863, two full days before the arrival of Princess Alexandra of Denmark for her wedding to the Prince of Wales, Arthur Munby went down to London Bridge to look at the decorations being erected: 'an huge [sic] mass of people of all kind [sic] was struggling to and fro'. The next day, 'The Strand was scarce passable', with 'Crowds all the way' from Inner Temple along Newgate and Cheapside to London Bridge, 'the crush increasing' with every step, 'till at the Monument I found I could get no further; being indeed borne backward by the mass of people coming the other way'. The attraction for these people was just the decorations and bunting, not even the arrival itself (see pp. 315–17).

Events of state, especially declarations of war and peace, produced more formal street ceremonies and celebrations. In 1853, at the start of the Crimean War, the City's mace bearer and the Lord Mayor's gate porter processed from the Mansion House to the Royal Exchange in their black robes of office, drawing a crowd of 300: 'The news spread in all directions, and a rush was made to the point of interest', to hear, and to cheer, as the queen's declaration of war with Russia was read aloud. Enthralled, spectators watched as the royal standard was raised and 'the sword of state belonging to the Corporation was unsheathed'. Over the next two years, battles were ceremonially marked: cannon were fired from the Tower and St James's Park throughout the day to celebrate the victory at Alma. In the City, the Lord Mayor carried the news first to the London Tavern, where 'the leading members of the Corporation' were to be found, and only then conveyed it to the Royal Exchange 'for the purpose of more publicly proclaiming the news. The civic trumpeter having sounded several times', he read the news of the victory to a crowd of 500.

The coming of peace had long been a street event. In 1814, the Peace of Paris had been marked by a festival, with all the central London parks decorated and lit up to resemble pleasure gardens, with mock battles enacted on the Serpentine, hot-air balloons and theatre booths at the fairs. After a 'Grand National Jubilee' on 1 August, however, the fairground people in

location, the statue was removed to Aldershot. The sculpture now on top of the arch is twentieth century, Adrian Jones' *The Angel of Peace Descending on the Chariot of War*.

Hyde Park refused to strike their very prosperous pitches and finally had to be evicted by soldiers. When the Crimean War ended in 1856, there were more fireworks in Hyde Park, but this time a stand was erected with seats costing 1s 6d apiece, to make the crowds easier to control.

Far more moving, and more involving for the populace, was the return of the soldiers from the Crimea. Just over two years after the first troops had embarked, four brigades of 3,200 men emerged from Nine Elms station in formation, still wearing their weather-beaten, battle-damaged uniforms, to a band playing 'Hail the Conquering Hero Comes', 'amidst a tremendous burst of cheering'. They marched along below balconies and windows thick with spectators: 'Every point on the route was positively thronged,' with the crowds nearly a couple of hundred yards deep in places. At Whitehall and Old Palace Yard, every window in the Houses of Parliament was crammed with MPs, peers and their families. The bells of St Margaret's, Westminster's parish church, pealed and guns were fired in the park. From the windows of the houses that lined Parliament Street, flags hung and flowers rained down on men ravaged by battle injuries and disease.

As they neared Buckingham Palace, the queen appeared at a window – the sole window not bursting with cheering men and women. The troops assembled in the forecourt as the queen and Prince Albert emerged, Albert accompanying the men as they marched up to Hyde Park, while the queen rode in her carriage to meet them. Up to 100,000 people had been waiting in the park for hours. The soldiers arrived at 12.30, after which Queen Victoria and Albert inspected the troops, before taking the salute. The troops then cheered the royal family, placing their bearskins on the tips of their bayonets and waving them high overhead. Once the royal party had left, the people lining the streets were expected merely to cheer the guards as they marched to their barracks. Instead, tens of thousands broke through the barriers to where the soldiers were mustered. At first the soldiers closed ranks, but this onslaught was not one of aggression, but an expression of gratitude. The crowds washed around the troops, hurrahing, waving their hats and handkerchiefs, reaching to clasp the shoulders of men who had seen thousands of their brother soldiers die, shaking their hands over and over, walking alongside them and cheering them all the way to their quarters.

Less emotional, but more frequent, was the Lord Mayor's Show, held every 9 November to celebrate the incoming Lord Mayor of the City of London.* Throughout the City, shops either didn't open at all or closed early, while 'streamers are hung out from the houses... amiable street-boys at every corner' waved flags, and all was 'brass bands and confusion and endless cheers!' The new Lord Mayor swore his oath before the aldermen of the City, then set off on a quasi-coronation procession, accompanied by the previous mayor, the aldermen and other City and guild officials, preceded by 'the city heralds, trumpeters, men in brass armour'. By tradition, the route passed through the parish in which the mayor was himself an alderman, a mark of favour celebrated by exceptional street decorations. Officials then went upriver on the City barges to Westminster, where the Lord Mayor swore another oath of allegiance before the judges at the Court of Exchequer and then returned by barge once more, to Blackfriars Bridge. Once ashore, the procession 'increases in splendour and magnificence', as the wives of the mayor and officials joined them in the City's state coaches, followed by 'Princes, Ministers of State, the Judges of the land, and the Foreign Ambassadors', all taking the road to the Mansion House, for the day's highlight: the civic dinner.

Prime ministers, Lord Mayors, even royalty were a regular sight in the streets, although the public response was not uniformly admiring. In his day the Prince Regent rarely showed himself to the unmediated populace, who had a nasty habit of shouting at him, 'You d—d rascal, where's your wife?'† Under Victoria, public response was more muted, to the point

* From the sixteenth century, the Lord Mayor's Show had taken place on 29 October; with the adoption of the Gregorian calendar in 1751, when eleven days were 'lost', it moved to 9 November. In 1959, the date became moveable, and the show is now held on the second Saturday in November. The only year the show has not been held was in 1852, when the Duke of Wellington's funeral prevented the event (see pp. 335–46). The Lord Mayor today has a mainly ceremonial role as mayor only of the Square Mile, and is not to be confused with the mayor of London.

† The sorry saga of the marriage of Caroline and the Prince Regent, later George IV, is too long to rehearse here: it is enough to say that before their wedding in 1794, the Prince had already secretly morganatically married Maria Fitzherbert. The royal couple separated within a year, after the birth of their daughter, Charlotte. The Regent made three formal attempts to find evidence of his wife's adultery, to enable a divorce; when their daughter died, her

where the presence of royalty excited little notice, much less enthusiasm. Leonard Wyon noted in his diary, 'as we were in the Edgware Road in an omnibus we saw P. Albert P. of Wales and Col. Grey riding behind us,' adding immediately afterwards, 'dear Mary bought me a handsome walking stick.'

Fluctuating attitudes to royalty could partly be gauged by the crowds in the streets. Victoria's reign began with scant public interest. In 1837, after William IV's death, the new queen was driven from Kensington Palace to St James's, an event that prompted so feeble a public reaction that one observer commented, 'I was surprised to hear so little shouting, and to see so few hats off as she went by.' When she appeared at the palace window for the formal proclamation, 'the people...did not...hurrah' until they were urged on by a courtier. Six months later, on her way to the House of Commons, 'not a hat [was] raised' as the new queen passed, and at Ascot she was 'tolerably well received; some shouting, not a great deal, and a few hats taken off'. The political diarist Charles Greville was clearly not impressed.*

Her coronation got off to a bad start. The original date had been set for 20 June 1838, which was the first anniversary of the death of William IV. The opposition claimed that a cheeseparing government had done this deliberately, as a way of saving money by claiming it was a day of mourning. The date was therefore moved to 28 June, provoking the trade element to complain again: first, that they had not been given adequate time to produce souvenirs; then, that by the time the date had changed, they had already produced souvenirs, all of which carried the wrong date. Disraeli,

---

mother was not notified but left to find out by chance. On the Regent's accession to the throne in 1820, Caroline, who was physically barred from his coronation, became a rallying point for opponents of the unpopular new king.

* Greville (1794–1865) was a minor political figure and a diarist of genius. When his expurgated diaries were published after his death, in 1874, even in this form they offended the queen, who recorded that she was '*horrified* and *indignant* at this dreadful and really scandalous book. Mr Greville's indiscretion, indelicacy, ingratitude, betrayal of confidence and shameful disloyalty towards his Sovereign make it *very important* that the book should be severely censored and discredited.' It was those very qualities, of course, that made Greville great.

a very new MP, was scarcely more enchanted even a week before the event. As MPs were obliged to wear formal court dress, he told his sister that he planned to save his money and stay away from the ceremony, sooner than attend 'dressed like a flunky'. However, a few days later he wrote wistfully, 'London is very gay,' with the processional route 'now nearly covered with galleries and raised seats', which he thought would look superb once they were decorated with 'carpets and colored hangings'. Diplomatic London, too, was seething with foreign dignitaries, 'visible every night with their brilliant uniforms and sparkling stars'. Unsurprisingly, Disraeli attended the ceremony 'after all', using it as an opportunity to store up droll episodes: Lord Melbourne 'looked very awkward and uncouth, with his coronet cocked over his nose', and clutching the sword of state 'like a butcher', while 'ribboned military officers and robed aldermen...were seen...wrestling like schoolboys...behind the Throne'. One elderly peer, Lord Rolle, having climbed the stairs to the throne to make his bow, caught his foot in his coronation robes and tumbled down them again. Wicked Disraeli solemnly told visitors that Lord Rolle's roll 'was a tenure by which he held his Barony'.

While the crowd loved a parade, it was not yet committed to loving those who paraded. Two years later, Victoria's fiancé was referred to in street songs as a 'German sausage' (lewd subtext intended). And while 'a countless multitude' stood in the driving rain to watch the royal bride pass by on her way to the wedding, they did so 'without any cheering'. Later, popular attitudes fluctuated with events. When a royal child was born (and there were nine of them), salutes were fired in the parks, while a greater or lesser number of private individuals and commercial premises marked the occasion with decorations. In 1842, few buildings bothered to display illuminations for the birth of the Prince of Wales (for more on illuminations, see pp. 363–9), and in 1848, after the queen gave birth to yet another child, when 'God Save the Queen' was played at the theatres, a number of 'ill-mannered' people refused to take off their hats. The 'sorry usage' shown by more fervent royalists was recorded by one journal as indicating 'loyal enthusiasm'. However, in the same magazine, when a miser named Neild died, leaving more than £250,000 to the queen, it was noted laconically that the will was most likely to be disputed 'on the ground of insanity'.*

It was the seven attempts to assassinate the queen that drew the strongest public displays of admiration, and then affection, until in time the monarch's advanced age and longevity on the throne eventually prompted veneration. The first such attempt was in 1840; in 1842 two more followed within days of each other. After the first, which occurred while she was out driving, the queen quickly visited her mother, to reassure her, then returned to the park, where 'she was received with the utmost enthusiasm by the immense crowd'; all the men on horseback 'formed themselves into an escort and attended her back to the Palace, cheer[ing] vehemently'. This may be the first time Greville recorded seeing active cheering for Victoria, adding that the incident had 'elicited whatever there was of dormant loyalty'. After the first of the two 1842 attempts, the following morning 'numbers of respectable persons' stood outside Buckingham Palace for hours until the queen and her party drove out for her regular airing in the park. The queen, despite the attack, still used her open barouche, which elicited 'one long, loud, and continued shout of hurrahs, accompanied by the waving of handkerchiefs and hats'. The road from the palace to Hyde Park Corner was lined with people, and the park, too, was dense with spectators: when the queen arrived, 'not a head was covered', which was a big change in a few years. By the time of the fifth assassination attempt, in 1850, theatregoers had become accustomed to welcoming the queen after such an episode. The young Sophia Beale was at Covent Garden that evening to see Meyerbeer's *The Prophet*:

> We were in a small box up at the top of the theatre opposite the royal box and all of a sudden every one stood up and cheered and made a great noise. Then we saw the Queen and Prince Albert come into the box, and they came to the front and bowed and looked very pleased. And then Madame Grisi rushed on the stage in evening dress from her box, she was not acting, and all the singers sang *God save the Queen*... Papa went out and asked the box keeper what had happened, and he said a man

* The queen did inherit the cash, using it to build Balmoral and buy extra land around Osborne House on the Isle of Wight.

had thrown a stick at the Queen when she was driving in the Park, but it did not hurt her.* So after they had sung *God save the Queen*, the opera went on.

Such imperturbability impressed everyone. Four years earlier, Dickens watched Louis Philippe, the king of the French, driving out in Paris. He too had survived an assassination attempt, but, wrote Dickens contemptuously, 'His [carriage] was surrounded by horseguards. It went at a great pace, and he sat very far back in a corner of it, I promise you. It was strange to an Englishman to see the Prefect of Police riding on horseback some hundreds of yards in advance...turning his head incessantly from side to side...scrutinizing everybody and everything, as if he suspected all the twigs in all the trees.'

But the public's affection waned as rapidly as it had grown, again precipitated by the queen's behaviour. After the death of Prince Albert in 1861, Victoria went into seclusion, observing a level of of widowly mourning considered extreme even by nineteenth-century standards. Although a year or even two of private grief would have been respected, the queen kept obstinately to Windsor and her two private homes, Osborne and Balmoral, year after year, refusing to live in London or to perform her ceremonial functions. Soon the public made it quite clear that they saw this as a dereliction of duty. In 1864, a notice was posted on the railings of Buckingham Palace: 'These commanding premises to be let or sold, in consequence of the late occupant's declining business.' Four years later, with no change in sight, less witty placards began to appear in the streets more generally:

> VICTORIA!
> Modest lamentation is the right of the dead;
> Excessive grief is the enemy of the living.
> —Shakespeare

* Robert Pate had actually managed to strike the queen with his stick: this was the one incident in which the queen was injured.

This quote was followed by a number of advertisements, which suggests a commercial source. Even later in the decade, when the queen did perform certain public duties, such as attending the opening of the great engineering project that was Holborn Viaduct in 1869, many thought she did so grudgingly. She arrived by train from Windsor and travelled in state to Blackfriars Bridge, which she formally opened, before moving in procession to the eastern end of Holborn Viaduct. Having opened this too, as the *Illustrated London News* noted sharply, she then 'quit the City', scuttling back to Paddington to catch a train to Windsor a few hours after arriving in the capital.

Perhaps it was this sense of London being abandoned by royalty that provoked the outpouring that greeted Princess Alexandra on her arrival in the city in 1863. All the way from the Bricklayers' Arms station in Camberwell, where the Danish party was scheduled to arrive, up to Paddington, where it was to re-embark for Windsor, 'every house has its balcony of red baize seats; wedding favours fill the shops, and flags of all sizes'.* A week beforehand, banners were already flying. London Bridge was festooned in scarlet hangings, with a triumphal arch 'as big as Temple Bar', and, in the recesses of the bridge, 'massive draped pedestals, surmounted by Mediaeval Knightly figures: rows of tall Venetian standards with gilt Danish elephants atop', while between them were placed 'great tripods of seeming bronze, from which incense is to arise'. None of this was to celebrate the wedding itself, which was to be a gloomy private occasion in Windsor, with the queen still in deep mourning. Rather, these decorations were merely to greet the soon-to-be Princess of Wales as she drove across the city from one railway station to another.

Despite the brevity of this visit, the day was a 'universal holiday', with crowds everywhere. Fleet Street and all the way along to Blackfriars Bridge 'was given up to Pedestrians, who filled the whole of it as far as one could

* Wedding favours were posies of flowers surrounded by leaves and ribbons for women; for men, silvered leaves and acorns, with more ribbons. They were worn pinned on the breast, usually by members of a wedding party and their households, although for royal weddings no family connection was required.

After the death of Prince Albert, Queen Victoria's never-ending seclusion at Windsor made her increasingly unpopular. A quarter of a century later, cartoons like this one continued to appear. Queen: 'What is that large empty building there?' Footman: 'Please, Your Majesty, that's Buckingham Palace!'

see'. Steamers were unable to dock at London Bridge, so congested were the steps. 'Every avenue to [the bridge] was barricaded with vehicles full of sightseers…every visible window and housetop on every side was filled with gay people, wearing…wedding favours or Danish colours: a vast and compact multitude filled the streets: banners and illumination devices appeared everywhere: the triumphal arch on the Bridge, now finished, was glorious with white & gold and bright colours.'

The carriages took an hour to cover the half-mile between the Bricklayers' Arms and London Bridge, slowed to a crawl by the dense jam of spectators.* The first coaches were cheered heartily by people pleased to be pleased. Then, 'when the last open carriage came in sight, the populace, who had been rapidly warming to tinder point, caught fire all at once. "Hats off!" shouted the men: "Here she is!" cried the women: and all…surging

* The Bricklayers' Arms, otherwise a station used by labourers as they travelled to Kent for the hop-picking, was more infrequently the place where grandees arrived by train from Dover, being convenient for Westminster Bridge, and then only a short ride up to Parliament or Buckingham Palace.

round the carriage, waving hats and kerchiefs, leaping up here and there and again to catch a sight of her…her carriage was imbedded in eager human faces, & not the scarlet outriders with all their appeals…could make way one inch.' On the day of the wedding itself, trains into London were 'decked with flowers and evergreens, and nearly all the passengers wore wedding favours…every station on the line was dressed with flags and flowers, and…there were sounds of guns and blazing of fireworks'. The crowds, estimated at 2.5 million people, were happy to enjoy the decorated streets even without the principal players.

However, it wasn't necessary for a visitor to be royal to receive an eager and passionate popular reception. The year after Alexandra's marriage, as much uproar was generated by the hero of Italian unification, Giuseppe Garibaldi, who was given a welcome every bit as tumultuous, with streets every bit as jam-packed, as were the houses overlooking the route. Garibaldi, too, arrived at the Bricklayers' Arms, where the band of the United Italians in London, all in red shirts, played on the platform, under banners reading: 'The Pure Patriot', 'The Hero of Italy' and 'The Man of the People'.* Unlike Alexandra, Garibaldi was staying in London, travelling in over Westminster Bridge and up to the now symbolic centre of Trafalgar Square. Sophia Beale, who was in the throng at the bottom of the Haymarket, watched him, 'standing up in the carriage in his historic red shirt and grey cloak, bareheaded' as onlookers 'clambered on to the carriage, and would have liked to have taken the horses out to drag it'. When Garibaldi visited the Crystal Palace on the following Saturday, 'Some thirty thousand people were present,' with many women wearing dresses in red, white and green, the Italian colours; his visit to Anthony Panizzi, the Italian political exile turned British Museum librarian, drew huge numbers of spectators all along Great Russell Street. (More enduringly, it was this trip that decided one manufacturer to name its new raisin biscuit the Garibaldi.)

* He lived up to this last slogan. At the station, as the crowd pressed forward, he reached over the barricades and shook hands indiscriminately, thanking members of the public for coming and calling workmen 'my brothers', before picking up and petting a child who offered him flowers. It is clear from the reports that this type of contact with people was unusual, possibly previously unknown.

Yet all these celebrated folk were minor diversions in a street life that was constantly filled with theatre. As well as the many unscheduled events, there were a number of days every year that the people celebrated entirely or primarily on the street.

Until 1837, one of the highlights of street life was the procession of the mailcoaches on the king's birthday. (George III was born in June; both George IV and William IV in August.) As this was the 'royal' mail, for the birthday procession the coaches were freshly painted and varnished; the horses' manes decorated with flowers, their harnesses with rosettes. The coachmen and guards all received new livery, and wore flowers in their hats, whips and buttonholes. Their families, in their Sunday best, had places of honour inside the mailcoaches as the parade wound its way from St James's Palace to the main post office. Friedrich von Raumer, quietly reading in the Athenaeum, was roused by the club secretary to watch the coaches pass, such was the popularity of this annual event. In Victoria's reign, the parade changed its date and was then discontinued, most likely as in the 1830s the mail began to be carried by rail.

Other events of greater or lesser formality, attracting popular attention in varying degrees, occurred throughout the year. On Ascension day (the fortieth day after Easter), 'the ceremony of beating the Parochial bounds' was enacted by the parish officials and churchwardens, to denote the limits of each district by walking along the boundary lines between parishes and, with staffs or tree branches, beating, or tapping, the markers that showed the boundaries.* In the City, well-behaved charity-school children were rewarded by being chosen to beat the bounds, and in Holborn an elaborate ceremonial pantomime was played out annually. The Inns of Court, under ancient statutes that gave them civic rights over their own land, ceremonially closed their gates to the parish authorities, who annually requested – and were refused – permission to enter to enact this civic ritual.

A more spontaneous festivity was the parading of the sweeps on May day. During the year, dirty-faced chimney sweeps were a necessary but not

* A few City parishes continue this tradition, but on different days, and sometimes only once every few years.

interesting part of London life. On May day, however, they cleaned themselves up and, with their wives and children dressed in their best, 'They go about [the streets] in parties of four or five.' Dickens recalled seeing them 'dancing…bedecked with pieces of foil, and with ribbons of all gay colours, flying like streamers in every direction…Their sooty faces were reddened with rose-pink, and in the middle of each cheek was a patch of gold-leaf, the hair was frizzed out, and as white as powder could make it, and they wore an old hat cocked for the occasion, and in like manner ornamented with ribbons, and foil, and flowers. In this array were they dancing through the streets, clapping a wooden plate…and soliciting money from all whom they met.' The women played tambourines or sang, and were traditionally accompanied by a Jack-in-the-Green, a man covered 'down to the boots with a circular wicker frame of bee-hive contour, carried on the shoulders, and terminating in a dome or pinnacle above his head. This frame was entirely concealed by green boughs and flowers, May blossoms preponderating', as he 'pranced, twirled, jumped and capered to the music, while the others danced round'.

As with so many folk customs, throughout the century people complained that the sweeps' celebration was no longer as it had been when they were children. Dickens in the mid-1830s was already recalling that the sweeps and their wives once used to dress as 'My Lord' and 'My Lady'. Although 'the "greens" are annually seen to roll along the streets…[and] youths in the garb of clowns, precede them', it seemed to him that these performers were no longer always sweeps, now being joined by brickmakers, costermongers and other labourers. And while everyone continued to lament the demise of the ritual they remembered, at the same time they reported its observance annually, right through to Dickens' death in 1870, with Munby that year seeing a 'May Day band of chimney sweepers' in Whitehall. Together with the traditional Jack-in-the-Green, there was a 'King in gilt cocked hat & gilt coat, and a Queen in a black velvet jacket with spangles…gay with ribbons, & pink stockings…All danced around the "Green", & the Queen…danced vigorously down the street by my side, till I gave her something.'

Derby Day was less of a ritual, but every bit as much a participation event. For many if not most people, going to the races was not the point:

watching those who were going was sport enough. By nine in the morning, 'Open carriages, with hampers lashed to the footboard, emerge from every turning...At the Regent-circus [now Piccadilly Circus], omnibuses and stage-coaches, "Defiances" and "Resolutions", "Paddingtons" and "Royal Blues", have clapped on four horses, and tout for passengers; men on the roofs play horns to attract notice.' Once on the road and into suburban London, residents could be seen 'seated on the tidy lawns, or leaning over the garden-walls, watching the mob of vehicles dart past. In front of all these...dwellings were seated mammas and daughters, and at the upper windows the servant-girls were leaning over the sills.' One journal even memorialized the outing in verse:

With lots of prog* and lots of grog
Away some thousands scampered,
I cannot tell how much with wine
Their carriages were *hampered*.

They went in gigs, they went in carts,
In coaches and in chaises;
And some in vans adorned by hands
With buttercups and daisies...

Oyster day came later in the year, to mark the start of the oyster season (then on 'Old St James's Day', 25 July, because a shell was the emblem of St James). On the day, boys and girls collected empty oyster shells and built them into little heaps on street corners, or in doorways, setting a candle or a reed light inside to illuminate it. Some children 'made windows with bits of coloured glass or tinsel' in their grottoes and stood beside them, soliciting the passers-by for halfpennies or farthings with, 'Please to remember the grotto.' (Plate 18 shows a grotto, bottom right.)

Similar solicitations came on 5 November, Guy Fawkes Night, commemorating the unravelling of the 1605 plot to blow up the Houses of Parliament and assassinate James I in order to install a Catholic monarch on the throne.

* Slang for food, particularly picnic food.

In the early decades of the nineteenth century, boys made 'guys' by stuffing suits of old clothes, which they carried about on chairs, calling out,

Please to remember,
The fifth of November,
Gunpowder, treason and plot.

With the proceeds they would buy fireworks. By the 1840s, Mayhew thought that 'the character of Guy Fawkes-day has entirely changed', with a festival, May-day-ish element creeping in. The guys had become much larger than life-sized and were paraded in barrows and carts by boys dressed as clowns, with musicians and dancers tagging along to serenade the guy.

In 1844, Mayhew saw his first 'celebrity' guy – that is, the first guy created as a caricature of a popular figure, rather than simply an upright ragbag. The evening had always had an element of anti-Catholic sentiment, owing to its origins, but in a renewed period of anti-Catholic unrest Cardinal Wiseman and the pope were both transformed into guys, with accompanying verses:

A penn'orth of cheese to feed the pope,
A twopenny loaf to choke him,
A pint of beer to wash it down,
And a good large fagot to smoke him!*

In the 1850s, during the Crimean War, a guy of Tsar Nicholas was also accompanied by a verse:

Poke an ingun in his eye –
A squib shove up his nose,† sirs;

* Cardinal Wiseman (1802–65) was made the first cardinal-archbishop of Westminster when Pius IX re-established the Catholic hierarchy in England, an action that provoked the hostility described above.

† I suspect when sung on the streets another portion of his anatomy was substituted here. I have no evidence, but see the songs on pp. 360–2.

Then roast him till he's done quite brown,
And Nick to old Nick [that is, the devil] goes, sirs.

Many of the costermongers' barrows that were used to parade the guys were marked with the names of battles in these years: Inkerman, Balaclava, Sebastopol. In one Peckham neighbourhood in 1855, the locals subscribed £250 for fireworks, in a celebration involving a procession of carriages, bands and possibly 200 people carrying torches, with guys in uniform representing the Crimean generals, all surrounding a guy of the Tsar. After the Indian Mutiny, many bonfires consumed guys with blackened faces bearing signs identifying them as 'Nana Sa hib, the murderer of women and children in Cawnpore'. By the early 1860s, supporters of both sides of the American Civil War carried guys, 'the sympathisers with the North exhibiting various phases of slavery', while southern supporters 'paraded Mr. President Lincoln in all sorts of vicious shapes'.

The symbols of death when it occurred at home were just as visible to the public on the streets and were designed to elicit a response from strangers. Blinds were drawn in a house of mourning and, for those who could afford it, mutes, men 'habited from top to toe in suits of sables, their faces composed to decent sympathy', were stationed outside on the day of a funeral, holding wands, large staffs from which depended black crape drapery, known as weepers.* Further public indications of family loss were swags of funeral drapery, 'black or white, as the sex and age of the defunct may be', hung across the ground-floor façade of the house. For the more prosperous, the fabric might be velvet or embroidered with silver; for the less well off, plain wool. An aristocratic death was marked by a hatchment – a large diamond-shaped shield of canvas with the family's coat of arms painted on it – hung over the doorway of the house in mourning.† A black funeral

* Crape was a silk that had been treated so that it had a wrinkled surface that absorbed rather than reflected the light, producing a dull, matte finish that was considered appropriate for mourning.

† They remained there for the full year of mourning, and if, noted one bemused foreigner, the house was let during that year, 'the tenants take on' the hatchment together with the

hearse and carriages, with coachmen and attendants in black and drawn by black-plumed black horses '(either by nature or dye-stuffs)', arrived to transport the coffin and the family. The only variant was when a young girl died, when by tradition the mourning accoutrements were all white, and the coffin was attended by her friends, also in white. For those for whom this level of expenditure was impossible, there were walking funerals, where the coffin was carried, followed by a train of mourners. Or, sadder still, 'the coffin of a child [was borne] aloft on the shoulders of a single bearer, and followed only by the sorrowing members of the family'.

For public figures in the first half of the nineteenth century, the ceremonial of death was a street event in which outsiders and passers-by were expected to take part. In 1831, an American tourist noticed a funeral procession in the yard of Westminster Abbey. There were just seven official mourners, but, he was happy to see, they were trailed by 'a respectful multitude' of strangers. In 1847, the 3rd Duke of Northumberland died. He had attempted to wreck the Slave Trade Abolition Bill, was vehemently anti-Catholic and anti-working-class, as well as being considered rather stupid and extremely arrogant by the public and his peers alike. Yet 'crowds of persons' lined the streets to watch his funeral procession travel from Northumberland House to Westminster Abbey.

It was after the mass orgy of ostentatious ceremonial that was the Duke of Wellington's funeral in 1852 (see pp. 335–46) that funerals of the great, the good and the not-so-good became for the most part quieter events, with less public participation. Less, that is, not none. When Prince Albert died in 1861 he had requested that his funeral be 'of the plainest and most private character' and was accordingly buried in a private ceremony at Windsor. Even so, the general public saw themselves as participants in the ritual. On the streets of London, 'Every one [is] in mourning; all shops boarded across with black; even brass door plates covered with crape'. Cab and bus drivers attached crape rosettes to their whips. Everyone, down to 'the very poorest and meanest...had put on "decent mourning", were it only in the shape of

---

lease. The hatchment for the Duke of Wellington remained outside Apsley House more than a decade after his death.

a ribbon or a crape bow', which custom dictated should be worn for two months. Palmerston's funeral in 1865 marked a brief return to the old style of bigger and more ostentatious funerals than had been seen for years on the streets of London: for him, White's, Boodle's and Brooks's clubs in St James's all covered their façades in black drapery. The Reform club topped that with 'a sable curtain, bearing a viscount's coronet and the letter "P", with yellow wreaths of immortelles tastefully festooned...and the pillars and balustrades dressed in black and white'.

This is so foreign to us today that Dickens' distaste for these elaborate ceremonies seems normal. At the time, however, it was the author's views that were unusual. Most people thought that outward show conveyed inward respect, even as they also recognized the mercenary spirit behind this trade in the artefacts of death. Mr Mould, the undertaker in *Martin Chuzzlewit*, is thrilled to discover that for one funeral 'there is positively NO limitation...in point of expense!' and he can 'to put on my whole establishment of mutes; and mutes come very dear', as well as 'any number of walking attendants, dressed in the first style of funeral fashion'. In his will, written the year before his death, Dickens rejected these attitudes once more: 'I emphatically direct that I be buried in an inexpensive, unostentatious and strictly private manner...that those who attend my funeral wear no scarf, cloak, black bow, long hatband, or any other such revolting absurdity.'*

These were symbols of death rather than death itself, but the actuality was also often seen on the street. The starving poor died publicly where they fell; transportation accidents were common; even more routine was violent death from natural, or man-made, disasters.

In 1857, Dickens was accused of basing his depiction of the collapse of Mrs Clennam's house in *Little Dorrit* on the recent fall of four houses that made up Maple's shop on Tottenham Court Road. Stung, he replied that that instalment of the novel had gone to press before the buildings fell,

* This clause caused problems on his death, when public opinion demanded that he be buried in Westminster Abbey. A compromise was reached: he was buried in the Abbey, but in a private ceremony.

adding that he had foreshadowed precisely this collapse at the very beginning of the novel, which had begun serialization eighteen months earlier. He need hardly have protested, nor was the Maple's collapse a one-off. In 1826, a German nobleman, Prince Pückler-Muskau, had written home: 'A house, by no means old, fell last night in St. James's-street, close by me, just like a house of cards.' In 1840, in *The Old Curiosity Shop*, Sampson Brass says: 'I am a falling house, and the rats... fly from me,' as we might say, 'Rats leave a sinking ship.' Dickens might equally have pointed to newspaper reports of the buildings that had fallen in St Paul's Churchyard in July 1852, or to the two in Seven Dials three months later, or to the 'great portion' of the Excise Office that collapsed in Old Broad Street, killing two, in 1854. Vast numbers of houses, in an arrested state of half falling and being shored up by timber struts, can be seen in almost any contemporary picture of the London streets.

The buildings collapsed because they were old, but modernity brought its own dangers. As gasworks grew ever bigger to supply more and more households, the perils increased too. In 1865, the meter house of the London Gasworks Company exploded at Nine Elms, in Battersea, killing several and injuring many more, even before two nearby gasometers were engulfed, one of which also exploded, killing another nine people. Newspapers began printing the locations of gasometers and fretting that the Houses of Parliament, or St Paul's, or other heritage sites, might be at risk. What was surprising was not the explosion, but the general response: there had been numerous gas-related explosions ever since gas arrived and, on the whole, they were thought of as a routine hazard.

Even more common, in the days of lighting with candles, oil and gas, where naked flames were used for heating and cooking, were house fires, a well-loved element of popular street entertainment. Fires in private houses – particularly chimney fires, when the old soot and chimney detritus ignited – accounted for nearly half of all such incidents in the city, with candles causing another 30 per cent. In 1848, one newspaper reported that in London's 644 fires (a much lower figure than in most years, which averaged around 1,000), 239 members of the public had been killed. However, this apparently did not include the children who had died when their clothes caught fire – evidently too common an event to warrant counting. Theatres, too, were always at risk, given the gas lighting, the female performers in gauzy dresses moving near stage lights and the crowded conditions. In the quarter-century between 1841 and 1867, nine major theatres burnt down.

Technology having made such conflagrations more rather than less likely, the focus was on controlling them, rather than preventing them. From 1774, each parish vestry was obliged to have ready two engines, leather 'pipes' (hoses), and ladders. Initially these engines were not for the most part horse-drawn but were literally manned, pulled by local street boys or 'by poor decrepit old men from the workhouse', under the supervision of the parish beadle. Dickens, who all his life hated men in petty authority with all the hatred of a formerly lower-middle-class child harassed by these minor tyrants, contemptuously satirized a parish response to a chimney fire: its engine 'came up in gallant style – three miles and a half an hour, at least'. Then 'Bang went the pumps...the beadle perspired profusely; but it was unfortunately discovered, just as they were going to put the fire out, that nobody understood the process by which the engine was filled with water; and that eighteen boys, and a man, had exhausted themselves in pumping for twenty minutes, without producing the slightest effect!' A quarter of a century later, the parish was no more efficient, their engine responding to a fire at the offices of *All the Year Round* 'like a drivelling Perambulator'. Dickens cheered up when the crowd, discovering that the fire had already been extinguished, 'Snowballed the Beadle'.

More usefully, and professionally, the city's insurance companies had their own fire brigades, and the façades of many buildings carried small metal tags to identify the company with which they were insured. This was an incomplete solution, leading to instances when a brigade failed to deal with a burning building because it was not insured with their company, only for the fire to spread to neighbouring ones that were their responsibility. Between the parish and the insurance companies, far too many buildings that could have been salvaged burnt down, and so in 1833 a single London Fire Engine Establishment was established by the ten largest insurance companies. (Another five joined soon after, and by 1846 just two did not belong.)

In its first year the Fire Engine Establishment employed seventy-seven men, with fourteen horse-drawn engines in thirteen stations, all under the superintendence of James Braidwood, aged thirty-three, who had already served as Edinburgh's Master of Fire Engines for nearly a decade. He divided the city into five districts; by 1846, the most easterly station was at the Ratcliffe Highway, the most westerly by Portman Square, with thirty-five engines controlled by ninety men in dark-grey uniforms trimmed with red and black leather helmets. (The glamour days of uniforms were behind them: the Sun Insurance company firemen had worn blue coats with metal buttons, double-breasted waistcoats, breeches, striped stockings and boots; the Hope Insurance company dressed its men in red short-skirted frock coats and waistcoats, blue breeches and top-boots.) Two years after the devastating Tooley Street fire (see pp.111–121), a Parliamentary Select Committee recommended that a new brigade supersede both the parishes and the insurance companies, to be paid for by taxation as a public good. In 1865, the old Fire Engine Establishment was put under the authority of the Metropolitan Board of Works. By 1869, this Metropolitan Fire Brigade had forty-four stations, three floating engines and 314 men.

As early as 1830, steam engines had been available: a 10-horsepower engine with high-pressure hoses spraying out nearly 170 gallons a minute, to a height of three yards – vastly more than the old manual engines had been able to produce. However, these inefficient predecessors were preferred, partly through innate conservatism, but more so because the general populace could make money from assisting. For seventy-seven – or even 314 – men were not going to extinguish London's fires all on their own, and volunteers played a major part. When a station was alerted to a major fire, all the men and engines from that district set off immediately, as did two-thirds of the men and engines from the districts on either side and one-third from districts further afield.* Fires were eagerly announced: a notification

* One particularly unfortunate display of the Northern Lights kept twelve engines and seventy-four men dashing about an entire night, attempting to locate the fire that kept being sighted over the horizon – a sobering indication of how street lights have altered our ideas of night.

This undated photograph (probably after 1866 from the uniforms) shows Willesden Fire Brigade with two engines and 'fire-escapes', extendable wheeled ladders used to rescue people from upper storeys.

from a policeman earned him 10s; a member of the public received a smaller sum. At the first cry of fire, 'away scamper the policemen to the nearest stations of the Fire Brigade, passing the word to other policemen as they run, till all the police force in the neighbourhood are clattering along the pavements... either towards an engine-station... or to pass the word to the policeman whose duty it will be to run to the engine-station next beyond. By this means of passing the word, somebody arrives at the gates of the Chief Office of the Fire Brigade, in Watling Street, and, seizing the handle of the night-bell, pulls away at it with vigour.' The fireman on duty took the immediate details – location and size – before ringing the 'singleman's bell', which rang in 'the division where the four unmarried men sleep', and heading for the stables to start harnessing the horses. By the time the engines were ready, Braidwood, if the fire was sufficient to warrant it, had mounted beside the driver, with the engineer, the foreman and firemen on board behind. Then they were off. If the fire was only a mile or two away, then the horses were set at full gallop, aiming for ten miles an hour, or 'the best royal mail pace'. If it was further, they could not go flat out, 'for fear of breaking down the horses', tiring them before they reached their destination. In the early part of the century, before gas lighting had become prevalent, men with lit torches ran alongside the horses, calling encouragement to the animals and shouting warnings to everyone else on the street by wild cries of 'Hi! yi! hi! yi!'* After gas lighting became more common, the torches were dispensed with, but two men on board the engine continued to stand by the driver and 'roar incessantly' to warn oncoming traffic.

As the horses were always at risk of slipping on their mad careen to the fire, the men were also there to help them up if it were possible or cut them out of their traces if not. A problem of a different kind was posed by the number of private streets in the capital, especially in Bloomsbury on the Bedford Estate, and in Mayfair, where the Westminster Estate ruled. These neighbourhoods marked their exclusivity by barriers at the ends of the roads, but they also prevented the entry of fire engines, increasing the danger to these neighbourhoods. Even with the risks to the horses and the detours, by the late 1840s Braidwood expected a response time of twenty-eight minutes for a fire within a half-mile of any station, from first receiving the report of a fire to the water being pumped. (In 2006, the average response time to fires in England was just under seven minutes.)

Metal plaques were affixed to buildings across London: 'W.M. 16 feet', for example, indicating the distance to the nearest water mains. As part of their charter, all water companies were obliged to give free access to their pumps in case of fire. Immediately the engine arrived, crowds collected and volunteers stepped forward to help hook up the pipes and especially to man the pumps, six or eight men per pump handle. (The two floating river engines required 100 men each.) The work was exhausting: every five minutes a fresh relay of pumpers was needed. The excitement of the fire made people want to join in; an added incentive was that those who pumped were paid 1s for the first hour of their labour and 6d for each

* In 1901, a journalist born in 1864 noted that the firemen still roared 'Hi! yi! hi! yi!' as they raced along. 'The suggestion so often made that the firemen should abandon their wild cries and substitute a gong is bitterly opposed' by the men: 'They have always yelled "Hi! yi!" and they will always do so.'

additional hour, as well as being supplied with bread, cheese and beer. A foreman for each engine chose from among the volunteers (while the hungry masses might want to work for the money, they weren't necessarily physically capable). Such was the enthusiasm that, 'if necessary [he] fought off the surplus with the aid of his crew', before acting as a coxswain, setting the tempo for pumping. 'Down with her,' he cried, 'down with the pump,' as the men worked to the chant of 'Beer-oh! Beer-oh!' Sometimes armbands were used to identify the volunteers, which they handed over in return for their 'creature comforts' of beer and food. Sometimes, if the fire were big enough to make it pay, nearby pubs opened up again, 'doing a roaring trade in beer, which is distributed to the volunteers at the pumps in sufficiently liberal quantities, a check being kept upon the amount consumed by means of tickets'. So that a pay office didn't have to be established with every fire, the volunteers were given metal tokens, to be exchanged for cash at the station the next day. While the volunteers were pumping, the Fire Engine Establishment employees, known as the 'brigade men', did the dangerous work, first clearing a working area for themselves by a fast squirt from their hoses to move the crowds back.

For those not actively assisting, fires were street theatre for all, from high to low. In 1830, a fire broke out at 2 a.m. at the English Opera House, in Covent Garden. Charles Greville, the political diarist, 'was playing at whist at the "Travellers" [club, a few hundred yards away]...when we saw the whole sky illuminated and a volume of fire rising in the air. We thought it was Covent Garden, and [he and two peers] set off to the spot...though it was three in the morning the streets filled with an immense multitude...All the gentility of London was there from Princess Esterhazy's ball and all the clubs; gentlemen in their fur cloaks, pumps, and velvet waistcoats mixed with...men and women half-dressed, covered with rags and dirt.' This was not at all unusual: when the Houses of Parliament were destroyed by fire in 1834, everyone who was anyone turned out to watch. The fire was probably caused by the overheating of flues from the furnace under the House of Lords, where the exchequer tally-sticks were burnt. The old, in many places medieval, wooden structure went up quickly, aided by a lack of fire-stops or party walls, as well as by the fact that Braidwood and his men, when they arrived, had no idea of the layout of the building. In private houses or warehouses, a basic floor-plan could be assumed, but faced with such a rabbit warren at no time did the firemen have any sense of where they were, or where the fire might break out next. The Fire Engine Establishment supplied twelve engines and sixty-four men, even though, technically, the Houses of Parliament were outside its remit, being uninsured government property. From the first they saw that they were too late to save Westminster Palace and St Stephen's Chapel; instead they concentrated on Westminster Hall, dragging their engines inside the walls and cutting away the roof where it adjoined the Speaker's house, which was already well alight.

Lord Melbourne, the prime minister, and other members of the government gathered to watch throughout the night. The philosopher Thomas Carlyle, also present, described the crowd as more gratified than awed or frightened: they '*whew'd* and whistled when the breeze came as if to encourage it: "there's a *flare-up*...A judgement for the Poor-Law Bill"...A man *sorry* I did not anywhere see.' The artist Benjamin Robert Haydon and his wife arrived by cab specifically to see the spectacle, sitting with 'the people', who were full of 'jokes and radicalism universal'. When Covent Garden theatre burnt down in 1856, Queen Victoria, Prince Albert, the Prince of Wales and the Princess Royal visited the smouldering site the next day, as did Dickens three days later, 'the moment' he returned to London from a trip. In adult life, the Prince of Wales did not wait until the flames were out to put in an appearance. He and his friends enjoyed attending fires, like the rest of the populace, and they even had replica fire-brigade uniforms made up, in which they bustled about at fire scenes, playing at firemen and getting in the way. (While volunteers were still needed, it is hard to imagine the already portly Prince of Wales taking his five-minute turn at the pumps.)

For those without titles and replica uniforms, it was the event itself that made good street theatre. In 1829, the young Hékékyan Bey, studying in England, heard 'sudden cries of "fire" and the noise of running footsteps'. Looking out, he saw a fire apparently a few hundred yards from the house. Despite the heavy rain, 'the street was crowded with people of both sexes hastening to the conflagration', and without any hesitation he too rushed out to join them. Sala, two decades later, would have understood this perfectly: at the call of 'Fire! fire!' he wrote, 'It matters not how late the hour be, how important the avocations of the moment, that magic cry sets all legs...in motion...A minute past, I was at Evans's [Supper Rooms], tranquilly conversing...now I find myself racing like mad up St. Martin's Lane, towards St. Giles's...running after that hoarse cry, and towards that awful Redness in the sky.' This particular fire was at an oil shop, which went up like a rocket, with 'columns of flame, and...billows upon billows of crimson smoke, the whole encircled by myriads of fiery sparks that fall upon the gaping crowd and make them dance and yell with terror and excitement.' Sometimes viewers set up to watch these blazes at a distance: in 1847, a fire in Battersea drew busloads of spectators who stood all along the north side of the river and on the bridges, even venturing out in small boats.

It is unsurprising, therefore, to find that in Dickens' day journalists 'prowl continually about London...in search of fires, fallings in and down of houses, runnings away of vicious horses, breakings down of cabs, carriages, and omnibuses; and, in fact, accidents and casualties of every description. But especially fires. Fatal accidents are not unnaturally preferred...and in the case of a fire a slight loss of life is not objected to.' Street theatre was, after all, discerning in its disasters.

PART FOUR

Sleeping and Awake

1852: The Funeral of the Duke of Wellington

The great duke was dying. In a way, the great duke had been dying for so long that no one believed he would actually die. He had had a stroke in 1839, which had been fairly successfully hidden from the public, and well into his seventies he continued to ride out, unaccompanied, in his quaintly old-fashioned clothes. Another stroke followed on one of these rides. Then another, in the House of Lords. These were harder to hide, and the end was coming.

The vanquisher of Napoleon was the man people remembered. Forgotten was the execrated politician, the public face of anti-Reform sentiment of the 1820s and 1830s. Forgotten was the man who was known to have long been on intimate terms with a married woman who was not his wife. In the late 1820s, one American tourist had seen him in the street, a man, he commented, 'who might have rendered himself the idol of the nation', but whose name, instead, was 'scarcely ever mentioned' except accompanied by 'some epithet of reproach', even his '*military* talents' being condemned, 'so strong is the dislike he has incurred' by his 'domestic habits'. At that time, there had been no admiration, much less veneration. In 1830, on the way to the Abbey for the coronation of William IV, his carriage 'rolled on in solemn silence, as if to a funeral', while that of Lord Brougham, the populist reforming chancellor, was 'hailed by the shouts and acclamation of all'.

By 1852, this had been forgotten and the old duke was once more part of the city's landscape. Apsley House, at Hyde Park Corner, his home since 1817, was known as 'Number 1, London', and by now people assumed that it was so-called because of its famous owner. (More prosaically, it had simply been the first house on the very western edge of the city in the eighteenth century.) Long forgotten too, or at least regarded as a foible of age, was the reason why the windows of Apsley House had been covered with sheets of iron since 1831. In that year the government's rejection of Reform had seen a mob surge down Piccadilly, breaking windows. Stones had been thrown at the windows of Apsley House, too, until the butler came out to remonstrate: the Duchess of Wellington had just died, and her body still lay inside, awaiting burial. The mob passed on, but the bitter, furious duke – who had been famously unpleasant to his wife throughout their marriage ('I was not the least in love with her. I married her because they asked me to do it') – ostentatiously had great iron shutters nailed over the windows and left them there for the remainder of his life. In 1852, many full-grown adults could not remember Apsley House with open windows, but they were seeing him now not as a statesman of disastrous political ineptitude but as the soldier, the hero of Salamanca and of Vittoria, of Badajoz and, of course, of Waterloo.

Yet, when the end finally came, on 14 September, at the duke's home at Walmer Castle, near Deal, in Kent, the public response was initially muted. Lord Stanley, parliamentary under-secretary at the Foreign Office, wrote to Disraeli that the duke's death had not produced 'the slightest impression out-of-doors… no crowd of enquirers round Apsley House… We telegraphed down to Balmoral without delay: but I don't imagine the Chief [the Earl of Derby: both prime minister and also Stanley's father] will find it worth his while to come up [to London].' It was another week before it was announced that a state funeral would take place, but that the date was to be decided by Parliament, which was in recess and would not reconvene until 11 November.

While the public initially displayed an interest that was devoid of emotion or excitement, the newspapers viewed it as a bigger event. The day after it was decided to hold a state funeral, the *Illustrated London News* was already advertising that its 'Regular Subscribers will receive GRATIS splendid large ENGRAVINGS of the PROCESSION and PUBLIC FUNERAL of the DUKE OF WELLINGTON, a lasting memorial of the national mourning'. Other papers were more ambivalent, at least at first. The *Daily News* noted that before Nelson's funeral in 1805 the vergers of St Paul's were said to have made over £1,000 by taking payments to let people in to see the preparations. And, it reminded its readers, that funeral had cost the country £14,698. It added, without comment, that the duke was earning nearly £10,000 a year. (This was made up of his salary as commander-in-chief, an allowance as colonel of the Grenadier Guards, a salary as colonel-in-chief, Rifle Brigade, a salary as Lord Warden, Cinque Ports, a salary as Constable of the Tower, and a 'Forage Allowance' of £700 a year. The article left unmentioned the fact that more than £400,000 had been voted him by Parliament as reward for his role in the Napoleonic wars, or the quarter of a million pounds paid by the nation for his country estate.) Instead, the newspaper stressed that the funeral should be in keeping with 'the simple, the severe spirit of the man', although, it added hastily, it didn't 'grudge' a 'penny'. Not that anyone knew how much anything would cost, because it was nearly two months before the Earl Marshal announced even the date of the funeral or its route.

Perhaps those intervening two months of uncertainty were what drove the public into such a frenzy. About ten days after the duke's death, advertisements began to be placed for Wellington-related entertainment: the Gallery of Illustration (a quasi-theatre, for people whose religious scruples did not permit them to attend real theatres) mounted 'The Diorama of Wellington's Campaigns', showing twice daily. Portraits and engravings, biographies and histories of his battles went on sale, together with a 'NATIONAL SONG' dedicated to his memory, and a copy of an equestrian sculpture (in plaster for five guineas, or bronze at fifty guineas), a Minton bust and likenesses in gold or silver, suitable for mounting in mourning rings and other jewellery.

By the middle of October, newspapers were running advertisements for seats along what was expected to be the procession's route. 'FUNERAL of the GREAT DUKE. – The Nobility and Gentry are informed that any number of SEATS or FLOORS, to view the Procession, may be obtained of MR. THEARLE, the masonic jeweller, 198, Fleet-street, near Temple-bar' was a fairly representative example. By the end of October, a single room in the Strand was offered for an astonishing 100 guineas, while a grocer in St Paul's Churchyard was reputed to have rented out the upper storeys of his house for £500. Most papers were carrying two or three of these advertisements daily; by early November, this had risen to half a dozen or so, and the tourist market was not overlooked: 'Sitze für die Beerdigung des Herzog von Wellington'. A lack of solemnity was apparent: those taking rooms, advertised Messrs Purssell of Cornhill, 'can be supplied with REFRESHMENTS of any kind, including wines, and the use of china, glass, cutlery, &c.'

The churches were determined not to be left behind. St Mary-le-Strand advertised one-guinea seats in a gallery to be erected in front of the church. St Clement Danes joined in in early November, its seats 'exclusively [for] ratepayers of the parish' for the first week, then available to the public at large. (At the end of the year St Clement's divided its takings of £223 among seven charities and made donations of 'many other...smaller amounts', all from this sale of seats for the funeral.)

An advertisement in the *Morning Post* warned, 'It has been computed that one million of individuals will visit London to witness the melancholy procession of departed greatness, and at this inclement season of the year...it is most important that the feet should be kept free from damp', for which, happily, it provided the solution: 'AMERICAN OVER-SHOES should be worn, both by those attending the funeral and those waiting, perhaps for hours, to see the procession pass.' Glenny's Irish Hand-knit Stockings and Socks reminded readers that 'THE FUNERAL of the DUKE OF YORK was attended with loss of life to several illustrious Statesmen, in consequence of taking cold in the feet.' Other establishments attempted to appear less openly commercial: Moses and Son, a well-known City firm selling ready-made, inexpensive men's clothing, produced a rare black-bordered notice: 'E. Moses and Son are no way desirous of making this a business affair, but, prompted by a disposition to offer every accommodation to their patrons...they have prepared for this occasion a Stock of Mourning Habiliments.'

It was becoming clear that this was an occasion that hundreds of thousands did not want to miss. Train schedules were revised to depart from towns and cities in the middle of the night, to get spectators to London first thing on the morning of the funeral. Even shipping was affected. The Mount Alexandra line announced that its packet ships, due to sail to Australia that week, would 'In consequence of the request of many of the passenger...not leave the East India Docks until after the day of the funeral of the Duke of Wellington'.

For by now the funeral was turning into an extravaganza. On 10 November the embalmed body of the duke was conveyed to London by special train from Kent. It arrived at the Bricklayers' Arms after midnight, a time when no spectators might have been expected. Nevertheless, 'a very considerable number of persons' waited there for hours, as they did all along the route, even though the train made only two stops, chugging without pause through the other stations. Even those platforms were 'lined with railway officials holding lamps in their hands, which served to show further back groups of spectators...every one...in mourning'.

The duke's body was taken, with military escort, to the Great Hall of Chelsea Hospital, where the hall was hung with his 'trophies of great military achievements...from the banners of the "Mysore Tiger" to the Eagles of the "Grand Army"'. The staging was dramatic: a vestibule was draped in black, with 'an enormous plume of black feathers, descending in the form of a chandelier', while the inner hall was lit by eighty-three candelabras displaying sable hangings that entirely covered the walls and ceiling. The niches were lined with soldiers from the duke's regiment in pairs, their arms reversed. A passageway led to a dais covered with cloth of gold under a canopy of black velvet, spangled with silver stars and a silver fringe, with, at the front, a heraldic mantle, the arms in gold, lined with black-spangled silver fabric, all looped up in festoons. The coffin itself was placed on a raised platform with 'an ornamental fence, massively silvered' around it, with lions rampant carrying shields on pedestals. Ten hollow columns, made to resemble bundles of spears bound with laurels, marched down the hall, containing reflectors to light the bier, on which stood another dozen smaller silver candelabra. Behind hung the flags of the conquered from all Wellington's battles; in front were displayed his military insignia and decorations, including the ones given by foreign governments, his marshal's batons and Waterloo sword. At the head of the coffin chairs were placed for the chief mourner and two 'assistant mourners', who changed by rota, the places being filled by 'some of the most distinguished personages in the kingdom'.

The first day of the lying-in-state was quiet, probably because potential visitors feared massive crowds; when none manifested, *everyone* came the following day. By seven in the morning, it was estimated that there were

100,000 people waiting. The actor Fred Belton commented, 'Barriers had been erected, and as soon as the first barrier was withdrawn another mob were [sic] admitted; then the shrieks, cries, and yells, were terrific. I felt that to stumble or fall would be death... When we entered by the hall... my wife's dress [was] in ribbons.' Even as this crowd was funnelled through the single narrow exit, packed steamers continued to drop off more and more passengers at Cadogan Pier, pressing the growing multitudes into the railings. Some people were saved only by being lifted over the high wrought-iron railings by Life Guards; two died.

Those who were to take part in the actual funeral procession were instructed on appropriate dress: 'in mourning, without weepers, but with mourning swords'. Those who had seats in St Paul's were to wear 'mourning frock dress', while their 'Servants (not in mourning) attending the carriages' should still have silk or crape hatbands and black gloves. Even those watching were advised as to appropriate dress: according to the *Post*, there had been 'considerable doubt' whether women were expected to continue to wear general mourning in the street after the funeral (it went without saying that mourning was expected on the day itself). Now, the editorial went on, 'we are in a position to state, upon the highest authority', that mourning should be worn for the single day, while 'The introduction of crape as a prominent feature of dress' could be 'left to the discretion' of each wearer, while 'velvet, we are informed, may be worn in cloaks'.

The buildings along the funeral route were equally carefully adorned for the occasion, with banners appearing, embroidered with '*Non sibi, sed Patriae*' ('Not for himself, but for his country'). Along Pall Mall and St James's, clubs draped their façades in black cloth and other appropriate decorations: the Oxford and Cambridge Club's balconies were 'tastefully hung with black cloth, festooned with silver lace, the letter "W." enclosed in laurel wreaths, being inserted in temporary hatchments'. Other clubs, as well as some of the mansions of the rich in this area, did not meet public expectations, with only a 'few mean and scanty black cloths... shabbily decorated'. That could not be said of Temple Bar: both sides of the stone gateway were 'covered with black cotton velvet, which was decorated with appropriate fringes. Each side was arranged with Roman cornices and frieze, in imitation of silver. On the summit was an immense funeral urn (of silver gilt), surrounded with 12 flambeaux of funeral torches. At each corner... was a funeral urn... somewhat smaller than... the central one... On the drapery were several monograms, with the initials "W.A.",' for Arthur Wellesley, together with shields and flags of the countries that had made the duke an honorary officer, with orders suspended from them. The whole was lit from 6 a.m. on the morning of the funeral by gas lighting that had been specially piped in.

At St Paul's, the great building contractor William Cubitt had been commissioned to build an interior grandstand to seat the thousands of mourners, as well as hanging the galleries and walls with mourning draperies. The City Corporation had laid down three large gas mains to ensure that the nave, the cornice and the Whispering Gallery above would be suitably lit: nearly 7,000 lamps were installed. St Paul's – as it had with Nelson, and as the newspapers had warned – had become a tourist site: Greville went to take a look two days before the funeral. He judged that the effect of the lights was very good 'but it was like a great rout [ball]; all London was there strolling and staring about in the midst of a thousand workmen going on with their business... all the fine ladies [were] scrambling over vast masses of timber, or ducking to avoid the great beams that were constantly sweeping along'.

On 17 November, the duke's remains were taken from Chelsea Hospital to the Audience Room at Horse Guards, the starting place for the funeral procession. The police had barred all traffic from the parade ground, and on the 18th the roads around St James's and Green Park were closed from 7 a.m. Those with tickets for St Paul's were permitted to drive through until fixed times, graded by their proximity to the cathedral. Everyone else in London had to walk that day. Sophia Beale and her family in central London ate breakfast at five to be in their places at Ludgate Hill before the barriers came down at eight.

At seven o'clock on the morning of the funeral, the ceremonial gilded coach of the Speaker of the House of Commons, together with six carriages of state each pulled by five horses, drew into Horse Guards to represent the royal family. At 7.45, 'the seventeen minute guns, which were the military salute due to the remains of the Duke of Wellington from his rank as a field-marshal, began to be fired'. Church bells throughout the city started to toll, as they would once every minute for the rest of the morning. The funeral car was uncovered, and its twelve horses harnessed three abreast. The catafalque itself was astonishing. Of solid bronze, it measured twenty-seven feet long and ten feet wide, with a carved and gilded canopy seventeen feet high, the sides of which carried the names of Wellington's victories, with replicas of some of his battle trophies and his coronet. On the car itself rested the bier, covered by a 'magnificent pall, with a silver fringe, six inches deep, and powdered with ornaments in the same metal', on which had been placed the coffin, covered with scarlet velvet, on which lay the duke's sword and cap. A silver and gold cloth formed a canopy above, supported by halberds. In even the most laudatory images, the car looks like a mobile shop window, gaudy and overstuffed, with the coffin diminished by the size of the car into a tiny little bump on the top of an excess of plush. One foreign correspondent merely wrote, 'I will not speak of it out of respect for him it carried.'

As the sides of the catafalque were drawn up to show the bier, the soldiers presented and then reversed their arms to a roll of muffled drums. Finally, at eight o'clock the procession began to move. The band of the Rifle Brigade, playing the 'Dead March' from Handel's *Saul*, went first, with troops following in sections eight deep with their arms reversed, followed in turn by '13 trumpets and kettle drums, two pursuivants-at-arms in a mourning coach', then by the long line of mourning coaches of the public bodies, ambassadors and state officials. The procession was so extensive that it was nearly an hour and a half before the funeral car itself moved out of Horse Guards, followed by the new Duke of Wellington and other family members, as well as Wellington's own horse, led riderless, saddled and with the duke's boots reversed in the stirrups. As more soldiers fell in behind, the procession moved slowly and steadily until it reached the Mall, where the funeral car became bogged down in a rut in the street. (It took ten minutes of 'active exertions' by the police and soldiers on duty to extricate it and get on the move again.)

The nearby parks – St James's and Green Park – were relatively empty, having been kept locked, reserved for the use of grandees. In the grounds of St James's Palace, scaffolding had been erected to create seating for the families and friends of the royal family, while the grounds of Marlborough House were filled with 'rows of seats…extending from the gate to Pall-mall back to the Chapel Royal'. At Stafford House, the family and friends of the Duke of Sutherland, 'dressed in deep mourning, watched…from an enclosed building raised at the bottom of the garden'. Before eight o'clock, Queen Victoria, in deep mourning, had emerged onto the central balcony of Buckingham Palace to stand with Prince Albert, their children and other foreign royals. She remained there as the procession passed – nearly two hours from start to finish – but after the mourning coaches had passed the Prince Consort and some of the other men in the party left to join in the procession themselves. After it had continued into Green Park, the queen and her family went to St James's Palace, to take up a new viewing position.

At Constitution Hill, the hordes of onlookers watched the procession appear just as the sun came out. At the Wellington Arch, the cavalcade paused; then, as the funeral car moved past Apsley House, someone in the throng shouted, 'Hats off!' and all the men in the vast crowd removed their hats, 'except in cases where the pressure [of people] did not permit the spectators to use their hands'. After another pause, soon after ten, the cortège moved slowly down Piccadilly, where possibly as many as 30,000 people had crammed themselves, having waited all night despite torrential rain and icy winds. In several of the mansions the blinds were drawn out of respect, but for the most part the windows and rooftops all along the route swarmed with spectators; many of the great mansions had built in extra viewing space. The many clubs in St James's and Pall Mall had placed tiers of seats in the windows, and some had even built platforms on their roofs, providing viewing spaces for their members, their families and friends: some clubs offered seating for 2,000 people. Only the Carlton had made no special provision: the duke had been a founder member, and it felt that strict mourning precluded spectators.

By the time the head of the procession reached Trafalgar Square, it was estimated that 10,000 people had squeezed into the space, filling the windows of all the surrounding buildings with crowds on the roof of the National

Gallery and even St Martin-in-the-Fields. ('One poor fellow, clinging to a chimney-pot, fell from a terrific height.') As the cortège neared, then passed interminably, 'whispered murmurs of "here comes the Duke!" met our ear', but 'no emotion was shown' until 'his favourite horse, led by his favourite groom, appeared, with the heads both of horse and men bent as if in deep grief, and the saddle to which were appended his boots…Then sobs, sighs, silent tears.' Here eighty-three Chelsea Pensioners, one for each year of the duke's life, were drawn up in formation between Nelson's Column and the statue of Charles I. As the long cavalcade marched by, the Pensioners fell in, joining their more active colleagues for the rest of the route.

With the exception of the house windows, the Strand was, curiously, the least crowded section, with people lining the pavements no more than two or three deep, although most of the buildings had additional seating on scaffolding. The procession slowed once more as the head of it reached Temple Bar: the soldiers, who had been marching six abreast, had to re-form into a double file to fit through the gateway; the canopy of the catafalque, too, had to be lowered to pass under the arch. (The week before, the car, suitably weighted to represent the real thing, had been taken on a trial run.) As the procession crossed the boundary into the City, the Lord Mayor joined it, together with members of the Common Council. At Ludgate Hill there was an involuntary pause once more: the steepness of the hill slowed the horses pulling the carriages and the catafalque, while the dense crowds, too, spilt over into the road, slowing things further. Nevertheless, the funeral car arrived at St Paul's exactly at noon and was immediately moved into a temporary shed 'where means had been supplied to move the ponderous bier into the body of the cathedral'. Meanwhile a blue light was flashed out from the dome of the cathedral, 'for the purpose of informing the Tower authorities when to begin the firing of the minute guns'.

The congregation had been instructed to arrive at St Paul's at 6 a.m., but the builders were then still frantically finishing, and it was eight o'clock before the doors opened; many people had been waiting outside for more than two hours in the rain. Once inside, the temporary tiers provided seats for 6,000, with another 7,000 squeezed in under the dome and more spaces found in the transepts and galleries – altogether, room for about 17,000 had been created.*

Around the coffin stood Prince Albert, bearing the duke's field marshal's baton; the Marquess of Anglesey, who had lost his leg at Waterloo and was himself eighty-four, carrying his marshal's baton; and the pall-bearers, all officers who had served under Wellington. Apart from Austria, every country for which the duke had held a marshal's baton had sent a representative: thirty-seven years after Waterloo the allies against Napoleon were reunited.† After the funeral service, the coffin was lowered into its tomb beneath the cathedral floor, forty trumpeters sounded a dirge at the west entrance to the cathedral, and the troops began to disperse, followed by the funeral car, Prince Albert, the foreign dignitaries and then the crowds. By five o'clock, the hundreds of thousands of spectators had vanished and only the black fabric remained, hanging damply across the buildings.

Soon, all trace of the spectacle was gone, but the man himself would continue to be remembered:

> Let the sound of those he wrought for,
> And the feet of those he fought for,
> Echo round his bones for evermore.

* Conditions can be imagined when comparing it to the last great state occasion in the cathedral, the marriage of the Prince of Wales and Diana Spencer: a mere 3,500 were seated then.

† The absence of Austria was in response to an ugly little episode. An Austrian general named Haynau had fought against Napoleon, but had later been involved in the atrocities against the revolutionaries of 1848 in Italy, stories of his vicious behaviour being widespread. In Belgium he had narrowly escaped attack in the street. In London in 1850 he was assaulted by some draymen working at the Barclays and Perkins brewery in Southwark, who shouted 'Down with the Austrian butcher!' threw mud and 'dirt' at him, threatened him with a beating and ultimately chased him down the Borough High Street until he hid in the George Inn. Austria was still smarting from this diplomatic humiliation two years later and refused to send a representative to the duke's funeral. On the other side, when Garibaldi visited London in 1864, he asked to be taken to see the brewery, so he could personally thank the draymen. The matter was a little delicate, as the men had committed criminal assault, although none had ever been identified. Finally it was suggested that if Garibaldi went to the brewery at a certain time, some men would be in the forecourt grooming the horses, and Garibaldi might wish to acknowledge, in particular, the man on the far right, which he did. Today a plaque marks the spot where Haynau was assaulted.

There, in St Paul's, instead of Westminster Abbey, usually the home of dead heroes, Wellington was placed for ever at the heart of the city, belonging to the people rather than the government, perhaps a suitable end for the man who rejected both Reform and the common people, but always did his duty for them nonetheless.

13.

NIGHT ENTERTAINMENT

There were thousands of places to go and be amused, on and off the street, in early- and mid-Victorian London – thousands of places, that is, if one happened to be a man. Public places for women's amusement were less easy to find and, for middle- and upper-class women, they verged on the non-existent. Clubs were, of course, entirely male. So were the coffee shops, chophouses and other public eating spaces; low-cost cookshops did a busy trade with working-class women, coming and going with their families' dinners, but eating there, although possible, was less common. Many West End theatres seated women in the boxes as well as in what later became known as the dress circle (for the prosperous) and the gallery (for the poor), but the pit and other low-priced areas were for men. Theatres in the East End and south of the river confined working-class women to the galleries and middle-class women to the boxes, although Astley's Amphitheatre, where hippodramas were staged, was an entirely family entertainment. Any woman anywhere in the Alhambra Music Hall, apart from working-class women in the gallery, was automatically assumed to have a dubious reputation, or none. The same went for most other nightspots of the city.

Perhaps the most masculine of all entertainment arenas was to be found in the variety of places where animal baiting occurred throughout the century. In theory, this was a Regency hangover that faded away with Victorian respectability. In reality, there are mentions of various types of baiting throughout the period, both in fixed venues and more loosely organized by individuals. One early memoirist recalled places for bull-baiting, badger-baiting, dogfighting 'and such like "manly sports"'. Lying between Parliament and Millbank was a house owned by William Aberfield, better known as

'Slender Billy', where bear-baiting and dogfighting were conducted, while the similarly characterfully named 'Harlequin Billy' presided over bear- and badger-baiting in a cellar in Whitechapel every Monday, Wednesday and Friday, at eight o'clock, all year round. The compiler of a notebook in the possession of the magistrate John Silvester recorded that Mrs Cummings, a fence, may have owned the cockpit in Bambridge Street, which had twice-weekly fights.* It also stated that Mrs Smith, near Blackfriars, 'has a Bear Bait twice a week, Mondays & Thursdays, in a Shed at the back part of the House'. Both places charged 6d admission. So although women could not attend, at least a few ran these activities.

A fictional bear-baiting was described in *Real Life in London* in 1821, where the two men on the razzle remind themselves to button their jackets tightly and 'be awake' for pickpockets in the audience they mix with, who 'bore the appearance of Butchers, Dog-fanciers and Ruffians, intermingled here and there with a few *Sprigs of Fashion... Coster-mongers*, Coal-heavers, Watermen, Soldiers, and Livery-servants'. The bear stands on his hind legs, chained to a wall by its neck. Dogs are loosed on him and bets laid as to 'how long the bow-wow would bother the ragged Russian'. (See Plate 19.) Each time a dog retreats wounded, a new dog is brought out, until at last the bear is taken away to be bandaged until he had healed enough to fight again. Pierce Egan's novel, *Life in London*, in the same year describes a monkey fighting dogs at Westminster Pit, near Tothill Fields, a famous location for all types of animal baiting.

Both these instances are fiction, but the Westminster Pit was a real place, and newspapers routinely carried advertisements for fights throughout the 1820s. In 1822, *The Times* ran an advertisement for 'A grand MAIN [match] of COCKS to be FOUGHT at the Cockpit Royal, Westminster', over three days, 'for 5 guineas a battle, and 100 the odds', with two fights scheduled daily, at two and five o'clock. As late as 1865, there were reports

* There are two small notebooks and they are a mystery. They contain a note dated 1952 (when they were acquired by the British Museum) stating that they previously belonged to the 1952 owner's father-in-law, who in turn had been Silvester's great-great-nephew; but while the notebooks may well have been in Silvester's possession, there is no knowing who compiled the information they contain, for what purpose, or how reliable it is.

of cockfighting, although by that time they were balanced by reports of police-court appearances of men arrested in raids on illegal fighting dens. (Fights were legal as long as the premises were licensed.) Dogfighting also continued throughout the century, together with ratting. In the late 1840s, handbills were distributed announcing a 'great hundred rat match' in a pub in Graham Street, off the City Road, for an audience of the familiar mix of sporting types, costers, soldiers and tradesmen. The 1s entry fee gave visitors access to an upstairs room, where wooden boards created a small ring six feet in diameter, 'about as large as the centre flower-bed', lit by a large gaslight and surrounded by benches and tables. A dozen or so rats were loosed and the dogs set on them. As the rats were killed, their bodies were flung into a corner, the little arena swept clean, and the process began again. Dogs also fought each other, generally on the sly, in the backyards of beer shops, or on Sundays in the fields and waste ground surrounding the city.

The purpose of animal baiting was gambling. There was a middle-class sense that London was full of gamblers, card-sharpers, extortionists and other conmen, all waiting to leap upon the young naïf up from the country. In *Martin Chuzzlewit*, Dickens mocked this foreboding when the rather simple Tom Pinch arrives in London for the first time and finds, to his surprise, that he was not once 'the prey of ring-droppers, pea and thimble-riggers, duffers, touters, or any of those bloodless sharpers... He fell into conversation with no gentleman who took him into a public-house, where there happened to be another gentleman who swore he had more money than any gentleman, and very soon proved he had more money than one gentleman by taking his away from him; neither did he fall into any other of the numerous man-traps which are set up without notice, in the public grounds of this city.' Despite these generalized fears for country bumpkins, some of the worst mantraps were designed for the upper classes. The fanciest gambling den in London in the first half of the century was Crockford's in St James's Street, founded in 1826 by a retired fishmonger. Crockford ensured that his club, apart from being a place where the rich could lose their shirts in decent privacy, in all other respects resembled the best gentlemen's club: it was exclusive and had a good chef. Indeed, it even laid on special late supper hours during the parliamentary season, when an exhausted legislator could stagger up the road from the Houses of Parliament and be refreshed at any hour from midnight to five in the morning.

There were thousands more clubs and drinking places to suit every socio-economic level and every purpose. The attitude to drinking was almost entirely class based. *Hints to Men About Town*, published in 1840, warned that 'as every Man about Town is liable to be placed in situations where it is almost impossible to escape perfectly sober', such a young man needed to learn how 'to take his glass...without making a fool of himself'. The author, who called himself 'The Old Medical Student', advised young men to eat as well as drink, to stick to one type of wine, not to get rowdy and, above all, 'Do not be prevailed upon to sing' (which is surely good advice today too). This was followed by a section on what to do when a friend passed out from drink and how to cure a hangover. It was all very matter-of-fact.

The Servant Girl in London: Showing the Dangers to which Young Country Girls are Exposed was published in the same year, but could not be further away in tone, even though its author had similarly pragmatic views. Readers were instructed that many pubs were entirely respectable, having been established by servants of gentry, and in them one could expect to meet 'some of the most pleasant company...The conversation is often very instructive, and well expressed...about politics, the news of the day, parish intelligence, and the like.' It was the taproom that was the danger: 'Here collect the working men, male servants in and out of place, hackney-coachmen, omnibus cads, &c.', who 'drink far more in proportion than those in the parlour...and frequently insult most grossly' the servant girls from local houses, the 'wives of mechanics [artisans], poor tradesmen, and the broken-down gentlewoman who keeps a school'. These blameless females, while waiting to collect the supper beer, were obliged meanwhile to mingle with 'the washerwoman, the market-woman, the basket-woman, the gaudily-attired courtesan, the sad street-walker'. This mixing, warned the author, was 'highly dangerous', but it was the mixing he was warning about, not the drinking.

From the mid-eighteenth century, there had been a shift from gin, the historic drink of the people, to beer. Bad harvests and the 1751 Gin Act had made the spirit much more expensive, while the licensing laws for beer were being gradually loosened. Pubs were also changing. Previously, a pub had been a terraced house like any other, its ground-floor front room the public area, laid out and decorated like any front room, where people who knew each other sat together, as if they were at home. With increasing urbanization came a greater anonymity; a counter was installed so that the pub workers had access to the drink, while the customers (who were strangers, after all) no longer did. As early as the 1830s, this homely space was becoming more formal, more businesslike. A plan for a model pub showed a 'shop', that is, the bar, with an area for customers to stand on one side. A counter divided it from the bar-parlour, which was still considered a private part of the house and was decorated as a private sitting room 'for the master and mistress', where customers ventured only by invitation. A 'company parlour' led off to the right; and behind the shop was the taproom, the largest of them all. Later on, pubs also had jug-and-bottle departments, where householders would go with their own jugs to collect beer for home consumption, instead of using the shop, which was given over to drinking on the premises. The rooms were socially graded by their

On Sundays, pubs were legally required to close during the hours of church services. It was not only drinkers who waited for opening hours: the child on the left in this 1850 illustration holds a jug to carry home the dinner beer.

furnishings: taprooms had cheap wooden tables and benches; furniture in the parlour was mahogany, perhaps with upholstered chairs; while the bar-parlour retained its domestic furnishings.

With different rooms serving different types of customers, most pubs also expected to attract a number of regular clients. In *Sketches by Boz*, two pubs, one in Henrietta Street, and one in Fleet Street, draw a group of 'steady old boys' who are 'always to be seen in the same taverns, at the same hours every evening', where they sit and smoke and drink and tell stories; or they meet there, go half-price to the theatre, and then return after the show, for steak and oysters.* These were central London pubs. Some were attached to coaching inns, both for passengers and for those meeting them, later providing the same function at railway stations. Some served those regular commuters walking past, who made up a substantial market. Pubs were therefore to be found on all the major arteries in and out of London, where possible on a corner site, to catch two streams of pedestrians. So essential were they to daily life that when speculative builders began to develop any area, a pub was routinely the first building to be erected, with the builder as licensee. The pub gave his workmen a place to eat and drink (as well as a place for their wages to be directed back into the contractor's own pocket); then, when a few houses had been built, the pub lease was sold off to provide more capital for further building. Augustus Mayhew's *Paved with Gold* described a new suburb in the mid-1850s: 'Of the residences already erected, the large majority were still unfinished [but]...Dotted all about was a thick sprinkling of public-houses.'

In the 1830s, pubs especially relied on a variety of customers when they began to face direct competition from a new type of drinking establishment, the gin palace. In 1834, a Select Committee on the Prevailing Vice of Drunkenness heard from a grocer in Tothill Street, near the Houses of Parliament, that a pub 'nearly opposite to my residence, where the consumption of

* Theatres had historically run long programmes, beginning with a five-act drama at 5 p.m., followed by an interlude of some sort, then an afterpiece – a farce or a comedy in one act. After the third act of the main play, entrance was reduced to half-price, and many people who worked long hours or had small incomes regularly attended only after the discounted prices came into effect.

spirits was very trifling' had been converted into a gin palace. From being 'a low dirty public-house, with only one doorway', it was transformed into 'a splendid edifice, the front ornamented with pilasters, supporting a handsome cornice and entablature, and balustrades, and the whole elevation remarkably striking and handsome; the doorways were increased in number from one, and that a small one…to three, and each of those eight to ten feet wide; the…doors and windows glazed with very large single squares of plate glass, and the gas fittings of the most costly description…when the doors were opened, the rush was tremendous; it was instantly filled with customers, and continued so till midnight.'

Gin palaces flourished with the arrival of gas lighting and plate-glass windows, making them a thing of wonder, places of light and warmth for those whose lives held little of either: undoubtedly, as Dickens observed, the poorer the neighbourhood, 'the more splendid do these places become'. In 1835, amid the filth and despair of St Giles, he recognized that the gin palaces were 'All…light and brilliancy…the gay building with the fantastically ornamented parapet, the illuminated clock, the plate-glass windows surrounded by stucco rosettes, and its profusion of gas-lights in richly-gilt burners, is perfectly dazzling when contrasted with the darkness and dirt we have just left.' Soon the enormous gaslights outside became the distinctive marker of a gin palace. One such place in the Ratcliffe Highway, in the East End, had 'a revolving light with many burners playing most beautifully' over one door; over a second, 'about fifty or sixty jets, in one lantern, were throwing out…brilliant gleams, as if from the branches of a shrub'; while a third had 'no less than THREE enormous lamps, with corresponding lights'. The man describing them was a temperance campaigner, so he might have been somewhat carried away by the enticements on offer, but not by much.

The decor, it seemed to Dickens, was, if possible, 'even gayer than the exterior'. 'A bar of French-polished mahogany, elegantly carved, extends the whole width of the place; and…Beyond the bar is a lofty and spacious saloon…with a gallery running round it, equally well furnished.' This luxury contrasted sharply with the gin palace's customers: two washerwomen; two old men who had 'finished their third quartern' – their third quarter of a pint – of gin and are 'crying drunk'; and some 'fat comfortable-looking elderly women' drinking rum shrub (rum with lemon and sugar). 'A throng of men, women, and children…have been constantly going in and out, [but late in the day this] dwindles down to two or three occasional stragglers – cold, wretched-looking creatures, in the last stage of emaciation and disease.' Dickens is both realistic and sympathetic here, ending by commenting that if temperance societies could provide against hunger and want, the gin palaces would vanish; since they could not, who could blame the drinkers for gravitating to the warmest, most attractive place available? (It is also worth considering that people who rarely had enough to eat would easily become drunk on very little alcohol.)

By the late 1840s, these drinking saloons were glamorous yet had no seating at all: 'every exertion is used to make the place as uncomfortable to the consumers as possible, so that they shall only stop in to drink, and pay; step out, and return to drink and pay again'. In the 1850s, Sala described one busy gin palace, with about fifty customers at two in the afternoon. Drinkers were invited to state their business by being separated into distinct sections, the 'Jug and Bottle Entrance', the 'Wholesale Bar' and the 'Retail Bar', while barrels lined the walls emblazoned with enticing slogans and brand names encouraging them with visions of delight: 'Choice Compounds', 'Cream of the Valley', or 'The Dew off Ben Nevis'. An advertisement for the 'Celebrated Balmoral Mixture, patronised by his Royal Highness Prince Albert' was accompanied by 'the illustrious personage, clad in full Highland costume…represented taking a glass of the "Mixture" with great apparent gusto'. And all to serve gin at a penny a glass, to people who were deciding between food and another tumbler of oblivion.

From the eighteenth century, pubs had been the natural home of all types of clubs and special-interest groups, and as gin palaces became more elaborate, these were increasingly encouraged. Mr Pickwick's journeys start at, and the novel is predicated on, the Pickwick Club, which holds its meetings in a pub. Its club room was the epitome of many an upstairs club room, containing little more than a long wooden table and Windsor chairs, with prints on the walls. Pubs found numerous ways of attracting regulars: in the

1860s, several along Fleet Street were known as sporting taverns, stocking sporting newspapers, posting up telegrams announcing race results and otherwise ensuring they were the meeting places for like-minded people. The actor Charles Macready and John Forster were members of a Shakespeare club in the 1830s that met at the Piazza Coffee House in Covent Garden to read and discuss literature; Dickens soon enrolled.

Pubs and clubs were also venues for people at times of distress, as well as at times of jollity. In Shoreditch in the 1860s, a pub sold black-bordered 'tickets' for 3d, to help the family of the recently deceased 'Jemmy Baldwin [who] had died sudden, leaving nothing to bury him...a few friends would meet that night at the Tinkers' Arms, Spicer Street, for the benefit of the widow and orphans'. On happier occasions, many of these pubs also held 'twopenny hops', or costermongers' dances, where anything up to a hundred men and women congregated to drink and dance to the music of a fiddle, 'sometimes with the addition of a harp and cornopean' (a cornet: a brass instrument that sounded like a trumpet). By the 1850s, many pubs had widened the scope of their club meetings, holding weekly discussion groups that were open to casual visitors, with a variety of subjects and different customer profiles being known and understood. The Cogers, in Bride Lane, Fleet Street, was a political forum; the Green Dragon, also in Fleet Street, held discussions on Tuesdays for 'Literary Loungers'; on Mondays and Thursdays for other 'popular subjects'. At the Blue Posts, in Shoe Lane, the Ruminators met on Wednesdays, with more miscellaneous discussions on Tuesdays and Fridays, while Mondays and Saturdays were given over to Harmonics.

Harmonic meetings, also known as free-and-easies, covered the social spectrum: men meeting for the purpose of drinking and singing, sometimes as a club or a group of friends, sometimes a group of strangers. When a free-and-easy was held in a pub, there were usually some professional performers, but all present were expected to contribute. In *Sketches by Boz*, Dickens described a late-night harmonic meeting, where as many as a hundred men sit at tables, listening to three 'professional gentlemen' sing a glee (a part-song for three or more voices), after which they drink and smoke, and listen once more to 'our friend, Mr Smuggins', who 'after a considerable quantity of coughing' sings a comic song, 'received with unbounded applause', followed by a recitation, before the group joins in another glee.

If the harmonic meeting was open to the public, the landlord of a pub frequently acted as the chairman, as is the case in *Oliver Twist* at the Three Cripples, the rogues' pub in Saffron Hill, where the landlord seemed 'to give himself up to joviality', but 'had an eye for everything that was done, and an ear for everything that was said'. *Bleak House*, too, includes a harmonic meeting at the Sol's Arms, with the professional Little Swills, the comic vocalist. But it was group singing that was the *raison d'être* of these evenings: 'it is only when one of the amateurs presently consents to oblige amidst a great rattling of glasses and thumping of pint pots, that the chorus develops its full perfections...with the united strength of some forty pairs of lungs.' So ubiquitous was the free-and-easy that in *Little Dorrit* even in the Marshalsea the prisoners hold a regular club night in their 'Snuggery', complete with 'presidential tribute...beery atmosphere, sawdust, pipe-lights, [and] spittoons'.*

Sometimes the meetings were more select, involving a group of friends or colleagues, as in *The Pickwick Papers*, when the legal clerks gather at the Magpie and Stump pub in Clare market: 'There's Samkin and Green's managing-clerk, and Smithers and Price's chancery, and Pimkin and Thomas's out o' doors† – sings a capital song, he does.' Sometimes harmonic meetings were held to celebrate specific events. In *Nicholas Nickleby*, when the strolling players, the Crummles family, plan to go abroad, a supper is given in their honour at a local pub, 'at which Mr Snittle Timberry would preside, while the honours of the vice chair would be sustained by the African Swallower'. A shoemaker attended a similar dinner that his employer held for his workers: the master 'occupied the chair himself, and requested that I would act as vice', as after the meal, 'we indulged in

* Spittoons, although usually unmentioned, were an important part of club furnishings. One pub in 1847 had four spittoons in the bar-parlour – and twenty-nine in its club room, which held only twenty-one chairs.

† 'Out o' doors' clerks are known as outside clerks today; they transport documents from legal chambers to court registry offices, serve papers and so on.

mirth and song'. In the early 1830s, John Barrow, the editor of the *Mirror of Parliament*, was trying to find work for his nephew, a young man named Charles Dickens, and asked the journalist John Payne Collier whether he might recommend him to the owners of the *Morning Chronicle*.* Barrow 'also informing me that [Dickens] was cheerful company and a good singer of a comic song', Collier 'agreed to meet Dickens at dinner'; Dickens was so young 'that he had no vestige of beard or whiskers' and had needed a 'good deal of pressing' before he sang 'The Dandy's Dog's-meat Man', as well as a song he had written himself, 'Sweet Betsy Ogle'.†

More common were regular club nights, whose exclusivity was an indicator of their desirability. In *The Old Curiosity Shop*, Dick Swiveller belongs to 'a select convivial circle called the Glorious Apollers' [sic], of which he had 'the honour to be Perpetual Grand'. This was a lower-middle-class version of Pip's club in *Great Expectations*, the Finches of the Grove: 'the object of which institution I have never divined, if it were not that the members should dine expensively once a fortnight, to quarrel among themselves as much as possible after dinner, and to cause six waiters to get drunk on the stairs'.

These young men met regularly in Covent Garden, in the heart of the song-and-supper-club neighbourhood. From the earliest part of the century, 'Supper Rooms' were places men went to in the evening after dinner, and among the most famous were Evans's, Offley's, the Garrick, the Coal Hole and the Cider (sometimes Cyder) Cellars, all in Covent Garden or near the Strand. Singing was automatically part of the evening.

* John Payne Collier's reputation today is primarily as a literary forger. However, at the time John Dickens approached him, he was an admired journalist, particularly for *The Times* and the *Morning Chronicle*, as well as the *Observer*'s theatre critic.

† Collier also wrote that Barrow had told him that the boy had 'assisted Warren…in the conduct of his extensive business', and 'referred…jocosely' to the rhyming advertisements, suggesting Dickens had written them. Biographers have wondered whether Barrow knew of Dickens' childhood disgrace, and why he would hint at it. But Collier's diary was published the year after Forster's biography of Dickens revealed to the world the events of Dickens' childhood, and it seems more likely that Collier retrospectively 'remembered' something that Barrow, forty years earlier, had never told him, to embellish his diary now that the young Dickens was famous.

An 1839 guidebook, in its listing of supper clubs, observes, in its entirety: 'At most of these houses some good singing is to be heard, they being attended by professional men': the quality of the song was more important than the food or the ambience, neither of which was mentioned. These clubs served breakfast fare, alcohol and cigars. In the intervals between the songs, the waiters rushed round, crying, 'Gentlemen, give your orders; give your orders, gentlemen; whiskey, brandy, gin, and rum – rum, gin, brandy, whiskey,' and taking orders for food: 'Fried-'am-an'-eggs for you, sir? Sassages, did that gentleman say? Sassages is all gone, sir... Tripe, sir? Yessir.' Then, when they heard 'Order, order! Silence, waiters. Gentlemen, if you please, I'll sing a song,' they vanished until it was finished, when it would be, 'Now, then, Waiter, bring that gentleman's kidneys. Chop and shallots for the man oppo-*site*. Look alive there – be brisk! Kidneys for you, sir? Copy of the song just sung, gentlemen – copy of the song; celebrated song, sir – thanky, sir. Song, gentlemen, song; orders, gentlemen, orders – gentlemen, give your orders!'

Evans's was one of the longest surviving and most famous of the supper rooms. Originally established in an old house overlooking Covent Garden

The Coal Hole, a supper and singing club, opened first as a working-class pub in 1817, and this drawing probably dates from those early days. The men on the left, however, appear to have a punch bowl on the table, and they may well be a social group gathered to sing.

piazza, it was a hotel until W. C. Evans became the landlord in the 1820s and turned it into a supper room.* In 1844, Evans retired, and Paddy Green later built a much more elegant galleried room, with gas lighting and a stage at the far end. Evans's had been known for singing 'erotic and bacchanalian' songs, but under Green it was said to have become much more respectable. The Cider Cellars, on Maiden Lane, was the supper room that Thackeray fictionalized as the Fielding's Head in *Pendennis* with a landlord who took the chair and sang 'profusely'. In the 1840s, one performer was known in particular for a song entitled 'Sam Hall', about a condemned man awaiting execution, with the refrain 'damn your eyes'. Late at night, the Cellar's tone changed, when 'the songs became decidedly equivocal in character' and not for '*virginibus puerisque*' – for girls and boys.

Even with that warning, the memoirists and novel writers apparently toned down their descriptions, if books like *The Nobby Songster*, *The Flash Chaunter* and *The Flash Songster* are to be believed. These claim to contain songs 'now singing' at Offley's, the Cider Cellar and the Coal Hole (see below), and most of the songs are headed, 'to be sung to the tune of —', which suggests group singing, or at the very least joining in the choruses. One volume gives a list of toasts 'as given at the Cider Cellar', which includes:

> 'Here's to the maid, who will take that in her hand which she longs for in her heart.'
>
> 'A clear house, good lodging, and in a hairy situation.'
>
> 'The bird in the hand and then in the bush.'
>
> 'A fine maid, a good plaice, and a large pair of cods.' [a 'good place' in the nineteenth century was a good job; cods were testicles, hence the fish pun]

* A memoirist records that the original building appears in Hogarth's *Morning* engraving in his *Four Times of the Day* series. Reading from right to left, Tom's Coffee-House, the entrance to St Paul's church, and then Evans's were depicted. But, he added, Hogarth had not reversed his original drawing to allow for the fact that the engraving would flip the image, so it appears backwards.

> 'May we always be able to insert a long article in the Ladies Magazine.'
>
> 'The Sea (c—) for ever; and he who would be afraid to dive into it, may he be jammed and d—d for ever.'
>
> 'Here's what every woman's got, what every man has not got, what we all get out of, and what we all like to get into.'

Even today, these do not fall into the 'respectable' category, and many of the songs were even smuttier. Others are outright obscene:

THE SWELL COVES [fashionable gent's] ALPHABET

A. stands for actresses who'll work as well as play.
B. for bilking bulleys [cheating the pimps], and old bawds [madams of brothels] of their pay,
C. for c—t, and crim. con.* deny it, ye who can.
D. for ladies dil—s when they cannot get a man.
So do not think me foolish, or think a flat [dupe] you see,
I've learnt the swell coves alphabet, just hear my A.B.C.

E. stands for Emmerson of bawds she is the queen
F. for fancy [sporting] fellows – did you ever see one green [inexperienced]
G, you know, is Goodereds in famous Piccadilly†
H is mother H's where I've covered many a filly.‡
Chorus &c.

I. next for Ives of St. Giles's petts the first
J. for *Joe* the Stunner, whose *Banks* may never burst§

* Crim. con. was an abbreviation for a legal term, 'criminal conversation'. As a wife was legally a man's property, if she committed adultery, her husband could sue her lover for damages, not for the adultery, but for reducing her 'value' by entering into 'criminal conversation' with her.

† Goodered's Flash Saloon was a 'hotbed of vice', according to a guidebook.

‡ Mother H. was a well-known madam; see p. 412.

§ I have not identified Ives of St Giles – a prostitute perhaps? Joe the Stunner was 'stunning Joe Banks' (fl. 1830–50), a well-known London publican and fence, whose pub was in St Giles.

K. stands for Kinchins, and kifer hung with hair,*
L. for lush [alcohol] and lechery, as well as Leicester Square.
Chorus &c.

M. stands for maidenhead, I often have drove through,
N, stands, for Nicholson, of 'Town' chaps few so true,†
O. you know is opera, where swells must keep a box,
P. stands for patent pills, Phoenix Alley and the P— [pox],
Chorus &c.

Q. is Q—m and Queen's-Bench, queer places to be in,
R. Rhodes rogering hole, where you'll always go again,‡
S. is sponging houses, Shire-lane, saloons, and s—ing.
T. you know is thimble-rigs, and Tattersalls [horse-auction rooms] low-cunning.
Chorus &c.

U is an uprighter or hunt with hasty dressing,
V. is the venereal that follows as a blessing,
W. stands for Waterford, of spreeing he's the king,§
X. is a *cross* [double-cross] so you must *square* it while I sing.
Chorus &c.

Y. you know are yokels, but if now there's any here, as
Z. is my last letter, why he must be a Zany.
My song now is ended, I hope you'll have not cause,
To say I am not wide awake, or grudge me your applause.

---

* 'Kinchen' were child thieves, more commonly boys, while 'kifer' was a woman as represented by her sex organs – 'plenty of kifer in that house'; so the sentence praises both young girls and those who had reached puberty.

† For more on 'Baron' Nicholson, see p. 363.

‡ This is John Rhodes, the owner of the Coal Hole (his brother William managed the Cider Cellars). It is interesting that the place is referred to in such sexual terms; for more on the overlap of entertainment halls and prostitution, see pp. 405–6.

§ This is the 3rd Marquess of Waterford, whom the *Dictionary of National Biography* describes as 'reprobate and landowner', itemizing some of his exploits: 'it amused him to challenge passers-by to fight him, to break windows, to upset (literally) applecarts. He painted the Melton Mowbray toll bar red; he fought a duel; he painted the heels of a parson's horse with aniseed and hunted him with bloodhounds.'

> So do not think me foolish, or think a flat you see,
> I know the swell coves alphabet, and say the A B C.

By comparison, some songs had only mildly bawdy elements: 'The Bill Sticker' describes how the bill-sticker of the title, 'Holloway's ointment and Paris pills, the last a great reformer, / I plaster'd to Miss Kembles tail the first night she play'd Normer'.* Or, to the tune of 'God Rest Ye, Merry Gentlemen', lyrics concerning

> some queer old gentlemen
> That nothing can dismay;
> Who crawl about the city,
> Almost every day;
> And look for game – I mean young girls,
> To lead them all astray,
> And rob them of comfort and joy.

Several were far less respectful about authority figures than we might assume today. *The Cockchafer* presented 'A Celebrated Parody on The King, God Bless Him', while a song about the burning of the Houses of Parliament told the story of Bill, a hackney coachman, who fell down the House of Commons privy: 'they said, Bill, are you dead, no I'm only *inturd.*'

The songbooks claim that all these songs were sung in many supper clubs, of which the Coal Hole had the worst reputation, while still being a place where a respectable man could be seen. The Coal Hole began life as the Wolf Club in 1817, a working-class pub down 'a dingy-looking alley' at the bottom of Southampton Street, near where it met the Strand, before moving to the Strand proper, where Simpson's restaurant is now. It was only when it began its harmonic meetings that it became fashionable. Thackeray depicted it as the Cave of Harmony in *The Newcomes*, where it is run 'by the celebrated Hoskins', a place where men go late at night when they want

* This is Adelaide Kemble, the now less-remembered opera-singer sister of the actress Fanny Kemble, both daughters of Charles Kemble.

'welsh-rabbits and a good old glee'. However, by the time *The Newcomes* appeared in the 1850s, it had changed radically. In 1841, at the Garrick pub, in Bow Street, Renton Nicholson had set up what came to be known as 'Judge and Jury' evenings, appointing himself 'the Lord Chief Baron' and presiding over mock trials, with audience members acting as the jury. Favourite subjects were current crim. con. cases, or trials for alienation of affection, adultery and divorce. Since the entertainment, like all of these supper rooms, was confined to men, there was also a certain amount of cross-dressing as the parts were acted out. The 1s fee bought entry, 'a glass of grog and a bad cigar'. 'Men about town, city clerks...betting men, and provincials ambitious of initiation into the shady side of London life' made up the audience. Three years later, Nicholson moved these Judge and Jury evenings to the Coal Hole, where they, and he, flourished until 1846, when they returned to the Garrick. The Coal Hole settled down to being a regular supper room, but kept up its risqué reputation, with *poses plastiques*: semi-draped women in tableaux recycling episodes from history and literature, while providing soft-core leering opportunities.

These evenings were all for men, and even the cheapest of them involved some cost. One amusement that was available to both men and women, city-wide and without charge, was to be found throughout the streets: illuminations. Long before Paris, London was known as the city of lights. In 1805, when Frederick Winsor began his experiment of lighting the streets by gas at Carlton House, he began not with the functional but with the decorative, erecting thirty-two gas burners, including a four-branched one shaped like the Prince of Wales feathers. Over the gateway he set up a transparency, a painting on a semi-opaque fabric, lit from behind to display the initials 'GR' and a crown, with, on the other side, an illuminated address beginning 'Rejoice, rejoice, 'tis George's natal day'.

Gas illuminations in the early days were a novelty strictly for free-spending princes, but they built on a popular tradition. For state celebrations and public events, illuminations were a regular part of London's night-time celebrations via hundreds and thousands of small oil lamps hung from windows and along the façades of buildings, with glass of different colours, to build up images and even words. These lamps appeared not only on government buildings and on shops, but also on private houses, offering an indicator – in the mind of one tourist, at least – of an individual's loyalty 'by the quantity of oil consumed'. Even he, cynic that he was, admitted that the 'effect on the whole was very pretty', even 'brilliant'.

As the long French wars drew to a close and Wellington roared across Europe, the two technologies for a time coexisted. In 1813, the victory at the battle of Vittoria was celebrated over three nights: 'The fronts of Carlton-house and Somerset-house, exhibited...a blaze of light, with the name of Wellington formed with [oil]-lamps, and allusions to the hero's exploits', while other oil lights spelt out 'The Grand Alliance'. In 1814, for the Grand National Jubilee marking the Peace of Aix-la-Chapelle, an illuminated Temple of Concord was set up on a revolving platform in Green Park, while St James's Park was lit by large paper lanterns hung from the trees, their painted paper shades illustrating battles, heroes 'and every variety of subject'. So bright were the illuminations, or so dark were cities more usually at the time, that their light was visible nearly fifteen miles away, in Bromley, Kent.

However great these celebrations were, they were surpassed when London became 'one continual scene of uproar and joy in consequence of the total defeat of Bonaparte at Waterloo by Lord Wellington... Friday and Saturday night all the public buildings and many private ones were illuminated. Many fanciful and beautiful devices were exhibited.' One house in St James's mounted a replica 'fortress with cannon, flags, etc... A publican who keeps a tavern with the sign of a cock, had a large transparency representing a game cock strutting over his fallen combatant with the inscription, "England, the cock of the walk!"'

By the coronation of William IV, in 1830, street illuminations had become even more elaborate, with 'various, most ingenious, and fantastic devices – always, however, representing in some form the initials or full names, of the king and queen – the principal centre of which ordinarily would be a crown'. Sometimes these would be created by the new technology, for private houses as well as palaces: 'Here and there a temporary gas machinery had been erected, on which the slightest breeze would occasion a sportful dance of lights and shadows by blowing out some portions, and lighting others, in rapid succession – at one moment showing the whole tracery in full blaze, and then only parts.' Seven years later, when Princess Victoria, heir to the throne, attained her majority, the streets, according to the footman William Tayler, were decorated by a 'grand ilumination'. Six months later the princess had become a queen and on the occasion of the Lord Mayor's installation made her first formal visit to the City as monarch. 'The sitisens are making great preperations to receve her. All the streets...will be very briliantly eluminated. It is said it will cost eight hundred pound to eluminate Temple Bar alone, and many thousands to eluminate the Citty.'

The illuminations varied in quantity and quality with the event being celebrated, and to a degree it is possible to trace popular enthusiasm for royalty, or lack thereof, through the reports. When the Prince of Wales was born in 1842, 'The illuminations on Wednesday night were few, and many of the club-houses were not illuminated at all. Pall-mall contained but one illumination.' The United Services Club in Trafalgar Square, however, was 'beautifully illuminated', complete with an illuminated 'Ich Dien' and a set of Prince of Wales feathers. Unfortunately, 'the night being wet the streets were nearly deserted'. In 1847, when Prince Albert had still not achieved the popularity that came in the last decade of his short life, his birthday was 'observed in the metropolis with the usual rejoicings. In the evening the Royal tradesmen illuminated their houses', making a business proposition of this supposed happy day. Attitudes were very similar in 1859 when the Prince of Wales turned eighteen: 'in the evening the theatres Royal and the houses of the purveyors to the Royal household were illuminated.'* And the ho-hum air continued even with the queen herself. For her fifty-first birthday in 1870, nearly a decade after Albert's death, at a time when her subjects were heartily tired of a seclusion that seemed to mean she could attend only the events she enjoyed, 'The various clubhouses, theatres, and residences of the members of the Ministry were

* Dickens three years later echoed this lack of enthusiasm, calling him a 'poor dull idle fellow'.

illuminated, as were also the establishments of the Royal tradesmen', but evidently there was nothing further.

It had not always been like this. In 1853, riding a wave of emotion after the success of the Great Exhibition, which Albert was seen to have steered so successfully, the illuminations on the queen's birthday were 'more than usually brilliant and the various devices in gas and coloured lamps [were]...worthy of the occasion...On no former anniversary of her Majesty's birthday has the illumination been so good.' Particularly worthy of mention were the illuminations at the Junior United Services Club, in Waterloo Place, which included 'A large bulging-crown' with a 'V' inside the order of the garter, and the motto *Honi soit qui mal y pense*, together with 'two irradiated stars of Brunswick, military flags and ensigns, wreaths of laurel, scrolls'.

A grand effort was made for the wedding of Princess Alexandra to the Prince of Wales. For the previous week the gas companies had been 'economising gas, and the street lamps were not lighted till long after the usual time...Circulars...were sent round...asking that the inhabitants would burn as little gas as possible inside, in order that there might be enough to supply the innumerable jets which were to blaze on the outside of their houses.' The results amply justified the scrimping. The dome of St Paul's was given 'a fiery coronet', while its base was surrounded by a ring of yellow lamps, with the supporting pillars having 'a ring of red lamps'. In addition to these gas illuminations, limelight was projected onto the dome, so that 'from a distance, the high fires darted out rays...and the streams of light thrown upon the building looked like the water forced from a fire-engine'.* The most spectacular displays in the City were at the Mansion House, the Bank and the Royal Exchange buildings. The Mansion House had strung lamps along all its cornices and pediments, as well as five large gas stars, and its columns were covered with crimson cloth, with illuminated swags of flowers hanging between the columns.

* Limelight was more commonly used in theatres for special effects. It was created by burning off the calcium in lime, which gave a red flame; when oxygen was mixed in, the gases together gave off an incandescent light.

At the Royal Exchange a row of lights ran along the pediments, 'and its columns [were] twined by thousands of small oil lamps of various colours'. The effect was enhanced by oil lamps spelling out: 'The earth is the Lord's, and the fulness thereof' in coloured lights. The West End did not lag behind. The National Gallery began with Prince of Wales feathers, moving on to a more ambitious transparency of two medallion portraits, with 'two guardian angels crowning them with wreaths' and a star of St George made of crystal, surmounted by a series of mottoes: 'Long Life to the Prince and Princess of Wales!' and 'England's Hope!' in 'amber-coloured crystal glass'. In addition the fountains in Trafalgar Square were lit by that dazzling new technology, 'the electric light, which was also at intervals directed upon the Nelson Monument'. That night the streets were so densely crowded by people out to see the illuminations that it was almost impossible to walk through them, and Hungerford Bridge was closed at six that evening, for fear it would collapse. All night there were 'dead locks' of pedestrians, 'during which no one progressed more than a dozen yards in an hour'.

Public events were celebrated by massive illuminations on public buildings and private houses alike. Here the Ordnance Office in Pall Mall marks the end of the Crimean War in 1856 with flags, an illuminated Order of the Garter and a giant VR, for Victoria Regina.

This physical impasse was not unprecedented. When Leonard Wyon set off with his wife from their house in St John's Wood to see the illuminations in the West End that marked the end of the Crimean War, they too had difficulty walking: 'the crowd was so great, and the carriages so thickly packed in Oxford Street that we could not cross the road without going a good deal out of the way.' They were deeply impressed by the illuminations on public buildings and on the mansions that lined Park Lane, including one that required 2,000 feet of gas a minute to light the coat of arms encircled with gas jets and the façade's eighteen pillars 'decorated with spiral twists and flags of all nations'. Even the railway stations were decorated, one having 'a beading of gas running along the top and sides of the principal face of the [station], with a monster reflecting star in the centre'. In Lincoln's Inn Fields, three large transparencies showed the Allies attacking Sebastopol, with the word 'Peace' next to the coats of arms of England and the Allies. A shopkeeper in the Strand proudly boasted a transparency that read:

MAY THE
DESTROYERS OF PEACE
BE DESTROYED BY US.
TIFFIN & SON,
BUG-DESTROYERS TO HER MAJESTY.

While individual choices were made by each resident or shopkeeper, the decision to illuminate at all came from the top. The end of the siege of Sebastopol in 1855 had led to many houses being decorated, but, admonished the *Illustrated London News* severely, 'this was not by any means general; no intimation having been given that any external marks of rejoicing on the part of the people would at present be expected'. Later in the week, the French ambassador's residence 'was splendidly illuminated' with 10,000 lamps, even though 'the order for illumination was not given until half-past six in the evening'.

When they first heard about the illuminations, Wyon and his wife had bought 'half a dozen French Lanterns' to tie to their balcony before they realized that only 'people of note' were obliged to join in. The danger must have been one factor – those vast quanitites of gas in temporary pipes cannot have been entirely safe; the cost another; and, finally, a heartfelt cry in *The Times* suggested that many people did not want to participate. 'Mr. (with the consent and approbation of Mrs.) GLASS' wrote in to say:

> I have not met with a single person in society who has not spoken of the illumination of private houses as a nuisance, which no one would incur if it were not for the fear of a stone through his drawing-room window… I rest my appeal on the absolute nastiness of smoke, grease, and gas… I agree most willingly to my share in the cost…of the public illuminations. I am perfectly willing, if any public or parochial boards will undertake to exhibit supplementary fireworks or transparencies in the open spaces of each quarter of the town, to be rated or to subscribe for that purpose; but I object, with all my heart, to be coerced into a piece of domestic dirt and discomfort.

On the one hand were the people in the street, public entertainment and street theatre; on the other, 'domestic dirt and discomfort'. In nineteenth-century London, there was no competition: the street won every time.

14.

STREET VIOLENCE

Entertainment and street theatre often met and, when they did, the result could be violent. Not all violence was condemned and suppressed by the state and its authorities. In fact, some violence was state-sanctioned; nor was it even seen as violence, but as the individual's just deserts. Some cruelties only gradually came to be seen as such: as the norms of behaviour and personal interaction changed, so what had been acceptable at one end of the century appeared shocking at the other.

In 1836, Dickens wrote 'The Great Winglebury Duel', presenting duelling as a relic from the past, a matter for farcical treatment – mistaken identities, runaway marriages and all. But even as he wrote, newspapers from time to time reported on duels still occurring. In 1842, two men from genteel St John's Wood trekked out to Putney Heath for a duel over a political disagreement. Both were wounded, but there was no hint of censure in the report of the incident, one magazine even calling it an 'affair of honour'. In the following year, an Anti-Duelling Association was formed, aiming to see 'the disgraceful practice' 'speedily exploded', but six weeks later two officers fought a duel in Camden Town and one died. The ensuing investigation produced an interesting set of mixed signals. The inquest found that the duellist had been murdered by his opponent; the seconds and the attending doctor were charged with murder in the second degree. Yet after a series of trials, only the duellist was convicted, with the jury giving a strong recommendation for mercy. This was endorsed by the judge, who even as he passed the death sentence assured the prisoner that it would not be carried out.

As late as 1869, what was in effect an upper-class brawl was treated as another affair of honour. Lord Carrington 'horsewhipped, or something like it', a man for writing a scurrilous article about Carrington's father. Carrington was charged with both common assault and for challenging the writer to a duel. Despite this, public opinion was obviously with him, and while he was found guilty of the assault, it was 'under circumstances of the greatest provocation'. He was merely bound over to keep the peace for a year, on his own recognizance. Four months after the conviction, in a sign of how the establishment regarded the incident, the Prince of Wales made a highly public visit to Carrington's country house. Yet at the same time, the lower orders found that their violent behaviour was seen as less acceptable. A few months before Carrington carried out his horsewhipping, a licensed victualler was charged with assaulting a policeman who had stopped him for furious driving. He was given two weeks' imprisonment, with hard labour, although the newspaper noted that, not that long before, he would have been let off with a minimal fine. This type of force, except for grandees, was now harshly punished.

This was a great change from the early years of the century, when mob rule was far more visible in the streets, beginning with the literally theatrical, and mostly non-violent, protests, the Old Price Riots. Covent Garden theatre had burnt down in 1808; when the new theatre opened in 1809, it was discovered that the galleries and pit – the lower-priced areas – had been reduced in extent to create more seating for the prosperous, while ticket prices had been raised throughout. On the first night, the noise from the pit and galleries was so loud that nothing at all could be heard of the performance above drumming feet and voices shouting, 'Old prices!' On subsequent nights, the demonstrations, both inside and outside the theatre, became more vehement, more focused and more purely theatrical, as the participants began to sing Old Price songs and dance the Old Price dance, stamping their feet and banging their sticks in tempo. A coffin bearing the epitaph 'Here lies the body of the New Price' was paraded through the streets and into the theatre. The manager, John Philip Kemble, hired Daniel Mendoza, the retired pugilist, to restore order. This was a major error, raising the emotional temperature and pushing the previously good-tempered crowds towards mayhem. After more than a month of performances where all the theatre took place in the auditorium, Kemble had the Riot Act read one night to disperse the audience.* This was another misjudgement, producing even greater fury as well as even less likelihood that the demonstrators would permit performances to proceed. It was another month before Kemble admitted defeat and returned to the old prices, whereupon the crowds held up a gracious banner: 'We are Satisfied.'

The Old Price riots, taking place at one of London's two patent theatres, attracted attention, but riotous assembly was not uncommon. What were called riots by those in authority were often just street brawls, sometimes organized as an accepted form of channelling popular aggression. In 1821, in St Giles, about 200 people assembled, 'armed with sticks and other weapons…each party being decorated with distinguishing colours'. They set on each other with a will; one side was gradually pushed back towards High Holborn before regrouping and in turn forcing its opponents back into St Giles. The two groups then made an unspoken alliance and turned on the parish watchmen who, with twenty flurried assistants, had been sent to deal with the problem. It took the Bow Street patrol – the precursors to the police – to charge with swords drawn, taking thirteen into custody, before the crowd dispersed, clearly feeling a good day had been had by all – or by all but the four dead and the twenty wounded badly enough to require hospitalization.

Some gangs were more permanently constituted and more focused on gain. In 1826, a gang of marauders gathered (and possibly lived) near a brickfield in Spitalfields, preying on the drovers on the road to Smithfield and Barnet markets, singling out and stealing prize cattle. Their looting was serious enough to be discussed in Parliament, with the Secretary of State questioning whether the men were 'distressed weavers' – the highly skilled silk weavers who had inhabited Bethnal Green for centuries who had recently been reduced to poverty by the lifting of import bans on luxury goods at the end of the French wars. The Spitalfields gangs were

* Now only an idiom, the Riot Act of 1715 was a legal formula used to break up 'tumults and riotous assemblies'. A strict procedure had to be followed: the Act had to be read aloud to those whom the officials wished to disperse, using a set form of words. The crowd then had one hour to leave the area, and no force was permitted until that hour had elapsed.

not weavers, although violence from them was not unusual either. In 1829, two men who had been hired to repossess some silk from a weaver felt it necessary to ask the patrol to accompany them. They were right to be afraid: they were followed by over 500 men, and when they repossessed the goods, 'bricks, stones, and whatever came to hand, were showered' on them. Even though they were greatly outnumbered by the outraged mob, which extended halfway down Bethnal Green Road, the patrol foolishly drew their weapons. They were immediately surrounded and themselves had to be rescued from the crowd of angry, semi-starving men.

In the late 1820s and early 1830s, riots became less random outbreaks of unfocused rage and more, as with the weavers, a desire to express a political and social point. Their being linked with these earlier outbreaks, however, permitted the perception that all political gatherings of the working classes were potential riots. Even so, the formation of Robert Peel's Metropolitan Police force in 1829 improved matters: no longer were armed soldiers brought out at the first intimation of danger. In November 1830, a political rally was held in Blackfriars Road. After the speeches, the crowd raised a flag with 'Reform' painted on it. To the cry of 'Now for the West End!' a thousand men, shouting 'Reform', 'Down with the police', 'No Peel' and 'No Wellington', crossed Blackfriars Bridge and surged down Fleet Street and the Strand, heading for Parliament. As they reached Downing Street, the New Police caught up with the action, forming a line at the end of King Street, to prevent the men reaching the Houses of Parliament. The novelty lay in the fact that this force, armed only with truncheons, could disperse crowds without resorting to killing.

Four months later, public expressions of anger were refocused. As cholera ravaged the city, the government nominated 21 March 1831 as a national Day of Fasting and Humiliation, when prayers would be offered and a twenty-four-hour fast observed as a sign of submission to divine will, in the hope that this would lift the epidemic. The Political Union of the Working Classes, representing the economic group that was bearing the brunt of the epidemic, issued a counter-proclamation, announcing 'their intention to distinguish that day by the distribution of bread and meat amongst the lower orders': as they so sharply pointed out, fasting was something they did all too routinely. By 11 a.m., nearly 15,000 workers, 'many of whom appeared to be in the greatest possible distress', had gathered in Finsbury Square, and three hours later the number had grown to 25,000. The plan had been to 'perambulate in procession into different parts of the metropolis', but the very fact of the gathering was considered dangerous, and the police were out in force, determined to clear the square and prevent the march, even though there had been few signs of incipient trouble.

This political response to the epidemic was unusual. Far more common were outbursts, even violent ones, aimed at medical personnel, for the epidemic had produced a strong link in the public mind between doctors and what were known as resurrection men. Over the previous decades, medical schools had expanded, while the supply of cadavers for study remained finite. Only the corpses of executed criminals were legally available for dissection, leaving most medical schools unable to teach anatomy or surgery. Resurrection men had therefore prospered by digging up freshly buried bodies to sell to the schools. In the first decade of the century, Joseph Naples, an ex-gravedigger and a member of a south London gang of resurrectionists, most unusually kept a diary, which showed how profitable the trade was. On 14 January 1812, he wrote: 'went to St Luke's [church graveyard and disinterred] 2 adults…1 large and 1 small, took them to barthow [St Bartholomew's Hospital]. Came home and went to St Thomas' [Hospital], afterwards went to the other end of town for orders.' The gang then met 'at the Hartichoak' pub, to divide their takings: £8 4s 7½d to each gang member, or about four months' income for a street seller. In 1831, two men who were tried for the murder of an Italian street boy admitted that they had sold more than 500 bodies to the London hospitals in the previous decade.

The 1832 Anatomy Act was passed in order to shut down this thriving business. Now medical schools were entitled to claim for dissection any bodies that were to be buried at the parish expense – in effect, the bodies of paupers, or the working poor whose families could not afford a funeral. By this Act, many thought, anatomization had been transformed from being a punishment for capital crime into being a punishment for poverty. When the first wave of cholera arrived simultaneously with the change in the law, some believed that this new disease was a pretext to lure the unwary poor to hospital, where they would be killed as a precursor to being anatomized. In June 1832, a hospital porter was attacked in Oxford Street as he carried a man dying of cholera to hospital; police were needed to disperse the crowd. On the same day, a woman was assaulted when bringing a patient to the Lime Street cholera hospital, the infuriated mob baying 'Burker!' at her.* Later a surgeon making a house call in Vauxhall was attacked; when the parish surgeon arrived after the patient's death, he found that the body had been hidden, for fear it would be taken for anatomization. Those gathered outside whispered that he and his colleagues 'merely wanted to get the poor into their clutches to burke them', and once more the police were called. Sala remembered as a child watching a similar incident from his nursery window in North Audley Street. One of the Earl of Clarendon's servants had died of cholera and 'a great crowd' had gathered before the earl's door, all 'violent and clamorous... My nurse says that they will have to send for the "padroll" with "cutlashes".'†

These small, irregular outbreaks were dealt with as isolated episodes, just as earlier street violence had been, but political protest continued to alarm the authorities. In April 1848, the Chartist Convention organized a mass meeting on Kennington Common, where the workers were to congregate before marching on Parliament to present a petition of nearly 2 million signatures from supporters of political reform. Even children were aware of the middle-class fear of popular disorder. Sophia Beale, aged about seven, recorded two days before the meeting: 'There is to be a great meeting of Chartists the day after tomorrow on Kenington Common. every one is very excited and peple are being made into speshal cunstabels... not papa because he is a docter and... if any one is shot he will have to bind them up. Papa is

* 'Burker' had become a term of abuse for any resurrectionist, although Burke and his partner Hare, were murderers rather than resurrectionists. Between November 1827 and 31 October 1828 William Burke and William Hare murdered sixteen or seventeen people in Edinburgh before selling their bodies to Dr Robert Knox's anatomy school.

† Sala very possibly did see this; it sounds as if he did. However, the 'nurse' and his 'nursery' appear to be adult inventions to make his background more middle-class: his mother was a singer and dancer and only just eked out a living.

going to take me to see the cannons tomorrow so good bye.' The next day, 'We went to the Common this morning but there was nothing to see. Papa talked to a polliceman and he said there were some big guns in some of the back yards and garden so we came home to tea and ever body thinks they will fight tomorrow out there on the Common.' In the event, while 100,000 'speshal cunstabels' were sworn in to prevent the protestors crossing the river, the 150,000 or so who gathered held a peaceful meeting on the Common, with the leadership taking the petition separately after the event.

It is noticeable in retrospect that, by the late 1840s and 1850s, what were termed 'riots' were generally nothing of the kind and were more likely merely large crowds with something on their minds. The earlier violence had to a great extent vanished. The Hyde Park riots over the ultra-Sabbatarian legislation were a prime example, only seven years after the Great Chartist meeting. In 1855, Lord Robert Grosvenor and others attempted to push a bill through the House of Commons to ban the Sunday selling of refreshments in places of amusement. This was widely seen as one law for the rich (whose servants worked on Sundays and whose clubs were open on Sundays) and another for the poor (whose single day of leisure was to be curbed). A demonstration was organized in Hyde Park. On the first Sunday the protestors stood along Rotten Row, waiting for the carriages of the fashionable and greeting them with 'loud hissing and groaning, accompanied by deafening cries of "Go to church!" "Why do you allow your servants to work on Sunday?" "Shame on you!" "Down with the Sabbatarians!"' One woman stood up in her carriage, holding her prayer book aloft to indicate her church-going, but its sole effect was to make the protestors shout, 'Walk, walk, and let your horses rest, and your coachman go to church!' Several people were forced out of their carriages and had to walk home, but there was nothing worse. As with Sophia Beale and her father on Kennington Common, many perfectly respectable middle-class people found the mass protest a matter of almost touristic interest. Leonard Wyon noted in his journal that 'a disturbance was expected ... [so] May [his wife] and I walked to Hyde Park in the evening, but everything seemed quite quiet.' The Wyons were an intensely respectable pair – they were sober, industrious, went to church twice every Sunday and then discussed the sermons afterwards. Furthermore, May was prone to panic attacks. Nonetheless they visited Hyde Park specifically to see a 'disturbance'.

Even *The Times*, that establishment paper, was with the workers, calling the proposed law 'unequal and onesided' and claiming that it 'interfered with the comforts and recreations of the working classes' while leaving the wealthy to do as they liked. The single episode of violence came the following week, when crowds once more assembled to hoot and jeer. Immediately they did so, 'the police rushed out from their ambuscades, and made unsparing use of their truncheons on every persons within their reach'. Even when the protestors scattered, the police continued to chase them, driving them into the Serpentine and indiscriminately sweeping up many unrelated passers-by out for their Sunday walks. This description of a police-sanctioned assault was unusual only in that it was a newspaper report, not fiction. Dickens had for some time expressed his ambivalence about unruly mobs and authority's response. In the late 1830s, in *Nicholas Nickleby*, he portrayed a meeting in the City, where 'the sterner spirits' barracked the speaker, stamping on the floor and shouting. A policeman 'immediately began to drag forth...all the quiet people...at the same time dealing out various smart and tingling blows with their truncheons, after the manner of that ingenious actor, Mr Punch: whose brilliant example, both in the fashion of his weapons and their use, this branch of the executive occasionally follows'.

This was only a decade after the old system of parish watchmen – which Dickens had grown up with – had been replaced by the police. Dickens soon became their ardent supporter, but his own background on the fringes of the lower middle classes meant that he always had a corner, sometimes quite a large corner, of distrust for petty authority. This was not unreasonable. The pre-1829 system had been notably corrupt. The notebook owned by the (also notably corrupt) magistrate Sir John Silvester contained a list of receivers of stolen goods. Several entries say a receiver 'is or lately was' an officer, while a 'well known Fence' is listed as having lived for fifteen years as the tenant of a 'Sheriffs Officer'. A second list suggests that receivers were a fact of life across the city and across social classes, including as it does goldsmiths, weavers, the widow of a Newgate turnkey and the 'watchman

[at] the corner of Cow Lane'. A separate page, which may (or may not) be a continuation of that list, includes a law stationer, two attorneys, a lieutenant in the East India Company, his servant, a lottery-office keeper, 'Smith [who] belongs to Chancery [court or bar]', a baronet, and 'Sir Brook Boothby memb. for Co. Stafford'.

In 1837–9, Dickens immortalized his distrust of officialdom in *Oliver Twist*, with his depiction of Fang, the magistrate, who was easily recognized by contemporaries as a portrait of Allan Stewart Laing, a Hatton Garden police magistrate notorious both for the savagery of his sentencing and for his intemperate outbursts. In the novel Fang has one street beggar arrested 'for playing the flute', just as Laing once had a muffin man arrested for ringing his bell. In 1838, a doctor accidentally bumped into Laing in the street and the magistrate assaulted him before having him arrested. Arresting doctors was a very different matter from arresting muffin men, so Laing's services were dispensed with. Two decades on, Fang had another real-life double, when in the Sabbatarian riots an ecclesiastical agent was caught up in the arrests. When he came up before the magistrate he was refused a hearing, as was his character witness, a barrister and the editor of the *Civil Service Gazette*.

For there was a curious attitude to petty crime. It was generally believed in middle-class society that crime was a constant, bubbling under, always waiting to erupt; at the same time, the pettiness of petty crime was visible to all, as was the fact that most thefts were undertaken purely for survival. A Select Committee on the Police heard testimony in 1816 that there were 'above two hundred regular flash-houses in the metropolis' – places where stolen goods were received and where the residents divided 'the plunder of the day', before 'sally[ing] forth from these houses to rob in the streets'. Yet the detail of the same report suggests nothing of the sort. One of these master criminals was a coster-woman who sold goods from a basket on the street, paying children a penny or two for stolen handkerchiefs, which she then pawned to buy stock for her basket. Another was a woman near Wigmore Street who 'buys chiefly Brushes, Pails, Coal-skuttles [sic], &c., which little Boys sneak from Gentlemen's Houses, down the areas and at the doors'.

Similarly, dog theft was spoken of as a highly lucrative criminal industry. In the late 1810s, one memoirist said that men 'leading poodles fantastically trimmed' haunted the Queen's Head pub in Chiswell Street (as Beech Street this is now the fluorescent-lit tunnel beside the Barbican Centre). The pub was said to be the nexus of a nationwide dog-theft underworld, where dogs that had been stolen in the countryside were brought to be sold, while dogs stolen in London were shipped from there to the country, so that no stolen dog was ever again seen near its home. This may have been the case, but if Jane Carlyle's experiences were anything to go by, things had changed radically in the intervening decades. Jane and Thomas Carlyle lived in Chelsea, by the river, and Jane's dog Nero was stolen twice in 1851: 'mercifully it was near home that he was twitched up...and the lads who are all *in my pay* for odd jobs – rushed out to look for him and stopt the man who had him till I came up and put my thumb firmly inside his collar...he said [he] had *found* the dog...and...I would surely "give him a trifle for his *trouble*"!! and I was cowardly enough to give him *twopence* to rid Nero and myself of his dangerous proximity.' Even after this, her husband believed that 'There is a large Fraternity...who live by stealing Dogs, chiefly women's, and selling them back at a ransom. I have heard some big sum, £10,000 I think, mentioned as their annual income from this fine act.' A lot of dogs, surely, would have to be 'twitched up' at 2d per dog to reach an income of £10,000.

Low-level crime remained a reality for much of the first half of the century, with the same causes, and the same perpetrators – the hungry poor, often children.* Nightly in Covent Garden, as Little Dorritt crossed the piazza, she saw 'the miserable children in rags...[who] like young rats, slunk and hid, fed on offal [refuse, or market waste], huddled together for warmth, and were hunted about'. These youngsters were little different from the sixteen-year-old prostitute interviewed by Mayhew, who had been on her own from the age of ten and had stolen 'cats' and 'kittens' – the pint and half-pint pots that were left on house-railings for the pubs – to

* As late as the 1850s the age of criminal responsibility was seven, compared to sixteen in France at the same time. Now ten in England and Wales, it remains among the lowest in Europe, where it ranges from fourteen to sixteen.

survive. In another interview a pickpocket told Mayhew how well he had done in a crowd at a double execution: he took, he said, a purse with 2s in it, and two handkerchiefs; at a fire he had stolen handkerchiefs worth 2s 3d and three pairs of gloves, worth 4d. Fires and executions were known to be particularly good spots for thieving, although this apparently noteworthy haul of, at most, a few shillings' worth of goods in a prime location puts into perspective the type of journalism that assured its readers that petty thieves were making over £100 a year, the wages of a well-employed clerk. John Silvester's notebooks instead make clear how little was earned from thieving, at least early in the century: Mr Baker, of One Tun Court, off the Strand, 'Keeps a Drag [a wheel-less cart] & lets it out to Thieves to convey Stolen Property'; Mr Garratt of Moor Street, Soho Square, rented out housebreaking tools; while Mr Zachariah Philips in White Hart Yard, Drury Lane, 'Lends out Pistols…by the Night at so much for their use'. There were criminals who earned so little they could not afford their own tools of their trades.

The police were not, however, misled by media sensationalism, concentrating doggedly on routine policing. One tourist heard a policeman say to a boy in the street: 'My lad, you have been here five minutes, looking at those goods, it is time you were off.' As Dickens went out on the beat with them, he saw how they spent much of their time 'push[ing] at doors; to try fastenings; to be suspicious of bundles' – the daily minutiae of low-level pilfering. River crime, which sounded so exciting, was equally trifling. The Thames River Police had ninety-eight men patrolling from Battersea to Barking Creek as 'a police of prevention', against tier-rangers, who crept onto boats at night and 'groped for the skippers' inexpressibles' [trousers], taking their 'watch, money, braces, boots and all'; lumpers, or unskilled labourers, who unloaded the ships and smuggled ashore small items, usually tobacco, for the crews; dredgermen, employed to unload barges, who threw stolen items overboard, dredging them up later while pretending to search for dropped bits of coal. These were the major thefts; the minor ones were of stolen 'copper nails, sheathing, hardwood, &c.', carried away by workmen to sell to marine-store dealers.

❧

Punishment for these crimes was visible in the street too. The centre of London itself, the point that marked the separation of the City and the West End, was Temple Bar. By the nineteenth century this was the one surviving gate marking the old City boundaries, the other seven – Aldgate, Aldersgate, Bishopsgate, Cripplegate, Ludgate, Moorgate and Newgate – having been demolished long before. It had also been the final destination for the heads of traitors, impaled on spikes and left to rot in full sight of the populace as a warning. Those who had been found guilty of involvement in the Jacobite uprising of 1745 were the last to be impaled, remnants of their heads surviving for decades, well within living memory at the beginning of the nineteenth century. Dickens, in *A Tale of Two Cities*, called the display one of 'an insensate brutality and ferocity'. These were, he wrote bitterly, 'those good old customs of the good old times which made England, even so recently as in the reign of the Third King George, in respect of her criminal code and prison regulations, one of the most bloody-minded and barbarous countries on the earth'.

While heads were no longer displayed for public amusement and edification, other forms of state-endorsed violence survived the arrival of the new century and were visible on the streets. One was the public pillorying of criminals. The pillory was an upright pole raised on a platform, having a cross-piece with holes in it for the victim's arms and head. 'The board moved on a pivot, and...the poor terrified delinquent...was required to perambulate round and round.' Today the perception of the pillory is that it was punishment by public humiliation. In fact, it was a punishment of both mental degradation and acute physical danger.

In 1810, the occupants of the White Swan, a gay brothel or molly-house, in Vere Street, Clare market, were arrested.* At the subsequent trial, six

* The White Swan is generally referred to as a brothel, that is, a place where a proprietor or hired supervisor controls resident prostitutes, collecting fees and paying the sex-workers either a percentage or a salary. But from the description that comes down to us it sounds as though it might have been an accommodation house, a place where rooms were rented for short periods of time to anyone who appeared: professional sex-workers or couples simply wanting a private space. For more on heterosexual accommodation houses, see pp. 411–2. Whatever type of house it was, a contemporary author claimed there were many similar houses in the Strand, in Blackman Street, in the Borough, near the Obelisk, at

men were found guilty of attempted sodomy and sentenced to the pillory, followed by penal servitude. On the day, 'All the windows and even the very roofs of the houses were crowded with persons.' Boys lined the route with cartloads of dung and supplies from the local slaughterhouses; 'a number of fishwomen attended with stinking flounders and the entrails of other fish'. At 12.30 the sheriff and City marshals appeared at the head of 100 mounted constables and 100 foot patrol. The men were taken in an open cart from Old Bailey Yard, beside Newgate, and swiftly received 'The first salute', 'a volley of mud, and a serenade of hisses, hooting, and execration', so that after a few yards they 'resembled bears dipped in a stagnant pool'. All the way along Fleet Street and the Strand, 'Dead cats and dogs, offal, potatoes, turnips, &c.' were flung at them with force.

At one o'clock the procession reached the Haymarket, where the men were placed in the pillory as the howling mob circled and bayed, continuing to pelt the prisoners with ordure. After an hour four of the men were removed to Coldbath Fields prison; the other two had been sentenced to an additional hour because of previous convictions. They were both barely conscious when they came to be released. This was not unusual, and they might even be said to have been fortunate. Some of those pilloried were blinded by flying stones, while in 1815 a man died in the pillory, causing MPs to call for its abolition. (However, this was not because of, or not entirely because of, the fatality. What shocked them was the uncertainty of the punishment: when a publisher was sent to the pillory for publishing Thomas Paine's banned work, *The Age of Reason*, the crowd cheered him wildly, offering him food and drink.)

Although the pillory wasn't immediately abolished, after 1816 the punishment was confined to perjurers, and the violence subsided, perhaps because this crime aroused fewer passions. The journalist Henry Vizetelly remembered seeing someone in the pillory in front of Newgate one evening when he was young. Although the crowd seemed to him as big as for any execution, the people were for the most part 'more curious than vindictive', and

---

the intersection of Kennington Lane and Kennington Road, in the Inns of Court, and in Bishopsgate Street, in the City.

they obeyed the ban on 'missiles being thrown'. The last man to be pilloried in Britain was a fishmonger who fell into debt and perjured himself during his trial. When he stood in the pillory in June 1830, *The Times* noted that it had been twelve years since the pillory had last been used.

The pillory was a temporary wooden erection in the street. Far more formidable was the seemingly eternal great stone wall of Newgate, next to the Old Bailey, the Central Court of Criminal Justice. Given the looming presence of the prisons in the city, it is perhaps not surprising that many of the prisons had nicknames that were recognized by much of the population, for they were part of everyone's daily life. Pentonville, built along new lines, to reform rather than punish, was ridiculed as 'the Model'; Millbank was the Tench, from 'Penitentiary'; Horsemonger Lane gaol was either the Lane or, more poetically, the Old Horse; Tothill Fields was, for some inscrutable reason, the Tea Garden; Clerkenwell was the Wells; and Coldbath Fields was the Steel, short for 'Bastille'. Newgate was known, from the eighteenth century, as the Stone Jug. And stone was the predominating element, its façade unpierced by any windows, with one 'small, black, iron-studded door...low and narrow as the entrance to a vaulted grave'. It was, said one twentieth-century architectural historian, 'an extraordinary building...a great Palace of Retribution'.

This was the place where the ultimate public state-sanctioned violence occurred: execution. Prisons and death were firmly linked. In the 1840s, one journalist wrote that the current slang word for 'prison' was 'sturbon', from '*gestorben*', German for dead, hence a place of execution. (A more likely derivation is from the Romany '*stariben*'; whichever the origin, 'sturbon' is the source of the word 'stir' for prison.) From 1784, London executions were held either outside Newgate, in the City of London, or in front of Horsemonger Lane gaol in Southwark (Horsemonger Lane is now Harper Road): in both cases, in the middle of densely populated neighbourhoods. Among connoisseurs of executions, it was considered that the crowds at Horsemonger Lane had the better view, as the prison had a specially built gallows on the roof. The scaffold at Newgate was not as easily viewed from the small clearing in front of the gaol, but viewers felt closer to events.

Newgate was just yards from Smithfield and not much further from St Paul's. 'There, at the very core of London, in the heart of its business and animation...upon the very spot on which the vendors of soup and fish and damaged fruit are now plying their trades – scores of human beings...have been hurried violently and swiftly from the world.' This was Dickens writing in the late 1830s, although he never became more used to either the idea or the actuality of public executions. In 1840, he attended an execution for the first time, when a valet, Benjamin-François Courvoisier, was hanged for the murder of his master. Dickens, who watched, sickened, among the crowd, thought he had spent 'a ghastly night in Hades with the demons'.

Dickens, like many middle-class commentators, often wrote of the crowds who witnessed the executions as though they were all criminals and vagrants, but that does not appear to have been the case. Nearly half a century earlier, in 1807, thirty people were killed in a crush at one execution, and the inquest listed their occupations. They included 'a respectable

Execution days at Newgate brought crowds so vast to the narrow City streets that for many the scaffold dwindled to a small element in the distance.

gentleman' (that is, a middle-class man of means), an apprentice piano manufacturer, a wine merchant's son and a shoemaker's child. Among the wounded were a tavern keeper, a pieman, a porter, a weaver, a brush maker, a carpenter's apprentice and a butcher's child – a good cross-section of the London streets. In the 1840s, Thackeray also attended an execution, writing later that the bystanders came from 'all ranks and degrees – mechanics, gentlemen, pickpockets, members of both Houses of Parliament, street-walkers, newspaper-writers... dandies, with mustachios and cigars... family parties of simple honest tradesmen and their wives'.

Until 1836, the condemned were executed forty-eight hours after their conviction, unless a Sunday intervened, in which case the hanging was seventy-two hours later. After this date, more time was allowed for legal arguments to be heard if there was a liklihood of clemency, or if there were petitions for mercy, or, later, if appeals were planned. Executions were traditionally held outside Newgate or Horsemonger Lane gaol on Monday mornings at eight. For crimes that had captured the public imagination, preparation might begin days before the execution. For the double execution of Maria and Frederick Manning in November 1849, convicted of the murder of her lover, landlords near Horsemonger Lane gaol erected scaffolding on their buildings overlooking the gallows to create additional seating. The police cleared the area in front of the gaol three full days before the hanging, putting up barricades and blocking off streets to prevent a repeat of those deaths by overcrowding.

The gallows was traditionally erected during the night before the execution, and crowds milled around, shouting encouragement or derision, depending on the attitude towards the convicted, while street sellers and pubs supplied their wants. In 1836, before the execution of James Greenacre, convicted of killing and dismembering his washerwoman fiancée, and scattering her in sections across London, the appearance of the scaffold 'was hailed with three cheers of deafening applause'. This was repeated when the great transverse beam was raised and yet again when the noose was put up. Throughout the night before each Newgate execution, the bell of St Sepulchre tolled for the dead man before he had died. Fagin listens to it from the condemned cell with 'despair. The boom of every iron bell came laden with the one deep hollow sound – Death.'* By six o'clock on an execution morning, the open space in front of the prison was thronged with bystanders, as were the surrounding streets, every window and every rooftop having been hired out long before. For the execution of the Mannings, Dickens and his friends paid ten guineas ('extremely moderate', in Dickens' view) for a rooftop vantage point.

After the French Revolution, the number of crimes punishable by death, and the consequent number of executions, had risen sharply. Prompted by fear of the mob, of the returning, now unemployed, soldiers, and of the unruly working classes, the number of people hanged in the thirty years between 1800 and 1830 was double the figure for those executed in the previous half-century. In 1837, the year of *Oliver Twist*, as well as the year Victoria came to the throne, 438 death sentences were passed in Britain. And in that novel, just as in that year, it seemed to be a subliminal idea in the minds of many of the middle-class upholders of the Poor Law that hanging was the natural fate of the poor. When Oliver asks for 'more', the Poor Law Guardian says, 'That boy will be hung... I know that boy will be hung'; and when Oliver is apprenticed, his master 'felt a strange presentiment from the very first, that that audacious young savage would come to be hung!'

However, 1837 was the peak, and a greatly exaggerated peak. Two years later the number of death sentences passed in Britain had declined by nearly 90 per cent, to just fifty-six. This was not because of establishment repugnance for the death penalty, but rather because those at risk of being victims

* Dickens' depiction of Fagin in the condemned cell on the night before his execution was artistic licence. By 1837, the year *Oliver Twist* began serialization, the only crimes punishable by death were high treason, murder, attempted murder, arson on inhabited premises, wrecking (causing a shipwreck), piracy, rape and 'unnatural offences', while Fagin was a receiver of stolen goods, for which the punishment was transportation. Isaac (Ikey) Solomon, on whom it has long been thought Dickens may have in part based Fagin, was found guilty of receiving at the Old Bailey in 1830, and transported to Van Diemen's Land (Tasmania). However, recently a more interesting possibility has emerged: Dickens may well have used someone even closer to home as his model for the Jewish fence. His maternal aunt had married into a Jewish family (it was her stepson who gave the young Charles work at the blacking factory), and in 1825 her husband's cousin-by-marriage, Henry Worms, was convicted of receiving stolen goods and transported, like Fagin and like Solomon, to Van Diemen's Land.

of property crime – the rich and the business classes – realized that juries were refusing to convict because of the harshness of the penalties. The number of crimes punishable by death was reduced, with transportation or penal servitude being imposed instead, in order to increase the number of guilty verdicts. From that time, the number of executions steadily decreased. Attending them, however, reached the height of its popularity from the late 1840s to the early 1860s: scarcity drove demand. As the century progressed, this was compounded by the railways, which enabled more people, from a wider area, to travel to see the fun; and by the spread of cheap newspapers, attracting more readers by drumming up interest in each crime. When the crowds were mixed and the events popular, their festival air disturbed many. A snippet of dialogue from Punch and Judy captures well the grisly good temper of many execution assemblies with its cheerful disregard for authority:

> LORD CHIEF JUSTICE: Hollo! Punch, my boy!
> PUNCH: Hollo! Who are you with your head like a cauliflower?...
> LORD CHIEF JUSTICE: You're a murderer, and you must come and be hanged.
> PUNCH: I'll be hanged if I do. [*Knocks down the Chief Justice and dances and sings.*]

Allowing for the exaggeration of a puppet show, it was demonstrably the case that this tone sometimes mirrored reality. In 1820, ten men were charged with conspiracy to assassinate the prime minister and his entire cabinet. It was said that the Cato Street conspirators, named for the street in Marylebone where they had met, had hoped to establish a 'Committee of Public Safety' modelled on the bloody French Revolutionary group that had sent so many to the guillotine less than three decades earlier. Ten men were found guilty and sentenced to be hanged, drawn (that is, eviscerated while still partially alive) and quartered (cut in four), as the statute book demanded for high treason. Five had their sentences commuted to transportation for life, but the other five were executed, their sentences being moderated to hanging and the beheading of their corpses. This was carried

In 1820, a plot to assassinate the entire cabinet was uncovered. When the conspirators were surprised in the loft where they met, a policeman was stabbed and killed. The day five of the men were executed – and subsequently beheaded – was one of Newgate's bloodiest.

out, on 1 May of that same year, in front of Newgate. Twenty years later Thackeray claimed that when the heads were held up to the huge gathering to show the fate that awaited all traitors, the executioner, his hands slippery with gore, fumbled the final head, at which a comedian in the crowd yelled, 'Butter-fingers!' – to the vast amusement of all. Indeed, the execution was a subject for jokes even before the event. When the fashionable fencing master Henry Angelo was in search of a window overlooking the scaffold, one landlord demanded a fee of one guinea. Angelo exclaimed: 'What! to see four men have their heads cut off? I'll give you half a crown a head.'*

More than anything else, it was jokes of this type that troubled many. Dickens was not against the death penalty, merely against the public levity that accompanied its enactment. After Courvoisier's execution, he wrote in the *Daily News*, 'From the moment of my arrival... down to the time when I saw the body with its dangling head, being carried on a wooden bier

* I can discover no reason for Angelo to refer to four men. Five were executed on 1 May 1820: Arthur Thistlewood, John Thomas Brunt, James Ings, William Davidson and Richard Tidd.

into the gaol – I did not see one token in all the immense crowd...of any one emotion suitable to the occasion...nothing but ribaldry, debauchery, levity, drunkenness, and flaunting vice.' This was not always the case: a great deal depended on who was being executed, and why. When the servant Eliza Fenning was hanged for attempted murder in 1815, the miscarriage of justice was so blatant that the working-class spectators, perhaps as many as 50,000 strong, stood, it was reported, in total silence as the victim in white appeared on the scaffold. But when the ex-lady's maid, Maria Manning, and her husband were executed at in 1849, greeted her with a raucous rendition of 'Oh Mrs Manning, don't you cry for me', sung to the tune of 'Oh Susannah'.

Thackeray, who had attended Courvoisier's execution too, wrote that 'I came away...that morning with a disgust for murder, but it was for *the murder I saw done*.' Two weeks later he still felt 'degraded at the brutal curiosity which took me to that brutal sight'. It is simplistic to present a picture of the savage unfeeling workers enjoying the sight of death, while the fastidious bourgeoisie recoiled. One upper-class man happily recalled an outing he and his friends had planned to the gallows as late as 1864, when they rented a window across from Newgate to watch the hangings of five men known as the 'Flowery Land pirates' (they had attacked a ship named the *Flowery Land*). These spectators were West End types, soldiers in fashionable regiments. On the day of the execution, they woke to morning-after-the-night-before headaches, grey skies and rain. Despite having paid possibly as much as fifty guineas for their window, they contemplated not going, until 'the sight of three or four cabs, a couple of servants, and a plentiful supply of provender decided the question, and the procession started'.* Food, drink, transport: their requirements were no different from those of the working-class onlookers.

As the century progressed, many of the middle and upper classes were likely to evince distaste, or shame, at least in public, at the mere notion

* If he recalled the price accurately, the cost of a rooftop spot had increased by 400 per cent from Dickens' rental in 1849. This may indicate how rarity drove prices up, although it may also be the memoirist's faulty recollection, or a desire to appear a big spender.

of executions, pillories and heads on spikes, which gradually ceased to be considered an acceptable part of city life. In 1819, a guidebook had highlighted Temple Bar as a place 'particularly *distinguished*' (my italics) by the 'exhibition of the heads of those who have been executed for treason'. By the 1839 edition, this was reduced to half a sentence in passing – 'The heads of persons executed for high treason were formerly exhibited on this gate' – before the authors hastened to focus on Temple Bar as the place where the City Corporation received the royal family on its visits to the City. Public displays of body parts were no longer something to promote to visitors.

The final public execution in Britain was not the fiesta that Courvoisier's or Mrs Manning's had been. The death of Michael Barrett took place against a background of the independence struggle in Ireland by the Fenians (named for the legendary Irish army, the Fianna). Richard O'Sullivan Burke, the Irish Republican Brotherhood's arms' agent in Britain, was arrested late in 1867. An escape plan was hatched to blast a hole in the wall of the Clerkenwell House of Correction, where Burke was being held; in the confusion, Burke was to make his escape. But the Home Office was tipped off by an informer and Burke was moved to a different part of the prison. Even now, the Fenians still had a chance, as the police had failed to act quickly enough to prevent their laying explosives. The rebels miscalculated the amount of gunpowder, however, and instead of a hole being neatly blown in one section of the wall, the whole thing was lifted from its foundations, while the façades of the entire row of houses across the road were ripped away like peel from an orange. And when the dazed conspirators peered through the gaping hole, they were confronted with armed guards taking up positions to defend the gaol. The Fenians scrambled away from the site of this humiliating debacle just as 3,000 Metropolitan police constables descended on the scene.

Six people had been killed by the blast, another six later died of their wounds, while 120 were seriously injured, with fifteen left permanently crippled. The bomb had plunged the streets into total darkness, and before any rescue attempts could begin, the paving had to be lifted to gain access to the gas mains. Fifty firemen and a regiment of the Household Guards, later joined by the Scots Fusiliers, worked all night, first putting out the blazes caused by burst gas mains and destroyed chimneys, then searching through the rubble for the dead and the injured, slightly hampered by sightseers. For as always, 'The streams of visitors, in spite of mud, and rain, and barriers, and walls of impassable police, have continued unabated...Corporation-lane was closed...although last night announcements were posted outside the end houses that the public would be admitted to them to view the ruins for sums varying from sixpence to a penny.' A greengrocer even set up a ladder so that people could peer over the hoardings to the destroyed prison wall: 'numbers of persons paid their money for the view'. Meanwhile, 'Photographers and artists were taking pictures and making sketches throughout the morning' for their newspapers and journals.

Michael Barrett was arrested in January 1868, along with five others. The Crown's case wasn't merely poor: it barely existed. One of the accused turned informer; another admitted on the witness stand that he was being paid by the police; against one of the accused, the Crown offered no evidence; against another, there was only the word of the informer. A single witness, the police informer, said he had seen Barrett in London on the day of the explosion, while several disinterested witnesses placed him in Glasgow at the relevant time. In the end, the jury found five not guilty, and Barrett guilty.

Fearing another Fenian rescue attempt at his execution, the police were armed with revolvers and cutlasses, rather than just truncheons, but, in the event, 'They never had easier work.' Surprisingly few turned out on 26 May 1868 to see what everyone knew would be the last public execution in Britain. Popular antipathy to such things was stronger than anti-Fenian outrage: one shopkeeper with premises overlooking the scaffold said 'he had not [fallen] so low as to let his windows to see a fellow creature strangled'. Some claimed that only 2,000 people were waiting at Newgate at dawn, in a gathering that was 'one of the smallest...that has for a long time assembled in front of the Old Bailey'. Most of the onlookers appeared to be respectable working men and tradesmen who had come because it was to be the last public execution, not for political reasons. So sparse was the assembly that some of the police, who had regularly done duty at Newgate and knew the '"hanging" crowds...as familiar acquaintances, were puzzled, and almost grieved'.

Yet the memory of Newgate as a place of violent public death lingered. The year after Barrett's execution, Dickens could still write that it was a setting of 'fire and fagot, condemned Hold, public hanging, whipping through the city at the cart-tail, pillory, branding-iron, and other beautiful ancestral landmarks'.

15.

THE RED-LIT STREETS TO DEATH

What struck most people on seeing London for the first – or the thousandth – time was its vastness, its unknowability, not merely in terms of its streets and buildings, but in terms of its people. Dickens referred to one of his characters in *Martin Chuzzlewit* as belonging to 'a race peculiar to the City; who are secrets as profound to one another, as they are to the rest of mankind'. Visitors from more sparsely populated nations felt this the most. Even if they lived in capital cities themselves, none was the size of London. One American wrote: 'How utterly lost a stranger feels in London. In the midst of that great mass of human life and activity, a stranger is perfectly alone', yet at the same time, 'No matter...how far he walks, he cannot get beyond the crowd.' In *A Tale of Two Cities*, the narrator, on entering 'a great city by night', considers how 'every one of those darkly clustered houses encloses its own secret...[and] every beating heart in the hundreds of thousands of breasts...is...a secret to the heart nearest'. Moreover, each stranger on the street was a secret, and London was filled with millions of strangers. Many of these strangers were women, going about lives that seemed incomprehensible to their fellow men. These women aroused fears by their number, as well as by their unknowability.

It cannot be stated too emphatically that we have *no* firm knowledge of the number of prostitutes on the streets of London for most of the nineteenth century. First, there is the question: what is a prostitute? Apart from a woman actively soliciting on the streets, does the term include a woman living with a man to whom she is not married, on a long-term, monogamous basis, who does not work and is supported by that man? Does it encompass a woman in employment, who intermittently or regularly is given additional cash by a long-term, or short-term, partner? Does it take into account a woman whose wages do not entirely support her, or who is temporarily out of work, who receives financial help from one or more men?* The rigid separation of 'good' and 'bad' women did not hold even according to Victorian morality. There were women who enjoyed a night-life that was not acceptable to moralists, but who pursued it for pleasure rather than money; equally, there were women in long-term relationships living in communities that traditionally did not resort to the church for sanctification. Many in the nineteenth century regarded any and all of these women as prostitutes. In *London Labour*, the widespread nature of this term could not be plainer: ballet girls, it was said, were 'in the habit of prostituting themselves when the occasion offers, either for money, or more frequently for their own gratification' – that is, they had sex outside marriage, which is not our definition of prostitution at all.

None of this stopped experts from attempting to enumerate the prostitutes of London as though they were a single, countable class. In 1791, the police magistrate Patrick Colquhoun had estimated (and it should be noted that he used the word 'estimate', as well as 'conjecture', although this element of doubt was later ignored) that there were 50,000 prostitutes in London. He then separated this figure into two groups, allowing that at least half were not what he called 'common prostitutes', by which he meant those who walked the streets soliciting. More than 25,000, he believed, were kept women, by which he meant those who fitted the commercial definition of this term, as well as those who lived with long-term partners outside wedlock. The remaining figure of 25,000 is still much higher than the police and court reports of the period indicate, yet by 1817, this was supposed to have soared to 80,000, although no source for it was ever given. It might be an extrapolation of Colquhoun's figure of 50,000, taking into account the rising population.

* The nineteenth-century view was that women in certain notoriously poorly-paid trades automatically became prostitutes, although modern historians have questioned this. Milliners, for example, routinely worked fourteen-hour days, and sixteen in the season. In view of the difficulties of life that we have seen – finding time to collect water and so on – it is worth questioning how much time, if not energy, they had for extra-curricular prostitution as well.

By 1851, William Acton, a surgeon specializing in genito-urinary disorders and one of the main contributors to the debate on prostitution, published statistics showing that there were 210,000 prostitutes in London, calculating this by taking as his starting point the 42,000 live births to unwed mothers recorded that year. These women had 'taken the first step in prostitution'. From that, he went on to posit that each one would go on to work as a prostitute for an average of five years, giving a total, over the five years, of 210,000 women, or one in every twelve unmarried females in Britain.

Similar claims were made by Michael Ryan, who wrote *Prostitution in London* (1839). Even with his background as the editor of the *London Medical and Surgical Journal* and a lecturer on midwifery and medical jurisprudence, he appeared even more credulous and every bit as innumerate. 'Every [fallen] girl, or woman, has her fancy man, or bully,' he wrote, 'who lives upon her prostitution, and seldom confines himself to one female.' Despite making their livings from these women, such men were 'thieves, pickpockets, and often murderers...Bullies spend the day in public-houses, and the night in brothels, in which they always assist in robbing, and often in murdering their victims.' He could make these assertions despite the fact that, a few pages earlier, he had discussed the police reports on brothels, in only one of which was anyone robbed and no one murdered.

Ryan then moved on from what these women did to how many there were: 'suppose that the number of prostitutes be 80,000, as already concluded, and that *each* has a bully [my italics: this despite writing a few lines earlier that a bully 'seldom confines himself to one female'], then there would be this great number of thieves and vagabonds let loose on the community.' As if that weren't enough, 'an enlightened medical gentleman' had told him that, near the Fleet Ditch, 'There is an aqueduct of large dimensions, into which murdered bodies are precipitated by bullies, and discharged at a considerable distance in to the Thames, without the slightest chance of discovery.'

Acton was more realistic: incidents of 'robbery and violence in brothels' were 'rare and scattered', he wrote, and the murderous aqueducts 'extraordinary inventions'. Mayhew's *London Labour* repeated the aqueduct story in order to reject it, but that didn't prevent the same volume citing Ryan as an authority elsewhere. On the streets, the police reported substantially lower numbers of streetwalkers and, what is more, Acton at least knew it. In 1838, the Commissioner of the Metropolitan Police believed that there were fewer than 7,000 prostitutes in London (excluding the City). On the page before Acton came up with his figure of 210,000, he noted that in 1841 the police had estimated that there were 9,409 prostitutes throughout the city (although that does seem an implausibly precise figure).

Preconceptions clouded the causes of prostitution, too. The Edinburgh surgeon William Tait, in his book *Magdalenism: An inquiry into the extent, causes and consequence of prostitution in Edinburgh** (1840), divided prostitutes into two groups: those 'naturally' inclined to a life of vice from 'Licentious Inclination – Irritability of Temper – Pride and Love of Dress – Dishonesty and Desire of Property – Indolence', and those who became prostitutes because of their personal circumstances, that is, poverty, lack of skills, abandonment by or the death of their parents. Yet once he had developed his theme, he concluded that all the middle-class women, such as governesses, were apparently led into prostitution by such life events – by being seduced and abandoned, for example – while all the working-class women ended up as prostitutes because they had 'a looseness in their characters'.

It is Mayhew's encyclopaedic work that ultimately reveals the real problem in discussing nineteenth-century prostitution. Although Mayhew relied on collaborators to produce many of the reports on street workers that he crafted into the first three volumes of *London Labour and the London Poor*, he interviewed many himself and wrote those volumes on his own. The fourth volume, on 'Those That Will Not Work, comprising Prostitutes, Thieves, Swindlers and Beggars', was different. (It is surely telling, too, that in his view, as is clear from the title alone, prostitutes

* Mary Magdalene was, of course, the follower of Christ to whom he appeared after his resurrection (John 20:1–18); she is frequently linked with the sinner in Luke 7:37, and thus represents a repentant prostitute. Asylums for 'fallen women' were therefore often called Magdalen homes.

did 'Not Work'.) This volume was the work of several contributors, about whom little is known. John Binny, probably a journalist, wrote the 'Thieves and Swindlers' section and later produced another volume with Mayhew. The Revd William Tuckniss, who wrote the section the charitable rescue societies, was chaplain to the Society for the Rescue of Young Women and Children and editor of *The Magdalen's Friend and Female Homes' Intelligencer*. Andrew Halliday, the author of the section on 'Beggars', who became a minor novelist and theatrical farceur, was the son of a Scottish minister; at the time of publication he was a journalist of just twenty, two years out of an Aberdeen school. Bracebridge Hemyng, who had recently left Eton, was reading for the bar. He later practised as a barrister of the Middle Temple and had a second career as the author of the *Jack Harkaway* Boys of England series. It is not clear what qualified Hemyng, who must have been barely nineteen when he was writing, as an expert on prostitution, but whatever it was, he was entirely responsible for that section in Mayhew's fourth volume.

While the subject was presented as magisterially as the style of the earlier volumes, only sixty of its 230-odd pages are actually about women on the London streets. The remainder contain either stories of prostitution as it was currently practised in Afghanistan, or Iceland, or other countries the contributors undoubtedly knew nothing about, or it was a historical retrospective of prostitution in Britain. In the London section, the information 'for certain facts, statistics, &c.' was derived from material published by the Society for the Suppression of Vice, the police, the Society for the Prevention of Juvenile Prostitution and other formal bodies whose aim was to eradicate the trade. This was in direct contrast to the other three volumes, which drew on direct interviews with the participants, reproducing their life stories and experiences in their own words. One of the sources for this section was even *The Life and Adventures of Col. George Hanger*, an 'autobiography' of the 4th Baron Coleraine, who wrote his highly coloured memoir in order to stave off his return to debtors' prison. He was satirically portrayed in caricatures of the day as pimping for the Prince of Wales, but, that apart, his only apparent experience of prostitution may have been in

Women were regularly mistaken for prostitutes merely because they were out on the streets. There were, however, ways of identifying 'unfortunates'. Location was one element, and here the Haymarket, the centre of the red-light district, is shown. Another marker was dress, and the illustrator has gone to town on hiked-up skirts; men, too, were not expected to smoke in front of 'respectable' women, so the inclusion of so many cigars sends a clear signal.

purchasing their services.* The real problem for us today is that the writings of these self-styled experts are all that we have.

One of their standard methods of assessing the number of prostitutes was purely visual. Acton wrote that he and a friend had 'counted 185 [prostitutes] in the course of a walk home from the Opera to Portland-place'. From Covent Garden, Acton most likely walked along to the top of the Haymarket, in the centre of the red-light district and London's most famous cruising ground, then continued up Regent Street, also known for its prostitutes; Portland Place itself was the site of several accommodation houses (see pp. 411–2) and lodgings for prostitutes. So Acton may have passed many working women, possibly even 185 of them. But short of his accosting each one, it is hard to judge how he *knew* the 185 he counted were sex-workers.

* According to the *Dictionary of National Biography*, Hanger was considered 'among the dregs of society' by his contemporaries.

Some, perhaps many, of the women may have spoken to him, offering their services. It is just as likely, though, that Acton made his assessments based on the women's clothes and manner: women who dressed or behaved in a way that he and other men considered inappropriate were seen as whores. This was standard. Dickens, too, wrote as if prostitutes were immediately recognizable. In 'The Pawnbroker's Shop' in *Sketches by Boz*, he describes the customers: first are a mother and daughter, respectable but fallen on hard times; then comes 'a young female', by whose dress the reader is to understand she is a prostitute: her clothing, 'miserably poor, but extremely gaudy, wretchedly cold, but extravagantly fine, too plainly bespeaks her station. The rich satin gown with its faded trimmings, the worn-out thin shoes, and pink silk stockings, the summer bonnet in winter…a daub of rouge…cannot be mistaken.'

It appears from the scant information we have that the majority of women who earned their living from selling sex were for the most part working-class women, many of whom had been servants or street sellers. Many more of them than the average population – perhaps as many as 70 per cent – had lost one or both parents. The average age for becoming sexually active was probably about sixteen, and most of the girls first took up with men of their own class, going out on the streets a couple of years later.

Despite many reports at the time and after, child prostitution may have been relatively rare. To stress that it was endemic, Ryan reproduced fourteen case studies from the London Society for the Protection of Young Females and Prevention of Juvenile Prostitution. Of those, one girl was twelve, one thirteen, another five were fifteen years old, and the remaining seven were older, including one woman whose age was not given but who had been married for six years. These girls may have been inveigled into prostitution, or become prostitutes for other reasons, and they had applied to the society for help – their suffering is undoubted – but none was at the time legally considered to be a child.* Judicial statistics collected by modern scholars

* The female age of consent had been twelve since the sixteenth century; in the nineteenth century, intercourse with a girl under the age of ten was a felony, with a girl aged between

suggest that, between 1849 and 1865, 6.5 per cent of female admissions to a venereal hospital were girls under sixteen.

Much more typical was the story a sixteen-year-old girl who had worked as a servant from the age of ten; when she was eleven or twelve, she moved to a post where her mistress beat her, and she ran away. She had nowhere to go, her mother being dead (she doesn't mention a father: perhaps he had died, disappeared or remarried, and she was no longer wanted). She met a fifteen-year-old boy, with whom she lived in a lodging house until he was arrested for pickpocketing. He had infected her with venereal disease, and so she broke a window in order to be sent to prison where a doctor would treat her. When she was released, having no possibility of returning to service because of her prison record, she became a streetwalker, living in a lodging house with others her age, up to fifty a room. 'Many a girl – nearly all of them – goes out into the streets... to get money for their favourite boys... If the girl cannot get money she must steal something, or will be beaten by her "chap" when she comes home.'

The older, more fortunate women, usually in the West End and the prosperous suburbs, worked as prostitutes for a few years, saving their money and then getting married – much the way the servant market operated, where service for many girls was a stage rather than a lifetime career. One day in Regent Street, Arthur Munby encountered a woman he had known when she was in service in a house in Oxford Street. Now she was 'arrayed in gorgeous apparel. How is this? said I. Why, she had got tired of service, wanted to see life and be independent; & so she had become a prostitute, of her own accord & without being seduced. She... enjoyed it very much, thought it might raise her & perhaps be profitable. She had taken it up as a profession... she had read books, and was taking lessons in writing and other accomplishments, in order to fit herself to be a companion of gentlemen.' After this, he saw her a few times on the street, finding that 'she continued to like it – she had some good friends, & was getting on nicely'. A few years later, when he encountered her again, she was dressed 'quietly &

ten and twelve a misdemeanour. The age of consent was raised to thirteen in 1875, and to sixteen in 1885. Historically there has never been a male age of consent for heterosexual sex.

well, like a respectable upper servant'. She told him that after three years as a prostitute she had saved up – 'I told you I should get on, you know' – and was the landlady of a coffee house on the south side of Waterloo Bridge.

> Now here is a handsome young woman of twentysix, who, having begun life as a servant of all work, and then spent three years in *voluntary* prostitution…invests the earnings of her infamous trade in a respectable coffeehouse, where she settles down in homely usefulness and virtuous comfort! That the coffeehouse *is* respectable, is clear I think from her manner: that she *did* invest her earnings…I believe, because she was not fashionable enough to be pensioned, & if she were, men do not pension off their whores in that way.

Munby noticed the changes in this woman's dress, from servant, to prostitute, to landlady of a respectable coffee house, and clothing played a great part in how prostitutes were recognized. Many walked the streets without a bonnet or shawl, a great breach of the dress code in displaying their hair and their figures as well as giving off indoor signals out of doors. The only description I have found of prostitutes overtly attempting to attract men in the street comes from 1870, in the notorious Boulton and Park case, when two men were arrested for dressing as women (see below, pp. 416–18). At their trial, the superintendent of the Alhambra theatre testified that they had been ejected from the theatre because they had been 'walking about as women looking over their shoulders as if enticing men' and had made 'noises with their lips, the same that I have heard made by females when passing gentlemen on the street'. The street keeper at the Burlington Arcade had also seen Boulton 'turn his head to two gentlemen who passed them, smile at them, and make a noise with his lips, the same as a woman would for inducement'. But apart from this one piece of evidence, and in unusual circumstances, it appears that streetwalkers rarely did even this, being content, as the Alhambra manager said, with looking over their shoulders.

Walter – who should have known a prostitute when he saw one, having, according to his own account at least, slept with eleven volumes'-worth of them (see note on p. 55 for my attitude to his evidence) – made it clear that identification was not straightforward. Walking one day down a muddy

Regent Street, he watched a woman 'holding her petticoats well up out of the dirt, the common habit of even respectable women...With gay ladies the habit was to hold them up just a little higher.' ('Gay' at the time meant a prostitute, probably from the connection with their wearing brightly – gaily – coloured clothes; it did not gain our current meaning until the 1920s, and then originally in the USA.) But how high was 'a little higher'? Walter was not sure. He walked ahead of her and 'turned round, and met her eye. She looked at me, but the look was so steady, indifferent, and with so little of the gay woman in her expression, that I could not make up my mind as to whether she was accessible or not.' He continued to follow her, and when she held up her skirts again, knowing he was behind her, he moved in, 'saying as I came close, "Will you come with me?"' It was only then, when she agreed, that he could be certain. The quality of women's clothes, too, was no indicator. 'Dress prostitutes' were lent clothes that they could otherwise not afford, usually by brothel madams. The *Yokel's Preceptor*, presented as a guidebook to young men fresh from the country, separated 'blowens' (prostitutes) from 'private blowens': respectably married women who 'are in the habit of walking out, neatly and modestly attired'. According to the author, 'should they be accosted by a gentleman', the private blowens might agree to go with him to an accommodation house to make a little spare cash. It is clear that those writers who thought they saw streets full of prostitutes really just saw streets full of women.

If prostitutes could be identified only when they were approached, then it becomes clear that women were indiscriminately importuned in the streets. That this was indeed the case emerged in a debate that played out in the pages of *The Times* in 1862. A gentleman calling himself 'Paterfamilias' wrote to the editor (letters from members of the public were often signed with a sobriquet, frequently in Latin, such as 'Pro Bono Publico') to complain that on a trip to London his daughters had been followed down Oxford Street by 'scoundrels' who stared at them and made remarks. 'Puella' ('Girl') replied two days later, saying that she frequented the same street and was never accosted; perhaps it was the girls' fault – had their country dress or outgoing rural manners encouraged these men? 'Paterfamilias', by return, was indignant: his daughters were wearing mourning following the death of Prince Albert. He was backed up by 'M', a day-governess (one who went from one pupil's house to another), who said she too had been accosted by 'middle-aged and older men'. Readers joined in, on both sides of the question. The following month the *Saturday Review* finally suggested that if women dressed attractively, they must expect to be looked at, but added this rider: 'the remedy is in their own hands...If they will be seen in the well-preserved coverts, it is for them to be careful that they do not look like game...Let them dress thoroughly unbecomingly. Let them procure poke bonnets, stint their skirts to a moderate circumference, and cultivate sad-looking underclothing. Any woman thus armed, and walking on without sauntering or looking about her, is perfectly safe even from amorous glances.' (Note that even badly dressed women still needed to keep their eyes down and walk briskly.) This was partly a satirical response, but the controversy made it clear that no one could tell a respectable woman from a prostitute by appearance alone, and barely by behaviour. The supposed signals that indicated a gay woman – slow walking, looking around, fashionable dress – were also natural behaviour on a shopping street. A lithograph of 1865, 'Scene in Regent Street', concurred: in it a 'Philanthropic Divine' attempts to hand an improving tract to a fashionably dressed woman. Perhaps she had been approached before, for in this parody she sounds remarkably tolerant as she replies, 'Bless me, Sir...I am not a social evil, I'm only waiting for a bus.'

The places where women were seen defined them: if women passed through certain places, they were automatically prostitutes, no matter how they behaved or dressed. It has been suggested that in *Great Expectations*, when Pip says the Finches of the Grove club meet at a hotel in Covent Garden, the mere words 'hotel' and 'Covent Garden' together suggested to contemporary readers that the young men were picking up women. Two decades later, when *All the Year Round* described a hotel down a side street between the Houses of Parliament and the Pye Street slum, where 'pretty girls' were 'always to be seen', readers would have known exactly what kind of pretty girls were meant.

Above all, from the beginning of the century a woman signalled her status by her mere presence in a place of public entertainment. *Life in London* was completely matter-of-fact about this. In this Regency romp there is no hesitation in calling prostitution by its name. The men go to Covent Garden, where they retire to the Saloon, colloquially known as the 'Mutton Walk', and are immediately surrounded 'by number of the gay *Cyprians*, who nightly visit this place'.* They have calling cards, which they hand to the visitor from the country, before 'The regular *covies* paired off with their *covesses*.' This fictional description was a reflection of the real world: a few years later Hékékyan Bey noticed that, in the theatre, 'Common strumpets sat near the respectable wives and daughters of the citizens of London.' In the 1830s, a visiting American added that streetwalkers got preferential treatment, being admitted 'at an inferior charge with season tickets'.

In the late 1830s or early 1840s, a series of small books was published to guide the 'swell' to various places where prostitutes were to be found, listing brothels and accommodation houses, as well as places of public amusement. The eighteenth century developed a tradition of such catalogues: Ned Ward's *The Secret History of London Clubs* (1709) listed a 'Bawds' Initiating Club', while the more notorious Harris's *List of Covent Garden Ladies* was published for at least three decades between 1764 and 1788, giving names, addresses, price and description of prostitutes. There appear to have been far fewer in the nineteenth century. *The Swell's Night Guides* were probably published in the 1840s; *The Bachelor's Pocket Book for 1851* may have been aimed at the (male) visitors in London for the Great Exhibition, but it was, at least in part, a reprint of the *Swell's* guides. Later in the 1850s, the *Yokel's Preceptor: or, More Sprees in London! Being a...Show-up of All the Rigs and Doings of the Flash Cribs in This Great Metropolis* delivered rather less than it promised. In its 'Roll Call of Some Celebrated Mots [prostitutes]', of the seven listed, two were dead, one had retired, one had the pox and another was 'as regular a fireship as ever sailed the coast. Take care' – which suggests she too was infected, so in reality only two women were available. Perhaps this volume was more for the

* In Greek mythology, Cyprus was devoted to the worship of Aphrodite, and so a Cyprian was a prostitute. If one wants to carp, 'gay Cyprian' is the equivalent of saying a prostituted prostitute.

young man who wanted to think himself a bit of a dog, but who had no intention of doing anything more than buying a dirty book.

The *Swell's Night Guides*, however, do seem to have contained solid information. One lists a number of theatres, presenting their advantages and their drawbacks for a man of pleasure. At Her Majesty's, on the Haymarket, 'An occasional trifle to the hall-keeper will get a gentleman behind the scenes.' In the Theatre Royal, Covent Garden, run by Mme Vestris (who later went on to run the Olympic as the first entirely respectable theatre), 'The private boxes... have snug and secret retiring anti-rooms [sic], with voluptuous couches, and all things requisite for the comfort and convenience of the *debauchée.*' The same could be said of Drury Lane, which boasted excellent arrangements in the rooms beside the boxes: 'The doors fastening on the inside, the visitors are not so liable to be intruded on.' (At almost the same date Dickens wrote that Drury Lane was no longer the 'temple of obscenity' it had once been, having banned prostitutes from its Grand Saloon.) The Haymarket possessed no retiring rooms, although the quality of female attractions in the Saloon was commended, while the English Opera House in the Strand was dismissed for its inferior girls. The Adelphi 'always contrives to have the prettiest women... There are more kept women, and open trading women of pleasure, in the female *corps dramatique* of the Adelphi... than in any other', yet 'the private boxes are ill-conditioned and enormously dear'. The Pavilion, in the East End, was 'well conducted', and the manager 'is not very particular as to his privacy behind the scenes. The entrée is to be obtained on very moderate terms'. There was little change more than a decade later, when a Parliamentary Select Committee on Public Houses heard that at the Eagle Tavern's theatrical performances, 'No gentleman, well dressed, can promenade there without being solicited by a female to go to houses of accommodation.' In the late 1860s, at the Alhambra theatre in Leicester Square, there were bars that charged special admission to men who wanted to mingle with the unaccompanied women who were regulars. There was another, private bar under the stage, where patrons could mix with the ballet girls from backstage.

The Swell's Night Guide also listed eighteen actresses, with notes on where they performed, where they lived and under whose protection (that is, the identity of their lover). It included the wife of the playwright Edward Stirling, who was supposedly under the protection of a doctor in Pall Mall; and the actor John Saville Faucit's wife, Elizabeth, who was living with the actor William Farren in Brompton. The book gave advice too on how to approach an actress. It warned the interested party not to offer her money directly, but to say he wanted to engage her as he was staging private theatricals. This throws some light on how Dickens' friends might have viewed his relationship with Nelly Ternan, for whom Dickens left his wife in 1858: Dickens, aged forty-five, had hired the eighteen-year-old actress to perform in some private theatricals. Soon after, he encouraged one theatre manager to give her work, sending a cheque for £50, either intended for her, or to pay the manager for taking her on. It was not long, however, before she retired from the stage, unlike the 'many' actresses who, said *The Swell's Night Guide*, 'frequent some of the French Introducing Houses' (see p.412–13); in those cases, it added, they could be dealt with on a commercial basis.

According to Dickens, when theatres became more respectable they were replaced by the 'Dancing Establishment'. He admitted that 'Great order is observed' in most of these venues, but few men resorted to them for anything other than what he referred to as 'allurement'. Although he didn't name it, the establishment he had in mind was most probably the Argyle (sometimes Argyll) Assembly Rooms in Windmill Street, near Regent Street and the Haymarket. Originally housed in a Nash-designed building that opened in the early 1820s, the Argyle was for many the epitome of a place of loose morals. In *London by Night*, by 'Anonyma', a risqué novel about a barmaid who becomes a prostitute, an illustration entitled 'Lost' shows her in front of the Argyle. The 1s admission charge gave entry to a dance floor downstairs; an additional 1s fee brought access to the upstairs galleries, which had private seating in alcoves. By the late 1860s, the upstairs was notable for its bright lighting and its fifty-piece band; by the bar hung panels depicting Europa and the bull, Leda and the Swan, and Bacchus and Silenus. Here the women met and sat drinking with their admirers until the Rooms closed at one.

Similar to the Argyle, but not as exclusive, was the Casino de Venise, more commonly referred to as the Holborn Casino, or even just the Holborn.

It too charged 1s, and was 'gorgeously fitted up with immense mirrors, and velvet covered sofas and seats, handsome carpets, gilding'; it too had a separate 'wine room'. A City clerk in *London by Night* lives in chambers at Furnival's Inn, as Dickens had in the early days of his marriage, but since the clerk is unmarried, he is freer to indulge himself: 'I call the Holborn my drawing-room. I believe I come here pretty well every night.' Dancing saloons could be found right across the city, each attuned to its particular audience. The Ratcliffe Highway one had a single long room with a bar, offering entertainment as well as dancing: 'a young lady in short muslin petticoats performs a ballet by herself, or with a little girl of some seven years old, dressed like a marine-store fairy'. In the intervals the child sold biscuits and cakes to the audience, before she was replaced by her father, who sang sentimental ballads.

There also existed public places for dancing that were respectable: Caldwell's, in Dean Street in Soho, was fequented by 'Lots of young men, clerks & apprentices, dancing with . . . shopgirls & milliners – also respectable'. These '*soirées dansantes*' were generally run by a dancing master, admission 6d; lists were readily available of the teachers and the evenings when they held assemblies. But dancing itself could make a place of doubtful propriety unless care was taken. Caldwell's also had a reputation as an establishment where middle- and upper-class men brought working-class women they had designs on: even if the women concerned were not already on the road to ruin, just being there could all too easily set them on that path.

After the dancing saloons closed (at 3 or 4 a.m. until mid-century; then at 1 a.m. later on), the dancers moved on to eating establishments such as the oyster houses and pastry-cooks that lined the night districts, or to the finishes, 'low taverns or large and luxurious public houses where people go to finish off the night'. Their exterior appearance could be deceptive. In the 1830s, one finish had a dingy little entrance; inside, however, 'the brilliance of hundreds of gas lights' revealed a large room divided lengthways, with booths, as in an eating house, down on one side; opposite was a raised area where prostitutes sat 'in their finest attire'. In the mid-1840s, a coffee house called the Finish, in James Street, Covent Garden, attracted a mixture of late-night revellers and early-morning market people. Many more finishes resembled Barnes's night house, 'an ordinary drinking-saloon' that also sold pastries, and steak and oysters.

Most prostitutes, however, did not while away their time rolling from the Argyle via the finishes to bijou villas paid for by their lovers. Most were streetwalkers, spending long hours in the wet and the cold. The areas in the West End where prostitutes were mostly to be found varied over the decades. In 1818, according to one guide, prostitutes could be seen walking from Aldgate Pump to St James's Street, that is, a two-and-a-half-mile stretch from where the Bank tube station is now, along Fleet Street, the Strand and Pall Mall to St James's. 'Another line extends along Newgate Street, into Lincoln's Inn-fields, across Covent Garden', and then to Piccadilly. The Strand, Holborn and Fleet Street were popular venues for streetwalkers in the 1820s, as were Leicester Square and Regent Street in the 1830s, and the Haymarket at almost all dates.* Mayfair was another favourite haunt; in *Dombey and Son* (written in the 1840s, set in the 1830s) Edith Dombey sees 'faded' women 'wander...past' outside the upper-class house in Brook Street, by Grosvenor Square.

Many streetwalkers, however, stayed in their own neighbourhoods, servicing the men who lived and worked near by. The areas by the dockyards supported a large population of prostitutes, and Granby Street, parallel to Lower Marsh Street, beside Waterloo station, was notorious. When Flora Tristan saw it in 1839, she found 'women were looking out of windows or seated on their doorsteps...half-dressed; several were bare to the waist'.†

* It is worth remembering, too, that at the beginning of this period, as well as being the main red-light district at night, the Haymarket was, in the daytime, just that: a market where hay was sold: 'The whole right hand side of the street going downwards, from the Piccadilly end to the Opera House, used to be lined with loads of hay', with the pavement 'crowded by salesmen and their customers'.

† I suspect that 'bare to the waist' here means without the handkerchief that would normally have been worn at the neck of a low-cut dress, thus with the breasts partially exposed, which Walter's 'half naked' in the next sentence appears to back up. (See also note on p. 184.) Although this passage is corroborated by Walter, I have found Flora Tristan unreliable on the subject of prostitution more generally. She replicates whole passages from Ryan's *Prostitution in London*, which cannot be taken at face value (see p. 395), and she doubles Colquhoun's estimate of the number of prostitutes in London, purely because, she writes, the population had doubled.

Walter agreed: on a Saturday night, the street was 'full of women who used to sit at the windows half naked', with more soliciting in the doorways. In the 1841 census, twenty-four houses on this street were occupied by fifty-seven young single women running their own households; their age and the absence of men suggests that prostitution may have been their primary source of income. Twenty years later nearly two-thirds of the single women were in their twenties, and a dozen in their teens. (The street was purchased in its entirety by the railway at the end of the 1860s, for company housing; when Waterloo station was extended it was built over, and no longer exists.)

Many of these women serviced clients at home, but just as many walked over the bridge to the West End each evening at about nine o'clock, reversing the trend of commuting, before heading back south over the river at eight the next morning. Haymarket prostitutes generally walked the streets from eleven at night until one in the morning: in other words, from the time the theatres closed to the opening of the finishes. According to Walter, in the daytime, 'Exceedingly nice women were... to be met... from eleven to one in the morning, and three till five in the afternoon' in Regent Street. The pattern varied from district to district. In the late 1830s, out at the western edge of suburban London – where the new, unlit roads were extending for the first time into what had recently been country and market gardens – 'Gay women of a poor class were then... about the darkest parts, or they used to walk there with those who met them where the roads were lighter.'

For the most part, notions of upper-class cads twiddling their moustaches and seducing working girls were fiction, not fact. Police returns suggest that 'a substantial majority' of working women serviced men of their own class and economic background, and their lives were far from novelistically glamorous. When Walter went looking for women towards the end of the 1840s, he 'began to walk through streets inhabited by very poor gay women', who stood at their doors from about two o'clock 'to catch passers by'. One of them, Mary, lived in a room, 'about twelve feet square', with a bed taking up a third of the space, a table, two chairs, a cupboard, a chest of drawers, a looking-glass, a coal cuttle and a slop pail. It was fairly well furnished by the standards of impoverished districts, yet so cold that

Walter kept all of his clothes on (this was unusual for him, and he mentions it specifically). This despite the fact that Mary did relatively well for herself. Walter began to visit her regularly, paying her £2 a week, although sometimes 'I left off for a while, and gave Mary a chance of keeping her other friends…mostly poor clerks…and married men better off, who gave her a pound.' If Walter's figures are accurate, Mary earned approximately £80 or £100 a year, the income of a minor clerk.

Evidence confirms that this was the way of things in the poorer areas. In Whitechapel there was little work available for women apart from domestic service or the local gin shops and coffee houses; in the aptly named Angel Alley, the best-paid work was providing sex for the men who brought hay and straw to Whitechapel market twice a week. Around the docks, many women had intermittent but long-term arrangements with sailors, living with them for the duration of their shore leave. One woman said she had 'six, eight, ten, oh! more…husbands. I am not married, of course not, but they think me their wife while they are on shore.' This was an entirely accepted way of life, barely regarded as prostitution by the women or their communities.

Not everyone could aspire even to Mary's existence. Most of the women around Granby Street were 'to be had for a few shillings' in the 1840s. Walter laid out the economics of streetwalking. Women of a 'superior class' charged a sovereign, but half that sum would pay for 'as nice a one as you needed'. 'Two good furnished rooms near the Clubs could be had by women for from fifteen to twenty shillings per week, a handsome silk dress for five or ten pounds'. Even if they couldn't afford the pleasant room, as long as they had the handsome dress, they could charge 'from five to ten shillings a poke' in an accommodation house.*

* Walter seems overly optimistic about their income. If a woman paid 15s a week for her rooms, and once a year bought a dress for £5, plus other items of clothing for another £5, food (7s a week), fuel (3s), candles or other lighting (3s) and laundry (1s), at a minimum her outgoings would be nearly £3, probably closer to £4 to cover only the necessities of life and her trade. This would require eight clients a week paying the maximum to cover the basics, leaving no room for anything to go wrong, no seasonal fall in trade, as in August, and with no money going towards dependants. That some women in the West End or prosperous locations could indeed make a living this way and set money aside for the future can be seen

Accommodation houses were places to take a woman for a brief period of time, or overnight. These might be rooms over coffee houses, or might even resemble private houses, the only difference being that the door to the street was left open, and inside there was a 'red or blue transparent blind' illuminated from behind by a gaslight. The quality of the houses varied according to price and location. Walter's first suburban accommodation house cost him 5s for a visit of 'some hours'; and the room was well furnished, with 'red curtains, looking-glasses, wax lights, clean linen, a huge chair, a large bed, and a cheval-glass'.* The Cross Keys coaching inn in Gracechurch Street cost 4s a night, or, for 'a short visit the mere calling for wine is deemed sufficient' – that is, the mark-up on the wine covered the cost of the room. But a short visit meant short: Walter and his friend had just fallen asleep at one house when there was a knocking at the door and a voice called, 'Shall you be long, sir, we want the room.' As Walter, said, 'I was having too much accommodation for my money.'

If the guides and Walter are to be relied on, it might be swifter to demarcate the places where there were no such houses than to list where they might be found. At the beginning of the century, according to the tailor Francis Place, there were three or four brothels around Charing Cross, in addition to two nearby courts almost entirely populated by prostitutes; by 1815, the courts had been cleaned up; by 1824, this 'improvement' had spread to the entire neighbourhood, probably owing to the Strand Western Improvements. Some districts were notorious throughout the century: this was particularly true of the area between Leicester Square and the Haymarket, north of the Strand around Panton Street; and around Exeter Street, off the Strand. In fact so disreputable was this area that when Walter took a girl there, 'the cabman insolently demanded about five times his fare' and added,

---

in the stories of women like the coffee-house proprietor Munby knew (see p. 400); but it was just as obviously not possible for everyone.

* Walter claimed in the 1850s that the overseer of a house in James Street, which had eight good rooms and two small, less desirable ones, took £20 a day. Eliminating the two small rooms, if we assume that the eight rooms charged 5s per customer, then to make £20 a day, each room would have to process ten customers a day, a hot-sheet hotel indeed. Even if the actual income were only half this, the house's turnover would be over £2,500 a year for a forty-six-week year.

'Think yourself lucky a peeler don't drop on you for taking a young gal like that' to such an address. Up around Portland Place was another well-known red-light district: Walter used a neighbourhood house in James Street, as well as another on Titchfield Street, the 'quietest house in London', known for having two entrances, so an ideal place to meet a married woman. In the 1840s, *The Swell's Night Guides* list a number of places, many of which were free-and-easies and supper rooms such as the Cider Cellars and Evans's. The guidebooks make little distinction between places where prostitutes might be found and those where they were the *raison d'être*. Undoubtedly some of the named houses were brothels: Mother H's was one. It was, the guide enthuses, 'the multibona casey for the swell donnas', and Mother H herself 'was complete mistress of her functions'. (She is named in the drinking song on p. 360.)

There were probably far more accommodation houses, catering to women who worked independently, than there were brothels, where women worked for an employer, were given a share of the fee or a salary, and were fed and lodged at the proprietor's expense. The number of accommodation houses is entirely unknown; we have a better sense of how many brothels existed, because the authorities attempted to keep track of them. In 1841, the police were aware of 933, and in 1857, 410. Even so, some of these may not have been brothels but places where a few women had chosen to lodge together, sometimes pooling their income, sometimes operating independently and sharing living expenses.

A secondary type of brothel, probably more common, was the introducing house. This did not employ resident prostitutes, but was where the women came to work. Pubs operated as introducing houses, with the women using the rooms upstairs, and *The New Swell's Night Guide* listed some of the 'ladies who are generally to be found' at specific addresses. More introducing houses masqueraded as respectable businesses, with a brass plaque – the sign of tradesmen and the professional middle classes – on the doors, claiming the premises to be a doctor's, or a male midwife's, or, if entirely run by women, a milliner's, or a stay- or corset-maker's. An introducing house in the Wandsworth Road announced itself as 'A Seminary for Young Ladies', while another in Villiers Street, run by the same woman, claimed to house a 'Professor of Pianoforte and Guitar'. Many were set up 'in the most stylish streets': St James's Place, Piccadilly, Jermyn Street, around Portman Square. At Mme Matileau's establishments for young ladies, in Dean Street and the Old Brompton Road, 'nothing is allowed to get stale...you may have your meat dressed to your own liking...if it suit your taste, you may kill your own lamb or mutton, for her flock is in prime condition, and always ready for sticking; when any of them are fried, they are turned out to grass, and sent to the hammer or disposed of by private contract...consequently the rot, bots, glanders, and other diseases incidental to cattle, are not generally known here.'

Some women worked on their own, and the guides printed long lists of such prostitutes, with their addresses. Sometimes these women were kept by men, named by the guides, although they also continued to be available to other male clients. *The Bachelor's Pocket Book* gave detailed directions to the house with 'Two Birds hanging in a Parlour Window', or the one with 'Amber Curtains to Windows'. It also listed the speciality of the women in detail: Jane Fowler, in Church Street, Soho, 'has a peculiar method of disrobing...for the purpose of enhancing the enjoyment', while Miss Alice Grey, New Street, Portland Road, 'frequently performs the rites...according to the *equestrian* order'. Miss Walbeck, of William Street, King's Cross, takes '*male parts*' on stage, and in the book is shown in her chemise, wearing a top hat and trousers and holding a whip: 'she has a piece of the termagant about her.' Such women could be found in every part of the city. Renton Nicholson, in his autobiography, remembered that in the early 1830s many 'dashing beaut[ies], gaily dressed' took lodgings in the district north of Oxford Street, and 'loud knockings late at night were frequently heard'. In general, the streets mentioned most often are around the Adelphi, south of the Strand, north of Oxford Street and south of the New Road, in most of Soho, and around Edgware Road at Marble Arch.

These guides to the night dealt entirely with heterosexual commercial sex. That there was a homosexual commercial world is known, but the surviving details are even scantier, and even less certain, than the unreliable information we have for the heterosexual world, and much of it comes from evidence given in court.* Of the cases that ended publicly, in the press and in court, a large proportion of offences through the century were enacted in public places: of a sample 105 cases, 22 per cent occurred in the street, 20 per cent in parks, 8 per cent in public urinals (which started to appear mid-century), 14 per cent in pubs or shops and only 3 per cent in theatres.

In 1806, David Robertson was arrested for sodomy; he had kept what may have been a gay brothel, or perhaps an accommodation house, in Charles Street, Covent Garden, although few details survive. More information can be gleaned from details of the arrest in 1810 of James Cook and his partner Yardley (whose first name does not appear to be known), the owners of the White Swan public house in Vere Street, Clare market. According to the single contemporaneous publication about the case, the pub was in part an accommodation house and in part what was described as a brothel, where 'The upper part of the house was appropriated to youths who were constantly in waiting for casual customers'. However, it seems more likely that this was an introducing house (that is, the men probably did not live on the premises). Whatever it was, within six months of opening it was raided and the owners arrested. (For their fates, see pp. 381–2.)

Pubs, despite the low number of arrests mentioned above, were an obvious place for like-minded men to meet. In 1825, the Barley Mow pub in the Strand was raided after information was received that it held gay free-and-easies twice weekly. The parks and the streets were also favoured gay cruising areas, particularly those near barracks. An 1813 publication reported that the author had attended a court case where a soldier on duty in the park 'under the wall of Marlborough-gardens' was approached by a man who, after speaking to him briefly, 'put his hand in his breeches'. And according to *The Times* in 1825, 'scarcely a week passes' without magistrates courts hearing cases of 'indecent assaults on the sentries in the park'. These men were generally arrested under the Vagrancy Act (1822), which required

* The cases relate entirely to male homosexual transactions; if there were female homosexual street encounters, we have no evidence: unlike male homosexual acts, which had been illegal from 1533, there have never been any legal constraints on female homosexual acts, and therefore the court records, which supply so much evidence for men, are of no assistance.

people to give 'a satisfactory account of themselves' and their reason for being in the street, making it a useful catch-all way to remove both beggars and sex-workers.

There are a few transient glimpses, however, of happy relationships formed from encounters in the streets that did not come within the purview of the magistrates. Edward Leeves was an Englishman living in Venice, who returned for a time to London in the late 1840s, socializing with the upper classes and cruising, from what we can tell from his heavily redacted diary: 'Fine. Tried my luck once more. I sat in the Park; but so shy that I cd make [illegible] nothing.' A few weeks later, 'Fun & Folly seems the order there for those who have money. Saw J.B. We went up to Albany St.' Later Leeves filled in the scanty details of his first meeting with a trooper named Jack Brand: 'This day year, Dear Boy, about this hour, I saw you in all your beauty, smiling as your gallant charger reared & pranced…And then in the [sentry] Box I spoke to you, & after Parade we met for five minutes, & you told me your name.' That evening, 'at the Arch at Hyde Park Corner met my poor Boy. We went together in a cab to Albany St, or one just by', presumably to an accommodation house, since the address was far from Leeves's own lodgings. The brief and sad story then continued:

> I saw J.B. on 3rd & 5th August, & on the 9th & 10th I think but not sure.
> 12 AUGUST: 'J.B. Gravesend.'
> 14 AUGUST: 'D[itt]o. and back to Town. [Inserted later: '& now on the 6th Septr what regrets & what recollections!!!', for on 5 September, Jack Brand died of cholera, aged twenty-two.]
> 18 DECEMBER: 'About this hour [fifteen weeks ago] I was arriving in London and anticipating our meeting…And I am alive – & He is gone & forgotten save by me – and nothing remains to tell of him save the cold stone which I have had placed by his Grave!'
> 28 DECEMBER: 'If it were not [for] the intense cold I think that I should make an escapade, & try to drown thought & grief…There would be found scope enough for even my appetite, I believe.'
> 26 JANUARY 1850: 'Twenty six weeks…since I first saw you in Hyde Park!'

> 6 FEBRUARY: 'Had a pleasant half hour after [military] parade & made some new, rollicking acquaintance.'
> 7 FEBRUARY: 'Rather a pleasant evening with my yesterday lads – or rather with two of them – rare boys, by God! & no mistake; but for gentleness & *simpatia* nothing like my own poor boy, who has no equal left.'
> 8 FEBRUARY: 'Repetition of evening party: two prime swells in their way; but the fun is expensive, & yet there is no grudging the blunt [cash] to such roaring boys.'

In the 1850s, the *Yokel's Preceptor* claimed that male prostitutes could be found on Regent Street, Fleet Street, Holborn and the Strand, looking into shop windows to give cover to their slow strolls, and also in coffee houses, dancing saloons and theatres – in effect, in the same places where women carried out the same business. But it is a matter of debate as to how reliable the book is: it speaks of 'the beasts... commonly designated *Margeries*, *Pooffs*, &c.' and appears to define male prostitutes exactly as Acton and his colleagues defined female ones – by assessing whether or not they visually conformed to the author's preconceptions.

In 1864, Arthur Munby had attended a commercial dance in Camberwell, ostensibly like those run by dancing masters, but one where the women dressed as men, and the men as women. Munby – who was sexually excited by masculine-looking, working-class women, especially dirty ones – found this 'simply disgusting'. But the event was not secret and, he admitted, 'only a lark'. Indeed, ten years earlier, at the Druid's Hall, Turnagain Lane, off Fleet Street, dances attended by cross-dressers were held over an eighteen-month period at least, untroubled by the police or anyone else.

The Boulton and Park case, in 1870, was an extension of this cross-dressing and was also a case of non-commercial sex, yet the stage it was performed on was still the street. That spring, Ernest Boulton and Frederick Park – the sons of, respectively, a wine merchant and a judge – were arrested as they left the Strand theatre dressed as women. It soon emerged that over the previous three years they had regularly appeared dressed as women, in the streets as well as at theatres, restaurants, even at the Oxford–Cambridge Boat Race. It seemed to have been fairly clear to everyone who saw them

Ernest Boulton and Frederick Park were arrested in 1870 for appearing in public dressed as women. 'Stella' and 'Fanny' even made their first court appearance in female dress, to the great amusement of the crowds who waited to see them.

that Boulton and Park were male, yet their ejections from various places of entertainment were rare.*

The two men initially seemed not to take the prosecution seriously. On his first court appearance Boulton wore 'a cherry-coloured evening dress rimmed with white lace' together with a wig giving him a demure chignon, while Park's gown was 'dark green satin…low-necked, trimmed in black lace', and covered by a shawl; he wore his hair in flaxen curls. (Both disappointed their followers by afterwards dressing as men and, apparently on legal advice, sporting moustaches and whiskers.) There was no public outrage: the crowds waiting by the police vans waved their hats and shouted encouragement; when the men's letters were read out in court, 'the audience in the body of the court appeared to be exceedingly amused'. There was little

* The man who was arrested with them swore in court that he had thought they were women, and that earlier, when he had seen them dressed as men, he had thought they were women in men's clothes. But as he was facing prosecution for intent to commit sodomy, to quote a more modern sex-trial witness, he would, wouldn't he?

sense that Boulton and Park were in any way a public danger or disgrace: this was just one more instance of street theatre. It shows a substantial shift in attitudes from 1835, when in his 'Visit to Newgate' in *Sketches by Boz*, Dickens reported on seeing the last two men to be executed for 'unnatural acts', or homosexual, consensual sex. They were unnamed by Dickens but have since been identified as John Smith and John Pratt. At the time, 'the nature of [their] offence rendered it necessary to separate them' from the prison's other convicted men.

The assumption in literature, and in all good books, was that women who transgressed the moral code by becoming sex-workers were sure to meet an untimely death. Flora Tristan was certain that 'Many die in hospitals from shameful diseases', or in neglect and poverty 'in their frightful hovels'. Dr Ryan wrote that up to 10 per cent of these women killed themselves, 'or become insane, or idiotic' through moral turpitude. William Tait agreed that prostitutes fell into a decline and rapidly died: this was a 'general law'. Acton, in contradiction, compiled figures to show that prostitutes did not commit suicide more often than any other group, but fiction supported the views of his colleagues. In *London by Night*, the barmaid Louisa, who was 'Lost' on entering the Argyle Rooms, was 'Found' at the end of the story, when her body was pulled from the river, where she had ended her life.

The Romantic notion of suicide was that it respresented the act of a rash and impetuous free (male) spirit. While few young men may have killed themselves for love, as Romantic literature had it, it was the case then, as now, that far more men than women committed suicide – up to four times as many. Despite these statistics, between the end of the eighteenth century and the coming of Victoria, there was a perceptual shift. From the late 1830s it was thought that it was women who killed themselves more frequently, and that they did so for love. This change is illustrated in the series of engravings of an eighteenth-century pond, known as Rosamond's Pond, in St James's Park, which was filled in in 1770. In 1780, an etching of it in its former state was captioned: 'This spot was often the receptacle of many unhappy Persons, who in the stillness of an Evening Plung'd themselves into Eternity.' In 1825, the etching was reissued and the caption altered:

'The South West corner of St. James's Park was enriched with this romantic scene... *its melancholy situation seems to have tempted more persons, (especially young women) to suicide by drowning than any other place about town.*' In 1859, Sala claimed that Rosamond's Pond had been the Waterloo Bridge of its day, for it was there that 'forsaken women' went to drown themselves.

For, a mere dozen years after Waterloo Bridge opened, it had become a byword for suicides. A political essay as early as 1829 used the bridge as an obvious synonym for suicide without feeling the need for any explanation: 'The man who loves his country with a sincere affection, unwilling to witness the decline of her prosperity and glory, already hesitates only between pistols and prussic acid, Waterloo-bridge and a running noose.' In a short story in the late 1830s, Dickens had a drunkard end his life on the bridge. By then, however, it was generally women abandoned by their lovers who were said to kill themselves there: the bridge was known as 'the English "Bridge of Sighs"... "Lover's Leap", the "Arch of Suicide"... a favourite spot for love assignations; and a still more favourite spot for the worn and the weary, who long to cast off the load of existence... To many a poor girl the assignation over one arch... is but a prelude to a fatal leap from another.'

Thomas Hood added a link to prostitution in his poem, 'The Bridge of Sighs' (1844), basing his story on a real incident, when Mary Furley, an impoverished seamstress faced with the workhouse, threw herself into the Regent's Canal, taking one of her two small children with her. Hood's poem altered the location to Waterloo and removed all the identifying details. Much later, Dickens described the death of a woman in the Regent's Canal that was probably much closer to reality. Walking at dusk through Regent's Park 'one day in the hard winter of 1861', he saw a cab driver speaking to the park keeper with 'great agitation', before rushing off, followed by the novelist. 'When I came to the right-hand Canal Bridge, near the cross-path to Chalk Farm, the Hansom was stationary, the horse was smoking hot', and, lying 'on the towing-path with her face turned up towards us, [was] a woman, dead a day or two, and under thirty, as I guessed, poorly dressed in black. The feet were lightly crossed at the ankles, and the dark hair, all pushed back from the face, as though that had been the last action of her desperate hands, streamed over the ground.'

That was journalism. In fiction it was the river rather than the canal that called to Dickens in his depictions of desperate prostitutes. In *Oliver Twist*, Nancy gestures to the Thames: 'How many times do you read of such as me who spring into the tide... It may be years hence, or it may be only months, but I shall come to that at last.' (Although compared to the end Dickens gave her, bludgeoned to death by Sikes, drowning might have been more merciful.) In *David Copperfield*, Martha, who had grown up in the small town of Great Yarmouth, flees to London to hide her shame after she 'falls'. David comes across her at Blackfriars Bridge and follows her along the river, past Waterloo Bridge, past Westminster Abbey, to Millbank – that is, along the streets frequented by prostitutes, through the slum around Westminster,

Hood's poem, 'The Bridge of Sighs', fixed Waterloo Bridge in the public mind as the place where women, especially prostitutes, committed suicide. This illustration by Gustave Doré reinforced the location, with its view of St Paul's looming in the background.

and then back to the river, where she cries: 'I know I belong to it. I know that it's the natural company of such as I am!' These prostitutes flit across London's bridges like the ghosts they would soon become. In *Little Dorrit*, begun five years later, in 1855, Little Dorrit and Maggie, her simple-minded companion, walk across London Bridge at night, where they meet a prostitute walking east, in the direction of Granby Street and Waterloo Road. Maggie asks her, 'What are you doing with yourself?' and the answer is stark: 'Killing myself.' This may be metaphorical, a conventional view of the natural destination of one who leads her life, or it may be literal. We don't know, as she vanishes into the morning mist.

Other locations for suicide were equally symbolic. A particular magnet for the desperate was the Monument to the Great Fire of London, a stone column 202 feet high topped by an urn in the shape of flames, standing 202 feet from the spot where the fire that devastated the City in 1666 first broke out. In low-rise, nineteenth-century London, the Monument was far more visible than it is today and was one of the most important sights of the City; many visitors climbed its 300-plus stairs for the view of London spreading beneath them. Yet negative connotations were ever-present. In *Barnaby Rudge*, set in the 1780s, a young man is sent off for a day in London with 6d to spend on 'diversions', and his father recommends passing the entire day at the top of the Monument: 'There's no temptation there, sir – no drink – no young women – no bad characters.' By the time Dickens wrote this, in 1841, the main temptation that people associated with the Monument was jumping over the edge, and this father, who is not a loving one, may be telling his son that he might kill himself for all he cared.

Even so, few chose it for this purpose. In 1788, a baker jumped off, followed in 1810 by a diamond merchant and, shortly afterwards, another baker. In 1839, a fifteen-year-old boy, thought to have lost his job, leapt from the platform, as did a baker's daughter. As a result, a guard was stationed at the top, but he failed to prevent Jane Cooper, a servant, throwing herself over. After her death a cage was placed around the platform, to prevent any others from following suit. Six people had plunged to their deaths here in forty-four years, four of whom were men, but it was still said that suicide by women crossed in love was 'a tradition of the Monument'.

But it was the river, always the river, to which Dickens returned. In 1860, his journalistic narrator stood at the riverside at Wapping, 'looking down at some dark locks in some dirty water', said to be the local 'Bridge of Sighs'. He comments to an 'apparition' that materializes beside him, 'A common place for suicide,' and the chilling answer is: 'Sue... And Poll. Likewise Emily. And Nancy. And Jane... Ketches off their bonnets or shorls, takes a run, and headers down here, they doos. Always a headerin' down here, they is. Like one o'clock.' The journalist conscientiously asks, 'And at about that hour of the morning, I suppose?' The apparition rejects this: 'They an't partickler. Two 'ull do for them. Three. All times o' night.' The poor, the hungry, the desperate: none was particular, just looking for an end.

At the beginning of the century, in 1801, the essayist Charles Lamb refused an invitation to the Lake District, unable to bear leaving behind 'all the bustle and wickedness round about Covent Garden, the very women of the Town, the Watchmen, drunken scenes, rattles, – life awake, if you awake, at all hours of the night, the impossibility of being dull in Fleet Street, the crowds, the very dirt & mud, the Sun shining upon houses and pavements, the print shops, the old book stalls... coffee houses, steams of soup from kitchens, the pantomimes, London itself a pantomime and a masquerade, – all these things work themselves into my mind and feed me... I often shed tears in the motley Strand from fulness of joy at so much Life.' Yet many others saw not life but death in what Arthur Clennam in *Little Dorrit* described as London's 'streets, streets, streets'. In Henry Wallis's *The Death of Chatterton* (1859), one of the most famous paintings of the nineteenth century, the main area of the picture is given to the image of the young poet who has committed suicide. Behind him, through the window, can be seen the dome of St Paul's, the symbol of the indifferent, anonymous city that has crushed him, and continues on, uncaring. This is what Dickens meant when he wrote, 'with how little notice, good, bad, or indifferent, a man may live and die in London... his existence... [is] a matter of interest to no one save himself; he cannot be said to be forgotten when he dies, for no one remembered him when he was alive.'

Yet in the same year that Dickens stood by that Wapping bridge, looking down into the water where so many women had met their end, he also created a fictional barrister who had chambers in Gray's Inn Square, precisely where the young Dickens himself had begun his writing life. The barrister, a dried-up man of fifty-five, fretted: 'What is a man to do? London is so small!... Then, the monotony of all the streets, streets, streets – and of all the roads, roads, roads – and the dust, dust, dust!' He gives his watch to a man who has chambers near by, asking him to look after it while he is out of town. And that is the last anyone sees of him until, after 'his letter-box became choked', the porter enters his rooms to find that he had hanged himself. Leaving London and leaving life were one and the same.

This was the refrain of Dickens' novels and journalism for thirty years. It was only with his very last work that there is any indication of a different view, perhaps a hint of how worn-out this dynamo of a man had become. In his twenties, Dickens had found happiness – as well as his career, and fame, and fortune – in the streets. By the mid-1860s, when Dickens was in his fifties, in *Our Mutual Friend* the 'great black river' is now seen to be 'stretching away to the great ocean, Death'; in the penultimate chapter of *Edwin Drood*, left on his desk unfinished at his demise in 1870, it comes even closer. Mr Tartar takes pretty Rosa Bud for a day out on the Thames: 'The tide bore them on in the gayest and most sparkling manner, until they stopped to dine in some everlastingly green garden.' Then, 'all too soon', they must head back, and once more 'the great black city cast its shadow on the waters, and its dark bridges spanned them as death spans life'. The river had been at the heart of London and the heart of Dickens' work. As early as *Oliver Twist* his writing had been compared to 'The surface of the stream [that] seems bright, and cheerfully bubbling as it rushes on – but in its windings you come ever and anon upon some place of death'. In his final novel, only the river represents life, while London – that never-equalled city, the city that was the motivating force behind one of the greatest novelists of all time – is shadowy and dark with death.

It is not possible, however, to leave Dickens there. He himself would not have done so voluntarily. Instead, let us leave him with Arthur Clennam and Little Dorrit, when they marry in the old church beside the Marshalsea, the scene of the Dickens family's terrible humiliation. After the ceremony the couple stand together on the church steps, looking down at the busy street below them. Then: 'They went quietly down in to the roaring streets, inseparable and blessed; and as they passed along in sunshine and shade, the noisy and the eager, and the arrogant and the froward, and the vain, fretted, and chafed, and made their usual uproar.'

DICKENS' PUBLICATIONS

	Publication date
Sketches by Boz	Newspaper sketches: November 1837–June 1839; in book form, 1836–7; in 1 vol., 1839
Pickwick Papers	Serial: April 1836–November 1837; book, 1837
Oliver Twist	Serial: February 1837–April 1839; book, 1838
Nicholas Nickleby	Serial: April 1838–October 1839; book, 1839
Old Curiosity Shop	Serial: April 1840–November 1841; book, 1841
Barnaby Rudge	Serial: February 1841–November 1841; book, 1841
American Notes	Book: 1842
A Christmas Carol	Book: December 1843
Martin Chuzzlewit	Serial: January 1843–July 1844; book, 1844
The Chimes	Book: December 1844
The Cricket on the Hearth	Book: December 1845
Dombey and Son	Serial: October 1846–April 1848; book, 1848
The Battle of Life	Book: December 1846
The Haunted Man	Book: December 1848
David Copperfield	Serial: May 1849–November 1850; book, 1850
Bleak House	Serial: March 1852–September 1853; book, 1853
Hard Times	Serial: April–August 1854; book, 1854
Little Dorrit	Serial: December 1855–June 1857; book, 1857
A Tale of Two Cities	Serial: April 1859–November 1859; book, 1859
Great Expectations	Serial: December 1860–August 1861; book, 1861
Our Mutual Friend	Serial: May 1864–November 1865; book, 1865
Edwin Drood	Serial: April 1870–September 1870 [left incomplete]

NOTES

INTRODUCTION

'merely life': Dickens, *The Posthumous Papers of the Pickwick Club*, ed. Mark Wormald (first published 1836–7; Harmondsworth, Penguin, 1999), p. 752; early citations of use of the term 'Dickensian': *Glasgow Herald*, 20 December 1859, *Hampshire Advertiser*, 31 December 1870, *Liverpool Mercury*, 23 November 1888.

'on Dickens himself': 'packed, like game': Dickens, 'Dullborough Town', in *All the Year Round*, 30 June 1860, *The Dent Uniform Edition of Dickens' Journalism*, vol. 4, *The Uncommercial Traveller and Other Papers*, ed. Michael Slater and John Drew (London, J. M. Dent, 2000), p. 140; John Forster, *The Life of Charles Dickens*, 3 vols (London, Chapman and Hall, 1872–4), vol. 1, p. 16; rent: Peter Ackroyd, *Dickens* (London, Vintage, 1999), p. 61.

'and kitchen ranges': Dickens, *David Copperfield*, ed. Jeremy Tambling (first published 1849–50; Harmondsworth, Penguin, 1996), p. 170.

'labouring hind': *David Copperfield*, p. 150; the chronology for Dickens' time in the blacking factory is uncertain. Dickens' friend and biographer John Forster says Dickens started work there around December 1823, while other writers believe that it was more likely to be January or February 1824. The date he left is equally uncertain, with one scholar, Michael Allen, *Charles Dickens and the Blacking Factory* (St Leonards, Oxford-Stockley Publications, 2011), pp. 92–4, suggesting it was as much as a year later. Most biographers think six months is more likely. It was certainly early 1825 before the boy returned to school. In his single known comment on the episode, Dickens himself claimed not to be able to remember; 'labouring hind': my thanks to Leslie Katz, Suzanne Daly, Susan Dean, Charles Hatten and Karla Waters for their help in tracking down the use of this phrase in the nineteenth century.

'far he had come': Forster, *Life*, vol. 1, pp. 47–8.

'shortened it to Boz': 'I walked down', Forster, *Life*, vol. 1, p. 76.

'find himself famous': sales figures for *Pickwick* are variously cited, ranging from 400–500 copies at the start, to 40,000–50,000 or even 60,000 by the end; I have followed the middle course of Michael Slater, *Charles Dickens* (New Haven, CT, Yale University Press, 2009), p. 215. For the chronology of Dickens' childhood and adolescence in the previous paragraphs, I have followed Michael Allen, *Charles Dickens' Childhood* (Basingstoke, Macmillan, 1988), passim, and Duane DeVries,

Dickens's Apprentice Years: The Making of a Novelist (Hassocks, Sussex, Harvester Press, 1976), passim.

'Vauxhall-bridge-road': 'Gone Astray', in *Household Words*, 13 August 1853; *The Dent Uniform Edition of Dickens' Journalism*, vol. 3: *'Gone Astray' and Other Papers*, ed. Michael Slater (London, J. M. Dent, 1998), pp. 155–65; Sala, cited in Forster, *Life*, vol. 3, p. 476; footnote on Dickens' walking pace: George Dolby, *Charles Dickens as I Knew Him: The Story of the Reading Tours in Great Britain and America, 1866–1870* (London, T. Fisher Unwin, 1885), p. 255.

'his final years': all but one of these descriptions of Dickens were compiled by Frederic G. Kitton, *Charles Dickens by Pen and Pencil*, and *A Supplement* (London, Frank T. Sabin, 1890); Sala's contribution appears on p. 93; the 'whipper-snapper' and the 'pretty-boy' are Thomas Trollope, p. 53; the light step and jaunty air, Arthur Locker, p. 173; the 'man of sanguine complexion' is from Derek Hudson, ed., *Munby, Man of Two Worlds: The Life and Diaries of Arthur J. Munby*, 1828–1910 (London, John Murray, 1972), p. 191.

'in the daylight': Forster, *Life*, vol. 2, p. 256; Dickens, *The Old Curiosity Shop*, ed. Angus Easson (first published 1840–41; Harmondsworth, Penguin, 1985), p. 43.

'accuracy of a cabman': 'Whenever we have an hour': this was the original opening for 'The Prisoner's Van', as printed in the newspaper *Bell's Life*, 29 November 1835, but it was replaced when it was collected into *Sketches by Boz*. Cited in John Butt and Kathleen Tillotson, *Dickens at Work* (London, Methuen, 1957), p. 44; the solicitor's clerk: Kitton, *Charles Dickens, by Pen and Pencil*, pp. 130–31; 'accuracy of a cabman': *Fraser's Magazine*, 21 (April 1840), p. 400.

'may interest others': 'lounging one evening': Dickens, 'The Parlour Orator', *Sketches by Boz*, ed. Dennis Walder (first published 1836–9; Harmondsworth, Penguin, 1995), p. 272; 'Suggest to him': Dickens to W. H. Wills, 27 September 1851, *The Letters of Charles Dickens: The Pilgrim Edition*, ed. Madeline House, Graham Storey, Kathleen Tillotson (Oxford, Clarendon, 1965–), vol. 6, p. 497; 'The Uncommercial Traveller: His General Line of Business', *All the Year Round*, 28 January 1860, *Dickens' Journalism*, vol. 4, p. 28.

'on the London streets': the charity children appear in *Illustrated London News* (hereafter cited as *ILN*), 28 May 1842, pp. 44–5; *Our Mutual Friend*, originals in Mayhew, noted in Harland S. Nelson, 'Dickens's *Our Mutual Friend* and Henry Mayhew's *London Labour and the London Poor*', *Nineteenth-Century Fiction*, 20: 3 (December 1965), pp. 207–22; Harvey Peter Sucksmith, 'Dickens and Mayhew: A Further Note', *Nineteenth-Century Fiction*, 24: 3 (December 1969), pp. 345–9, and Richard J. Dunn, 'Dickens and Mayhew Once More', *Nineteenth-Century Fiction*, 25: 3 (December 1970), pp. 348–53; the woman in white: Dickens, 'Where We Stopped Growing', *Household Words*, 1 January 1853, *Dickens' Journalism*, vol. 3, p. 111.

'been in 1800': size of London, numbers of inhabitants and houses: Jeremy Tambling, *Going Astray: Dickens and London* (Harlow, Pearson Longman, 2009), p. 18, and Jerry White, *London in the Nineteenth Century: 'A Human Awful Wonder of God'* (London, Jonathan Cape, 2007), p. 77.

'impression so nicely': Walter Bagehot, 'Charles Dickens', in *The Works and Life of Walter Bagehot*, ed. Mrs Russell Barrington (London, Longmans, Green, and Co., 1915), vol. 3, pp. 84–5; 'fanciful photograph': Dickens to W. H. Wills, 24 September 1858, *Letters*, vol. 8, p. 669; footnote: I owe this idea to Tambling, *Going Astray*, pp. 21–2.

'he marvelled': Henry James, 'The Art of Fiction', 1884, cited in F. O. Matthiesson, *The James Family* (New York, Knopf, 1947), p. 360; 'English Traits', in Emerson, *The Prose Works of Ralph Waldo Emerson* (Boston, Fields, Osgood & Co., 1870), vol. 2, p. 278; Parkman, *The Journals of Francis Parkman*, ed. Mason Wade (London, Eyre and Spottiswoode, 1949), vol. 1, p. 221.

'created Dickens': J.-K. Huysmans, *Against Nature*, trans. Robert Baldick (Harmondsworth, Penguin, 1959), p. 138; Walter Benjamin citing G. K. Chesterton, *Dickens*, in *The Arcades Project*, trans. Howard Eiland and Kevin McLaughlin (Cambridge, MA, Belknap, Harvard University Press, 1999), p. 438.

'the nearest way': *David Copperfield*, p. 153.

1810: THE BERNERS STREET HOAX

'aged family retainer': 'piano-fortes by dozens': [Theodore Hook], *Gilbert Gurney* (London, Whittaker & Co., 1836), vol. 1, pp. 298–9.

'left in peace': verse: 'The Hoax: An Epistle from Solomon Sappy, Esquire, in London, to his brother Simon at Liverpool', *Satirist, or, Monthly Meteor*, 1 January 1811, pp. 59–61.

'the fun in comfort': the details of the episode are given by Hook's biographer, Bill Newton Dunn, *The Man Who Was John Bull: The Biography of Theodore Edward Hook, 1778–1841* (London, Allendale, 1996), p. 12, citing an article from the *Morning Post*, which he does not date and I have been unable to trace. However, the *Examiner*, 2 December 1810, p. 768, 'Principal Occurrences in the Year 1810', in the *New Annual Register* [January 1811?] and 'Principal Occurrences in the Year 1810', in the *Edinburgh Annual Register* [January 1811?], all seem to be reprints, with some additional information.

'of Bedford Street': this and the next two paragraphs: Mrs [Nancy] Mathews, *Tea-Table Talk, Ennobled Actresses, and Other Miscellanies* (London, Thomas Cautley Newby, 1857), pp. 158–62.

'those in the street': epilogue to *Lost and Found*: cited in *Literary Panorama*, February 1811, pp. 379–90; the *European Magazine, and London Review*, January 1811, p. 46, names the play and authors.

1. EARLY TO RISE

'are rapidly filling': [William Moy Thomas], 'Covent Garden Market', *Household Words*, 175, 30 July 1853, pp. 505–11.

'side of the river': long lines of men and women: Charles Dickens, 'The Streets – Morning', *Sketches by Boz*, p. 70.

'leathern leggings': Augustus Mayhew, *Paved with Gold, or, The Romance and Reality of the London Streets* (London, Chapman and Hall, 1858), p. 75. This is a novel, but Augustus Mayhew acted as one of his brother Henry's primary researchers on *London Labour and the London Poor*, and not only does he use here the material he gathered for background, but some of it shows up in the same words in both works. I have therefore, with caution, treated some descriptive passages in the novel as non-fiction.

'from nightwork': Dickens, *Bleak House*, ed. Norman Page (first published 1852–3; Harmondsworth, Penguin, 1985), p. 96.

'ready for customers': [Thomas Wright], *The Great Unwashed*, 'by a Journeyman Engineer', p. 185; footnote on Wright: Alastair J. Reid, 'Wright, Thomas', *Oxford Dictionary of National Biography*, Oxford University Press, October 2006 [http://www.oxforddnb.com.ezproxy.londonlibrary.co.uk/view/article/47426, accessed 7 January 2011]; Camberwell: Alfred Rosling Bennett, *London and Londoners in the Eighteen-fifties and Sixties* (London, T. Fisher Unwin, 1924), p. 54; Covent Garden: George Augustus Sala, *Gaslight and Daylight, with Some London Scenes They Shine Upon* (London, Chapman & Hall, 1859), p. 13; footnote: biographical information on G. A. Sala: P. D. Edwards, 'Sala, George Augustus', *Oxford Dictionary of National Biography*, Oxford University Press, 2004; online edn, May 2005 [http://www.oxforddnb.com.ezproxy.londonlibrary.co.uk/view/article/24526, accessed 17 June 2011]; Islington: James Greenwood, *Unsentimental Journeys: or, Byways of the Modern Babylon* (London, Ward, Lock, & Tyler, 1867), pp. 32–3.

'worse off than themselves': [Thomas Wright], *Some Habits and Customs of the Working Classes*, 'by a Journeyman Engineer' (London, Tinsley Brothers, 1867), p. 255.

'for a street seller': Greenwood, *Unsentimental Journeys*, pp. 34ff.

'journalist Charles Dickens': 'The Streets – Morning', *Sketches by Boz*, p. 73.

'his little finger': middle-aged clerks: Leman Rede, 'The Lawyer's Clerk', in Kenny Meadows [illus.], *Heads of the People: or, Portraits of the English*, 'with original essays by distinguished writers' (London, Willoughby & Co., [1840]), vol. 1, pp. 28ff; younger clerks: George Augustus Sala, *Twice Round the Clock: or, The Hours of the Day and Night in London* (London, Houlston and Wright [1859]), p. 83; *Bleak House*, p. 173.

'to the City': Anon., *The London Conductor* (London, John Cassell, 1851), p. 1; 'reduced to a system': *The London Guide, and Stranger's Safeguard*... 'by a Gentleman' (London, Bumpus, 1818), p. 27; newspaper reader: W. E. Adams, *Memoirs of a Social Atom* (London, Hutchinson, 1903), vol. 2, p. 313.

'one shop alone': 1850 figures: Parliamentary Select Committee report, cited in John R. Kellett, *The Impact of the Railways on Victorian Cities* (London, Routledge and Kegan Paul, 1969), pp. 45–6; 1866 figures: White, *London in the Nineteenth Century*, p. 42; Robert Southey, cited in David Barnett, *London, Hub of the Industrial Revolution: A Revisionary History, 1775–1825* (London, Tauris, 1998), p. 1.

'four and a half miles': musician's children: Rosamund Gotch Brunel (ed.), *Mendelssohn and his Friends in Kensington: Letters*... *1833–36* (London, Oxford University Press, 1934), pp. 24–5; Leonard Wyon: Journal, BL Add MS 59,617, 21 January 1854; Maria Cust, cited in Heather Creaton (ed.), *Victorian Diaries: The Daily Lives of Victorian Men and Women* (London, Mitchell Beazley, 2001), p. 39; Dickens to the Hon. Mrs Richard Watson, 11 July 1851, *Letters*, vol. 6, p. 429.

'was the norm': Peepy: *Bleak House*, p. 109; the page references for the rest of the walks in this paragraph are respectively: pp. 224, 260, 921, 750, 375, 718, 867, 247, 356; Dickens, *Our Mutual Friend*, ed. Adrian Poole (first published 1864–5;

Harmondsworth, Penguin, 1997), pp. 446, 452; Dickens, *Little Dorrit*, ed. John Holloway (first published 1855–7; Harmondsworth, Penguin, 1985), p. 830.

'at the termini': Mayhew on working hours: Henry Mayhew, *London Labour and the London Poor* (New York, Dover, 1968; facsimile of Griffin, Bohn edn, 1861–2), vol. 2, p. 174; the cab and bus employees: John Garwood, *The Million Peopled City, or, One-half of the People of London Made Known to the Other Half* (London, Wertheim and Macintosh, 1853), pp. 177–9, 220–24; the cab horses: William John Gordon, *The Horse-World of London* (London, Leisure Hour Library, 1893), p. 36.

'employment practices': the draper: *ILN*, 12 October 1844, p. 230; Henry Vizetelly, *Glances Back through Seventy Years: Autobiographical and Other Reminiscences* (London, Kegan Paul, Trench, Trübner & Co., 1893), vol. 1, p. 116; Dickens, *Nicholas Nickleby*, ed. Michael Slater (first published 1838–9; Harmondsworth, Penguin, 1978), p. 539; footnote on Foreign Post nights: the days are taken in this instance from *Leigh's New Picture of London…* (London, Leigh and Co., 1839 edn), but other handbooks carry the same information.

2. ON THE ROAD

'running along': Dickens, *Oliver Twist, or, The Parish Boy's Progress*, ed. Philip Horne (first published 1837–8; Harmondsworth, Penguin, 2002), p. 330.

'crashing roar': Max Schlesinger, *Saunterings in and about London*, trans. Otto Wenckstern (first published 1852; London, Nathaniel Cooke, 1853), p. 70; Mrs Gaskell, *The Life of Charlotte Brontë* (London, Smith, Elder & Co., 1870), pp. 270–71; Henry Mayhew and John Binny, *The Criminal Prisons of London and Scenes of Prison Life* (London, Charles Griffin [1862]), p. 53; 'crashing roar': Charles Manby Smith, *The Little World of London* (London, Arthur Hall, Virtue and Co., 1857), p. 395.

'hear each other': American clergyman: Nathaniel S. Wheaton, *A Journal of a Residence during Several Months in London…in the Years 1823 and 1824* (Hartford, CT, H. & F. J. Huntington, 1830), p. 41; Jane Carlyle to Eliza Stodart, 1 August 1834, *The Collected Letters of Thomas and Jane Welsh Carlyle* (hereafter referred to as *Carlyle Letters*), ed. Charles Richard Sanders, Kenneth J. Fielding, et al. (Durham, NC, Duke University Press, 1977), vol. 7, pp. 250–54. The complete letters are available online, at http://carlyleletters.dukejournals.org; *Bleak House*, p. 823.

'in Holborn today': footnote: the location of Ellis and Blackmore is slightly opaque, as Dickens, in *Sketches by Boz*, claimed that the solicitors' offices were at 1 Raymond Buildings, 'originally off Gray's Inn Square'. However, Geoffrey Fletcher, *The London Dickens Knew* (London, Hutchinson, 1970), p. 48, states that Ellis and Blackmore was definitely at Holborn Court, now South Square, and the company moved to Raymond Buildings later; survival of Number 1: Andrew Goodman, *The Walking Guide to Lawyers' London* (London, Blackstone, 2000), p. 205; Dickens, *David Copperfield*, p. 754.

'on his boots': Doctors' Commons: *David Copperfield*, p. 327; Dickens, *The Life and Adventures of Martin Chuzzlewit*, ed. P. N. Furbank (first published 1843–4; Harmondsworth, Penguin, 1986), p. 693; *Our Mutual Friend*, pp. 99–100;

Dickens, *The Mystery of Edwin Drood*, ed. Arthur Cox (first published 1870; Harmondsworth, Penguin, 1993), p. 133.

'day nor night': Robert Southey, *Letters from England*, ed. Jack Simmons (first published 1807; Gloucester, Alan Sutton, 1984), p. 46; footnote on the Temple watchman: Hudson, *Munby*, pp. 191–2; church bells: Mayhew and Binny, *The Criminal Prisons*, pp. 23, 32; dockyards: James Freeman Clarke, *Eleven Weeks in Europe; and, What May be Seen in that Time* (Boston, Ticknor, Reed, and Fields, 1852), p. 59.

'poorly or not at all': [Louis Simond], 'A Day in London', in *The National Register*, vol. 2, no. 4, 21 September 1816, p. 59; footnote on Louis Simond: the contemporary academic's work from whom Simond's biographical information also derives is Xavier Baron (ed.), *London 1066–1914: Literary Sources and Documents*, vol. 2: *Regency and Early Victorian London, 1800–1870* (Robertsbridge, Helm Information, 1997), p. 143; reasons for street noise: Ralph Turvey, 'Street Mud, Dust and Noise', *London Journal*, 21: 2 (1996), pp. 131–48.

'fall in unison': this and the following two paragraphs come from Turvey, 'Street Mud', unless otherwise stated; 'iron or stone cylinders': Bennett, *London and Londoners*, p. 90; sticky streets: Parliamentary Papers, 1868, XII, Select Committee on Metropolitan Local Government Q1866–72; 'quagmires': [Alexander MacKenzie], *The American in England* (New York, Harper & Brothers, 1835), p. 103; adhesive qualities: cited in James Winter, *London's Teeming Streets, 1830–1914* (London, Routledge, 1993), p. 119; the mob and the roads: *ILN*, 7 July 1855, p. 7.

'with the granite': London Bridge navvies: Bennett, *London and Londoners*, p. 98; footnote on Alfred Rosling Bennett: Ronald M. Birse, 'Bennett, Alfred Rosling', rev. Brian Bowers, *Oxford Dictionary of National Biography*, Oxford University Press, 2004 [http://www.oxforddnb.com.ezproxy.londonlibrary.co.uk/view/article/37181, accessed 17 June 2011]; horses' hooves: *ILN*, 7 January 1854, pp. 7, 10; Wilkie Collins, *Basil* (London, Richard Bentley, 1852), vol. 2, pp. 155, 194.

'windows were open': *Journal of the Society of Arts*, cited in Turvey, 'Street Mud', p. 139.

'into the twentieth century': Cheapside petition: *ILN*, 29 October 1842, p. 391; wood in the City: *ILN*, 28 January 1843, p. 59, but this story runs and runs: see also 4 and 18 February, 2 September, 7 October and 18 November 1843, 7 December 1844, p. 359; locations retaining use of wood: *ILN*, 20 June 1846, p. 398, lists the Old Bailey, and it was still wood paved when Mayhew was writing *London Labour*, in which he also notes 'some churches and other public buildings', but does not itemize them, vol. 2, p. 181; post-1870s wooden paving: Walter Besant, *London in the Nineteenth Century* (London, Adam & Charles Black, 1909), p. 344.

'paved at all': New Yorker: Fanny W. Hall, *Rambles in Europe*… (New York, E. French, 1839), vol. 2, p. 143; the date of her trip is not stated, but appears from the context to be before 1837, possibly as early as the late 1820s; *Leigh's New Picture* (1839 edn), p. 29, although this quote and some of the accompanying text in fact repeat almost verbatim C. F. Partington, *National History and Views of London…from Original Drawings*… (London, Allan Bell and Co., 1834), p. 4.

'in every suburb': Hector Gavin, *Sanitary Ramblings: Being Sketches and Illustrations of Bethnal Green* (London, John Churchill, 1848), pp. 14–17; western suburbs: 'Walter', *My Secret Life* (5 vols., first published 1888–94; Ware, Herts, Wordsworth,

1995), vol. 2, p. 241; Anthony Trollope, *Castle Richmond* (London, Chapman & Hall, 1860), vol. 3, p. 196.

'throughout his life': the memoirist: S. and E.-A. Whyte, *Miscellanea Nova* (Dublin, Edward-Athenry Whyte, 1800), p. 49; [Louis Simond], *Journal of a Tour and Residence in Great Britain during the Years 1810 and 1811...* (Edinburgh, Archibald Constable and Company, 1815), vol. 1, p. 18; Wheaton, *Journal of a Residence*, p. 191; 1835 guidebook: Partington, *National History and Views of London*, p. 4; macadamization and pavements: Winter, *London's Teeming Streets, 1830–1914*, p. 37.

'and certain progress': traffic islands: Andrew Dickinson, *My First Visit to Europe...* (New York, George P. Putnam, 1851), p. 119; Schlesinger, *Saunterings*, p. 16; the view from the bus: Henry Colman, *European Life and Manners; or, Familiar Letters to Friends* (Boston, Charles C. Little and James Brown, 1850), vol. 1, p. 163.

'but still faster': Fordyce: cited in Dana Arnold, *Re-Presenting the Metropolis: Architecture, Urban Experience and Social Life in London, 1800–1940* (Aldershot, Ashgate, 2000), p. 38; *Little Dorrit*, p. 690.

'Kennington Gate': factor in traffic problems: T. C. Barker and Michael Robbins, *A History of London Transport...*, vol. 1: *The Nineteenth Century* (London, George Allen & Unwin, 1975), p. 64; turnpike locations: Arthur Hayward, *The Days of Dickens: A Glance at Some Aspects of Early Victorian Life in London* (London, George Routledge and Sons, 1926), p. 84. This book appears to be in many places an unacknowledged compilation of contemporary accounts, occasionally conflating information from more than one account. I therefore cite Hayward only when I have been unable to identify an original.

'one for tickets': Old Brompton toll gate: S. C. Hall, *Retrospect of a Long Life, 1815–83* (London, Bentley and Son, 1883), vol. 1, p. 68; Oxford Street gates: Thomas Adolphus Trollope, *What I Remember* (London, Richard Bentley, 1887), p. 31; footnote on pockets: Phillis Cunnington and Catherine Lucas, *Occupational Costume in England, from the Eleventh Century to 1914* (London, Adam & Charles Black, 1967), p. 353.

'returned the money': keeping travellers waiting: Hall, *Retrospect of a Long Life*, vol. 1, pp. 68–9.

'the rest themselves': clockwork mechanism: MacKenzie, *The American in England*, vol. 1, p. 217; Dickens on its inventor: Dickens, 'Down with the Tide', in *Dickens' Journalism*, vol. 3, p. 115; taking goods instead of money: ibid., p. 117.

'of verisimilitude': number of tickets: Revd R. H. Dalton Barham, *The Life and Remains of Theodore Edward Hook* (London, Richard Bentley, 1849), vol. 1, pp. 61–2; *Oliver Twist*, p. 365.

'river were abolished': 1830 toll removal: Barker and Robbins, *A History of London Transport*, vol. 1, p. 13; the 178 toll bars: Bennett: *London and Londoners*, p. 90; Vauxhall: Edmund Yates, *Edmund Yates: His Recollections and Experiences* (London, Richard Bentley and Son, 1885), p. 96; the campaign to lift the tolls: *ILN*, 23 March 1857, 6 June 1857, 15 August 1857, 8 and 29 May 1858; 'Great Open-Air Demonstration': *ILN*, 27 July 1857, p. 632; abolition of tolls: G. A. Sekon, *Locomotion in Victorian London* (London, Oxford University Press, 1938), p. 40.

'defied the night': Southwark Bridge: *ILN*, 19 November 1864, p. 513; *Little Dorrit*, pp. 135, 260, 305; Waterloo Bridge: 'Night Walks', in *All the Year Round*, 21 July 1860, in *Dickens' Journalism*, vol. 4, p. 151.

'private matter': straps on buses: Barker and Robbins: *A History of London Transport*, vol. 1, p. 32; Magazine Day: Smith, *Little World of London*, p. 47; police notice: *ILN*, 31 July 1852, p. 71.

'given to the police': Westminster Bridge: *ILN*, 10 March 1860, p. 235; traffic light: cited in William Kent, *London for Dickens Lovers* (London, Methuen, 1935), p. 48; 1871 treatise: Henry Carr, *Metropolitan Street Traffic: Suggested Improvements* (London, R. J. Mitchell and Sons, 1871), p. 3.

'weighing machine': weights of horses and carts, lack of turning space: Gordon, *The Horse-World of London*, pp. 54, 84, 127, 77; brewers' dray horses: J. E. Bradfield, *The Public Carriages of Great Britain: A Glance at their Rise, Progress, Struggles and Burthens* (London, Piper, Stephenson & Spence, 1855), p. 69; six horses harnessed in line: David W. Bartlett, *What I saw in London, or, Men and Things in the Great Metropolis* (Auburn [CT?], Derby and Miller, 1852), p. 69; Nelson's Column: *ILN*, 2 July 1842, p. 121; carters lending horses: Albert Smith (ed.), *Gavarni in London: Sketches of Life and Character* (London, David Bogue, 1849), p. 39.

'twenty-five yards': Half-way House: plans for destruction in *ILN*, 16 July 1842, p. 150; Middle Row: Percy Edwards, *History of London Street Improvements, 1855–1897* (London, London County Council, 1898), facing p. 35, and map, Yates, *Recollections*, p. 35, Edward Callow, *Old London Taverns: Historical, descriptive and Reminiscent…* (London, Downey & Co., 1899), p. 224, Walter Thornbury, *Old and New London*, 6 vols (London, Cassell, Petter, & Galpin [?1887–93]), vol. 1, pp. 51ff.

'pornography industry': this paragraph and the next draw on Barker and Robbins, *A History of London Transport*, vol. 1, pp. 10–11, 64ff.

'blocked by traffic': Park Lane widening: *ILN*, 10 December 1864, p. 591, 17 December 1864, p. 603; footnote: *ILN*, 11 August 1866, p. 127.

'several hours' duration': Wheaton, *Journal of a Residence*, pp. 243–4.

'into shop-windows': tourist: MacKenzie, *The American in England*, pp. 73–4; 'Passage in the Life of Mr Watkins Tottle', *Sketches by Boz*, p. 511.

'the crossing-sweepers': Schlesinger, *Saunterings* (and at the end of the paragraph), pp. 231–2; licensed horse-killing: Gordon, *The Horse-Sense of London*, p. 184ff.; road deaths: *ILN*, 4 January 1868, p. 7, gives a figure of 170 deaths in 1867.

'and umbrellas': Tambling, *Going Astray*, p. 264, identifies the church and therefore suggests that Holborn is the site of Tom-all-Alone's, but I am not persuaded that the description is not a composite: the routine of Jo's day suggests a location closer to Drury Lane. It is also Tambling who identifies the Society for the Propagation of the Gospel; Dickens, *Bleak House*, pp. 274–5.

'for their customers': Venice: Smith (ed.), *Gavarni in London*, p. 36; footnote on crossing-sweepers: Hudson, *Munby*, p. 143; *Bleak House*, p. 200; different types of sweeps: Charles Manby Smith, *Curiosities of London Life: or, Phases, Physiological and Social, of the Great Metropolis* (London, William and Frederick G. Cash, 1853), pp. 44–9, and Smith, *Little World of London*, p. 84; police and companies: Mayhew, *London Labour*, vol. 2, pp. 465.

'are all shown': the Select Committee, undated, is cited in Mayhew, *London Labour*, vol. 2, pp. 193; ingredients of street dirt, and scavengers: ibid., vol. 2, pp. 185, 193, 196–7, 217, and Turvey, 'Street Mud, Dust and Noise', p. 134; dustmen's clothes: Cunnington and Lucas, *Occupational Costume*, p. 277, and *Our Mutual Friend*, p. 770.

'scuttle or trough': William Tayler, *The Diary of William Tayler, Footman, 1837*, ed. Dorothy Wise (London, Westminster City Archives, 1998), p. 17; sweeping by machine: Dickinson, *My First Visit to Europe*, p. 119.

'private households': *David Copperfield*, p. 183; Derby wear: A. Mayhew, *Paved with Gold*, pp. 218–19; effect of dust on shops and houses: Mayhew, *London Labour*, vol. 2, p. 213.

'a dusty roadway': tank-like carts: Mayhew and Binny, *The Criminal Prisons*, p. 173; mechanics of pumps, and footnote: Bennett, *London and Londoners*, pp. 46–7.

'indicative of light': tallow lights: William T. O'Dea, *The Social History of Lighting* (London, Routledge and Kegan Paul, 1958), p. 96; John Gay, 'Of Walking the Streets by Night', in *A Complete Edition of the Poets of Great Britain* (London, John and Arthur Arch [1792–5]), vol. 8, p. 293, ll. 139–43; City oil lamps: O'Dea, ibid.; *Pickwick Papers*, p. 50; Simond, *Journal of a Tour and Residence*, vol. 1, pp. 26–7.

'shares her concern': Carlton House illuminations: Hugh Barty-King, *New Flame: How Gas Changed the Commercial, Domestic and Industrial Life of Britain...* (Tavistock, Graphmitre, 1984), p. 28; visitors to Pall Mall: Wolfgang Schivelbusch, *Disenchanted Night: The Industrialisation of Light in the Nineteenth Century*, trans. Angela Davies (Oxford, Berg, 1988), p. 115; Rowlandson: Arnold, *Re-Presenting the Metropolis*, p. 33, but note that she has confused the 1805 and 1807 displays, thinking the latter three-month display was the temporary display for the birthday of George III (she says it is the Regent's).

'could be accessed': lights spanning the lane: *Athenaeum*, cited in O'Dea, *Social History of Lighting*, pp. 29ff.; lamp-posts and pavements: David Hughson, *Walks through London...* (London, Sherwood, Neely and Jones, 1817), p. 396.

'their own lamp': dress: Cunnington and Lucas, *Occupational Costume*, p. 286.

'roads were lighter': Wheaton, *Journal of a Residence*, p. 38; 'Walter', *My Secret Life*, vol. 1, p. 143.

'they had finished': Sala, *Twice Round the Clock*, p. 43; Parliament Square: O'Dea, *Social History of Lighting*, pp. 29ff.; Camberwell: H. J. Dyos, *Victorian Suburb: A Study of the Growth of Camberwell* (Leicester, Leicester University Press, 1973), p. 147; closure of Fleet Street: *ILN*, 15 August 1846, p. 99; Strand closure: *ILN*, 7 August 1858, p. 128.

'end of the street': *ILN*, 23 November 1850, p. 403.

'for the upkeep': demolitions: Peter Jackson, *George Scharf's London: Sketches and Watercolours of a Changing City, 1820–50* (London, John Murray, 1987), pp. 110–11; Upper Thames Street: *ILN*, 28 May 1842, p. 42; Piccadilly: ibid., and 20 July 1844.

'if generally adopted': 'The Wants of London': *ILN*, 30 September 1854, p. 291; descriptive addresses: Silvester notebooks, British Library, Egerton 3710; Dickens autobiographical fragment in Forster, *Life of Charles Dickens*, vol. 1, p. 41; lack of signage: *ILN*, 5 March 1853, p. 183.

'also took place': repeated street names: [W. H. Wills], 'Streetography', *Household Words*, 38, 14 December 1850, pp. 275–6; synonyms for slum streets: John Hollingshead, *Ragged London in 1861* (London, Smith, Elder, 1861), p. 96; George Streets: *ILN*, 1 February 1868, p. 103; street renaming: *ILN*, 25 July 1846, p. 54, and reprinted Metropolitan Board of Works announcements, 13 August 1864, p. 163, 25 February 1865, p. 175, 1 July 1865, p. 627, 11 November 1865, 16 February 1867, 20 February 1869, p. 175, among many others.

'mammoth unknowability': Ordnance Survey: *ILN*, 29 January 1848, p. 53; 1850 publication: Ackroyd, *London*, p. 117.

'Fyodor Dostoyevsky': Byron, *Don Juan*, ed. Leslie A. Marchand (Boston, Houghton Mifflin, 1958), Canto 10, v. 82; Philadelphia visitor: Orville Horwitz, *Brushwood Picked Up on the Continent: or, Last Summer's Trip to the Old World* (Philadelphia, Lippincott, Grambo & Co., 1855), pp. 21–2; Dostoevsky: *Winter Notes on Summer Impressions*, trans. David Patterson (Evanston, IL, Northwestern University Press, 1997), p. 37.

'pageant of phantoms': Heine: cited in Hugh and Pauline Massingham, *The London Anthology* (London, Spring Books [n.d.]), pp. 474–5; de Quincey: *De Quincey's Writings*, fol. 23, 'Life and Manners' (Boston, Ticknor, Reed and Fields, 1851), p. 53.

'the prime minister': Bagehot: 'Charles Dickens', vol. 3, pp. 82–5; number of new roads: *ILN*, 2 January 1869, p. 3, 15 September 1849, p. 186; Downing Street and environs: John Thomas Smith, *An Antiquarian Ramble in the Streets of London*, ed. Charles Mackay (London, Richard Bentley, 1846), vol. 1, pp. 180–81.

'the building trade': development of Euston, and footnote: Alan A. Jackson, *London's Termini* (London, Pan, 1969), pp. 18–20; Wellington House Academy: 'Our School', *Household Words*, 11 October 1851, *Dickens' Journalism*, vol. 3, p. 35; Dickens, *Dombey and Son*, ed. Peter Fairclough, intro. Raymond Williams (first published 1846–48; Harmondsworth, Penguin, 1985), pp. 120–21; building trade: John Summerson, *The London Building World of the Eighteen-Sixties* (London, Thames and Hudson, 1973), p. 9.

'Grosvenor Estate': hill at Piccadilly: *ILN*, 19 September 1846, p. 182; Oxford Street: *ILN*, 5 October 1850, p. 273; Grosvenor Basin: *ILN*, 7 July 1860, p. 13.

'frames of timber': Hudson, *Munby*, p. 175; *Daily News*, cited in Richard Altick, *The Presence of the Present: Topics of the Day in the Victorian Novel* (Columbus, OH, Ohio State University Press, 1991), pp. 414–15; description of Viaduct site: *ILN*, 30 March 1867, p. 303.

3. TRAVELLING (MOSTLY) HOPEFULLY

'City by boat': *Dombey and Son*, pp. 362 and 725 for example; Yates, *Recollections*, p. 63.

'of the river': number of boats: White, *London in the Nineteenth Century*, pp. 14–15; 'Sculls, sir!': MacKenzie, *The American in England*, vol. 2, p. 56; 'The Steam Excursion', *Sketches by Boz*, p. 447; *The Old Curiosity Shop*, p. 86.

'in the east': the development of steamers in this and the next five paragraphs, unless otherwise noted, is from: Frank L. Dix, *Royal River Highway: A History of the Passenger Boats and Services on the River Thames* (Newton Abbot, David and Charles, 1985), pp. 51–84 and passim, Sekon, *Locomotion in Victorian London*, pp. 56–64 and passim, and Barker and Robbins, *A History of London Transport*, vol. 1, pp. 43ff.; *Leigh's New Picture of London…* (London, Leigh and Co, 1819 edn), pp. 420–22, and the 1839 edition, p. 350; river stairs: David Paroissien, *The Companion to Great Expectations* (Robertsbridge, Helm Information, 2000), p. 217.

'boat to another': *Our Mutual Friend*, p. 539; 'half a dozen': Schlesinger, *Saunterings*, pp. 31–2.

'people took boat': Hungerford Stairs: Mayhew and Binny, *The Criminal Prisons*, p. 233–4; *David Copperfield*, pp. 150–51.

'man at the wheel': the dimensions are taken from Allison Lockwood, *Passionate Pilgrims: The American Traveller in Great Britain, 1800–1914* (NY, Cornwall Books, 1981), p. 175; operating procedure: Bennett, *London and Londoners*, pp. 113–14; call boy, John Forney, *Letters from Europe* (Philadelphia, T. B. Peterson & Brothers, 1867), p. 362.

'filthy to a degree': schedules: George Frederick Pardon, *Routledge's Popular Guide to London and its Suburbs* (London, Routledge Warne & Routledge, 1862), pp. 44–5; onboard conditions: Revd A. Cleveland Coxe, *Impressions of England; or, Sketches of English Scenery and Society* (New York, Dana & Co., 1856), p. 37, *ILN*, 23 May 1846, p. 339, [Elias Derby], *Two Months Abroad: or, A Trip to England, France, Baden, Prussia, and Belgium, in August and September, 1843*, 'by a Rail-road Director of Massachusetts' (Boston, Redding & Co., 1844); Henry Morford, *Over-Sea, or, England, France and Scotland, as Seen by a Live American* (NY, Hilton and Co., 1867), p. 76, and Forney, *Letters from Europe*, pp. 360–61.

'Ramsgate on Fridays': names: Bennett, *London and Londoners*, pp. 108–110.

'of manslaughter': shoe-leather: Smith, *Curiosities*; the *Cricket*: *ILN*, 27 July 1844, p. 51.

'may have died': number of accidents: Barker and Robbins, *A History of London Transport*, vol. 1, pp. 41; *Our Mutual Friend*, p. 436.

'by the City short-stage': Schlesinger, *Saunterings*, p. 161; short-stage in 1825: Michael Freeman and Derek H. Aldcroft (eds), *Transport in Victorian Britain* (Manchester, Manchester University Press, 1988), p. 139; *Pickwick Papers*, p. 615; *David Copperfield*, pp. 563, 565; *Great Expectations*, ed. Charlotte Mitchell, intro. David Trotter (first published 1860–61; Harmondsworth, Penguin, 1996), pp. 186, 269.

'seven or eight miles': 'A Dinner at Poplar Walk' was retitled 'Mr Minns and His Cousin' when it was collected into *Sketches by Boz*, p. 367; Simond, *Journal of a Tour and Residence*, vol. 1, p. 17.

'costing 2s': personal service: Bradfield, *Public Carriages*, p. 38; Mr Minns: 'A Dinner at Poplar Walk', *Sketches by Boz*, p. 372; cost: G. A. Thrupp, *The History of Coaches* (London, Kerby & Endean, 1877), p. 121.

'Bardell omnibus company': bus speed and width of three-horse buses: Bradfield, *Public Carriages*, pp. 35, 37; seating capacity and number of horses, John Gloag, *Victorian Comfort: A Social History of Design from 1830–1900* (Newton Abbot, David and Charles, 1973), p. 128; footnote on library of books: Gordon, *The Horse-World of London*, p. 11; names of buses: Schlesinger, *Saunterings*, p. 161; the Bardell omnibus company: William F. Long, 'Mr Pickwick Lucky to Find a Cab?', *Dickensian*, Autumn 1991, pp. 167–70.

'as they left': number of box seats: Bennett, *London and Londoners*, p. 82; the author also notes their popularity, as do other writers of the period (Thrupp, *The History of*

Coaches, p. 122, is the only one to describe them as 'unpopular', and he seems to be outnumbered in this); how to mount: Sekon, *Locomotion in Victorian London*, p. 33; the width: Garwood, *The Million Peopled City*, p. 204.

'to the top': the interior height: *ILN*, 12 August 1854, p. 130, but this may have been journalistic exaggeration. Certainly the height was limited, but no other source claims that those seated had to stoop. According to an earlier paragraph in the *ILN*, 1 May 1847, p. 288, a new design was being promoted, whereby passengers would be able to enter and exit 'without stooping': however, this doesn't suggest that, once inside, tall men still needed to stoop; the Frenchman: Francis Wey, *A Frenchman Sees London in the 'Fifties*, 'adapted from the French' by Valerie Pirie (London, Sidgwick and Jackson, 1935), pp. 69–70.

'own umbrellas': drivers' dress and manner, and leather covering: Schlesinger: *Saunterings*, pp. 163–4, 168; Bennett, *London and Londoners*, p. 81.

'to the suburbs': decline of the short-stagecoach: Barker and Robbins, *A History of London Transport*, vol 1, p. 26; incomes: *Penny Magazine*, 31 March 1837, cited in Freeman and Aldcroft (eds), *Transport in Victorian Britain*; suburban routes: Dyos, *Victorian Suburb*, p. 67; the 37.5 million passengers: *ILN*, 19 September 1857, p. 287.

'along their routes': dress: Bennett, *London and Londoners*, pp. 81–2, and Schlesinger, *Saunterings*, p. 164; cad's step and behaviour, Bennett, *London and Londoners*, p. 82; the height of the step, Sekon, *Locomotion in Victorian London*, p. 33.

'up to 9d': 'Omnibuses', *Sketches by Boz*, p. 169; S. Sophia Beale, *Recollections of a Spinster Aunt* (London, William Heinemann, 1908), p. 20; impact of snow: Wyon, Journal, BL Add MS 59,617, f.29; increased costs: *ILN*, 7 January 1854, p. 3.

'the increased work': 'Omnibuses', *Sketches by Boz*, p. 169; driving on the pavement: *ILN*, 7 September 1844, p. 155; ignoring passengers: Watts Phillips, *The Wild Tribes of London* (London, Ward and Lock, 1855), p. 17.

'emptied roads': use of skids: Yates, *Recollections*, p. 35, and Schlesinger, *Saunterings*, p. 58–9; drivers strapped in: Sekon, *Locomotion in Victorian London*, p. 33; falling horses: Phillips, *Wild Tribes*, p. 17; boys skating: Bennett, *London and Londoners*, p. 98.

'their own doors': *Nicholas Nickleby*, p. 673; Smith, *Curiosities*, pp. 337–8.

'begin in 1859': this outline is drawn from Freeman and Aldcroft (eds), *Transport in Victorian Britain*, p. 145, and Alan A. Jackson, *London's Metropolitan Railway* (Newton Abbot, David and Charles, 1986), pp. 14ff.

'natural disaster': *Daily News*, 23 June 1862, p. 5.

'regained control': locomotive explosion: Anthony Clayton, *Subterranean City: Beneath the Streets of London* (London, Historical Publications, 2000), p. 99; landslide: Jackson, *London's Metropolitan Railway*, p. 23; Fleet Ditch disaster: *Daily News*, 19 and 20 June, 18 July 1862, *Standard*, 19, 20, 25 and 26 June 1862, *ILN*, 28 June 1862.

'ventured underground': VIP trip and photograph: ChristianWolmar, *The Subterranean Railway: How the London Underground was Built, and How it Changed the City Forever* (London, Atlantic, 2004), pp. 37–8, 41; layout and lighting: Mayhew, *The Shops and Companies of London*, p. 150; fares and numbers of passengers: *ILN*, 27 December 1862, p. 687, 17 and 24 January 1863, pp. 57, 91.

'passengers annually': Kensington Canal: Hugh Meller, *London Cemeteries: An Illustrated Guide and Gazetteer* (2nd edn, Godstone, Surrey, Gregg, 1985), p. 75; otherwise, this paragraph: Christian Wolmar, *The Subterranean Railway*, pp. 66, 71, 81.

'at King's Cross': John H. B. Latrobe, *Hints for Six Months in Europe...* (Philadelphia, J. B. Lippincott, & Co., 1869); Anthony Trollope, *The Way We Live Now*, ed. Frank Kermode (first published 1875; Harmondsworth, Penguin Books, 1994), p. 696.

'you are reduced': *ILN*, 13 February 1869, p. 155.

'besides six persons': number of coaches: Long, 'Was Mr Pickwick Lucky...?', p. 167; broughams: Thrupp, *History of Coaches*, p. 118.

'temper of the drivers': American tourist: Charles Stewart, *Sketches of Society in Great Britain and Ireland* (2nd edn, Philadelphia, Carey, Lea & Blanchard, 1835), vol. 1, pp. 93–4; 'The Last Cab-driver, and the First Omnibus Cad', *Sketches by Boz*, pp. 171–2; the driver's breath: Fred Belton, *Random Recollections of an Old Actor* (London, Tinsley Brothers, 1880), p. 4.

'in a hurry': Schlesinger, *Saunterings*, p. 158; 'Coach!': 'Hackney-coach Stands', *Sketches by Boz*, p. 107; footnote: Mayhew, *London Labour*, vol. 3, p. 353; 'I'm in a hurry': Bradfield, *Public Carriages*, p. 49, is one example of this joke among many.

'1 per 300 residents': numbers and fares, 1830: Thrupp, *History of Coaches*, p. 118; hansom design, ibid.; Hudson, *Munby*, p. 147; *Pickwick Papers*, p. 290; *ILN*, 29 January 1864, p. 83; cab numbers: F. M. L. Thompson, 'Nineteenth-century Horse Sense', *Economic History Review*, 29: 1 (February 1976), p. 65; the number of black cabs today is given as 25,000 on the government's official Transport for London website: http://www.tfl.gov.uk./businessandpartners/taxisandprivatehire/1364.aspx, accessed on 29 July 2011.

'noise and dirt': description of stands: [Dickens, W. H. Wills and E. C. Grenville-Murray], 'Common-Sense on Wheels', *Household Words*, 12 April 1851, in Harry Stone (ed.), *Charles Dickens' Uncollected Writings from Household Words, 1850–59*, 2 vols (Bloomington, Indiana University Press, 1968), vol. 1, pp. 243–4, Smith, *Curiosities*, pp. 103, 105, and Phillips, *Wild Tribes of London*, p. 17; horse manure: Smith, *Curiosities*, p. 66.

'checked outfits': watermen's dress: *Pickwick Papers*, p. 21, *Sketches by Boz*, 'The Last Cab-Driver', p. 178, and Diana de Marly, *Working Dress: A History of Occupational Clothing* (London, B. T. Batsford, 1986), p. 88; coachman's dress: Cunnington and Lucas, *Occupational Dress*, p. 226, and Gloag, *Victorian Comfort*, p. 136.

'to the pubs': reputations of cabstands, and railway approach: Garwood, *The Million Peopled City*, pp. 180–81; watermen: Mayhew, *London Labour*, vol. 3, p. 353.

'£46 a year': economics of cabs: Garwood, *The Million Peopled City*, pp. 175–6, and James Greenwood, *The Wilds of London* (London, Chatto and Windus, 1874), p. 113.

'between specific points': bucks extorting fares: Garwood, *The Million Peopled City*, p. 176; Dickens, Wills, Grenville-Murray, 'Common-Sense on Wheels', p. 242; 1853 legislation: Sekon, *Locomotion in Victorian London*, pp. 76–9.

'is a magistrate': in snow: Wyon, Journal, BL Add MS 59,617, f. 29; Schlesinger, *Saunterings*, p. 159; *Dombey and Son*, p. 107.

'Mayfair and Belgravia': Trollope, *Phineas Redux*, ed. John C. Whale (first published 1873–4; Oxford, Oxford University Press, 2000), pp. 184, 212–13.

'to need stables': *Our Mutual Friend*, p. 249; 'Anonyma', *London by Night*, 'by the author of 'Skittles' (London, William Oliver [?1862]), p. 52. The British Library catalogue suggests that 'Anonyma' may be the journalist W. S. Hayward; 10,000 carriages: Mayhew and Binny, *The Criminal Prisons*, p. 55; builders and mews in 1860s: Freeman and Aldcroft (eds), *Transport in Victorian Britain*, p. 142.

'treated as mendicants': footnote: William Kitchiner, *The Traveller's Oracle; or, Maxims for Locomotion: Containing Precepts for Promoting the Pleasures... of Travellers* (London, Henry Colburn, 1828), vol. 2, pp. 78–9; *Martin Chuzzlewit*, p. 637; Schlesinger, *Saunterings*, p. 5.

'cockade in your hat': livery: Zachariah Allen, *The Practical Tourist...* (Providence, RI, A. S. Beckwith, 1832), vol. 2, pp. 250–51, Cunnington and Lucas, *Occupational Costume*, pp. 182–5; *Martin Chuzzlewit*, p. 487.

'control the horse': descriptions, benefits and drawbacks of carriages and cabs: Thrupp, *History of Coaches*, pp. 82–3, 118, William Bridges Adams, *English Pleasure Carriages; Their Origin, History, Varieties...* (London, Charles Knight, 1837), pp. 240–43, Ross Murray, *The Modern Householder: A Manual of Domestic Economy in all its Branches* (London, Frederick Warne and Co., [1872]), pp. 456ff.

'of the hood': lack of noise: Adams, *English Pleasure Carriages*, p. 241; number of street lights: John Hollingshead, *Underground London* (London, Groombridge, 1862), p. 199; mailcoaches' lighting: Edward Corbett, 'Colonel late Shropshire Militia', *An Old Coachman's Chatter, with some Practical Remarks on Driving*, 'by a semi-professional' (facsimile of 2nd edn [first published ?1894], Wakefield, EP Publishing, 1974), pp. 46–7; hansom's light: A. Mayhew, *Paved with Gold*, p. 110.

'one with a light': carriage lamps: Kitchiner, *Traveller's Oracle*, vol. 2, p. 100, and O'Dea, *Social History of Lighting*, pp. 76–7, which also contains the 'harvest moon' quote; Queen Victoria in Paris: *ILN*, 8 September 1855, pp. 308–9.

'something altogether different': Corbett, *Old Coachman's Chatter*, pp. 46–7.

4. IN AND OUT OF LONDON

'glared away': *Nicholas Nickleby*, pp. 89–90.

'hours straight': Dickens' trip to Yorkshire: Ackroyd, *Dickens*, p. 265.

'o'clock at night': post-chaises and system: Hayward, *Days of Dickens*, p. 84; guidebook: *Leigh's New Picture of London* (1819 edition), pp. 419–20; *Pickwick Papers*, pp. 122–5.

'the mail moving': decoration and running of mailcoaches: Hayward, *Days of Dickens*, pp. 76–80; dress: Cunnington and Lucas, *Occupational Costume*, pp. 239–40.

'at a gallop': MacKenzie, *The American in England*, vol. 1, p. 118, 128–9.

'per mile inside': *Little Dorrit*, pp. 203–4; fares: Hayward, *The Days of Dickens*, p. 80.

'of burning joy': this paragraph and the next: Thomas de Quincey, *The English Mail-Coach and Other Essays* (London, J. M. Dent, 1961), pp. 17–18.

'coaches were late': *Pickwick Papers*, p. 306; twelve miles an hour: Calvin Colton, *Four Years in Great Britain, 1831–5* (2nd edn, New York, Harper & Brothers, 1836), pp. 54–5; coach names: Thomas Burke, *Travel in England, from Pilgrim and Pack-Horse to Light Car and Plane* (London, T. Batsford, 1942), p. 92; brass clock: Lockwood, *Passionate Pilgrims*, pp. 45–6; London–Brighton refund: Burke, *Travel in England*, p. 100.

'called the Flyer': *Martin Chuzzlewit*, pp. 141, 174; *David Copperfield*, p. 123.

'and to locals': Trollope, *What I Remember*, p. 5; *Bleak House*, p. 74.

'fire being stirred': mouldy-looking room: 'Early Coaches', *Sketches by Boz*, p. 161; *Pickwick Papers*, pp. 432, 469.

'only bare boards': booking procedure: Hayward, *The Days of Dickens*, pp. 76–80; tipping: Colman, *European Life and Manners*, vol. 1, p. 142; 1837 capacity: Bradfield, *Public Carriages*, p. 30; mailbags and benches: Trollope, *What I Remember*, p. 34.

'of your Ride': Kitchiner, *Traveller's Oracle*, vol. 1, pp. 162–3.

'at the same time': coachmen's salutations: Heman D. D. Humphrey, *Great Britain, France and Belgium: A Short Tour in 1835* (NY, Harper & Brothers, 1838), vol. 1, p. 24; *Pickwick Papers*, p 570.

'course of a day': *Pickwick Papers*, p. 362–4.

'his own nephew': greatcoats and Brighton coach: Yates, *Recollections*, pp. 32–4.

'to the reader': the 'Taglioni': Corbett, *Old Coachman's Chatter*, pp. 75–6; [Jonathan Badcock and Thomas Rowlandson], *Real Life in London, or, The Rambles and Adventures of Bob Tallyho* . . ., 2 vols (London, Jones & Co., 1821), vol. 1, p. 12.

'mitigate the cold': Constable: cited in Burke, *Travel in England*, p. 95; forward versus backward seating, and 'calefacient': Kitchiner, *Traveller's Oracle*, pp. 164–5, 167; open window: *Pickwick Papers*, p. 674.

'prepared oilskin': [Thomas Hughes], *Tom Brown School Days*, 'by an Old Boy', (Cambridge [?MA], Macmillan & Co., 1857), pp. 82–3; Frederick von Raumer, *England in 1835: Being a Series of letters Written to Friends in Germany* . . ., trans. Sarah Austin (London, John Murray, 1836), vol. 2, p. 94; Xavier Baron (ed.), *London 1066–1914*, p. 235, suggests that these are not in fact letters at all, but were written by von Raumer for publication; *Pickwick Papers*, p. 676.

'appearance dead': *Nicholas Nickleby*, p. 116; *Martin Chuzzlewit*, pp. 723–4.

'left off raining': Dickens travelling for the *Morning Chronicle*: Forster, *Life*, vol. 1, p. 247.

'with some difficulty': W. Outram Tristram, *Coaching Days and Coaching Ways* (London, Macmillan and Co., 1888), p. 13.

'positively understated': possible accidents: Corbett, *Old Coachman's Chatter*, pp. 48ff.; *Pickwick Papers*, p. 725; 'I do verily': Forster, *Life*, vol. 1, p. 79.

'passing, or past': 'Dullborough Town', in *All the Year Round*, 30 June 1860, in *Dickens' Journalism*, vol. 4, p. 140. The SER was the South-Eastern Railway, which ran from Folkestone to Dover from 1844, and to London from 1850.

'is secure': Thackeray, 'De Juventute', *Roundabout Papers* (London, Smith, Elder and Co., 1869), pp. 73–4; *Pickwick Papers*, p. 107; *Dombey and Son*, pp. 289–90.

'over twelve miles': Dickens, Preface to 1847 Cheap Edition of *Pickwick Papers*, p. 762; exasperated commuter: Barker and Robbins, *History of London Transport*, vol. 1, p. 66; Schlesinger, *Saunterings*, pp. 169–70; 160 million rail journeys: White, *London in the Nineteenth Century*, p. 79; railway to Sydenham: Bennett, *London and Londoners*, p. 181; afternoon concert trains: ibid., p. 187.

'Victoria at six': Railway Regulation Act: H. J. Dyos, *Exploring the Urban Past: Essays in Urban History*, ed. David Cannadine and David Reeder (Cambridge, Cambridge University Press, 1982), p. 89; shunted trains: Justin McCarthy, *Reminiscences* (London, Chatto & Windus, 1899), vol. 1, p. 1; Ludgate Hill to Victoria: Dyos, ibid., p. 89.

'later with gas': second- and third-class carriage descriptions: Wey, *A Frenchman Sees London*, pp. 278–9, Burke, *Travel in England*, p. 117, and John Hollingshead, *My Lifetime*, 2 vols (London, Sampson Low, Marston, 1895), vol. 1, p. 50; Beale, *Recollections*, p. 10; second-class carriage description: Daniel C. Eddy, *Europa, or, Scenes and Society in England, France, Italy and Switzerland* (Boston, N. L. Dayton, Higgins & Bradley, 1856), pp. 42–3; accommodation train price: Revd John E. Edwards, *Random Sketches and Notes of European Travel in 1856* (New York, Harper and Brothers, 1857), p. 35; Harriet Beecher Stowe, *Sunny Memories of Foreign Lands* (London, George Routledge & Co., 1854), p. 21; lamps: Gloag, *Victorian Comfort*, pp. 161ff.; seats and light: James M. Hoppin, *Old England: Its Scenery, Art, and People* (New York, Hurd and Houghton, 1867), pp. 2–3.

'were City commuters': range of commuting: Freeman and Aldcroft (eds), *Transport in Victorian Britain*, p. 144.

'to this loop': the development of railway stations in London and the ideas in this paragraph: Susan Ryley Hoyle, *London Journal*, 'The First Battle for London: A Case Study of the Royal Commission on Metropolitan Termini 1846', 8: 2 (1982), pp. 140–41.

'a mean structure': Euston: Jackson, *London's Termini*, pp. 20–24; King's Cross: Jackson, ibid., p. 67; London Bridge: Bennett, *London and Londoners*, p. 97.

'parcels office': Euston: Jackson, ibid., pp. 26–7; Bibles: Hippolyte Taine, *Notes on England*, trans. W. F. Rae (London, Strahan, 1872), p. 15; booking tickets: Forney, *Letters from Europe*, p. 38.

'brick wall': reserving seats, place for luggage: [R. S. Surtees], *Hints to Railway Travellers and Country Visitors to London*, 'by an Old Stager' (London, Bradbury and Evans, 1851), pp. 7–8; luggage vans: Fitzroy Gardner, *Days and Ways of an Old Bohemian* (London, John Murray, 1921), p. 15; checking tickets: at Waterloo: Mayhew and Binny, *The Criminal Prisons*, p. 21; at Euston: ibid.; at London Bridge: Bennett, *London and Londoners*, p. 139; Wey, *A Frenchman Sees London*, p. 279.

'speeding up': Dickens, *Bleak House*, p. 211; Wyon, Journal, BL Add MS 59,617, 16 November 1853.

1861: THE TOOLEY STREET FIRE

The main narrative of the fire has been drawn from newspaper reports, in particular *Birmingham Daily Post* (which reprinted the *Observer*'s eyewitness accounts), 24 June 1861, *Daily News*, 24 and 25 June, 1 July 1861, *Lloyd's*, 7 July 1861, *Morning Chronicle*, 24, 25, 26, 27 and 28 June, 2 July 1861, *Morning Post*, 27 and 29 June, 9 July 1861, and *Standard*, 26 June 1861. The only exceptions are: Munby quotations: Hudson, *Munby*, pp. 100–101, except the people salvaging fat, which is cited in Rick Allen, 'Observing London Street-Life: G. A. Sala and A. J. Munby', in Tim Hitchcock and Heather Shore (eds), *The Streets of London: From the Great Fire to the Great Stink* (London, Rivers Oram Press, 2003), p. 208; the fat on the river as far as Erith: Bennett, *London and Londoners*, p. 85; funeral of Braidwood: *Morning Chronicle*, 1 July 1861, *The Times*, 1 July 1861.

5. THE WORLD'S MARKET

'cabbages and turnips': Mayhew, *London Labour*, vol. 1, p. 81.

'Borough market': Bedford Estate development: W. J. Passingham, *London's Markets: Their Origin and History* (London, Sampson Low, Marston [1935]), p. 63; the market's appearance in 1829: Celina Fox (ed), *London – World City, 1800–1840* (London, Yale University Press, 1992), p. 296; Piazza Hotel and Floral Hall: *ILN*, 10 April 1858, p. 367, 15 May 1858, p. 483.

'cart in front of them': waggoners' dress: Christobel Williams-Mitchell, *Dressed for the Job: The Story of Occupational Costume* (Poole, Blandford Press, 1982), p. 66; Bob: Smith, *Curiosities*, pp. 112ff.

'with a breastwork': 'crowd, bustle, hum': [William Moy Thomas], 'Covent Garden Market', *Household Words*, 175, 30 July 1853, pp. 505–11; dress: Cunnington and Lucas, *Occupational Costume*, p. 148; divisions of produce sellers: Charles Knight (ed.), *London*, 6 vols (London, Charles Knight, 1841–4), vol. 5, p. 141; *Martin Chuzzlewit*, p. 696.

'around their necks': subsidiary sellers: Thomas, 'Covent Garden Market'; basket sellers, and perambulating sellers in the next paragraph: Mayhew, *London Labour*, vol. 1, pp. 82–3; dress: Cunnington and Lucas, *Occupational Costume*, p. 148.

'and dust protection': porters' knots: Lucas, *Occupational Costume*, pp. 367–8, De Marly, *Working Dress*, p. 88.

'indoors only in 1849': [Dickens and W. H. Willis], 'A Popular Delusion', *Household Words*, 1 June 1850, in Stone, *Uncollected Writings*, vol. 1, pp. 113–22.

'hours of being caught': destruction of Thames fisheries: Parliamentary Select Committee report, 1810, in Passingham, *London's Markets*, p. 46; deliveries: Dickens and Willis, 'A Popular Delusion'.

'switched to oilskin': Cunnington and Lucas, *Occupational Costume*, pp. 148, 328ff.; 'almost fashionable': Dickens and Willis, 'A Popular Delusion'; *Our Mutual Friend*, pp. 208–9.

'or to costermongers': drinks, 'swallow you up else', and bummarees: Sala, *Twice Round the Clock*, pp. 12–13, 16, 19–23; auction: Dickens and Willis, 'A Popular Delusion'.

'confounded the senses': *Oliver Twist*, p. 171.

'jolt of the vehicle': numbers of animals: Alec Forshaw and Theo Bergström, *Smithfield Past and Present* (London, Heinemann, 1980), p. 54; access roads: Greenwood, *Unsentimental Journeys*, p. 18; Wheaton, *Journal of a Residence*, pp. 285–6.

'or sieves': size of Smithfield: Passingham, *London's Markets*, p. 8; Carlyle's estimate: Thomas Carlyle to Alexander Carlyle, 14 December 1824, *Carlyle Letters*, vol 3, pp. 217–22; [Charles Dickens and W. H. Wills], 'The Heart of Mid-London', *Household Words*, in Stone (ed.), *Dickens' Uncollected Writings*, vol. 1, pp. 101–11.

'long as possible': [Dickens], 'A Monument of French Folly', *Household Words*, 8 March 1851, in *The Dent Uniform Edition of Dickens' Journalism*, vol. 2: *The Amusements of the People and Other Papers*, ed. Michael Slater (London, J. M. Dent, 1996), p. 328.

'amok regularly': 'A Monument of French Folly', p. 330.

'in the journals': *Dombey and Son*, p. 128; 'The Heart of Mid-London', p. 110.

'with wet dirt': Mayhew, *London Labour*, vol. 1, pp. 27–8.

'hides or meat': new Smithfield: Passingham, *London's Markets*, pp. 10–12, and Daniel Joseph Kirwan, *Palace and Hovel: or, Phases of London Life*..., ed. A. Allan (first published 1870; London, Abelard-Schuman, 1963), p. 128; Leadenhall: ibid., p. 78; *Dombey and Son*, p. 778.

'be a nuisance': John Weale, *London Exhibited in 1852…* (London, John Weale, 1852), pp. 610ff.

'as the child': ice cream and poultry at Hungerford: Mayhew and Binny, *The Criminal Prisons*, pp. 232–3; reconstruction: Thomas Allen, *The History and Antiquities of London, Westminster and Southwark, and Parts Adjacent* (London, Cowie & Strange, vols 1–4, 1827, vol. 5, 1837), vol. 5, pp. 286–7; Dickens and the cherries: John Payne Collier, *An Old Man's Diary, Forty Years Ago*, 'for strictly private circulation', in 2 vols (London, Thomas Richards, 1871–2), p. 15.

'gory to the elbows': Lumber Court and Newport markets: Weale, *London Exhibited*, pp. 610ff.; number of barrels: John Hogg, *London as it is, Being a Series of Observations on the Health, Habits, and Amusements of the People* (London, John Macrone, 1837), p. 222; Greenwood, *Unsentimental Journeys*, p. 23.

'to six people': Clare market: Phillips, *Wild Tribes*, p. 78; street with tripe boiler: George Godwin, *London Shadows: A Glance at the 'Homes' of the Thousands* (London, George Routledge, 1854), p. 62.

'from birth to death': William Waight: Health of Towns Association, *The Sanitary Condition of the City of London…with the Sub-Committee's Reply…* (London, W. Clowes, 1848), p. 16; St Giles slaughterhouses: [Henry Morley], 'Life and Death in St Giles', *Household Words*, 13 and 18 November 1858, p. 526; 'cattle-driving, cattle-slaughtering': 'A Monument to French Folly', p. 331.

'sold it wholesale': [R. H. Horne], 'The Cattle Road to Ruin', *Household Words*, 14 and 29 June 1850, pp. 325–30.

'and fire-wood': types of lighting: Mayhew, *London Labour*, vol. 1, p. 9. 'great jets': Phillips, *Wild Tribes*, p. 78; 'primitive tubes': Sala, *Gaslight and Daylight*, pp. 260–2.

'*Here's* your turnips': St Luke's: Greenwood, *Unsentimental Journeys*, p. 10; Bethnal Green: Greenwood, *Wilds of London*, p. 32; New Cut: Mayhew, *London Labour*, vol. 1, pp. 9–10.

'trailing behind': Wright, *The Great Unwashed*, pp. 208–15.

'meagre and unwashed': the women without bags: 'Rough Sketches of London Life', 'II: The Brill', *Church of England Temperance Magazine*, 2 April 1866, p. 102; church bells: Mayhew, *London Labour*, vol. 1, pp. 11–12; Whitecross market: Smith, *Curiosities*, pp. 250ff.

'Saturday-night heads': barbers: Wright, *Some Habits and Customs of the Working Class*, pp. 219–23; *Nicholas Nickleby*, pp. 780–81, 784.

'to paper mills': the Exchange: Smith, *Curiosities*, pp. 250–56; breaking and turning: Mayhew, *London Labour*, vol. 1, pp. 368–9, vol. 2, pp. 26–7; wholesale market: Mayhew and Binny, *The Criminal Prisons*, p. 40.

'military suppliers': admission, and subsidiary markets: Mayhew, *London Labour*, vol. 1, pp. 368–9, vol. 2, pp. 26–7.

'the cheapest shops': Mayhew, *London Labour*, vol. 1, p. 369, vol. 2, p. 35.

'horses and manure': smell of Rag Fair: Mayhew and Binny, *The Criminal Prisons*, p. 39; quantities that horses eat: Asa Briggs, *Victorian Things* (Harmondsworth, Penguin Books, 1990), p. 415; Pickford's, coal deliveries, and lack of quantifiable data: Thompson, 'Nineteenth-century Horse Sense', pp. 60–81; footnote on pub names:

from 'The Signs of the Times', in Smith, *Little World of London*, pp. 129ff., although it is troubling that there is no information about how, or when, or why, this list was compiled.

'at a great rate': this paragraph and the next: Diana Donald, '"Beastly Sights": The Treatment of Animals as a Moral Theme in Representations of London, c.1820–1850', in Dana Arnold (ed.), *The Metropolis and its Image: Constructing Identities for London, c.1750–1950* (Oxford, Blackwell, 1999), pp. 60–62, Mayhew, *London Labour*, vol. 1, p. 181, Mayhew and Binny, *The Criminal Prisons*, p. 20, Wheaton, *Journal of a Residence*, p. 128.

6. SELLING THE STREETS

'something outdoors': number of street sellers: the discrepancy is noted in White, *London in the Nineteenth Century*, p. 198. It is to be expected that this trade, carried out by the very poor, would be difficult for the authorities to quantify, and in any case Mayhew's statistics are notoriously unreliable (see, among others, Gertrude Himmelfarb, 'Mayhew's Poor: A Problem of Identity', *Victorian Studies*, 14 (March 1971), pp. 307–20); one out of every 150: the census gives a population of 2,363,341 in London in 1851.

'Humrellars to mend': income: Mayhew, *London Labour*, vol. 1, pp. 54–5; housewives in the rain: Smith, *The Little World of London*, p. 90.; umbrella sellers and repairers: Smith, *Curiosities*, pp. 68–71.

'4d a day': 'a full market hand': A. Mayhew, *Paved with Gold*, p. 73; Hackney markets: Greenwood, *Wilds of London*, p. 183; general details of trade, and next paragraph: Greenwood, *Unsentimental Journeys*, pp. 118ff.

'lettuces and onions': number of stalls: Mayhew, *London Labour*, vol. 1, p. 6; costers' carts: ibid., vol. 1, pp. 26–7; Lamb's Conduit Street: Hudson, *Munby*, p. 227.

'o'clock at night': costers' boys: Mayhew, *London Labour*, vol. 1, pp. 33–4; their schedule: ibid., vol. 1, p. 36.

'without some result': Mayhew, *London Labour*, vol. 1, p. 346.

'fronds in their carts': draught excluders and fly-catchers: Bennett, *London and Londoners*, p. 52; flowers in spring: Mayhew and Binny, *The Criminal Prisons*, pp. 172–3; gravellers: Smith, *Curiosities*, p. 339; ice sellers: *ILN*, 5 January 1850, p. 2; other seasonal greenery: Charles Hindley, *History of the Cries of London, Ancient and Modern* (London, Reeves and Turner, 1881), p. 221.

'regarded as his': Hyde Park: Amy Grinnell Smith and Mary Ermina Smith, 'Letters from Europe, 1865–6', ed. David Sanders Clark (Washington, DC, 1948; typescript in British Library), p. 24; *Our Mutual Friend*, pp. 52–3.

'as fertilizer': Mayhew, *London Labour*, vol. 2, pp. 343, 357, 360.

'and her meals': Welsh dress: John Leighton, *London Cries & Public Edifices from Sketches on the Spot* (London, Grant and Griffith [1847]), p. 19; dress otherwise: Bennett, *London and Londoners*, p. 40, and Sala, *Twice Round the Clock*, p. 72; cans, yokes, lowering milk, working hours and pay: Hudson, *Munby*, pp. 167, 99, 178–9.

'all wearing caps': costers: Mayhew, *London Labour*, vol. 1, pp. 51ff.; butchers' boys: Bennett, *London and Londoners*, p. 41.

'for resale': footnote on clothing: *Our Mutual Friend*, p. 72, *Bleak House*, p. 180.

'miles a day': Mayhew, *London Labour*, vol. 1, p. 367.

'respectable householders': hats: Bennett, *London and Londoners*, p. 39; secrecy: Phillips, *Wild Tribes*, p. 58.

'lately swept up': *Great Expectations*, p. 196; wash men: Mayhew, *London Labour*, vol. 2, p. 132; hare skin sellers: Bennett, *London and Londoners*, p. 39; tea leaves: Mayhew, *London Labour*, vol. 2, p. 133. Mayhew claims this trade is 'extensive', yet his is the only mention of it I have found.

'1d a door': chairs to mend: Bennett, *London and Londoners*, p. 52; prices for grinders: Jackson, *George Scharf's London*, p. 53; sharpening penknives for office workers etc.: Leighton, *London Cries*, p. 21; knife-cleaning machine: Mayhew, *London Labour*, vol. 1, p. 27; step washing: Garwood, *Million Peopled City*, p. 80.

'GOES MAD': *Punch*, 'The Demons of Pimlico', 21 November 1857, p. 215.

'from the damp': Thomas Rowlandson, *Rowlandson's Characteristic Sketches of the Lower Orders* (London, Samuel Leigh, 1820), no page; carrying methods: Mayhew, *London Labour*, vol. 1, pp. 26–50, 367; delivery boys' containers: A. Mayhew, *Paved with Gold*, p. 2.

'penny a bit': Schlesinger, *Saunterings*, p. 23.

'Underground for it': three o'clock: Sala, *Twice Round the Clock*, pp. 160–63; Shepherdess Walk seller: *ILN*, 18 January 1845, pp. 34–5, and a similar case in the Queen Street police office, ibid.; underground: *Punch*, 'Metropolitan Improvements', 17 January 1885, p. 34.

'the public streets': Drury Lane: MacKenzie, *The American in England*, vol. 1, p. 207; rhubarb seller: Phillips, *Wild Tribes*, p. 80. Phillips states the man was not a Turk, but an East End cadger. I can find no evidence either way, but throughout his book Phillips finds all the poor he writes about distasteful: the Irish, the Jews, or the plain poverty-stricken are all dubious at best, or thieves most likely.

'an oil-painting': stagecoach offices: 'The Streets – Morning', *Sketches by Boz*, p. 72; railway stations and penknives: Bennett, *London and Londoners*, p. 149; *Dombey and Son*, p. 237.

'or a bird-warbler': jewellery: Mayhew, *London Labour*, vol. 1, pp. 346, 348; *Oliver Twist*, p. 400; malacca canes etc.: Andrew Tuer, *Old London Street Cries* (London, Field & Tuer, 1885), p. 50–51.

'scraped them in return': water pistol: Tuer, *Old London Street Cries* , p. 44; 'All the Fun of the Fair' is frequently reported: Tuer, ibid., p. 50; 'a mischievous little': David Masson, *Memories of London in the 'Forties*, ed. Flora Masson (Edinburgh, William Blackwood & Sons, 1908), p. 145, 'These are for sale': Colman, *European Life and Manners*, vol. 2, pp. 73–4, also reported by Nathaniel Hawthorne in *Hawthorne in England: Selections from Our Old Home and The English Note-books*, ed. Cushing Strout (Ithaca, NY, Cornell University Press, 1965), p. 172.

'on their earnings': 'Japan your shoes': Tuer, *Old London Street Cries*, p. 44; footnote on the two Warrens: Altick, *Presence of the Present*, p. 232; Shoeblack Society: Garwood, *Million Peopled City*, pp. 74–9.

'on their rounds': two currents: J. MacGregor, 'Ragamuffins', *Leisure Hour*, 15 (1856), pp. 455–60; number of London papers: Richard Altick, *The English Common Reader: A Social History of the Mass Reading Public, 1800–1900* (Chicago, University of Chicago Press, 1957), p. 329; newsboys' day, in this paragraph and the next two: Smith, *Curiosities*, pp. 90ff.; rental prices: Schlesinger, *Saunterings*, p. 213.

'possibility of truth': *Old Curiosity Shop*, pp. 162, 594; *Dombey and Son*, p. 383; Badcock and Rowlandson, *Real Life in London*, vol. 1, p. 522.

'householders' buckets': the chemist's shopboy: A. Mayhew, *Paved with Gold*, p. 85; Haymarket boys: ibid., p. 108; the crippled knife cleaner: Mayhew, *London Labour*, vol. 1, p. 171; water boys: Smith, *Little World of London*, p. 66.

'y'r honor pleases': G. A. Sekon, *Locomotion in Victorian London*, pp. 90–91, which reflects the attitude that the boys were aggressive bullies; the American tourist: Joshua White, *Letters on England, Comprising Descriptive Scenes* (Philadelphia, privately printed, 1816), vol. 1, p. 5.

'tear on his boots': Smith, *Curiosities*, pp. 138–9.

'state of exhaustion': porters: Freeman and Aldcroft (eds), *Transport in Victorian Britain*, p. 136, and Walter M. Stern, *The Porters of London* (London, Longmans, Green, 1960), pp. 181ff.; Dickens, 'The Chimes', in *The Christmas Books*, vol. 1: 'A Christmas Carol' and 'The Chimes', ed. Michael Slater (first published 1843, 1844; Harmondsworth, Penguin, 1985); *David Copperfield*, p. 340.

'out the rags': the history of the development of the match in this and the next paragraph: Hall, *Retrospect of a Long Life*, vol. 1, p. 2, Hayward, *Days of Dickens*, p. 14, *ILN*, 13 October 1860, p. 352, [Charles Knight], 'Illustrations of Cheapness: The Lucifer Match', *Household Words*, 13 April 1850, pp. 54–6, and Trey Philpotts, *The Companion to Little Dorrit* (Robertsbridge, Helm Information, 2003), p. 306.

'with magical rapidity': lament for tinderbox: Sala, *Gaslight and Daylight*, p. 61.

'the café door': Rosamond Street explosion: *ILN*, 12 August 1843, p. 103; Haymarket street children: A. Mayhew, *Paved with Gold*, p. 108.

'but as beggars': cost of matches: Knight, 'Illustrations of Cheapness'.

'lucifers and onions': outside the gin palace: John Fisher Murray, 'Physiology of London Life', *London Journal*, 16 October 1847, p. 103; Godwin, *London Shadows*, p. 22.

'a living unviable': John Thomas Smith, *Vagabondiana; or, Etchings of Remarkable Beggars, Itinerant Traders and other Persons…in London and its Environs* (London, no publisher, 1817), pp. 41–3, and Mayhew, *London Labour*, vol. 2, pp. 136–40.

'to the cold: *ILN*, 14 December 1844, p. 371.

'for their donkeys': the Watford labourers: Smith, *Vagabondiana*, p. 32; groundsel, chickweed and duckweed sellers: Smith, *Curiosities*, pp. 20–22; groundsel sellers also appear in Bennett, *London and Londoners*, p. 53; rheumatic chickweed seller: Smith, *Cries of London*, pp. 73–4; simplers: ibid., pp. 77–8; reeds for donkeys: Smith, *Curiosities*, p. 142.

'a bare living': pins and ink: Hindley, *History of the Cries of London*, p. 101; the idea of modernism pushing street sellers aside is elaborated in Richard Maxwell, 'Henry Mayhew and the Life of the Streets', *Journal of British Studies*, 17: 2 (spring 1978), pp. 87–105.

'the financial system': Weale, *London Exhibited in 1852*, p. 107.

'Road among others': skilled-labour clubs: [T. Carter], *Memoirs of a Working Man* (London, Charles Knight, 1845), p. 122; hiring stands: Smith, *Vagabondiana*, p. 46.

'4d an hour': dockyards: Mayhew and Binny, *The Criminal Prisons*, p. 35.

'to the post': W. Warrell, *Scribes Ancient and Modern (Otherwise Law Writers and Scriveners),* (1880), cited in Michael Paterson, *Voices from Dickens' London* (Cincinnati, OH, David and Charles, 2006), p. 93; the night officer: Dickens, 'A Sleep to Startle Us', *Household Words*, 13 March 1852, in *Dickens' Journalism*, vol. 3, pp. 55–6.

'more in demand': pea-picking: Raphael Samuel, 'Comers and Goers', in H. J. Dyos and Michael Wolff (eds), *The Victorian City: Images and Realities* (London, Routledge, 1973), vol. 1, p. 135.

'the fair season': the trampers' life here and in the next two paragraphs: Samuel, 'Comers and Goers', vol. 1, pp. 123–60 unless otherwise stated; footnote on brickmaking pubs: Smith, *Little World of London*, pp. 129ff.

'twopence for it': occasioning: John Brown, *Sixty Years' Gleanings from Life's Harvest: A Genuine Autobiography* (Cambridge, J. Palmer, 1858), p. 31; William Lovett, *The Life and Struggles of William Lovett, in His Pursuit of Bread, Knowledge, and Freedom...* (London, Trübner & Co., 1876), pp. 24–5; sackmakers: Knight (ed.), *London*, vol. 3, p. 31; 'she can't carry': 'Walter', *My Secret Life*, vol. 2, p. 33.

7. SLUMMING

'of slums themselves': word derivations and citation from *Oxford English Dictionary*, with interdating from the British Library's Nineteenth-Century Newspaper database.

'capital every day': population figures and percentages in urban and rural districts: F. S. Schwarzbach, *Dickens and the City* (London, Athlone Press, 1979), pp. 7–9.

'author and his readers': Rowlandson, in R. Ackermann, *Microcosm of London*, 3 vols. (London, Ackermann's Repository of Arts [1808–10]), vol. 3, p. 240; *Oliver Twist*, p. 14; Mayhew, *London Labour*, vol. 1, p. 338; the ideas in this paragraph and the next two draw heavily on Lynn Hollen Lees, 'Poverty and Pauperism in Nineteenth-century London', The H. J. Dyos Memorial Lecture, May 1988 (Leicester, University of Leicester, 1988), pp. 2–9, 13, 37–52.

'into the workhouse': this paragraph and the next draw on Stephen Halliday, *The Great Stink of London: Sir Joseph Bazalgette and the Cleansing of Victorian London* (Stroud, Sutton, 1999), pp. 128–9; *Oliver Twist*, p. 59.

'with a Pauper': Dickens, *Little Dorrit*, pp. 416, 418.

'off to the workhouse': responsibilities and payment of workhouse masters: Lees, 'Poverty and Pauperism', pp. 115ff.; *A Christmas Carol*, pp. 50–51.

'friendless and unprotected': Dickens' Norfolk Street lodgings and the Cleveland Street Workhouse: Ruth Richardson, *Dickens and the Workhouse:* Oliver Twist *and the London Poor* (Oxford, Oxford University Press, 2012), *passim*. The workhouse, until the 2005 closure of the Middlesex Hospital, was the hospital's Outpatients' Department. There is an account of its rescue at http://clevelandstreetworkhouse.org. Although the workhouse in *Oliver Twist* is outside London, it seems difficult to believe that the one in Cleveland Street could not have been, at least in part, in Dickens' mind as he wrote; *Our Mutual Friend*, pp. 199–200, 498; *The Times*, 6 December 1836, p. 4.

'these slum dwellings': Pierce Egan [and George and Robert Cruikshank], *Life in London, or, The Day and Night Scenes of Jerry Hawthorn, Esq., and his Elegant*

Friend Corinthian Tom… (London, Sherwood, Neely, & Jones, 1821), pp. 344–5; Bermondsey slum: 'Every Man's Poison', *All the Year Round*, 13, 11 November 1865, pp. 372–6.

'would give him': pub saveall: J. C. Loudon, *An Encyclopaedia of Cottage, Farm, and Villa Architecture and Furniture…* (London, Longman, Rees, Orme, Brown, Green, & Longman, 1833), p. 689; Henry Dupuis: *ILN*, 21 August 1852, p. 135, and many cases of child stealing, e.g., *ILN*, 27 November 1869, p. 535; workhouse clothes: *ILN*, 9 September 1843, p. 167; sheets: Dickens, 'On Duty with Inspector Field', in *Household Words*, 14 June 1851, in *Dickens' Journalism*, vol. 2, p. 365 and vol. 2, p. 369; breaking street lights: *ILN*, 21 March 1868, p. 271.

'small air-hole': Geo. Alfd Walker, *The First of a Series of Lectures…on the Actual condition of the Metropolitan Grave-Yards* (2nd edn, London, Longman, Brown, Green, and Longmans, 1849), p. 30.

'be none the wiser': views of Tothill prison: Hepworth Dixon, *The London Prisons* (London, Jackson and Walford, 1850), p. 248; 9 Fleet Market: J. F. C. Phillips, *Shepherd's London* (London, Cassell, 1976), p. 18.

'benefits of modernity': *Great Expectations*, p. 165; Thurlow Weed, *Letters from Europe and the West Indies, 1843–1862* (Albany, NY, Weed, Parsons and Co., 1866), p. 82; Pardon, *Routledge's Popular Guide*, p. 50; Sun Fire-Office and Pentonville: *ILN*, 18 August 1842, p. 217.

'to have money': verse: [Frederic William Naylor Bayley], '*Scenes and Stories by a Clergyman in Debt…* (London, A. H. Baily and Co., 1835); costs: Brothers Mayhew, *Living for Appearances* (London, James Blackwood, 1855), pp. 181–2, Dickens, 'Passage in the Life of Mr Watkins Tottle', in *Sketches by Boz*, p. 519, and [Anna Atkins], *The Colonel* 'by the author of "The perils of fashion"' (London, Hurst and Blackett, 1853), p. 68.

'in *Bleak House*': Benjamin Disraeli, *Henrietta Temple: A Love Story* (Leipzig, Bernhard Tauchnitz, 1859), p. 376; Thackeray, *Vanity Fair*, ed. J. I. M. Stewart (first published in 1848; Harmondsworth, Penguin, 1985), p. 614.

'most of London's debtors': White, *London in the Nineteenth Century*, p. 219.

'in his pocket': Dickens, *Pickwick Papers*, p. 565; footing and chummage: James Grant, *Sketches in London* (London, W. S. Orr, 1838), p. 52; *Pickwick Papers*, p. 563; *Oliver Twist*, p. 363.

'and a pie seller': *Great Expectations*, p. 260; *Nicholas Nickleby*, pp. 695–6; deputy coachman: Revd J. Richardson, *Recollections…of the Last Half-century* (London, Savill & Edwards, 1855), p. 22; Lovett, *Life and Struggles*, pp. 28–9; Queen's Bench shops: Grant, *Sketches in London*, pp. 54–6.

'carried to the kitchen': 'oblong pile': *Little Dorrit*, p. 97; *Pickwick Papers*, p. 279; description of the Marshalsea and its rules in this paragraph and the next: Trey Philpotts, 'The Real Marshalsea', *Dickensian*, Autumn 1991, pp. 133–46. Ackroyd, *Dickens*, p. 76, gives a slightly smaller size of rooms: eight by twelve feet; this may well be correct, but as Ackroyd lists no sources, it cannot be verified; Philpotts uses the Select Committee Report on the State and Management of Prisons in London and Elsewhere, which covers the Marshalsea in 1815–18.

'those of any slum': the extent of the rules, and liberty tickets: Dixon, *London Prisons*, pp. 114–15.

'the whole place': Pentonville: Dixon, *London Prisons*, pp. 150–56; Millbank, ibid., pp. 132ff.; *David Copperfield*, pp. 625ff.

'with paid workers': Dixon, *The London Prisons*, p. 127.

'of homelessness': 'thrown away': Forster, *Life*, vol. 1, p. 49; 'but for the mercy of God', ibid., vol. 1, p. 2; *David Copperfield*, p. 192.

'let us go': 'A Nightly Scene in London', *Household Words*, 26 January 1856, in *Dickens' Journalism*, vol. 3, pp. 346–51.

'been one of them': 'On an Amateur Beat', 27 February 1869, *All the Year Round*, in *Dickens' Journalism*, vol. 4, p.318; the source of Dickens' identification with the beggars I owe to Michael Slater, *Intelligent Person's Guide to Dickens* (London, Duckworth, 1999), p. 103.

'the new suburbs': destruction of houses: Lees, 'Poverty and Pauperism', p. 9.

'an alien race': population density: Mayhew and Binny, *The Criminal Prisons*, p. 15.

'rogues and thieves': *Oliver Twist*, pp. 63, 153, 417; Hockley-in-the-Hole: ibid., p. 63; link to *Beggar's Opera*: Tambling, *Going Astray*, p. 64.

'knight errant style': 'Seven Dials', *Sketches by Boz*, p. 92; [G. A. Sala], 'Bright Chanticleer', in *Household Words*, 11, 31 March 1855, p. 204; [Donald Shaw], *London in the Sixties (With a Few Digressions)* 'by one of the Old Brigade' (London, Everett and Co., 1908), pp. 92–4. I have approached these memoirs with more than usual caution. While there is little that can be verifiably checked in them, what there is tends to be misremembered. For example, Shaw writes of Valentine Baker, who was discharged from the British army after a scandal; he joined the Ottoman army, before becoming head of the Egyptian police. Shaw claimed to have seen him in Egypt in 1894 and, seemingly unaware of his post-British career, described his friend as 'a broken man', as well he might have been, for when Shaw supposedly saw him Baker had been dead for seven years. I have therefore relied on Shaw not for facts, but simply for how people remembered, or wanted to remember, people or events; Dickens to Daniel Maclise, 20 November 1840, *Letters*, vol. 2, p. 152.

'believed such stories': Field Lane: Trollope, *What I Remember*, p. 11; Dickens, 'On an Amateur Beat', in *Dickens' Journalism*, vol. 4, pp. 380–81.

'the blacking factory': *Bleak House*, pp. 683–4; St Giles: Dickens, 'On Duty with Inspector Field', in *Dickens' Journalism*, vol. 2, pp. 356–69; *Nicholas Nickleby*, p. 228.

'desperately overcrowded': *Pickwick Papers*, pp. 212–13.

'and a sink': small terraced houses: Thomas Beames, *The Rookeries of London: Past, Present, and Prospective* (London, Thomas Bosworth, 1850), p. 79; Holborn lodging house: Thomas Archer, *The Pauper, the Thief, and the Convict: Sketches of Some of their Homes, Haunts, and Habits* (London, Groombridge and Sons, 1865), pp. 140–41.

'without a parent': Hudson, *Munby*, p. 248; Flower and Dean Streets: White, *London in the Nineteenth Century*, pp. 236, 324.

'working people's lodgings': 'a covered alley': Archer, *The Pauper, the Thief, and the Convict*, p. 11; Field Lane: Smith, *Little World of London*, p. 135 (Smith calls it Lagmansbury, but it is clearly Field Lane); Frying-pan Alley: Godwin, *London Shadows*, p. 13; *Bleak House*, p. 263.

'off Holborn': footnote: *Bleak House*, p. 215; it is Tambling, *Going Astray*, pp. 136ff., who suggests Forster's house; E. Beresford Chancellor, *London's Old Latin Quarter, Being an Account of Tottenham Court Road and its Immediate Surroundings* (London, Jonathan Cape [1930]), p. 206, suggests the Inigo Jones house next door.

'misery to misery': James Elmes, *Metropolitan Improvements; or, London in the Nineteenth Century*... (London, Jones & Co., 1829), pp. 1–3; *The Times*, 2 March 1861, p. 8.

'the Devil's Acre': Select Committee: cited in Donald J. Olsen, 'Victorian London: Specialization, Segregation and Privacy', *Victorian Studies*, 17: 3 (March 1974), pp. 265–78.

'order, very like': 'their bread': Hollingshead, *Ragged London*, p. 118; Westminster: Anthony S. Wohl, *The Eternal Slum: Housing and Social Policy in Victorian London* (New Brunswick, NJ, Transaction, 2002), p. 30; Church Lane: Roy Porter, *London: A Social History* (London, Hamish Hamilton, 1994), p. 268; 1838–56 figures: White, *London in the Nineteenth Century*, pp. 32–4; 'Life and Death in St Giles's', in *Household Words*, 18, 13 November 1858, pp. 524–8; *Bleak House*, pp. 319–20; footnote: an earlier mention of 'gonoph' that Dickens may have seen occurs in W. A. Miles, *Poverty, Mendicity and Crime*, Report, 1839, p. 168: 'Cocum gonnofs flash by night the cooters in the boozing kens, and send their lushy shicksters out to bring the ruin in', cited in Jonathon Green, *Green's Dictionary of Slang* (London, Chambers, 2010); New Oxford Street: Dickens, 'On Duty with Inspector Field', in *Dickens' Journalism*, vol. 2, p. 363; *Bleak House*, p. 275.

'to all parties': *Our Mutual Friend*, p. 143.

'smell of a graveyard': Sir Peter Laurie: Simon Joyce, *Capital Offenses: Geographies of Class and Crime in Victorian London* (Charlottesville, University of Virginia Press, 2003), p. 102; Dickens, *Oliver Twist*, pp. 416–17; Henry Mayhew, 'Home is Home, be it never so Homely', in [Lord Shrewsbury], *Meliora: or, Better Times to Come* (1852), pp. 276–7.

'the sixteenth century': extent of St Giles: Lynn Hollen Lees, *Exiles of Erin: Irish Migrants in Victorian London* (Manchester, Manchester University Press, 1979), p. 84.

'drunkards and thieves': 'Seven Dials', *Sketches by Boz*, pp. 94–5; Flora Tristan, *Flora Tristan's London Journal: A Survey of London Life in the 1830s*, trans. Dennis Palmer and Giselle Pincetl (London, George Prior, 1980), p. 135.

'to journalists': Jennings' Buildings: 'Jennings' Buildings and the Royal Borough: The Construction of the Underclass in Mid-Victorian England', in David Feldman and Gareth Stedman-Jones (eds), *Metropolis: London Histories and Representations since 1800* (London, Routledge, 1989), pp. 11–39.

'enough to work': Bemerton Street: George Godwin, *Another Blow for Life* (London, Wm H. Allen, 1864), pp. 36–7; Nichol Street: ibid., pp. 12–13; Covent Garden porter: ibid., p. 22.

'obviously to mind': *Oliver Twist*, p. 69; cleaning the privy: James Greenwood, *Wilds of London*, p. 75; letter to *The Times*: *The Times*, 5 July 1849, p. 5, follow-up, 9 July, p. 3; footnote: the contemporary historian is James Winter, *London's Teeming Streets*, pp. 130–31.

'about to begin': *ILN*, 13 and 27 February 1847, pp. 103, 144.

'there's nowhere else': House of Commons Select Committee, Royal Commission on Metropolis Railway Termini, 1846, cited in Kellett, *Impact of the Railways on Victorian Cities*, p. 36; Farringdon Street alley: Greenwood, *Wilds of London*, p. 72.

'to walk down': clearance for Royal Courts of Justice: *ILN*, 18 August 1866, p. 155, and 15 December 1866, p. 575–7.

'very worst conditions': this paragraph and the next: starvation, private charity and Poor Law statistics: Hollingshead, *Ragged London*, pp. 3–4, and Mayhew and Binny, *The Criminal Prisons*, p. 44.

'one for life': Ragged School: Garwood, *Million Peopled City*, p. 61; dormitory: Dickens, 'A Sleep to Startle Us', in *Household Words*, 15 March 1852, in *Dickens' Journalism*, vol. 3, pp. 54–6; 'a large crowd': Mayhew and Binny, *The Criminal Prisons*, p. 31.

'casual hiring stands': Mayhew and Binny, *The Criminal Prisons*, p. 44; Greenwood: 'A Night in a Workhouse', reprinted in pamphlet form from the *Pall Mall Gazette* (first published 1866; London, F. Bowering [n.d.]), passim. Greenwood based his pamphlet on trips he and another man made to the workhouse, but Greenwood's is the narrative voice.

'and were fed': Some of the shocked response to Greenwood's depiction appeared the next day: Frederick Greenwood, 'Casual Wards', *Pall Mall Gazette*, 16 January 1866, p. 1. I am grateful to Matthew Rubery for this reference, and to Patrick Leary and Clare Clarke for other information.

'around us every day': influence on *Our Mutual Friend*: Seth Koven, *Slumming: Sexual and Social Politics in Victorian London* (Princeton, NJ, Princeton University Press, 2004), p. 35; inquests: *ILN*, 19 December 1846, pp. 390–91, among many; incidence of rickets: Stephen Halliday, *The Great Filth: The War Against Disease in Victorian England* (Stroud, Sutton, 2007), p. 43; Ragged School deaths: 'A Sleep to Startle Us', in *Dickens' Journalism*, vol. 3, p. 56; *Bleak House*, p. 705.

8. THE WATERS OF DEATH

'on the river': Carter, *Memoirs of a Working Man*, pp. 125, 128.

'Muswell Hill': I am grateful to Ravi Mirchandani and Frank Wynne, who helped me come up with this well of place names.

'inlet at Blackfriars': I owe much of my description of the underground rivers in this and the next two paragraphs to N. J. Barton, *The Lost Rivers of London* (London, Phoenix House, 1962), pp. 26–7, 30ff., 37ff., and to Halliday, *Great Stink*, pp. 26–7.

'Westminster Abbey': the Serpentine: Edward John Tilt, *The Serpentine 'as it is' and 'as it ought to be'*... (London, John Churchill, 1848), pp. 4–8.

'new phenomenon': outline of creation of fogs: Dale H. Porter, *The Thames Embankment: Environment, Technology, and Society in Victorian England* (Akron, OH, University of Akron Press, 1998), p. 57, and Peter Brimblecombe, *The Big Smoke: A History of Air Pollution in London Since Medieval Times* (London, Methuen, 1987), pp. 109ff.

'as usual': Benjamin Robert Haydon, *Life of Benjamin Robert Haydon...from his Autobiography and Journals*..., ed. Tom Taylor, 3 vols (New York, Harper and Bros, 1853), vol. 1, p. 52; Byron, *Don Juan*, ed. Leslie A. Marchand (first published 1823–4, Boston, Houghton Mifflin, 1958), Canto 10, v. 82; Wheaton, *Journal of a Residence*, p. 117.

'London particular': *A Christmas Carol*, pp. 47, 52; *Bleak House*, pp. 75–6.

'of the sun': St Paul's: Wheaton, *Journal of a Residence*, pp. 40–1; *Bleak House*, p. 49.

'any circumstances': bottle-green: Hogg, *London as it is*, pp. 186–7; yellow: Thomas Miller, *Picturesque Sketches of London, Past and Present* (London, National Illustrated Library, [?1851]), p. 243; *Our Mutual Friend*, p. 417; Hawthorne, *English Note-Books*, vol. 2, p. 381; Italian friend: Dickens to Angela Burdett-Coutts, 13 December 1858, *Letters*, vol. 8, p. 718.

'Cayenne pepper': sulky gas: Miller, *Picturesque Sketches*, p. 243; effect on candles: *Bleak House*, p. 76; haggard light: *Bleak House*, p. 50; *Edwin Drood*, p. 136.

'be run over': 'Implacable November': *Bleak House*, p. 49; 'You step gingerly': Miller, *Picturesque Sketches*, pp. 244–7.

'lasted four minutes': Allen, *History and Antiquities of London*, vol. 5, pp. 60–61, vol. 4, p. 102.

'was raw sewage': Porter, *London*, p. 56, except for the 150 sewers: Anne Hardy, 'Parish Pump to Private Pipes: London's Water Supply in the Nineteenth Century', in W. F. Bynum and Roy Porter, *Living and Dying in London, Medical History*, Supplement No. 11 (London, Wellcome Institute, 1991), p. 82.

'sold as fertilizer': Bill of Sewers: Halliday, *Great Filth*, p. 27; night-men's operations: Mayhew, *London Labour*, vol. 2, pp. 450–51, 446.

'nearly six inches': West End: Michael Durey, *The Return of the Plague: British Society and the Cholera, 1831–2* (Dublin, Gill and Macmillan, 1979), p. 56; St Giles: Halliday, *Great Filth*, pp. 133–4.

'zincing establishment': Hékékyan Bey, Journal, British Library Add MS 37,448; 10,000 cows: Hogg, *London as it is*, pp. 224–5; 1850 figures: [Richard H. Horne], 'The Cow with the Iron Tail', *Household Words*, 33, 9 November 1850, p. 147; St James's cowsheds: Beames, *Rookeries*, pp. 166–7.

'local hackney stands': Millbank: Mayhew and Binny, *The Criminal Prisons*, p. 235; parks and Westminster Abbey: Wey, *A Frenchman Sees London*, p. 166; grazing rights: Schlesinger, *Saunterings*, p. 181; Old Bailey: A. Mayhew, *Paved with Gold*, p. 26; Carlyle: the references in his letters abound: among others, Carlyle to George Remington, 12 November 1852, *Carlyle Letters*, vol. 27, pp. 356–7; *Nicholas Nickleby*, pp. 227–8; *David Copperfield*, p. 324.

'worth the expenditure': Mayhew, 'Home is Home', pp. 278–80.

'at all to take it': Halliday, *Great Filth*, pp. 132–3, 202, 203, except for the farmers taking the soil for free: Mayhew, *London Labour*, vol. 2, p. 446.

'per cent was reached': 270,000 houses: John Liddle, *On the Moral and Physical Evils Resulting from the Neglect of Sanitary Measures*... (London, Health of Towns Association Depot, 1847), pp. 16–18; Fulham and water supply by neighbourhood: Anne Hardy, 'Parish Pump to Private Pipes', pp. 79–82.

'so little water': Savile Row: Dickens, 'Arcadian London', *All the Year Round*, 29 September 1860, in *Dickens' Journalism*, vol. 4, p. 188; thieving shopkeeper: [Henry Morley], 'Death's Doors', *Household Words*, 9, 10 June 1854, pp. 398–402.

'the waste back out': East London Water Co., and frequency of standpipes: Gavin, *Sanitary Ramblings*, p. 88, 92.

'get some water': communal casks: Godwin, *London Shadows*, p. 62; Rose Street: ibid., p. 42; footnote on contemporary water consumption: by data360.org; water for fires: Morley, 'Death's Doors'.

'cup of coffee': baths for the prosperous: *Leigh's New Picture of London* (1839 edn), p. 350, and Pardon, *Routledge's Popular Guide to London*, p. 45; Jermyn Street Baths: Henry Mayhew, *The Shops and Companies of London, and the Grades and Manufactories of Great Britain* (London, The Second Printing and Publishing Co., 1865), p. 62.

'hour of the night': *Great Expectations*, p. 366.

'of the Epidemic': bathhouses: White, *London in the Nineteenth Century*, p. 457; Goulston Square Bath and free entry during epidemics: Beames, *Rookeries*, pp. 56–7; footnote: Halliday, *Great Filth*, p. 49.

'of old age': life expectancy: Andrew Sanders, *Charles Dickens, Resurrectionist* (London, Macmillan, 1982), p. 4; 1869 deaths: *ILN*, 30 January 1869, p. 128.

'the killing ennui': *ILN*, 13 February 1858, p. 159.

'relation to it': Sir John Simon: Halliday, *Great Filth*, p. 119.

'health was established': this and the next paragraph: Edwin Chadwick, *Report on the Sanitary Condition of the Labouring Population of Great Britain*, ed. M. W. Flinn (first published 1842; Edinburgh, Edinburgh University Press, 1965), passim, Anthony Brundage, *England's 'Prussian Minister': Edwin Chadwick and the Politics of Government Growth, 1832–1854* (University Park, PA, Pennsylvania State University Press, 1988), passim, and Halliday, *Great Filth*, passim.

'250 Acts': Parliament: *ILN*, 21 October 1848, p. 247; Christchurch rector: Halliday, *Great Filth*, p. 28; governmental multiplicity: Francis Sheppard, *London: A History* (Oxford, Oxford University Press, 1998), p. 280.

'typhus and typhoid': epidemic figures: Charles Creighton, *A History of Epidemics in Britain*, vol. 2, *From the Extinction of the Plague to the Present Time* (first published 1891–4; London, Frank Cass, 1965), pp. 793–4; Tayler, *Diary*, pp. 19, 22; Prince Albert in footnote: Stanley Weintraub, 'Albert [Prince Albert of Saxe-Coburg and Gotha]', *Oxford Dictionary of National Biography*, Oxford University Press, 2004; online edn, Sept 2010 [http://www.oxforddnb.com.ezproxy.londonlibrary.co.uk/view/article/274, accessed 7 May 2011].

'cannot smell': City sewers: Health of Towns Association, *The Sanitary Condition*, passim.

'people died there': Spitalfields Workhouse: Lovett, *Life and Struggles*, pp. 70–71; Minories death: Health of Towns Association, *The Sanitary Condition*, p. 12.

'were worst affected': the information in this paragraph: Creighton, *A History of Epidemics*, vol. 2, pp. 793–4, apart from the list of parishes, Durey, *Return of the Plague*, p. 28; footnote on mortality rate: Durey, *Return of the Plague*, p. 125; cholera south of the river: White, *London in the Nineteenth Century*, pp. 50–51.

'his handkerchief': Coldbath Field: George Laval Chesterton, *Revelations of Prison Life* (3rd edn, London, Hurst and Blackett, 1857), p. 116; the hulks: Mayhew and Binny, *The Criminal Prisons*, pp. 199–200.

'sound of voices': the description is of Golden Square, Soho: Hollingshead, *My Lifetime*, vol. 1, pp. 190–91.

'first-floor windows': 'a solemn consideration': 'Night Walks', in *Dickens' Journalism*, vol. 4, p. 154; *Oliver Twist*, p. 43, and the information on Chatham: ibid., p. 493n.; *Nicholas Nickleby*, p. 898; Drury Lane graveyards: Geo. Alfd Walker, *Gatherings from Graveyards, Particularly those of London ...* (London, Longman, 1839), p. 162.

'bones for fertilizer': St Ann's: Walker, *The First of a Series ... Metropolitan Grave-Yards*, pp. 14–16; sale of bones: ibid., pp. 16–17.

'dead citizens': St Clement Danes: Walker, *Gatherings*, pp. 158–9; 'rot and mildew': 'City of London Churches', in *All the Year Round*, 5 May 1860, in *Dickens' Journalism*, vol. 4, p. 115.

'or even weeks': Bunhill Fields: Geo. Alfd Walker: *The Second of a Series…Metropolitan Grave-Yards* (London, Longman, Brown, Green, and Longmans, 1847), p. 9; St Martin's and Mr Foster: Walker, *The First of a Series…Metropolitan Grave-Yards*, pp. 26–8.

'a reeking fluid': Portugal Street ground: Walker, *The Second of a Series…Metropolitan Grave-Yards*, p. 6; *A Christmas Carol*, p. 124.

'for the privilege': protesting undertaker: Walker, *The First of a Series…Metropolitan Grave-Yards*, p. 19; Enon chapel: Walker, *Gatherings*, pp. 154–5 and *The Second of a Series…Metropolitan Grave-Yards*, pp. 15–16, and David L. Pike, *Subterranean Cities: The World Beneath Paris and London, 1800–1945* (Ithaca, Cornell University Press, 2005), p. 221; advertisement for dancing: 'Lord' George Sanger, *Seventy Years a Showman: My Life and Adventures…* (London, C. Arthur Pearson [1908]), p. 79; viewings: *ILN*, 27 November 1847, p. 343.

'using the grounds': *ILN*, 1 March 1845, p. 131.

'were the dead': 'Address': [Percival Leigh], 'Address from an Undertaker to the Trade', *Household Words*, 13, 22 June 1850, pp. 301–4; poem: [John Delaware Lewis], 'City Graves', *Household Words*, 38, 14 December 1850, p. 277; Nemo's burial spot: *Bleak House*, pp. 202, 276. The location is debated. Tambling, *Going Astray*, p. 139, says it is in the churchyard of St Mary-le-Strand, while the editors of Dickens' *Letters* suggest St Martin-in-the-Fields. I am with Tambling in this matter; *Our Mutual Friend*, pp. 386–7.

'water-borne coffins': Hugh Meller, *London Cemeteries: An Illustrated Guide and Gazetteer* (2nd edn, Godstone, Surrey, Gregg, 1985) lists all the new cemeteries, and their most famous residents. Mary Hogarth's burial site and footnote: Tambling, *Going Astray*, p. 292.

'fine, and river': [Richard H. Horne], 'Father Thames', *Household Words*, 45, 1 February 1851, pp. 446–7; *Little Dorrit*, p. 68.

'it won't do': 'head-and-stomach': Dickens to W. W. F. de Cerjat, 7 July 1858, *Letters*, vol. 8, p. 599; 'smell rushes up': *ILN*: 19 June 1858, p. 603, and 26 June, p. 631; Dickens: to de Cerjat, 7 July 1858, ibid.

'of sheer stench': Disraeli: *The Times*, 3 July 1858, p. 9; 'compelled to legislate': ibid., 18 June 1858, p. 9.

'makes us clean': Hollingshead, *Underground London*, pp. 58, 68, which is a collection of pieces from *All the Year Round*; Anon., *The Wild Boys of London, or, Children of the Night. A Story of the Present Day* (London, no publisher, [1866?]), p. 8.

'doing properly': Duke of Buccleuch's house: *ILN*: 6 September 1862, p. 265, 30 May 1868, p. 535, 28 May 1870, p. 554. The embanking of the Thames in this and the next paragraph: Porter, *The Thames Embankment*, passim.

'stage of transition': military campaign: *ILN*, 30 July 1864, p. 114; Hudson, *Munby*, pp. 175, 191, 203, 221; Dickens to W. W. F. de Cerjat, 1 February 1861, *Letters*, vol. 9, p. 383.

'form and colour': Hudson, *Munby*, p. 265; the historian: Porter, *The Thames Embankment*, p. 34.

1867: THE REGENT'S PARK SKATING DISASTER

'off a cold': *Pickwick Papers*, pp. 396ff.

'end of the water': numbers and Humane Society: *ILN*: 14 December 1844, pp. 375–6.

'tunnel as usual': Express Train: *ILN*, 17 February 1855, p. 151; skating in the tunnel: ibid., 3 March 1855, p. 197.

'of a serious nature': the paragraphs that follow have been compiled from newspaper reports. The eyewitness evidence is from the inquest transcripts, reprinted in *The Times* over the next two weeks of January, with further information from the *Daily News*, 16 and 17 January 1867, and the *Morning Post*, 16 January 1867. One of the most complete reports appears in the *Standard*, 22 January 1867. The number of icemen on duty is taken from these reports; however, according to Wendy Neal, *With Disastrous Consequences: London Disasters 1830–1917* (Enfield Lock, Hisarlik Press, 1992), p. 111, there were nineteen.

'to us, are *dead*': The diary of Shirley Brooks is in the British Library; I am grateful to Patrick Leary for this transcript, and for pointing me to the skating disaster in the first instance.

9. STREET PERFORMANCE

'occupy his day': Pantheon description: Allen, *History and Antiquities of London*, vol. 5, pp. 281–3; footnote on the Pantheon: Alison Adburgham, *Shops and Shopping, 1800–1914: Where, and in What Manner the Well-dressed Englishwoman Bought her Clothes* (London, Allen and Unwin, 1981), p. 22; Thackeray, 'De Juventute', 'Roundabout Papers from the *Cornhill Magazine*', in *The Works of William Makepeace Thackeray* (London, Smith Elder & Co., 1887), vol. 22, p. 73.

'confectioners and milliners': fashionable hours: Badcock and Rowlandson, *Real Life in London*, vol. 1, p. 104; carriages: Wey, *A Frenchman Sees London*, p. 72; 'sparkling jewellery': *Nicholas Nickleby*, pp. 488–9; Sala, *Twice Round the Clock*, pp. 132–3, 157.

'clients also vanished': Dickens to Catherine Dickens, 7 September 1853, *Letters*, vol. 7, p. 138; shop assistants and milkmaids: Dickens, 'Arcadian London', in *All the Year Round*, 29 September 1860, in *Dickens' Journalism*, vol. 4, p. 183, 185; prostitutes: Hudson, *Munby*, p. 69.

'they had been given': Dickens, 'Arcadian London', *Dickens' Journalism*, vol. 4, p. 189.

'Rag Fair market': marine stores and rag-and-bottle shops: Mayhew, *London Labour*, vol. 2, p. 108, *Bleak House*, pp. 98–9, *David Copperfield*, p. 177; Susan Shatto, *The Companion to Bleak House* (London, Unwin Hyman, 1988), pp. 59–64, on reselling.

'sort: see below': *Martin Chuzzlewit*, p. 280; West End: Greenwood, *Unsentimental Journeys*, p. 14; St Giles: Sala, *Twice Round the Clock*, pp. 264ff.; carpenter's tools, and outline of pawning: Dickens with W. H. Willis, 'My Uncle', in *Household Words*, 6 December 1851, in Stone (ed.), *Uncollected Writings*, vol. 2, pp. 367–78.

'for a consideration': trickery and sympathy: Renton Nicholson, *Autobiography of a Fast Man* (London, published 'for the Proprietors', 1863), pp. 11, 97.

'a broken plate': dolly shops: Dickens, 'Brokers' and 'Marine-store Shops', in *Sketches by Boz*, pp. 211–13, A. Mayhew, *Paved with Gold*, p. 10; leaving shops: Greenwood, *Unsentimental Journeys*, p. 15; *Our Mutual Friend*, p. 346; Southwark shop: Anon., 'Turpin's Corner', *Household Words*, 17, 8 May 1858, pp. 493–6.

'5 shillings': Cranbourne Alley: Sala, *Gaslight and Daylight*, p. 60, Smith, *An Antiquarian Ramble*, vol. 1, pp. 124–5; Beale, *Recollections*, p. 20.

'massive pie sign': shop signs: Badcock and Rowlandson, *Real Life in London*, vol. 1, p. 170; *Little Dorrit*, p. 258; *Dombey and Son*, p. 88; *Martin Chuzzlewit*, p. 377.

'nibbling the cheese': pub signs: Bennett, *London and Londoners*, p. 96; all others: Smith, *Little World of London*, pp. 233ff.

'on the pavements': Warren's Blacking: Colton, *Four Years in Great Britain*, p. 63; 'Try Warren's': R. S. Surtees, *Ask Mamma, or, The Richest Commoner in England* (London, Bradbury and Evans, 1858), p. 18; use of pavements: Altick, *Presence of the Present*, p. 232.

'at any height': Regency bills: John Thomas Smith, *Ancient Topography of London...* (London [no publisher], 1815), facing p. 32, Smith, *Vagabondiana*, final plate, Leighton, *London Cries*, facing p. 2, and Thomas H. Shepherd [and James Elmes], *London and its Environs in the Nineteenth Century, Illustrated by a Series of Views from the Original Drawings by Thomas H. Shepherd, with... Notes* [by James Elmes], (London, Jones & Co., 1829), facing p. 114, are only a few examples; 'a fresh supply': Knight (ed.), *London*, vol. 5, pp. 33–4; dress: ibid., p. 36.

'excursion advertisements': Dickens, 'Bill-Sticking', *Household Words*, 22 March 1851, in *Dickens' Journalism*, vol. 2, pp. 339–50; Mr Guppy: *Bleak House*, p. 175; Schlesinger, *Saunterings*, p. 24.

'any other way': Southey, *Letters from England*, p. 51; Egan, *Life in London*, 158; *Old Curiosity Shop*, p. 282; 'seedy personages': Bennett, *London and Londoners*, p. 55.

'a bigger impression': Regent Street: MacKenzie, *The American in England*, vol. 1, p. 172; 'animated sandwich': 'The Dancing Academy', *Sketches by Boz*, p. 299; 'piece of human flesh': Knight (ed.), *London*, vol. 5, p. 37; *ILN*: *ILN*, 14 May 1842, p. 16.

'and even weeks': the itch: MacKenzie, *The American in England*, vol. 1, pp. 172–3; bootmaker: Wey, *A Frenchman Sees London*, p. 207; Mr Falcon: Schlesinger, *Saunterings*, p. 15.

'gilding and pictures': Boz ads: Mark Wormald, introduction to *Pickwick Papers*, p. xiii; Bardell bus company: Long, 'Mr Pickwick Lucky to Find a Cab?'; wellington boot: engraving in the *Weekly Chronicle*, reproduced in Jackson, *George Scharf's London*, p. 36; models of houses and steamboats: MacKenzie, *The American in England*, pp. 73–4; hat, obelisk and gothic windows: Knight (ed.), *London*, vol. 5, p. 38; Schlesinger, *Saunterings*, pp. 15, 18–19.

'whiskers with him afterwards': auctions: Greenwood, *Wilds of London*, pp. 152–3; bear grease: Lockwood, *Passionate Pilgrims*, p. 129, Bennett, *London and Londoners*, pp. 100–101; *Nicholas Nickleby*, p. 131.

'his wet things': shop bells: Phillips, *Wild Tribes*, p. 97; tailors: Badcock and Rowlandson, *Real Life in London*, vol. 1, pp. 530–31; *Pickwick Papers*, pp. 431–2; coffee rooms: Hudson, *Munby*, p. 85; *Great Expectations*, p. 446.

'early dinner-beer': delivery boy's dress: Frank Bullen, *Confessions of a Tradesman* (London, Hodder and Stoughton, 1908), p. 22; *Pickwick Papers*, pp. 417–18, 424; Kentish Town newspaper: Yates, *Recollections*, p. 28.

'in St Martin's Lane': *ILN*, 2 June 1854, pp. 562, 564.

'spoil – spile': *Pickwick Papers*, pp. 131, 163; *Bleak House*, pp. 278, 422–3.

'Menshun Ouse': Badcock and Rowlandson, *Real Life in London*, vol. 1, p. 457; Bennett, *London and Londoners*, pp. 140–41, and Hollingshead, *My Lifetime*, vol. 1, p. 49, agrees with him here; location names: Tuer, *Old London Street Cries*, pp. 70, 73.

'had all vanished': *Edwin Drood*, pp. 254–5; 'Metropolitan Miss' and upper-class gent: Mayhew and Binny, *The Criminal Prisons*, p. 5; Trollope, *What I Remember*, p. 49.

'clothes get tight': the Stilton: Mayhew and Binny, *The Criminal Prisons*, p. 5; costers' backslang: Mayhew, *London Labour*, vol. 1, p. 23, and Mayhew and Binny, ibid.

'Oliver Twist (fist)': rhyming slang: Mayhew and Binny, ibid., Hayward, *Days of Dickens*, pp. 16–17; novel: A. Mayhew, *Paved with Gold*, p. 70.

'Romany for speak': Mayhew and foreign languages: Mayhew and Binny, *The Criminal Prisons*, p. 6; Dickens, *Oliver Twist*, pp. 79, 29; Romany: Mayhew and Binny, ibid.

'your poor feet': 1830s catchphrases: Hayward, *Days of Dickens*, p. 17 and Vizetelly, *Glances Back*: vol. 1, p. 103; 1860s catchphrases: Bennett, *London and Londoners*, pp. 41–2.

'Hookey estates from': 'Do you see any green': Hayward, *Days of Dickens*, p. 17; *A Christmas Carol*, p. 129; *David Copperfield*, p. 307.

'cocking a snook': *Pickwick Papers*, p. 405; *Old Curiosity Shop*, p. 365.

'a dancing girl': bands: Mayhew: *London Labour*, vol. 3, p. 159; types of organists in the following three paragraphs: Smith, *Curiosities*, pp. 2–15.

'extremely unusual': Hudson, *Munby*, p. 276; Stabbers's Band: 'An Unsettled Neighbourhood', *Household Words*, 11 November 1854, in *Dickens' Journalism*, vol. 3, p. 243.

'in such circumstances': 'The Streets – Night', *Sketches by Boz*, p. 77; Hudson, *Munby*, pp. 157–8; Joseph Johnson: Smith, *Vagabondiana*, facing p. 33; sailor with child: Jackson, *Scharf's London*, p. 56; sailors: Bennett, *London and Londoners*, p. 53.

'brazen instruments': Robert Seymour, *Seymour's Humorous Sketches…*, with text by Alfred Crowquill (2nd edn, London, Henry G. Bohn, 1866), sketch 22; Leech and Dickens, cited by John M. Picker, *Victorian Soundscapes* (Oxford, Oxford University Press, 2003), p. 42.

'with the quality': Mayhew, *London Labour*, vol. 3, p. 44; 'An Unsettled Neighbourhood', *Household Words*, 11 November 1854, in *Dickens' Journalism*, vol. 3, p.243; *Punch*'s summer holiday: Mayhew, *London Labour*, vol. 3, pp. 45–7.

'and Christmas pantomimes': puppets: Bennett, *London and Londoners*, p. 61; Sanger, *Seventy Years*, pp. 12–13, 18, 50; subjects for peep-shows: Sanger, and Mayhew, *London Labour*, vol. 3, pp. 88–9.

'to Queen Victoria': bear: Mayhew, *London Labour*, vol. 3, p. 72; Sanger, *Seventy Years*, p. 54; Happy Families: Mayhew, *London Labour*, vol. 3, p. 179, Bennett, *London and Londoners*, p. 67; exhibitor to Queen Victoria: *ILN*, 29 August 1842, p. 237.

'a funny dance': 'Hal. Lewis, Student at Law, 'The Street-Conjuror', in Meadows, *Heads of the People*, vol. 1, p. 275, Mayhew, *London Labour*, vol. 3, pp. 90ff., 98, 104, 107, 110, 117, Smith, *Little World of London*, pp. 6–7.

'day-trippers obeyed': Cackler Dance: Sanger, *Seventy Years*, p. 60; the 'it forms' man: Sala, *Gaslight and Daylight*, p. 62; profile cutters: Mayhew, *London Labour*, vol. 3, p. 210; pavement chalkers: ibid., vol. 3, p. 214; street boys tumbling: A. Mayhew, *Paved with Gold*, p. 92; riverside boys: Mayhew and Binny, *The Criminal Prisons*, p. 233; Greenwich children: Bennett, *London and Londoners*, p. 139.

10. LEISURE FOR ALL

'the masses out': Anthony Trollope, *The Warden*, ed. David Skilton (Oxford, Oxford University Press, 1998), Chapter 16, pp. 210ff., itemizes Mr Harding's dispiriting day; St James's and Green Parks: Susan Lasdun, *The English Park: Royal, Public and Private* (London, André Deutsch, 1991), pp. 126, 129.

'risen to 461': fifty squares: Knight (ed.), *London*, vol. 6, p. 194; 200 squares: *Leigh's New Picture* (1839 edn), p. 221; 461 squares: White, *London in the Nineteenth Century*, p. 71.

'centuries of growth': *Leigh's New Picture* (1819 edn): p. 259, 1839 edition, p. 221; greenery visible: Henry W. Lawrence, *City Trees: A Historical Geography from the Renaissance through the Nineteenth Century* (Charlottesville, VA, University of Virginia Press, 2006), p. 179.

'and middle class': Knight (ed.), *London*, vol. 6, p. 199.

'around central London': Mayhew and Binny, *The Criminal Prisons*, pp. 59–60.

'over his horse': 'Leicester-square adventurer': *ILN*, 7 January 1860, p. 3; *Bleak House*, p. 356; Reynolds and Hogarth: *ILN*, 11 January 1868, p. 42; Savile House: E. Beresford Chancellor, *The Squares of London, Topographical and Historical* (London, Kegan Paul, Trench, Trübner & Co., 1907), pp. 167ff.; foreignness of Leicester Square: Smith, *Antiquarian Ramble*, vol. 1, pp. 119–20; gas explosion: Halliday, *Great Stink*, p. 175; George I: Beale, *Recollections*, pp. 41–2.

'their great trays': Belgrave Square villas: Charles Knight (ed.), *London*, vol. 6, p. 194; Pantechnicon: *Leigh's New Picture* (1839 edition), p. 222; Berkeley Square occupants: Chancellor, *The Squares of London*, p. 20; Pardon, *Routledge's Popular Guide*, lists Thomas's Hotel as still there in 1862, p. 46; 'clatterings': Mrs Gore, *Cecil, or, The Adventures of a Coxcomb* (London, Richard Bentley, 1841), vol. 3, p. 214.

'landowner's revenue': Nash, cited in Dyos, *Exploring the Urban Past*, p. 82.

'*rus in urbe* setting': the three paragraphs on the development of Regent's Park: Arnold, *Re-Presenting the Metropolis*, p. 39, J. Mordaunt Crook, *London's Arcadia: John Nash and the Planning of Regent's Park*, Fifth Annual Soane Lecture ([n.p., no publisher] 2000), pp. 4–14, J. Mordaunt Crook, 'Metropolitan Improvements: John Nash and the Picturesque', in Fox (ed.), *London – World City*, pp. 77–96, Terence Davis, *The Architecture of John Nash* (London, Studio, 1960), pp. 9–16, Anne Saunders, *Regent's Park: A Study of its Development of the Area from 1086 to the Present Day* (Newton Abbot, David and Charles, 1969), passim, Anne Saunders, *The Regent's Park Villas* (London, Bedford College, 1981), passim, and White, *London in the Nineteenth Century*, pp. 23–6, 73–4.

'of great magnificence': Wheaton, *Journal of a Residence*, p. 222; Henry Vizetelly, *Glances Back*, vol. 1, p. 27; MacKenzie, *The American in England*, pp. 169–71, 176–7.

'until 1857': Lasdun, *The English Park*, pp. 124–5, 128–9, 149–65. The purchase of Primrose Hill: Lasdun says the land (fifty-eight acres) was bought for £300; according to Saunders, it was a land swap with the owners of the land, Eton College, in which the college acquired more land in Windsor.

'to have attended': Victoria Park: Winter, *London's Teeming Streets*, p. 164; carriage driving: Wey, *A Frenchman Sees London*, pp. 162, 165; Wyon, Journal, BL Add MS 59,617; *ILN*, 8 September 1855, p. 287, 17 May 1856, pp. 527, 615, 13 September 1856, p. 265.

'street from Westminster': Nash, cited in Rodney Mace, *Trafalgar Square: Emblem of Empire* (London, Lawrence and Wishart, 1976), pp. 23–9, 31–46, and Tambling, *Going Astray*, p. 31.

'the front lawn': lion: Knight (ed.), *London*, vol. 6, p. 207; description from text and images in E. Beresford Chancellor, *Lost London: Being a description of Landmarks which have disappeared pictured by J. Crowther circa 1879–87…* (London, Constable, 1926), pp. 30ff.

'an open piazza': except where noted, this and the next eight paragraphs are derived from: Allen, *History and Antiquities of London*, vol. 5, pp. 291–2, Fox (ed.), *London – World City*, pp. 94ff., Mace, *Trafalgar Square*, pp. 126ff.

'a cold plunge': Ely Place and its jurisdiction: my thanks to Lee Jackson for pointing this out; 'Roman' pool: Clayton, *Subterranean City*, p. 21.

'of his scheme': footnote: the architectural historian is John Summerson. I thank Jonathan Foyle for alerting me to this, and for his views of the project.

'bare-headed': the Nelson monument: Felix Barker and Ralph Hyde, *London as it Might Have Been* (London, John Murray, 1982), pp. 65–70 (it is they who thought that the mermaids were playing water-polo), Mace, *Trafalgar Square*, p. 65; Nelson's hat: Smith, *An Antiquarian Ramble*, vol. 1, p. 135; footnote on statues apart from the empty plinth: Mace, ibid., p. 111.

'a clean one': Sala, *The Hats of Humanity, Historically, Humorously and Aesthetically Considered…* (Manchester, James Gee, 'Hatter', [?1880]), pp. 16–17; *Martin Chuzzlewit*, p. 796; doctors' boys: Sala, *Hats of Humanity*, pp. 15–16; man leaving prison: J. Ewing Ritchie, *Days and Nights in London; or, Studies in Black and Gray* (London, Tinsley Brothers, 1880), p. 267; paper caps: Cunnington and Lucas, *Occupational Costume*, pp. 86–7; *Martin Chuzzlewit*, p. 225.

'Landseer was about': artesian wells: *ILN*, 24 August 1844, p. 119; 29 March 1845, p. 199, and 14 March 1846, p. 174; bathing in the fountains: A. Mayhew, *Paved with Gold*, p. 85; Nelson's column and granite arrival: *ILN*, 2 July 1842, p. 121; arrival of statue: ibid., 4 November 1843, p. 288; reliefs, and non-completion: ibid., 23 October 1858, p. 380, 17 March 1860, p. 251.

'that was that': unveiling: Hudson, *Munby*, pp. 236–7; lack of ceremony: *ILN*, 2 February 1867, pp. 111–12.

'outdoor sitting room': Boucicault: *Illustrated Times*, cited in Lynda Nead, *Victorian Babylon: People, Streets and Images in Nineteenth-Century London* (London, Yale University Press, 2000), p. 99.

'by the waiter': Dickens, 'London Recreations', *Sketches by Boz*, p. 120; the Eagle: 'Miss Evans and the Eagle', *Sketches by Boz*, p. 269; Highbury Barn: 'Anonyma', *London by Night*, pp. 77ff.; *Little Dorrit*, p. 417.

'main attraction': *Pickwick Papers*, p. 614; Hornsey and Epping: Archer, *The Pauper, the Thief, and the Convict*, p. 22; vans: Colman, *European Life and Manners*, vol. 2, p. 78; vehicles and types: Sala, *Looking at Life; or, Thoughts and Things* (London, Routledge, Warne, and Routledge, 1860), pp. 189–90; the Welsh Harp: White, *London in the Nineteenth Century*, pp. 266–7.

'river excursion': tea gardens south of the river: [G. A. Sala], 'Sunday Tea-Gardens', *Household Words*, 10, 30 September 1854, p. 147.

'by the tide': Dolphin and Swan taverns: Mayhew and Binny, *The Criminal Prisons*, p. 233; swimming match: *ILN*, 14 July 1849, p. 23; cholera deaths: ibid., 28 July 1849, p. 55; rowing matches: ibid., 24 July 1852, p. 62, for the Thames Watermen's Royal Regatta; others reported: ibid., 2 July 1842, p. 115, 8 July 1843, pp. 27–8, 4 July 1846, p. 9, and passim; championship of the Thames, ibid., 22 September 1860, p. 269; Astley's clown: ibid., 28 September 1844, p. 193.

'financial resources': Yates, *His Recollections*, pp. 106–7.

'dinner at Greenwich': Barry dinner: *ILN*, 6 July 1850, p. 3; Crimea dinner: *ILN*, 12 August 1854, p. 131.

'wedding breakfast': Dickens dinner: Michael N. Stanton, 'Dickens' Return from America; A Ghost at the Feast', *Dickensian*, Autumn 1991, p. 148; *Our Mutual Friend*, pp. 313, 649.

'day on the river': *Princess Alice* excursion and footnote: Ritchie, *Days and Nights in London*, pp. 197ff.; Dickens' excursion: Claire Tomalin, *Charles Dickens: A Life* (Harmondsworth, Viking, 2010), p. 316.

'flagrant evils': number of fairs and fair-days: *Leigh's New Picture* (1819 edn), pp. 176–8; (1839 edn), p. 120.

'and nothing else': Bartholomew Fair: Thomas Frost, *The Old Showmen, and the Old London Fairs* (London, Tinsley Brothers, 1874), pp. 214ff., Henry Morley, *Memoirs of Bartholomew Fair* (London, Frederick Warne & Co., [n.d.]), pp. 375ff., Badcock and Rowlandson, *Real Life in London*, vol. 1, pp. 528–9, Grant, *Sketches in London*, pp. 289ff.; last days in 1848: *ILN*, 9 September 1848, p. 150.

'draw the crowds': Greenwich Fair in this and the next two paragraphs from: Masson, *Memories*, pp. 145–7, Smith (ed.), *Gavarni in London*, pp. 76–80, Grant, *Sketches in London*, pp. 289–317, Hawthorne, *Hawthorne in England*, pp. 172–5; footnote on roundabouts: Sanger, *Seventy Years*, p. 16.

11. FEEDING THE STREETS

'or a tea': *David Copperfield*, p. 153.

'of their lodgings': hot-eel sellers: Mayhew, *London Labour*, vol. 1, pp. 160–2; whelk sellers: ibid., vol. 1, p. 164, and their calls, vol. 1, p. 76.

'steadily declined': *Pickwick Papers*, p. 294; Mayhew on oyster selling and in footnote: *London Labour*, vol. 1, pp. 75–6; Bennett, *London and Londoners*, p. 71.

'over a meal': wink men: Mayhew, *London Labour*, vol. 1, p. 76; footnote on American tourist: James N. Matthews, *My Holiday: How I Spent it…in the Summer of 1866* (Buffalo, Martin Taylor, 1867), p. 197; cabbage plants, chickweed and cresses: Smith, *Cries of London*, pp. 7–8.

'potatoes – right away': Mayhew, *London Labour*, vol. 1, pp. 173–5.

'was not profitable': economics of muffin men: Greenwood, *Wilds of London*, p. 184; caps: Bennett, *London and Londoners*, p. 44.

'piemen even further': description of piemen, and economic reasons for decline: Smith, *Curiosities*, pp. 202–5; *Pickwick Papers*, p. 252.

'manner of a pieman': *Pickwick Papers*, p. 294, *David Copperfield*, p. 314, *Martin Chuzzlewit*, p. 284.

'around their necks': Greenwich Fair: *Sketches by Boz*, p. 140, and Smith (ed.), *Gavarni in London*, pp. 78–9; fried-fish sellers at Epsom: Mayhew, *London Labour*, vol. 1, p. 166.

'had arrived': Smith, *Little World of London*, pp. 51–2; hoboys: Mayhew, *London Labour*, vol. 1, p. 85;

'for a meal': Sunday excursionists: elder wine: ibid., vol. 1, p. 189; peppermint water: ibid., vol. 1, p. 191, and Sanger, *Seventy Years*, p. 57; curds-and-whey and rice milk: Mayhew, ibid., vol. 1, pp. 192–3.

'mashed turnip': Sanger, *Seventy Years*, p. 57; 'coolers': Mayhew and Binny, *The Criminal Prisons*, p. 41; hokey-pokey men and ingredients: Tuer, *Old London Street Cries*, pp. 58–60.

'repeat performance': dress and wooden frames: Bennett, *London and Londoners*, pp. 43–4; sticks: Sekon, *Locomotion in Victorian Britain*, p. 18; *Old Curiosity Shop*, p. 331; 'The Streets – Night', *Sketches by Boz*, p. 75.

'with a pewter-pot': *Nicholas Nickleby*, p. 228; *Dombey and Son*, p. 143; Miss Tox's location is not pinpointed, but on p. 144 it is in the West End, although not a good house – 'think of the situation!' says Miss Tox, surely implying it lies in Mayfair.

'on the town': 'The Amusements of the People (II)', *Household Words*, 13 April 1850, in *Dickens' Journalism*, vol. 2, pp. 195–6.

'take gravy away': ham-and-beef shop: Sala, *Gaslight and Daylight*, p. 5; *Martin Chuzzlewit*, p. 288; Badcock and Rowlandson, *Real Life in London*, vol. 1, p. 388; window display: A. Mayhew, *Paved with Gold*, pp. 81–2; newspaper and dishes: Callow, *Old London Taverns*, pp. 82, 292–3.

'sit and eat': hours: Yates, *Recollections*, p. 107; locations, Yates, ibid., and *London by Night, or, The Bachelor's Facetious Guide to All the Ins and Outs and the Nightly Doings of the Metropolis*... (London, William Ward [?1857]), pp. 44–6; Holborn oyster house: 'Misplaced Attachment of Mr John Dounce', *Sketches by Boz*, pp. 286–7.

'its roller afterwards': Scott's: 'Anonyma', *London by Night*, p. 82, and Kirwan, *Palace and Hovel*, pp. 181–2; 'lobsters, crabs': Sala, *Twice Round the Clock*, p. 324.

'their names suggest': Sala, *Twice Round the Clock*, p. 147.

'conducted houses': *David Copperfield*, p. 335; 'Refreshments for Travellers', 24 March 1860, *All the Year Round*, in *Dickens' Journalism*, vol. 4, p. 78; Pardon, *Routledge's Popular Guide to London*, p. 48.

'coming and going': earthenware dishes: Smith, *Curiosities*, p. 255; thieving cookshops: Wright, *Habits and Customs*, pp. 216–17; Christmas Day: Forster, *Life*, vol. 3, p. 477.

'twenty-four hours': *Little Dorrit*, p. 283; Bethnal Green: Archer: *The Pauper, the Thief*, p. 17; pea soup: Bullen, *Confessions of a Tradesman*, pp. 40–41.

'and doze indoors': workers, newspapers: Carter, *Memoirs of a Working Man*, p. 186; Greville Street: Lovett, *Life and Struggles*, p. 88; Egan, *Life in London*, p. 181; Sala, *Gaslight and Daylight*, p. 15.

'knife and fork': number of coffee shops: Knight (ed.), *London*, vol. 1, p. 317, vol. 1, p. 140; working-class coffee house: ibid., vol. 4, pp. 317–18; customers bringing food: Hugh Miller, *First Impressions of England and its People* (London, John Johnstone, 1847), p. 354; 'Night Walks', in *All the Year Round*, 21 July 1860, in *Dickens' Journalism*, vol. 4, pp. 155–6; footnote on hats: these references are in:

Pickwick Papers, p. 397; *Oliver Twist*, pp. 30, 69, 202; *Nicholas Nickleby*, pp. 482, 672, 809; *Old Curiosity Shop*, p. 544; *Martin Chuzzlewit*, pp. 98, 630; *Little Dorrit*, pp. 321, 833; and *David Copperfield*, p. 455; the Sherlock Holmes story is 'A Scandal in Bohemia' (1891).

'particularly successful': Brontës: Mrs Gaskell, *Life of Charlotte Brontë*, pp. 270–71; *Little Dorrit*, p. 68, *Our Mutual Friend*, p. 35; American newspapers: Wheaton, *Journal of a Residence*, p. 120; business connections: Tambling, *Going Astray*, pp. 283–4; Garraway's and coffee-house boxes: Callow, *Old London Taverns*, p. 6; footnote on boxes: Dickens, 'A Sleep to Startle Us', *Dickens' Journalism*, vol. 3, p. 52; *David Copperfield*, p. 754.

'in such a place': cigar divans: Masson, *Memories*, p. 124, and *London by Night: The Bachelor's…*, pp. 50–52; Trollope, *The Warden*, pp. 226–7.

'nothing at all: post-office clerk: Yates, *Recollections*, p. 80; *Our Mutual Friend*, p. 590; speed, and bread and cheese lunches: Sala, *Twice Round the Clock*, p. 140.

'a fourpenny': Yates, *Recollections*, pp. 80–81; beef with carrots: Callow, *Old London Taverns*, p. 84; Boiled-Beef House: Badcock and Rowlandson, *Real Life in London*, vol. 2, p. 158; 'Which would you please': ibid., vol. 1, p. 388; lesser houses: Knight (ed.), *London*, vol. 4, p. 314.

'something like meat': display and prices: Knight (ed.), *London*, vol. 4, p. 314; Raumer, *England in 1835*, vol. 2, p. 113.

'down to eat': menu: Hollingshead, *My Lifetime*, vol. 1, pp. 57–8; Old Fleece and Sun, and the Bay Tree: Callow, *Old London Taverns*, pp. 2–3, 29–30, and John Murray Fisher, *The World of London*, 2 vols. (Edinburgh, William Blackwood, 1843), vol. 2, pp. 4–5.

'the day before': system of waiting staff: Seymour, 'The Eating House', in *Seymour's Humorous Sketches*, [no page]; footnote on income and outgoings: *The Servant Girl in London: Showing the Dangers to which Young Country Girls are Exposed…* (London, R. Hastings, 1840), pp. 34–6; *Bleak House*, p. 337; police-court report: *ILN*, 25 June 1842; Dickens, 'Thoughts about People', *Sketches by Boz*, p. 252.

'quarter-hour break': Edmund Yates, *After Office-Hours* (London, W. Kent and Co., 1861), p. 251; *Great Expectations*, p. 383; Reeves' Luncheon Rooms: Pardon, *Routledge's Popular Guide to London*, prelims.

'sustained coo': Yates, *After Office-Hours*, pp. 246–7.

'its turtle soup': menu: Knight (ed.), *London*, vol. 4, p. 313; specialities: Forney, *Letter from Europe*, p. 345.

'the carving-knife': *Bleak House*, p. 337; *Pickwick Papers*, p. 584.

'implore or threaten': location, description of Bell Alley, reputation: Callow, *Old London Taverns*, pp. 120–21; guidebook: Knight (ed.), *London*, vol. 4, p. 314; description: [Dickens with W. H. Willis], 'A Popular Delusion', *Household Words*, 1 June 1850, in Stone (ed.), *Uncollected Writings*, vol. 1, p. 120 and Callow, ibid., pp. 120–22.

'civil and quick': new Simpson's: Callow, ibid., pp. 125–6, and Yates, *After Office-Hours*, p. 243; the Albion: Yates, ibid., p. 105.

'box and all': *Martin Chuzzlewit*, p. 767.

'meat and drink': *Old Curiosity Shop*, pp. 108–9.

'of its time': Postmaster General: Yates, *Recollections*, pp. 80–81; Reeves' Luncheon Rooms: Pardon, *Routledge's Popular Guide to London*, prelims.

12. STREET THEATRE

'a drunken man': original opening for 'The Prisoner's Van', in Butt and Tillotson, *Dickens at Work*, p. 44.

'in my life': Forster, *Life*, vol. 3, p. 141.

'summoned a throng': boys' comments: A. Mayhew, *Paved with Gold*, pp. 333, 109; prisoners' van jokes: ibid., p. 1; Bow Street prisoners: Sala, *Twice Round the Clock*, p. 215, also mentioned by Kirwan, *Palace and Hovel*, p. 175; mailcoaches, Wheaton, *Journal of a Residence*, p. 400, and Mayhew and Binny, *The Criminal Prisons*, pp. 19–20.

'landlord's men': *Martin Chuzzlewit*, p. 829; Ritchie, *Days and Nights in London*, p. 257; Serpentine: *ILN*, 16 October 1869, pp. 379, 392; *Dombey and Son*, p. 790; Peel: Wey, *A Frenchman Sees London*, pp. 263–4; Clerkenwell eviction: *ILN*, 11 January 1843, p. 19.

'part of a week': the earthquake: from the *Era*, *Examiner*, *Morning Post*, *Observer*, *Standard* and *Morning Chronicle*, as well as some local papers: *Aberdeen Journal*, *Belfast News-Courant*, *Berrow's Worcester Journal*, *Bradford Observer*, *Bristol Mercury*, *Caledonian Mercury*, *Cornwall Royal Gazette*, *Derby Mercury*, *Freeman's Journal*, *Hampshire Advertiser and Salisbury Guardian*, *Hull Packet*, *Ipswich Journal*, *Jackson's Oxford Journal*, *Liverpool Mercury*, *Manchester Times and Gazette*, *Newcastle Courant*, *Preston Chronicle*, *Sheffield and Rotherham Independent* between 2 March and 8 April 1842; Whitechapel Church ghost: *ILN*, 15 October 1842, p. 359.

'the arrival itself': Wyatt's sculpture: Mrs E. M. Ward, *Mrs. E. M. Ward's Reminiscences*, ed. Elliott O'Donnell (London, Sir Isaac Pitman & Sons, 1911), pp. 65–6; Hudson, *Munby*, p. 150.

'crowd of 500': *ILN*, 8 April 1854, p. 329, 7 October 1854, pp. 340–41.

'easier to control': 1814: White, *London in the Nineteenth Century*, p. 261; Crimean War: Creaton (ed.), *Victorian Diaries*, p. 39.

'injuries and disease': this paragraph and the next: *ILN*, 12 July 1856, p. 31. I am grateful to Michael Hargreave Mawson for attempting to instil in me some rudimentary knowledge of military terminology.

'the civic dinner': Schlesinger, *Saunterings*, pp. 90–92.

'handsome walking stick': Prince Regent: Joseph Ballard, *England in 1815: A Critical Edition of The Journal of Joseph Ballard*, ed. Alan Rauch (Basingstoke, Palgrave Macmillan, 2009), p. 54; Prince Albert: Wyon, Journal, BL Add MS 59,617, 27 April 1855.

'not impressed': Charles Greville, *The Greville Diary*..., ed. Philip Whitwell Wilson (London, William Heinemann, 1927), vol. 2, pp. 14–15, 28, 41; footnote on Greville: Christopher Hibbert (ed.), *Queen Victoria in Her Letters and Journals: A Selection* (London, John Murray, 1984), pp. 237–8.

'held his Barony': Disraeli, *Benjamin Disraeli, Letters*, ed. M. G. Wiebe et al. (Toronto, University of Toronto Press, 1987, 1997), vol. 3, *1838–1841*, pp. 54–5, 67, 69, 70, 72.

'ground of insanity': German sausage: there are a number of broadsides with these songs. An example, 'The Queen's Marriage', can be seen in Charles Hindley, *The Life and Times of James Catnach, Ballad Monger* (London, Reeves and Turner, 1878), p. 326, while James Hepburn, *A Book of Scattered Leaves: Poetry and Poverty in Broadside Ballads of Nineteenth-Century England* (London, Associated University Presses,

2001), vol. 2, p. 453, contains more. I am grateful to Suzanne Daly and Inktwala Meredith for pointing me in the direction of these volumes; Victoria's wedding day: Greville, *Diary*, vol. 2, pp. 130–31; birth of Prince of Wales: *ILN*, 12 November 1842, p. 423; refusal to remove hats, and miser Neild: *ILN*, 25 March 1848, p. 201, and 18 September 1852, p. 222; amount of bequest: Stanley Weintraub, *Victoria, Biography of a Queen* (London, Unwin Hyman, 1987), p. 201.

'opera went on': 1840 assassination attempt: Greville, *Diary*, vol. 2, pp. 203–4; first 1842 attempt: *ILN*, 4 June 1842, pp. 49–50; fifth attempt: Beale, *Recollections*, p. 13.

'all the trees': Dickens to John Forster, ?30 November 1846, *Letters*, vol. 4, p. 669.

'arriving in the capital': Buckingham Palace notice: Elizabeth Longford, *Victoria R.I.* (London, Weidenfeld & Nicolson, 1964), p. 321; Shakespeare notice: in Agnes E. Claflin, *From Shore to Shore: A Journey of Nineteen Years* (Cambridge, MA, Riverside Press, 1873), p. 154. My thanks to Abigail Burnham Bloom for copying the pages of this book for me; Holborn Viaduct opening: *ILN*, 6 November 1869, p. 451.

'station to another': this paragraph and the next two: Hudson, *Munby*, pp. 149–52.

'biscuit the Garibaldi': Beale, *Recollections*, pp. 118–19; Hudson, *Munby*, pp. 186–9; McCarthy, *Reminiscences*, vol. 1, p. 133; footnote on Garibaldi: *ILN*, 16 April 1864, p. 374.

'carried by rail': the mailcoaches on the king's birthday: Bradfield, *Public Carriages*, p. 21, Corbett, *Old Coachman's Chatter*, pp. 43–4, Mayhew and Binny, *The Criminal Prisons*, pp. 19–20, Raumer, *England in 1835*, vol. 2, p. 52 and Thrupp, *History of Coaches*, p. 113.

'this civic ritual': Smith, *Little World of London*, p. 109; Holborn: *ILN*, 23 May 1857, p. 493.

'danced round': 'They go about': Southey, *Letters from England*, p. 78; 'The First of May', *Sketches by Boz*, pp. 205–8.

'gave her something': Dickens, 'The First of May', ibid.; Hudson, *Munby*, p. 285.

'and daisies': 'open carriages': A. Mayhew, *Paved with Gold*, pp. 217–18; verse: *ILN*, 28 May 1842, p. 41.

'remember the grotto': Bennett, *London and Londoners*, pp. 70–71; *ILN*, 10 August 1850, p. 115.

'serenade the guy': this paragraph and the next from: Bennett, *London and Londoners*, pp. 126, 166, *ILN*, 10 November 1855, p. 547, 7 November 1857, p. 458, 7 November 1863, p. 462, Mayhew, *London Labour*, vol. 3, pp. 64–8.

'of the family': mutes: Hall, *Retrospect of a Long Life*, vol. 1, pp. 70–71, Mrs Gore in Meadows, *Heads of the People*, vol. 2, p. 38, Bennett, *London and Londoners*, pp. 58–9; funeral drapery: Mrs Gore, ibid.; hatchments: Smith, *Little World of London*, p. 59; footnote on hatchments: Wey, *A Frenchman Sees London*, p. 50, and Smith, *Letters from Europe*, p. 34; funeral carriages and horses: Hall, ibid.; walking funerals: Smith, *Little World of London*, p. 59.

'Westminster Abbey': 1831 funeral: McLelland, *Journal of a Residence*, p. 229; Duke of Northumberland's funeral: *ILN*, 27 February 1847, p. 137.

'black and white': mourning for Prince Albert: Hudson, *Munby*, p. 111, *ILN*, 4 January 1862, p. 7; Palmerston: *ILN*, 4 November 1865, p. 447.

'revolting absurdity': *Martin Chuzzlewit*, pp. 380, 386–7; Dickens' will: cited in Ackroyd, *Dickens*, p. xiii.

'of the London streets': Maple's: *ILN*, 8 August 1857, p. 150; Prince Pückler-Muskau, *A Regency Visitor: The English Tour of Prince Pückler-Muskau, described in his letters, 1826–1828*, trans. Sarah Austin, ed. E. M. Butler (London, Collins, 1957), p. 87; *Old Curiosity Shop*, p. 606; St Paul's Churchyard: *ILN*, 17 July 1852, p. 44; Seven Dials, ibid., 2 October 1852, p. 279; Old Broad Street: ibid., 21 January 1854, p. 63.

'a routine hazard': Nead, *Victorian Babylon*, pp. 93–4.

'theatres burnt down': types of fires: Timbs, *Curiosities*, vol. 1, p. 299; 1848 figures: *ILN*, 6 January 1849, p. 7; the nine theatres are: 1841, Astley's; 1846, Garrick, Leman Street; 1849, Olympic; 1853, Islington Circus; 1846, Pavilion, Whitechapel, and Covent Garden; 1865, Surrey; 1866, Standard; 1867, Haymarket.

'Snowballed the Beadle': workhouse men: G. V. Blackstone, *A History of the British Fire Service* (London, Routledge and Kegan Paul, 1957), p. 106; Dickens, 'The Beadle – The Parish Engine . . .', *Sketches by Boz*, p. 20. The history of the Fire Engine Establishment that follows in the next four paragraphs, unless otherwise noted, is drawn from: Blackstone, ibid.; P. G. M. Dickson, *The Sun Insurance Office, 1710–1960: The History of Two and a Half Centuries of British Insurance* (London, Oxford University Press, 1960), pp. 129–30, and Knight (ed.), *London*, vol. 4, pp. 178–88; Dickens to Miss Mary Boyle, 28 December 1860, *Letters*, vol. 9, p. 354.

'and 314 men': insurance company uniforms: Cunnington and Lucas, *Occupational Costume*, p. 260.

'warn oncoming traffic': Northern Lights footnote: this was claimed by Bartlett, *What I Saw in London*, pp. 50–51; 'away scamper the policemen': [Richard H. Horne], 'The Fire Brigade of London', *Household Words*, 7, 11 May 1850, pp. 145–7; horses' speed: Mayhew, *London Labour*, vol. 2, p. 381; 'hi! yi!' and footnote: Massingham, *London Anthology*, p. 170; speed modified by horses' capacity, and standing by driver: R. M. Ballantyne, *Fighting the Flames: A Tale of the London Fire Brigade* (London, James Nisbet, 1868), pp. 30–31.

'seven minutes': private roads: Hogg, *London as it is*, p. 216; nineteenth-century speed of response: Mayhew, *London Labour*, vol. 2, p. 381. 2006 response times: CLG, 'Review of Fire and Rescue Service response times' – Fire Research Series 1/2009, www.communities.gov.uk/documents/fire/pdf/frsresponsetimes.pdf, accessed 16 February 2012.

'the crowds back': metal signs: Weale, *London Exhibited in 1852*, p. 112; volunteers and wages: Bartlett, *What I Saw in London*, pp. 47–8; Bartlett translates the pay into US dollars, but many other sources bear him out; number per pump on land: Bennett, *London and Londoners*, pp. 84–5, and Blackstone, *British Fire Service*, p. 114; river engines: Bartlett, ibid., pp. 47–8; payment methods: Bartlett, ibid., p. 114, and Sala, *Twice Round the Clock*, p. 355.

'well alight': Greville, *Diary*, vol. 1, pp. 307–8; Houses of Parliament fire: Blackstone, *British Fire Service*, pp. 118–19.

'turn at the pumps': Carlyle: *Carlyle Letters*, vol. 7, pp. 318–19; Haydon, *Memoirs*, cited in Massingham, *London Anthology*, p. 167; visitors to Covent Garden ruins: *ILN*, 15 March 1856, p. 275; Dickens, to W. C. Macready, 22 March 1856, *Letters*, vol. 8, p. 75; Prince of Wales: John A. Walker, 'The People's Hero: Millais's *The Rescue* and the Image of the Fireman in Nineteenth-century Art and Media', *Apollo,* December 2004, p. 59.

'in small boats': Hékékyan Bey, Journal, British Library, Add MS 37,448; Sala, *Twice Round the Clock*, p. 348; Battersea: *ILN*, 20 March 1847, pp. 177–8.

'in its disasters': journalists on the prowl: Sala, *Twice Round the Clock*, p. 353.

1852: THE FUNERAL OF THE DUKE OF WELLINGTON

'acclamation of all': the American tourist: Wheaton, *Journal of a Residence*, p. 161; the coronation crowd: Colton, *Four Years in Great Britain*, p. 71.

'of Waterloo': shutters: Stewart, *Sketches of Society*, vol. 1, p. 170; butler: Haydon, *Life of Benjamin Robert Haydon…*, vol. 2, p. 275; attitude to his wife: Francis Bamford and the Duke of Wellington (eds), *Journal of Mrs Arbuthnot, 1820–1832* (London, Macmillan & Co., 1950), vol. 1, p. 169.

'until 11 November': Disraeli, *Letters*, vol. 6, p. 148, and I am grateful to Mary Millar for identifying the dramatis personae of this letter; the death, the lying-in-state and the preparations for the funeral that follow are all described from newspaper reports, especially the *Daily News*, *Morning Chronicle*, *Morning Post* and *The Times*.

'or its route': advertisement for *Illustrated London News* supplement in *Morning Post*, 23 September 1852; vergers of St Paul's and income of Wellington: *Daily News*, 27 September 1852.

'and other jewellery': these advertisements, among many others, can be found in *Morning Post*, 23 and 25 September, *Morning Chronicle*, 25 September and 16 October 1852.

'glass, cutlery, &c.': Mr Thearle: *Morning Post*, 16 October 1852; grocer: *Era*, 24 October 1852; German advertisement: *Morning Post*, 5 November 1852; Messrs Purssell: *Morning Chronicle*, 10 November 1852.

'for the funeral': St-Mary-le-Strand: *Daily News*, 23 October 1852, and on many other days; St Clement Danes: *Era*, 3 November 1852; charitable giving: *Illustrated London News*, 25 December 1852, p. 555.

'Mourning Habiliments': American overshoes: *Morning Post*, 20 October 1852; Glenny's Irish stockings: *Morning Post*, 10 November 1852; Moses and Son: *Examiner*, 13 November 1852.

'Duke of Wellington': special trains: *Daily News*, 10 November 1852; *Era*, 14 November 1852; Mount Alexandra: *Daily News*, 13 November 1852.

'one…in mourning': *Morning Chronicle*, 11 November 1852.

'in the kingdom': 'Official Programme of the Public Funeral of the late Field-Marshal, Arthur Duke of Wellington, K. G., as Issued by the Authority of the Earl-Marshal (London, N. Pearce [1852], BL shelfmark 812.e.2).

'two died': Belton, *Random Recollections*, pp. 146–7; crush outside: *Morning Chronicle*, 15 November 1852; *Daily News*, 16 November.

'worn in cloaks': mourning wear at St Paul's: 'Official Programme', and *Morning Post*, 30 October 1852; mourning wear for observers: *Morning Post*, 9 November 1852.

'specially piped in': '*Non sibi*': *ILN*, 27 November 1852, p. 467; clubs and Temple Bar: *The Wellington News* (London, E. Appleyard [1852], BL shelfmark 1764 E8).

'constantly sweeping along': Cubitt: *Morning Post*, 19 October 1852; lighting: *Standard*, 27 October 1852; Greville, *Diary*, 16 November 1852, vol. 2, p. 346.

'barriers came down at eight': general organization: 'Police Regulations. Funeral of the late Field Marshal, Arthur Duke of Wellington, K. G., November 18, 1852' (London, Metropolitan Police Office, 1852, BL shelfmark 1309 l.14, f.117); Beale, *Recollections*, p. 26.

'for him it carried': from this paragraph, unless otherwise noted, the details come from *The Wellington News*; description of catafalque: 'Official Programme' with additions from printed images; the foreign correspondent: in the *Independence Belge*, reprinted in the *Illustrated London News*, 27 November 1852, p. 467.

'rest of the route': falling man: Belton, *Random Recollections*, p. 147; Chelsea Pensioners: 'The Order of Proceeding in the Public Funeral of the Late Field-Marshal Arthur Duke of Wellington …' ([n.p.] 1852, BL shelfmark 813.cc44).

'the minute guns': testing the catafalque: *Illustrated London News*, 13 November 1852, p. 399.

'Haynau was assaulted': footnote on assault: *The Times*, 5 September 1850, p. 4; Garibaldi and the Barclay's brewers: *The Times*, 2 June 1932, p. 15.

'bones for evermore': 'Ode on the Duke of Wellington', Alfred, Lord Tennyson, *The Poems of Tennyson*, ed. Christopher Ricks (London, Longman, 1969), pp. 1007–17.

13. NIGHT ENTERTAINMENT

'ran these activities': animal baiting in Westminster: Richardson, *Recollections*, vol. 1, pp. 6, 9. The flyleaf of the copy in the British Library is inscribed 'Son of the great [illegible] actor' and then 'Eton school list'. The Eton School Lists show a John Richardson attending *c.*1805–8, describing him as the 'son of the great Lottery contractor'. If they are the same person, this dates the baiting arenas to *c.*1810s. The biographical information of the book's inscription and the Eton School List otherwise seem incompatible. The 'great' showman John Richardson had no known children; the keeper of the lottery office in the eighteenth century was at one point a man named Richardson. (If this Revd John Richardson is his son, he was also a cousin of Beau Brummel.) I am grateful to Penny Hatfield, Eton College Archivist, for her help; Notebook of Sir John Silvester, British Library, Egerton 3710, ff. 3–4, 9, 29.

'of animal baiting': Badcock and Rowlandson, *Real Life in London*, vol. 1, pp. 596–7; monkey fight: Egan, *Life in London*, p. 222.

'surrounding the city': *The Times*, 28 March 1822, p. 1; police court: *ILN*, 29 April 1865, p. 391, is one account among many; ratting: Mayhew, *London Labour*, vol. 3, p. 7; the report is used almost verbatim by A. Mayhew, *Paved with Gold*, pp. 149ff., which I have cited here; dogfights: Mayhew, *London Labour*, vol. 1, p. 15, Smith, *Little World of London*, p. 52.

'in the morning': *Martin Chuzzlewit*, p. 651; Crockford's: Donald A. Low, *The Regency Underworld* (Stroud, Sutton, 1999), pp. 145–6, and Anita McConnell, 'Crockford, William', *Oxford Dictionary of National Biography*, Oxford University Press, 2004; online edn, January 2008 [http://www.oxforddnb.com.ezproxy.londonlibrary.co.uk/view/article/6713, accessed 16 May 2011].

'matter-of-fact': *Hints to Men about Town*, by 'The Old Medical Student' (Liverpool, George Davis, 1840), pp. 35, 42.

'not the drinking': *The Servant Girl in London*, pp. 14–17.

'domestic furnishings': model pub: Loudon, *An Encyclopaedia of Cottage, Farm, and Villa Architecture*, pp. 686–7.

'of public-houses': 'Misplaced Attachment of Mr John Dounce', *Sketches by Boz*, pp. 284–6; suburban building and pubs: Mark Girouard, *Victorian Pubs* (London, Studio Vista, 1975), p. 38; A. Mayhew, *Paved with Gold*, p. 41.

'so till midnight': Select Committee: Parliamentary Papers, 1834, pp. 8, 121.

'not by much': 'Gin-shops', *Sketches by Boz*, pp. 217–18; temperance reformer in East End: cited in Brian Harrison, 'Pubs', in Dyos and Wolff, *Victorian City*, vol. 1, p. 170.

'very little alcohol': 'Gin-shops', *Sketches by Boz*, pp. 217–18.

'of oblivion': discomfort of gin palaces: John Fisher Murray, 'Physiology of London Life', *London Journal*, 16 October 1847, p. 103; Sala, *Gaslight and Daylight*, p. 72.

'soon enrolled': sporting pubs: Archer, *The Pauper, the Thief*, p. 64; Shakespeare club: Tomalin, *Charles Dickens*, p. 90.

'to Harmonics': Tinkers' Arms: Greenwood, *Wilds of London*, pp. 25–6; costermongers' dances: Mayhew, *London Labour*, vol. 1, p. 12; discussion groups: Adams, *Memoirs of a Social Atom*, vol. 2, p. 315 and *London by Night, or, The Bachelor's...*, pp. 42–3.

'another glee': *Sketches by Boz*, pp. 78–9.

'and spittoons': *Oliver Twist*, p. 207; *Bleak House*, p. 196; 'forty pairs of lungs': Archer, *The Pauper, the Thief*, p. 101; *Little Dorrit*, p. 128; footnote: Girouard, *Victorian Pubs*, p. 43.

'Sweet Betsy Ogle': *Pickwick Papers*, p. 272; *Nicholas Nickleby*, p. 724; shoemaker: Brown, *Sixty Years' Gleanings*, p. 233; Collier, *An Old Man's Diary*, vol. 2, pp. 12–14.

'drunk on the stairs': *Old Curiosity Shop*, p. 159; *Great Expectations*, p. 273.

'give your orders': 'some good singing': *Leigh's New Picture* (1839 edn), p. 348; waiters: Paul Prendergast, 'The Waiter', in Meadows, *Heads of the People*, vol. 2, p. 223.

'girls and boys': Evans's: Hollingshead, *My Lifetime*, vol. 1, pp. 154–5, Masson, *Memories*, p. 149, Girouard, *Victorian Pubs*, p. 46, and Hayward, *Days of Dickens*, p. 112; footnote on Hogarth: Hollingshead, ibid.; Thackeray, *The History of Pendennis* (Leipzig, Bernh. Tauchnitz, 1849), vol. 2, p. 136; Sam Hall: Masson, *Memories*, p. 153; 'equivocal': Vizetelly, *Glances Back*, vol. 1, p. 171; *virginibus puerisque*: Masson, *Memories*, p. 153.

'they include': the toasts and songs come from the following, all anonymous: *The Cockchafer. A Choice Selection of Flash, Frisky, and Funny Songs...Adapted for Gentlemen Only...* (London, W. West [?1865]), *The Cuckold's Nest, of Choice, Flash, Smutty and Delicious Songs...Adapted for Gentlemen Only* (London, W. West [?1865]), *The Flash Chaunter...now singing at Offley's, Cider Cellers* [sic], *Coal Hole, &c....* (London, W. West [?1865]), *The Nobby Songster, A Prime Selection as now Singing at Offleys Cider Cellar: Coal Hole &c...* (London, W. West [?1842]), *The Rambler's Flash Songster...now singing at Offley's, Cider Cellars, Coal Hole, &c....* (London, W. West [?1865]). The publication dates are those suggested by the British Library catalogue. However, the publisher William West died in 1854, by which time he was eighty-four, and had been retired for some years. These British Library copies may be reprints, or the dates may be incorrect. Edward Cray, Patrick

Spedding and Paul Watt, editors of the *Bawdy Songbooks of the Romantic Period* (London, Pickering and Chatto, 2011), have dated *The Cockchafer* to *c.*1836, *The Cuckold's Nest* to *c.*1837, *The Flash Chaunter* to *c.*1834, *The Nobby Songster* to *c.*1842, and *The Rambler's Flash Songster* to *c.*1838. I am grateful to them for their generosity in offering advice on these songbooks, and to Patrick Spedding and Edward Cray for allowing me to read their introductions and notes in manuscript; D. E. Latané identified John Rhodes for me, and Mary Millar Joe the Stunner. I am grateful to them both; footnote on Waterford: K. D. Reynolds, 'Beresford, Henry de la Poer, third marquess of Waterford', *Oxford Dictionary of National Biography*, Oxford University Press, 2004 [http://www.oxforddnb.com.ezproxy.londonlibrary.co.uk/view/article/56726, accessed 17 May 2011].

'leering opportunities': Coal Hole address: *Every Night Book; or, Life After Dark*, 'by the author of "The Cigar"' (London, T. Richardson, 1828), p. 55; Thackeray: *The Newcomes: Memoirs of a Most Respectable Family* (London, Bradbury and Evans, 1854), p. 6; admission and programme: Vizetelly, *Glances Back*, vol. 1, p. 169; *poses plastiques*: *London by Night: The Bachelor's…*, p. 121, and Greenwood, *Wilds of London*, p. 105.

'natal day': Barty-King, *New Flame*, p. 28.

'even brilliant': Wheaton, *Journal of a Residence*, p. 222.

'Bromley, Kent': Vittoria: Allen, *History and Antiquities of London*, vol. 2, p. 187; 1814 celebrations: Pardon, *Routledge's Popular Guide*, pp. 106–7, O'Dea, *Social History of Lighting*, p. 47; Bromley: *ILN*, 4 August 1865, p. 142.

'cock of the walk': Joseph Ballard, *England in 1815, as seen by a Young Boston Merchant…*, ed. J. G. Crocker (Cambridge, MA, Riverside, 1913), pp. 115–17.

'the Citty': William IV: Colton, *Four Years in Great Britain*, p. 77; Tayler, *Diary of William Tayler*, pp. 48, 71.

'nothing further': Prince of Wales's birth: *ILN*, 12 November 1842, p. 423; Prince Albert's birthday: ibid., 18 August 1847, p. 139; Prince of Wales' eighteenth birthday: ibid., 12 November 1849, p. 464; footnote: Dickens to de Cerjat, 16 March 1862, *Letters*, vol. 10, pp. 64–5; the queen: *ILN*, 4 June 1870, p. 571.

'of laurel, scrolls': *ILN*, 28 May 1853, p. 415.

'coloured lights': this paragraph and the next: *ILN*, 14 May 1863, p. 263, 4 April 1863, p. 374.

'TO HER MAJESTY': Wyon, Journal, British Library Add MS 59,617; *ILN*, 31 May 1856, p. 579; bug-destroyers: Mayhew, *London Labour*, vol. 3, p. 37.

'six in the evening': *ILN*, 15 September 1855, p. 323.

'dirt and discomfort': 'The Horrors of Peace', *The Times*, 21 May 1856, p. 5.

14. STREET VIOLENCE

'be carried out': 'The Great Winglebury Duel', *Sketches by Boz*, pp. 463–82; Putney Heath duel: *ILN*, 23 July 1842; Camden Town duel: ibid., 8 July 1843, p. 30, 22 July 1843, p. 55, 21 July 1847, p. 114.

'harshly punished': *ILN*, 10 July 1869, p. 27; 31 July 1869, p. 103, 6 November 1869, p. 451; victualler: *ILN*, 9 January 1869, p. 27.

'are Satisfied': footnote: the Riot Act is, formally, 1 Geo. I St.2. c.5.

'require hospitalization': there are few reports on these street brawls, which are mentioned in the newspapers only in passing, if at all. A good modern study is Rob Sindall, *Street Violence in the Nineteenth Century: Media Panic or Real Danger?* (Leicester, Leicester University Press, 1990); this account draws from Allen, *History and Antiquities of London*, vol. 5, p. 59.

'semi-starving men': Spitalfields gang: Allen, ibid., vol. 5, p. 90, weavers: ibid. vol. 4, pp. 111–12.

'resorting to killing': Allen, ibid., vol. 4, pp. 129–30, reports the incident, but the interpretation of it, as well as the role of police, is my own.

'incipient trouble': Allen, ibid., vol. 5, pp. 129–30.

'the previous decade': Naples' diary: cited in Durey, *Return of the Plague*, pp. 172–3.

'padroll with cutlashes': assaults on medical personnel: Durey, ibid., pp. 162–3; Sala, *Twice Round the Clock*, p. 146; footnote with the biographical information on Sala's mother: P. D. Edwards, 'Sala, George Augustus', *Oxford Dictionary of National Biography*, Oxford University Press, 2004; online edn, May 2005 [http://www.oxforddnb.com.ezproxy.londonlibrary.co.uk/view/article/24526, accessed 28 February 2011].

'after the event': Beale, *Recollections*, pp. 9–10; the number of Chartists on Kennington Common is disputed. I have followed David Goodway, *London Chartism, 1838–1840* (Cambridge, Cambridge University Press, 1982), p. 76.

'see a disturbance': the Sabbatarian riots in this and the next paragraph: *ILN*, 30 June 1855, pp. 646–7, and then passim, to 27 July 1855; Wyon, Journal, British Library, Add MS 59,617.

'executive occasionally follows': *The Times*, 27 June 1855, p. 8, 2 July 1855, p. 8; Dickens, *Nicholas Nickleby*, p. 71.

'for Co. Stafford': Notebooks of John Silvester, British Library, Add MSS 47,466 and Egerton MS 3710, passim.

'*Civil Service Gazette*': Dickens, *Oliver Twist*, pp. 79–80, 102–3; biographical information on Laing: *Oliver Twist*, p. 499n.; arrest of ecclesiastical agent: *ILN*, 28 July 1855, p. 99.

'at the doors': Select Committee on the Police, 1816, in Low, *Regency Underworld*, p. 67.

'income of £10,000': 1810s: Brown, *Sixty Years Gleanings*, pp. 248–9; Jane Welsh Carlyle to John Carlyle, 31 January 1850, *Carlyle Letters*, vol. 25, pp. 15–17; Thomas Carlyle to Jean Carlyle Aitken, 23 January 1851, ibid., vol. 26, p. 2204.

'tools of their trades': Dickens, *Little Dorrit*, p. 208; the sixteen-year-old: Mayhew, *London Labour*, vol. 1, p. 413; pickpocket: Mayhew, *London Labour*, vol. 1, p. 411; £100 a year: *Leigh's New Picture* (1839 edn), p. 81; Notebook of John Silvester: British Library, Egerton MS 3710.

'marine-store dealers': 'My lad': Derby, *Two Months Abroad*, p. 12; pushing at doors: *Bleak House*, p. 499; river thefts: 'Down with the Tide', *Household Words*, 5 February 1853, *Dickens' Journalism*, vol. 3, pp. 119–21.

'countries on the earth': Dickens, *A Tale of Two Cities*, ed. George Woodcock (first published 1859; Harmondsworth, Penguin, 1985), p. 84; 'those good old customs': Dickens, *American Notes* (New York, Modern Library, 1996), p. 68.

'physical danger: Vizetelly, *Glances Back*, vol. 1, pp. 9–10.

'them with force': the summary and quotations from the White Swan case in this paragraph and the next are from Rictor Norton, *Mother Clap's Molly House: The Gay Subculture in England, 1700–1830* (London, GMP Publishers, 1992), pp. 187–90; footnote on other locations of molly-houses: [Robert Holloway], *The Phoenix of Sodom . . . the Gambols Practised by the Ancient Letchers of . . . The Vere St Coterie* (London, J. Cook [1813]), p. 14.

'food and drink': the shocked MPs: *The Times*, 7 April 1815, p. 3; Paine's publisher: V. A. C. Gatrell, *The Hanging Tree: Execution and the English People, 1770–1868* (Oxford, Oxford University Press, 1994), p. 89n.

'had last been used': the forger: Vizetelly, *Glances Back*, vol. 1, p. 10; the fishmonger: *The Times*, 5 June 1830, p. 6.

'of Retribution': prison nicknames appear in both Chesterton, *Revelations of Prison Life*, p. 13, and Mayhew and Binny, *The Criminal Prisons*, p. 82. Where they differ, I have relied on Chesterton, who was a prison governor, rather than Mayhew and Binny, who were journalists; the wall and door: Archer, *The Pauper, the Thief*, p. 173; the architectural historian is John Summerson, *The Microcosm of London*: [reproductions of pictures] by T. Rowlandson and A. C. Pugin (London, Penguin, 1943), p. 12.

'closer to events': '*gestorben*': Mayhew and Binny, *The Criminal Prisons*, p. 82, while Partridge, *A Dictionary of Slang and Unconventional English* (London, Routledge and Kegan Paul, 1961) suggests the Romany source. The OED is unhelpful: 'origins unknown'.

'with the demons': executions at Newgate: Dickens, *Nicholas Nickleby*, pp. 89–90; Dickens at Courvoisier's execution: cited in Philip Collins, *Dickens and Crime* (3rd edn, Basingstoke, Macmillan, 1994), pp. 224–5.

'and their wives': Cited in Gatrell, *The Hanging Tree*, pp. 62–4.

'deaths by overcrowding': time between conviction and execution: Martin J. Wiener, 'Judges v. Jurors: Courtroom Tensions in Murder Trials and the Law of Criminal Responsibility in Nineteenth-century England', *Law and History Review*, 17: 3 (1999), pp. 467–506.

'rooftop vantage point': Greenacre: Camden Pelham [pseud.], *The* New *Chronicles of Crimes, or, The Newgate Calendar* (London, Reeves & Turner, 1886), vol. 2, p. 446; Fagin in the condemned cell: *Oliver Twist*, p. 445; footnote on capital crimes: 'unnatural offences', incorporating both sodomy and bestiality, was regulated by the Buggery Act of 1533 until 1861, when it was replaced by the Offences against the Person Act of 1861. The Act did not include incest, which was dealt with by the ecclesiastical rather than the criminal courts until 1908. As late as 1908 there was some discussion about the undesirability of criminalizing such acts on the interesting grounds that doing so might give people ideas. My thanks to Dr Sharon Bickle for this helpful summary; Dickens' Jewish relatives: Michael Allen, *Charles Dickens and the Blacking Factory*, p. 36; Dickens' rooftop: Dickens to John Leech, 12 November 1849, *Letters*, vol. 5, p. 643.

'come to be hung': *Oliver Twist*, pp. 15, 52.

'crown a head': rates of executions, Philip Horne, *Oliver Twist*, pp. xv–xvi; analysis of reduction in numbers hanged: Collins, *Dickens and Crime*, p. 4; rarity increasing audiences: Thomas W. Laqueur, 'Crowds, Carnival and the State in English

Executions, 1604–1868', in A. L. Beier, David Cannadine and James M. Rosenheim (eds), *The First Modern Society: Essays in English History in Honour of Lawrence Stone* (Cambridge, Cambridge University Press, 1989), p. 308; Punch and Judy: cited in Gatrell, *The Hanging Tree*, p. 121; William Thackeray, 'Going to See a Man Hanged', *Fraser's Magazine*, 22: 128 (August 1840), pp. 150–58; Henry Angelo, *Reminiscences of Henry Angelo* … (London, Kegan, Paul & Co., 1904), vol. 2, p. 139.

'Oh Susannah': Dickens, letter to the editor, *Daily News*, 28 February 1846, p. 6.

'working-class onlookers': Thackeray, 'Going to See a Man Hanged'; *Flowery Land* pirates: Shaw, *London in the Sixties*, p. 130.

'promote to visitors': *Leigh's New Picture* (1819 edn), p. 252, (1839 edn), p. 209.

'descended on the scene': The details of the Clerkenwell bombing, and the execution of Michael Barrett in this paragraph and the next two: Patrick Quinlivan and Paul Rose, *The Fenians in England, 1865–1872: A Sense of Insecurity* (London, John Calder, 1982), K. R. M. Short, *The Dynamite War: Irish-American Bombers in Victorian Britain* (Dublin, Gill and Macmillan, 1979), *Daily News*, 14, 16 and 25 December 1867, 27 May 1868; *Morning Post*, 16 December 1867; special constables: *Daily News*, 25 December 1867; *Era*, 29 December 1867.

'ancestral landmarks': 'On an Amateur Beat', *Dickens' Journalism*, vol. 4, p. 382.

15. THE RED-LIT STREETS TO DEATH

'their unknowability': *Martin Chuzzlewit*, p. 517; 'How utterly lost': Horwitz, *Brushwood Picked*, pp. 21–2; *A Tale of Two Cities*, p. 44.

'prostitution at all': the modern historian in the footnote is Judith R. Walkowitz, *Prostitution and Victorian Society: Women, Class and the State* (Cambridge, Cambridge University Press, 1980), p. 14; Mayhew, *London Labour*, vol. 4, p. 255. Although the author here is Hemyng, see p. 397, I will continue to refer to 'Mayhew' in these notes, for bibliographical clarity.

'the rising population': from 50,000 to 80,000: Michael Mason, *The Making of Victorian Sexuality* (Oxford, Oxford University Press, 1994), pp. 76–8, although the suggestion as to how the 80,000 figure was achieved is my own.

'females in Britain': this and the next three paragraphs: William Acton, *Prostitution, Considered in its Moral, Social, & Sanitary Aspects* (London, John Churchill, 1857), p. 18; Michael Ryan, *Prostitution in London, with a comparative View of that of Paris and New York* … (London, H. Bailliere, 1839), pp. 176–7.

'precise figure': 'robbery and violence': Acton, *Prostitution*, p. 95; Mayhew, *London Labour*, vol. 4, p. 224; Metropolitan police commissioner: Philpotts, *Companion to Little Dorrit*, p. 200; 1841 figures: Acton, p. 17.

'in their characters': Lynda Nead, *Myths of Sexuality: Representations of Women in Victorian Britain* (Oxford, Basil Blackwell, 1988), pp. 103–4.

'Mayhew's fourth volume': I am grateful to Eileen Curran, Robert Douglas-Fairhurst, Priti Joshi and Scott Rogers for their help in piecing together the few scraps of evidence that remain relating to these men, and to Penny Hatfield, Eton College Archivist, for confirming Bracebridge Hemyng's time at Eton (which he attended as the less exotically named Samuel Bracebridge Heming).

'all that we have': Hanger: Stuart Reid, 'Hanger, George, fourth Baron Coleraine', *Oxford Dictionary of National Biography*, Oxford University Press, 2004; online edn, January 2008 [http://www.oxforddnb.com.ezproxy.londonlibrary.co.uk/view/article/12195, accessed 18 May 2011]; caricatures of Hanger pimping for the Prince of Wales: Elizabeth Cooke, *The Damnation of John Donellan: A Mysterious Case of Death* (London, Profile, 2011), p. 64; the citation in Mayhew, *London Labour*, is at vol. 4, p. 215.

'cannot be mistaken': Acton, *Prostitution*, p. 18; 'The Pawnbroker's Shop', *Sketches by Boz*, pp. 228–9.

'of years later': Walkowitz, *Prostitution*, pp. 15–19.

'girls under sixteen': Ryan, *Prostitution in London*, pp. 119, 125–9, 139–41; footnote on the felony/misdemeanour distinction: Sindall, *Street Violence*, p. 21; venereal hospital figures: Walkowitz, *Prostitution*, p. 17.

'she comes home': sixteen-year-old: *Mayhew, London Labour*, vol. 1, p. 413.

'whores in that way': Hudson, *Munby*, pp. 40–41.

'over their shoulders': bonnets and shawls: Walkowitz, *Prostitution*, p. 26; Boulton and Park: Morris B. Kaplan, '"Men in Petticoats": Border Crossings in the Queer Case of Mr. Boulton and Mr. Park', in Pamela Gilbert (ed.), *Imagined London* (Albany, NY, State University of New York Press, 2002), pp. 53–4.

'full of women': 'Walter', *My Secret Life*, vol. 2, p. 94; *Yokel's Preceptor: or, More Sprees in London! Being a... Show-up of All the Rigs and Doings of the Flash Cribs in This Great Metropolis...* (London, H. Smith [?1855]), p. 3.

'for a bus': Paterfamilias' letter: *The Times*, 7 January 1862; responses on subsequent days; 'Rape of the Glances', *Saturday Review*, 1 February 1862, pp. 124–5; lithograph: [C. J. Culliford], 'Scene in Regent Street', *c.*1865, in Nead, *Victorian Babylon*, p. 63.

'girls these were': *Great Expectations*, p. 273; the historian who makes the suggestion is Michael Slater, 'The Bachelor's Pocket Book for 1851', in Don Richard Cox (ed.), *Sexuality and Victorian Literature* (Knoxville, TN, University of Tennessee Press, 1984), p. 139; pretty girls: 'Home Sweet Home', *All the Year Round*, 15, 7 April 1866, p. 303.

'with season tickets': Egan, *Life in London*, pp. 173, 211, 214; Hékékyan Bey, Journal, British Library, Add MSS 37,448; MacKenzie, *The American in England*, vol. 1, p. 211.

'dirty book': The three British Library volumes are: *The New Swell's Night Guide to the Bowers of Venus...* (London, J. Paul [?1840]), *The Swell's Night Guide Through the Metropolis*, 'by the Hon. F. L. G.' (London, 'printed for the author, for private circulation, by Roger Funnyman', [?1841]), and *The Swell's Night Guide Through the Metropolis, or, A Peep through the Great Metropolis...*, 'by Thelord [sic] Chief Baron' [which suggests Renton Nicholson] ([place and publisher cut away], [?1846]). The dates of the first two are the suggestions of the British Library catalogue; the last has '1846' written on its flyleaf. Neither Copac nor WorldCat lists a copy of *The Bachelor's Pocket Book for 1851*; my information and citations come from Slater, 'The Bachelor's Pocket Book for 1851'. In this essay Slater does not appear to be aware of the *Swell's Guides*, so it is only from the material that he cites that I can see the overlap/copying of material. There may of course be much more, or none apart from the few citations; *Yokel's Preceptor*, pp. 7–9.

'from backstage': *The New Swell's Night Guide*, 'Saloons of the Theatres' [no page]; 'Theatrical Examiner', *Examiner*, 26 July 1840, in *Dickens' Journalism*, vol. 2, p. 42; Eagle Tavern: in Tracy C. Davis, *Actresses as Working Women: Their Social Identity in Victorian Culture* (London, Routledge, 1991), p. 81; Alhambra: Kirwan, *Palace and Hovel*, pp. 138–9, 143.

'commercial basis': Dickens writing a cheque for £50: Tomalin, *Charles Dickens*, p. 293, although she has no doubt that the cheque is for Nelly, while it seems to me just as likely to have been for the manager, to subsidize her salary; *The New Swell's Night Guide*.

'closed at one': Dickens to Lord Lyttelton, 16 August 1855, *Letters*, vol. 7, p. 691; Argyle Rooms: Henry H. Wellbeloved, *London Lions, for Country Cousins and Friends about Town…* (London, William Charlton Wright, 1827), p. 31; 'Anonyma', *London by Night* (1862), pp. 34, 37, 40, 42; decor: Kirwan, *Palace and Hovel*, pp. 147–9.

'sentimental ballads': Holborn Casino: *London by Night*, pp. 56, 59; Ratcliffe Highway saloon: Archer, *The Pauper, the Thief*, p. 117.

'on that path': Caldwell's: Hudson, *Munby*, p. 22; dancing master's assemblies: *London by Night, the Bachelor's…*, pp. 1–5, gives one such list; Caldwell's reputation: Hayward, *Days of Dickens*, pp. 122–3.

'steak and oysters': 1830s' finish: Tristan, *London Journal*, pp. 75–7; the Finish, James Street: Vizetelly, *Glances Back*, vol. 1, p. 170; Barnes's: Kirwan, *Palace and Hovel*, p. 150.

'Grosvenor Square': streetwalking locations: in 1818, *The London Guide, and Stranger's Safeguard…*, 'by a Gentleman' (London, Bumpus, 1818), p. 134; other locations: Mason, *The Making of Victorian Sexuality*, p. 89; footnote on the Haymarket: Trollope, *What I Remember*, p. 55; *Dombey and Son*, p. 514.

'no longer exists': Tristan, *London Journal*, pp. 74–5; footnote: Flora Tristan uses Ryan, p. 91, and Colquhoun's statistics, p. 79; 'Walter', *My Secret Life*, vol. 1, p. 146; 1841 and 1861 censuses: White, *London in the Nineteenth Century*, pp. 295ff.

'roads were lighter': walking to the West End: Tristan, *London Journal*, p. 75; Haymarket hours: Davis, *Actresses as Working Women*, pp. 144–5; Regent Street hours: 'Walter', *My Secret Life*, vol. 1, p. 345; western suburbs: ibid., vol. 1, p. 143.

'a minor clerk': police returns: Walkowitz, *Prostitution*, p. 23; Mary: 'Walter', ibid., vol. 1, pp. 369, 372.

'or their communities': Whitechapel: Hollingshead, *Ragged London*, p. 49; sailors' wives: Walkowitz, ibid., p. 29.

'accommodation house': 'a few shillings': 'Walter', *My Secret Life*, vol. 1, p. 173; economics: ibid., vol. 1, p. 145; footnote on streetwalkers' income: the room and dress are costed by Walter, but the remaining figures are my own, based on the working-class budgets outlined in my *The Victorian House: Domestic Life from Childbirth to Deathbed* (London, HarperCollins, 2003), passim.

'for my money': light: 'F. L. G.', *The Swell's Night Guide*, 'Accommodation Houses' [no page]; Walter's first accommodation house: *My Secret Life*, vol. 1, p. 72; footnote: ibid., vol. 2, p. 124; Gracechurch Street: Slater, 'The Bachelor's Pocket Book', p. 131; short visit: 'Walter', ibid., vol. 1, p. 75.

'on p. 360': Francis Place and reasons for improvement: Mason, *Making of Victorian Sexuality*, p. 28; cabman: 'Walter', *My Secret Life*, vol. 2, p. 56; Titchfield Street: 'Walter', *My Secret Life*, vol. 1, p. 263 and passim; Mother H: 'The Lord Chief Baron', *The Swell's Night Guide*, p. 33.

'sharing living expenses': Walkowitz, *Prostitution*, p. 24.

'generally known here': 'F. L. G.', *The Swell's Night Guide*, pp. 42–3, NB, these passages, and the names and addresses of several introducing houses, reappear verbatim in 'The Bachelor's Pocket Book', cited by Michael Slater, p. 137.

'at Marble Arch': Slater, 'The Bachelor's Pocket Book', p. 133.

'frequently heard': Nicholson, *Autobiography of a Fast Man*, p. 96.

'per cent in theatres': location and percentage of offences: H. G. Cocks, *Nameless Offences: Homosexual Desire in the Nineteenth Century* (London, I. B. Tauris, 2003), p. 29. For this section I am indebted to Dr Alison Hannegan for providing me with many helpful references, and to Peter Parker for guiding me to Dr Hannegan in the first instance.

'the owners arrested': Rictor Norton is the acknowledged expert in this area. David Robertson: Rictor Norton, 'The Vere Street Coterie', The Gay Subculture in Georgian England. Updated 7 August 2009 <http://rictornorton.co.uk/vere.htm>, accessed 21 May 2011; the White Hart: Norton, *Mother Clap's Molly House*, pp. 187–90, [Anon.], *Religion and Morality Vindicated…or, an Account of the Life and Character of John Church, the Obelisk Preacher, who was formerly a frequenter of Vere-street* (second edn, London R. Bell, [?1813]), and Holloway, *The Phoenix of Sodom*, passim.

'and sex-workers': Cocks, *Nameless Offences*, p. 68; soldier in court: Holloway, *The Phoenix of Sodom*, p. 29; *The Times*, 16 August 1825, p. 3; Vagrancy Act: Cocks, *Nameless Offences*, p. 56.

'such roaring boys': Edward Leeves, *Leaves from a Victorian Diary*, intro. by John Sparrow (London, Secker & Warburg, 1985), passim.

'author's preconceptions': *Yokel's Preceptor*, pp. 5–7.

'or anyone else': Hudson, *Munby*, p. 188; Druid's Hall dances: Charles Upchurch, *Before Wilde: Sex Between Men in Britain's Age of Reform* (Berkeley, University of California Press, 2009), p. 75.

'were rare': Boulton and Park in this paragraph and the next: Kaplan, '"Men in Petticoats"', pp. 45–68, and Cocks, *Nameless Offences*, pp. 105ff. The fashion information is from *The Times*, 30 April 1870, p. 11; 'A Visit to Newgate', *Sketches by Boz*, p. 244.

'ended her life': Tristan, *London Journal*, p. 79; Ryan and Tait: Nead, *Myths of Sexuality*, pp. 145ff.; Acton, *Prostitution*, p. 38; 'Anonyma', *London by Night*, p. 176.

'drown themselves': incidence of suicide and gender, and engraving: L. J. Nicoletti, 'Morbid Topographies: Placing Suicide in Victorian London', in Lawrence Phillips, (ed.), *A Mighty Mass of Brick and Smoke: Victorian and Edwardian Representations of London* (Amsterdam, Rodopi, 2007), pp. 10–12; Sala, *Twice Round the Clock*, p. 70.

'leap from another': 'The man who loves': 'The Millennium', *Blackwood's Edinburgh Magazine*, 153: 25 (June 1829), p. 703; Dickens, 'The Drunkard's Death', *Sketches by Boz*, p. 565; 'English Bridge of Sighs': Charles Mackay, 'Rambles Among the Rivers, no. 1: The Thames and its Tributaries', *Bentley's Miscellany*, April 1839, p. 378.

'over the ground': Hood: 'The Bridge of Sighs', *The Poetical Works of Thomas Hood* (NY, James Miller, 1867), vol. 1, pp. 151–4; details of Mary Furley: *The Times*, 1 April 1844, p. 7; 'Some Recollections of Mortality', *All the Year Round*, 16 May 1863, in *Dickens' Journalism*, vol. 4, p. 224.

'the morning mist': *Oliver Twist*, p. 389; *David Copperfield*, pp. 317, 625ff.; *Little Dorrit*, p. 217.

'all he cared': Dickens, *Barnaby Rudge*, ed. Gordon Spence (first published 1841; Harmondsworth, Penguin Books, 1986), p. 153.

'of the Monument': suicides from the Monument: Nicoletti, 'Morbid Topographies', pp. 13–14; Bartlett, *What I Saw in London*, pp. 182–3.

'for an end': 'Wapping Workhouse', *All the Year Round*, 18 February 1860, in *Dickens' Journalism*, vol. 4, p. 44.

'he was alive': Charles Lamb, cited in Baron (ed.), *London 1066–1914*, p. 25; *Little Dorrit*, p. 67; Henry Wallis, *Death of Chatterton*, is in the Tate; 'Thoughts about People', *Sketches by Boz*, p. 251.

'one and the same': 'Chambers', *All the Year Round*, 18 August 1860, in *Dickens' Journalism*, vol. 4, p. 164.

'dark with death': *Our Mutual Friend*, p. 77; *Edwin Drood*, p. 258; 'The surface': *Carlton Chronicle*, 40, 8 April 1837, p. 635.

'their usual uproar: *Little Dorrit*, p. 895.

BIBLIOGRAPHY

Works by Dickens

FICTION

Barnaby Rudge, ed. Gordon Spence (first published 1841; Harmondsworth, Penguin Books, 1986)

Bleak House, ed. Norman Page (first published 1852–3; Harmondsworth, Penguin, 1985)

The Christmas Books, vol. 1: 'A Christmas Carol' and 'The Chimes', ed. Michael Slater (first published 1843, 1844; Harmondsworth, Penguin, 1985)

David Copperfield, ed. Jeremy Tambling (first published 1849–50; Harmondsworth, Penguin, 1996)

Dombey and Son, ed. Peter Fairclough, intro. Raymond Williams (first published 1846–8; Harmondsworth, Penguin, 1985)

Great Expectations, ed. Charlotte Mitchell, intro. David Trotter (first published 1860–61; Harmondsworth, Penguin, 1996)

The Life and Adventures of Martin Chuzzlewit, ed. P. N. Furbank (first published 1843–4; Harmondsworth, Penguin, 1986)

Little Dorrit, ed. John Holloway (first published 1855–7; Harmondsworth, Penguin, 1985)

The Mystery of Edwin Drood, ed. Arthur Cox (first published 1870; Harmondsworth, Penguin, 1993)

Nicholas Nickleby, ed. Michael Slater (first published 1838–9; Harmondsworth, Penguin, 1978)

The Old Curiosity Shop, ed. Angus Easson (first published 1840–41; Harmondsworth, Penguin, 1985)

Oliver Twist, or, The Parish Boy's Progress, ed. Philip Horne (first published 1837–8; Harmondsworth, Penguin, 2002)

Our Mutual Friend, ed. Adrian Poole (first published 1864–5; Harmondsworth, Penguin, 1997)

The Posthumous Papers of the Pickwick Club, ed. Mark Wormald (first published 1836–7; Harmondsworth, Penguin, 1999)

A Tale of Two Cities, ed. George Woodcock (first published 1859; Harmondsworth, Penguin, 1985)

NON-FICTION

American Notes (first published 1842; New York, Modern Library, 1996)

Charles Dickens' Uncollected Writings from Household Words, 1850–59, ed. Harry Stone, 2 vols (Bloomington, Indiana University Press, 1968)

The Dent Uniform Edition of Dickens' Journalism, vol. 2: *The Amusements of the People and Other Papers*, ed. Michael Slater (London, J. M. Dent, 1996)

The Dent Uniform Edition of Dickens' Journalism, vol. 3: *'Gone Astray' and Other Papers*, ed. Michael Slater (London, J. M. Dent, 1998)

The Dent Uniform Edition of Dickens' Journalism, vol. 4: *The Uncommercial Traveller and Other Papers*, ed. Michael Slater and John Drew (London, J. M. Dent, 2000)

The Letters of Charles Dickens. The Pilgrim Edition, ed. Madeline House, Graham Storey and Kathleen Tillotson (Oxford, Clarendon, 1965–)

Sketches by Boz, ed. Dennis Walder (first published 1836–9; Harmondsworth, Penguin, 1995)

Primary Sources

Ackermann, R., *Microcosm of London*, 3 vols (London, Ackermann's Repository of Arts [1808–10])

Acton, William, *Prostitution, Considered in its Moral, Social, & Sanitary Aspects* (London, John Churchill, 1857)

Adams, W. E., *Memoirs of a Social Atom*, 2 vols (London, Hutchinson, 1903)

Adams, William Bridges, *English Pleasure Carriages: Their Origin, History, Varieties...* (London, Charles Knight, 1837)

Adshead, Joseph, *Prisons and Prisoners* (London, Longman, Brown, Green, and Longman, 1845)

Aiken, Henry, *The Funeral procession.* [sic] *of Arthur Duke of Wellington* (London, Ackermann and Co., 1853)

All the Year Round, 'The Genii of the Lamps', 6, 12 October 1861, pp. 55–8

—, 'Every Man's Poison', 13, 11 November 1865, pp. 372–6

—, 'Home Sweet Home', 15, 7 April 1866, pp. 303–6

Allbut, Robert, *London Rambles 'En Zigzag', with Dickens* (London, Edward Curtice, [1886])

Allen, Thomas, *The History and Antiquities of London, Westminster and Southwark, and Parts Adjacent* (London, Cowie & Strange, vols 1–4, 1827, vol. 5, 1837)

Allen, Zachariah, *The Practical Tourist...* (Providence, RI, A. S. Beckwith, 1832)

'Anonyma', *London by Night*, 'by the author of 'Skittles' [BL suggests W. S. Hayward] (London, William Oliver [?1862])

'Anonyma, Companion to', *Skittles: A Biography of a Fascinating Woman* (London, George Vickers, 1864)

Apperson, G. L., *Bygone London Life* (London, Elliot Stock, 1903)

Archer, Thomas, *The Pauper, the Thief, and the Convict: Sketches of Some of their Homes, Haunts, and Habits* (London, Groombridge and Sons, 1865)

[Badcock, Jonathan, and Thomas Rowlandson], *Real Life in London, or, The Rambles and Adventures of Bob Tallyho ...*, 2 vols (London, Jones & Co., 1821)

Bagehot, Walter, 'Charles Dickens', in *The Works and Life of Walter Bagehot*, ed. Mrs Russell Barrington, vol. 3 (London, Longmans, Green, and Co., 1915)

Ballantyne, Michael, *Fighting the Flames: A Tale of the London Fire Brigade* (London, James Nisbet, 1868)

Bamberger, Louis, *Bow Bell Memories* (London, Sampson Low, Marston, 1931)

Barham, R. H., *The Life and Remains of Theodore Edward Hook*, London, Richard Bentley, 1849)

Bartlett, David W., *What I saw in London, or, Men and Things in the Great Metropolis* (Auburn [CT?], Derby and Miller, 1852)

Beale, S. Sophia, *Recollections of a Spinster Aunt* (London, William Heinemann, 1908)

Beames, Thomas, *The Rookeries of London: Past, Present, and Prospective* (London, Thomas Bosworth, 1850)

Bee, J. [pseud. of John Badcock], *A Living Picture of London, for 1828…* (London, W. Clarke, 1828)

Belton, Fred, *Random Recollections of an Old Actor* (London, Tinsley Brothers, 1880)

Bennett, Alfred Rosling, *London and Londoners in the Eighteen-fifties and Sixties* (London, T. Fisher Unwin, 1924)

Besant, Walter, *London in the Nineteenth Century* (London, Adam & Charles Black, 1909)

Blanc, Louis, *Letters on England*, trans. James Hutton and L. J. Trotter (London, Sampson, Low, Son, and Marston, 1867)

Boys, Thomas Shotter, *Original Views of London as it is* (London, Thomas Shotter Boys, 1842)

Bradfield, J. E., *The Public Carriages of Great Britain: A Glance at their Rise, Progress, Struggles and Burthens* (London, Piper, Stephenson & Spence, 1855)

Brown, John, *Sixty Years' Gleanings from Life's Harvest: A Genuine Autobiography* (Cambridge, J. Palmer, 1858)

Bullen, Frank, *Confessions of a Tradesman* (London, Hodder and Stoughton, 1908)

Callow, Edward, *Old London Taverns: Historical, descriptive and Reminiscent…* (London, Downey & Co., 1899)

Carlyle, Thomas and Jane, *The Collected Letters of Thomas and Jane Welsh Carlyle*, ed. Charles Richard Sanders, Kenneth J. Fielding, et al., vol. 7 (Durham, NC, Duke University Press, 1977)

Carr, Henry, *Metropolitan Street Traffic: Suggested Improvements* (London, R. J. Mitchell and Sons, 1871)

[Carter, T.], *Memoirs of a Working Man* (London, Charles Knight, 1845)

—, *A Continuation of the Memoirs of a Working Man* (London, Charles Cox, 1850)

Chadwick, Edwin, *Report on the Sanitary Condition of the Labouring Population of Great Britain*, ed. M. W. Flinn (first published 1842; Edinburgh, Edinburgh University Press, 1965)

Chesterton, George Laval, *Revelations of Prison Life* (3rd edn, London, Hurst and Blackett, 1857)

Clarke, James Freeman, *Eleven Weeks in Europe: and, What May be Seen in that Time* (Boston, Ticknor, Reed, and Fields, 1852)

[Clarke, W. S.], *The Suburban Homes of London, A Residential Guide…* (London, Chatto and Windus, 1881)

The Cockchafer. A Choice Selection of Flash, Frisky, and Funny Songs...Adapted for Gentlemen Only... (first published 1836; London, W. West [?1865])

Collier, John Payne, *An Old Man's Diary, Forty Years Ago*, 'for strictly private circulation', 2 vols (London, Thomas Richards, 1871–2)

Colman, Henry, *European Life and Manners; or, Familiar Letters to Friends* (Boston, Charles C. Little and James Brown, 1850)

Colton, Calvin, *Four Years in Great Britain, 1831–5* (2nd edn, New York, Harper & Brothers, 1836)

Cooper, J. Fenimore, *Recollections of Europe* (London, Richard Bentley, 1837)

Corbett, Edward, 'Colonel late Shropshire Militia', *An Old Coachman's Chatter, with some Practical Remarks on Driving*, 'by a semi-professional' (facsimile of 2nd edn [?1894], Wakefield, E. P. Publishing, 1974)

Coxe, Revd A. Cleveland, *Impressions of England; or, Sketches of English Scenery and Society* (New York, Dana & Co., 1856)

Cruikshank, George, *Metropolitan Grievances; or, A Serio-Comic Glance at Minor Mischief in London...*, 'by one who thinks for himself' (London, Sherwood, Neely, and Jones, 1812)

—, *Scraps and Sketches* (London, published by the artist, 1828)

The Cuckold's Nest, of Choice, Flash, Smutty and Delicious Songs...Adapted for Gentlemen Only (first published *c.*1837; London, W. West, [?1865])

[Derby, Elias], *Two Months Abroad: or, A Trip to England, France, Baden, Prussia, and Belgium, in August and September, 1843*, 'by a Rail-road Director of Massachusetts' (Boston, Redding & Co., 1844)

De Quincey, Thomas, *The English Mail-Coach and Other Essays* (London, J. M. Dent, 1961)

Dickinson, Andrew, *My First Visit to Europe...* (New York, George P. Putnam, 1851)

Disraeli, Benjamin, *Benjamin Disraeli, Letters*, ed. M. G. Wiebe et al., vol. 3, *1838–1841*; vol. 6, *1852–1856* (Toronto, University of Toronto Press, 1987, 1997)

Dixon, Hepworth, *The London Prisons* (London, Jackson and Walford, 1850)

Dostoevsky, Fyodor, *Winter Notes on Summer Impressions*, trans. David Patterson (Evanston, IL, Northwestern University Press, 1997)

[Duncombe, J.], *The Dens of London Exposed* (London, privately printed, 1835), in Marriott (ed.), *Unknown London*, pp. 271–383

Eddy, Daniel C., *Europa, or, Scenes and Society in England, France, Italy and Switzerland* (Boston, N. L. Dayton, Higgins & Bradley, 1856)

Edwards, Percy, *History of London Street Improvements, 1855–1897* (London, London County Council, 1898)

Edwards, Revd John E., *Random Sketches and Notes of European Travel in 1856* (New York, Harper and Brothers, 1857)

Egan, Pierce, *Grose's Classical Dictionary of the Vulgar Tongue* (London, 'printed for the editor', 1823)

—, [and George and Robert Cruikshank], *Life in London, or, The Day and Night Scenes of Jerry Hawthorn, Esq., and his Elegant Friend Corinthian Tom...* (London, Sherwood, Neely, & Jones, 1821)

Elmes, James, *Metropolitan Improvements; or, London in the Nineteenth Century...* (London, Jones & Co., 1829)

Elson, George, *The Last of the Climbing Boys: An Autobiography* (London, John Long, 1900)

Emerson, Ralph Waldo, 'English Traits', in *The Prose Works of Ralph Waldo Emerson* (Boston, Fields, Osgood & Co., 1870)

Every Night Book; or, Life After Dark, 'by the author of "The Cigar"' (London, T. Richardson, 1828)

The Flash Chaunter...now singing at Offley's, Cider Cellers [sic], *Coal Hole, &c....* (first published *c.*1834; London, W. West [?1865])

Fletcher, Hanslip, *London Passed and Passing: A Pictorial Record of Destroyed and Threatened Buildings* (London, Sir Isaac Pitman & Sons, 1908)

Forbes, Mrs E. A., *A Woman's First Impressions of Europe...* (New York, Derby & Miller, 1865)

Forney, John, *Letters from Europe* (Philadelphia, T. B. Peterson & Brothers, 1867)

Forster, John, *The Life of Charles Dickens*, 3 vols (London, Chapman and Hall, 1872–4)

Frost, Thomas, *The Old Showmen, and the Old London Fairs* (London, Tinsley Brothers, 1874)

Gardner, Fitzroy, *Days and Ways of an Old Bohemian* (London, John Murray, 1921)

Garwood, John, *The Million Peopled City, or, One-half of the People of London Made Known to the Other Half* (London, Wertheim and Macintosh, 1853)

Gavin, Hector, *Sanitary Ramblings: Being Sketches and Illustrations of Bethnal Green* (London, John Churchill, 1848)

Godwin, George, *London Shadows: A Glance at the 'Homes' of the Thousands* (London, George Routledge, 1854)

—, *Another Blow for Life* (London, Wm H. Allen, 1864)

Gotch, Rosamund Brunel (ed.), *Mendelssohn and his Friends in Kensington: Letters... 1833–36* (London, Oxford University Press, 1934)

Grant, James, *Sketches in London* (London, W. S. Orr, 1838)

Greenwood, James, *Unsentimental Journeys: or, Byways of the Modern Babylon* (London, Ward, Lock, & Tyler, 1867)

—, *The Seven Curses of London* (London, Stanley Rivers [1869])

—, *In Strange Company: Being the Experience of a Roving Correspondent* (Edinburgh, Henry S. King & Co., 1873)

—, *The Wilds of London* (London, Chatto and Windus, 1874)

—, *Low-Life Deeps: An Account of the Strange Fish to be Found There* (London, Chatto and Windus, 1876)

[—], 'A Night in a Workhouse', reprinted in pamphlet form from the *Pall Mall Gazette* (London, F. Bowering [n.d.])

Greville, Charles, *The Greville Diary...*, ed. Philip Whitwell Wilson (London, William Heinemann, 1927)

Gronow, Captain, *Reminiscences of Captain Gronow...* (London, Smith, Elder, 1862)

Hall, Fanny W., *Rambles in Europe...* (New York, E. French, 1839)

Hall, S. C., *Retrospect of a Long Life, 1815–83* (London, Bentley and Son, 1883)

Harben, Henry, *A Dictionary of London: Being Notes Topographical and Historical Relating to the Streets... in the City of London* (London, Herbert Jenkins, 1918)

Hare, Augustus, *Walks in London* (London, Daldy, Isbister & Co., 1878)

Harling, Robert (ed.), *The London Miscellany: A Nineteenth Century Scrapbook* (London, William Heinemann, 1937)

[Harvey, William], *London Scenes and London People…*, 'by Aleph' (London, W. H. Collingridge, 1863)

Hawthorne, Nathaniel, *Hawthorne in England: Selections from Our Old Home and The English Note-books*, ed. Cushing Strout (Ithaca, NY, Cornell University Press, 1965)

Haydon, Benjamin Robert, *Life of Benjamin Robert Haydon…from his Autobiography and Journals*, ed. Tom Taylor, 3 vols (New York, Harper and Brothers, 1853)

Hayward, Arthur, *The Days of Dickens: A Glance at Some Aspects of Early Victorian Life in London* (London, George Routledge and Sons, 1926)

Headley, Joel, *Rambles and Sketches* (New York, Baker and Scribner, 1850)

Health of Towns Association, *The Sanitary Condition of the City of London…with the Sub-Committee's Reply…* (London, W. Clowes, 1848)

[Heath, Henry], *The Caricaturist's Scrap Book: Omnium Gatherum* ([London], no publisher [1840])

Hékékyan, Joseph, Journal, 1829–30, British Library, Add MSS 37,448

Hindley, Charles, *History of the Cries of London, Ancient and Modern* (London, Reeves and Turner, 1881)

—, (ed.), *The Life and Adventures of a Cheap Jack, by One of the Fraternity* (London, Tinsley Brothers, 1876)

Hints to Men about Town, 'by The Old Medical Student' (Liverpool, George Davis, 1840)

Hogg, John, *London as it is, Being a Series of Observations on the Health, Habits, and Amusements of the People* (London, John Macrone, 1837)

Hollingshead, John, *Underground London* (London, Groombridge, 1862)

—, *My Lifetime,* 2 vols (London, Sampson Low, Marston, 1895)

[Holloway, Robert], *The Phoenix of Sodom…the Gambols Practised by the Ancient Letchers of… The Vere St Coterie* (London, J. Cook [1813])

Hook, Theodore Edward, *Gilbert Gurney* (London, Whittaker & Co., 1836))

Hoppin, James M., *Old England: Its Scenery, Art, and People* (New York, Hurd and Houghton, 1867)

[Horne, Richard H.], 'The Fire Brigade of London', *Household Words,* 7, 11 May 1850, pp. 145–51

[—], 'Address from an Undertaker to the Trade', *Household Words,* 13, 22 June 1850, pp. 301–4

[—], 'Dust, or Ugliness Redeemed', *Household Words,* 16, 13 July 1850, pp. 379–84

[—], 'The Cow with the Iron Tail', *Household Words,* 33, 9 November 1850, pp. 145–51

[—], 'Father Thames', *Household Words,* 45, 1 February 1851, pp. 445–9

Horwitz, Orville, *Brushwood Picked Up on the Continent: or, Last Summer's Trip to the Old World* (Philadelphia, Lippincott, Grambo & Co., 1855)

Household Words, 'Heathen and Christian Burial', 1, 6 April 1850, pp. 43–8

—, 'Penny Wisdom', 6, 16 October 1852, pp. 97–101

—, 'Piping Days', 10, 14 October 1854, pp. 196–9

—, 'Important Rubbish', 11, 19 May 1855, pp. 376–9

—, 'Wild Court Tamed', 12, 25 August 1855, pp. 85–7

—, 'Turpin's Corner', 17, 8 May 1858, pp. 493–6

—, 'Dirty Cleanliness', 18, 24 July 1858, pp. 121–3

—, 'Life and Death in St Giles's', 18, 13 November 1858, pp. 524–8

Hughes, William R., *A Week's Tramp in Dickens-Land: Together with Personal Reminiscences of the 'Inimitable Boz'* (London, Chapman & Hall, 1891)

Hughson, David [pseud. of David Pugh], *Circuit of London*, in 6 vols (London, James Robins [?1825])

Humphrey, Heman D. D., *Great Britain, France and Belgium: A Short Tour in 1835* (NY, Harper & Brothers, 1838)

Hunt, Leigh, *Leigh Hunt's London Journal*, vol. 1 (London, Charles Knight, 1834)

Jerrold, Blanchard, and Gustave Doré, *London: A Pilgrimage*, intro. by Peter Ackroyd (first published 1872; London, Anthem Press, 2005)

Kirkland, Mrs [Caroline], *Holidays Abroad; or, Europe from the West* (New York, Baker and Scribner, 1849)

Kirwan, Daniel Joseph, *Palace and Hovel: or, Phases of London Life…*, ed. A. Allan (first published 1870; London, Abelard-Schuman, 1963)

Kitchiner, William, *The Traveller's Oracle; or, Maxims for Locomotion: Containing Precepts for Promoting the Pleasures… of Travellers* (London, Henry Colburn, 1828)

Kitton, Frederic G., *Charles Dickens by Pen and Pencil*, and *A Supplement* (London, Frank T. Sabin, 1890)

Knight, Charles (ed.), *London*, 6 vols (London, Charles Knight, 1841–4)

[—], 'Illustrations of Cheapness: The Lucifer Match', *Household Words*, 3, 13 April, pp. 54–6

Lamb, Charles, *The Essays of Elia* (London, Edward Moxon, 1849)

Latrobe, John H. B., *Hints for Six Months in Europe…* (Philadelphia, J. B. Lippincott, & Co., 1869)

Leeves, Edward, *Leaves from a Victorian Diary*, intro. by John Sparrow (London, Secker & Warburg, 1985)

Leigh's New Picture of London… (London, Leigh and Co., 1818 and 1839)

Leighton, John, *London Cries & Public Edifices from Sketches on the Spot* (London, Grant and Griffith [1847])

[Lewis, John Delaware], 'A Voice from a 'Quiet' Street', *Household Words*, 31, 26 October 1850, pp. 143–4

[—], 'City Graves', *Household Words*, 38, 14 December 1850, p. 277

Liddle, John, *On the Moral and Physical Evils Resulting from the Neglect of Sanitary Measures…* (London, Health of Towns Association Depot, 1847)

Lillywhite, Bryant, *London Coffee Houses: A Reference Book of Coffee Houses of the Seventeenth, Eighteenth and Nineteenth Centuries* (London, George Allen and Unwin, 1963)

London by Night, or, The Bachelor's Facetious Guide to All the Ins and Outs and the Nightly Doings of the Metropolis… (London, William Ward [?1857])

The London Guide, and Stranger's Safeguard …, 'by a Gentleman' (London, Bumpus, 1818), in J. Marriott (ed.), *Unknown London*

Loudon, J. C., *An Encyclopaedia of Cottage, Farm, and Villa Architecture and Furniture…* (London, Longman, Rees, Orme, Brown, Green, & Longman, 1833)

Lovett, William, *The Life and Struggles of William Lovett, in His Pursuit of Bread, Knowledge, and Freedom…* (London, Trübner & Co., 1876)

McCarthy, Justin, *Reminiscences* (London, Chatto & Windus, 1899)

[MacKenzie, Alexander], *The American in England* (New York, Harper & Brothers, 1835)
McLelland, Henry B., *Journal of a Residence in Scotland and Tour through England…* (Boston, Allen and Ticknor, 1834)
Marriott, John (ed.), *Unknown London: Early Modernist Visions of the Metropolis, 1815–45*, 6 vols (London, Pickering and Chatto, 2000)
Marriott, John, and Masaie Matsumura (eds), *The Metropolitan Poor: Semi-factual Accounts, 1795–1910* (London, Pickering and Chatto, 1999)
Masson, David, *Memories of London in the 'Forties*, ed. Flora Masson (Edinburgh, William Blackwood & Sons, 1908)
Mathews, Mrs [Nancy], *Tea-Table Talk, Ennobled Actresses, and Other Miscellanies* (London, Thomas Cautley Newby, 1857)
Matthews, James N., *My Holiday: How I Spent it…in the Summer of 1866* (Buffalo, Martin Taylor, 1867)
Mayhew, Augustus, *Paved with Gold, or, The Romance and Reality of the London Streets* (London, Chapman and Hall, 1858)
Mayhew, Henry, *London Labour and the London Poor* (New York, Dover, 1968; facsimile of Griffin, Bohn edition, 1861–2)
—, *The Shops and Companies of London, and the Grades and Manufactories of Great Britain* (London, The Second Printing and Publishing Co., 1865)
—, *The Unknown Mayhew: Selections from the Morning Chronicle, 1849–50*, ed. E. P. Thompson and Eileen Yeo (Harmondsworth, Penguin, 1973)
—, 'Home is Home, be it never so Homely', in [Lord Shrewsbury], *Meliora: or, Better Times to Come* ([?London], no publisher [?1852])]
— and John Binny, *The Criminal Prisons of London and Scenes of Prison Life* (London, Charles Griffin [1862])
Meadows, Kenny [illus.], *Heads of the People: or, Portraits of the English*, 'with original essays by distinguished writers' (London, Willoughby & Co. [1840])
Melville, Herman, *Journal of a Visit to London and the Continent, 1849–1850*, ed. Eleanor Melville Metcalf (London, Cohen & West, 1949)
Miller, David Prince, *The Life of a Showman…* (London, Lacy, 1849)
Miller, Hugh, *First Impressions of England and its People* (London, John Johnstone, 1847)
Miller, Thomas, *Picturesque Sketches of London, Past and Present* (London, National Illustrated Library [?1851])
Morley, Henry, *Early Papers and Some Memories* (London, George Routledge, 1891)
—, *Memoirs of Bartholomew Fair* (London, Frederick Warne & Co. [n.d.])
[—], 'Death's Doors', *Household Words*, 9, 10 June 1854, pp. 398–402
Munby, Arthur, *Munby, Man of Two Worlds: The Life and Diaries of Arthur J. Munby, 1828–1910*, ed. Derek Hudson (London, John Murray, 1972)
Murray, John Fisher, *The World of London*, 2 vols (Edinburgh, William Blackwood, 1843)
—, 'Physiology of London Life', *London Journal*, 16 October 1847, p. 103
Murray, Ross, *The Modern Householder: A Manual of Domestic Economy in all its Branches* (London, Frederick Warne and Co. [1872])
[Nash, John, and John White], *Some Account of the Proposed Improvements of the Western Part of London…* (London, W. & P. Reynolds, 1814)
The New Swell's Night Guide to the Bowers of Venus… (London, J. Paul [?1840])

Nicholson, Renton, *Cockney Adventures, and Tales of London Life* (London, W. M. Clark, 1838)

—, *Autobiography of a Fast Man* (London, published 'for the Proprietors', 1863)

The Nobby Songster, A Prime Selection as now Singing at Offleys Cider Cellar: Coal Hole &c... (London, W. West 1842)

'Official Programme of the Public Funeral of the late Field-Marshal, Arthur Duke of Wellington, K. G., as Issued by the Authority of the Earl-Marshal (London, N. Pearce [1852]; British Library shelfmark 812.e.2)

'The Order of Proceeding in the Public Funeral of the Late Field-Marshal Arthur Duke of Wellington...' ([n.p., no publisher], 1852; British Library shelfmark 813.cc44)

Pardon, George Frederick, *Routledge's Popular Guide to London and its Suburbs* (London, Routledge Warne & Routledge, 1862)

Partington, C. F., *National History and Views of London...from Original Drawings...* (London, Allan Bell and Co., 1834)

Phillips, Watts, *The Wild Tribes of London* (London, Ward and Lock, 1855)

'Police Regulations. Funeral of the late Field Marshal, Arthur Duke of Wellington, K.G., November 18, 1852' (London, Metropolitan Police Office, 1852; British Library shelfmark 1309 l.14, f. 117)

Poyntz, Albany, 'The Physiology of London Life: The London Hotel-Keeper', *Bentley's Miscellany*, 15, 1844, pp. 52–7

Pratt, A. T. Camden, *Unknown London: Its Romance and Tragedy* (London, Neville Beeman [1897])

Prime, Samuel Irenæus, *Travels in Europe and the East*... (London, Sampson Low, Son, & Co., 1855)

The Rambler's Flash Songster...now singing at Offley's, Cider Cellars, Coal Hole, &c .... (first published *c.*1838; London, W. West [?1865])

Remarks on the Buildings and Improvements in London, and Elsewhere (Bath, Richard Cruttwell, 1816)

Raumer, Frederick von, *England in 1835: Being a Series of Letters Written to Friends in Germany* ..., trans. Sarah Austin (London, John Murray, 1836)

Richardson, Revd J., *Recollections...of the Last Half-century* (London, Savill & Edwards, 1855)

Ritchie, J. Ewing, *Days and Nights in London: or, Studies in Black and Gray* (London, Tinsley Brothers, 1880)

Rowlandson, Thomas, *Rowlandson's Characteristic Sketches of the Lower Orders* (London, Samuel Leigh, 1820)

Ryan, Michael, *Prostitution in London, with a comparative View of that of Paris and New York*... (London, H. Bailliere, 1839)

Sala, George Augustus, *Gaslight and Daylight, with Some London Scenes They Shine Upon* (London, Chapman & Hall, 1859)

—, *Twice Round the Clock: or, The Hours of the Day and Night in London* (London, Houlston and Wright [1859])

—, *Looking at Life; or, Thoughts and Things* (London, Routledge, Warne, and Routledge, 1860)

—, *The Hats of Humanity, Historically, Humorously and Aesthetically Considered*... (Manchester, James Gee, 'Hatter' [?1880])

[—], 'Sunday Tea-Gardens', *Household Words*, 10, 30 September 1854, pp. 145–8
[—], 'Bright Chanticleer' *Household Words*, 11, 31 March 1855, pp. 204–9
Sanger, 'Lord' George, *Seventy Years a Showman: My Life and Adventures…* (London, C. Arthur Pearson [1908])
Saturday Review, 'The Rape of the Glances', 1 February 1862, pp. 124–5
Schlesinger, Max, *Saunterings in and about London*, trans. Otto Wenckstern (first published 1852; London, Nathaniel Cooke, 1853)
The Servant Girl in London: Showing the Dangers to which Young Country Girls are Exposed… (London, R. Hastings, 1840)
Seymour, Robert, *Seymour's Humorous Sketches…*, with text by Alfred Crowquill (2nd edn, London, Henry G. Bohn, 1866)
[Shaw, Donald], *London in the Sixties (With a Few Digressions)*, 'by one of the Old Brigade' (London, Everett and Co., 1908)
Shepherd, Thomas H. [and James Elmes], *London and its Environs in the Nineteenth Century, Illustrated by a Series of Views from the Original Drawings by Thomas H. Shepherd, with…Notes* [by James Elmes] (London, Jones & Co., 1829)
—, [and James Elmes], *The World's Metropolis, or, Mighty London…* (London, published 'for the Proprietors' [?1855])
'Silvester, Sir John (d. 1822), Notebook of, containing notes on London criminals; *circ.* 1812.' (1) 'A List of Houses of resort for Footpads & Housebreakers'… (2) 'Numbers of Hackney Coaches'… (3) 'Coach-Masters'… (4) 'Names & Places of Abode of Receivers of Stolen Goods'… (5) 'Men or *(sic)* Town who have been Transported, Jany. 1812'… (6) 'Short accounts of the careers of Aaron Barrow, receiver… and Benjamin Farmer al. Solomon …' (British Library, Add MS 47,466)
'Silvester, Sir John (d. 1822), Notebook of, containing notes on the London criminal underworld …' (1) 'Receivers of Stolen Property'… (2) 'List of Receivers'… (3) 'A List of Houses of resort for Thieves'… (4) 'A List of Cant Words… with their Meaning'… (British Library MS, Egerton 3710)
[Simond, Louis], *Journal of a Tour and Residence in Great Britain during the Years 1810 and 1811…* (Edinburgh, Archibald Constable and Company, 1815)
Sinks of London Laid Open: A Pocket Companion for the Uninitiated, to which is added, A Modern Flash Dictionary… (London, J. Duncombe, 1848)
Smeeton, George, *Doings in London, or, Day and Night Scenes of the Frauds, Frolics, Manners, and Depravities of the Metropolis* (Southwark, G. Smeeton [1828])
Smith, Albert (ed.), *Gavarni in London: Sketches of Life and Character* (London, David Bogue, 1849)
Smith, Amy Grinnell, and Mary Ermina Smith, 'Letters from Europe, 1865–6', ed. David Sanders Clark (Washington, DC, 1948; typescript in British Library)
Smith, Charles Manby, *Curiosities of London Life: or, Phases, Physiological and Social, of the Great Metropolis* (London, William and Frederick G. Cash, 1853)
—, *The Working Man's Way in the World*, 'Being the Autobiography of a Journeyman Printer' (London, William and Frederick G. Cash [1853])
—, *The Little World of London* (London, Arthur Hall, Virtue and Co., 1857)
Smith, John Thomas, *Ancient Topography of London…* (London, no publisher, 1815)

—, *Vagabondiana; or, Etchings of Remarkable Beggars, Itinerant Traders and other Persons…in London and its Environs* (London, no publisher, 1817)

—, *The Cries of London…Itinerant Traders of Antient and Modern Times* (London, John Bowyer Nichols, 1839)

—, *An Antiquarian Ramble in the Streets of London*, ed. Charles Mackay (London, Richard Bentley, 1846)

Some Olde London Cries & Street Noises of the XV, XVI, XVII, XVIII and XIXth Centuries (London, privately printed, 1908)

Southey, Robert, *Letters from England*, ed. Jack Simmons (first published 1807; Gloucester, Alan Sutton, 1984)

Stewart, Charles, *Sketches of Society in Great Britain and Ireland* (2nd edn, Philadelphia, Carey, Lea & Blanchard, 1835)

[Surtees, R. S.], *Hints to Railway Travellers and Country Visitors to London*, 'by an Old Stager' (London, Bradbury and Evans, 1851)

The Swell's Night Guide Through the Metropolis ,'by the Hon F. L. G.' (London, 'printed for the author, for private circulation, by Roger Funnyman' [?1841])

The Swell's Night Guide Through the Metropolis, or, A Peep through the Great Metropolis…, 'by Thelord [sic] Chief Baron' ([place and publisher cut away], 1846)

Taine, Hippolyte, *Notes on England*, trans. W. F. Rae (London, Strahan, 1872)

Tait's Edinburgh Magazine, untitled review (anon.) of Herbert Spencer, *Railway Morals and Railway Policy*, November 1855, pp. 695–6

Tayler, William, *The Diary of William Tayler, Footman, 1837*, ed. Dorothy Wise (London, Westminster City Archives, 1998)

[Thackeray, William Makepeace], 'Mr Brown's Letters to a Young Man About Town', *Punch*, 18 August 1849, pp. 4, 6

[Thomas, William Moy], 'Covent Garden Market', *Household Words*, 175, 30 July 1853, pp. 505–11

Thomson, John, and Adolphe Smith, *Victorian London Street Life in Historic Photographs* (NY, Dover, 1994; facsimile reprint of *Street Life in London* (London, Sampson Low, Marston, Searle & Rivington [1877]))

Thornbury, Walter, *Haunted London* (London, Hurst and Blackett, 1865)

—, *Old and New London*, 6 vols (London, Cassell, Petter, & Galpin [?1887–93])

Thrupp, G. A., *The History of Coaches* (London, Kerby & Endean, 1877)

Tilt, Edward John, *The Serpentine 'as it is' and 'as it ought to be'…* (London, John Churchill, 1848)

Timbs, John, *Curiosities of London…* (London, David Bogue, 1855)

Tinsley, William, *Random Recollections of an Old Publisher* (London, Simpkin, Marshall, Hamilton, Kent & Co., 1900)

'Titus' [William Maginn?], 'The Night Walker', *Blackwood's Edinburgh Magazine*, 14, November 1823, pp. 507–11

Tristan, Flora, *Flora Tristan's London Journal: A Survey of London Life in the 1830s*, trans. Dennis Palmer and Giselle Pincetl (London, George Prior, 1980)

Tristram, W. Outram, *Coaching Days and Coaching Ways* (London, Macmillan and Co., 1888)

Trollope, Thomas Adolphus, *What I Remember* (London, Richard Bentley, 1887)

Tuer, Andrew, *Old London Street Cries* (London, Field & Tuer, 1885)

Vizetelly, Henry, *Glances Back through Seventy Years: Autobiographical and Other Reminiscences* (London, Kegan Paul, Trench, Trübner & Co., 1893)

Walker, Geo. Alfd, *Gatherings from Graveyards, Particularly those of London…* (London, Longman, 1839)

—, *The First of a Series of Lectures…on the Actual condition of the Metropolitan Grave-Yards* (London, Longman, Brown, Green, and Longmans, 1847); also the *Second, Third* and *Fourth Series* (London, Longman, Brown, Green, and Longmans, 1847–9)

—, *The First of a Series* . . . (2nd edn, London, Longman, Brown, Green, and Longmans [sic], 1849)

'Walter', *My Secret Life* (first published 1888–94; Ware, Herts, Wordsworth, 1995)

Ward, Mrs. E. M. [Henrietta Mary Ada], *Mrs. E. M. Ward's Reminiscences*, ed. Elliott O'Donnell (London, Sir Isaac Pitman & Sons, 1911)

Ward, Matt. F., *English Items: or, Microscopic Views of England and Englishmen* (New York, D. Appleton and Co., 1853)

Weale, John, *London Exhibited in 1852…* (London, John Weale, 1852)

Weed, Thurlow, *Letters from Europe and the West Indies, 1843–1862* (Albany, NY, Weed, Parsons and Co., 1866)

Wellbeloved, Henry H., *London Lions, for Country Cousins and Friends about Town…* (London, William Charlton Wright, 1827)

The Wellington News (London, E. Appleyard [1852]; British Library shelfmark 1764 E8)

Wey, Francis, *A Frenchman Sees London in the 'Fifties*, 'adapted from the French' by Valerie Pirie (London, Sidgwick and Jackson, 1935)

Wheaton, Nathaniel S., *A Journal of a Residence during Several Months in London…in the Years 1823 and 1824* (Hartford, CT, H. & F. J. Huntington, 1830)

[Wilkinson, Robert], *Londina Illustrata: Graphic and Historic Monuments…* (London, Robert Wilkinson [1819])

[Wills, W. H.], 'Streetography', *Household Words*, 38, 14 December 1850, pp. 275–6

[Wright, Thomas], *Some Habits and Customs of the Working Classes*, 'by a Journeyman Engineer' (London, Tinsley Brothers, 1867)

[—], *The Great Unwashed*, 'by a Journeyman Engineer' (London, Tinsley Brothers, 1868)

Wyon, Leonard, Engraver at the Mint, Journal, 1853–67; British Library Add MS 59,617

Yates, Edmund, *After Office-Hours* (London, W. Kent and Co., 1861)

—, *Edmund Yates: His Recollections and Experiences* (London, Richard Bentley and Son, 1885)

Yokel's Preceptor: or, More Sprees in London! Being a…Show-up of All the Rigs and Doings of the Flash Cribs in This Great Metropolis… (London, H. Smith [?1855])

Secondary sources

Ackroyd, Peter, *London: The Biography* (London, Chatto & Windus, 2000)

Alber, Jan, and Frank Lauterbach, eds, *Stones of Law, Bricks of Shame: Narrating Imprisonment in the Victorian Age* (Toronto, University of Toronto Press, 2009)

Allen, Michael, *Charles Dickens and the Blacking Factory* (St Leonards, Oxford-Stockley Publications, 2011).

—, *Charles Dickens' Childhood* (Basingstoke, Macmillan, 1988)

Allen, Michelle, *Cleansing the City: Sanitary Geographies in Victorian London* (Athens, OH, Ohio University Press, 2008)

Allen, Rick, *The Moving Pageant: A Literary Sourcebook on London Street-Life, 1700–1914* (London, Routledge, 1998)

Altick, Richard, *The English Common Reader: A Social History of the Mass Reading Public, 1800–1900* (Chicago, University of Chicago Press, 1957)

—, *The Presence of the Present: Topics of the Day in the Victorian Novel* (Columbus, OH, Ohio State University Press, 1991)

Anderson, Olive, *Suicide in Victorian and Edwardian England* (Oxford, Clarendon Press, 1987)

Andrews, Malcolm, *Dickens on England and the English* (Hassocks, Harvester Press, 1979)

Arnold, Dana, *Re-Presenting the Metropolis: Architecture, Urban Experience and Social Life in London, 1800–1940* (Aldershot, Ashgate, 2000)

— (ed.), *The Metropolis and its Image: Constructing Identities for London, c.1750–1950* (Oxford, Blackwell, 1999)

Aycock Metz, Nancy, *The Companion to Martin Chuzzlewit* (Robertsbridge, Helm Information, 2001

Ball, Michael, and David Sunderland, *An Economic History of London, 1800–1914* (London, Routledge, 2001)

Banks, J. A., 'Population Change and the Victorian City', *Victorian Studies*, 11: 3, March 1968, pp. 277–89

—, '*My Secret Life*: Theme and Variations (A Symposium on the Obscenity Case)', *Victorian Studies*, 13: 2 (December 1969), pp. 204–15

Banks, Stephen, *A Polite Exchange of Bullets; The Duel and the English Gentleman, 1750–1850* (Woodbridge, Boydell, 2010)

—, 'Killing with Courtesy: The English Duellist, 1785–1845', *Journal of British Studies*, 47 (2008), pp. 528–58

—, 'Very Little Law in the Case: Contests of Honour and the Subversion of the English Criminal Courts, 1780–1845', *King's Law Journal*, 19: 3 (2008), pp. 575–94

—, 'Dangerous Friends: The Second and the Later English Duel', *Journal of Eighteenth Century Studies*, 32: 1 (2009), pp. 87–106

Barker, Felix, and Ralph Hyde, *London as it Might Have Been* (London, John Murray, 1982)

Barker, T. C., and Michael Robbins, *A History of London Transport ...*, vol. 1: *The Nineteenth Century* (London, George Allen & Unwin, 1975)

Barnett, David, *London, Hub of the Industrial Revolution: A Revisionary History, 1775–1825* (London, Tauris, 1998)

Baron, Xavier (ed.), *London 1066–1914: Literary Sources and Documents*, vol. 2: *Regency and Early Victorian London, 1800–1870* (Robertsbridge, Helm Information, 1997)

Barret-Ducrocq, Françoise, *Love in the Time of Victoria: Sexuality, Class and Gender in Nineteenth-Century London*, trans. John Howe (London, Verso, 1991)

Barton, N. J., *The Lost Rivers of London* (London, Phoenix House, 1962)

Barty-King, Hugh, *New Flame: How Gas Changed the Commercial, Domestic and Industrial Life of Britain...* (Tavistock, Graphmitre, 1984)

Betjeman, John, *Victorian and Edwardian London from Old Photographs* (London, Portman, 1987)

Blackstone, G. V., *A History of the British Fire Service* (London, Routledge and Kegan Paul, 1957)

Blount, Trevor, 'Dickens's Slum Satire in *Bleak House*', *Modern Language Review*, 60 (July 1965), pp. 340–51

Briggs, Asa, 'The Victorian City: Quantity and Quality', *Victorian Studies*, 11, Supplement (Summer 1968), pp. 711–30

Brimblecombe, Peter, *The Big Smoke: A History of Air Pollution in London Since Medieval Times* (London, Methuen, 1987)

Brundage, Anthony, *England's 'Prussian Minister': Edwin Chadwick and the Politics of Government Growth, 1832–1854* (University Park, PA, Pennsylvania State University Press, 1988)

Burke, Thomas, *Travel in England, from Pilgrim and Pack-Horse to Light Car and Plane* (London, T. Batsford, 1942)

Bynum, W. F., and Roy Porter, *Living and Dying in London, Medical History*, Supplement No. 11 (London, Wellcome Institute, 1991)

Cameron, David Kerr, *The English Fair* (Stroud, Sutton, 1998)

Chadwick, George F., *The Park and the Town: Public Landscape in the 19th and 20th Centuries* (London, Architectural Press, 1966)

Chalklin, C. W., 'The Reconstruction of London's Prisons, 1770–1779: An Aspect of the Growth of Georgian London', *London Journal*, 9: 1 (1983), pp. 21–34

Chancellor, E. Beresford, *The Squares of London, Topographical and Historical* (London, Kegan Paul, Trench, Trübner & Co., 1907)

—, *The London of Charles Dickens: being an account of the haunts of his characters and the topographical setting of his novels* (London, Grant Richards, 1924)

—, *Lost London: Being a description of Landmarks which have disappeared pictured by J. Crowther circa 1879–87…* (London, Constable, 1926)

—, *Disappearing London*, ed. Geoffrey Holme (London, 'The Studio', 1927)

—, *London's Old Latin Quarter, Being an Account of Tottenham Court Road and its Immediate Surroundings* (London, Jonathan Cape, [1930])

Chandler, James, and Kevin Gilmartin (eds), *Romantic Metropolis: The Urban Scene of British Culture, 1780–1840* (Cambridge, Cambridge University Press, 2005)

Chittick, Kathryn, *Dickens and the 1830s* (Cambridge, Cambridge University Press, 1990)

Choi, Tina Young, 'Writing the Victorian City: Discourses of Risk, Connection and Inevitability', in *Victorian Studies*, 42: 4 (2001), pp. 561–89

Clark, Cumberland, *Dickens' London. A Lantern Lecture* (London, Wass, Pritchard, 1923)

Clayton, Anthony, *Subterranean City: Beneath the Streets of London* (London, Historical Publications, 2000)

Cocks, H. G., *Nameless Offences: Homosexual Desire in the Nineteenth Century* (London, I. B. Tauris, 2003)

Cohen, William A., and Ryan Johnson (eds), *Filth: Dirt, Disgust and Modern Life* (Minneapolis, University of Minnesota Press, 2005)

Collins, Philip, *Dickens and Crime* (3rd edn, Basingstoke, Macmillan, 1994)

—, 'Trollope's London', The H. J. Dyos Memorial lecture, May 1982 (Leicester, Victorian Studies Centre, University of Leicester, 1982)

Conway, Hazel, *People's Parks: The Design and Development of Victorian Parks in Britain* (Cambridge, Cambridge University Press, 1991)

Cotsell, Michael, *The Companion to Our Mutual Friend* (London, Allen & Unwin, 1986)

Creaton, Heather, ed., *Victorian Diaries: The Daily Lives of Victorian Men and Women* (London, Mitchell Beazley, 2001)

Creighton, Charles, *A History of Epidemics in Britain*, vol. 2, *From the Extinction of the Plague to the Present Time* (first published 1891–4; London, Frank Cass, 1965)

Crook, J. Mordaunt, *London's Arcadia: John Nash and the Planning of Regent's Park*, Fifth Annual Soane Lecture ([n.p., no publisher] 2000)

Crowther, M. A., *The Workhouse System, 1834–1929: The History of an English Social Institution* (London, Batsford Academic and Educational, 1981)

Cunnington, Phillis, and Catherine Lucas, *Occupational Costume in England, from the Eleventh Century to 1914* (London, Adam & Charles Black, 1967)

Dart, Gregory, '"Flash Style": Pierce Egan and Literary London, 1820–28', *History Workshop Journal*, 51 (Spring 2001), pp. 180–205

Daunton, M. J., *House and Home in the Victorian City: Working-Class Housing 1850–1914* (London, Edward Arnold, 1983)

Davis, Graham, *The Irish in Britain, 1815–1914* (Dublin, Gill and Macmillan, 1991)

Davis, Terence, *The Architecture of John Nash* (London, Studio, 1960)

Davis, Tracy C., *Actresses as Working Women: Their Social Identity in Victorian Culture* (London, Routledge, 1991)

DeVries, Duane, *Dickens's Apprentice Years: The Making of a Novelist* (Hassocks, Sussex, Harvester Press, 1976)

Dexter, Walter, *The London of Dickens* (London, Cecil Palmer, 1923)

Dickson, P. G. M., *The Sun Insurance Office, 1710–1960: The History of Two and a Half Centuries of British Insurance* (London, Oxford University Press, 1960)

Dix, Frank L., *Royal River Highway: A History of the Passenger Boats and Services on the River Thames* (Newton Abbot, David and Charles, 1985)

Drew, John M. L., *Dickens the Journalist* (Basingstoke, Palgrave, 2003)

Dunn, Richard J., 'Dickens and Mayhew Once More', *Nineteenth-Century Fiction*, 25: 3, December 1970, pp. 348–53

Durey, Michael, *The Return of the Plague: British Society and the Cholera, 1831–2* (Dublin, Gill and Macmillan, 1979)

Dyos, H. J., *Victorian Suburb: A Study of the Growth of Camberwell* (Leicester, Leicester University Press, 1973)

—, *Exploring the Urban Past: Essays in Urban History*, ed. David Cannadine and David Reeder (Cambridge, Cambridge University Press, 1982)

—, 'The Slums of Victorian London', *Victorian Studies*, 11: 1 (September 1967), pp. 5–40

—, 'The Speculative Builders and Developers of Victorian London', Summer 1968, Supplement, pp. 641–90

—, and D. H. Aldcroft, *British Transport: An Economic Survey from the Seventeenth Century to the Twentieth* (Harmondsworth, Penguin, 1969)

—, and Michael Wolff (eds), *The Victorian City: Images and Realities* (London, Routledge, 1973)

Emmerson, Andrew, *The Underground Pioneers: Victorian London and its First Underground Railways* (Harrow Weald, Capital Transport, 2000)

Escott, T. H. S., *Social Transformations of the Victorian Age* (London, Seeley and Co., 1897)

Feldman, David, and Gareth Stedman Jones (eds), *Metropolis: London Histories and Representations since 1800* (London, Routledge, 1989)

Finn, Margot, 'Being in Debt in Dickens' London: Fact, Fictional Representation and the Nineteenth-Century Prison', *Journal of Victorian Culture*, 1: 2 (1996), pp. 203–26

Fletcher, Geoffrey, *The London Dickens Knew* (London, Hutchinson, 1970)

Forshaw, Alec, and Theo Bergström, *Smithfield Past and Present* (London, Heinemann, 1980)

Fox, Celina, *Londoners* (London, Thames and Hudson, 1987)

— (ed.), *London – World City, 1800–1840* (London, Yale University Press, 1992)

Freeman, Michael, and Derek H. Aldcroft (eds), *Transport in Victorian Britain* (Manchester, Manchester University Press, 1988)

Fryer, Peter (ed.), *The Man of Pleasure's Companion: A Nineteenth Century Anthology of Amorous Entertainment* (London, Arthur Barker, 1968)

Gibson, Ian, *The Erotomaniac: The Secret Life of Henry Spencer Ashbee* (London, Faber and Faber, 2001)

Gillooly, Eileen, and Deirdre David (eds), *Contemporary Dickens* (Columbus, OH, Ohio State University Press, 2009)

Girouard, Mark, *Victorian Pubs* (London, Studio Vista, 1975)

Gledhill, David, *Gas Lighting* (Princes Risborough, Shire, 1981)

Gloag, John, *Victorian Comfort: A Social History of Design from 1830–1900* (Newton Abbot, David and Charles, 1973)

Goodman, Andrew, *The Walking Guide to Lawyers' London* (London, Blackstone, 2000)

Gorham, Maurice, and H. McG. Dunnett, *Inside the Pub* (London, The Architectural Press, 1950)

Greaves, John, *Dickens at Doughty Street* (London, Elm Tree/Hamish Hamilton, 1975)

Green, David R., 'A Map for Mayhew's London: The Geography of Poverty in the Mid-Nineteenth Century', *London Journal*, 11: 2 (1985), pp. 115–26

Haddon, Archibald, *The Story of Music-Hall: From Cave of Harmony to Cabaret* (London, Cecil Palmer, 1924)

Halliday, Stephen, *The Great Stink of London: Sir Joseph Bazalgette and the Cleansing of Victorian London* (Stroud, Sutton, 1999)

—, *Newgate: London's Prototype of Hell* (Stroud, Sutton, 2006)

—, *The Great Filth: The War Against Disease in Victorian England* (Stroud, Sutton, 2007)

Hamlin, Christopher, *Public Health and Social Justice in the Age of Chadwick: Britain, 1800–1854* (Cambridge, Cambridge University Press, 1998)

Harper, Charles G., *Queer Things about London: Strange Nooks and Corners of the Greatest City in the World* (London, Cecil Palmer, 1923)

Harrison, Brian, 'Underneath the Victorians', *Victorian Studies*, 10: 3 (March 1967)

Harrison, Fraser, *The Dark Angel: Aspects of Victorian Sexuality* (London, Fontana/Collins, 1979)

Himmelfarb, Gertrude, 'Mayhew's Poor: A Problem of Identity', *Victorian Studies*, 14 (March 1971), pp. 307–20

Hitchcock, Tim, and Heather Shore (eds), *The Streets of London: From the Great Fire to the Great Stink* (London, Rivers Oram Press, 2003)

Hollington, Michael, 'Dickens the Flâneur', *Dickensian*, 77: 2 (1981), pp. 71–87

Hopkins, Albert A., and Newbury Frost Read, *A Dickens Atlas: Including Twelve Walks in London with Charles Dickens* (New York, Hatton Garden Press, 1923)

Hoyle, Susan Ryley, 'The First Battle for London: A Case Study of the Royal Commission on Metropolitan Termini 1846', *London Journal*, 8: 2 (1982), pp. 140–55

Humpherys, Anne, *Travels into the Poor Man's Country: The Work of Henry Mayhew* (Firle, Sussex, Caliban [1982])

Jackson, Alan A., *London's Termini* (London, Pan, 1969)

—, *London's Metropolitan Railway* (Newton Abbot, David and Charles, 1986)

Jackson, Peter, *George Scharf's London: Sketches and Watercolours of a Changing City, 1820–50* (London, John Murray, 1987)

—, *Drawings of Westminster by Sir George Scharf* (London, London Topographical Society, 1994)

Jordan, John O. (ed.), *The Cambridge Companion to Charles Dickens* (Cambridge, Cambridge University Press, 2001)

Joyce, Simon, *Capital Offenses: Geographies of Class and Crime in Victorian London* (Charlottesville, University of Virginia Press, 2003)

Kaplan, Morris B., '"Men in Petticoats": Border Crossings in the Queer Case of Mr. Boulton and Mr. Park', in Pamela Gilbert (ed.), *Imagined London* (Albany, NY, State University of New York Press, 2002), pp. 45–68

Kellett, John R., *The Impact of the Railways on Victorian Cities* (London, Routledge and Kegan Paul, 1969)

Kent, William, *London for Dickens Lovers* (London, Methuen, 1935)

Korg, Jacob, *London in Dickens' Day* (Englewood Cliffs, NJ, Prentice-Hall, 1960)

Koven, Seth, *Slumming: Sexual and Social Politics in Victorian London* (Princeton, NJ, Princeton University Press, 2004)

Kynaston, David, *The City of London*, vol. 1, *A World of Its Own, 1815–90* (London, Chatto & Windus, 1994)

Lasdun, Susan, *The English Park: Royal, Public and Private* (London, André Deutsch, 1991)

Lawrence, Henry W., *City Trees: A Historical Geography from the Renaissance through the Nineteenth Century* (Charlottesville, VA, University of Virginia Press, 2006)

Lees, Lynn Hollen, *Exiles of Erin: Irish Migrants in Victorian London* (Manchester, Manchester University Press, 1979)

—, 'Poverty and Pauperism in Nineteenth-Century London', The H. J. Dyos Memorial Lecture, May 1988 (Leicester, University of Leicester, 1988)

Lockwood, Allison, *Passionate Pilgrims: The American Traveller in Great Britain, 1800–1914* (NY, Cornwall Books, 1981)

Long, William F., 'Mr Pickwick Lucky to Find a Cab?', *Dickensian* (Autumn 1991), pp. 167–70

Low, Donald A., *The Regency Underworld* (Stroud, Sutton, 1999)

Luckin, Bill, *Pollution and Control: A Social History of the Thames in the Nineteenth Century* (Bristol, Adam Hilger, 1986)

Lynch, Tony, *Dickens's England: A Travellers' Companion* (London, B. T. Batsford, 1986)

McCarthy, Patrick J., 'Dickens at the Regent's Park Colosseum: Two Uncollected Pieces', *Dickensian*, 79: 3 (1983), pp. 154–60

Mace, Rodney, *Trafalgar Square: Emblem of Empire* (London, Lawrence and Wishart, 1976)

Maidment, Brian, *Dusty Bob: A Cultural History of Dustmen, 1780–1870* (Manchester, Manchester University Press, 2007)

Marcus, Steven, *The Other Victorians: A Study of Sexuality and Pornography in Mid-Nineteenth-Century England* (2nd edn, London, Transaction, 2009)

Maré, Eric de, *Victorian London Revealed: Gustave Doré's Metropolis* (Harmondsworth, Penguin, 2001)

Marly, Diana de, *Working Dress: A History of Occupational Clothing* (London, B. T. Batsford, 1986)

Mason, Michael, *The Making of Victorian Sexuality* (Oxford, Oxford University Press, 1994)

Massingham, Hugh and Pauline, *The London Anthology* (London, Spring Books [n.d.])

Meller, Hugh, *London Cemeteries: An Illustrated Guide and Gazetteer* (2nd edn, Godstone, Surrey, Gregg, 1985)

Metz, Nancy Aycock, '*Little Dorrit*'s London: Babylon Revisited', *Victorian Studies,* 33: 3 (Spring 1990), pp. 465–86

Moreland, Arthur, *Dickens Landmarks in London* (London, Cassell, 1931)

Nadel, Ira Bruce, and F. S. Schwarzbach, *Victorian Artists and the City: A Collection of Critical Essays* (New York, Pergamon, 1980)

Nead, Lynda, *Myths of Sexuality: Representations of Women in Victorian Britain* (Oxford, Basil Blackwell, 1988)

—, *Victorian Babylon: People, Streets and Images in Nineteenth-Century London* (London, Yale University Press, 2000)

Neal, Wendy, *With Disastrous Consequences: London Disasters 1830–1917* (Enfield Lock, Middlesex, Hisarlik Press, 1992)

Nelson, Harland S., 'Dickens's *Our Mutual Friend* and Henry Mayhew's *London Labour and the London Poor*', *Nineteenth-Century Fiction,* 20: 3 (December 1965), pp. 207–22

Newton Dunn, Bill, *The Man Who Was John Bull: The Biography of Theodore Edward Hook, 1778–1841* (London, Allendale, 1996)

Nord, Deborah Epstein, *Walking the Victorian Streets: Women, Representation and the City* (Ithaca, NY, Cornell University Press, 1995)

—, 'The City as Theater: From Georgian to Early Victorian London', *Victorian Studies,* 31: 2 (1988), pp. 159–88

Norton, Rictor, *Mother Clap's Molly House: The Gay Subculture in England, 1700–1830* (London, GMP Publishers, 1992)

O'Dea, William T., *The Social History of Lighting* (London, Routledge and Kegan Paul, 1958)

Olsen, Donald J., *The Growth of Victorian London* (London, B. T. Batsford, 1976)

—, 'Victorian London: Specialization, Segregation and Privacy', *Victorian Studies,* 17: 3 (March 1974), pp. 265–78

Panayi, Panikos, *Immigration, Ethnicity and Racism in Britain, 1815–1945* (Manchester, Manchester University Press, 1994)

Paroissien, David, *The Companion to Oliver Twist* (Edinburgh, Edinburgh University Press, 1992)

—, *The Companion to Great Expectations* (Robertsbridge, Helm Information, 2000)

—, *A Companion to Charles Dickens* (Malden, MA, Blackwell, 2008)

Passingham, W. J., *London's Markets: Their Origin and History* (London, Sampson Low, Marston [1935])

Paterson, Michael, *Voices from Dickens' London* (Cincinnati, OH, David and Charles, 2006)

Pattinson, John Patrick, 'The Man who was Walter', *Victorian Literature and Culture*, 30: 1 (2002), pp. 19–40

Pelling, Margaret, *Cholera, Fever and English Medicine, 1825–65* (Oxford, Oxford University Press, 1978)

Pemberton, T. Edgar, *Dickens's London, or, London in the Works of Charles Dickens* (London, Samuel Tinsley, 1876)

Phillips, J. F. C., *Shepherd's London* (London, Cassell, 1976)

Phillips, Lawrence (ed.), *A Mighty Mass of Brick and Smoke: Victorian and Edwardian Representations of London* (Amsterdam, Rodopi, 2007)

Philpotts, Trey, *The Companion to Little Dorrit* (Robertsbridge, Helm Information, 2003)

—, 'The Real Marshalsea', *Dickensian* (Autumn 1991), pp. 133–46

Picker, John M., *Victorian Soundscapes* (Oxford, Oxford University Press, 2003)

Pike, David L., *Subterranean Cities: The World Beneath Paris and London, 1800–1945* (Ithaca, Cornell University Press, 2005)

Porter, Dale H., *The Thames Embankment: Environment, Technology, and Society in Victorian England* (Akron, OH, University of Akron Press, 1998)

Pritchard, Allan, 'The Urban Gothic of *Bleak House*', *19th-Century Fiction*, 45: 4 (March 1991), pp. 432–52

Quinlivan, Patrick, and Paul Rose, *The Fenians in England, 1865–1872: A Sense of Insecurity* (London, John Calder, 1982)

Reeder, David A., *Suburbanity and the Victorian City* (Leicester, University of Leicester, 1980)

Richard, Maxwell, 'Henry Mayhew and the Life of the Streets', *Journal of British Studies*, 17: 2 (Spring 1978), pp. 87–105

Robinson, Alan, *Imagining London, 1770–1900* (Basingstoke, Palgrave Macmillan, 2004)

Rule, Fiona, *The Worst Street in London* (Hersham, Ian Allen, 2008)

Sanders, Andrew, *Charles Dickens, Resurrectionist* (London, Macmillan, 1982)

—, *Dickens and the Spirit of the Age* (Oxford, Clarendon Press, 1999)

Saunders, Ann, *Regent's Park: A Study of its Development of the Area from 1086 to the Present Day* (Newton Abbot, David and Charles, 1969)

—, *The Regent's Park Villas* (London, Bedford College, 1981)

Schivelbusch, Wolfgang, *Disenchanted Night: The Industrialisation of Light in the Nineteenth Century*, trans. Angela Davies (Oxford, Berg, 1988)

Schlicke, Paul, *Dickens and Popular Entertainment* (London, Unwin Hyman, 1985)

— (ed.), *Oxford Reader's Companion to Dickens* (Oxford, Oxford University Press, 1999)

Schwarzbach, F. S., *Dickens and the City* (London, Athlone Press, 1979)

Sekon, G. A., *Locomotion in Victorian London* (London, Oxford University Press, 1938)

Shatto, Susan, *The Companion to Bleak House* (London, Unwin Hyman, 1988)

Sheppard, Francis, *London, 1808–1870: The Infernal Wen* (London, Secker & Warburg, 1971)

—, *London: A History* (Oxford, Oxford University Press, 1998)

Shesgreen, Sean, *Hogarth and the Times-of-Day Tradition* (Ithaca, NY, Cornell University Press, 1983)

—, *Images of the Outcast: The Urban Poor in the Cries of London* (Manchester, Manchester University Press, 2002)

Short, K. R. M., *The Dynamite War: Irish-American Bombers in Victorian Britain* (Dublin, Gill and Macmillan, 1979)

Sicher, Efraim, *Rereading the City, Rereading Dickens: Representation, the Novel and Urban Realism* (NY, AMS Press, 2003)

Simpson, Anthony E., 'Vulnerability and the Age of Female Consent: Legal Innovation and Its Effect on Prosecutions for Rape in 18th Century London', in G. S. Rousseau and Roy Porter (eds), *Sexual Underworlds of the Enlightenment* (Chapel Hill, University of North Carolina Press, 1987)

Slater, Michael, *The Intelligent Person's Guide to Dickens* (London, Duckworth, 1999)

—, 'The Bachelor's Pocket Book for 1851', in Don Richard Cox (ed.), *Sexuality and Victorian Literature* (Knoxville, TN, University of Tennessee Press, 1984)

Spiller, Brian, *Victorian Public Houses* (Newton Abbot, David and Charles, 1972)

Stamp, Gavin, *The Changing Metropolis: Earliest Photographs of London, 1839–1879* (Harmondsworth, Viking, 1984)

Stanton, Michael N., 'Dickens' Return from America; A Ghost at the Feast', *Dickensian* (Autumn 1991), pp. 147–52

Stapleton, Alan, *London Alleys, Byways and Courts, Drawn and Described* (London, John Lane the Bodley Head, 1924)

Stedman Jones, Gareth, *Outcast London: A Study in the Relationship Between Classes in Victorian Society* (Harmondsworth, Penguin, 1971)

Stern, Walter M., *The Porters of London* (London, Longmans, Green, 1960)

Sucksmith, Harvey Peter, 'Dickens and Mayhew: A Further Note', *Nineteenth-Century Fiction*, 24: 3 (December 1969), pp. 345–9

Summerson, John, *The London Building World of the Eighteen-Sixties* (London, Thames and Hudson, 1973)

Tambling, Jeremy, *Going Astray: Dickens and London* (Harlow, Pearson Longman, 2009)

Thompson, E. P., 'The Political Education of Henry Mayhew', *Victorian Studies*, 11 (September 1967), pp. 41–62

Thompson, F. M. L., 'Nineteenth-Century Horse Sense', *Economic History Review*, 29: 1 (February 1976), pp. 60–81

Thurston, Gavin, *The Clerkenwell Riot: The Killing of Constable Culley* (London, George Allen & Unwin, 1967)

Turvey, Ralph, 'Street Mud, Dust and Noise', *London Journal*, 21: 2 (1996), pp. 131–48

Upchurch, Charles, *Before Wilde: Sex Between Men in Britain's Age of Reform* (Berkeley, University of California Press, 2009)

Walker, John A., 'The People's Hero: Millais's *The Rescue* and the Image of the Fireman in Nineteenth-century Art and Media', *Apollo* (December 2004), pp. 56–62

Walkowitz, Judith R., *Prostitution and Victorian Society: Women, Class and the State* (Cambridge, Cambridge University Press, 1980)

Weinreb, Ben, and Christopher Hibbert (eds), *The London Encyclopaedia* (London, Macmillan, 1983)

Welsh, Alexander, *The City of Dickens* (Oxford, Clarendon Press, 1971)

—, 'Satire and History: The City of Dickens', *Victorian Studies*, 11: 3 (March 1968), pp. 379–400

White, Jerry, *London in the Nineteenth Century: 'A Human Awful Wonder of God'* (London, Jonathan Cape, 2007)

Wigley, John, *The Rise and Fall of the Victorian Sunday* (Manchester, Manchester University Press, 1980)

Williams-Mitchell, Christobel, *Dressed for the Job: The Story of Occupational Costume* (Poole, Blandford Press, 1982)

Winter, James, *London's Teeming Streets, 1830–1914* (London, Routledge, 1993)

Wohl, Anthony S., *The Eternal Slum: Housing and Social Policy in Victorian London* (New Brunswick, NJ, Transaction, 2002)

Wolmar, Christian, *The Subterranean Railway: How the London Underground was Built, and How it Changed the City Forever* (London, Atlantic, 2004)

Woolf, Larry, 'The Boys are Pickpockets, and the Girl is a Prostitute: Gender and Juvenile Criminality in Early Victorian England from Oliver Twist to London Labour', *New Literary History*, 27: 2 (1996), pp. 227–49

INDEX

NOTE: Page numbers in *italic* refer to illustrations and captions. Works by Charles Dickens (CD) appear directly under title; other works under author's name)